I0519176

Reading Matthew, Trusting Jesus

Christian Tradition and First-Century Fulfillment within Matthew 24-25

—

Jonathan E. Sedlak

Reading Matthew, Trusting Jesus
Christian Tradition and First-Century Fulfillment within Matthew 24-25
Copyright © 2024 by Jonathan E. Sedlak

Theopolis Books
An imprint of Athanasius Press
715 Cypress Street
West Monroe, Louisiana, 71291
athanasiuspress.org | (318) 323-3061

Cover design and typesetting: Rachel Rosales

ISBN: 978-1-957726-09-0

Contents

Foreword

PETER J. LEITHART

Many years ago, I became convinced of a preterist reading of Jesus' Olivet Discourse (Matt. 24; Mark 13; Luke 21) and of the book of Revelation. Preterists believe the events Jesus predicted were fulfilled before the end of the "wicked and perverse generation" in which He lived (Matt. 24:34; cf. Matt. 23:36). Revelation greatly complicates the picture, but it also portrays events that were fulfilled "soon" after John saw his visions (Rev. 1:1; 22:6).

In the preterist framework, neither the Olivet Discourse nor the book of Revelation are about the "end of *the* world." Rather, they are concerned with the looming end of *a* world, the geopolitical system Yahweh organized following the Babylonian exile. At the center of what James B. Jordan calls "the *oikoumene*" stood Jerusalem and the temple, but the restoration community of Israel was nestled within, scattered throughout, and often dominated by a series of imperial frenemies—Babylon, Persia, Alexandrian Greece, and Rome. *That* world ended in the first century, with the Roman obliteration of Jerusalem and the temple and the upheaval throughout the empire that accompanied it.

Jesus wasn't like the crank on the street corner with the mortar board announcing "The End Is Near." He was more like a cultural critic or prophetic pundit warning about the end of the world as we know it. Jesus warned His disciples about the end of the *oikoumene*, and He was *right*. As N.T. Wright has emphasized, events vindicated Jesus as *the* prophet of Israel.

Both liberal and conservative Christians have misread the Discourse as a prophecy of the end of all things. This is not a minor issue. If Jesus expected the end of the world, He was mistaken, and that mistake has significant implications for the reliability of Jesus and/or of the Gospels. Based on their misinterpretation, liberals reconstruct the early development of the church under the heading of a mythical "delay of the Parousia." Reading the Discourse with a newspaper in hand, Fundamentalists misidentify current events as signs of Jesus' return. Ironically, liberal and Fundamentalist errors arise from the *same* misinterpretation of Jesus' prophecy.

Jonathan Sedlak's study demonstrates in great detail that there has been a persistent preterist element in classic Christian eschatology. To take one example more or less at random: Commenting on the "abomination of desolation" and the flight from Jerusalem (Matt. 24:15-22), the Venerable Bede writes:

> [The abomination of desolation] may either be said simply of Antichrist, or of the statue of Caesar, which Pilate put into the temple, or of the equestrian statue of Adrian, which for a long time stood in the holy of holies itself. An idol is also called abomination according to the Old Testament, and he has added of desolation, because it was placed in the temple when desolate and deserted. [...] It is on record that this was literally fulfilled, when on the approach of the war with Rome and the extermination of the Jewish people, all the Christians who were in that province, warned by the prophecy, fled far

> away, as Church history relates, and retiring beyond Jordan, remained for a time in the city of Pella under the protection of Agrippa, the king of the Jews, of whom mention is made in the Acts, and who with that part of the Jews, who chose to obey him, always continued subject to the Roman empire.

At the same time, patristic and medieval commentators left an opening for the blunders of modern liberals and Fundamentalists. The final chapters of Revelation move beyond the first century to sketch the end of the millennium, the final judgment, and the descent of the bridal city from heaven. Many have claimed the Olivet Discourse makes a similar "transition" to the end of all things (at Matt. 24:36). Jon argues this is a misreading, the product of confusion about the overall logic of the Discourse. Through a meticulous structural analysis, he answers the question of whether or not there is any "transition" in the text.

Jonathan Sedlak is an unusual author. A licensed electrician lacking formal theological training and academic credentials, Jon (or, as we at Theopolis like to call him, Sedlak) has written the most comprehensive historical review of preterism I know of, and has isolated and rebutted a persistent error that affects the very heart of Christian eschatology. I hope this volume will receive the wide attention it deserves, which would be fair repayment for the sizable theological debt we now owe to Jonathan Sedlak.

To my children, Ignatius Jadon,
Philothea Eden, and Barnabas Gaius,
that they would know Jesus and
trust his promises.

γενώμεθα ναὸς τέλειος τῷ θεῷ.
— *Ep. Barn.* 4.11 —

For my father:
Some walls cannot a prison make.

In memory of my mother:
A witness to the worth of hiddenness.

Mistakes are wondrous and simple, like life
and death, like a small child's arithmetic book.

—Yehuda Amichai

Preface & Acknowledgments

This book has been over ten years in the making. It began in the winter of 2010 as I assembled notes in preparation for bible studies with friends and family in Slinger, Wisconsin. It developed even further in the spring of 2011, after stumbling across Peter Leithart's essay, *Jesus as Israel: The Typological Structure of Matthew's Gospel*, in preparation for a lengthy group-study of Matthew's Gospel, scheduled to begin in August of that year. That group of friends and family met once a week for two years, and each time we gathered our discussions lasted two, sometimes three hours each evening. I am grateful for the patience, good will, and sincere faith of friends in that group who encouraged me in my studies.

By the time that study in Matthew's Gospel began, I had already dug deeply into the text and become increasingly convinced of Leithart's thesis in comparison with other scholarly approaches to Matthew's Gospel. One year later, in the fall of 2012, a friend asked me to compile my notes and share them, which then led to a full decade more of note taking and sharing. In need of greater philosophical and exegetical sharpening, I signed up for the Fall 2013 certificate program at the *Theopolis Institute* in Birmingham, AL, and remained a devoted student for years while also juggling a growing family and career. Elements of my early research and later "Theopolitan" sharpening are contained in this book, and have been presented to the Theopolis Institute in the form of completed assignments pertaining to biblical studies, now published online at Academia.edu. By the Spring of 2021, I completed my course work and submitted a proposal to Peter Leithart for a final thesis in order to graduate with a certificate in Biblical, Liturgical, and Cultural Studies. In March 2022, I successfully defended my thesis and graduated. All but chapter three and the appendices of this book were contained, in one form or another, within that final thesis.

Because the history of Christian interpretation covers so much, it would be naïve to claim I have read everything regarding Matthew's Gospel. Nevertheless, a concerted effort was made to include as much as was feasible and useful. While researching and writing, a number of people helped me remain on task. Darin Fawley and Jeffrey Jones reviewed an early draft and a near-complete version of manuscripts, along with conversations between to keep me motivated. I am very grateful for their friendship throughout this whole process. Also, Matthew Colvin supplied his own scholarly English translation of three important Reformation-era works only available to me in Latin at the time I began research on chapter three: Cardinal Cajetan's *Evangelia cum Commentariis*, Heinrich Bullinger's *In Sacrosanctum Iesu Chrisi Domini Nostri Evangelium Secundum Matthaeum Commentariorum Libri XII*, and Martin Bucer's *In Sacra Quatuor Evangelia, Enarrationes Perpetuae*. Colvin's scholarly acumen is exceptional, and so I am not only honored by his willingness to provide a modern translation of such previously untranslated works, but I am also grateful for his great care and skill in that process.

David Shaw also deserves special mention. He digested the whole manuscript in multiple phases, offering many suggestions and corrections that have been enormously helpful and productive. I honestly cannot thank him enough for his support and friendship. In many ways, David embodies the ideal pastor-theologian, in which intellectual curiosity, hermeneutical sensitivity, wide-ranging knowledge, and assiduous attentiveness to literary details are brought together, creating a space where wisdom is nurtured. This project would not have reached its final form without his help. Thank you, David. All remaining errors to be discovered throughout this book are, of course, my own.

Sincere gratitude is also due to my friend and sister-in-Christ, Katie Schlosser, who once stormed out of my living room in the fall of 2016 during a study of Matthew's five discourses because she deemed first-century fulfillment to be heretical and damaging to Catholic sensibilities. I would have never investigated patristic tradition or its methodologies if she never offered both a memorable contribution to Christian fellowship and a direct challenge to provide evidence in support of first-century fulfillment within the Catholic tradition.

Fostering healthy fellowship and dialogue within the household of Christian faith—especially across denominational boundaries and through tribalistic misunderstandings—underlines the spirit of this entire project. Very few philosophical topics are as unwittingly systemic and troublesome as *eschatology*. The fulfillment of prophecy in "end-time" events always has and always will remain a hot-button-topic to press. Christians subconsciously live, move, and sustain their daily existence in order to ultimately reach God, see their Savior face-to-face, and live forever with Him in new creation. Our notions of what the future holds for each and every one dear to us is also intimately tied with our trust in Jesus' promises, especially those described in the Gospels. For many Christians, both today and throughout past generations, it is commonly imagined that Jesus promised one thing for certain: that he would be returning *soon*. Jesus also did not know—so I have been told—*which* generation he would return in. Consequently, successive generations of Christians have been left with conflicting messages of hope, many of which encourage the faithful to patiently endure tribulations under the increased reign of Satan while spreading that most assured message of our Savior's delay until the Last Day. And when Jesus does finally come, I am told it will be sudden like lightning, with signs and portents of doom everywhere; our planet will become pitch-black, and stars will fall from the sky, accompanied by a host of angels blasting trumpets to announce Jesus' majestic return. As I hope to show throughout this book, I have no interest in debating how soon Jesus will return or what that event will look like. My interests are much more modest. I merely wish to highlight historical interpretations, ask relevant questions, and offer suggestions that are frequently overlooked or neglected across the field of Matthean studies.

Aside from this book's focal point on Christian interpretations of the Olivet Discourse, this study also indirectly offers a plea to humbly examine our own human limitations as interpreters while enjoying the humor underlining God's good providence. With a dozen years of pointed research under my belt, along with countless conversations about eschatology across a wide array of Christian denominations, I occasionally jest that someday we will all be with Jesus together, laughing about how mistaken many of us were. I jest because some Christians do not realize that they have imbibed too many cartoonish eschatological interpretations and not enough realistic, well-documented, first-century history. Thus, many unfortunate reactions to interpretations of first-century fulfillment continue to range widely among Christian brethren—from indifference, ignorance, or naïveté on the one hand, to hubris, vitriol, and superciliousness on the other. Nevertheless, I firmly believe that hope still remains for the people of God. In God's good providence, centuries of traditional assumptions and questionable methodologies have become more accessible now than ever before in history, thereby inviting some hardy self-reflection on the part of Christian exegetes and arm-chair theologians to chuckle about how mistaken many of us have been. A revival of healthy, irenic dialogue and fellowship among people of faith should be the result of such joy and peace with the Lord, which is as greatly needed in this generation as it was in the generation denounced by Jesus. As one Dominican motto expresses, *contemplata aliis trader*, my sincere hope is that this work leads many to discover and attain such joy and peace.

Finally, because the development of healthy Christian communion underlines the spirit of this project, I cannot thank my wife, Alison, enough for modeling the profoundest spirit of Christian fellowship and dialogue in my life. I owe the greatest debt to her for being the listening ears, questioning eyes, challenging mind, and supporting arms in all my endeavors to remain loyal to Jesus Christ, ἐν ᾧ εὑρεθείημεν ἄμωμοι.

The Feast of Matthew the Evangelist
Milwaukee, Wisconsin

Abbreviations

ACT	Ancient Christian Texts
ACW	Ancient Christian Writings: The Works of the Fathers in Translation
ANCT	Ashgate New Critical Thinking in Religion, Theology, and Biblical Studies
AUSDDS	Andrews University Seminary Doctoral Dissertation Series
AYB	The Anchor Yale Bible Series
AYBRL	The Anchor Yale Bible Reference Library
BATCB	Belief: A Theological Commentary on the Bible
BBRS	Bulletin for Biblical Research Supplement
BETL	Bibliotheca Ephemeridum Theologicarum Lovaniensium
BIS	Biblical Interpretation Series

BS	Bibliotheca Sacra
BTCB	Brazos Theological Commentary on the Bible
BTS	Biblical Tools and Studies
BTTS	Bonaventure Texts in Translation Series
BZNW	Beihefte zur Zeitschrift für die Neutestamentliche Wissenschaft
CBNTS	Coniectanea Biblica New Testament Series
CCSS	Catholic Commentary on Sacred Scripture
COQG	Christian Origins and the Question of God
CTCS	Christian Theology In Context Series
EBS	Expositor's Bible Commentary
EBTC	Evangelical Biblical Theology Commentary
EC	Early Christianity
ECIL	Early Christianity and Its Literature
ESS	Emerging Scholars Series
FS	Franciscan Studies
HCHCB	Hermeneia—A Critical and Historical Commentary on the Bible
HTS	Harvard Theological Studies
IBCTP	Interpretation: A Biblical Commentary for Teaching and Preaching
IRUSC	Interpretation: Resources for the Use of Scripture in the Church
ICC	The International Critical Commentary on the Holy Scriptures of the Old and New Testaments
JBL	Journal of Biblical Literature
JCTS	T&T Clark Jewish and Christian Texts Series

JSNTSS	Journal for the Study of the New Testament Supplement Series
JSSS	Journal of Semitic Studies Supplement
LCC	Library of Christian Classics
LCL	Loeb Classical Library
LMS	Lexham Methods Series
LNTS	Library of New Testament Studies
LW	Luther's Works
LXX	Septuagint
MBCINT	The Mellen Biblical Commentary Intertextual New Testament Series
MBI	Methods in Biblical Interpretation Series
NCBC	New Cambridge Bible Commentary
NGS	New Gospel Studies
NITCNT	The New International Commentary on the New Testament
NPNF	Nicene and Post-Nicene Fathers
NTSSA	Journal of the New Testament Society of Southern Africa
OBSCS	The Orthodox Bible Study Companion Series
OECS	Oxford Early Christian Studies
OSHT	Oxford Studies in Historical Theology
PBM	Paternoster Biblical Monographs
PTMS	Princeton Theological Monograph Series
RABS	Routledge Ancient Biography Series
RCSNT	Reformation Commentary on Scripture: New Testament

REC	Reformed Expository Commentary
SASRH	St. Andrews Studies in Reformation History
SBLDS	Society of Biblical Literature Dissertation Series
SBLSS	Society of Biblical Literature Symposium Series
SJSJ	Supplements to the Journal for the Study of Judaism
SNT	Supplements to Novum Testamentum
SNTSMS	Society for New Testament Studies Monograph Series
SNTWS	Studies of the New Testament and Its World Series
SOTSM	Society for Old Testament Study Monographs
SPS	Sacra Pagina Series
TFC	The Fathers of the Church
THNTC	The Two Horizons New Testament Commentary
TMSS	The Masterpiece Study Series
TNTL	The New Testament Library
WBBC	Wiley Blackwell Bible Commentaries
WBC	Word Biblical Commentary
WGRW	Writings from the Greco-Roman World
WUNT	Wissenschaftliche Untersuchungen zum Neuen Testament

Introduction

Around the dawn of the fifth century, an interesting trend emerged among influential Christian exegetes of the Roman Empire. The so-called Olivet Discourse in the Gospel of Matthew had received a peculiar methodology for its interpretation, which could follow one of two paths. Either Jesus was asked *three* questions, and he answers all three of them *in order*, beginning with his answer to the first question, "When will these things be?"; or, Jesus is asked *two* questions consisting of two distinct parts, which he, in turn, answers in the same order. Ultimately, this methodology illustrated that some kind of transition took place between Jesus' response to his disciples' first question, "When will these things be?" and his response to their other questions, "What will be the sign of your *Parousia* and the end of the age?" (Matt. 24:3).

I describe this methodology as emerging centuries after the Gospels were composed *not* because I imagine it to be a novel interpretation within the fourth or fifth century. Rather, it appears to be the widespread beginning of a prominent methodology among commentaries of that era. Certainly, other commentaries were available prior to the fifth century, yet they are not as uniform or clear as what later emerged and remained popular.

Origen's commentary on the Gospel of Matthew, which was composed in Caesarea between 232–254 CE, most likely toward the end of his life,[1] appears to be a seminal source of interpretation for Gospel commentaries produced shortly thereafter.[2] Origen also seems to be the first on record to highlight a distinction within the Olivet Discourse between first-century events and futuristic end-of-the-world events. Due in part to his awareness with the first-century works of Josephus,[3] Origen was aware that many of Jesus' promises

---

1. Ronald Heine offers this range of time in which Origen was in Caesarea. Toward the end of his introduction, Heine also says it was likely among "the last works Origen composed." On this, see Origen, *The Commentary of Origen on the Gospel of St Matthew*, Volume II, trans. Ronald E. Heine (Oxford, UK: Oxford University Press, 2018), 4, 24ff.

2. Heine's comments about biblical commentaries before Origen are helpful: "When Origen began writing commentaries on Scripture there was a long tradition of commentary literature preceding him. The museum at Alexandria had been producing commentaries on Homer, the Greek dramatists, and the Attic orators for several centuries. Philosophers were producing commentaries on the writings of Plato, Aristotle, and the Stoics, and there were the writings of Hellenistic Jews such as Philo of Alexandria commenting on sections of the Torah. Among Christians, Hippolytus of Rome had written commentaries on Scripture prior to Origen, though he appears to have written only on some books of the Old Testament. . . . Origen is the first person, however, from whom we have actual texts of continuous commentary on the Gospels." Ronald E. Heine, "Origen's Gospel Commentaries" in *The Oxford Handbook of Origen*, ed. Ronald E. Heine, Karen Jo Torjesen (Oxford, UK: Oxford University Press, 2022), 211.

3. Various scholars have noted Origen's familiarity with the works of Josephus. According to Frederick Norris, who carefully cross-references numerous sources cited by Eusebius of Caesarea (among whom Origen is but one), Origen's commentary on the *Gospel of Matthew* shows familiarity with the works of Josephus. On that, see Frederick W. Norris, "Eusebius on Jesus as Deceiver and Sorcerer" in *Eusebius, Christianity, and Judaism*, ed. Harold W. Attridge and Gohei Hata (Detroit, MI: Wayne State University Press, 1992), 539n22.
Bas ter Haar Romeny goes one step further in connecting Origen with Josephus, claiming that Origen "re-interpreted a number of suitable passages from the

about soon-coming wrath and judgment were clearly fulfilled in that generation.[4]

A.J. [*Antiquities of the Jews*, by Josephus]" for the purpose of expressing "clearly anti-Jewish" sentiment. Romeny's justification for this claim appears shallow. His grounds for attributing "clearly anti-Jewish" sentiment to Origen is his belief "that the Jews lost their homeland and their Temple on account of their crimes and their rejection of Jesus. Bas ter Haar Romeny, "Hypotheses on the Development of Judaism and Christianity in Syria in the Period after 70 C.E." in *Matthew and the Didache: Two Documents from the Same Jewish-Christian Milieu?*, ed. Huub van de Sandt (Minneapolis, MN: Fortress Press, 2005), 16. Aside from Romeny's conjecture about Origen's "anti-Jewish" motives—which are entirely incorrect according to Ronald E. Heine, *Origen: Scholarship in the Service of the Church* (CTCS; New York, NY: Oxford University Press, 2010), 147-151, 172-9, 227-231—it seems certain that Origen did connect the destruction of Jerusalem with God's judgment for rejecting Jesus and persecuting his disciples thereafter.

However, because I agree with Romeny (and others) that anti-semitism is a seriously abhorrent inclination, my view on this matter needs to be stated at the outset of this book: Although I will demonstrate that many Christians throughout history have reached this same conclusion as Origen (i.e., that Jerusalem's destruction was by Divine appointment, and one consequence, among others, for crucifying Jesus unjustly), I have no "anti-Jewish" motives in sharing this history, nor am I endorsing or encouraging any person to have such evil "anti-Jewish" inclinations. As can be seen across this entire book, my motive for tracing a history of what might mistakenly be perceived as an "anti-Jewish" message is to understand Matthew's Gospel and Jesus' Olivet Discourse, despite how Christians have abused its message. Numerous notes throughout this book highlight evidence about "Matthew's" literary intentionality (and by extension, his motives), which are difficult to construe as being "anti-Jewish," especially insofar as the broad range of Matthean scholarship acknowledges that "Matthew" himself and his Gospel were Jewish.

4. Commenting on Jesus' statement in Matthew 24:2 ("Truly I say to you a stone will not be left here on a stone which is not destroyed"), Origen says that "Christ had predicted everything that was to come to Jerusalem . . . in accordance with the word that he had spoken, 'The kingdom of God will be taken from you and will be given to a nation producing its fruit.'" Origen, *Matthew*, 585. Immediately prior to his remarks about Matthew 24:1-3, Origen points out again that "Christ prophesied above of its future destruction and thus threatened its desertion in the words, 'Behold now your house is left to you deserted' . . . . They [i.e., his disciples] want, of course, to persuade him to show mercy on

However, it remains unclear what methodology Origen himself used to transition from first-century fulfillment to "end-of-the-world" fulfillment within the Olivet Discourse.[5] Although he does not propose any so-called transitional verse between the two, he does propose

---

that place, and not do what he had threatened to do." Origen, *Matthew*, 586. Commenting on the fulfillment of the "abomination of desolation," he says, "But at that time also the abomination of desolation of the temple and the city was upon the temple that was in Jerusalem, at that time, of course, 'when they saw Jerusalem surrounded by an army', so that (as the Savior had prophesied) they might know 'that its desolation was at hand.'" Origen, *Matthew*, 603.

5. J. A. McGuckin describes the "dominant exegetical character and method" of Origen's eschatology as "the sense that there are always various 'levels of meaning' in a biblical text . . . a meaning that it has in the past, a meaning it has for the present life of faith, and a meaning that it will have for the future (its *telos*)"; These "varieties of meanings" are, strictly speaking, "perceived according to the level of spiritual acuity of the observer." J. A. McGuckin, "Origen's Eschatology" in *The Oxford Handbook of Origen*, 412.

Although Origen offers plenty of "figurative" interpretations (see Origen, *Matthew*, 18-20), he nonetheless provides a variety of clear remarks regarding the literal sense of certain passages. On one occasion he offers this literal sense primarily for "the simple" in order to provide clarification to those paying attention to what Jesus meant in response to "when these things will be." According to Roukema's explanation, the "simple" were "Christians who preferred a literal reading of Scripture and were opposed to his allegorical explanations." Riemer Roukema, "Origen, the Jews, and the New Testament" in *The 'New Testament' as a Polemical Tool: Studies in Ancient Christian Anti-Jewish Rhetoric and Beliefs*, ed. Riemer Roukema and Hagit Amirav (Gottingen: Vandenhoeck & Ruprecht Gmbh & Co., 2018), 244. A few examples of Origen's "literal" sense for "the simple" will suffice to show his own awareness of first-century fulfillment as a well-known interpretation among other Christians. Commenting on Matthew 24:34, Origen says, "Let us see what 'this generation' is of which Christ speaks. The simple refer the words to the destruction of Jerusalem and think it said of that generation that lived at the time of Christ and witnessed his passion and which is not to pass on before the destruction of that city occurs. But I do not know if they are able to explain word for word what is said: 'Do you not see all these things? Truly I say to you, stone will not be left here on stone which will not be destroyed' up to that which says: 'It is near, at the door.' For perhaps they can in some passages, but in others not at all, and I do not know if, pressed sufficiently, they can say anything." Origen, *Matthew*, 635. These remarks about

one implicitly by only offering interpretations of first-century fulfill-ment among verses 4–35 within Matthew 24. There are no explicit references to first-century historical fulfillment to be found from verse 35 to the end of the discourse. Therefore, it can be deduced from what remains of Origen's commentary that the *first* question from Jesus' disciples pertained in some sense to historical, first-century events. Jesus then answered that first question *first*, between verses 4 and 35. The remainder of Origen's commentary on the discourse also main-

---

"the simple" follow a lengthy exposition of the "literal sense" in verses 15-24. On those verses he commented:

"But now let us explain the text of the Gospel. We said that the 'abomi-nation of desolation' standing 'in the holy place' is the prince who surrounded Jerusalem with an army. And so, because such terrible things happened to those who were in Judea at that time, therefore the Lord, prophesying these future events, says to the people, 'Let those who are in Judea at that time flee to the mountains.' And the things that happened at that time were so bad that we say that the person who was 'on the roof of the house' would not have had time to descend and 'take anything from his house,' and the one 'who was in the field' would not have been able to return to the city and 'take his garment.' And there was no time then for mercy, not even for the pregnant, nursing mothers, or their infants. Therefore, he says (*I mean as far as the literal sense goes*): 'Woe to those who are pregnant and to those who are nursing in those days.' And as if speaking to Jews who thought it not lawful on the Sabbath to be active or walk more than a Sabbath day's journey, he says: And pray that your flight not occur in winter or on 'the Sabbath,' but also in 'winter.' And it is related by those who have written a Jewish history about the things that happened at that time, that the people suffered a 'great tribulation such as had never occurred from the beginning of the world up to' the time of Christ. . . . And at that time when the people were experiencing great calamities and the elect in Judea were suffering dangers, many deceivers were saying: 'Behold, Here is the Christ; behold, there.' Jesus, teaching his disciples to watch out for such people, said, 'If at that time someone shall say to you, Behold, here is the Christ; behold there, do not believe them; for false Christs and false prophets will arise and perform great signs and portents. And someone can mention Simon Magus who used to claim to be the great power of God, or anyone like him, who wanted 'to deceive, if possible, the elect.'" Origen, *Matthew*, 606; italics added. Regardless of Origen's attempt to exposit varying levels of meaning across the Olivet Discourse, ultimately, there can be no doubt that he recognized some level of first-century fulfillment in these passages.

tains some sense of historical fulfillment. Following verse 35, historical fulfillment seems to occur in a "final consummation of all things" scenario because no first-century events related to the destruction of Jerusalem are mentioned.[6]

It is the validity of this basic methodology, developed in more detail by later church fathers, that I plan to address within this book. The basic assumptions of this paradigm are as follows: **(1)** Jesus was asked two (or three) questions and **(2)** Jesus answered each question in the order of first to last.

It should be noted from the outset that this book is not primarily exegetical, although elements of exegesis certainly apply. Nor will I be offering my own detailed interpretation of the Olivet Discourse (hereafter referred to as the "OD").[7] The ultimate goal of this study

---

6. Origen's futuristic interpretation of the latter half of Matthew 24 reflects familiarity with ideas proposed by Hippolytus (170—235 CE), who saw everything from Matthew 24:15 onward "as referring to the future time of the Antichrist, and the Parousia which will swiftly follow." Ian Boxall, *Matthew Through the Centuries* (WBBC; Hoboken, NJ: Wiley-Blackwell, 2019), 251-2. Tradition also suggests that Hippolytus was familiar with the works of Irenaeus (130–202 CE), who combined the deceiver figure of Matthew 24:5 and 24:24 with the *second* beast of Revelation (13:13-14) and the "man of lawlessness" in 2 Thessalonians 2:3-4 (Boxall, *Matthew*, 351). Interestingly, both Hippolytus and Irenaeus seem to imagine that those New Testament letters are predicting end-of-the-world events and figures to arise *in each of their own futures,* and not in first-century figures.

7. I will be using "OD" throughout this book as shorthand to describe Matthew's *fifth* discourse in its entirety, as well as Luke 21 and Mark 13 respectively. Some scholars prefer to limit Jesus' "OD" to a so-called Eschatological Discourse in Matthew 24-25, thereby separating Jesus' location within the temple in Matthew 23 from eschatology proper. For reasons that will become clear in later chapters [see **2.1.1, 2.1.2, 2.1.2 (b), 2.2, 4.1.5**], labeling Matthew 24-25 as a separate "eschatological" discourse is unhelpful for understanding Matthew's literary purpose. My reason for using "OD" consistently as shorthand for one discourse (instead of "ED" for "Eschatological Discourse") has less to do with technicalities of where Jesus is located at every moment of his discourse and more to do with each author's literary design for the discourse itself. This approach is adequate when Matthew's version is compared with Luke's version. Luke 20:1

is to address the *historical* anomaly of this interpretive methodology and its influence upon later generations. In doing so, I will need to compare historical interpretations of this notable methodology with the literary structure offered to us in Matthew's Gospel, which clarifies the order in which Jesus answers each question. By comparing historical interpretations with Matthew's literary structure, we will address one elephant in the room throughout the ages: Did Jesus answer these questions sequentially or chronologically, as many Christians throughout the ages have assumed? If Matthew's version of the OD clearly arranges the sequence or chronology of the OD differently than historical assumptions that began with early church fathers, how might Christian eschatological explications require reformulation today?

In particular, this investigation will address three chief issues: **(1)** How common has it been for church fathers, theologians, historians, and pastors to interpret the content of Matthew 24:4-35 (and by extension, its parallels in other synoptic gospels) as referring to first-century events and their fulfillment, but interpret the remainder of the Discourse as referring to the *Parousia* and the "end of the world"? **(2)** Does Matthew's version of the OD allow for such theoretical divisions? **(3)** Given the numerous and varied interpretive trends among contemporary scholars,[8] which tend to justify the "de-

---

mentions that Jesus was teaching the people *inside* the temple compounds, and Luke 21:37 says Jesus was teaching in the temple every day and *lodging* on the Mount of Olives at night. Since there are no other indicators of Jesus' location at that time, according to Luke's version the OD appears to be located within the temple, even though no precise location is specifically indicated.

8. Many contemporary scholars assert that the date of Matthew's composition, especially in relation to Mark and Luke, is critical for interpreting the OD "properly." Although this assertion is only one of many interpretive trends, it is considered foundational for most modern academic approaches to the OD. In this book I take no position about the priority or posteriority of Matthew's Gospel. As far as I am concerned, Matthew's Gospel could have been composed after 70 CE, and that would not change the intended meaning or message of Matthew's version of the OD. My justification for this will become considerably evident by **2.1.2 (c)** and elucidated even further in **4.1**, **4.1.8**, and the **con-**

lay" of Christ's Parousia, have they, too, overlooked what Matthew's

---

clusion. Two excellent resources supporting the priority of Matthew's Gospel are B. C. Butler, *The Originality of Matthew: A Critique of the Two-Document Hypothesis* (1951, repr., Cambridge, UK: Cambridge University Press, 2011) and John Wenham, *Redating Matthew, Mark & Luke* (Downers Grove, IL: Intervarsity Press, 1992). For many reasonable arguments *against* the priority of Mark's Gospel, which is a position utilized to advocate a late date for Matthew's composition, I have found three works to be thorough and helpful, with limited reservations: David B. Peabody, Lamar Cope, and Allan J. McNicol, eds., *One Gospel from Two: Mark's use of Matthew and Luke* (Harrisburg, PA: Trinity Press International, 2002); Hans-Herbert Stoldt, trans. Donald L. Niewyk, *History and Criticism of the Markan Hypothesis* (Macon, GA: Mercer University Press, 1980); George Wesley Buchanan, *The Gospel of Matthew, Volumes 1-2*, Mellen Biblical Commentary New Testament (Eugene, OR: Wipf & Stock Publishers, 2006 reprint). For reasonable, but highly technical arguments in favor of Matthean *posteriority*, I consider MacEwen's work to be the most concise, although it assumes great familiarity with numerous overlapping discussions within contemporary Synoptic studies. On that, see Robert K. MacEwen, *Matthean Posteriority: An Exploration of Matthew's Use of Mark and Luke as a Solution to the Synoptic Problem* (New York: Bloomsbury T&T Clark, 2016). Steve Mason and Tom Robinson also provide a constructive overview of the so-called "Synoptic problem," arguing favorably for a post-70 CE composition of Matthew as the simplest solution. On that, see Steve Mason and Tom Robinson, *Early Christian Reader: Christian texts from the first and second centuries in contemporary English translations including the New Revised Standard Version of the New Testament* (Atlanta, GA: Society of Biblical Literature, 2013), 243-82. Robert Gundry's technical essay on Luke's use of Matthew is another beneficial resource for appreciating disputes about Matthean posteriority. On that early essay, see Robert H. Gundry, "Matthean Foreign Bodies in Agreements of Luke with Matthew Against Mark: Evidence that Luke used Matthew," in *The Four Gospels: Festschrift Frans Neirynck*, BETL, C, ed. F. Van Segbroeck, C.M. Tuckett, G. Van Belle, and J. Verheyden (Leuven, Belgium, Leuven University Press, 1992), 1467-95. David Sim also offers a helpful sampling of evidence in favor of Matthean posteriority. On that, see David C. Sim, *The Gospel of Matthew and Formative Judaism: The History and Social Setting of the Matthean Community*, SNTIW Series (Edinburgh, Scotland: T&T Clark LTD, 1998), 31-40. For some scrupulous insights navigating between views of Matthean priority and posteriority, see John A.T. Robinson, *Redating the New Testament* (1976, repr., Eugene, OR: Wipf & Stock, 2000). Finally, one valuable and practical resource for assessing the date of Matthew's composition, placing it between 45-59 CE, is Jonathan Bernier's

literary structure has made clear?

Admittedly, this is an ambitious project, but I hope to show that both ancient and modern Christian traditions have overlooked an obvious alternative methodology. As a result, some significant speculations permeating through purported eschatological dogmas may need to be reevaluated in light of what has been overlooked. That way, Matthew's Gospel may be re-encountered as a reliable and relevant artifact of apostolic tradition.

This study proceeds in four parts, each one building on the previous. In chapter one we will consider how various church fathers interpreted first-century fulfillment contained in Matthew 24 and observe the common methodology they utilized in transitioning between first-century fulfillment and future, end-of-the-world fulfillment. This will also include a survey of highly influential church fathers who seem to be aware of, and in significant ways agree with, this methodology.[9]

---

detailed investigation, *Rethinking the Dates of the New Testament: Evidence for Early Composition* (Grand Rapids, MI: Baker Academic, 2022).

9. Because this book focuses heavily upon the *methodology* utilized or underscored throughout Christian tradition, the citations of various church fathers that I will be presenting in chapter one will have to be limited. For the sake of brevity, I will not include direct citations from Eusebius of Caesarea, whose remarks about biblical prophecy connected with the destruction of Jerusalem and the events leading up to it are so numerous and extensive that an entire research project could be written about that subject. Eusebius is also referenced many times in the comments of many church fathers and theologians whom I will be citing throughout this book, thereby showing familiarity with his views. For the works of Eusebius in which such interpretations are presented extensively, see Eusebius, *The Proof of the Gospel: Being the Demonstratio Evangelica of Eusebius of Cæsarea*, vol. 1, Society for Promoting Christian Knowledge, ed. W. J. Sparrow-Simpson and W. K. L. Clark, trans. W. J. Ferrar (London: Macmillan Co., 1920); Eusebius, *The Ecclesiastical History: English Translation*, vol. 1, LCL, no. 153, ed. T. E. Page, E. Capps, W. H. D. Rouse, L. A. Post, and E. H. Warmington, trans. Kirsopp Lake (London: William Heinemann; New York: G. P. Putnam's Sons; Cambridge, MA: Harvard University Press, 1974); Eusebius,

This will set the stage for chapter two, which will trek through the literary themes and structure of Matthew's Gospel, perusing for clues related to Matthew's intended design for interpreting the OD. Chapter two will end with special attention to why the OD occurs as Jesus' *fifth* discourse in Matthew's Gospel. Chapter two will also inevitably address the question of whether the final version of Matthew's fifth discourse shows any literary intentionality of transitioning from first-century events to "end-of-the-world" events.

The third part will attempt to illustrate the reception of the methodology discovered in chapter one, picking up where its historical timeline finished, and then spanning all the way into the nineteenth century. The third part will also manifest a conspicuous handful of important Christian scholars who expounded upon the literary intentionality proposed in chapter two.

In the fourth part we will take a cursory glance across the broad landscape of modern scholarship and contemporary explications of the OD, beginning in the nineteenth century and working our way up into the present, while noting either **(1)** their skeptical reactions to the more traditional methodology of the church fathers, or **(2)** their adoption or adaptation of it.

Bracketing this entire project, I will conclude with some comparative remarks about the unity and cogency of my thesis, focusing especially upon the continued importance of Matthew's Gospel for appreciating and adjusting traditional eschatological expectations.[10]

The Theophany or Divine Manifestation of our Lord and Savior Jesus Christ, trans. Samuel Lee (London: University Press at Cambridge, 1843).

10. I also will not be offering an analysis of New Testament *Apocrypha* or *Pseudepigrapha*, even though many of them clearly contain "apocalyptic" expectations related to Jesus' Olivet Discourse, and sometimes appear to quote verbatim from it. Christian apocrypha and pseudepigrapha offer neither a methodology derived from nor a commentary *per se* on the Olivet Discourse, and so will not be pertinent for this study. It should be noted, however, that a few influential works among them did shape some Christian imagination *contrary* to Matthew's literary design. Among the most noteworthy in their embellished interpolations

of statements made within the Olivet Discourse, six appear to have been instrumental in shaping apocalyptic imagination throughout the first millennium: **(1)** *The Apocalypse of Peter* (second century), **(2)** the *Epistula Apostolorum* (second century), **(3)** the *Sibylline Oracles: Book 2* (third century), **(4)** the *Tiburtine Sibyl* (fourth century), **(5)** the *Apocalypse of Thomas* (fifth century), and **(6)** the *Apocryphal Apocalypse of John* (eighth century). Among all those just listed, it is worth pointing out that the earliest among them—the Apocalypse of Peter—was immensely influential, if not foundational for later apocalyptic interpretations. According to Dennis Buchholz, the Greek/Ethiopic Apocalypse of Peter was not only "well known in the early church of the third and fourth centuries," but was also referred to by some church fathers and quoted as authoritative scripture. Dennis Buchholz, *Your Eyes Will Be Opened: A Study of the Greek (Ethiopic) Apocalypse of Peter*, SBL Dissertation Series, no. 97 (Atlanta, GA: Scholars Press, 1988), 17. According to Buchholz, the early evidence suggests that "perhaps the Apocalypse of Peter was so well known that it was unnecessary to name it, as is also often true of the other Scriptures" (Buchholz, 36). The *Muratorian Canon*—the oldest list of the New Testament canon—also includes the Apocalypse of Peter seemingly favorably. Even the fifth-century Palestinian lawyer of Constantinople, Sozomen, who compiled an ecclesiastical history between 439 and 450 CE, pointed out that the *Apocalypse of Peter* had "proved entirely spurious by the ancients" yet was still, unfortunately, "being read in some churches of Palestine even now once each year during the day of preparation on which the people most reverently fast in commemoration of the saving passion" (Buchholz, 40). For more about its early Christian reception, see Buchholz, *Apocalypse of Peter*, 20-81. For texts, translations, and the historical influence of the other five works listed above, see Francis Watson, *An Apostolic Gospel: The "Epistula Apostolorum" in Literary Context*, SNTSMS, 179 (Cambridge, UK: Cambridge University Press, 2020); Milton S. Terry, *The Sibylline Oracles* (New York: Eaton & Mains, 1899); Stephen J. Shoemaker, "The Tiburtine Sibyl: A New Translation and Introduction" in *New Testament Apocrypha: More Noncanonical Scriptures*, vol. 1, ed. Tony Burke and Brent Landau (Grand Rapids, MI: William B. Eerdmans Publishing Company, 2016), 510–25; Bernard McGinn, *Visions of the End: Apocalyptic Traditions in the Middle Ages* (New York: Columbia University Press, 1979), 18-21, 43-50; Rick Brannan, "1 Apocryphal Apocalypse of John: A New Translation and Introduction" in *New Testament Apocrypha: More Noncanonical Scriptures*, vol. 2, ed. Tony Burke (Grand Rapids, MI: William B. Eerdmans Publishing Company, 2020), 378—98; Matthias Geigenfeind, "The Apocalypse of Thomas: A New Translation and Introduction" in *New Testament Apocrypha: More Noncanonical Scriptures*, vol. 2, ed. Tony Burke (Grand Rapids, MI: William B. Eerdmans Publishing Company, 2020), 580–604.

CHAPTER 1

Patristic Methodology and its Reception

1.1 INTRODUCTION

To illustrate the emergence of a striking methodology around the dawn of the fifth century, I will limit its explicit presentation to commentaries of Matthew's Gospel by four scholars of that era. In this chapter I have chosen to begin by focusing upon the writings of St. Hilary of Poitiers (310-367 CE), whose influence spread throughout Gaul; St. Jerome of Stridon (345-420 CE), whose life of study influenced various regions of Asia minor, Syria, Palestine, and northern Egypt; St. John Chrysostom (347-407 CE), whose influence was widespread throughout the Byzantine empire; and finally, the anonymous author of *Opus Imperfectum* (396-450 CE) referred to as Pseudo-Chrysostom, whose commentary on Matthew's Gospel also influenced the surrounding empire for almost a millennium.

1

1.1.1 ST. HILARY OF POITIERS

Beginning with Hilary of Poitiers, the leading apologist of Nicene theology in the fourth century,[1] we find a lengthy exposition of the OD in which his audience is presented with the order of the disciples' questions along with the order of Jesus' answer to such questions. Hilary wrote:

> "And as He was walking away from the Temple, his disciples approached and beckoned him to look at the structure of the Temple." After threatening that Jerusalem would be forsaken, he is shown the grandeur of the Temple's stature, as if it were necessary to stir him by its splendor. . . . Once the Lord had withdrawn to the mountain, his disciples came and asked him privately when this would happen [to the Temple] and by what sign they would recognize his coming and about the end of the age.
>
> *Here we have three questions* in one [setting], separated by chronology and distinguished by the [degree of] significance in their meaning. *The Lord answers the first question concerning the destruction of the city* [Jerusalem], an event confirmed by the truth of his teaching so that they should not be deceived by an imposter because of their ignorance. For there would come, even in the disciples' day, imposters who would claim they were the Christ. He therefore warns them that the faith could be undermined by a pernicious lie. In fact, it happened that Simon the Samaritan, bolstered with diabolical works and words, led many astray by his miracles.

---

1. John Anthony McGuckin, *The Path of Christianity: The First Thousand Years* (Downers Grove, IL: IVP Academic, 2017), 432.

2

> *And because this happened during the time of the apostles*, the Lord said, *the end is not yet.*[2]

Following this, Hilary makes numerous remarks about those disciples of Christ in the first century who had endured suffering, famine, scourging, public hatred, and death as "apostolic men are scattered throughout all parts of the world."[3] "All of this," Hilary remarks, "*happened in Jerusalem, just as it had been foretold*; the city was consumed—ruined by her stoning, by her expulsions, by her murder of the apostles, by her hunger, by war, and by her captivity."[4] Surprisingly, though, Hilary suddenly slips into a futuristic application for his own audience once he comes across Matthew's reference to the "abomination of desolation" in 24:15. There he writes:

> Then there follows a sign of his future advent. When they see the abomination of desolation standing in the holy place, we should understand his glorious return. Concerning this matter, I think that our comment is superfluous given the teaching of the most blessed Daniel and Paul. That which is spoken by each writer concerns the times of the Antichrist. . . . Because the Antichrist was received by the Jews, he will stand in the holy place, where God used to be invoked.[5]

At this point in the discourse Hilary has chosen to interpret a revival of the Jews in Jerusalem at some future point in history. Hilary then continues expositing Jesus' words as though the remainder of the OD applied directly to him and his own audience, exhorting *them* to do

---

2. Hilary of Poitiers, *Commentary on Matthew*, TFC, vol. 125, trans. D. H. Williams (Washington, D.C: The Catholic University of America Press, 2012), 248-9. The words in brackets are original. Italics added.

3. Hilary, *Matthew*, 249.

4. Hilary, *Matthew*, 249. Italics added.

5. Hilary, *Matthew*, 250.

what Jesus warned about. For example, when seemingly first-century references are made to Judeans[6] in Jesus' generation (Matt. 24:16-20), Hilary says that *"we* are urged to pray that *our* flight be neither in the winter nor on the Sabbath. That is, *we* should not be found in the coldness of *our* sins or indifferent to good works."[7]

This is not the last time Hilary would attempt to apply the remaining remarks of the discourse to his own audience. He also says that in Christ's future advent,

> he will be present everywhere and in the sight of everyone just as lightning, coming from the east, spreads its light towards the west. As it flashes from any one place it is seen everywhere. Lest *we remain ignorant* of the place of his coming, he says, "Wherever there is a body, there the eagles will gather." He calls the saints "eagles" from the spiritual flight of their bodies. . . . There *we will rightly wait* for the brightness of his advent, where he wrought for us eternal glory.[8]

---

6. I agree with Anthony Saldarini, who argues that the generic word for "Jews" is better understood across the New Testament in more nuanced terminology, such as Jewish leaders, Judeans, or specific groups within Judaism. On that, see Anthony J. Saldarini, "Reading Matthew without Anti-Semitism," in *The Gospel of Matthew in Current Study: Studies in Memory of William G. Thompson, S.J.*, ed. David E. Aune (Grand Rapids, MI: William B. Eerdmans Publishing Company, 2001), 166-84. Jason A. Staples, *The Idea of Israel in Second Temple Judaism: A New Theory of People, Exile, and Israelite Identity* (Cambridge, UK: Cambridge University Press, 2021), also offers a thorough historical and sociological reconstruction of the ancient data pertaining to three terms: "Jews," "Hebrews," and "Israelites." He concludes that "the evidence is overwhelming that the three terms and the concepts they represent are neither synonymous nor coextensive in the Second Temple period, with each having its own specific nuance, overlapping with but not identical to the meaning of the others" (Staples, 339).

7. Hilary, *Matthew*, 252. Italics added.

8. Hilary, *Matthew*, 253. Italics added.

Beginning with such subtle shifts of interpretation in Matthew 24:15, it is no surprise to learn that Hilary interpreted the tribulation and cosmic imagery that follows as indicating Christ's "glorious advent and majestic return."[9] Indeed, Hilary remains so convinced of this interpretation that he even interprets verse 34 as applicable to his own generation, saying:

> In order that there would be complete assurance about these future events, and by saying *Amen* in declaring the truth, the Lord adds that *our generation* will not pass away until every one of these things has happened.[10]

In summary, it is clear that Hilary interpreted Jesus' answer to the disciples first question ("When will these things be?") as being largely fulfilled in first-century events leading up to the destruction of Jerusalem in 70 CE. Jesus' answer to that *first* question is contained in the *first* remarks of Matthew 24, within verses 4–14. Everything contained in verses 15 and following refer to Christ's *future* advent—during or beyond Hilary's own generation—and the events surrounding it.

1.1.2 ST. JEROME

Jerome was one of the most important biblical scholars of the early Western church.[11] In his commentary on Matthew's Gospel, St. Jerome writes about the questions Jesus is asked upon the Mount

---

9. Hilary, *Matthew*, 254.

10. Hilary, *Matthew*, 255. Italics of "our generation" added for emphasis.

11. McGuckin, *The Path of Christianity*, 456. McGuckin also notes that Jerome was a "devoted Origenian scholar" for many years before officially denouncing Origen, and that even after Jerome began denouncing Origen he continued "to use vast amounts of unacknowledged exegetical material from Origen." On this, see McGuckin, *The Path of Christianity*, 457-8.

of Olives and the way in which each question should be interpreted. He says:

> *Now as he was sitting on the Mount of Olives, the disciples came to him privately, saying: "Tell us, when will these things be and what will be the sign of your coming and of the consummation of the world?"*
>
> He is sitting on the Mount of Olives where the true light of knowledge was rising. The disciples come to him privately. They were longing to know mysteries and revelation about the future. *And they ask three questions: At what time is Jerusalem to be destroyed,* when is Christ going to come, and when is the consummation of the world going to happen?[12]

Here we find another clear reference to the disciples asking three questions but with the *first* question being interpreted as the time when Jerusalem was to be destroyed in the first century. Jerome takes a slightly different approach than Hilary with regard to a transition between Jerusalem's destruction in 70 CE and Christ's future advent. All the way up through Matthew 24:25, Jerome regularly makes remarks about the possibility of first-century fulfillment. For example, when referring to the abomination of desolation standing in the holy place, he says that "this can be interpreted either literally of the Antichrist, or of the image of Caesar that Pilate placed in the temple, or of the equestrian statue of Hadrian, which stands to the present day in the very location of the holy of holies."[13] Commenting on verses 19 and 20, his conjecture goes even further:

---

12. Jerome, *Commentary on Matthew*, TFC, vol. 117, trans. Thomas P. Scheck (Washington, D.C.: The Catholic University of America Press, 2008), 269. Italics added.

13. Jerome, *Matthew*, 272.

6

"And woe to pregnant women and nursing mothers in those days".... This can also be explained in the following manner. During the persecution of the Antichrist *or of the Roman captivity*, pregnant women and nursing mothers, being weighed down by the burden in their womb or of their children, will be unable to escape very easily.

"Pray that your flight may not be in winter or on a sabbath." *If we want to take this of the captivity of Jerusalem when it was captured by Titus and Vespasian, the meaning is that they should pray that their flight will not be in winter or on a sabbath.* For in the former season, the harshness of the cold hinders from traveling in the wastelands and hiding in the mountains and deserts. On the sabbath either it is a transgression of the Law if they wanted to escape, or there would be imminent death if they remain. But if it is understood of the consummation of the world, he is commanding that our faith in and love for Christ not grow cold, and that on the sabbath of the virtues we may not grow torpid and lazy in the work of God.[14]

Jerome continues this blend of first-century fulfillment and future fulfillment all the way up through verses 23–25, where he says that Jesus' prophecy referred to "the time of the Judaic captivity" when "the Romans were conducting their siege."[15] Nevertheless, immediately after these final remarks about first-century fulfillment, Jerome opines frankly: "But it is understood *better* of the consummation of the world."[16]

In summary, it is clear that Jerome, much like Hilary, interpreted Jesus' answer to the disciples' first question ("When will these

14. Jerome, *Matthew*, 273. Italics added.

15. Jerome, *Matthew*, 274.

16. Jerome, *Matthew*, 274. Italics added.

things be?") as containing fulfillment in first-century events leading up to the destruction of Jerusalem in 70 CE. Likewise, Jesus' answer to that first question is contained within Matthew 24:4-25, which immediately follows the disciples' questions.

The major differences between Jerome and Hilary seem to be that Jerome is *not* willing to commit to any transitional verse in favor of the future consummation of the world. Rather, Jerome blends first-century fulfillment along with contemporary expectations of fulfillment as a possible interpretation of verses 4–25 while maintaining that many of those verses are "better" understood when imagined in relation to the consummation of the world. According to Jerome, everything could *technically* be interpreted as being fulfilled in the future consummation of the world, but the only clear references to first-century fulfillment occur within the first 25 verses of Matthew 24; that is because the disciples asked Jesus three questions, and it was the *first* question about the Roman siege and the destruction of Jerusalem that Jesus answered *first*.

1.1.3 ST. JOHN CHRYSOSTOM

Chrysostom was the Archbishop of Constantinople and one of the most voluminous expositors of Christian Scriptures in his era. In a series of sermons on Matthew's Gospel, Chrysostom devotes more attention than any patristic source of his generation, making all kinds of detailed remarks about the fulfillment of the disciples' first question in first-century events.[17] Chrysostom also presents a similar paradigm

---

17. Chrysostom's comments could not be clearer about first-century fulfillment in the passages of 24:4-29, where he says, "And if thou art minded to learn these things more distinctly, I mean, the famines, the pestilences, the earthquakes, the other calamities, peruse the history about these things composed by Josephus, and thou wilt know all accurately." Chrysostom, *Homilies on the Gospel of St. Matthew*, NPNF, vol. 10, ed. Philip Schaff (1888, repr., Peabody, MA: Hendrickson Publishers, Inc., 1999), 453. For the influence of Josephus' works, see the footnotes of **1.1.4** below.

to what Hilary and Jerome suggested about the questions asked of Jesus and the order in which Jesus responded. His comments in that regard are as follows:

> And as He sat upon the mount of Olives, the disciples came unto Him privately, saying, Tell us when shall these things be? And what shall be the sign of Thy coming, and of the end of the world? Therefore did they come unto Him privately, as it was of such matters they meant to inquire. For they were in travail to know the day of His coming, because of their eager desire to behold that glory, which is the cause of countless blessings. And these two things do they ask him, *when shall these things be? that is, the overthrow of the temple*; and, what is the sign of thy coming? But Luke saith (Luke 21: 6.7), the question was one concerning Jerusalem, as though they were supposing that then is His coming. And Mark saith, that neither did all of them ask concerning the end of Jerusalem, but Peter and John, as having greater freedom of speech.[18]

After multiple pages in which he makes clear that the eventual overthrow of Herod's temple is in view and that the "wars" and tumults mentioned are "surely not" those outside of what brought the Roman siege upon Jerusalem,[19] he insists that only verses 4 through

---

18. Chrysostom, *Matthew*, 450. Italics added.

19. Chrysostom also noted parallels between Matthew's OD and statements in the apostle Paul's writings: "Therefore He added moreover, 'And this gospel shall be preached in the whole world for a witness to all nations, and then shall the end come,' of the downfall of Jerusalem. For in proof that He meant this, and that before the taking of Jerusalem the gospel was preached, hear what Paul saith, 'Their sound went into all the earth;' and again, 'The gospel which was preached to every creature which is under Heaven.' And seest thou him running from Jerusalem unto Spain? And if one took so large a portion, consider what the rest also wrought. For writing to others also, Paul again saith concerning the gospel, that 'it is bringing forth fruit, and growing up in every creature which is

28 find their fulfillment in first-century events. There, in verse 29, he transitions away from first-century fulfillment: *"Having finished what concerned Jerusalem, He passes on to His own coming, and tells the signs of it, not for their use only, but for us also, and for all that shall come after us."*[20]

Most notably for our purposes, then, is Chrysostom's interpretation of the order in which Jesus responds to his disciples' questions. Jesus' initial response is to their *first* question. The events leading up to the "overthrow of the temple" are answered by Jesus *first*, in verses 4–28. The events surrounding the "second coming" and "end" of the world follow after Jesus' *first* response to his disciples' *first* question.

1.1.4 OPUS IMPERFECTUM

Around that same general time in which Jerome, Hilary, and Chrysostom influenced Christians with their teaching, an *anonymous* commentary on the Gospel of Matthew became highly influential and was promulgated widely as a composition of St. Chrysostom throughout the latter half of the first millennia CE, thereby "exerting a signif-

---

under Heaven.' But what meaneth, 'For a witness to all nations?' Forasmuch as though it was everywhere preached, yet it was not everywhere believed. It was for a witness, He saith, to them that were disbelieving, that is, for conviction, for accusation, for a testimony; for they that believed will bear witness against them that believed not, and will condemn them. And for this cause, after the gospel is preached in every part of the world, Jerusalem is destroyed, that they may not have so much as a shadow of an excuse for their perverseness. For they that saw His power shine throughout every place, and in an instant take the world captive, what excuse could they then have for continuing in the same perverseness? For in proof that it was everywhere preached at that time, hear what Paul saith, 'of the gospel which was preached to every creature which is under Heaven.' Which also is a very great sign of Christ's power, that in twenty or at most thirty years the word had reached the ends of the world. 'After this therefore,' saith He, 'shall come the end of Jerusalem'" (Chrysostom, *Matthew*, 452).

20. Chrysostom, *Matthew*, 458. Italics added.

icant influence on many medieval gospel commentaries."[21] This commentary on Matthew is known today as the *Opus imperfectum,* whose author is now referred to by scholars as Pseudo-Chrystostom due to its false attribution to St. Chrysostom. In it the anonymous exegete comments on these very questions addressed to Jesus in Matthew 24:

> As he sat on the Mount of Olives, the disciples came to him privately, saying, "Tell us, when will this be, and what will be the sign of your coming and of the close of the age?" *That is, when will these things be so that stone will not remain on stone, as you say?* And they add also another item to their questions, namely, to indicate to them even the end of the age, which Christ had not mentioned. *But they ask that first question of their own accord and for their own sake,* but they ask the second question at our prompting and for our sake. . . .
>
> I think that this ought not to be overlooked so that we consider what the apostles asked and so understood better what Christ answered. For the apostles asked these two things: "What is the sign of the destruction of Jerusalem?" and "What is the sign of the end of the world?"[22]

Beginning with commentary on Matthew 24:4 and continuing through verse 20, Pseudo-Chrysostom continually makes references to first-century events being fulfilled within the first century, as well as over twenty *direct* references to the destruction of Jerusalem in 70 CE. All of these references are determined according to other New Testament passages and historical records outside of the Bible, such as

---

21. Kevin Madigan, *Olivi and the Interpretation of Matthew in the High Middle Ages* (Notre Dame, Indiana: University of Notre Dame Press, 2003), 177n56.

22. James A. Kellerman, trans., *Incomplete Commentary on Matthew,* Opus imperfectum, ACT, vol. 2 (Downers Grove, IL: IVP Academic, 2010), 372. Italics added.

Josephus' account of the first-century *Jewish Wars*,[23] which was written

---

23. As will be seen in later chapters (especially **Chapter 3**), Josephus' *Jewish Wars* is frequently referenced by commentators according to its Latin title, *Bellum Judaicum*. For a highly accessible, modernized English version of this work, see Bob Beasley, *Flavius Josephus: The Jewish Wars* (Hartville: OH, Living Stone Books, 2015). For a concise account and classic translation of the portion pertaining to Jerusalem's destruction, see Josephus, *The Fall of Jerusalem*, trans., G. A. Williamson (London: Penguin Group, 2006). For a succinct application of Josephus' *Jewish Wars* to the Olivet Discourse and other Scriptures, see George Peter Holford, *The Destruction of Jerusalem: An Absolute Irresistible Proof of the Divine Origin of Christianity*, 6th ed. (1814, repr., Nacogdoches, TX: Covenant Media Press, 2001) and John L. Bray, *Matthew 24 Fulfilled*, 5th ed. (Powder Springs, GA: American Vision Press, 2008).

The influence and importance of Josephus' works cannot be overstated. His account of first-century events leading up to the destruction of Jerusalem was so influential in the early Christian church that book six of Josephus' *Jewish Wars*, which describes Jerusalem's actual destruction and a brief account of its aftermath, became included in the oldest, complete Old Testament canon of the Syriac Church (seventh century CE, *Codex Ambrosianus 7al*), where it takes the place of the Old Testament's *last* book. For more information about *Codex Ambrosianus 7al*, see Edmund L Gallagher and John D. Meade, *The Biblical Canon Lists from Early Christianity: Texts and Analysis* (Oxford, UK: Oxford University Press, 2017), 242-254. S.G.F. Brandon explains how vital the destruction of Jerusalem was for "apostolic times" of Christ-followers to blossom and flourish into *Christianity*. Having argued extensively for the significance of Alexandrian Christianity's influence in early Christian history with regard to Christianity moving beyond various Judaisms of that era, he begins by addressing the near-complete silence of early Christian tradition about the origins of faith in Alexandria, and then concludes: "Our picture of the evolution of Christianity in apostolic times is almost completely derived from the narrative of the Acts. But this is demonstrably an *ex parte* statement, and when we remember that the New Testament bears witness to many other interpretations of the Christ, or that the beginnings of the Church at Rome are almost equally obscure, we see that this silence is not really serious. The most crucial factor of all, however, is undoubtedly the destruction of Jerusalem in A.D. 70. This tremendous event, the effect of which has been so curiously ignored by New Testament scholars, produced a situation which really caused Christianity to be reborn." S.G.F. Brandon, *The Fall of Jerusalem and the Christian Church: A Study of the Effects of the Jewish Overthrow of A.D. 70 on Christianity*, 2nd ed. (1951, repr., Eugene, OR: Wipf & Stock, 2010), 243.

within the decade of the Temple's demise.[24] Nevertheless, he points out that it is not clear "which signs pertain to the destruction of Jerusalem and which to the end of the world." His reason for such a disclaimer is because "the Lord does not say [which] distinctly."[25] Consequently, following verse 20, all remarks to first-century fulfillment become finalized and he begins his transition toward interpretations about the "end of the world" thereafter.

1.2 THE TRAJECTORY OF THIS INFLUENTIAL PARADIGM

My point here is not to debate possible interpretations. I simply wish to highlight that there was certainly a common and widespread methodology emerging around the dawn of the fifth century that included first-century fulfillment in response to the disciples' first question, "When will these things be?" That is to say, Jesus answered his disciple's *first* question *first*, and the remaining parts of their questions are answered in succession. Jesus answered the second question (about the sign of his *Parousia*) second, followed by answers to the third question (about "the end") last.

Since the focus of this book is upon the way in which the OD *transitions* from first-century fulfillment to doctrines of futuristic, end-of-the-world fulfillment beyond even our own lifetime, it will be helpful to recognize how common this view evidently remained for centuries. However, because lengthy commentaries on the Gospel of Matthew are relatively scarce over the first thousand years of Christendom, it will be necessary to incorporate comments from various Church fathers in relation to the OD generally.[26] This will necessar-

---

24. Jonathan Klawans, *Josephus and the Theologies of Ancient Judaism* (New York, NY: Oxford University Press, 2012), 18; David M. Jacobson, *Agrippa II: The Last of the Herods*, RABS (2019, repr., New York: Routledge, 2021), 7.

25. Kellerman, *Opus imperfectum*, 372-73.

26. Lactantius (250–325 CE), who I will not be listing in the pages that follow, is a good example of an early church father, theologian, and historian who mere-

ily entail commentary about passages in Mark and Luke that share

ly touched upon statements from the OD, and without much clarification. He deserves mention due to being a contemporary of Eusebius of Caesarea who, likewise, showed extraordinary familiarity with the New Testament scriptures, the works of Josephus, and first-century history in general. Although Lactantius provided no formal commentary on Matthew's Gospel, he did make some historical remarks that clearly echo the interpretation of Eusebius in connection with Josephus' *Jewish Wars* and the destruction of Jerusalem: "[Jesus] also made known to them all that would take place. Peter and Paul preached these things at Rome, and that preaching has remained in writing unto their memory. In this they have told both many other marvels and that this also would take place, that after a short time God would send a king who would attack the Jews and raze their cities to the ground and lay siege to them after they had been consumed with hunger and thirst. Then it would happen that they would feed on their own bodies and consume one another, and, at length captured, they would come into the hands of the enemy. And before their very eyes they would behold their wives most bitterly attacked, virgins violated and prostituted, boys snatched up, little ones torn from them and marred, and everything finally destroyed by fire and sword, the captives being taken away from their land forever. This, because they have exulted over the most loving and most noble son of God. And so, after their death, when Nero had dispatched them, Vespasian brought to nought the name and race of the Jews, and he did all the things which those who had foretold would come to pass." Lactantius, *The Divine Institutes*, TFC, Books I-VII, trans. Sister Mary Francis McDonald, O.P. (Washington, D.C.: The Catholic University of America Press, 1964), 301.

Another notable exegete worth mentioning briefly is Ephrem the Syrian (306-373), who wrote a commentary on Tatian's *Harmony of the Gospels*. In the section that immediately follows the "woes" indicting scribes and Pharisees (Matt. 23:13-39; cf. Luke 11:37-53), St. Ephrem addresses the question of "When you will see the sign of its terrible destruction?" Although the question of a "sign" alludes to a unity of all three questions asked in Matthew 24:3, Ephrem begins his commentary of this section with explicit reference to Matthew 24:15 (cf. Luke 21:20) and Daniel's "prophecy" therein, saying, "Jerusalem was destroyed many times and then rebuilt, but here it is a question of its [total] upheaval and destruction and the profanation of its sanctuary, after which it will remain in ruins and fall into oblivion. The Romans placed standards representing an eagle within this temple just as [the prophet] had said, *On the wings of impurity and ruination. The sign of its terrible destruction, foretold by the prophet Daniel.* Some say that the sign of its destruction was the pig's head which the Romans gave Pilate to carry into the interior of the temple to place there. [The Lord] also said, *The one who stands on the housetop* [Matt. 24:17; cf. Luke 17:31], for they

nearly identical sayings of Jesus in Matthew's version. It will also be helpful to include influential church fathers prior to the fifth century who shared similar views, even though their remarks are not explicitly about a transition from first-century fulfillment to later events in world history.

One assumption I will be making along the way, which seems indisputable, is that these Christian theologians throughout the centuries were aware of the synoptic gospels[27] and parallel passages between them.[28] Therefore, many of their remarks about Luke's or

---

were not to escape in the usual way, since the concern of [God's] solicitude was not over them. He also said, *Woe to those who will be with child* [Matt. 24:19; cf. Luke 21:23]. [He was speaking] of those who were tortured during the siege of Jerusalem by the Romans. *There will be distress for this people* [Luke 21:23], he said, such that women will eat their children. [...] *If God had not shortened these days, no human being would have been saved* [Matt. 24:22; cf. Mark 13:20]. It was not the number of days or hours that was shortened, but time itself was lessened, *for the sake of the elect* [Matt. 24:22; cf. Mark 13:20], in order that their tribulations would not be multiplied, but rather shortened, so that redemption might reach them." Ephrem the Syrian, *Saint Ephrem's Commentary on Tatian's Diatessaron: An English Translation of Chester Beatty Syriac MS 709 with Introduction and Notes*, JSSS, no. 2, trans., Carmel McCarthy (1993, repr., Oxford, UK: Oxford university Press, 2000), 276-8. Interestingly, when Ephrem arrives at the section of Tatian's *Harmony* that parallels Matthew 24:32-25:30, he transitions into end-of-the-world speculations beyond 70 CE and offers only one brief reference to Jerusalem's destruction in the verses that parallel Matthew 24:40-41 and Luke 17:34-35 (Ephrem, 280).

27. The "Synoptic Gospels" refer to Matthew, Mark, and Luke. The adjective "synoptic" (συνοπτικός) refers to the similarities which can be seen (ὀπτικός, "optical") together (συν, "with") among these three gospels.

28. Increased awareness and focused attention to parallel passages between the Synoptic Gospels began in the fourth century with Eusebius of Caesarea's invention of the *Gospel Apparatus*. Jeremiah Coogan's research in this regard is profoundly important for appreciating the influence of Eusebius' invention. He writes, "Devised by Eusebius of Caesarea (ca. 260-339/340 CE) in the fourth century, the Eusebian apparatus became a standard feature of the Gospel manuscripts and transformed subsequent Gospel reading. While it originated in Greek, the apparatus accompanied the Gospels into many other languages. It circulated in Latin, Gothic, Syriac, Ethiopic, Armenian, Coptic, Georgian, Sla-

Mark's OD will be considered relevant for understanding their interpretation of Matthew's OD. Another factor which I will be taking for granted, which needs no further explanation, is that in addition to first-century events being prophesied *somewhere* in the OD, all of the theologians cited below believed that Jesus *also* prophesied about his coming at the "end" of the world.

I hope all of this historical evidence below will clearly illustrate that many of the earliest church fathers shared at least one view in common with the methodology proposed above: Jesus prophesied about first-century events and the catastrophic destruction of Jeru-

---

vonic, Arabic, even Caucasian Albanian. For well over a millennium, the vast majority of people who encountered a Gospel manuscript encountered the Gospels in their Eusebian form." Jeremiah Coogan, *Eusebius the Evangelist: Rewriting the Fourfold Gospel in Late Antiquity* (New York: Oxford University Press, 2022), 3. Coogan also writes, "Eusebius created the first consistent system for the Gospels. This map of the Gospels is exceptionally precise. . . . Eusebius made it possible to reference and locate specific Gospel passages. This system of textual division exceeds Eusebius' cross-referential objectives. . . . [L]ater readers structured both liturgical reading and commentary using the Eusebian sections. For a wide range of textual practices, the sections became standard reference points like modern chapters and verses" (Coogan, 33). As Coogan illustrates in later chapters of his thesis, the widespread usage of the Eusebian apparatus was almost immediate. For example, even though St. Augustine does not mention his own use of the Eusebian apparatus, he mentions his use of Jerome of Stridon's revised edition of the gospels, which were completed around 384 CE. "This new edition," Coogan says, "transposed the Eusebian apparatus into Latin—although Augustine does not explicitly call attention to that fact. Nonetheless, Augustine's dependence on Eusebius is clear, especially from his repeated recourse to Eusebius' creative juxtapositions" (Coogan, 35). Coogan also notes that St. Bede and Rabanus Maurus (see **1.2.7** and **1.2.9** below) utilized Eusebius' apparatus (Coogan, 127-9). For further research on this topic, including Augustine's use of the Eusebian apparatus, see Matthew R. Crawford, *The Eusebian Canon Tables: Ordering Textual Knowledge in Late Antiquity*, OECS (New York: Oxford University Press, 2019). For a fascinatingly detailed study about systems of organization and division (e.g., paragraphs, chapters, etc.) within gospel manuscripts that predate the Eusebian apparatus, see Charles E. Hill, *The First Chapters: Dividing the Text of Scripture in Codex Vaticanus and its Predecessors* (New York: Oxford University Press, 2022).

salem somewhere within Matthew 24:4-29 or those parts of other Synoptic Gospels which parallel Matthew 24:4-29.

1.2.1 AMBROSE OF MILAN

Commenting on Luke 21:5–8, which parallels Matthew 24:1–5, St. Ambrose, the Archbishop of Milan (374 CE) shows his familiarity with Jesus' predictions about the destruction of Herod's Temple in 70 CE.[29] He writes, "It was spoken then of the temple made with hands, that it should be overthrown."[30] Ambrose also refers to the order presented in Matthew's OD. Whereas Mark and Luke only contain two questions, Matthew's version adds a third question:

> Matthew adds a third question, that both the time of the destruction of the temple, and the sign of His coming, and the end of the world, might be inquired into by the disciples. But our Lord being asked when the destruction of the temple should be, and what the sign of His coming, instructs them as to the signs, but does not mind to inform them as to the time. It follows, 'Take heed that ye be not deceived.'[31]

In these remarks, St. Ambrose recognized that the initial portion of Jesus' response to his disciples' first question pertained, in some sense,

---

29. Commenting on Luke 21:6, Ambrose writes, "Yet there is also another Temple, made from precious stones and adorned with gifts, the ruin of which the Lord seems to proclaim." Ambrose of Milan, *Exposition of the Holy Gospel According to Saint Luke*, 2nd ed., trans. Theodosia Tomkinson (Etna, CA: Center for Traditionalist Orthodox Studies, 2003), 393.

30. Cited in Thomas Aquinas, *Catena Aurea: Commentary on the Four Gospels, Collected out of the Works of the Fathers: St. Luke*, vol. 3, ed. J. H. Newman (Oxford: John Henry Parker, 1843), 675.

31. Aquinas, *Catena: Luke*, 674.

to first-century events.[32] Jesus was asked "when the destruction of the temple should be," and in his remarks paralleling Matthew 24:15, Ambrose sees Jesus commencing with a reply about "the temple then made with hands."

1.2.2 TITUS OF BOSTRA

Commenting on those same verses of Luke's OD which parallel Matthew 24:1–5, Titus, the Bishop of Bostra (363 CE), clearly implies that he, too, was aware of other theologians who interpreted Luke 21:5–8 as having first-century fulfillment. He wrote, "perhaps He [i.e., Jesus] does not speak of false Christs coming before the end of the world, but of those who existed in the Apostles' time."[33]

Titus recognized that first-century apostles existed alongside "false Christs." This explanation is also set in contrast with "false Christs" near the "end of the world."

---

32. Although Ambrose's commentary on Luke's version of the OD is focused mainly on contemporary application, he intersperses references from Matthew's OD along the way, thereby illustrating a clear connection between each version. For example, commenting on Luke 21:8-20, Ambrose inserts a reference from Matthew 24:14 about preaching the gospel to the whole world, which, in his mind, began in "the cities of Judaea" and advancing through "the Goths and the Armenians," and even into his own context of empire (Ambrose, *Luke*, 396). In doing so, he seems to view first-century events as merely the beginning of prophetic fulfillment that leads into his own generation at "the end" of the age, for he adds that "we are at the end of the age" (Ambrose, *Luke*, 395). Regardless of how Ambrose envisioned the OD to apply to his own generation, his commentary is speckled with occasional first-century references, such as Luke 21:20, in which he says, "Truly, Jerusalem was besieged and taken by the Roman army" (Ambrose, *Luke*, 397). In his interpretation of this passage, he also brings "the desolation of abomination" from Matthew 24:15 into the picture, likening it to the "Devil . . . in the midst of the Temple," who is the "Antichrist." This antichrist is further likened to "Arius or Sebellius" who are "beguiled" like "the Jews who denied the True Christ" (Ambrose, *Luke*, 398).

33. Aquinas, *Catena: Luke*, 675.

1.2.3 CYRIL OF ALEXANDRIA

Commenting upon Luke 21:9–19, which parallels Jesus' remarks in Matthew 24:6, 7, and 29 (and also Matt. 10:17–18), Cyril of Alexandria (376–444 CE) shows that he, too, was well aware that the New Testament scriptures addressed the Jewish wars and persecutions which culminated in the destruction of Jerusalem in 70 CE:

> He says this, because before that Jerusalem should be taken by the Romans, the disciples, having suffered persecution from the Jews, were imprisoned and brought before rulers; Paul was sent to Rome to Caesar, and stood before Festus and Agrippa.[34]

Luke 21:9–19 mentions nations and kingdoms opposing each other, wars and tumults, great earthquakes, famine, signs from heaven, persecutions, deliverance of Christians to authorities in synagogues, and even their summons before kings and governors, some of whom would receive confinement in prison. Parents, brothers, relatives, and friends will even seek out reasons to put their Christian neighbors to death. Yet Cyril assigns to these descriptions offered by Jesus a place of first-century fulfillment.

1.2.4 ST. AUGUSTINE

Commenting on Luke 21:20–24 and its clear parallels with Matt. 24:15–21, St Augustine (354–430 CE) wrote:

> These words of our Lord, Luke has here related to show, that the abomination of desolation which was prophesied by Daniel, and of which Matthew and Mark had spoken, *was*

---

34. Aquinas, *Catena: Luke,* 678.

fulfilled at the siege of Jerusalem. . . . But where Matthew and Mark have written, *Neither let him which is in the field return back to take his clothes,* Luke adds more clearly, *And let not them that are in the countries enter thereinto, for these be the days of vengeance, that all the things which are written may be fulfilled.* . . . Then Luke follows in words similar to those of the other two; *But woe to them that are with child, and them that give suck in those days;* and thus has made plain what might otherwise have been doubtful, namely, that what was said of the abomination of desolation belonged not to the end of the world, but the taking of Jerusalem.[35]

Augustine states this again in his comments about the OD in Mark 13:14–20:

But Luke, in order to show that *the abomination of desolation happened when Jerusalem was taken,* in this same place, gives the words of our Lord, *And when ye shall see Jerusalem compassed with armies, then know that the desolation thereof is nigh.* It goes on: *Then let them that be in Judaea flee to the mountains.* . . . For Josephus, who has written the history of the Jews, relates that such things were suffered by this people.[36]

It is evident that Augustine viewed the siege of Jerusalem as fulfilling prophecy that Matthew and Luke elaborated. In those passages of Luke which parallel Matthew's version of the OD, first-century fulfillment took place where Jesus seemed to respond to his disciples' first question.

---

35. Aquinas, *Catena: Luke,* 681-82. See bibliography.

36. Cited in Thomas Aquinas, *Catena Aurea: Commentary on the Four Gospels, Collected out of the Works of the Fathers: St. Mark,* vol. 2, ed. J. H. Newman (Oxford: John Henry Parker, 1843), 260-61.

1.2.5 PAULUS OROSIUS

Paulus Orosius (375–418 CE) was a Catholic priest, historian, and theologian, as well as a close friend and student of St. Augustine. Among his works he composed a seven-volume history of important events in life of the Christian church. In one of his works, he quotes Luke 21:9–12, which parallels Matthew 24:6–9. Orosius wrote:

> But when at that time the city of Jerusalem had been captured and overthrown, as the prophets foretold, and after the complete destruction of the Jewish people, Titus, who had been ordained by the judgment of God to avenge the blood of our Lord Jesus Christ, as victor, holding a triumph with his father, Vespasian, closed the temple of Janus. Thus, although the temple of Janus was opened in the last days of Caesar, nevertheless, for long periods of time thereafter there were no sounds of war, although the army was in readiness for action. The Lord Jesus Christ Himself, then, in the Gospels, when in those times the whole world was living in the greatest tranquility and a single peace covered all peoples and He was asked by His disciples about the end of the coming times, among other things said this: *"You shall hear of wars and rumors of wars. Take care that you do not be alarmed, for these things must come to pass, but the end is not yet. For nations will rise against nation, and kingdom against kingdom; and there will be pestilences and famines and earthquakes in various places. But all those things are the beginnings of sorrows. Then they will deliver you up to tribulation, and will put you to death; and you will be hated by all nations for my name's sake."* Moreover, Divine Providence, by teaching this, strengthened the

believers by giving warning and confounded the unbelievers by His predicting.[37]

Orosius was clearly familiar with first-century people and events mentioned outside of the New Testament. He mentions Titus and Vespasian alongside the "complete destruction" of Jerusalem and its people living there at that time. This destruction, he says, is "as the prophets foretold." According to Orosius, Jesus also predicted those events, and his predictions parallel Matthew 24:6-9. Jesus even prophesied such tribulations in order to strengthen the faith of his disciples and confound those remaining in unbelief after the prophecies were fulfilled.

1.2.6 THEODORET OF CYRUS

Commenting on the book of Daniel, Theodoret, bishop of Cyrus (423–457 CE), clearly interpreted the "abomination of desolation" mentioned in Daniel's prophecy as foreshadowing a future, first-century fulfillment of the "abomination of desolation" mentioned by Jesus in Matthew 24:15. Theodoret wrote:

> an abomination of desolation on the temple: as a result of this sacrifice not only will the other sacrifice cease but as well an abomination of desolation will be inflicted on the temple— that is, that formerly venerable and fearsome place will be made desolate. A sign of the desolation will be the introduction into it of certain images forbidden by the law; Pilate was guilty of this by introducing into the divine temple by night the imperial images in violation of the law. The Lord also in the sacred Gospels foretold to his holy disciples, "When you

---

37. Paulus Orosius, *The Seven Books of History Against the Pagans*, FC 50, trans. Roy J. Deferrari, 289–90. Cited in Francis X. Gumerlock, *Revelation and the First Century: Preterist Interpretations of the Apocalypse in Early Christianity* (Powder Springs, GA: American Vision Press; 2012), 171.

22

see the abomination of desolation." *He said this to highlight the rapidity of the disaster about to overtake them.*[38]

Theodoret understood Jesus' remarks about the "abomination of desolation" in "the sacred Gospels" to foretell a rapid disaster about to overtake *that* generation of people. For our purposes here, it is important to notice where this "abomination" is mentioned within Matthew's OD. It takes place within Jesus' *initial* response to the three questions asked of him.

1.2.7 ST. BEDE

The Venerable Bede (672–735 CE) is considered by many historians to be the "Father of English exegesis."[39] Among all the theologians of the eighth century, Bede was "the only exegete of this period who could compare with the fathers in terms of the coherence and range

---

38. Theodoret of Cyrus, *Commentary on Daniel*, WGRW, trans. Robert C. Hill (Atlanta: Society of Biblical Literature, 2006), 257-58, cited in Gumerlock, *Revelation and the First Century,* 174-75. Italics added. In Theodoret's commentary on the twelve prophets, Theodoret makes other similar connections. When discussing the prophecy of Zechariah about the Lord's feet standing on the Mount of Olives (Zech. 14:4), Theodoret describes the fulfillment of such promises as the victory given to Jesus as the Lord of armies, and even of the Roman armies as they surrounded the Judeans during the siege of Jerusalem. He wrote, "'*On that day his feet will stand on the Mount of Olives, which is opposite Jerusalem from the east.'* From where he ascended into heaven, *from there he gives the victory to those fighting against the Jews.* He then says the mountain would be divided into four parts, one going to the east, one to the west, one to the north, and one to the south. . . . *By 'mountain' he refers to the cohort of the enemy divided for the purpose of besieging Jerusalem,* some occupying its eastern part, some its western, others guarding the north, others the south." Gumerlock, *Revelation and the First Century*, 203.

39. John J. Contreni, "The Patristic Legacy to c. 1000" in *The New Cambridge History of the Bible*, vol. 2, *From 600 to 1450*, ed. Richard Marsden and E. Ann Matter (Cambridge, UK: Cambridge University Press, 2017), 522.

of his exegetical activity."[40] "Bede respected the patristic tradition and throughout his life described himself as following in the footsteps of the fathers."[41] The importance of Bede's influence cannot be overstated, especially in light of the profound institutional changes that swept across Western civilization—especially those that supported biblical exegesis—by Bede's time.[42] Although he rose to prominence well beyond the Patristic Age, we will see in chapter three that Bede was to become ranked among the most cherished biblical commentators among all the holy fathers.

Commenting on Luke 21:5–24, which parallels Matthew 24:6–7, Bede wrote extensively about its fulfillment in first-century events:

> For it was ordained by the dispensation of God that the city itself and the temple should be overthrown, lest perhaps someone yet a child in the faith, while wrapt in astonishment at the rites of the sacrifices, should be carried away by the mere sight of the various beauties.[43]
>
> For there were many leaders when the destruction of Jerusalem was at hand, who declared themselves to be Christ, and that the time of deliverance was drawing nigh. Many heresiarchs also in the Church have preached that the day of the Lord is at hand, whom the Apostles condemn.[44] Many Antichrists also came in Christ's name, of whom the first was Simon Magus, who said, *This man is the great power of God....*[45]

---

40. Contreni, *Patristic Legacy*, 513.

41. Contreni, *Patristic Legacy*, 520.

42. Contreni, *Patristic Legacy*, 512.

43. Aquinas, *Catena: Luke*, 674.

44. 2 Thessalonians 2:2.

45. Acts 8:10. Cited in Aquinas, *Catena: Luke*, 675.

Hitherto our Lord had been speaking of those things which were to come to pass for forty years, the end not yet coming. He now describes the very end itself of the desolation, which was accomplished by the Roman army; as it is said, *And when ye shall see Jerusalem compassed, &c.* . . . But how, while the city was already compassed with an army, were they to depart out? except that the preceding word "then" is to be referred, not to the actual time of the siege, but the period just before, when first the armed soldiers began to disperse themselves through the parts of Galilee and Samaria. . . . And these are the days of vengeance, that is, the days exacting vengeance for our Lord's blood.[46]

Bede also commented on various passages contained within Mark 13:1–31, which parallel Matthew 24:1–34. In the expansive statements that follow, Bede's historical precision of first-century historical details is worth noting:

For many came forward, when destruction was hanging over Jerusalem, saying that they were Christs, and that the time of freedom was now approaching. Many teachers of heresy also arose in the Church even in the time of the Apostles; and many Antichrists came in the name of Christ, the first of whom was Simon Magus, to whom the Samaritans, as we read in the Acts of the Apostles, listened, saying, *This man is the great power of God*: wherefore also it is added here, *And shall deceive many.* (Acts 8:10) Now from the time of the Passion of our Lord there ceased not amongst the Jewish people, who chose the seditious robber and rejected Christ the Savior, either external wars or civil discord; wherefore it goes on: *And when ye shall hear of wars and rumors of wars, be ye*

46. Aquinas, *Catena: Luke*, 681-2.

25

not troubled. And when these come, the Apostles are warned not to be afraid, or to leave Jerusalem and Judaea, because the end was not to come at once, nay was to be put off for forty years.[47] And this is what is added: *for such things must needs be; but the end shall not be yet,* that is, the desolation of the province, and the last destruction of the city and temple. It goes on: *For nation shall rise against nation, and kingdom against kingdom. . . .* Now it is on record that this literally took place at the time of the Jewish rebellion. But kingdom against kingdom, the pestilence of those whose word spreads as a canker, dearth of the word of God, the commotion of the whole earth, and the separation from the true faith, may all rather be understood of heretics who, by fighting one against the other, bring about the triumph of the Church. . . .[48]

The Lord shows how Jerusalem and the province of Judaea merited the infliction of such calamities, in the following words: *But take heed to yourselves: for they shall deliver you up to councils; and in the synagogues ye shall be beaten.* For the greatest cause of destruction to the Jewish people was, that after slaying the Savior, they also tormented the heralds of His name and faith with wicked cruelty. . . . Ecclesiastical historians testify that this was fulfilled, for they relate that all the Apostles long before the destruction of the province of Judaea were dispersed to preach the Gospel over the whole world, except James the son of Zebedee and James the brother of our Lord, who had before shed their blood in Judaea for the word of the Lord. Since then the Lord knew that the hearts of the disciples would be saddened by the fall and destruction of their nation, He relieves them by this consolation, to let them know that even after the casting away of the

---

47. Around 70-73 CE, roughly forty years after Jesus' death.
48. Aquinas, *Catena: Mark,* 256–7.

Jews, companions in their joy and heavenly kingdom should not be wanting, nay that many more were to be collected out of all mankind than perished in Judaea. . . .[49]

When we are challenged to understand what is said [about the "abomination of desolation"], we may conclude that it is mystical. But it may either be said simply of Antichrist, or of the statue of Caesar, which Pilate put into the temple, or of the equestrian statue of Adrian, which for a long time stood in the holy of holies itself. An idol is also called abomination according to the Old Testament, and he has added *of desolation*, because it was placed in the temple when desolate and deserted. . . . It is on record that this was literally fulfilled, when on the approach of the war with Rome and the extermination of the Jewish people, all the Christians who were in that province, warned by the prophecy, fled far away, as Church history relates, and retiring beyond Jordan, remained for a time in the city of Pella under the protection of Agrippa, the king of the Jews, of whom mention is made in the Acts, and who with that part of the Jews, who chose to obey him, always continued subject to the Roman empire. . . .[50]

Some however refer this to the time of the Jewish captivity, where many, declaring themselves to be Christs, drew after them crowds of deluded persons.[51]

Bede's keen eye to historical detail is worthy of our rumination. In those portions of the OD which parallel Matthew 24:1-34, Bede speaks of God ordaining Israel's city and temple to be destroyed in the first century. Following that, various antichrists are mentioned,

---

49. Aquinas, *Catena: Mark*, 258-9.

50. Aquinas, *Catena: Mark*, 260-1.

51. Aquinas, *Catena: Mark*, 264.

among whom Simon Magus is offered as an explicit example from the New Testament. All of the warnings preceding "the end" offered by Jesus within the opening remarks of the OD are said to take place within a forty-year span of time (i.e., from the general time of Jesus' crucifixion to the destruction of Jerusalem). The "end" was to be put off for forty years while the disciples prepared for it. Nations and kingdoms rising against each other are emphatically placed within the archives of first-century history: *"Now it is on record that this literally took place at the time of the Jewish rebellion."* This would even include the persecution of Christian Jews and their deliverance up to ecclesiastical and civil authorities, which resulted from apostolic preaching and teaching, referred to first-century events: *"Ecclesiastical historians testify that this was fulfilled."*

1.2.8 ST. PHOTIUS THE GREAT

The Patriarch of Constantinople, St. Photius the Great (858–886 CE), also referenced Jesus' prophecy in Matthew 24 while describing the Jewish wars of the first century. He wrote:

> The city [of Jerusalem] suffered so grievously from famine that the inhabitants were driven to all kinds of excesses; a woman even ate the flesh of her own son. Famine was succeeded by pestilence, a clear proof that it was the work of divine wrath, in fulfillment of the Lord's proclamation and threat that the city should be taken and utterly destroyed.[52]

In this statement, Photius refers to "a woman" who, out of starvation, cannibalized her own infant child during the siege of Jerusalem. This reference comes from *The Jewish Wars* (6.3.4) as recorded by Josephus, a first-century Jew who lived through the tribulations that culminated

---

52. Cited in Gumerlock, *Revelation and the First Century*, 172. Words in brackets are mine.

in the destruction of Jerusalem in 70 CE. According to Photius, Jesus' predictions in Matthew's OD about soon-coming famine, pestilence, and suffering had become "clear proof" that he was a true prophet of God, since those events are recorded in first-century history. For Photius, the divinely appointed wrath of God reached its climactic fulfillment, as promised, in the utter destruction of the city and its inhabitants.

1.2.9 RABANUS AND REMIGIUS

Rabanus Maurus Magnentius was a Benedictine monk who became the archbishop of Mainz in 847 CE during the Carolingian age. The Carolingian age was when Western civilization saw an exponential rise in resources for biblical interpretation. As one recent historian has shown, Biblical commentaries and ancillary studies *tripled* in production during the Carolingian age in order to respond to exponentially rising needs of students, priests, monks, nuns and laypeople.[53] Rabanus became immensely influential because he "completed the task of providing Carolingian students with a complete series of commentaries on the Bible. His prodigious work survives in over 280 manuscript copies—an amount greater than that of any other Carolingian exegete." Rabanus "excerpted, abbreviated and simplified to provide his readers with commentaries based on the best patristic texts, all collected between the covers of one book."[54] His "one volume anothology of patristic commentaries," one historian says, "became the dominant form of exegesis in the 820s and 830s. The anthology commentary integrated the fathers and European culture."[55]

Remigius of Auxerre (841-908 CE) was also a Benedictine monk during the Carolingian age, but his influence grew through

---

53. Contreni, *Patristic Legacy*, 527.

54. Contreni, *Patristic Legacy*, 529.

55. Contreni, *Patristic Legacy*, 530.

his own compositions of Biblical exegesis and Christian philosophy. As the 'tradition of the holy fathers' became an increasingly acknowledged category among librarians between 900–1100 CE, Remigius's works grew in popularity among them.[56]

Each of these holy fathers had many things to say in response to Matthew's version of the OD. Thomas Aquinas extracted various comments from the works of Rabanus and Remigius and recorded their commentary on Matthew's version of the OD as follows:

> *And Jesus went out, and departed from the temple: and his disciples came to him for to shew him the buildings of the temple. And Jesus said unto them, See ye not all these things? verily I say unto you, There shall not be left here one stone upon another, that shall not be thrown down.*

> Rabanus: The historical sense is clear, that in the forty-second year after the Lord's passion, the city and temple were overthrown under the Roman Emperors Vespasian and Titus.

---

56. According to Guy Lobrichon, "the common repertoire of biblical exegesis stocked in their libraries was reduced to the essential minimum. Jerome, Augustine, and the Venerable Bede dominated the bulk of patristic commentaries, and were followed by the masters of the ninth century, Haimo and Remigius of Auxerre. These five covered all needs and satisfied the masters of the tenth century and the beginning of the eleventh." Guy Lobrichon, "The Early Schools, c. 900–1100" in *The New Cambridge History of the Bible*, vol. 2, *From 600 to 1450*, ed. Richard Marsden and E. Ann Matter (Cambridge, UK: Cambridge University Press, 2017), 541. According to Lesley Smith, biblical exegetes of later generations relied heavily upon comments left in glossed bibles. One "major source" of biblical interpretation in glossed bibles "was the biblical commentaries of Rabanus Maurus, who commented on almost the entire Bible whilst master of the school at the abbey of Fulda, and there are contributions by other Carolingian authors such as . . . Remigius . . . of Auxerre." Lesley Smith, "The Glossed Bible" in *The New Cambridge History of the Bible*, vol. 2, *From 600 to 1450*, 368.

Remigius: So it was ordained of God, that as soon as the light of grace was revealed, the temple with its ceremonies should be taken out of the way, lest any weakling in the faith, beholding all the things instituted of the Lord and hallowed by the Prophets yet abiding, might be gradually drawn away from the purity of the faith to a carnal Judaism.[57]

And as he sat upon the mount of Olives, the disciples came unto him privately, saying, Tell us, when shall these things be? and what shall be the sign of thy coming, and of the end of the world? And Jesus answered and said unto them, Take heed that no man deceive you. For many shall come in my name, saying, I am Christ; and shall deceive many.

Remigius: The Lord continuing His walk arrives at Mount Olivet, having by the way foretold the destruction of the temple to those disciples who had shown and commended the buildings. When they had reached the Mount they came to Him, asking Him further of this. [...] For Mount Olivet has no unfruitful trees, but olives, which supply light to dispel darkness, which give rest to the weary, health to the sick. And sitting on Mount Olivet over against the temple, the Lord discourses of its destruction, and the destruction of the Jewish nation, that even by His choice of a situation He might show, that abiding still in the Church He condemns the pride of the wicked.[58]

---

57. Cited in Thomas Aquinas, *Catena Aurea: Commentary on the Four Gospels, Collected out of the Works of the Fathers: St. Matthew*, vol. 1, trans. J. H. Newman (1841, repr., Veritas Splendor Publications, 2012), 594-5.

58. Aquinas, *Catena: Matthew*, 595.

And ye shall hear of wars and rumors of wars: see that ye be not troubled: for all these things must come to pass, but the end is not yet. For nation shall rise against nation, and kingdom against kingdom: and there shall be famines, and pestilences, and earthquakes, in diverse places. All these are the beginning of sorrows.

Rabanus: Or, this is a warning to the Apostles not to flee from Jerusalem and Judaea in terror of these things, when they should begin to come upon them; because the end was not immediately, but the desolation of the province, and the destruction of the city and temple should not come till the fortieth year. And we know that most grievous woes, which spread over the whole province, fell out to the very letter. [...] Nation shall rise against nation, shows the disquietude of men's minds; pestilences, the affliction of their bodies; famines, the barrenness of the soil; earthquakes in diverse places, wrath from heaven above.[59]

Then shall they deliver you up to be afflicted, and shall kill you: and ye shall be hated of all nations for my name's sake. And then shall many be offended, and shall betray one another, and shall hate one another. And many false prophets shall rise, and shall deceive many. And because iniquity shall abound, the love of many shall wax cold. But he that shall endure unto the end, the same shall be saved. And this Gospel of the kingdom shall be preached in all the world for a witness unto all nations; and then shall the end come.

---

59. Aquinas, *Catena: Matthew*, 598.

32

Rabanus: For what desert so many evils are to be brought upon Jerusalem, and the whole Jewish province the Lord shows, when He adds, Then shall they deliver you up, &c.

Remigius: As the capture of Jerusalem approached, many rose up, calling themselves Christians, and deceived many; such Paul calls false brethren, John Antichrists. . . .[60] Whoso shall endure unto the end, i.e., to the end of his life; for whoso to the end of his life shall persevere in the confession of the name of Christ, and in love, he shall be saved. . . . For the Lord knew that the hearts of the disciples would be made sad by the destruction of Jerusalem, and overthrow of their nation, and He therefore comforts them with a promise that more of the Gentiles should believe than of the Jews should perish. . . . But the whole passage might be referred to the end of the world. For then shall many be offended, and depart from the faith, when they see the numbers and wealth of the wicked, and the miracles of Antichrist, and they shall persecute their brethren; and Antichrist shall send false Prophets, who shall deceive many; iniquity shall abound, because the number of the wicked shall be increased; and love shall wax cold, because the number of the good shall diminish.[61]

Included in this "Catena" of interpretations by various church fathers, Thomas Aquinas (1225-1274 CE) added a marginal gloss of his own alongside Remigius' last remark, saying:

---

60. Aquinas, *Catena: Matthew*, 599-600.

61. Aquinas, *Catena: Matthew*, 600-1.

But it is possible to maintain both applications of the passage, if only we will take this diffusion of Gospel preaching in a double sense. If we understand it of fruit produced by the preaching, and the foundation in every nation of a Church of believers in Christ, as Augustine expounds it, then it is a sign which ought to precede the end of the world, and which did not precede the destruction of Jerusalem. But if we understand it of the fame of their preaching, then it was accomplished before the destruction of Jerusalem, when Christ's disciples had been dispersed over the four quarters of the earth. Whence Jerome says, I do not suppose that there remained any nation which knew not the name of Christ; for where preacher had never been, some notion of the faith must have been communicated by neighboring nations.[62]

It is worth noting that Aquinas attempts to solidify the either/or interpretation of Remigius by offering further clarification about endurance to "the end." Aquinas recommends a "double sense" for understanding the *primary* meaning of these passages in order to maintain

---

62. Aquinas, *Catena: Matthew*, 601-2. This marginal note by Aquinas makes sense in light of the common methodology he adopted in his more 'official' commentary on Matthew's Gospel. Commenting on the disciples' questions there, he writes, "*Dixerat destruendum templum, ideo tria quaerunt. Primum de templo; secundum de adventu; tertium de fine saeculi. Unde dicunt dic nobis quando haec erunt, scilicet consummatio tuae comminationis; et de adventu tuo: et quod signum adventus tui; item de fine saeculi: et consummationis saeculi.*" The English translation is as follows: "He had said that the temple was to be destroyed, so they ask three things: first, about the temple; second, about the coming; third, about the end of the age. Hence they say, *tell us when these things will be*, namely the consummation of your threats; and about your coming: *and what will be the sign of your coming*, likewise about the end of the age, *and of the consummation of the world?*" Thomas Aquinas, *Commentary on the Gospel of Matthew, Chapters 13-28*, Biblical Commentaries, vol. 34, *Latin/English Edition of the Works of St. Thomas Aquinas*, trans. Jeremy Holmes (Lander, WY: The Aquinas Institute for the Study of Sacred Doctrine, 2013), 287.

first-century fulfillment and futuristic fulfillment, even though Remigius expresses greater certainty about its first-century historical setting associated with the destruction of Jerusalem. According to Remigius, the primary meaning pertains to either first-century fulfillment or futuristic fulfillment, but not necessarily both; Jesus might have referred to the end of the world, but greater certainty is ascribed to the Lord knowing the hearts of his disciples and the "overthrow of their nation."

Continuing with one more comment about Matthew 24:15–22, Aquinas notes the following from Regimus' expository treatise:

> *When ye therefore shall see the abomination of desolation, spoken of by Daniel the prophet, stand in the holy place, (whoso readeth, let him understand:) Then let them which be in Judaea flee into the mountains: Let him which is on the housetop not come down to take any thing out of his house. Neither let him which is in the field return back to take his clothes. And woe unto them that are with child, and to them that give suck in those days! But pray ye that your flight be not in the winter, neither on the sabbath day: For then shall be great tribulation, such as was not since the beginning of the world to this time, no, nor ever shall be. And except those days should be shortened, there should no flesh be saved: but for the elect's sake those days shall be shortened.*

> Remigius: And this we know was so done when the fall of Jerusalem drew near; for on the approach of the Roman army, all the Christians in the province, warned, as ecclesiastical history tells us (Euseb. H.E. iii. 5.),[63] mirac-

---

63. Notice that *both* Remigius and Aquinas utilized the *Ecclesiastical History* of Eusebius (and by extension, Josephus and Hegessipus as well, whom Eusebius references throughout his works) to show that Christians in Judaea were warned "miraculously from heaven" about the destruction of Jerusalem. "This," Remigius writes, "we know was so done when the fall of Jerusalem drew near."

> ulously from heaven, withdrew, and passing the Jordan, took refuge in the city of Pella; and under the protection of that King Agrippa, of whom we read in the Acts of the Apostles, they continued some time; but Agrippa himself, with the Jews whom he governed, was subjected to the dominion of the Romans.[64]

When the comments of Remigius and Rabanus are compared with the passages quoted from Matthew's Gospel, a first-century context of fulfillment is unmistakable. Although no distinctive methodology is acknowledged, all of their remarks about first-century fulfillment take place within Jesus' *first* response to the question, "'When will these things be?"

1.2.10 THEOPHYLACT OF OHRID

Theophylact (1055–1108 CE), the Archbishop of Ohrid, had many interesting things to say about Jesus' promises regarding his "coming" in the gospels, particularly those mentioned in Luke 21 and Mark 13 (which parallel Matthew 24). Commenting on Luke 21:9–11, which parallels Matthew 24:6–7, he writes:

> Now some have wished to place the fulfillment of these things not only at the future consummation of all things, but at the time also of the taking of Jerusalem. For when the Author of peace was killed, then justly arose among the Jews wars and sedition. But from wars proceed pestilence and famine, the former indeed produced by the air infected with dead bodies, the latter through the lands remaining uncultivated. Josephus also relates the most intolerable distresses to have occurred from famine; and at the time of Claudius Caesar there was a

---

64. Aquinas, *Catena: Matthew*, 602-3.

severe famine, as we read in the Acts, (Acts 11:28) and many terrible events happened, foreboding, as Josephus says, the destruction of Jerusalem.[65]

Commenting on Luke 21:20–24, which parallels Matthew 24:15–22, he also wrote, "But some say that the Lord hereby signified the devouring of children, which Josephus also relates."[66] His comments about Mark 13:3–13, which parallel Matthew 24:4-8 (and 10:17-22), are similar:

> That is, the Romans against the Jews, which Josephus relates happened before the destruction of Jerusalem. For when the Jews refused to pay tribute, the Romans arose, in anger; but because at that time they were merciful they took indeed their spoils, but did not destroy Jerusalem. What follows shows that God fought against the Jews, for it is said, *And there shall be earthquakes in divers places, and there shall be famines. . . .*[67]
>
> Fitly also did He premise a recital of those things which concerned the Apostles, that in their own tribulations they might find some consolation in the community of troubles and sufferings. There follows: *And ye shall be brought before rulers and kings for my sake, for a testimony against them.* He says *kings and rulers*, as, for instance, Agrippa, Nero, and Herod. Again, His saying, *for my sake*, gave them no small consolation, in that they were about to suffer for His sake. *For a testimony against them*, means, as a judgment beforehand against them, that they might be inexcusable, in that though the Apostles were laboring for the truth, they would not join themselves to it. Then, that they might not think

---

65. Aquinas, *Catena: Luke*, 677.

66. Aquinas, *Catena: Luke*, 682.

67. Aquinas, *Catena: Mark*, 257. Italics are original.

that their preaching should be impeded by troubles and dangers, He adds: *And the Gospel must first be published among all nations.*[68]

Commenting on Mark 13:14–20, which parallels Matthew 24:15–22, his comments are, again, crystal clear:

That is, if the Roman war had not been soon finished, *no flesh should be saved*; that is, no Jew should have escaped; *but for the elect's sake, whom he hath chosen*, that is, for the sake of the believing Jews, or who were hereafter to believe, *He hath shortened the days*, that is, the war was soon finished, for God foresaw that many Jews would believe after the destruction of the city; for which reason He would not suffer the whole race to be utterly destroyed.[69]

---

68. Aquinas, *Catena: Mark*, 258.

69. Aquinas, *Catena: Mark*, 260. Intriguingly, Aquinas notes elsewhere that Theophylact made a passing comment about the "coming" of Jesus at the end of John's Gospel (21:18-24), saying that, "Some have understood, *Till I come*, to mean, Till I come to punish the Jews who have crucified Me, and strike them with the Roman rod. For they say that this Apostle [John] lived up to the time of Vespasian, who took Jerusalem, and dwelt near when it was taken" (Aquinas, *Catena: Mark*, 630). According to John 21:18-24, Theophylact's comments seem justified: "'Truly, truly, I say to you [Peter], when you were young, you used to dress yourself and walk wherever you wanted, but when you are old, you will stretch out your hands, and another will dress you and carry you where you do not want to go.' (This he said to show by what kind of death he was to glorify God.) And after saying this he said to him, 'Follow me.' Peter turned and saw the disciple whom Jesus loved following them, the one who also had leaned back against him during the supper and had said, 'Lord, who is it that is going to betray you?' When Peter saw him, he said to Jesus, 'Lord, what about this man?' Jesus said to him, 'If it is my will that he remain until I come, what is that to you? You follow me!' So the saying spread abroad among the brothers that this disciple was not to die; yet Jesus did not say to him that he was not to die, but, 'If it is my will *that he remain until I come*, what is that to you?' This is the disciple who is bearing witness about these things, and who has written these things,

1.3 CONCLUSION

A wide variety of church fathers were familiar with Jesus' OD prophecies containing first-century fulfillment. Interestingly, some of their interpretations included an indeterminate mixture of future fulfillment beyond the first century. It is unfortunate that many of them do not explain why they assume there is a transition from first-century fulfillment to future, end-of-the-world fulfillment.

Hilary, Jerome, Chrysostom, and Pseudo-Chrysostom are the clearest about their distinctive methodology. They insist that first-century fulfillment takes place somewhere within Jesus' initial response to his disciples' first question, but they also do not justify why Jesus' response to subsequent questions should refer to events still in their future. They simply explain the latter portions of the OD as containing facts about end-of-the-world fulfillment without a reasonably consistent defense of why such interpretive decisions occur. They are not even uniform with one another in how they offer futuristic interpretations of fulfillment. Some church fathers try to impose a sense of double fulfillment to Jesus' initial response. Some do not. A handful of them give the impression that Jesus' initial response pertained exclusively to first-century fulfillment. Uniformly, all of the church Fathers mentioned so far agree that some measure of Jesus' prophecy was fulfilled in the first century in response to the disciples' *first* question.[70] We must ask, however, does the interpreta-

---

and we know that his testimony is true." I have offered further commentary on these and other similar remarks elsewhere. See Jonathan Sedlak, *The Epexegetical Gospel: Parenthetical remarks and their usage in the Gospel of John* (unpublished manuscript, available at https://www.academia.edu/79043884/The_Epexegetical_Gospel_Parenthetical_remarks_and_their_usage_in_the_Gospel_of_John).

70. It is worth mentioning that in a recent publication edited by a leading Roman Catholic scholar, Robert Louis Wilkin, consisting entirely of early patristic comments on Matthew's Gospel, fails to select excerpts that clearly exposit the relevance of first-century fulfillment within Matthew 24:4-29. On that, see Robert Louis Wilkin, ed., *The Church's Bible: Matthew Interpreted by Early Christian*

tion of first-century fulfillment in these verses comport with Jesus' answer to his disciples' *first* question in Matthew's version?

Commentators, trans. D.H. Williams (Grand Rapids, MI: William B. Eerdmans Publishing Company, 2018), 444-53.

CHAPTER 2

Literary Themes and Structures of Matthew's Discourses

2.1 INTRODUCTION

We can see a common and notable methodology in the early church about the order of Jesus' responses to his disciples within the OD of Matthew's Gospel. Many influential church fathers recognized first-century fulfillment in the words spoken by Jesus that parallel Matthew 24:4-29. We will now compare this methodology with the literary structure and themes of Matthew's OD.

In order to appreciate Matthew's literary design for the OD, it will be helpful to peruse the structure of Matthew's Gospel as a whole first. We will begin this process by highlighting the unique placement of the five distinctive discourses of Jesus within it. After identifying Matthew's peculiar arrangement of all five discourses, many other unique literary themes and structures will emerge, bearing witness to the special and intentional positioning of its fifth discourse, which

41

frames the OD. At that time, we will be prepared to focus upon and analyze the literary structure and themes of the OD in detail. This will be necessary in order to discover what warrant there is for the distinctive, influential methodology found throughout early Christian tradition.

2.1.1 GENERAL LITERARY THEMES AND PATTERNS

According to Peter J. Leithart's essay, *Jesus as Israel: The Typological Structure of Matthew's Gospel*,[1] Matthew has "organized his account of the life of Jesus as an Irenaean recapitulation of Israel's history, in which Jesus replays both major individual roles of that history (Moses, David, Elisha, Jeremiah) as well as the role of the nation herself."[2] Leithart expands upon the studies of B. W. Bacon and Dale C. Allison Jr. regarding Matthew's literary structure in general and typological framework in particular. By interacting with some deficiencies presented in their works and building upon their strengths, Leithart defends his case convincingly. Leithart begins with the way Matthew bookends his Gospel. Phrases clearly echo the beginning and ending of the Old Testament Scriptures.[3] By means of these bookends, Matthew indicates that he has crafted a gospel of God that "begins like Genesis and ends like Chronicles, and thus encompasses the entirety of the Hebrew canon."[4]

---

1. Peter J. Leithart, *Jesus as Israel: The Typological Structure of Matthew's Gospel*, BH Occasional Paper, no. 38 (Niceville, FL: Biblical Horizons, Dec. 2010).

2. Leithart, *Typological Structure*, 2. In accordance with Leithart's thesis, David L. Turner affirms that "Matthew views both the historical patterns and prophetic oracles of the Hebrew Bible as filled with ultimate significance through the ministry and teaching of Jesus." David L. Turner, *Israel's Last Prophet: Jesus and the Jewish Leaders in Matthew 23* (Minneapolis, MN: Fortress Press, 2015), 123.

3. Leithart, *Typological Structure*, 8, 12.

4. Leithart, *Typological Structure*, 12. It is worth noting that the canonical ordering of the Hebrew Scriptures ends with 2 Chronicles. This ordering also corresponds with the tractate *Baba Bathra* (Folio 14b) of the Babylonian Talmud [see

Matthew introduces his Gospel with the phrase, "The book of the genealogy (βίβλος γενέσεως) of Jesus Christ, the son of David, the son of Abraham." This opening phrase incorporates an exact quotation from multiple introductory remarks found in the earliest parts of Genesis. There we find the βίβλος γενέσεως of heaven and earth (Gen. 2:4, LXX)[5] and the βίβλος γενέσεως of the first man, Adam (Gen. 5:1, LXX). Accordingly, when Matthew structured the beginning of his composition, he clearly seems to have designed it to echo the beginning of Israel's holy Scriptures.[6]

Gallagher and Meade, *The Biblical Canon Lists,* 68-9] and seems to be intentional on the part of the final canonical compilers. Accordingly, this canonical arrangement ends with an intimation of Israel being restored to its homeland by the Persian monarch, Cyrus; whereas, chronologically, the history of Ezra-Nehemiah takes place after Cyrus' decree in 2 Chronicles 36. For an argument in defense of the ordering of the Masoretic manuscripts, see Timothy J. Stone, *The Compilational History of the Megilloth: Canon, Contoured Intertextuality and Meaning in the Writings* (Tübingen, Germany: Mohr Siebeck, 2013). Furthermore, in rabbinical tradition Nehemiah the son of Hachaliah was considered to be the final author of 2 Chronicles, which sets a certain limit on the time in which the documents for the Hebrew canon were finalized. That tradition was also classified as *baraita* (oral law not incorporated in the Mishnah) from the Tannaitic period onward. On that, see Lee Martin McDonald, *The Biblical Canon: Its Origin, Transmission, and Authority* (Peabody, MA: Hendrickson Publishers, 2007), 164-5. However, according to more recent scholarship, which deflects attention away from such *baraita*, the Hebrew canonical arrangement is explained well if two factors are taken into consideration: **(1)** the final form of Chronicles (as a compilation of its contents from previous sources) originated under Hasmonean rule, and **(2)** the final order was solidified as a post 70 CE Pharisaic canon. On factor **(1)**, see David M. Carr, *The Formation of the Hebrew Bible: A New Reconstruction* (New York: Oxford University Press, 2011), 195-201. On factor **(2)**, see Timothy H. Lim, *The Formation of the Jewish Canon* (New Haven, CT: Yale University Press, 2013).

5. LXX refers to the Septuagint (i.e., the Greek Old Testament) commonly utilized by first-century Israelites and Christians.

6. In the revised version of his doctoral dissertation about textualized oral narratives within Hellenistic Judaism and early Christianity, focusing especially upon *The Gospel of Mark* and *Joseph and Aseneth,* Nicholas Elder compares and contrasts the "residually oral" tendencies of Mark's Gospel with the "consistently lit-

Similarly, Matthew *ends* his gospel with scriptural markers that would have been familiar to Israelites in the first century. The very last words of the Hebrew scriptures are found in 2 Chronicles, where we read Cyrus' "great commission" to rebuild the walls of Jerusalem and the temple of Israel's God (2 Chron. 36:22-23; cf. Ezra 6:3-9):

> Now in the first year of Cyrus king of Persia, that the word of the Lord by the mouth of Jeremiah might be fulfilled, the Lord stirred up the spirit of Cyrus king of Persia, so that he made a proclamation throughout all his kingdom and also put it in writing: "Thus says Cyrus king of Persia, '*The Lord, the God of heaven, has given me all the kingdoms of the earth, and he has charged me to build him a house* at Jerusalem, which is in Judah. Whoever is among you of all his people, *may the Lord his God be with him. Let him go up!*'" (2 Chron. 36:22-23, italics added).

The last words of Matthew's gospel echo this "great commission" closely:

> And Jesus came and said to them, "*All authority in heaven and on earth has been given to me. Go therefore and make disciples*

---

eraturized" stylistic features of Matthew and Luke's Gospels. On this, see Nicholas A. Elder, *The Media Matrix of Early Jewish and Christian Narrative*, LNTS, 612 (New York: T&T Clark, 2019), 164-5. In the midst of Elder's analysis, he points out that "Matthew's first two words, βίβλος γενέσεως ('book of the genealogy,' RSV), mirror a phrase that appears in Gen. 2:4 and 5:1, likely associating the First Gospel with that text of Jewish Scripture. By calling the narrative a βίβλος ('book'), Matthew has placed it into a category of written literature that has 'biblical-like' importance" (*Media Matrix*, 162). As a book of "biblical-like" literary intentionality, Matthew's γενέσεως Ἰησοῦ χριστοῦ ("genealogy" or "beginning" of Jesus Christ) in 1:1 pairs well with τῆς συντελείας (the "end" or "conclusion") in 28:20, thereby enveloping a theme of Israel's life-story from beginning to end. With an intentional framework of this sort, Matthew's Gospel is comparable to a final volume within the overall library of Israel's story.

of all nations, baptizing them in the name of the Father and of the Son and of the Holy Spirit, teaching them to observe all that I have commanded you. *And behold, I am with you always,* to the end of the age" (Matt. 28:18-20, italics added).

According to Leithart's summary,[7] there are three common elements between those two bookends: **(1)** There is a statement by God's "anointed one" (cf. Isaiah 44:28; 45:1) regarding universal authority, **(2)** a statement regarding the source of his authority, and **(3)** a commission to "Go!" and build God's House.[8]

These clear typological associations are important to recognize from the outset because they illustrate that Matthew's Gospel was *not* haphazardly designed. In its beginning and end, the history of Jesus is portrayed as the beginning and end of Israel's story.[9] Scribes like

---

7. See Leithart, *Typological Structure*, 12, which I have expanded slightly.

8. Buchanan, *Matthew,* vol. 2, 1023-4, covers these similarities as well: "Jesus is portrayed here as the new Son of man and the new leader of the return from Babylon. This concluding passage in Matthew was also based on the concluding verse of Second Chronicles. It called attention to the release of the Babylonian Jews who were taken captive. In keeping with sabbatical eschatology and in fulfilment of the prophecy of Jeremiah, Cyrus made an announcement pass through the land providing release of the captive Jews. He also gave permission to the Jews in Persia to return to their land, and reconstruct the temple at Jerusalem, just as Lev 25:10-17 commanded for the Jubilee observance." Buchanan, *Matthew,* vol. 2, 1024. Buchanan also positively cites the work of B. J. Malina, saying, "Malina has astutely shown that Matt 28:16-20 is a literary form similar to the official decree of 2 Chron 36:23, reportedly made by Cyrus of Persia." Buchanan, *Matthew,* vol. 2, 1025.

9. On this, Grant Macaskill writes, "much of the imagery often regarded as reflecting a *New Moses*-typology may actually reflect a *New Israel*-typology." Grant Macaskill, *Revealed Wisdom and Inaugurated Eschatology in Ancient Judaism and Early Christianity,* SJSJ, vol. 115 (Leiden, Netherlands: Brill, 2007), 124. Speaking holistically of Jesus as the fulfillment of Israel's life-story and scriptural hope, Mothy Varkey writes, "Matthew employs the fulfillment citations to 'ground' God's continuing saving activity. As Hays fittingly argues, these passages not only 'frame Israel's Scripture as a *predictive* text pointing to events in the life of

Matthew[10] would have had a keen awareness of what their Jewish au-

---

Jesus . . . but also 'validate' the claims about the status of Jesus, which Matthew makes for Jesus, by 'grounding' them in Jewish Scriptures. This means, for Matthew, whatever happened in the life of Jesus was 'intended to happen,' which genuinely situates him within the messianic hopes of the people of Israel, something that would be valued by those holding Jewish Scriptures in high esteem. For Matthew, the purpose of fulfillment citation is, therefore, both 'historical' (to situate Jesus's saving in history) and 'theological.' Clearly then, Matthew uses the fulfillment quotations to portray Jesus as the fulfillment of God's saving plans and promises." Mothy Varkey, *Salvation in Continuity: A Reconsideration of Matthew's Soteriology*, ESS (Minneapolis, MN: Fortress Press, 2017), 55.

10. M.D. Goulder offers a wide selection of literary evidence in favor of Matthew's familiarity with Rabbinic scribal methodology, including midrash, poetry, and parables. On that, see M.D. Goulder, *Midrash and Lection in Matthew* (London: S.P.C.K. 1974), 3-136. For a scholarly, evangelical examination of Matthew as a well-trained scribe, see Patrick Schreiner, *Matthew, Disciple and Scribe: The First Gospel and Its Portrait of Jesus* (Grand Rapids, MI: Baker Academic, 2019). See also Aaron M. Gale, *Redefining Ancient Borders: The Jewish Scribal Framework of Matthew's Gospel* (New York: T&T Clark International, 2005), 87-110, which balances a lot of Schreiner's oversimplified explanations. One major difference between the Schreiner and Gale is that Gale argues for a first century, *post*-70 CE date of scribal composition. Gale's work is a significant contribution to Matthean studies, especially in his defense of Matthew's Gospel being composed in Lower Galilee in the city of Sepphoris (not Antioch, as is commonly conjectured by advocates of "formative Judaism" hypotheses), and his target audience being "city churches" of well-educated and wealthy Jewish communities. The evidence Gale presents regarding the role of Matthew as a scribe in this context is convincing. To my knowledge, David Sim is the only Matthean scholar to intensely scrutinize Gale's proposal. In my appraisal, Sim's scrutiny is clever, but noticeably petty, and largely based on counter-arguments that require false dilemmas. On that, see David C. Sim, "Reconstructing the Social and Religious Milieu of Matthew: Methods, Sources, and Possible Results" in *Matthew, James, and Didache: Three Related Documents in Their Jewish and Christian Settings*, SBLSS, no. 45, eds. Huub van de Sandt and Jurgen K. Zangenberg (Atlanta, GA: Society of Biblical Literature, 2008), 21-5. No matter what time and location scholars imagine for the composition of "Matthew's" Gospel, virtually all agree that the author was familiar with Jewish scribal techniques. Regarding the speculative nature of determining "Matthew's" life situation after 70 CE, Romeny's description of such scholarly pursuits are important to keep in mind. He writes, "Discussions of the place and time of origin of

dience would recognize by way of design,[11] considering that *Israel* was considered to be God's firstborn "son" (Exod. 4:22; Hos. 11:1). Such basic typological hermeneutics even seem to be taken for granted,[12] since Matthew begins by highlighting *Jesus* as God's firstborn "Son" (Matt. 2:13-14).

Adding to these basic elements of Matthew's literary structure, Leithart has also pointed out that the narrative of Jesus' young life in Matthew's gospel, as contained in chapters one through four, closely parallels the Pentateuch where we find the young life of Israel be-

---

this gospel often pair speculation with simplification. Thus, Kummel denies a Palestinian origin because the author had intended the work for Greek-speaking Christians. However, what we know about the linguistic situation of Palestine at the end of the first century does not warrant this denial. The arguments for an Antiochene origin, put together by Davies and Allison, form a rather pitiful collection of circumstantial evidence, which impresses the reader more because of its size than its content – as the authors themselves seem to realize" (Haar Romeny, "*Hypotheses,*" 15).

11. Allan McNicol's observations are on point: "As one can immediately determine something of the educational skills and background of the writer by the style of his or her letters . . . the first gospel definitely, in terms of its general structure, bears the imprint of one who was knowledgeable about the conventions of Hellenistic rhetoric." Allan J. McNicol, *Jesus' Directions for the Future: A Source and Redaction-History Study of the Use of the Eschatological Traditions in Paul and in the Synoptic Accounts of Jesus' Last Eschatological Discourse*, NGS, no. 9 (Macon, GA: Mercer University Press, 1996), 69n5.

12. It should be stated from the outset that as with Leithart, I believe the authors of both the Old and New Testament scriptures employed typology in their hermeneutical methodologies. In defense of this, see G. W. H. Lampe, "The Reasonableness of Typology," in *Essays on Typology*, ed. Lampe and K. J. Woollcombe (London: SCM Press, 1957), 9-38, and especially 18-27; see also Warren A. Gage, *Theological Poetics: Typology, Symbol and the Christ* (Fort Lauderdale, FL: Warren A. Gage, 2010), 24-31; Richard M. Davidson, *Typology in Scripture: A Study of Hermeneutical* τύπος *Structures*, AUSDDS, vol. 2 (Berrein Springs, MI: Andrews University Press, 1981), 191-424; Peter J. Leithart, *BI111 Typological Hermeneutics: Finding Christ in the Whole Bible*, Logos Mobile Education (Bellingham, WA: Lexham Press, 2016), especially the sections titled "The Bible is about Jesus," Parts 1 and 2.

ginning with a *genealogy* akin to Adam's genealogy,[13] followed by the *birth* of Israel, and continuing with an *exodus* out of Egypt all the way to Moses's ascension on Mount Sinai to receive and to distribute God's Law.[14] Numerous other scholars have noticed these parallels as well.[15] For example, in his book, *The New Testament Documents: Are They Reliable?*, F. F. Bruce highlights this typological framework while summarizing the overall story of Matthew's Gospel:

> [Matthew] the evangelist is . . . at pains to show how the story of Jesus represents the fulfillment of the Old Testament Scriptures . . . that the experiences of Jesus recapitulate the experiences of the people of Israel in Old Testament times. Thus, just as the children of Israel went down into Egypt in their national infancy and came out of it at the Exodus, so Jesus in His infancy must also go down to Egypt and come out of it, that the words spoken of them in Hosea 11:1 might be fulfilled in His experience, too: "Out of Egypt have I called my son" (Mt. 2:15).[16]

These introductory themes of Israel's humble beginnings are only a few brush-strokes of the entire gospel-landscape which Matthew has painted. As Matthew's narrative continues up through chapter five, we can see that a new and unique sort of texture has been added to this landscape. In chapter five we find Jesus teaching extensively for the

---

13. Leithart, *Typological Structure*, 9.

14. Leithart, *Typological Structure*, 8-9. Leithart adds, "Much of this is old hat, and so self-evident that even scholars who resist typological interpretation have a hard time ignoring it" (Leithart, *Typological*, 9).

15. Perhaps the most notable work on this topic is Dale C. Allison Jr., *The New Moses: A Matthean Typology* (1993, repr., Eugene, OR: Wipf & Stock, 2013), which Leithart utilizes and critiques.

16. F. F. Bruce, *The New Testament Documents: Are They Reliable?* (1943, repr., Grand Rapids, MI: William B. Eerdmans Publishing Company, 1981), 38.

first time. In fact, if one were to flip through a "red-letter" bible a few times, it is very noticeable that once Jesus ascends the "mountain" in 5:1, a very lengthy discourse begins, leaving page after page with only red-lettering that does not end for a few chapters until Jesus *descends* that same mountain at the end of chapter seven.

Peter Leithart has noted in his book *The Four: A Survey of the Gospels* that the first discourse (commonly described as "the Sermon on the Mount") is clearly modeled on the revelation of God the law-giver at Sinai.[17] As Moses and Israel before him, Jesus passes through waters before ascending the Mountain (Matt. 3, c.f. Exod. 16) and spends forty days in the wilderness (Matt. 4:1-2; cf. Exod. 17-19).[18] From this mountain, Jesus quotes from the Ten Commandments and Torah, teaching his disciples that they must develop a godly ethos that surpasses the scribes and Pharisees. In this first discourse, Jesus is the new Moses on the Mount of the Lord delivering divine law to God's people. But according to Leithart—in distinction from Dale Allison's

---

17. Peter J. Leithart, *The Four: A Survey of the Gospels* (Moscow, ID: Canon Press, 2010), 132-47. For a thorough survey of the mountain motif across Matthew's Gospel and its connection with Sinai, see also Terence L. Donaldson, *Jesus on the Mountain: A Study in Matthean Theology*, JSNTSS, vol. 8 (Sheffield, England: 1985), 111-18.

18. Michael Knowles, *Jeremiah in Matthew's Gospel: The Rejected-Prophet Motif in Matthaean Redaction*, JSNT 68 (Sheffield, England: Sheffield Academic Press, 1993), 237-8, points out the importance of beginning Matthew's Gospel with Moses-typology. He writes, "Moses typology in Matthew's infancy narrative provides a starting point for the discussion of Moses' place within the Gospel as a whole. Even the language of Matthew's infancy narrative seems intended to recall the biblical story of Moses' birth and providential protection (e.g., 2.14, 16 . . . cf. LXX Exod. 2.15). . . . It has also been suggested that the account of Jesus' forty days of temptation in the wilderness (4:1-11) owes something to Israel's forty years in the wilderness, when the people put Moses—and God—to the test. If, however, this were so, it would seem more appropriate to a depiction of Jesus as the new Israel than as a new Moses."

thesis[19]—Mosaic typology is not the only way in which Matthew has designed the typological structure of his Gospel about Jesus.

As can be seen with any "red-letter" New Testament, chapters five through seven begin the first of *five* lengthy discourses spaced throughout Matthew's Gospel. Leithart argues that, "One of the most obvious things about Matthew is that it includes five large sections of teaching."[20] In each of the five discourses we find an identical phrase that marks and concludes each discourse: "*when Jesus had finished*" (7:28, 11:1, 13:53, 19:1, 26:1). Such markers indicate that Matthew structures his gospel *around* these five discourses.

Many scholars have acknowledged this general structure.[21] For example, D. A. Carson mentions that "the five discourses are sufficiently well-defined that it is hard to believe that Matthew did not plan them as such."[22] And even though R. T. France finds the "geographical outline of the story" to be "more satisfying" than discerning Matthew's narrative structure through "verbal division markers",[23] he nevertheless admits in his extensive commentary that,

> Recent discussion has often focused on the search for fomulae which may be taken to mark structural divisions. By far

---

19. See footnotes above in this section (**2.1.1**).

20. Leithart, *The Four*, 121.

21. According to Knowles, *Jeremiah in Matthew's Gospel*, 238, general disagreement about Matthew's five-part division involves forcing all five discourses into typological resemblance with the five books of the Pentateuch. Knowles notes, "Of central importance to a Moses typology is the much-controverted question of whether Matthew's division of Jesus' teaching into five discourses . . . is intended to reflect the fivefold division of the Mosaic Torah." This approach among scholars is flawed insofar as it assumes an over-arching "Moses" typology and not a Jesus-as-Israel typology.

22. D. A. Carson, *Matthew*, EBC, vol. 8 (Grand Rapids, MI: Zondervan Publishing House, 1984), 51.

23. R. T. France, *The Gospel of Matthew*, NICNT (Grand Rapids, MI: William B. Eerdmans Publishing Company, 2007), 4.

the most prominent is the slightly varying formula which concludes Matthew's five main collections of Jesus' teaching . . . (7:28; 11:1; 13:53; 19:1; 26:1).[24]

As with R.T. France, Craig Keener remains skeptical about how to interpret the five-fold structure of Matthew. Nevertheless he points out its plausibility in his socio-rhetorical commentary on Matthew's gospel:

> This Gospel may divide chronologically into three sections; the teaching material divides topically into five. . . . Most scholars identify five discourses by the closing formula "when he had finished speaking" in 7:28; 11:1; 13:53; 19:1; 26:1.[25]

I agree with Peter Leithart that these five discourses of Jesus are intentionally highlighted by Matthew and "are like five pillars that hold up the book of Matthew,"[26] set between the Gospel's opening and closing statements—statements which echo the βίβλος γενέσεως ("Book of Genesis") and closing "Decree of Cyrus" in the *Tanakh*.[27] In his book,

---

24. France, *Matthew*, 2.

25. Craig S. Keener, *The Gospel of Matthew: A Socio-Rhetorical Commentary* (Grand Rapids, MI: William B. Eerdmans Publishing Company, 2009), 36-7.

26. Leithart, *The Four*, 121. McNicol, who, along with Leithart, is critical of B. W. Bacon's literary structure of Matthew's Gospel, nonetheless highlights that "the Baconian view of Matthew's structure has one abiding feature that continues to commend it. It is clear that Matthew does contain five great bodies of Jesus' teachings: the Sermon on the Mount (5:1-7:27); the Mission Discourse (1-:5-42); the Parable Discourse (13:1-52); the Rules for the Community (18:1-35); and the Discourse on the Last Things (24:3-25:46). *This observation has to be foundational for any analysis of the structure of Matthew*" (McNicol, *Jesus' Directions*, 70; italics added). Although McNicol initially states that Matthew's version of the "Discourse on the Last Things" is confined to 24:3-25:46 alone, he later concedes that "the Discourse is an integral part of an entire unit that goes from 23:1 to 25:46" (McNicol, *Jesus' Directions*, 75).

27. Leithart, *The Four*, 121.

Matthew: His Mind and His Message, Peter Ellis provides a helpful symmetrical (chiastic) outline of Matthew's gospel that illustrates the way in which Matthew has framed the entirety of his message[28]:

Sermon	**(f) ch 13**	
Narratives	(e) 11-12	(e') 14-17
Sermons	**(d) 10**	**(d') 18**
Narratives	(c) 8-9	(c') 19-22
Sermons	**(b) 5-7**	**(b') 23-25**
Narratives	(a) 1-4	(a') 26-28

Ellis rightly observes that the sermons (i.e., discourses) woven through-out this gospel are

> artfully balanced both in length and subject matter, with the first (5-7) and the last (ch 23-25) concerned principal-ly with the theme of "discipleship"; the second (ch 10) and the fourth (ch 18) with the mission of the Apostles and the use of apostolic authority in the community, and the central discourse (ch 13) with the Church as Kingdom of heaven on earth. Such an arrangement and symmetry can hardly be a matter of chance.[29]

In light of these intentional literary designs, this ought to lead us to ask further questions. For example, if the first discourse—the Sermon on the Mount—is "artfully balanced" with the Sermon on the Mount of Olives (i.e., the OD), and the first "Sermon on the Mount" is in-tentionally modeled after the revelation at Sinai where Israel's God de-livered His law to them, *what portions of Israel's history are the remain-*

---

28. Peter F. Ellis, *Matthew: His Mind and Message* (Collegeville, MN: The Litur-gical Press, 1985), 12. I have slightly modified his layout.

29. Ellis, *Matthew,* 14.

ing four discourses modeled after? And for the purposes of this project, what portion of Israel's history is the OD specifically modeled after?

In order to appreciate the larger picture which Matthew has painted for us, more details from Leithart's essay are worth noting.[30] According to Leithart, the five major discourses or "pillars" of Matthew's literary structure are as follows:

1. Matt. 5–7 = Sermon on the Mount
2. Matt. 10 = Mission of the Twelve: Preparation
3. Matt. 13 = Parables, Proverbs, and Wisdom of the coming Kingdom
4. Matt. 18 = Instructions for a Divided Kingdom
5. Matt. 23–25 = Olivet Discourse: Woes and Prophecy about the House of Israel

If we then take into account the theme of the first four narrative chapters as well as the three closing narrative chapters of the gospel, the five "pillars" of discourse would be sandwiched in the middle as follows:

Narrative: Matt. 1-4 = Beginnings, Birth, and Youth of God's Son

Discourse 1: Matt. 5-7 = Sermon on the Mount

Discourse 2: Matt. 10 = Mission of the Twelve: Preparation

Discourse 3: Matt. 13 = Parables, Proverbs, and Wisdom for the coming Kingdom

Discourse 4: Matt. 18 = Instructions for a Divided Kingdom

---

30. In what follows, I have changed some words which Leithart used, but all of the essential content remains the same. See Leithart, *Typological Structure;* see especially page 15 of that essay for the "pillars" described above. Leithart also expands upon these findings in his book, *The Gospel of Matthew Through New Eyes,* vol. 1, *Jesus as Israel* (Monroe, LA: Athanasius Press, 2017); see especially 8-41. Another recent work which utilizes Leithart's thesis is Schreiner, *Matthew, Disciple and Scribe,* 210-39.

Discourse 5: Matt. 23-25 = Olivet Discourse: Woes and Prophecy about the House of Israel
Narrative: Matt. 26-28 = Death, Resurrection, and Great Commission of God's Son

If we translate this general structure of Matthew's gospel *from* Israel's history and expand it according to a typological framework contained in Israel's Scriptures, as Leithart suggests, its chiastic arrangement would look something like the following:

A) Beginnings, Birth, and Youth of God's Son = Israel's Genesis—Mount Sinai

  B) Sermon on the Mount = Giving the Law at Mt. Sinai

    C) Mission of the Twelve: Preparation = Deuteronomy / Preparation for Conquest

      D) Parables, *etc.*, for the coming Kingdom = Wisdom / Solomonic Kingdom

    C') Instructions for a Divided Kingdom = Israel's Kingdom is Hopelessly Divided

  B') Olivet Discourse: Woes and Prophecy about the House of Israel = The End of the Judaean Kingdom / Warnings of Temple Destruction and Babylonian Exile

A') Death, Resurrection, and Great Commission of God's Son = Death and Resurrection of Israel, and the "Great Commission" of the Lord's "Anointed" (Cyrus)

As will soon become evident while examining the fifth discourse (section B' above), there seem to be intentional parallels between each corresponding section within this chiastic framework. The only portions that have not been shown so far are chapters 8–9, 11–12, 14–17, and 19–22, which are the remaining *narrative* segments that provide continuity between each of the five "pillars" of discourse above. With a few minor alterations to the descriptions used by Leithart, the inclusion of those narrative segments completes the typological framework of Matthew's design and is portrayed as follows:

Narrative – Matt. 1-4 = Israel's Genesis–Mount Sinai

Discourse 1: Matt. 5-7 = Giving the Law at Mt. Sinai

Narrative – Matt. 8-9 = Wilderness Wandering / Moses–Joshua

Discourse 2: Matt. 10 = Deuteronomy / Preparation for Conquest

Narrative – Matt. 11-12 = Entrance into Land & the Rise of a King / Joshua–David

Discourse 3: Matt. 13 = Parables, Proverbs, and Wisdom / Solomonic Kingdom

Narrative – Matt. 14-17 = Prophetic Ministry in the Northern Kingdom / Elijah–Elisha

Discourse 4: Matt. 18 = Israel's Kingdom is Hopelessly Divided

Narrative – Matt 19-22 = Prophetic Ministry in the Southern Kingdom / Jeremiah, *et al.*

Discourse 5: Matt. 23-25 = The End of the Judaean Kingdom / Warnings of Temple / Destruction & Babylonian Exile

Narrative – Matt. 26-28 = Death & Resurrection of Israel, and the "Great Commission" of the Lord's "Anointed" (Cyrus)

Since all of the literary segments have now been displayed along with their typological associations, it should be clear that it is at least *possible*, if not probable, that Matthew has organized his gospel in an intentionally intricate manner.[31] By recognizing that Matthew has

---

31. **Appendix A** outlines this typological framework in greater detail.

framed the story of Jesus in this intricately typological manner, the scope of prophetic fulfillment within Matthew's OD is likely limited to themes within Israel's history, namely, in that generation which Jesus lived and taught.

2.1.2 THE LITERARY THEMES AND PATTERNS OF THE FIFTH DISCOURSE

As we have seen, the larger literary structures and themes of Matthew's Gospel illustrate that the author has intentionally framed the OD in a particular setting that prophesies the end and exile of Israel along with the destruction of their temple.[32] By means of this framework, Matthew has prepared his audience for the death, resurrection, and "great commission" of Israel (i.e., God's "Son") contained in the narrative section immediately thereafter. It is this fifth discourse, encasing the OD, that we must now focus upon in detail in order to determine whether or not Matthew's literary features sustain the patristic methodology that emerged thereafter.

Because this fifth discourse begins in chapter 23,[33] its most notable feature is its context and audience. It begins in the context of

---

32. In addition to the typological framework proposed by Leithart, which associates the fifth discourse (Matt. 23-25) with prophetic denunciation upon Jerusalem's temple, David Moffitt offers an extensive series of intertexual links between Matthew 23 and the book of Lamentations, which prophetically laments the temple's first destruction. Moffitt also develops a case for such intertextual relationships being an integral part of understanding Matthew's death and resurrection narrative in Matthew 27. On that, see David M. Moffitt, *Rethinking the Atonement: New Perspectives on Jesus's Death, Resurrection, and Ascension* (Grand Rapids, MI: Baker Academic, 2022), 211-26.

33. By means of subtle technicalities, mostly focused on Matthew's transition between a *public* audience in Herod's Temple and a *private* audience on the Mount of Olives, some contemporary scholars have insisted that Matthew 23 is an entirely separate literary unit and discourse than chapters 24–25. For example, Jeannine K. Brown and Kyle Roberts, *Matthew*, THNTC (Grand Rapids, MI: Wm. B. Eerdmans Publishing Co., 2018), 214-15, present a superficial case

Jesus within the confines of Herod's Temple (cf. 21:23), which was the epicenter of second temple Judaism.[34] Here Jesus poignantly addresses two groups of people: Jesus' own disciples and also the hypocritical

---

in favor of this approach. Initially, they state clearly that "the *first* section of the Eschatological Discourse (24:1-35) focused on Jesus's predictions about the fall of the temple" (italics added). Immediately thereafter, they assert that "The narrative audience of this discourse is specified as Jesus's (twelve) disciples *in contrast* to the crowds with the disciples, who have been the storied audience for Matthew 23" (italics added). By means of this evidence—and this meager evidence alone—they conclude that "In this way, the evangelist *distinguishes* Jesus's teaching about the scribes and Pharisees in Matthew 23 from the Eschatological Discourse, and the two *should* be understood as distinct though connected by the theme of announcement of judgment" (italics added). For reasons which should become obvious by the end of this chapter, I will treat Matthew 23–25 as one intentionally unified literary unit and discourse, which I believe (and hope to convince) is the way Matthew has arranged it. Various footnotes throughout **Chapter 4** will contain further elaboration of contemporary scholarly reasons for separating these chapters into multiple discourses, as well as my responses to them. For that, see especially the footnotes of **4.1.5**.

34. According to N.T. Wright, *Jesus and the Victory of God*, COQG, vol. 2 (Minneapolis, MN: Fortress Press, 1996), 406, "The Temple was, in Jesus' day, the central symbol of Judaism, the location of Israel's most characteristic praxis, the topic of some of her most vital stories, the answer to her deepest questions, the subject of some of her most beautiful songs. And it was the place Jesus chose for his most dramatic public action. It has long been recognized that the evangelists were alive to the symbolic value of Jerusalem, Mount Zion, and the Temple itself—so much so, in fact, that they were able to weave it as a theme into their writings in a fairly sophisticated manner. It would be very strange if Jesus himself were not equally aware of the significance of the place described by the psalmist as 'the joy of the whole earth.'"

Akiva Cohen also points out that, "In continuity with the Hebrew Bible, the Second Temple—preceded by the tabernacle and First Temple—plays a central role in Matthew's narrative as the locus of God's name, presence, and holiness . . . . The Second Temple served as the institutional and symbolic center of Jewish identity for all Jews, whether they lived in Israel or the farthest reaches of the diaspora." Akiva Cohen, "Matthew and the Temple" in *Matthew Within Judaism: Israel and the Nations in the First Gospel*, Early Christianity and Its Literature, no. 27, ed. Anders Runesson and Daniel M. Gurtner (Atlanta, GA: SBL Press, 2020), 76].

rulers and disciples of Israel's cultus.[35] This context and audience, as we have seen, was clearly noticed by patristic exegetes. What remains to be seen is whether Matthew introduces any different context or audience; that is to say, any other context than Judaism's cultic epicenter or the people of Israel within the first century. The literary structure of Matthew's OD is as follows:

A) Those seated in Moses' seat: *not* doing what *they* do (23:1–12)

    B) Jesus denounces those seated in Moses' seat: *eight* sections of "woes" (23:13,14,15–39)[36]

        C) Jesus asks his disciples a question about the temple, and then promises its desolation (24:1-2)

        C') The disciples ask Jesus questions (24:3)

    B') Jesus answers the disciples' questions: *eight* sections of prophetic response (24:4–25:30)

A') The Son of Man seated on his own throne: doing what *they* did *not* do (25:31-46)

---

35. Explicit remarks are made to "scribes" and "Pharisees." However, Jesus repeatedly uses the term "hypocrites" in Matthew 23, which refers elsewhere in Matthew's Gospel to *the ruling class* along with the priests and elders of the Judean communities. For a helpful analysis of the wide-ranging problems of the ruling class in Judaea at that time, of which various scribes and peculiar factions within the wide-ranging sect of Pharisees played no small part, see Martin Goodman, *The Ruling Class of Judaea: The Origins of the Jewish Revolt against Rome, A.D. 66-70* (1987, repr., New York: Cambridge University Press, 1993). Also, Steve Mason offers a well-balanced survey of the Chief Priests, Sadducees, Pharisees, and Sanhedrin in Josephus' works, as compared with Luke-Acts. On that, see Steve Mason, *Josephus, Judea, and Christian Origins: Methods and Categories* (Peabody, MA: Hendrickson Publishers, 2009), 343-73. Especially noteworthy are his observations about there being "no stronger Judaean credentials than alliance with the Pharisees" in Jesus' generation (Mason, 361). For a detailed history of Second Temple high priests from 37 BCE to 70 CE, see James C. VanderKam, *From Joshua to Caiaphas: High Priests after the Exile* (Minneapolis, MN: Fortress Press, 2004), 394-490.

36. I have separated verse 14 from its surrounding verses for reasons which I explain in the following pages below.

There are a few things worth noting at this point before we dive into the really controversial sections. First of all, it is worth noticing that sections A and A' are relatively short, covering less than 16 verses for each section. Compositionally, then, the length within each of these sections is of comparable size. There is also an explicit theme between them: the theme of "sitting" on a throne or "seat."[37] The enthroned Jesus sitting (καθίσει) within the heavenly temple of section A' is closely connected with Jesus' introductory remarks about the scribes and Pharisees who "sit (ἐκάθισαν) on Moses' seat" of authoritative lawgiving.[38]

37. The relationship between these two "seats" in Matthew's OD was first brought to my attention in James B. Jordan's essay, *Structures of The Gospel According to Matthew*, BH Occasional Paper, no. 38 (Niceville, FL: Biblical Horizons, Dec. 2010), 15. John Kampen also highlights the relationship between the scribes and Pharisees sitting in Moses' seat (Matt. 23:1) and Jesus sitting down to begin his "Sermon on the Mount" (Matt. 5:1). On that, see John Kampen, *Matthew within Sectarian Judaism* (New Haven, CT: Yale University Press, 2019), 161.

38. Anders Runesson suggests that Moses' seat can be considered "as a fixed institution related to Torah and teaching (and thus, implicitly to the public synagogues, and therefore, also to the scribal office)." Anders Runesson, *Divine Wrath and Salvation in Matthew: The Narrative World of the First Gospel* (Minneapolis, MN: Fortress Press, 2016), 212. In addition to the broad scholarly recognition that "sitting in Moses' seat" referred to being recognized as having authority to interpret the Torah, John Nolland, *The Gospel of Matthew: A Commentary on the Greek Text* (Grand Rapids, MI: William B. Eerdmans Publishing Company, 2005), 922-23, also suggests that this phrase, which is unique to Matthew, finds one explicit parallel among Second Temple literature in the *Exagoge of Ezekiel* with its reference to a "heavenly throne" for Moses. If that image of a heavenly throne was part of Matthew's (or Jesus') meaning, then this adds to the heavenly thematic correlation between the two "seats" mentioned in sections A and A' of Matthew's OD. Nolland thinks the phrase more likely referred to a stone seat found in ancient synagogue remains of the first century that held scrolls of Scripture. The question remains, according to Nolland, as to whether influential leaders of Judaean communities ever sat on such seats. For archeological evidence of "Moses' seat" in ancient synagogues, along with photos and sketches, see Anders Runesson, Donald D. Binder, and Birger Olsson, *The Ancient Synagogue from Its Origins to 200 C.E.: A Sourcebook* (Leiden, Netherlands: Brill, 2010), 132-3; Donald D. Binder, *Into the Temple Courts: The Place of the Synagogues in the*

Secondarily, it is important to notice that sections B and B' each contain *eight* subsections, *not* seven. I include verse 14 (which completes the total of eight subsections) in this literary structure because many *modern* translations of Matthew's Gospel remove verse 14 entirely on the alleged grounds that:

1) It is an "interpolation" derived from Mark 12:40 or Luke 20:47.

2) A handful of very "early" manuscripts omit the verse altogether.

3) In those manuscripts which do contain verse 14, it is inserted both *before and after* verse 13, thereby leaving its authenticity in doubt because of its supposed spurious placement within the narrative.[39]

In the ESV, Matthew 23:14 is translated, "*Woe to you, scribes and Pharisees, hypocrites! For you devour widows' houses and for a pretense you make long prayers; therefore you will receive the greater condemnation.*"[40] The reasons I consider this variant reading to be genuine and have

---

Second Temple Period, SBL Dissertation Series, no. 169 (Atlanta, GA: Society of Biblical Literature, 1999), 299-303.

39. In Bruce Metzger's work, *A Textual Commentary on the Greek New Testament*, 2nd ed. (Stuttgart, Germany: United Bible Societies, 1994), he simply asserts the following "facts" dogmatically: "That ver. 14 is an interpolation derived from the parallel in Mk 12.40 or Lk 20.47 is clear (*a*) from its absence in the earliest and best authorities of the Alexandrian and Western types of text, and (*b*) from the fact that the witnesses that include the passage have it in different places, either after ver. 13 (so the Textus Receptus) or before ver. 13" (Stuttgart, 50). In *A Textual Guide to the Greek New Testament* (Stuttgart, Germany: German Bible Society, 2012), Roger L. Omanson repeats Metzger's reasons almost verbatim, claiming that "Verse 14 is not included in the earliest and best manuscripts of the Alexandrian and Western types of text. Copyists have clearly added it from the parallel text in Mark 12:40 or Luke 20:47; this is confirmed by the fact that some copyists added it before v. 13, and others added it after v. 13."

40. This translation of the omitted verse—v. 14—is taken from the footnotes of the ESV.

incorporated it into the literary structure above are numerous and varied. However, a detailed excursus on the subject would be beyond the scope of this part of the study. Nevertheless, a brief explanation of my own conclusions may help encourage further investigation into what I believe to be an unnecessary omission from modern translations. Those reasons of my own can be summarized in four points:

    i)   The allegations of "interpolation" are, at best, conspicuously inconsistent, and at worst, demonstrably arbitrary in light of popular and official explanations given.[41]

---

41. I believe such explanations of "interpolation" from Mark 12:40 or Luke 20:47 (see above) are demonstrably arbitrary for *at least* two reasons:

(1) Matthew 23:14 is an obvious example of *Homoeoteleuton*, i.e., when a clause ends in the same word as that which ended the preceding sentence, or when two or more sentences begin with the same words, and "the transcriber's eyes have wandered from the one to the other, to the entire omission of the whole passage lying between them." Frederick Henry Ambrose Scrivener, *A Plain Introduction to the Criticism of the New Testament* (1961, repr., New York: Cambridge University Press, 2009), 9. Each of the eight subsections in Matthew 23:14-16 begin with the same words, Οὐαὶ ὑμῖν ("woe to you"), and the omission of verse 14 is easily explained by copyists who accidentally skipped over the Οὐαὶ ὑμῖν of verse 14. Scrivener, a well-respected NT textual scholar, concluded that Matthew 23:14 became lost in some manuscripts as a result of *Homoeoteleuton*.

(2) In light of the way Metzger and other editors of the UBS *Greek New Testament* have treated other verses *within the same discourse,* "interpolation" is *not* very obvious in Matthew 23:14. For example, only ten verses prior to this alleged "interpolation," in Matthew 23:4 we find variants in their critical apparatus which *expand* that verse, even though Matthew 23:14 and 23:4 share nearly identical manuscript support. The apparatus of Matthew 23:4 is *not* treated with certainty as an "interpolation," whereas 23:14 is treated with *absolute* certainty. The *expanded* variant reading of 23:4 remains approved within the final UBS Greek text. According to Kurt Aland, Matthew Black, Carlo M. Martini, Bruce Metzger, and Allen Wikgren, ed., *The Greek New Testament*, 2nd ed. (Stuttgart, Germany: United Bible Societies, 1968), 88, the inclusion and approval of this *longer* variant reading in 23:4 (instead of the shorter, *omitted* phrase among variants) is allegedly well-testified and justified by manuscripts K, W, Δ, II, 0107, 1038, 28, 565, 1009, 1071, 1079, 1195, 1216, 1230, 1241, 1242, 1253, 1365, 1546, 1646, 2148, 2174, *Byz Lect*, it(f), syr, cop, eth, Chrysostom, and

ii) Not all of the "earliest" or "best" manuscripts omit this verse.[42]

John-Damascus. Intriguingly, *those exact same manuscripts* are listed on the very next page as evidence which supports the *inclusion* of Matthew 23:14 in its entirety (which they conspicuously disapproved and omitted). In other words, the UBS committee chose to approve and include the *longer* reading of verse 4 and disapprove and omit the *longer* reading (i.e., the entire verse) of 23:14, even though the majority of manuscript witnesses for decisions about both verses are nearly identical.

Furthermore, Metzger's *Textual Commentary* on Matthew 23:4 shows that the *expanded* variants in 23:4 were considered an instance of *Homoeoteleuton* (Metzger, *Textual Commentary*, 49). After highlighting that "the majority of the Committee" favored the longer reading because they were "impressed by the weight of the external evidence supporting the longer text," Metzger states one of their reasons for keeping it: because its *absence* is explainable by "accidental oversight (the eye of the copyist passing from one καὶ to the other)." In response to this, one might suspect that a few more extremely "weighty" manuscripts were used by the UBS committee to support the *longer* reading of Matthew 23:4. And they do so in their textual apparatus. Yet, even that approach does not justify their conclusions, for in support of including the longer reading of 23:4, they prioritized codices *Vaticanus* (fourth century), *Bezae* (fifth century), and Θ *(Tbilisi,* eighth century*);* whereas the *shorter* (omitted) readings of that same verse are prioritized by codex *Sinaiticus* (fourth century) and *L* (seventh century). Such "weightiness" is seemingly arbitrary once one compares these decisions with their justification for *omitting* Matthew 23:14 in its entirety, just ten verses later. In support of *omitting* Matthew 23:14 entirely, their apparatus prioritizes all of the same "weighty" manuscripts above, i.e., codices *Sinaiticus, Vaticanus, Bezae, L,* and *Tbilisi.*

To summarize these facts stated above, the *majority* of the UBS committee members decided to keep the longer reading of Matthew 23:4 (omitted in some manuscripts) within their *Greek New Testament* because of how "impressive" the manuscript evidence was to support the longer reading. Yet when all of the exact same manuscripts seem to favor the longer reading of Matthew 23:14 (by not omitting it), the editors of the UBS (Metzger included) considered it best to delete the verse entirely. As far as I am concerned, if the "weight of external evidence" is impressive enough to *not* omit the longer reading of Matthew 23:4, it should also be impressive enough to *not* omit Matthew 23:14 entirely.

42. For understanding many of the reasons why I believe the "earliest" manuscripts (i.e., the Alexandrian and Western text-types, contra Omanson's claim above) are *not* necessarily—and certainly not *always*—the "best," see Jakob Van

iii) The insertion of verse 14 before and after verse 13 indicates scribal *awareness* of its authenticity.

iv) The eight subsections of sections *B* and *B'* within the Olivet Discourse *mirror* the eight subsections of *B* and *B'* in Matthew's "Sermon on the Mount."[43]

Bruggen, *The Ancient Text of the New Testament* (Winnipeg: Premier Publishing, 1936). Also, see Harry A. Sturz, *The Byzantine Text-Type & New Testament Textual Criticism* (Nashville, TN: Thomas Nelson Publishers, 1984).

43. The literary structure of the Sermon on the Mount is as follows:

A) Jesus ascends mountain surrounded by crowds, 4:25-5:2
  B) Eight blessings, 5:3-10
    C) Response to persecution on Jesus' account: Not destroying "the law and prophets," but glorifying "your Father in Heaven," 5:11-20
      D) Two triads about law-keeping, 5:21-48
        E) One triad about spiritual discipline, 6:1-18
      D') Two triads about kingdom prioritization, 6:19-7:6
    C') Response to persecution on Jesus' account: "*This is* the law and prophets," that "your Father in Heaven" provides, 7:7-12
  B') Eight warnings, 7:13-27
A') Jesus descends mountain surrounded by crowds, 7:28-8:1

The literary structure of sections *B* and *B'* (using the ESV translation) are as follows:

Section B: Blessings (5:3-10)

1) Blessed are the poor in spirit, *for theirs is the kingdom of heaven.*
2) Blessed are those who mourn, for they shall be comforted.
3) Blessed are the meek, for they shall inherit the earth.
4) Blessed are those who hunger and thirst for righteousness, for they shall be satisfied.
5) Blessed are the merciful, for they shall receive mercy.
6) Blessed are the pure in heart, for they shall see God.
7) Blessed are the peacemakers, for they shall be called sons of God.
8) Blessed are those who are persecuted for righteousness' sake, *for theirs is the kingdom of heaven.*

Section B': Warnings (7:13-27)

1a) Enter by *the narrow gate*, for the gate is wide and the way is easy that leads to destruction, and *those who will enter by it* are many.
1b) For *the gate is narrow* and the way is hard that leads to life, and *those who find it* are few.

The layout of eight subsections (see point **iv** above) is pertinent to Matthew's balanced literary *design* and *intentionality*, and therefore requires greater explanation.[44] I believe section *B* (Matt. 23:13-39)

2a) Beware of false prophets, who come to you in sheep's clothing but inwardly are ravenous wolves. *You will recognize them by their fruits.*

2b) Are grapes gathered from thornbushes, or figs from thistles? So, every healthy tree bears good fruit, but the diseased tree bears bad fruit. A healthy tree cannot bear bad fruit, nor can a diseased tree bear good fruit. Every tree that does not bear good fruit is cut down and thrown into the fire. *Thus you will recognize them by their fruits.*

3a) Not *everyone who says to me, "Lord, Lord,"* will enter the kingdom of heaven, but the one who does the will of my Father who is in heaven.

3b) On that day *many will say to me, "Lord, Lord,* did we not prophesy in your name, and cast out demons in your name, and do many mighty works in your name?" And then will I declare to them, "I never knew you; depart from me, you workers of lawlessness."

4a) *Everyone then who hears these words of mine and does them* will be like a wise man who built his house on the rock. And the rain fell, and the floods came, and the winds blew and beat on that house, but it did not fall, because it had been founded on the rock.

4b) And *everyone who hears these words of mine and does not do them* will be like a foolish man who built his house on the sand. And the rain fell, and the floods came, and the winds blew and beat against that house, and it fell, and great was the fall of it.

44. Jason Hood's essay, "Matthew 23-25: The Extent of Jesus' Fifth Discourse," JBL, vol. 128, no. 3 (2009), presents one of the most thorough and scathing critiques of contemporary Matthean scholars who divide Matthew 23 from chapters 24-25 and treat each of them as separate discourses. Among Hood's many proposals to illustrate the unity of Matthew 23-25, he illustrates the unity of chapters 5-7 (the first discourse) and its parallels with chapters 23-25 (the fifth discourse). Hood identifies "a number of significant links between chs. 5–7 and chs. 23–25, including the most important complex of links—the correspondence between the Beatitudes and the woes" (Hood, 540). Hood's insights about the beatitudes and woes are worth citing at length. He writes, "Although it is rarely noted, when viewed in tandem, the blessings of Matthew 5:3-12 and the curses of 23:13-36 present an important cluster of parallels. The Beatitudes open with a reference to the reception of the kingdom (5:2); the woes open with a reference to the loss of, and prevention of entry into, the kingdom (23:13; cf. 5:20). The scribes and Pharisees are *cursed* 'children of hell' leading their prose-

within the Olivet Discourse completes a *sequence* of eight "woes" total (not seven, as many scholars assert),[45] which can be divided into two

lytes to become twice the same (23:15) and the 'brood of vipers' (23:23), which contrasts with the parentage of Jesus' blessed followers, who are the 'children of God' (5:9). The Beatitudes commend mercy (5:5) and inner purity (5:8), while the woes condemn the lack of both traits in Jesus' opponents (23:23-26). The Beatitudes conclude with an extended reference to the persecution the righteous will experience 'for righteousness' sake' just as earlier generations 'persecuted the prophets' (5:10-12). The woes conclude with an extended discussion of judgment on the scribes and Pharisees for joining their ancestors in bringing such miseries on God's representatives, those who 'persecute' the 'prophets' (23:29-35). Both passages identify the persecuting scribes and Pharisees with earlier generations. . . . Both conclusions are immediately followed by passages in which Jesus addresses a city. Moreover, as with the Beatitudes and woes, there is *contrast* between the two cities, with one describing the vocation of true disciples and the other describing the judgment of those who have rejected Jesus" (Hood, 540-1).

45. Many scholars assert that only seven "woes" are genuine, without offering much evidence to support that claim. For multiple examples of this oft-parroted conjecture, see Nolland, *Matthew*, 932; Keener, *Matthew*, 547; France, *Matthew,* 867; Ulrich Luz, *Matthew 21–28: A Commentary*, HCHCB, vol. 3 of Matthew, trans. James E. Crouch (Minneapolis, MN: Fortress Press, 2005), 112; Carson, *Matthew,* 477; Donald A. Hagner, *Matthew 14–28*, WBC, 33B (Nashville, TN: Nelson Reference, 1995), 665; W.D. Davies and D.C. Allison, *The Gospel According to Saint Matthew*, ICC, vol. 3 (1997, repr., New York: Bloomsbury T&T Clark, 2012), 285; Alistair I. Wilson, *When Will These Things Happen? A Study of Jesus as Judge in Matthew 21-25*, PBM (2004, repr., Eugene, OR: Wipf & Stock Publishers, 2006), 102.

Butler, *The Originality of St Matthew*, 72-85, presents an argument for the likelihood of eight woes. First, he offers convincing evidence that Mark excerpted Matthew's version of the OD. After presenting a case for Mark's dependence on Matthew, he offers one further bit of evidence pertaining to Mark 12:40 and Mark's source for it (keeping in mind that Luke used Mark as a source). Butler imagines a curious difficulty with "cross-harmonizing" if Matthew used Mark 12:40 as a source to create an independent "woe" in 23:14. Although he accepts the possibility that Mark could have used an independent source for 12:40, and Matthew 23:14 might be a later scribal addition (i.e., not authentic, and therefore not a source for Mark), Butler suggests that Mark 12:40 is more easily explained if Matthew was Mark's source and Matthew 23:14 was actually original to Matthew. According to Butler, the alleged lack of manuscript support for Matthew 23:14 can be explained easily "by the early omission of the verse in

halves. The first three "woes" of each half are followed immediately by a much longer and detailed fourth "woe" that explicitly links the "scribes and Pharisees" with the "blind guides" overseeing God's people. Thematically, it is because of these blind guides and their ungodly oversight that the God of Israel who sits enthroned in His temple is misunderstood and mocked by many. Matthew organizes these eight subsections (23:13–39) in the following way:

---

one line of the MS tradition" (Butler, 75). The real difficulty, according to Butler, is convincing modern scholars to accept the likelihood that Markan priority is an overly-complicated, speculative, and unnecessary theory. Ironically, Butler's *only reservation* for accepting the authenticity of Matthew 23:14 is *not* textual, grammatical, or syntactical, but rather an "inconvenience" of eight woes instead of what he describes as "the (Semitic) seven." Butler suspects that the number seven is more *stylistically* appropriate for a Jewish author to record (Butler, 75). Strangely, Butler does not highlight that the eight *beatitudes* (Matt. 5:3-10) are lacking in Jewish style as well. Nevertheless, even when some scholars acknowledge eight legitimate "woes" across Matthew 23, it could still be argued that there is no numerical parallel with the Beatitudes in Matthew 5 because there are technically *nine* beatitudes (not eight). Such would then break the symmetry between each discourse. To this, David Wenham's observations are worth noting at length. He writes, "What is immediately clear from setting out the beatitudes in this way is that they are very carefully arranged. There are eight beatitudes in the third person, 'Blessed are so and so . . . ,' and the ninth is in the second person, 'Blessed are you.' The ninth is the odd one out, and is arguably a sort of bridge from the general statements in beatitudes 1-8 into the rest of the Sermon, which is addressed directly to the disciples. Beatitudes 1-8 may therefore be taken as a group. When they are, various things are notable: first, numbers 1 and 8 have the same promise, 'for theirs is the kingdom of heaven.' This probably suggests that all the beatitudes are about the kingdom of heaven, and about those who will receive it. In Matthew's gospel Jesus' message has just been summed up in 4:17: 'Repent, for the kingdom of heaven has come near.' And it is this kingdom that Jesus' ministry is about and that the Sermon on the Mount is about." David Wenham, "The Rock on Which to Build: Some Mainly Pauline Observations about the Sermon on the Mount," in *Built Upon The Rock: Studies in the Gospel of Matthew*, ed. Daniel M. Gurtner and John Nolland (Grand Rapids, MI: William B. Eerdmans Publishing Company, 2008), 198-9.

1) **But woe to you, scribes and Pharisees, hypocrites!** For you shut the kingdom of heaven in people's faces. For you neither enter yourselves nor allow those who would enter to go in.

2) **Woe to you, scribes and Pharisees, hypocrites!** For you devour widows' houses and for a pretense you make long prayers; therefore you will receive the greater condemnation.

3) **Woe to you, scribes and Pharisees, hypocrites!** For you travel across sea and land to make a single proselyte, and when he becomes a proselyte, you make him twice as much a child of hell as yourselves.

4) **Woe to you, blind guides**, who say, "If anyone swears by the temple, it is nothing, but if anyone swears by the gold of the temple, he is bound by his oath." You blind fools! For which is greater, the gold or the temple that has made the gold sacred? And you say, "If anyone swears by the altar, it is nothing, but if anyone swears by the gift that is on the altar, he is bound by his oath." You blind men! For which is greater, the gift or the altar that makes the gift sacred? So whoever swears by the altar swears by it and by everything on it. And whoever swears by the temple swears by it and by him who dwells in it. And whoever swears by heaven swears by the throne of God and by him who sits upon it.

5) **Woe to you, scribes and Pharisees, hypocrites!** For you tithe mint and dill and cumin, and have neglected the weightier matters of the law: justice and mercy and faithfulness. These you ought to have done, without neglecting the others. You blind guides, straining out a gnat and swallowing a camel!

6) **Woe to you, scribes and Pharisees, hypocrites!** For you clean the outside of the cup and the plate, but inside they are

full of greed and self-indulgence. You blind Pharisee! First clean the inside of the cup and the plate, that the outside also may be clean.

7) **Woe to you, scribes and Pharisees, hypocrites!** For you are like whitewashed tombs, which outwardly appear beautiful, but within are full of dead people's bones and all uncleanness. So you also outwardly appear righteous to others, but within you are full of hypocrisy and lawlessness.

8) **Woe to you, scribes and Pharisees, hypocrites!** For you build the tombs of the prophets and decorate the monuments of the righteous, saying, "If we had lived in the days of our fathers, we would not have taken part with them in shedding the blood of the prophets." Thus you witness against yourselves that you are sons of those who murdered the prophets. Fill up, then, the measure of your fathers. You serpents, you brood of vipers, how are you to escape being sentenced to hell? Therefore I send you prophets and wise men and scribes, some of whom you will kill and crucify, and some you will flog in your synagogues and persecute from town to town, so that on you may come all the righteous blood shed on earth, from the blood of righteous Abel to the blood of Zechariah the son of Barachiah, whom you murdered between the sanctuary and the altar. Truly, I say to you, all these things will come upon this generation. O Jerusalem, Jerusalem, the city that kills the prophets and stones those who are sent to it! How often would I have gathered your children together as a hen gathers her brood under her wings, and you were not willing! See, your house is left to you desolate. For I tell you, you will not see me again, until you say, "Blessed is he who comes in the name of the Lord."

Immediately after these "woes" are pronounced, Jesus abandons the temple and lucidly forecasts its destruction, saying, "there is not a layer of stone left behind in this place that will not be demolished" (Matt. 24:1).[46] Then he "walks over to the Mount of Olives east of the city (24:3), where God's presence had previously lodged after having left the first temple before its destruction (Ezek. 11:23)."[47] Much like Ezekiel's vision of God's glory finally departing the temple (Ezek. 10-11), Jesus' departure "initiates the process of abandonment of the temple" because "the temple cannot be destroyed as long as God dwells there."[48]

Equally important is the way in which the eighth subsection of "woes" ends. Underlined above (Matt. 23:36), Jesus declares emphatically that "*all these things* (ταῦτα πάντα) *will come upon this generation* (τὴν γενεὰν ταύτην)." Such distinctive phrases will become important to recall when deciphering later eschatological remarks in chapter 24, because they are echoed in the corresponding section (*B'*) of this fifth discourse, thereby implying the same objective audience and context in Jesus' repeated admonition:

> *Truly, I say to you, all these things* (ταῦτα πάντα) *will come upon this generation* (τὴν γενεὰν ταύτην). O Jerusalem! Jerusalem, the city that kills the prophets and stones those who are sent to it! How often I have gathered your children together as a

---

46. This is my translation. Jesus responds with an emphatic double-negation: "οὐ μὴ ἀφεθῇ ὧδε λίθος ἐπὶ λίθον ὃς οὐ καταλυθήσεται." In addition to this, I have stretched out ἀφεθῇ ὧδε beyond its typical usage (i.e., "left here"), and interpreted λίθος ἐπὶ λίθον ("a stone upon stone") as a course of stones, in order to provide a sense of place for the final verb in relation to the temple's construction. The final verb, καταλυθήσεται ("demolished" or "torn down"), is a relatively rare but important term used across Matthew's Gospel. It is only mentioned a handful of times. Matthew places Jesus' last use of καταλύω in the "Sermon on the Mount" (5:17): "Do not think I have come to *demolish* (καταλῦσαι) the Torah or the Prophets; I have not come to *demolish* (καταλῦσαι) them, but to fulfill them." The only other references to καταλύω used by Matthew are in 26:61 and 27:40, both of which repeat this temple-deconstruction and reconstruction theme.

47. Runesson, *Divine Wrath and Salvation*, 127.

48. Runesson, *Divine Wrath and Salvation*, 127.

hen gathers her brood under her wings, and you were not willing! See, your house is left to you desolate! (Matt. 23:36-38).

From the fig tree learn its lesson: as soon as its branch becomes tender and puts out its leaves, you know that summer is near. So also, *when you see all these things* (πάντα ταῦτα), you know that he is near, at the very gates. *Truly, I say to you, this generation* (ἡ γενεὰ αὕτη) *will not pass away until all these things* (πάντα ταῦτα) *take place* (Matt. 24:32-34).

The phrase "this generation" in Matt. 23:36 could theoretically refer to lots of ideas.[49] For example, some scholars draw attention to the notion that "this generation" is used *qualitatively* throughout Mat-

---

49. Runesson offers a wide variety of ways in which "this generation" could be (and has been) understood. On that, see *Divine Wrath and Salvation*, 271-307. Runesson also offers many helpful insights about "this generation" in relation to the eschaton. He writes, "Matthew shows an interest in the generations of Israel already in the genealogy, counting fourteen of them between Abraham and David, fourteen between David and the Babylonian exile, and fourteen between the exile and the Messiah (1:17). For Matthew, time is not a neutral phenomenon or a label used to define a series of events. Rather, time is something which is invested with theological and revelatory meaning; it can be structured to demonstrate God's plan and intent for the future, revealing the deeper meaning behind the fundamentally important question, 'What time is it?' 'This generation,' as shown by 24:34 and indirectly by 16:28, is a designation that refers to the last generation before the final judgment and the coming of the kingdom, i.e., the time immediately preceding the fulfillment of the promised eschatological salvation to be set in motion by the Messiah" (Runesson, *Divine Wrath*, 274). He also says, "the core meaning of 'this generation,' which is stable throughout the Gospel, is that it represents a theo-chronological marker, indicating that the present time is the time of the last generation before the eschatological end and the final judgment" (Runesson, *Divine Wrath*, 275); "the stated primary purpose of the Gospel, to save the Jewish people from their sins as the eschaton is approaching (1:21; 4:17), this is also exactly what we find in relation to the expression 'this generation'" (Runesson, *Divine Wrath*, 275).

thew's Gospel,[50] describing any generation that is distinctly worthy of God's judgment. Regardless of whether or not this qualitative distinction is adopted, many scholars are still content with acknowledging its most natural point of reference,[51] meaning *that particular generation* in which Jesus and his disciples were living. In Matthew 23:36, "this generation" described the populous who would endure up to the old covenant's *terminus*, when Jerusalem and Israel's temple within it would become desolate.[52]

50. See Robert Gundry's explanation in *Matthew: A Commentary on His Literary and Theological Art* (1982, repr., Grand Rapids, MI: William B. Eerdmans Publishing Company, 1983), 491. I interact with Gundry's remarks in **4.1.6**.

51. Nolland, *Matthew*, 989; France, *Matthew*, 930. Adela Yarbro Collins says, "The term 'this generation' refers to the contemporaries of John the Baptist, Jesus, and his followers (Matt. 11:16; 12:38-42, 45; 24:34)" and that "The lament of Jesus over Jerusalem that follows the woe sayings supports this inference that the destruction of the city is the punishment implied here." Adela Yarbro Collins, "Polemic against the Pharisees in Matthew 23" in *The Pharisees*, ed. Joseph Sievers and Amy-Jill Levine (Grand Rapids, MI: William B. Eerdmans Publishing Company, 2021), 167. Luz, *Matthew 21–28*, 208, goes a different direction, making a few interesting remarks along the way. First, he says that the clear meaning of γενεὰ is "generation." Second, he says, "Reinterpretations, of which there have been many even to the present, are useless." This opinion is interesting because it seems to arise from a careful reading of the discourse in its first-century historical context. However, because Luz *assumes* that the author of Matthew's Gospel is describing events *after* 70 CE that are imagined to be within the author's own immediate future, Luz is only willing to interpret "this generation" to mean what he imagines "Matthew" to have expected, which allegedly was "the parousia [to occur] within the space of at most one lifetime."

52. Commenting on Matthew's use of temple terminology, Daniel Gurtner points out that among all the terms available to describe the "Temple," the term ναός does not appear in Matthew's Gospel *until* the woes of chapter 23. This is noteworthy because the LXX "overwhelmingly" uses ναός to translate the Hebrew term for the main room of Jerusalem's Temple. In classical Greek, Gurtner says it referred to the "abode of the gods" within temples. On that, see Daniel M. Gurtner, "Matthew's Theology of the Temple and the 'Parting of the Ways': Christian Origins and the First Gospel" in *Built Upon The Rock,* ed. Gurtner and Nolland, 131-132. In contrast with prevalent scholarly views that relate temples with "house" terminology, Eyal Regev seriously questions whether "your

An interesting specimen of scholarly interpretation over the last

house" in Matthew 23:38 originally referred to the temple in Jerusalem. Instead, he claims that "your house" originally referred "to a house in the city" and *not* the temple within Jerusalem. Regev posits this on the basis of two factors: **(1)** modern scholars allocate the saying in Matthew 23:38 among an alleged "Q" source for the synoptic gospels, and **(2)** similar terminology is found in Jeremiah 22:5. On this, see Eyal Regev, *The Temple in Early Christianity: Experiencing the Sacred* (New Haven, CT: Yale University Press, 2019), 131-2. Aside from ignoring the fact that an alleged "Q" source notoriously strips statements of Jesus out of each Gospel's literary context, Regev's minimalistic argument at this point is noticeably brief and dodgy because he insists that the "house" mentioned in Jeremiah 22:5 only refers to the king's palace within Judaea (and not the temple or any of its precincts). Such minimalistic and convenient interpretations are not surprising considering that Regev frames his entire book around the tendentious notion that a loss of allegiance to the Jewish temple was *never* endorsed by Jesus. Needless to say, his prejudicial conjecture in this regard is irresponsible at best and duplicitous at worst. I contend, instead, along with many hundreds of scholars, that Jesus describes the temple when he mentions the future desolate-state of Jerusalem's "house" (οἶκος) in Matthew 23:38. In contrast with Regev's dubious propositions, Gurtner's observations about Jesus' actions in Matthew 23 are worth quoting at length. Gurtner writes:

Traditionally, scholars have seen this as a reference to God's abandonment of the First Temple, just as prior to its destruction (Ezek. 8:6, 12; 9:3, 9; 11:23; cf. Bar. 4:12) and perhaps looking back to the departure of the *Shekinah* from the Temple (cf. 1 Kgs. 9:6-9; Isa. 64:10-11). While Knowles is correct that these texts describe God's *departure* from the Temple, not its destruction, the departure of God's presence from the Temple was surely a prelude to the city's destruction (Josephus, *War* 5.412-13; 6.295-300; Tacitus, *Histories* 5.13; 2 *Bar.* 8.2; 64.6-7; *Par. Jer.* 4.1). But the destruction of the Temple was seen as subsequent to God's departure, both of which were inescapably the result of the sins of God's people. This is apparent in a similar use of Matthew's "desolation" (ἔρημος) saying, which occurs in *T. Levi* 15.1, announcing that "the sanctuary which the Lord chose shall become desolate through your uncleanness, and you shall be captives in all the nations." Similarly, Josephus says, "God himself . . . turned away from our city . . . because he deemed the Temple to be no longer a clean dwelling place for Him" (*Ant.* 20.166; cf. *War* 5.19). This view is underscored by the departure of Jesus' presence, which Matthew has already identified with the Shekinah (Matt. 18:20; cf. m. 'Abot 3.2), from the temple (ἱερόν) in prophetic fashion going toward the Mount of Olives (24:1; cf. Zech. 14:4). This is significant, Knowles contends, because God's presence in that shrine was an affirmation of Israel's election, sanctification and protection. Yet the realities of 586 B.C.E. indicate

two millennia is that the meaning of "this generation" in 23:36 is *rarely* disputed; only its meaning in 24:34 has remained hotly disputed,[53] because it is stated in a context which scholars *assume* to be in response to questions about future, "end-of-the-world" events. Some scholars acknowledge the oddity of widespread agreement pertaining to "this generation" in 23:36 followed by dissonant interpretations of "this generation" in 24:34. That is because the placement of this peculiar phrase in both 23:36 and 24:34 appears to be intentional on Matthew's part, since both take place within the same literary context.

"that the covenantal sanction afforded by God's 'presence' was not inviolable." It would seem natural, then, for a first-century Jewish reader to see Jesus' departure as a similar act of abandonment and, perhaps, the removal of the mark of Israel's identity as the people of God. Again, though, fault lies with the misuse and corruption of an otherwise perfectly legitimate Temple. Gurtner, "*Matthew's Theology of the Temple*," 144-6.

53. In his monograph about the peculiar phrase "this generation" (ἡ γενεὰ αὕτη) in the New Testament and its roots in early Judaism, Evald Lövestam shares the same opinion as Joseph Fitzmyer, who says that ἡ γενεὰ αὕτη "has been characterized as 'in the long run the most difficult phrase to interpret in this complicated eschatological discourse.'" Evald Lövestam, *Jesus and 'this Generation': A New Testament Study*, CBNTS, 25, trans. Moira Linnarud (Stockholm, Sweden: Almqvist & Wiksell International, 1995), 82. In contrast with Lövestam and Fitzmyer, I contend that this phrase only appears difficult because of presuppositional commitments to futuristic, end-of-*our*-world scenarios. In addition to that root cause, such apparent difficulties are perpetuated in commentaries that fail to mention the *possibility* of first-century fulfillment as well as the Christian tradition underlining it. This deflection is most glaring in Daniel Harrington's commentary on Matthew in which his only comments about "this generation" in 24:34 completely ignore Christian tradition that incorporates first-century fulfillment in 70 CE. He writes, "*this generation*: The phrase 'all these things' would most obviously refer to the events leading up to the coming of the Son of Man, though some interpreters connect it with Jesus' death and resurrection. The warning would therefore tie in the Son of Man's coming to the generation close to Jesus, though some interpreters understand *genea* as 'race' or 'people' (=Israel). At any rate the warning about the closeness of the Son of Man's coming is balanced by Matt 24:36." Daniel Harrington, *The Gospel of Matthew*, SPS, vol. 1 (Collegeville, MN: Liturgical Press, 2007), 342.

As a matter of literary design, it seems odd to imagine one author (or "final" redactor) placing two identical terms within the same discourse without any regard to the meaning shared between them. Moreover, if we take into account the literary structure in which these phrases take place, they are clearly established in sections that are parallel with each other (B and B'), thereby leaving an impression that they each share the same historical point of reference.

Following section B, we now approach sections C and C', which address the questions asked by Jesus and his disciples:

C) Jesus asks his disciples a question about the temple and then promises its desolation (24:1–2)
Jesus left the temple and was going away, when his disciples came to point out to him the buildings of the temple. But he answered them, "You see all these, do you not? Truly, I say to you, there will not be left here one stone upon another that will not be thrown down."

C') The disciples ask Jesus questions (24:3)
As he sat on the Mount of Olives, the disciples came to him privately, saying, "Tell us, when will these things be, and what will be the sign of your coming, and of the end of the age?"

Because this section of the fifth discourse is the center of its chiastic structure, where its design hinges, it is the most obvious transitional section to be expected therein. Even though there has been no hint of anticipating events taking place *beyond that generation*, it is here where contemporary scholars nevertheless opine about a "transitional verse" that supposedly divides first-century fulfillment from future "end-of-the-world" fulfillment yet to come.

When approaching ways in which to interpret these questions of section C', most agree that the first question of Jesus' disciples referred to Jerusalem's destruction in 70 CE. By supplementing the disciples' questions (or Jesus' enigmatic responses to them) with a foreign

74

objective, such as a very distant, futuristic prophecy about the "end of the world," the reader is suddenly presented with a dilemma: from where *in the discourse* did such a foreign idea about a transition into the future *beyond that generation* arise? This question is important to reflect upon because Matthew has not structured the fifth discourse in a way that shows the disciples' questions transitioning from first-century events to end-of-the-world events. If one assumes that they must have (which is not obvious at all), it is highly suspect that such a transition would take place *after* a question that clearly relates to the destruction of Jerusalem and its temple *in that generation*.

It seems even more disjointed to imagine, as some scholars have,[54] that all of the disciples' questions referred to first-century expectations, but Matthew (or an alleged "final" redactor) supposedly placed a transitional verse about the "end of the world" *halfway through* section *B'*, to clarify or correct their alleged misunderstandings, even though such a transition in the midst of section *B'* is not even close to the central "hinge" of his chiastic structure in sections *C* and *C'*. If "Matthew" intended to convey clear literary intentionality of such a transition, the *middle* of section *B'* is, perhaps, the most unlikely place to expect it.[55]

---

54. On this, see **4.1.6**, **4.1.7**, and **4.1.8**.

55. This makes even more sense if Nicholas Elder's suggestion is taken into account, that the length of Matthew's Gospel would have likely prevented it from being read aloud *in one sitting*. From this, I surmise that Matthew's Gospel was composed to be studied primarily as a written text, and possibly only read aloud communally (and scrutinized) according to its various literary segments; whereas reading Mark's Gospel aloud in one sitting fits within the "custom duration" of audiences in that era (Elder, *Media Matrix*, 162n149). Challenging this "custom duration," Brian Wright presents a case that communal reading events were not only the prevailing form of social media across a wide geographical region of the Roman empire within the first century, including locations with active synagogues, but such communal readings were also frequent *and lengthy*. Communal reading also involved studying, engaging, scrutinizing, and reciting related works in the process. On that, see Brian J. Wright, *Communal Reading in the Time of Jesus: A Window into Early Christian Reading Practices* (Minneapolis,

At this point we ought to recall that not only is Matthew's OD considerately crafted, but *his entire Gospel* is as well. Even the larger literary structure and typological hermeneutic does not seem to allow for such a transition, since Matthew's OD recapitulates the message of Judaean destruction and exile. Why, then, would Matthew suddenly supplement Judaean destruction and exile with a foreign concept, such as events leading into a futuristic end-of-Heaven-and-Earth,[56]

MN: Fortress Press, 2017). My point here is to highlight the likely format in which the coherence of Matthew's OD would have been scrutinized, i.e., in written format. If people in the first-century *merely* listened to Matthew's OD within communal settings, Matthew's structural intentionality could be misunderstood. However, upon close examination of *the text*, misunderstandings are not as easily excused. Brian Wright's research also adds a new dimension to the evidence provided by James Carleton Paget, who offers a litany of direct references to Jewish uses of New Testament Gospels. Paget argues tentatively for non-Christian Jews possessing copies of Christian Gospels. On that, see James Carleton Paget, *Jews, Christians and Jewish Christians in Antiquity*, WUNT, 251 (Tubingen, Germany: Mohr Siebeck, 2010), 268-86. In my evaluation, Paget's observations and conclusions need some readjustment according to Wright's thesis. With regard to communal reading within Rabbinic (non-Christian) communities, it is also worth noting that numerous references in the Talmud which slander Jesus and his reputation evince awareness of, if not also the possession of, New Testament Gospels to carefully scrutinize their literary and historical integrity. On that, see Peter Schafer, *Jesus in the Talmud* (Princeton, NJ, Princeton University Press, 2007).

56. It is often suggested that Jesus clearly refers to the "end" of *our* world in Matthew 24:34-35 when he says, "Truly, I say to you, this generation will not pass away until all these things take place. *Heaven and earth will pass away*, but my words will not pass away." Because "heaven and earth" passing away is imagined to be literal (or, at least *more* literal than figurative) "heaven and earth" have obviously not passed away yet, and the fulfillment of this promise has not yet occurred. However, there are two alternative interpretations to this approach. One is to interpret Matthew 24:34-35 as a figure of speech that establishes assurance about Jesus' "words" and their inevitable futuristic fulfillment as stated. In this view, an "end" of "heaven and earth" is *not* explicitly prophesied; rather, it is used rhetorically to contrast and amplify *the certainty* of everything else that has been prophesied within this discourse. To paraphrase this approach to vv. 34-35: "Certainly, this generation will not pass away until all these things occur.

thousands of years after the first-century destruction of Jerusalem and the definitive end of its old covenant administration?
If you think these words of mine will pass away, compared to heaven and earth the certainty of what I just mentioned will outlast them both."

There is a second alternative, too. Even if one assumes that an "end" of "heaven and earth" is promised here alongside Jesus' "words," some notable scholars have pointed out that "heaven and earth" is actually an allusion to *Jerusalem along with its temple* elsewhere within biblical literature. Isaiah 65 is but one of many examples, and it clearly illustrates God "creating" a new "heaven and earth" in parallel with God "creating" a new *city of Jerusalem* (Isa. 65:17-18) along with its temple as a "holy mountain" (v. 25). Even the poetic imagery of clean and unclean animals dining together in Isaiah 65 invites the reader to imagine this re-creation of "heaven-and-earth" as a *new covenant* administration, where Jew and Gentile are both welcome to dine *without* old covenant liturgical barriers (v. 25; cf. Acts 10:9-23). Regarding this interpretive connection between Jerusalem's temple and the location of "heaven and earth," Fletcher-Louis argues that "[T]he Jerusalem Temple always had a complex mythological and cosmological significance which was the heart of the apocalyptic spirituality and the formative context of its theology and literature. . . . in both the biblical and post-biblical periods the Temple is invested with a set of cosmological meanings: the Temple stands at the center of the universe; it is the place from which creation began; it is the meeting point of heaven and earth—the 'Gate of Heaven'; it is the place where, at the end of days, as at the dawn of creation, the forces of chaos would be defeated and, most importantly for our purposes, it is a miniature version of the whole universe—a microcosm of heaven and earth." Crispin H. T. Fletcher-Louis, "Jesus, the Temple and the Dissolution of Heaven and Earth," in *Apocalyptic in History and Tradition*, ed. Christopher Rowland and John Barton (London: Sheffield Academic Press, 2002), 123. Fletcher-Louis then comments on the parallel passage of Matthew 24:35, arguing that "Any Jew familiar with these texts would be inclined to read Mk 13 in the same way" (Fletcher-Louis, 139). In a different article, Fletcher-Louis says, "The implications of the appreciation of Judaism's temple-centered mythology for the description of its histories and theologies, including that of early Christianity, are far reaching. That mythology thought of the temple as the point at which the creation had taken place and around which it now revolved—the Navel of the Earth (*Jub.* 8:19; *1 Enoch* 26:1, cf. Ezk. 38:12); the meeting point of heaven and earth—the Gate of Heaven. As such the temple cult exist in a mythological space and time, closely identified with both Eden and the future 'eschatological paradise.' Most importantly of all for our purposes was the belief that the temple was regarded as the 'epitome of the world, a concentrated form of its essence, a miniature of the cosmos.' The temple was far more than the point at which heaven and earth met. Rather, it was thought to correspond to, represent, or, in some sense, to be 'heaven and

The focus here, in this central section of Matthew's OD, seems to remain upon the *particularity of* Herod's temple in Judaea and the city of Jerusalem "that kills the prophets and stones those who are sent to it" (23:37). Nothing within the close-context of this discourse indicates or anticipates Jesus transitioning into two *completely* different "generations" of time-related topics. Only "this generation" (singular) is mentioned twice. In context, Jesus and his disciples have just walked out of Herod's temple, and it is that temple which is *pointed at* and *asked about* by Jesus and his disciples. In this central section we are shown that as Jesus sat down, across from and in plain sight of the temple that he just promised would be destroyed, his disciples come

---

earth' in its totality." Crispin H. T. Fletcher-Louis, "The Destruction of the Temple and the Relativization of the Old Covenant: Mark 13:31 and Matthew 5:18" in *The Reader Must Understand': Eschatology in Bible and Theology*, ed. K. E. Brower and M. W. Elliott (Downers Grove, IL: Intervarsity Press, 1997), 156-7. Likewise, Jon Levenson points out that "The association of the Temple in Jerusalem with 'heaven and earth' is not without Near Eastern antecedents, nor is it limited in the Hebrew Bible to texts whose subject is creation." Jon D. Levenson, "Cosmos and Microcosm" in *Cult and Cosmos: Tilting Toward a Temple-Centered Theology*, ed. L. Michael Morales (Leuven: Peeters, 2014), 238. Soon after those remarks, Levenson mentions the "tantalizing possibility that 'heaven and earth' . . . in the Hebrew Bible may, on occasion, be an appellation of Jerusalem or its temple" (Levenson, 239). Levenson also concludes his chapter with some extensive interpretive remarks from Rabbinic literature to confirm the validity of this heaven-and-earth-as-Temple correlation (Levenson, 244-6). For further studies on biblical temple cosmology, see Morales, *Cult and Cosmos* (cited above) and his published doctoral dissertation, L. Michael Morales, *The Tabernacle Pre-Figured: Cosmic Mountain Ideology in Genesis and Exodus* (Leuven: Peeters, 2012). Some other valuable resources are: Robin A. Parry, *The Biblical Cosmos* (Eugene, OR: Cascade Books, 2014), 139-150; G.K. Beale, *The Erosion of Inerrancy in Evangelicalism: Responding to New Challenges to Biblical Authority* (Wheaton IL: Crossway Books, 2008), 161-192. For a detailed survey of two distinctive ideas among variations of first-century Judaism, namely, the temple as a symbol of the cosmos, and the earthly temple as an analogue to a sanctuary located in heaven, see Jonathan Klawans, *Purity, Sacrifice, and the Temple: Symbolism and Supersessionism in the Study of Ancient Judaism* (New York, NY: Oxford University Press, 2006), 111-44.

to him privately, asking some questions about that promise. Their questions are framed within the close-context of leaving Herod's *temple*, pointing to Herod's *temple*, discussing Herod's *temple*, and sitting on a hill while viewing that same *temple*. There is no indication of any object in view other than Herod's *temple* along with the disciples of that "generation" who coveted it.

It is at this point where the questionable methodology of various church fathers, illustrated in chapter one, comes into play. I have already shown how common it was for influential Christians of the ancient church to interpret Matthew 24:4-29 as referring (in whole or in part) to first-century events and their fulfillment. Curiously, they often interpreted the remainder of the OD in light of Christ's "second coming" near the end of the world. They assumed that (1) Jesus is asked (two or three) distinctive questions,[57] and (2) that Jesus answers the first question *first*, followed with a response to their other questions, all in *chronological* order.

It is at this transitional point in the OD where we must ask and answer the question: Does the literary structure or narrative design suggest or allow for a division between first century and end-of-*our-*

---

57. Some scholars argue that Jesus is asked two questions, with the second question divided into two parts. Conceptually, this means that Jesus is asked two questions consisting of *three* total parts. For simplicity, I will be describing all three "parts" of their questions as three distinctive *questions*. It also needs to be stated clearly that although I am presenting a literary structure with three questions, there is no doubt in my mind that the second and third questions are *conceptually* unified. In reference to these questions, Hagner, *Matthew 33B*, 688, states that "The conceptual unity of the parousia and the end of the age is indicated by the single Greek article governing both. (Granville Sharp's Rule [see S. E. Porter, Idioms of the Greek New Testament, 2nd ed. (Sheffield: JSOT, 1994), 110-11])." Gundry, *Matthew*, 466, also notes this ellipsis between the second question and its two parts: "Because a single definite article modifies the twofold reference, the sign deals with the coming and consummation considered as a unit." Therefore, it must be noted from the outset that neither the grammatical unity nor the conceptual unity of the questions *negatively* effects the argument I am making.

world events? To answer that question, we must look at the structure of section C:

The disciples then ask, "Tell us…
1) …when will these things be[58]

---

58. Notice carefully that "these things" (ταῦτα) is used again, only this time is it by Jesus' disciples. McNicol's insights about this repeated phrase are on point. He writes: "There is no doubt that the first part of the question, 'When will all these things be?' (πότε ταῦτα ἔσται) refers back to Matt 24:2, the harsh announcement of the destruction of the entire temple complex (ταῦτα πάντα). The rest of the composition of Matthew 24:3 is based on the fundamental presupposition that the actual destruction of the temple (ταῦτα) and the end of the age are coterminous events. The disciples ask, 'When will these things (i.e., the previously discussed destruction of the temple), *and at the same time* (καὶ), what will be the sign of your parousia and the end of the age?' (24:3b)" (McNicol, *Jesus' Directions*, 91). "Thus," McNicol reaffirms, "the destruction of the temple, as coterminous with the end of the age, provides narrative continuity for the entire unit" (McNicol, *Jesus' Directions*, 92). It is also worth pointing out that McNicol presumes the first καὶ within this series of questions is functioning exegetically and not as a conjunction. By means of this exegetical function of καὶ, McNicol posits that no matter when "Matthew" finalized this fifth discourse, the destruction of Jerusalem is conceptually unified with the parousia mentioned therein. His thoughts about this conceptual unity are worth citing extensively. McNicol writes, "The position that the author of Mathew argues that the temple will be destroyed at the parousia of the Son of Man, which will take place at the end of the age, is very compatible with the view that this work was composed in the late 60's of the first century, perhaps after the commencement of the revolt against Rome. The Matthean Jesus anticipates a final crisis at the temple (24:15-21). This is labelled in 24:21 as the 'Great Tribulation.' For this to happen, by definition, the temple is still standing at the time of composition. Then, immediately after the anticipated crisis of the Tribulation in 24:9a (εὐθέως), comes the parousia of the Son of Man (24:29-31). Presumably, at this time, the temple is to be destroyed . . . and the Son of Man is revealed in his glory (cf. 19:28; 25:31-46). The alternative view (often dictated by the presumed priority of the Markan version of the Discourse) is that Matthew was composed sometime after 70 CE. This inevitably leads the interpreter into a maze of painful exegetical choices, none of which have been found to be widely convincing in the academy. For example, those who take the position that, after 24:2, a major caesura takes place with respect to this verse being the end of discussion about

2) and what will be the sign of your coming[59]

3) and [*what will be the sign*] of the end of the age?"[60]

---

the temple (it is now presumed destroyed) and 24:3-31 refers entirely to post 70 events, have to explain why Matthew included 24:15-16 in his composition. . . . Without question, as the post-70 Jewish apocalypse 4 Ezra makes us well aware, the destruction of the temple sent shock waves among the Jewish community throughout the Eastern Mediterranean. It is very difficult to conceive that in the environment of post-70 Greater Syria the words of Matt 24:15-22 could have been written and read without some connection to the Fall of Jerusalem (24:1-2?) being made. But, even if . . . Matthew was composed some years after 70, this position still faces the difficulty of explaining the use of εὐθέως in 24:29. After what set of events does the parousia immediately follow? Finally, the other major alternative position in favor of post-70 authorship is that the parousia of the Son of Man of Matt 24:3 is the destruction of Jerusalem (24:29-31)." McNicol, *Jesus' Directions*, 91n45.

59. The word commonly translated as "coming" here is *parousia* (παρουσία), which means "presence," as opposed to *apousia*, which means "absence." This *parousia* or "presence" is different than other words for "coming" (as opposed to "going"). N.T. Wright has demonstrated that *parousia* was a distinct term that referred to a solemn "visitation" associated with the enthronement of a king, usually *after dethroning* authorities who were occupying a city. On that, see N.T. Wright, *Jesus and the Victory of God*, 341-6. Paul O'Callaghan highlights the frequency of παρουσία and its meaning across Greco-Roman literature: "The future coming in glory is generally called the *Parousia* (a Greek term derived from the verb *pareimi*, "to be present"). . . . In Greek and Roman literature *Parousia* often refers to the solemn entrance of a king or emperor into a province or city, as a conqueror proclaiming victory, or as a quasi-divine savior-figure inaugurating a new age." Paul O'Callaghan, *Christ our Hope: An Introduction to Eschatology* (Washington, DC: The Catholic University of America Press, 2011), 39. Contrary to this thoroughly supported meaning within the first-century, some scholars have translated παρουσία as "reappearing." This translation is offered frequently in Brown and Roberts, *Matthew*, 213, 215, 217-19. Unfortunately, their interpretive bias in translation is self-evident, for neither of them offer evidence in support of their interpretation disguised as a valid translation. Whatever παρουσία meant in the first century, there is no lexical support I am aware of for translating it as they have (i.e., "*re*-appearing").

60. The words in brackets are implied by the grammar, both in Greek and in English.

Church fathers and many Christian scholars have taught that the first question (and Jesus' response to it) referred to events fulfilled within the first century. They also maintained that the remaining questions referred to 'end-of-the-world' expectations. There are *at least* two significant misunderstandings related to their methodology built around this transition. The most important misunderstanding will be the first concern I address below.

2.1.2 (A) THE FIRST MISUNDERSTANDING

The first and most influential misunderstanding is this: Jesus does *not* answer the first question first. Jesus answers the *third* question first and the *first* question third. This is evident in both the language, structure, and conceptual nature of the answers given. I will begin by laying out the literary structure of section *B'* below:

B') Jesus answers all three questions: *eight* sections of prophetic response (24:4—25:30)

1) Answering the *third* question (**part one**): signs *preceding* "the end" of the age (24:4-14)

2) Answering the *third* question (**part two**): the sign *of* "the end" of the age (24:15-22)

3) Answering the second question (**part one**): signs *preceding* Christ's Parousia (24:23-29)

4) Answering the second question (**part two**): the sign *of* Christ's Parousia (24:30-35)

5) Answering the *first* question (**part one**): "Watch therefore" / "You do not know" the "day" or "hour" (24:36-44)

6) Answering the *first* question (**part two**): The "Master" and his "Servants" / "Wailing and gnashing of teeth" (24:45-51)

7) Answering the *first* question (**part three**): "Watch therefore" / "You do not know" the "day" or "hour" (25:1-13)

8) Answering the *first* question (**part four**): The "Master" and his "Servants" / "Wailing and gnashing of teeth" (25:14-30)

There are multiple aspects of this literary structure that reinforce its connection with the disciples' questions, as shown above. First of all, just as the third question asked specifically about the "end" or "conclusion" of the "age" they had in mind (24:3),[61] it is readily apparent

---

61. The Greek in 24:3 is συντελείας τοῦ αἰῶνος ("conclusion of the age"). As noted by Gundry, *Matthew,* 477, the exact phrase (or the association of these two words, "conclusion" and "age," in close proximity to each other) is used in various writings around the first century. Gundry seems to imagine that they all refer to a cataclysmic end of the world at the end of history. The examples he provides are *1QpHab* 7:1-2; *1 Enoch* 16:1; *Testament of Levi* 10:2; *Assumption of Moses* 1:18; *2 Apocalypse of Baruch* 13:3; 27:15; 29:8; 30:3; 54:21; 56:2; 59:8; 82:2; 83:7, 22. Unfortunately, it is assumed—not proven—by Gundry that any of those references intended to describe a time at the "end" of human history. Upon closer inspection of those passages, none of them explicitly teach an end of the "world," and they all seem to refer to the "conclusion" of an age where generations past (some of whom are awaiting deliverance out of Sheol) are *finally* judged, at which time the wicked are destroyed. But there is no explicit mention or obvious implication, even in pseudepigraphic literature with portions ascribed as *vaticinium ex eventu,* that such an event was (**1**) not expected to occur in the first century or (**2**) did not occur as a past event. Some of Gundry's ref-

erences are even clear about the "conclusion" taking place at the "end" of *Israel's* reign in history. For example, The *Testament of Levi* 10:2 says, "See, I am free of responsibility for your impiety or for any transgression which you may commit *until the consummation of the ages,* in leading Israel astray and in fomenting in it great evils against the Lord. And you shall act lawlessly in Israel, with the result that Jerusalem cannot bear the presence of your wickedness, but the curtain of the Temple will be torn, so that it will no longer conceal your shameful behavior. You shall be scattered as captives among the nations, where you will be a disgrace and a curse." H.C. Kee, "Testaments of the Twelve Patriarchs" in *The Old Testament Pseudepigrapha*, vol. 1, ed. James H. Charlesworth (New York, NY: Doubleday, 1983), 792. Such post-Christian *vaticinium ex eventu* pseudepigraphal remarks *could* have been intended to mean first-century fulfillment. Also, what are we to make of the Qumran *Commentary on Habakkuk* (1QpHab) 7:1 ff, which explicitly describes this "end" in reference to the "final generation" of the "House of Judah"? No matter how scholars date *1QpHab*, the end of *Israel's* kingdom is in view. Indeed, even Gundry's references to *2 Baruch* don't align with his assumptions about the end of the world, considering that he passes over numerous references in context to the "conclusion" of the "age" in the generation when Israel's Messiah 'arrives' immediately after twelve symbolic calamities fall upon Israel (cf. *2 Bar.* 26:1—30:5). On this, see A.F.J. Klijn, "2 (Syriac Apocalypse of) Baruch" in Charlesworth, *OT Pseudepigrapha*, 630-1. *2 Baruch* and *4 Ezra* (the latter of which Gundry does not cite as an example in this instance) are especially noteworthy, considering that they seem to be clear examples of *vaticinium ex eventu*, while also attempting to authoritatively interpret past events such as the destruction of Jerusalem in 70 CE immediately preceding the "end" or "great judgment" of God.

As noted adroitly by Andre Feuillet, it should be no surprise to those investigating the phrase συντελείας τοῦ αἰῶνος that it is used by the author of Hebrews (in 9:26) to describe, *not* the end of the Messianic age which later Christian tradition ascribed to the end of the world, but the end of *an old covenant age.* This language about the "conclusion of the age," Feuillet points out, is simply going back to the conceptual schema of Israel's prophets under the old covenant. He writes, "Quoi d'étonnant dès lors si l'Epitre aux Hébreux place 'la consommation du siècle', non pas à la fin de l'ère messianique lors de la résurrection et du jugement général, mais à la fin de l'ancienne alliance, ce qui est tout simplement revenir à la conception des prophètes. 'Il s'est manifesté maintenant , à la consommation des siècles (ἐπὶ συντελείᾳ τῶν αἰώνων) une seule et unique fois, pour abolir le péché par le sacrifice de lui-même' (ix. 26)." Andre Feuillet, "Le sens du mot Parousie dans l'Evangile de Matthieu. Comparaison entre Matth. xxiv et Jac. V. 1-11" in *The Background of the New Testament and its Eschatology: Studies*

84

that the only place in which *that* "end" is addressed by Jesus is in his initial response (subsections 1 and 2 above; Matt. 24: 4-14, 15-22). There is no other mention of an "end" (τέλος, "end" or "goal")[62] to this

---

in Honour of C. H. Dodd, ed. W. D. Davies and D. Daube (Cambridge, NY: Cambridge University Press, 1954), 270.

62. In Matthew 24:13 Jesus uses the phrase εἰς τέλος (*"into* [the] end"). The εἰς with the accusative τέλος typically expresses an extension in time. Since Jesus addresses *them* with second-person plural pronouns (vv. 9-13), in this case the endurance of those living extends *into* the goal that was promised to occur *within* that span of time. In other words, the "end" referred to here is expected to occur within the lifetime of the disciples whom Jesus was addressing (i.e., those addressed grammatically in the second-person). On Matthew's intended reference to a first-century audience, Alistair Wilson underlines a significant error among contemporary critics: "It is significant that throughout the section comprising verses 4-35 the second person is used extensively. While it could be argued (assuming a post-70 CE composition) that this is Matthew's editorial work serving to apply the passage specifically to the readers within his community, the more natural reading, on the assumption that Matthew is a faithful recorder of traditional material, is that it is the disciples who will witness and experience the events described." Wilson, *When Will These Things Happen?*, 139.

In addition to these insights, many credible scholars identify an explicit first-century connection between the συντελείας τοῦ αἰῶνος ("conclusion of the age") in 24:3 and the τέλος ("end") mentioned in 24:6, 13-14. For example, Alfred Plummer does so in Matthew 24:14, saying, "'And then the end shall come'(14) . . . 'The end' of course means the end of the age, and in interpreting that we must remember the subject of this discourse and the persons to whom it is addressed. Our Lord is speaking of the overthrow of Jerusalem and of the Temple to men who would inevitably think of such an overthrow as the end of the age." Alfred Plummer, *An Exegetical Commentary on the Gospel According to S. Matthew* (New York: Charles Scribner's Sons, 1909), 331-2. In predictable academic fashion, Plummer still questioned whether *Jesus intended* his words to be understood in this sense, even if "the Apostles and Evangelist understood the Messiah's words in this sense" (Plummer, *An Exegetical Commentary*, 332). Plummer then posited that the most important sense "for them to know was that the Temple was doomed and its end near", while fulfillment pertaining to the end of the *world* would have to be learned only by experience (Plummer, *An Exegetical Commentary*, 332).

Contrary to Plummer's common-sense approach to first-century fulfillment by linking συντέλεια with τέλος—συντέλεια being a combination of συν ("to-

"age" in the remainder of this OD. An "end" to the "age" they had in mind only occurs in Jesus' first response, which clearly suggests that Jesus is responding to their *third* question first.

Secondarily, based on the grammatical structure of the second question, which implies a conceptual unity of both the *sign* ($\sigma\eta\mu\epsilon\tilde{\iota}o\nu$) of Christ's *Parousia* and the *sign* of "the end," subsections one and two above are the *only* other places where Jesus responds by offering *signs* to be observed. This is evident in his repeated use of prophetic descriptions of cataclysmic events to be heard and/or seen. *Subsections 5–8 illustrate nothing of the sort*, and are universally accepted as parables (e.g., the days of Noah, a thief breaking into a home, the master with wise and wicked servants, the ten virgins, etc.). Subsections 5–8 are *not* historical signs to be observed and fulfilled as precursors to "the end";[63] whereas subsections 1–4 are prophetic descriptions of

---

gether with") and $\tau\epsilon\lambda\epsilon\omega/\tau\epsilon\lambda o\varsigma$—Brown and Roberts, *Matthew*, 216, both *claim* that Matthew (not Jesus!) uses $\tau\epsilon\lambda o\varsigma$ to describe a *temporal* horizon approaching in the near-future (i.e., the end of Jerusalem and its temple in 70 CE) while $\sigma\upsilon\nu\tau\epsilon\lambda\epsilon\iota\alpha$ describes a *very distant* horizon at the end of the world. This clever distinction is also adopted by others who, like Brown and Roberts, advocate R.T. France's exegesis of the OD and its "transitional" verse (see **4.1.8**). Still, many others continue to steer clear of Plummer's first-century connection between $\sigma\upsilon\nu\tau\epsilon\lambda\epsilon\iota\alpha$ and $\tau\epsilon\lambda o\varsigma$ while retaining substantial first-century fulfillment across the remainder of Jesus' initial response (i.e., across a lot of 24:4-35). For example, see Greg Carey, *Death, The End of History, and Beyond: Eschatology in the Bible* (IRUSC; Louisville, KY: Westminster John Knox Press, 2023), 170-4. As we shall discover across the following chapters of this book (especially in **chapter 3**), Christian tradition is loaded with contrived, conflicting, and unnecessary distinctions about "the end" in Matthew's OD.

63. The parables within subsections 5–8 have a notorious history of cartoonish exegesis stretching from the modern-era all the way back to the early patristic era. Among the most misunderstood "parables" here, Matthew 24:40-42 remains prominent. Some modern theologians and pastors imagine these parables to describe a "rapture" of saints into heaven before the end of the world, because Jesus says that "one person will be taken and one left" behind. (The infamous, sixteen-volume *Left Behind* series of novels by Tim LaHaye and Jerry Jenkins stems from this section of parables.) Somewhat amusingly, modern proponents of a "rapture" in the "end times" frequently assume that the people "left behind"

historical events *that are observable* and also function as precursors to "the end."[64]

Thirdly, it is evident that Matthew has provided very close parallels between subsections 1–2 *and* 3–4, by beginning with multiple signs of tribulation that precede "the end" (in part one), followed by a singular sign of the end with its "great tribulation" (v. 21) in part two.[65] This shares an identical structure with subsections 3–4, which

are the ones to suffer, while those "raptured" away are safe and secure. Ironically, in Jesus' *actual* context of the OD, which includes soon-coming judgment by first-century military forces, the people "left behind" could presumably be *more* safe and secure than those "taken away" because those taken away by military forces would go away to a foreign land, and even to their own execution or be sold into slavery. In the early church, at least as far back as the late fourth-century, this "rapture" was imagined differently; the parables of Matthew 24:40-42 and its parallels in Luke 17:34-37 were occasionally imagined to promise a "resurrection" of saints into heaven in the darkest hours of nighttime, leaving behind "Jews" to suffer on earth and then in hell for eternity. On this occasional, early patristic interpretation, see Maximus of Turin, *The Sermons of St. Maximus of Turin*, ACW, no. 50, trans. Boniface Ramsey (Mahwah, NJ: Newman Press, 1989), 46-9.

64. Commenting on subsections 1–4 above, McNicol observes that, "In 24:2-31 the Matthean Jesus will set forth a careful picture of the days after he has gone which will culminate with the parousia of the Son of Man. In many ways this is a conventional first-century Palestinian scenario for the end involving a great crisis in Judea, apostasy, tribulation, and shortly thereafter, the last judgment. But above all, the focus is on the need to be humbly obedient to Jesus' word and not to be led away by various prophets with their false signs and fantastic calculations. Having given this warning, in a brief parenthesis (24:32-36) the author of Matthew reinforces his belief in the sure and certain outworking of these events" (McNicols, *Jesus' Directions*, 93).

65. In his doctoral dissertation, Brant Pitre provides a detailed survey of the concept of *eschatological tribulation* in late Second Temple Judaism and how this was understood in extant literature of that period. His conclusion was that the expectation of a "final tribulation" period was very widespread in ancient Jewish literature, and was also intrinsically tied to several other important beliefs within early Jewish eschatology, the most notable of which were the attack and/or destruction of Jerusalem and its temple, the advent of the Messiah, the arrival of the Messiah's kingdom, and the gathering of the "lost tribes" of Israel in the

is also divided in two parts (like it is with subsections 1–2). The first part describes multiple signs preceding the *Parousia*, where multiple false prophets and false messiahs are reported to perform great σημεῖον ("signs") and wonders.[66] Jesus then tells his disciples *not* to believe those multiple reports (v. 23); whereas the second part describes what is to take place "immediately after the tribulation of those days" mentioned at the end of part one: the appearance of the *sign* (σημεῖον) of the Son of Man.[67] Conjointly, subsections 1–2 and 3–4 comport well with the commonly conceptualized "bi-partite" structure of the so-called second question,[68] "What will be the sign of your coming

---

"end" of exile. On that, see Brant J. Pitre, *The Historical Jesus, The Great Tribulation, and the End of Exile: Restoration Eschatology and the Origin of the Atonement* (PhD diss., University of Notre Dame, Notre Dame, IN, 2004), 41-142.

66. Regarding the context for such fulfillment, R. Alan Culpepper, *Matthew: A Commentary*, TNTL (Louisville, KY: Westminster John Knox Press, 2021), 467, notes that "The later NT writers also warn of false prophets in the last days (2 Tim 4:3-4; 2 Pet 2:1-3; 1 John 2:18; 4:1; 2 John 7)." Culpepper also highlights the historical records of Josephus, the first-century Jewish historian, who "names a succession of messianic pretenders in this period" (Culpepper, *Matthew*, 467). Among them are "Judas, son of the 'brigand-chief' Hezekiah (*Ant.* 17.271–272; *J.W.* 2.56; Acts 5:37," "Simon of Perea (*Ant.* 17.273-276; *J.W.* 2.57-59)," "Athronges the Shepherd of Judea (*Ant.* 17.278-284; *J.W.* 2.60-65)," Theudas (*Ant.* 20.97-98; Acts 5:36)," "an Egyptian false prophet (*Ant.* 20.169-170; *J.W.* 2.261-263)," Menahem son of Judas of Galilee (*J.W.* 2.433-448)," John of Gischala (*J.W.* 4.106-111, 126-128, 208," and "Simon bar-Giora (*J.W.* 4.503-544, 556-565)" (Culpepper, *Matthew*, 467).

67. Culpepper, *Matthew*, 476-7, comments on Matthew 24:29, saying, "Verse 29 contains three chronological references: 'immediately,' 'after the suffering,' and 'of those days.' The first, 'immediately,' is hard to reconcile with other chronological references, especially if 24:15-28 describes the destruction of Jerusalem and not events still in the future." Unsurprisingly, Culpepper argues that this first-century reference of "immediately" does not "control Matthew's view of the future," which is allegedly (as Culpepper imagines it) about the end of *our* world many thousands of years after Matthew recorded such remarks (Culpepper, *Matthew*, 477).

68. On this, see the footnotes near the end of **2.1.2** above (a few footnotes prior to those of **2.1.2 [a]**), and also **4.1.7** below.

and [*what will be the sign*] of the end of the age?" Subsections 3–4 are also where Jesus echoes a familiar phrase that he used while standing inside Herod's temple before announcing its destruction: "Truly, I say to you, *this generation*[69] will not pass away until *all these things*[70] take

---

69. Compare Jesus' reference to this "generation" (γενεὰ) with all the other passages in Matthew's Gospel that utilize the same word (1:17; 11:16; 12:39, 41, 42, 45; 16:4; 17:17; 23:36) and notice how the term is repeatedly used to describe a *singular* generation in which the people of Israel lived. In all of the places where Jesus is recorded to have specifically said "*this* generation" (11:16; 12:41, 42, 45; 23:36), the time-sensitive meaning within *that* generation is obvious. A consistent reading should conclude that the same is true for 24:34. Plummer, *Exegetical Commentary*, 338, says that "It is not satisfactory to extend the meaning of 'this generation' to future generations of either the Jewish or the whole human race. 'This generation' (ἡ γενεὰ αὕτη) is an expression of common and definite meaning; viz. 'the generation which was alive when the words were spoken,' many of whom did live to see 'the abomination of desolation' and the subsequent desolation of Jerusalem." Culpepper, *Matthew*, 479, summarizes the core dilemma here. He writes, "The interpretation of this saying [in Matt. 24:34] hinges on the meaning of 'this generation' and 'all these things.' Lurking in the background is the concern that Jesus' claims were not fulfilled if (1) 'this generation' literally means those alive during Jesus' lifetime and (2) 'all these things' includes the coming of the Son of Man. In context, there is little reason to search for other meanings. Beasley-Murray notes that elsewhere in the Gospels, 'this generation' designates Jesus' contemporaries and always carries an implicit criticism (cf. 12:39, 45; 16:4; 17:17). The more difficult question is whether 'all these things' includes the events just before the coming of the Son of Man or only the destruction of Jerusalem. The phrase brackets verses 2 and 3 at the beginning of the discourse in Matt 24. The natural interpretation is that Jesus expected the Parousia within that generation (cf. 10:23), just as he foresaw the coming judgment on Jerusalem."

70. Plummer, *Exegetical Commentary*, 338, says that "The meaning of 'all these things' . . . seems to be determined by the disciples' question in ver. 3, and this in Mt. includes not merely the destruction of Jerusalem, but the Coming and the consummation of the age. . . [W]e need not make 'all these things' refer to anything beyond the judgment on Jerusalem and the tribulation which preceded the execution of it." As with Plummer's earlier remarks about "the end" in verse 14 (see the footnotes above in this section), he questions whether Jesus meant this much in 24:34, even though Matthew seems to have meant it. According to Plummer, the end of the *world* (not *merely* "the end" of the age) was also part of Jesus' teaching (especially in the latter half of this discourse). Therefore, as implied by Plummer's exegesis, Matthew's intended meaning is presumably

place" (v. 34; cf. 23:36). All of these literary details indicate that the generation in which Jesus taught these things would hear and/or observe signs preceding "the end" and the *Parousia*, as well as a particular sign (σημεῖον) for its near-fulfillment.[71]

---

separable from Jesus' intended meaning, and modern scholars are somehow privy to Jesus' intended meaning in ways that the apostles and evangelists allegedly were not.

71. Tacitus, *Histories,* 5:13, seems to have recorded these σημεῖον in his account of the Roman siege upon Jerusalem in 70 CE. He says that after possession of the Temple was finally gained, "In the sky appeared a vision of armies in conflict, of glittering armor. A sudden lightening flash from the clouds lit up the Temple. The doors of the holy place abruptly opened, a superhuman voice was heard to declare that the gods were leaving it, and in the same instant came the rushing tumult of their departure. Few people placed a sinister interpretation upon this. The majority were convinced that the ancient scriptures of their priests alluded to the present at the very time when the Orient would triumph and from Judaea would go forth men destined to rule the world." Unsurprisingly, Tacitus concluded that this "mysterious prophecy *really* referred to Vespasian and Titus" (italics added). Tacitus, *The Histories: A New Translation,* trans. Kenneth Wellesley (1964, repr., New York, NY: Penguin Books, 1978), 279. In addition to Tacitus, the works of Josephus also report such signs. Commenting on Matthew 24:29-31, Charles L. Quarles, *Matthew,* EBTC (Bellingham, WA: Lexham Academic, 2022), 631, highlights some incredible remarks made by Josephus. Quarles writes, "Josephus reports that the fall of Jerusalem was presaged by several omens and oracles (*J. W.* 6.5.3 §288-315). Two of these portents are reminiscent of Jesus's teaching here. Shortly before the Jewish revolt, 'a star, resembling a sword, stood over the city' (*J. W.* 6.5.3 §289). Later on the twenty-first day of the month Artemisium, people all over the land of Israel saw chariots and armed battalions in the sky charging through the clouds to surround the cities. Josephus describes the event as an incredible, miraculous phenomenon, which would, 'I imagine, have been deemed a fable, were it not for the narratives of eyewitnesses and for the subsequent calamities which deserved to be so signalized' (*J. W.* 6.5.3 §297-99). He regards these events as 'manifest portents that foretold the coming desolation' and 'the plain warnings of God' (*J. W.* 6.5.3 §288). Those familiar with Jesus's reference to the sign of the Son of Man appearing in the sky and signaling the destruction of Jerusalem could understand the gleaming sword as the sword of the Lord, who would bring judgment on the city. They could recognize the armed battalions as the heavenly armies marching under the banner of the Messiah, who would crush the rebellion of Jerusalem. Josephus himself recog-

These close literary parallels provide sufficient evidence that Jesus was responding to the *third* question first. Biblical scholars do not typically dispute that the "end" of the age is intimately connected with the "coming" of Christ, which immediately follows according to Matthew's literary structure. Why, then, have so many of them imagined that Jesus responded *first* to his disciples' *first* question? As I have suggested, it is because that methodology is *assumed* from the outset in order to conceptually *divide* first-century fulfillment from end-of-the-world *Parousia* fulfillment.[72] It is *presupposed* by exegetes

---

nized that these armies were those of the Lord of hosts because, in his speech to the people of Jerusalem, he declared, 'God it is then, God himself, who with the Romans is bringing the fire to purge His temple and exterminating a city so laden with pollutions' (*J.W.* 6.2.1 §110)."

72. Greg Carey illustrates well how this conceptual division has developed since the days of the early church fathers. His own scholarly assessment is as follows: "The so-called delay of the Parousia poses another serious challenge for eschatological thinking. Neither Jesus, as presented by the Gospels, nor Paul claims to know when the Son of Man would arrive, but early Christians lived with a sense of urgency, reminding one another to keep alert. Most scholars agree that Jesus believed he was living in history's final days. He proclaimed that the Son of Man would come soon to set things right. His followers understood Jesus himself to be that Son of Man, and some, notably Paul, openly announced the expectation of Jesus' return in their own lifetimes. Jesus and Paul were wrong. . . . Modern readers already struggle to get our minds around the notion that a heavenly redeemer figure will suddenly come from the sky to set things right. If Jesus and Paul were wrong about the *timing* of the Son of Man's arrival, why should we take the concept seriously at all? . . . I do not believe modern Christians should imagine it [the Parousia] in the same ways we encounter it in the Gospels, and in Paul" (Carey, *Death, the End of History and Beyond*, 265-6).

Contrary to such modern, novel interpretations, early rabbinical tradition shows some expectation that their Messiah was expected to come *with* the destruction of Jerusalem in 70 CE. That coming, of course, can be understood in a multiplicity of theoretical ways according to the development of doctrine over past millennia. It could have been imagined as being bodily or angelic, but it also could have been imagined as the Messiah's powerful presence in judgment. We simply do not know because the available evidence to decipher their exact expectations is very limited. Moreover, much conjecture surrounds such topics. We merely know that some early rabbinic traditions evince a connection between

that only the disciples' *first* question and Jesus' initial response to it referred most clearly to first-century fulfillment.[73] However, it seems

the Messiah's "coming" and Jerusalem's destruction in 70 CE. Given the infrequent expression of this view among rabbinic sources, such was almost certainly a minority position as well. On this, see Lloyd Gaston, *No Stone On Another: Studies in the Significance of the Fall of Jerusalem in the Synoptic Gospels* (Leiden: Netherlands: E.J. Brill, 1970), 463-8. Bauckham highlights this same rabbinical tradition of early prophecy regarding Jerusalem's destruction in the first century and the supposed delay of their Messiah's *parousia*, but he does so with a seemingly furtive glance. Although his assessment is both dense and very brief, his insights seem misleading because he does not address the expected *40-year period* of messianic reign *preceding* Jerusalem's destruction, as elucidated by Gaston. Instead, Bauckham focuses on the rabbinic view that such ancient remarks merely conveyed a need for Israel's repentance before "the end" arrives. On this, see Richard Bauckham, *The Jewish World Around the New Testament: Collected Essays 1*, WUNT, 233 (Tubingen, Germany: Mohr Siebeck, 2008), 71-3.

73. Even when credible biblical scholars attempt to deflect attention away from first-century fulfillment within Matthew 24, they nonetheless frequently admit that the first question relates to first-century fulfillment. Perhaps the most noteworthy example of this comes from Douglas Hare, who attempts to interpret the entirety of Matthew 24-25 as containing *zero* first-century references or expectations of fulfillment. In order to accomplish this futuristic aim of his, he begins by asserting that Jesus never answers the first question! Hare writes, "Matthew, accordingly, edits the disciples' request in order to distinguish clearly between this past historical event and the apocalyptic signs and events that for him still lay in the future: 'Tell us when this [the destruction of the Temple] will be, and what will be the sign of your coming and the completion of the age.' In what follows, *no answer is given to the first of these two questions, since it is no longer of any interest to Matthew's readers*; all attention is paid to the second" (brackets are original; italics added, for emphasis). Douglas R. A. Hare, *Matthew*, IBCTP (Louisville, KY: Westminster John Knox Press, 2009), 274-5. Another noteworthy example of deflection comes from Craig Evans, who acknowledges that the first question relates to first-century events, but then continues to offer one *indecisive* historical interpretation after another, never seeming to present any confidence in historical fulfillment across Matthew 24 *unless* it pertains to the end of the world in *our* future. On that, see Craig A. Evans, *Matthew*, NCBC (New York: Cambridge University Press, 2012), 402-12. Interestingly, and somewhat surprisingly, among all the popular scholarly commentaries on Matthew's Gospel I have investigated, Daniel Harrington's commentary is the only resource I have found that *completely* ignores the questions asked by Jesus' disciples *and* constantly

Matthew has structured this discourse so that such presuppositional commitments are evidently mistaken.[74]

The fourth factor worth considering is that subsections 5–8 *explicitly answer* the first question, "*when* will these things be?", by pro-

---

deflects attention away from first-century interpretations of fulfillment, even though he shows in numerous *notes* his own familiarity with such views among credible scholars. On that, see Harrington, *Matthew*, 331-41. Harrington even goes so far in his futurist exegesis to allege dogmatically that Matthew "resists" identifying the "abomination" of desolation in 24:15 "with the destruction of Jerusalem in A.D. 70" (Harrington, *Matthew*, 339-40).

74. A good example of such presuppositional commitments is found in David R. Bauer's interpretation of Matthew 24-25. Although he points out that "The eschatological discourse [of Matthew 24-25] is notoriously resistant to straightforward structural analyses," the "key" to interpreting it properly "is to adopt an understanding of the structure that raises the fewest problems." David R. Bauer, *The Gospel of the Son of God: An Introduction to Matthew* (Downers Grove, IL: IVP Academic, 2019), 209-10. Because one of my purposes in writing this book is to provide a straightforward structural analysis of Matthew 24-25 that accomplishes this "key" proposed by Bauer (i.e., understanding a wide variety of structural proposals and presenting one that raises the fewest problems), I cannot help but notice that Bauer begins his interpretation of Matthew 24 with very clear presuppositional commitments that *perpetuate* "resistance" to "straightforward structural analyses." Bauer's presuppositional commitments are obvious and worth citing at length. He says, "The *most satisfying* way to understand the eschatological discourse is to see it as an answer to the questions posed by the disciples in Matthew 24:3, *but with the recognition that Jesus' answer corrects two false premises lying behind the questions* from the disciples. The first *false premise* is that the destruction of the temple will coincide with 'the close of the age.' Jesus is *careful* in his answer to *separate* these two events, while still indicating a *deep connection* between them. The second *false premise* is that Christ's coming (parousia) and the 'close of the age' will be presaged by a sign. Jesus will indicate that although *signs will hearken the approach of the destruction of the temple*, the end of the age will occur suddenly, with no signs" (Bauer, *The Gospel*, 210; italics added). According to Bauer, Matthew 24:1-14 describes "phenomena surrounding the destruction of Jerusalem" (Bauer, *The Gospel*, 210), and those phenomena "will characterize the period *between* the destruction of Jerusalem and the close of the age" (Bauer, *The Gospel*, 211; italics added). Matthew 24:15-35 then *backtracks in time* to describe the destruction of the temple in 70 CE, followed by Matt. 24:36-25:46, which describes the Parousia (Bauer, *The Gospel*, 211).

viding a noticeable sequence of parables related to *time* (24:45; 25:19) coupled with exhortations and commands related to *time*, including multiple, parallel references to a *day* and an *hour*. Although many scholars claim that Jesus does not answer his disciples' first question in subsections 5–8 (because they assume Jesus answered the disciples' first question first), Matthew has arranged all of these subsections (5–8 above) together in order to answer their first question *last*.

Subsections 5–8 clearly maintain this theme of *time*, being framed in a symmetrically parallel, a-b-a'-b' pattern. Thus, they clearly pair together as one distinctive answer to the same question. The parables of verses 24:36–44 and 25:1–13 are demonstrably parallel with each other,[75] being punctuated with imperatives to "watch" (γρηγορεῖτε; 24:42; cf. 25:13) along with hortatory remarks about his disciples not knowing (οἶδα; 24:42; cf. 25:13) the "day" (ἡμέρα; 24:36, 38, 42[76]; cf. 25:13) or the "hour" (ὥρα; 24:44; cf. 25:13).

Likewise, the parables of 24:45–51 and 25:14–30 are framed in such a way that maintain *thematic unity about time* between subsections 5–8; for it is only in these parallel subsections (6 and 8 above) where we find parables about a "Master" (κύριος, "Lord"; 24:45, 48,

---

75. John Breck has provided the clearest breakdown of this second, parallel pericope (Matt. 25:1-13), showing that there is considerable literary intentionality underlying its structure within the surrounding discourse. He also shows that it is arranged chiastically. On this, see John Breck, *The Shape of Biblical Language: Chiasmus in the Scriptures and Beyond* (Crestwood, NY: St Vladimir's Seminary Press, 2008), 151.

76. It is worth highlighting that in the so-called "Byzantine Text-type," Matthew 24:42 contains a variant reading of "hour," not "day." The prioritization of "day" (instead of "hour") comes from the so-called "Alexandrian Text-type," which contains "day," not "hour." Most modern bibles prioritize the Alexandrian over the Byzantine textual tradition. In this instance, I consider this "Byzantine" variant noteworthy because **(1)** "hour" makes far more sense within the pin-pointed illustration used by Jesus, which mentions a "*time*-of-the-night" (φυλακή, 24:43) and ends with a supposition (δοκεῖτε) about the Son of Man coming "at an hour" (ὥρα, 24:44) they don't expect, and **(2)** the previous illustration (about Noah and the Flood) already focused upon "days" and a "day."

50; cf. 25:18-26) and his "servants" (δοῦλος; 24:45-46, 48-50; cf. 25:14, 19, 21, 23, 26, 30), some of whom are "faithful" (πιστὸς, "loyal"; 24:45; cf. 25:21, 23) and others who are "wicked" or "evil" (κακὸς, 24:48; πονηρός, cf. 25:26). Each of those subsections also ends with an identical declaration, pairing them together: "In that place there will be weeping and gnashing of teeth" (ἐκεῖ ἔσται ὁ κλαυθμὸς καὶ ὁ βρυγμὸς τῶν ὀδόντων; 24:51; cf. 25:30). The last place in Matthew's Gospel where "a place of weeping and gnashing of teeth" occurs is in the chapter *immediately preceding* the fifth discourse (Matt. 22:13),[77] in the parable of the wedding feast (Matt. 22:1-14). As Knowles points out incisively, the parable of the wedding feast proposes a "murderous rejection of the 'king's envoys'" and pronounces "commensurate judgment on those responsible." "More specifically," Knowles adds, "the fate of 'those murderers and…their city' suggests that the focus of Matthew's . . . interests is the destruction of Jerusalem in 70 CE, which he explains as a consequence of the rejection of God's envoys and of his 'son' in particular."[78] In light of all this, it seems clear that

---

77. The "place" of "weeping and gnashing of teeth" also occurs in Matthew 13:50, indicating that the eschatologically-oriented "parable of the net" in Matthew 13 is connected with a cataclysmic first-century event. Although no conceptual or thematic relationship between Matthew 13 and the temple's destruction is offered in her pastoral commentary, Anna Case-Winters, *Matthew*, BATCB (Louisville, KY: Westminster John Knox Press, 2015), 278-9, nevertheless connects the "parable of the net" in Matthew 13 with the "final sorting" pericope of Matthew's OD (25:31-46) and the three parables preceding that "last judgment."

78. Knowles, *Jeremiah in Matthew's Gospel*, 115. The parable of the wedding feast (22:1-14) is also preceded by another parable (of the master and his vineyard, Matt. 21:33-44), which is connected with first-century characters and events surrounding the temple's destruction. There, Jesus declares emphatically that the kingdom of God will be stripped away from the chief priests and Pharisees; alongside that, a metaphor is used to describe those who reject the "cornerstone" (i.e., the chief priests, Pharisees, and their disciples) and are subsequently "crushed" by the edifice that collapses as a result (21:42, 44). Commenting on this peculiar stone metaphor which Jesus utilizes, Blaine Charette says, "The appearance of the verb λικμάω in this verse may be significant, in view of its

subsections 5–8 are to be understood as one literary unit and the only verses within Matthew's OD where Jesus answers the *singular* "when" question of his disciples. In context, subsections 5–8 also clearly anticipate first-century fulfillment.

Finally, as far as literary design and intentionality is concerned, Matthew seems to have *unified* all three answers of Jesus by dividing section *B'* into *eight* distinctive subsections which stylistically mirror the eight subsections of *B* earlier on within the same discourse.[79] *These*

---

basic meaning 'to winnow.' The theme of fruit which had been introduced by the words of John the Baptist, concerning the coming one who stands with the winnowing fork in his hand ready to separate the wheat from the chaff, is now concluded with this related image of the coming one who, like a stone, pulverizes and destroys what is useless. The prophets had explained the rejection and destruction of Israel as the consequence of the nation's failure to produce fruit befitting its chosen status. The nation was to be fruitful, so that it might bring glory to Yahweh and blessing to the nations, but in the end it was made desolate. In a similar way, Matthew employs the image of fruit in order to explain why the Jewish nation of his day, exemplified in its leaders, was rejected by God." Blaine Charette, *The Theme of Recompense in Matthew's Gospel*, JSNTSS, vol. 79 (Sheffield, England: Sheffield Academic Press, 1992), 139.

79. See point "**iv**" in section **2.1.2** above. Although Mervin Eloff points out that "N. T. Wright sees these 'woes' as the chiastic antithesis of the beatitudes in Matt. 5:3-10," Eloff prefers instead to link these woes to the prophetic denouncements of Isaiah 1–39, indicating that the nation of Israel and its leaders were under threat of judgment and exile according to Matthew's literary framework. On that see Mervyn Eloff, "ἀπὸ ... ἕως and Salvation History in Matthew's Gospel" in *Built Upon The Rock*, 102. In my opinion, the theme of prophetic denouncements upon Israel and its leaders is obvious and undeniable. Nevertheless, the literary parallels proposed by N.T. Wright are far more convincing than mere echoes scattered throughout Isaiah 1–39. Leithart, *The Four*, 122, also lists some thematic parallels between the eight "blessings" (section *B*) of Matthew's second discourse and the eight "woes" (section *B*) of Matthew's fifth discourse, thereby showing even greater literary intentionality on Matthew's part than what I presented in point **iv** of **2.1.2** above):

Beatitudes—Blessings	Woes
poor in spirit—kingdom	shut up kingdom
mourn—comfort	devour widows
meek—earth	travel to make proselytes

eight subsections also mirror subsections B and B' in Jesus' Sermon on the Mount (the first discourse of Matthew's Gospel, which corresponds chiastically with this fifth discourse),[80] thereby highlighting, yet again, that Matthew's entire Gospel was thoughtfully crafted and shaped. If Matthew intended to differentiate between first-century fulfillment and future, end-of-human-history fulfillment, we should not find such close literary parallels between all of these discourses, that clearly describe a first-century audience within a catastrophic first-century context.[81] The "woes" of Matthew's OD are against the leadership of Israel *at that time* in history. Furthermore, since no scholar that I am aware of disputes the fact that the eight "blessings" (section *B*) in the

hunger and thirst—filled	blind guides: swear by temple
merciful—mercy	tithes
pure in heart—see God	clean outside
peace—sons of God	whitewashed tombs: lawlessness
persecuted (prophets)—kingdom	prophets

80. Steve Mason and Tom Robinson (*Early Christian Reader*, 332) underline this intentional symmetry and design, saying, "if it is correct that the author intended five main speeches, the first (A, chs. 5–7) and last (A', chs. 23–25) are symmetrical in length, and the middle speech (C, ch. 13), which has no match, is featured." Kampen, *Sectarian Judaism*, 128-9, highlights some thematic parallels between section *B'* of the "Sermon on the Mount" and section *B'* of Matthew's OD: "In 7:21-23, those who do not do the will of the Father are not recognized by the Son (of Man) in the occasion of judgment: 'Go away from me, you evildoers' (literally 'you who do the works of unlawfulness'). The point is clear in the final parable of the Sermon (7:24-27), where it is the *phronimos* (wise or thoughtful man) who built his house upon the rock, while the *moros* (foolish) built upon the sand. A similar emphasis is apparent in the eschatological chapters leading into the account of the trial, where the wise and the foolish are contrasted in the parables of both the wise and evil slaves (24:45-51) and the wise and foolish maidens (25:1-13)."

81. In support of my not-so-subtle suggestion that Matthew has permeated Jesus' "Sermon on the Mount" with language and concepts about the temple as much as he has with the OD, thereby linking sections *B* and *B'* of each discourse even more definitively, see John W. Welch, *The Sermon on the Mount in the Light of the Temple*, SOTSM (New York: Routledge, 2016), 45-65 and 173-82.

first discourse (i.e., the "Sermon on the Mount," Matt. 5–7) are clearly differentiated *in time or historical reference* from the eight warnings at the end of that Sermon (section *B'*), why then would any of them imagine that Matthew has done so with this literarily parallel sermon on the Mount of Olives?

By taking all of this evidence into account, it is difficult to imagine Matthew (or his alleged "final redactor") being accused of haphazard editing, especially if he intended to communicate, as various church fathers have asserted, a clear differentiation between first-century events and end-of-the-world events beyond the first century. Furthermore, it is equally difficult to imagine how a simple and unfortunate assumption might lead others to abandon this orderly account of Jesus' sayings. Must we assume that Jesus answered each question in the order he was questioned, beginning with a response to the first question?

This evaluation of Matthew's literary design brings us back around to the implications of the church fathers and the emergence of their questionable methodology. Not only has there been a misunderstanding of the *sequence* in which Jesus responds, but there has also been at least one more unfortunate misunderstanding worth mentioning. That other misunderstanding needs to be addressed before we examine the "final judgment" scene of section *A'*.

2.1.2 (B) THE SECOND MISUNDERSTANDING

Due to the deeply entrenched presuppositions among Christian exegetes, it is often taken for granted that *Jesus* taught and predicted details about the future of this world beyond the first century. Although it is reasonable to believe that Jesus taught his disciples such things at some point in his earthly ministry, the focus of this enterprise is upon Matthew's Gospel and how it has remained a foundational source for justifying such interpretations, especially as they relate to Christ's own purported *Parousia* therein. Hundreds of books, thousands of pages, and millions of words have been predicated on the assumption that Christ's *Parousia* in Matthew's Gospel occurs at the end (or near the end) of human history. Such voluminous expositions of traditional faith-commitments may be philosophically compelling and healthy in large measure, but a close examination of *Matthew's* Gospel does not seem to endorse such fanciful speculation. This assumption about Jesus prophesying an "end" to *our* world scenario in Matthew's OD is the second misunderstanding. Leithart's remarks about this are perceptive, probing to the core of our present dilemma in biblical and historical scholarship:

> When faced with this significant evidence that the early Christians believed there was a great catastrophe imminent, one that would end the world as they knew it, we have several options. We can, with much scholarship of the past two centuries, conclude that their expectations were mistaken, and that Jesus too was wrong about the future. The early Christians formed communities agitated by apocalyptic expectation. Jesus had promised to end it all, and they believed Jesus. When it did not happen, they adjusted their expectations, along with their theology and church practice, to conform to the longer time perspective. Disappointed apocalyptic is the motivation behind the church's decision to settle for "early Catholicism," one of many mythical constructs of modern New Testament scholarship. We can, with some conservative scholarship, attempt to explain away the temporal indicators as atemporal propositions or as rhetorical devices. Or we can say that the temporal statements are indeed temporal, and that the expectations of the early Christians were *fulfilled*. That last option, though, requires us to understand "the end" quite differently.[82]

---

82. Peter J. Leithart, *Delivered from the Elements of the World: Atonement, Justification, Mission* (Downers Grove, IL: IVP Academic, 2016), 134.

As far as I can decipher, Christian tradition has always relied heavily upon Matthew's lengthy version of the OD in order to interpret the "end times" of human history. Yet every other reference within Matthew's Gospel that corresponds to the "end" or Christ's "coming" in judgment is explicitly framed in contexts with first-century people expecting cataclysmic events to occur *within that generation*.[83] It is even worth consideration to note that the entire corpus of New Testament literature seems to envision a seamless historical context anticipating imminent events within the first century. The gospel authors along with the apostle Paul all seem to be sufficiently clear enough.[84] However, when the

---

83. The kingdom of the heavens has approached (Matt. 3:2; cf. 4:17; 10:7; Mark 1:15); Who warned you to flee from the wrath coming soon? (Matt. 3:7; cf. Luke 3:7); but the axe is already placed against the root of the trees (Matt. 3:10; cf. Luke 3:9); You might not even make it through the cities of Israel completely before the Son of Man comes (Matt. 10:23); The Son of Man is about to come in the glory of His Father with His angels, and at that time he will reward each man according to his deeds (Matt. 16:27); there are some men standing here who might not taste death until they have seen the Son of Man coming in his Kingdom (Matt. 16:28; cf. Mark 9:1; Luke 9:27); When the Lord of the vineyard comes, what will he do to those farmers of his? . . . He will badly ruin those evil men, and will lease the vineyard to other farmers who will give him the fruits their seasons. . . . Therefore, I say to you that the kingdom of God will be taken away from you and be given to a nation producing its fruits. . . . When the Chief priests and Pharisees heard His parables, they knew He was speaking about them (Matt. 21:40-41, 43, 45; cf. Mark 12:9, 12; Luke 20:15-16, 19); This generation will not pass away until all these things take place (Matt. 24:34; cf. Mark 13:30; Luke 21:32). Translations are mine and are derived from Michael W. Holmes, *The Greek New Testament, SBL Edition* (Bellingham, WA: Lexham Press, 2013).

84. These are the days of vengeance, in order for all things written to be fulfilled (Luke 21:22); Daughters of Jerusalem, do not weep for me; Weep only for yourselves and for your children. Pay attention, because days are coming when they will say, 'Blessed are the barren, and the wombs that did not give birth, and the breasts that did not nurse.' Then they will begin to say to the mountains, 'Fall on us,' and to the hills, 'Cover us' (Luke 23:28-30; cf. Rev. 6:14-17); We were hoping that He was the One about to redeem Israel (Luke 24:21). But this is what was spoken of through the prophet Joel: 'And it will be in the last

remainder of New Testament letters are also closely examined, an expectation of first-century fulfillment just seems undeniably obvious.[85]

days' (Acts 2:16-17); There is about to be a resurrection of both the just and the unjust (Acts 24:15); while He was conversing about justice and self-control and the judgment that is about to come (Acts 24:25). It is the last hour. Even now many rival-christs exist; from this we know that it is the last hour (1 John 2:18; cf. Matt. 24:23-34); This spirit is of the rival-christ, of which you have heard that it is coming, and is now already in the cosmos (1 John 4:3; cf. 2 Thess. 2:7); The hour is already here for you to be awakened from sleep, for now our deliverance is nearer than when we believed. The night has progressed, and the day is drawing near (Rom. 13:11-12); The God of peace will soon crush the adversary under your feet (Rom. 16:20); These things happened as an example to those people, but they have been written for our instruction, to whom the ends of the ages have arrived (1 Cor. 10:11); which are a shadow of those things about to come (Col. 2:16-17); Since it is just in the sight of God to pay back those who are oppressing you, with affliction, and to pay back all of you who are oppressed, with rest, along with us in the unveiling of the Lord Jesus from heaven, along with His powerful angels in fiery flame (2 Thess. 1:6-7); Observe the commandment without stain, above criticism, until the appearance of our Lord Jesus Christ (1 Tim. 6:14); I urge you before God and Christ Jesus, and his appearance and his kingdom, who is about to judge the living-ones and the dead-ones: preach the word (2 Tim. 4:1). As noted above, these translations are mine and are derived from Holmes, *Greek New Testament.*

85. In these last days he has spoken to us by a Son, whom He made heir of all things, through whom, also, He appointed the ages (Heb. 1:1-2); By this the Holy Spirit indicates that the way into the holy places is not yet opened as long as the first section is still standing, which is a parable for that time into the present (Heb. 9:8-9); Now once at the conclusion of the ages He has appeared to annul the sin-offering by the sacrifice of himself (Heb. 9:26); As you see the Day approaching (Heb. 10:25); The fury of a fire which is about to consume the adversaries (Heb. 10:27); . . . in order that you may receive what was promised. For [it is said], 'Still, in a very, very short while, the Coming-One will be here and not delay' (Heb. 10:36-37); For here we do not have a lasting city; instead, we are seeking the one that is about to come (Heb. 13:14); Come now and weep, you wealthy men, howling over the troubles coming upon you . . . . You stored up treasures in these last days (Jas. 5:1, 3); Be patient, therefore, brethren, until the *parousia* of the Lord (Jas. 5:7); You, too, be patient. Strengthen your hearts, for the *parousia* of the Lord has approached (Jas. 5:8); He has been revealed in these last times for the sake of you-all (1 Pet. 1:20); The end of all things has approached (1 Pet. 4:7); I, your fellow elder and witness of the sufferings of

In other words, Matthew's Gospel is not unique in this regard.[86]

For example, Matthew begins his gospel with a clear message from John the baptizer that is directed *at the scribes and Pharisees*, who are also the chief influential enemies on display throughout Matthew's OD:[87]

Christ—the one, also, who is a sharer of the glory that is about to be unveiled (1 Pet. 5:1); what sort of people ought you to be in holy conduct and godliness, looking for and hastening the Day of the *parousia* of God (2 Pet. 3:10-12); But you, beloved, ought to remember the words that were spoken beforehand by the apostles of our Lord Jesus Christ, that they were saying to you: 'In the last time there will be mockers, following after their own ungodly lusts.' These are the ones who cause divisions (Jude 1:17-19); To show to His bond-servants, the things which must take place soon (Rev. 1:1; 22:6); The time is near (Rev. 1:3); The things you have, hold fast to them until I come (Rev. 2:25); I also will keep you from the hour of testing which is about to come upon the whole empire (Rev. 3:10); I am coming quickly (Rev. 3:11; 22:7, 12, 20); Do not seal up the words of the prophecy of this book, for the time is near (Rev. 22:10). As noted above, these translations are mine and are derived from Holmes, *Greek New Testament.*

86. Some scholars imagine that the authority of the Gospels is diminished when interpreted in light of embedded cultural and historical limitations, such as first-century fulfillment of promises. Benny Liew is one such scholar who makes this claim. He writes, "Seeing the Gospels as culturally embedded and histor-ically particular—that is, as cultural products as well as cultural interventions at a particular moment of history—diminishes their transcendent status, and thus their authority." Tat-siong Benny Liew, *Politics of Parousia: Reading Mark Inter(con)textually*, BIS, vol. 42 (Leiden, Netherlands: Brill, 1999), 29. I am not convinced by such claims. In my view, interpreting all literature—not just sacred Scriptures—in light of their own historical and cultural contexts is foundational for understanding and appreciating their "transcendent statuses" and authority (or lack thereof).

87. For appreciating Matthew's literary purpose in focusing upon the "scribes and Pharisees" and how that categorization compares with his limited focus upon the Sadducees, Herodians, high priests, "crowds," and other perceived op-ponents, see Runesson, *Divine Wrath and Salvation*, 233-59. Despite the gener-ally pejorative reception of the label "pharisee" over the last two millennia, many helpful essays have been produced within the last century on the first-century sect of Pharisees. Many essays also show clearly that positive attributes of Phari-

> But when he saw many of the Pharisees and Sadducees coming to his baptism, *he said to them*, "You brood of vipers! *Who warned you* to flee from *the wrath to come?*" (Matt. 3:7)

When exactly will this "wrath" come upon them? The text does not say explicitly. But it does clearly state that it will come upon *them*, and by implication in *that* generation.

In the second discourse, Jesus addresses his twelve disciples and commissions them to go to the "lost sheep of the house of Israel" (10:6). Indeed, the entirety of Matthew's second discourse seems to only address Jesus's twelves disciples as though *some of them* would experience the tribulations mentioned therein just before the promised "end" comes (compare Matt. 10:22 with 24:9, 13).[88] Jesus not

---

sees have been frequently overlooked. In my opinion, there is no more thorough, singular resource on the topic than Sievers and Levine, *The Pharisees*.

88. With all the resources available today for theological and literary analyses, it seems increasingly unreasonable to blindly imbibe the passing presumptuous comments of Matthean scholars about "the end" and its allegedly 'unknown' timeframe. For example, in an article by George Njeri about the theme of imminent judgment throughout Matthew's Gospel, he presumes that the timeframe for the "end" mentioned in Matthew 10:22 is *not* clear at all. He writes, "In Matt. 10:22, the phrase ["the end"] is used in the context of sending out the disciples. Jesus motivates them to persevere to the end, for their reward thereafter is guaranteed. Although the end is coming, there is no clear timeframe." George Njeri, "Surprise on the Day of Judgment in Matthew 25:31-46 and The Book of Watchers" in *Neotestamentica, 54.1* (NTSSA; 2020), 93. He also writes, "The exact time of judgment in Matthew . . . remains unknown. Although the coming judgment is known to be imminent, no one knows when it will take place. . . . Matthew is clear about the imminent coming of the judge, who at the appointed time will judge his people. . . . Earlier, the disciples had asked Jesus in private: 'Tell us, when will these things be, and what will be the sign of your coming and the end of the age?' (Matt. 24:3b). Jesus' long response to the question is equally apocalyptic. He uses apocalyptic symbolism to describe the nearness of the judgment (Matt. 24:15-34). Regarding the 'when,' no one knows, not even the angels of heaven, nor the son, but the father only (Matt. 24:36)" (Njeri, 98). One is left wondering, based on such passing remarks, why such passages like Matthew 10:22 and 24:15-34 are clear enough to recognize

only exhorts his twelve disciples to seek and establish peace among their neighbors while teaching them that "the kingdom of heaven *is at hand*" (10:7), but he also remarks as though "that house or town" (10:14) which spurns Jesus' message will face God's wrath on "the day of judgment." Such remarks imply a "day" that is *as near* as the kingdom of heaven is to them in that generation. Furthermore, Jesus emphasizes this nearness by pointing out in 10:23 that:

> When they persecute *you*[89] in one town, flee to the next, for truly, *I say to you*,[90] *you*[91] *will*[92] not have gone through all the towns of Israel before the Son of Man comes.

"imminent" expectations, yet the timeframe in which such expectations are exposited are allegedly unknown, even though Matthew 10:23 and 24:34-35 (i.e., the statements *immediately* surrounding such verses) are equally clear about *the generation* in which such expectations will certainly take place.

Another example comes from Thomas Hatina who posits that although the disciples may have assumed a "certain connection" between the destruction of the temple in 70 CE and the "end" of the age, "it remains uncertain whether the discourse itself confirms or rejects this point of view, and the chapter demonstrates a certain chronological imprecision." Thomas R. Hatina, "From History to Myth and Back Again: The Historicizing Function of Scripture in Matthew 2" in *Biblical Interpretation in Early Christian Gospels: Volume 2: the Gospel of Matthew*, LNTS, ed. Thomas R. Hatina (New York: 2008), 92. Hatina also describes this "chronological imprecision" as a "disappointing ambiguity" that "serves only to heighten the admonitions emphasized in the discourse" (Hatina, 92). Again, based on Matthew's *visible* literary intentionality, I contend that assertions about "chronological imprecision" and "ambiguity" are the result of misunderstandings on the part of interpreters who presume a chronological disconnect between 70 CE and the "end of the age."

89. The pronoun "you" is second-person plural.

90. Another second-person plural.

91. Yet another second-person plural.

92. The Greek here uses an emphatic construction alongside a subjunctive tense for τελέω (the verbal cognate of τέλος), indicating that it could be understood differently than what is found here (above) while still retaining its future sense (without using the future tense). Typically, the emphatic subjunctive preceded by μὴ is construed to confirm certainty (e.g., "you *will* not even make it through

These pronouns are all addressed in the second-person plural (in Greek), indicating that Jesus specifically referred to the twelve disciples in front of him. It is difficult to imagine why Matthew or his alleged "final redactor" would include such remarks if he did not intend on conveying a message of first-century fulfillment that was utterly certain of being accomplished (or having been accomplished) alongside *them* as stated.[93]

In the third discourse we find more references to soon-coming events, only its nearness is couched in parables. All of the parables describe first-century Israel, as can be seen by *Jesus' own justification* for speaking in parables (13:13-15):

> This is why I speak to them in parables, because seeing they
> do not see, and hearing they do not hear, nor do they un-

the cities…"). However, it is also possible to interpret this subjunctive of potentiality, οὐ μὴ τελέσητε τὰς πόλεις τοῦ Ἰσραὴλ ἕως ἂν ἔλθῃ ὁ υἱὸς τοῦ ἀνθρώπου, as "you *might* not even make it through the cities of Israel completely before the Son of Man comes," thus indicating realistically how soon the "coming" of Christ should have been expected within that generation. This "coming" was so near in the future, they might not even make it through the cities of Israel completely before it occurs.

93. David Sim points out the slippery rhetoric of modern scholars who emphasize and prioritize a message of consolation in Matthew 10:23, thereby minimizing its obvious message of imminence in the process. He writes, "scholars also focus on the consolatory nature of 10:23 by arguing that the evangelist intends more to offer comfort to those who are on the receiving end of persecution and to exhort them to steadfastness than to make any definitive statement about the time of the end. Yet it is obvious that we cannot so easily separate the two elements. It stands to reason that the consolatory aspect of this tradition is conveyed precisely by the temporal theme. What gives hope and encourages steadfastness is the information that the persecution will cease with the arrival of the Son of Man. Consolation without an imminent end expectation is no consolation at all! This is the point of 24:13-14 and we should not read Matthew 10:22-3 any differently. It is clear then that the plain temporal meaning of this verse cannot be so easily dismissed." David C. Sim, *Apocalyptic Eschatology in the Gospel of Matthew*, SNTS Monograph Series, 88 (1996, repr., Cambridge, UK: Cambridge University Press, 2005), 173.

derstand. Indeed, in their case the prophecy of Isaiah is *fulfilled* that says:

'You will indeed hear but never understand, and you will indeed see but never perceive. For this people's heart has grown dull, and with their ears they can barely hear, and their eyes they have closed, lest they should see with their eyes and hear with their ears and understand with their heart and turn, and I would heal them.'

By appealing to Isaiah 6:9, Jesus speaks to his own generation because *they* need to prepare for soon-coming judgment just as Isaiah spoke in preparation for the same.[94] In Isaiah 6, God commissioned Isaiah to go to Israel and preach to a deaf and dull generation *whose desolation was near*. Isaiah asks the Lord about how long he must preach to such a senseless generation (Isa. 6:11); the Lord replies, until northern Israel's cities "lie waste without inhabitant, and houses without people, and the land is a desolate waste." Such a cataclysmic event occurred within *that generation*, as promised by Isaiah. According to Anders Runesson, the purpose of citing Isaiah in Matthew 13:13-15 is straightforward because Isaiah's message is uncomplicated:

The purpose of this passage is to prepare the people for God's judgment, which will, inescapably, come. The situation has reached a point of no return, and the prophet's task is to make sure God's judgment can be carried out. God is thus,

---

94. Interestingly, the Greek verb translated here as "fulfilled" ($\pi\lambda\eta\rho\acute{o}\omega$) is not the common term used throughout Matthew's Gospel (e.g., Matt. 1:22; 2:15; 17, 23; 3:15; 4:14; 5:17; 8:17; 12:17; 13:35; 21:4; 26:54, 56; 27:9). Instead, in Matthew 13:14 Jesus uses the term $\dot{\alpha}\nu\alpha\pi\lambda\eta\rho o\tilde{\upsilon}\tau\alpha\iota$, which is only used once in Matthew's entire gospel. Although the foundational verbal root ($\pi\lambda\eta\rho\acute{o}\omega$) remains, its prepositional prefix ($\dot{\alpha}\nu\alpha$) is unique insofar as it denotes a sense of added movement, either *upward* or *again*. In this context, the term could then be understood as "re-fulfilled" or "filled-fully." In their case, Jesus says, the prophecy of Isaiah is "re-fulfilled" (or "filled-fully").

at this point, the active force behind the dulling of the people's mind, which is done in order to prevent the possibility of the people repenting; repentance, in turn, would have risked influencing God and making him reconsider the coming punishment. The resultant lack of understanding (seeing and hearing) is thus not the people's doing; their crimes had already been committed, generating the guilt which had created this unsustainable situation.[95]

As with the warnings issued from the outset of Jesus' ministry (Matt. 5:11–7:12),[96] northern Israel's systemic corruption and guilt was "revealed already from the outset" of Isaiah's prophetic ministry:[97] *Wash yourselves; make yourselves clean; remove the evil of your doings from before my eyes; cease to do evil, learn to do good; seek justice, correct oppression, bring justice to the fatherless, plead the widow's cause* (Isa. 1:16-17).

After Jesus finished preaching exclusively in parables to the public, *Matthew* informs us that Jesus' actions fulfilled the prophetic speech of Asaph the Psalmist (Ps. 78:2; cf. Matt. 13:34-35). Asaph's psalm of "parables" therein *rehearses* the life-story of Israel as God's "Son" along with their *repeated* failures, God's *repeated* warnings, God's *repeated* judgments as the consequence of their foolishness, and each generation's *repeated* need to remember God's covenant fidelity, which includes both blessings *and curses*.

---

95. Runesson, *Divine Wrath and Salvation*, 279. Runesson adds: "Both Mark's version, which aligns with the meaning of the Hebrew text, and Matthew's version, which adopts the perspective of the Septuagint, signal, by their very reference to this Isaianic passage, their own time as a time of imminent divine judgment" (282-3).

96. One major difference between Isaiah's warnings and Jesus' warnings is that Jesus offers specific solutions alongside his warnings as well, so that a remnant of God's people could be saved from the coming judgment.

97. Runesson, *Divine Wrath and Salvation*, 279n169. Runesson also suggests comparing these warnings with Isaiah 10:1-4.

This parabolic sense of rehearsing Israel's covenant fidelity with God illuminates why the "kingdom of heaven" is described as near to *that* generation, "like a net" thrown into the sea that gathers fish of every kind. Jesus was the one who sent his disciples (among whom, we are told, were fishermen; cf. Matt. 4:18-22) out into the sea of Israel's surrounding nations to proclaim soon-coming judgment upon that generation and the subsequent arrival of Jesus' reign as their long-awaited King. At the conclusion of their mission, when *their* net is full, the good creatures will be sorted and separated from the bad (13:47-48).

It is often assumed that this parable refers to the end of human history, at the end of the world. The end of the world (or something akin to it) is often assumed to be its historical point of reference because of what Jesus says next about angels separating the wicked from the righteous at this "end of the age" (13:49).[98] But in its close-con-

---

98. Here again, Matthew records Jesus as using the distinctive phrase, συντελείᾳ τοῦ αἰῶνος, which is repeated in Matthew's OD (24:3). This imagery is also echoed in Matthew 25:31-46 to describe the "final judgment" (13:49-50), which reinforces the narrative coherence of Matthew's OD in relation to first-century events and their fulfillment. Outside of Matthew's Gospel, the only other places where an "end of the age" is mentioned in the New Testament are in 1 Corinthians 10:11 ("Now these things happened to them as an example, but they were written down for *our instruction, on whom the end of the ages has come*") and Hebrews 9:26 ("for then he [Jesus] would have had to suffer repeatedly since the foundation of the world. But as it is, *he has appeared once for all at the end of the ages* to put away sin by the sacrifice of himself"). Those places clearly imply an "end of the age(s)" that was certain to reach its goal within their generation, *i.e.,* within the first century.

In addition to this, Buchanan's intertextual notes support this kind of interpretation. Commenting on Matthew 24:3, he writes, "The expression, 'the end of the age,' was used originally to describe the last of the Greek age of rule over Palestine. It was later used to anticipate the antitype of the end of the common era under the control of Antiochus Epiphanes. That end began when Antiochus defiled the temple. There followed a 3 ½ year period between the desolation of the temple (ca. 168 B.I.A.) until the temple was rededicated by Judas the Maccabee (ca. 164 B.I.A.). This was not the end of time or the world as Patte, Walvoord, Plummer, and others supposed. It was the beginning of the end of the

text, the separation mediated by angels still refers to a time within the first century when the ministry of Jesus' disciples can show results from their services to the Lord. One must *presuppose* an end-of-the-world history scenario in order to interpret it differently than what its own historical context portrays. The gathering and sorting by angels took place at the end of *the apostle's* mission (Matt. 10:5-23),[99] which began in cities, villages, and synagogues *of Israel* (Matt. 9:35) and only

---

pagan age and the beginning of the holy age when Jews would again have their own national leader and were free to worship in their own temple that was not under foreign control." Buchanan, *Matthew Vol 2*, 896.

99. Although Stanton's studies in Matthew are extremely theoretical while trying to be practical, I agree with him that "The closing logia of the missionary discourse, 10.40-2, foreshadow the closing pericope of the final discourse" in Matthew 25:31-46. Graham N. Stanton, *A Gospel for a New People: Studies in Matthew* (Louisville, KY: Westminster/John Knox Press, 1993), 214-17. Noticing these conceptual parallels helps appreciate Matthew's overall message of soon-coming judgment upon Israel within the first century. Regarding Matthew's second discourse, Mason and Robinson propose a similar thematic connection with the OD, albeit in simpler and more prosaic verbiage. They propose that Matthew chapter ten functions as a "manual for later missionaries" that could presumably extend beyond 70 CE: "One of the most important bases for the Son of Man's judgment is the reception of Jesus' missionaries, those sent out to bring people into salvation. The second major speech (ch. 10) is devoted to the theme of mission. Although the speech is set in Jesus' lifetime, the language shows that it is really a manual for later missionaries, since it predicts fierce persecution, appearances before governors and kings, and the coming of the Son of Man before the mission concludes—none of which applied to Jesus' lifetime (10:17, 23)" (Mason and Robinson, *Early Christian Reader*, 336). For our purposes here, it is worth highlighting that their conjecture is accurate as stated, but their insights only appear to apply beyond 70 CE once one assumes, as they seem to, that "the coming of the Son of Man" did not occur within that generation as promised. The difference between what they propose and what I am proposing in this book is that this second discourse was a "manual for later missionaries" up to the "coming" of the Son of Man in 70 CE, and not beyond it. Although Christian missionary activities certainly extended beyond 70 CE, and not without good reasons for doing so, I am not convinced that was *Matthew's* literary point within the second discourse. For more about what I mean by this, see **Appendix B**.

launched throughout the surrounding *diaspora* after the death, resurrection, and great commission of Jesus (Matt. 28:18-20).[100] There, in Jesus' "great commission," we find the last mention of this "end of the age," and the first-century context could not be stated more plainly. Jesus reassured the disciples who were present before him that he would be with *them*[101] in "all the days" of *their* mission,[102] even to the conclusion of the age (τῆς συντελείας τοῦ αἰῶνος).

---

100. Although Matthew 10:5-6 is frequently juxtaposed with Matthew 28:16-20 by critical scholars (see Kampen, *Sectarian Judaism*, 184), Jesus' warning in 10:5-6 is clearly a temporary commission in its localized, Matthean context. Although the ESV translates 10:5 as "Go nowhere among the Gentiles and enter no town of the Samaritans," the underlying Greek text of 10:5 can be translated as, "Do not go off into a road leading to Gentiles, and do not go into a city of Samaritans" (Εἰς ὁδὸν ἐθνῶν μὴ ἀπέλθητε καὶ εἰς πόλιν Σαμαριτῶν μὴ εἰσέλθητε), thereby suggesting the twelve apostles were to focus upon densely populated areas of Jews around Jerusalem during their time with Jesus before a greater commission from him was supplied. On the injunction regarding "Samaritans" in relation to "Gentile" cities within first-century parlance, see Kampen, *Sectarian Judaism*, 185.

101. Again, the phrase ἰδοὺ ἐγὼ μεθ' ὑμῶν (Matt. 28:20) is addressed in the second-person plural, referring to those present before him at that time.

102. The Greek text of Matthew 28:20 is καὶ ἰδοὺ ἐγὼ μεθ' ὑμῶν εἰμι πάσας τὰς ἡμέρας ἕως τῆς συντελείας τοῦ αἰῶνος, which can be casually interpreted as "Also, keep-in-mind: I am with those of you—those here with me now—all the days of your mission to disciple the nations until the conclusion of the age." With this interpretation in mind, I agree wholeheartedly with Andrew Perriman's comments about this "great commission," saying, "It would be a hard-hearted exegete who would deny that this remains a valid promise for the church today; nevertheless, it should be read in the first place as an immediate and highly pertinent assurance regarding the crisis in Judea and the emergence of the church into the Roman world. The one who has suffered and overcome death promises to be with those who will suffer for his sake during the turmoil of the coming years. In this way, we recover the narrative context, we reconnect Jesus' words with the experience of the disciples, the concrete circumstances that they faced, and the particular story of Israel." Andrew Perriman, *The Coming of the Son of Man: New Testament Eschatology for an Emerging Church* (Eugene, OR: Wipf & Stock, 2005), 85.

In context, there is no explanation for when this "end" or "conclusion" will take place *if* we assume that all the other references to soon-coming events within the first-century are *not* related to the "end" mentioned here. From Jesus' humble beginnings, all the way up to this third discourse, there has been no indication of any time beyond that generation when such an event should be expected to take place.

Jesus even began this third discourse with a parable that he ends up explaining in connection with the "end." At the very beginning, Jesus is the "Son of Man" (13:37; cf. vv. 1–9); the "Son of Man" is the one who sows good seeds throughout the land; the good seeds are his disciples (13:38);[103] the "weeds" are those who are not his disciples; the *harvest* which grows out of the efforts of his disciples is the "end of the age." As Jesus had already taught his disciples at the humble beginnings of *their* mission (Matt. 9:37-38), "The *harvest* is plentiful, but the laborers are few; therefore, pray earnestly to the Lord of the harvest to send out laborers into his harvest." This theme of harvesting makes complete sense if their season of labors in the land ended with a *gathering and sorting* (13:40-43; cf. 25:31-34).

After assessing all of what Matthew says up through this third discourse, there are no obvious indications of "the end" extending beyond *that* generation. Presuppositional commitments might incite us to imagine other "generations," but such is not actually the case when Matthew's Gospel is examined closely on its own terms. The age

---

103. The Greek text of Jesus' parables are more illustrious than what most English translations offer. For example, in Matthew 13:19, Jesus actually says "This is *the one having been sown* along the path" (οὗτός ἐστιν ὁ παρὰ τὴν ὁδὸν σπαρείς). The same construction is repeated in what follows: "But *the one having been sown* upon rocky ground, this is he who hears the word and immediately receives it with joy . . . . Now *the one having been sown* into the thorns is he who hears the word . . . . But *the one having been sown* upon the good land is he who hears the word and understands it" (13:20, 22, 23). In Matthew's version of the parable, Jesus is sowing *disciples* across the land of Israel.

in which his disciples were dispersed like seed was the period immediately prior to the "end."

Moving on to the only remaining reference in which Jesus mentions his "coming," we can see that the same expectation of first-century fulfillment is true there as well. Shortly before his transfiguration (Matt. 16:27-28), Jesus addresses his first-century disciples in front of him, saying:

> For the Son of Man *is going to come with his angels* in the glory of his Father, and then he will repay each person according to what he has done. Truly, I say to you,[104] *there are some standing here who will not taste death until they see the Son of Man coming in his kingdom.*

After combing through Matthew's Gospel in detail and noticing the overwhelming number of consistent references to Jesus' immediate audience, imaginary speculations about the "end of the world" ought to appear dubious. Why would Matthew (or an imaginary "final" redactor) intersperse *these* statements in a passage designed to communicate a unified message of first-century expectation and fulfillment?[105] Passages of soon-coming judgment each share a close resemblance with the "wrath to come" upon John the baptizer's first-century audience and also with the activities of the twelve apostles going through

---

104. This is another second-person plural.

105. David Sim's comments are, again, insightful. After covering various arguments of modern scholars who emphasize a drastic "editing" of sources on Matthew's part, Sim offers a counter-argument: "We must presume that in doing so he [Matthew] was creating a chronology of events which was both applicable and meaningful to the particular situation of his readers. This in itself severely weakens the alternative positions regarding Matthew's temporal expectations. Why would he so drastically and deliberately alter this material, if he either was not particularly interested in the timing of the end or had deferred it to the distant future?" Sim, *Apocalyptic Eschatology*, 161.

homes and cities of "Israel" until the "Son of Man" comes.[106] The explicit remark that "there are some standing here" means those in the presence of Jesus "who will not taste death until they see" the Son of Man "coming in his kingdom."[107] Such statements were *not* intended to convey the message that these disciples would actually die *once they saw* this "coming," nor is it reasonable to deduce that they must die first *in order* for Jesus to finally come as promised. Such statements would certainly be awkwardly unnecessary to mention if his "coming" would be fulfilled *thousands* of years after they all died. Instead, these statements unite a message that anticipates first-century fulfillment.

No matter how literally or figuratively these remarks about Christ's "coming" in 16:28 are taken, one aspect of their meaning seems undeniable: the coming of Jesus should soon fulfill his promises within that generation. Because of how apparent this aspect of the message is, some early church fathers and modern scholars have suggested that this particular "coming" mentioned in 16:28 referred to Jesus' *transfiguration*, not his *Parousia*.[108] Their interpretation is perceptive because it is based on the "glorious appearance" of Jesus that

---

106. As I mentioned in the footnotes of **1.1.1**, the research of Jason Staples is very helpful for understanding eschatological references to "Israel" (not "Jews" or "Hebrews") in Second Temple Judaism. On that, see Staples, *The Idea of Israel in Second Temple Judaism.*

107. The Greek text of Matthew 16:28 is εἰσίν τινες τῶν ὧδε ἑστώτων οἵτινες οὐ μὴ γεύσωνται θανάτου ἕως ἂν ἴδωσιν τὸν υἱὸν τοῦ ἀνθρώπου ἐρχόμενον ἐν τῇ βασιλείᾳ αὐτοῦ, which could be translated, "there are some men standing here who *might* not taste death until they have seen the Son of Man coming in his Kingdom." This emphatic subjunctive construction, along with its similarities to Matthew 10:23, indicates realistically how soon the "coming" of Christ would be, i.e., in *that* generation.

108. Bruner notes that many early church fathers suggested this explanation. He also lists modern scholars advocating this view. On this, see Frederick Dale Bruner, *Matthew: A Commentary,* vol. 2, *The Churchbook,* rev. ed. (Grand Rapids, MI: William B. Eerdmans Publishing Company, 1990), 161. Also, Nolland, *Matthew,* 695, suggests that the transfiguration pericope functions more like a "foretaste" than a fulfillment.

takes place immediately after the remarks of 16:28. However, it is not convincing because Matthew framed the narrative surrounding 16:28 so that there would be no *confusion* between Jesus' "coming" and his transfiguration.

In Matthew 17:9 Jesus commands his apostles *not* to tell anyone what they saw on the mount "until the Son of Man is raised from the dead." Once Jesus died and ascended to glory, *then* they could tell others about his transfiguration on the mountain. Notice carefully that they could still continue telling everyone about his "coming" in judgment before he rose from the dead, but they could *not* mention his transfiguration until after his resurrection. This indicates clearly that Jesus did not want the two events confused, conflated, or twisted by others. Furthermore, in the surrounding narrative, Jesus has all sorts of disciples out in the cities who are attempting to heal and perform miracles in his name. They know his message about soon-coming judgment; they know he performs miracles and conveys gifts of healing by his power; they are also zealous to do the works of Jesus and his apostles, but they cannot (17:14-21). As a result of their repeated failures (17:14-16) and "little faith" (17:20), bystanders in the cities are disappointed and confused, and that generation remains "faithless" and "twisted" (17:17) without Jesus' immediate assistance. The literary logic of all this within the surrounding narrative structure of the transfiguration[109] indicates that Jesus did not want others to

---

109. The chiastic structure with literary parallels surrounding Matthew's version of the Transfiguration is as follows:

A) 16:13-23 – "Simon," "Peter," "earth," "give," βασιλεία ("kingdom"), σκάνδαλον ("stumbling-block"), Jesus will "be killed" and "be raised on the third day"

    B) 16:24-28 – Jesus speaks (εἶπον) to his disciples, "truly I say to you" some here won't die until the Son of Man comes in His kingdom

        C) 17:1-2 – Ascending the high "mountain" / "He was transfigured before them"

            D) 17:3-4 – Behold! Moses & Elijah appear / Peter speaks

            D') 17:5-8 – Behold! The Father appears / Jesus speaks

C') 17:9-13 – Descending the "mountain" / "Tell no one the vision until the Son of Man is raised from the dead."

B') 17:14-21 – Disciples speak (εἶπον) to Jesus, and Jesus replies: "truly I say to you" / faith of a mustard seed moves this mountain

A') 17:22-27 – "Simon," "Peter," "earth," "give," βασιλεύς ("kings"), σκανδαλίσωμεν (cause them to "stumble"), Jesus will "be killed" and "be raised on the third day"

Matthew has also sandwiched this chiastic-section between the fourth discourse (chapter 18) and another distinctive set of literary sections that mirror each other, showing clearly that 16:13—17:27 (above) comprise one distinctive literary structure:

A) 11:1-19 John the Baptizer & prophet, a witness in prison

B) 11:20-24 Warnings of kingdom division & judgment

C) 11:25-30 All things handed over to the Son of God, the "wise" men of Israel are blind to this truth

D) 12:1-8 Pharisees accuses Jesus' disciples of breaking the Sabbath/Jesus responds

E) 12:9-14 Jesus withdraws and enters "their synagogue"/ Pharisees display great hatred

F) 12:15-21 Jesus withdrew "from there," and "many followed him," and "he healed them"

G) 12:22-37 Warnings of kingdom division & judgment

H) 12:38-45 Jesus asked to show a "sign." Sign of (prophet) Jonah is promised. House cleansed of demon, 7 more return

a) 12:46-50 – Jesus' mothers, brothers, and sisters

b) 13:1-52 – **DISCOURSE #3:** Parables, *etc.*, for the coming Kingdom

a') 13:53-58 – Jesus' mothers, brothers, and sisters

A') 14:1-12 John the Baptizer & prophet, a martyr (witness)

B') 14:13-21 Jesus feeds 5,000 with five loaves of bread (acts of compassion & unity)

C') 14:22-36 Jesus walks on water, declared to be the Son of God

D') 15:1-20 Pharisees accuses Jesus' disciples of breaking the Elder's traditions/ Jesus responds

confuse the promise of his *glorious coming* with his *glorious transfiguration* on the mountain.

Because of that generation's "little faith," people might mistakenly conflate descriptions of the *Parousia* with eye-witness testimony of the transfiguration and thereby possibly twist the message of Jesus' coming that his disciples had been preaching everywhere. That possible misunderstanding is why Jesus told those who witnessed his transfiguration not to tell anyone what they saw and heard until after his resurrection. It is only after his resurrection that they would receive great insight and power from him, because it is only after his resurrection that he is given all authority over the new-covenant administration of the cosmos (Matt. 28:18-20). Such would also explain, at least *literarily*, why, immediately after the transfiguration, Matthew records his disciples asking Jesus about the teaching of the scribes, who claimed that Elijah must "come" first as promised *before* the "coming" of the Lord (17:10-11). Jesus' response to them was that Elijah *had come*, and he had come in *that* generation (17:12).[110]

E') 15:21-28 Jesus withdraws and enters the district of Tyre and Sidon/Canaanite woman displays great faith

F') 15:29-31 Jesus withdrew "from there," and "great crowds came to him," and "he healed them"

G') 15:32-39 Jesus feeds 4,000 with 7 loaves of bread (acts of compassion & unity)

H') 16:1-12 Jesus asked to show a "sign". Sign of (prophet) Jonah is promised. Warning of leaven, teaching of Pharisees

110. Knowles, *Jeremiah in Matthew's Gospel*, 151, points out that "The designation of Jesus as a 'prophet' is often thought to have carried with it profound eschatological implications. This view is based on an apparent consensus in first-century Judaism that the prophetic spirit had departed from Israel, only to return at the end of the age, particularly in the person of Elijah or the 'prophet-like-Moses' of Deut. 18:15-18. On such a view, any manifestation of a pro-

2.1.2 (C) SUMMARY OF THESE MISUNDERSTANDINGS

Everything within the broad context of Matthew's Gospel suggests one cataclysmic event *culminating* with the end of that generation, at the end of the age in which many people of Israel still lived under the old covenant that was, according to the author of the Epistle to the Hebrews, "becoming obsolete and growing old . . . ready to vanish away" (Heb. 8:13). Jesus is the one portrayed as connecting his "coming" with the destruction of the Israel's temple. *Jesus* is the one who had come in the flesh to fulfill all the Torah and the prophets. *Jesus* is the one who had come to end the old covenant administration of atonement and consummate the pre-messianic age.[111] *Jesus* is the one who had come to make all things new in heaven and on earth. *Jesus* is the one who had come to finally raise the dead from Hades, destroy the wicked, and grant eternal life to those whose righteousness exceeded the scribes and pharisees. Matthew has "weaved his story so intricately that whatever is meant by 'good news' cannot be communicated beyond judgment discourses."[112] Therefore, in light of what Jesus came to accomplish *in that generation*, it seems presumptuous to insist that later on within the same Gospel, Matthew inserted a discourse that begins with first-century events (like the temple being destroyed

---

phetic ministry would have been understood to signal the 'end-time' and messianic era." In a couple footnotes within the same page, Knowles justifies these remarks with references to "Ps. 74:9; LXX Dan 3.38; 1 Macc. 4.46; 9:27; 14.41; *2 Bar.* 85.3; *T. Benj.* 9.2; 1QS 9:10-11 (*Manual of Discipline*); *b. Sanh.* 11a; *b Yom.* 9b; *b. Sot.* 48b; *t. Sot.* 13:2; *S. 'Ol. R.* 30; cf. Joel 2:28-29 [MT 3:1-2]; *Sib. Or.* 3.781; Josephus, *War,* 1.35", and "Cf. Mal 4:5-6 [MT 3:23-24]; Sir. 48:10; *Gen R.* 71:9; 99.11," and also "Cf. 4Q Testim 5-8."

111. For a fascinating study of Matthew's theology of atonement, including its intersection with Jerusalem's eschatological judgment in 70 CE, see Hans M. Moscicke, *The New Day of Atonement: A Matthean Typology,* WUNT, 517 (Tubingen, Germany: Mohr Siebeck, 2020), wherein he argues (among other things) for 70 CE as an atoning, purgative event in light of Yom Kippur typology.

112. Runesson, *Divine Wrath and Salvation,* 24.

and the hypocrites being judged, e.g., Matthew 23), followed by Jesus suddenly changing the subject in order to predict futuristic, end-of-the-world events in *our* future, many thousands of years later.[113]

Many modern scholars assume that various levels of redaction occurred in order to complete the final form of Matthew's Gospel (as we have it today).[114] Following their conjecture, it makes little sense to imagine a redactor intentionally placing such remarks within a given discourse in order to teach that Jesus was mistaken or did not mean what was recorded. Because of the difficulties this creates, modern scholars have chosen an alternate route. They assume that "Matthew"

---

113. Charles Price, *Matthew: The King and His Kingdom* (1998, repr., Scotland, UK: Christian Focus Publications Ltd., 2020), 340, acknowledges the difficulty underlying this sudden change in subject, but nevertheless comments as though end-of-*our*-world predictions are scattered throughout the discourse. He writes, "Chapter 24 is not an easy chapter to interpret. It begins with Jesus elaborating on his initial statement about the destruction of the temple itself (which took place a generation later in AD 70) and moves on to talk about his own second coming at 'the end of the age,' the second issue the disciples had introduced in their question. . . . To distinguish where Jesus ceased talking about one and began talking about the other is a difficulty for the interpreter of this passage. It seems there is a combination of statements about the immediate and the long term future, with some detail applying to the destruction of Jerusalem, some to the second coming of Christ and some to both." In a similar manner, Leon Morris, *The Gospel According to Matthew* (1992, repr., Grand Rapids, MI: William B. Eerdmans Publishing Company, 1995), 593-4, says that "The intermingling of prophecies [in Matthew 24] referring to the events leading up to A.D. 70 with those applying to the end of all things make this discourse particularly difficult to interpret."

114. Runesson's remarks in this regard are on point. He writes, "There is . . . no consensus regarding the sources used by Matthew. While most agree that Mark was the earliest Gospel, and that, in some form, it was used by the author of Matthew, the existence of the hypothetical source Q is disputed. . . . it makes best sense in light of the purpose of the present study to build an understanding of Matthew's narrative on the text as we have it, rather than relying too heavily on hypothetical redactional activity, based on a disputed hypothetical source (Q) or on the assumed restricted access to Markan traditions from the Markan text alone" (Runesson, *Divine Wrath and Salvation*, 20-1).

or Jesus' disciples were the mistaken ones while enlightened scholars who are thousands of years distant from the text in question are the ones with divine insight and expertise.[115]

As we shall see in chapter four, some influential scholars have imagined as much. Some think Jesus taught such things, but because the Son of Man has not yet "come" in our lifetime as promised, his disciples probably passed on another misunderstanding of their own and tied such views together with first-century events. This theory of transmission would imply, as far as literary intentionality goes, that "Matthew" might have even intended to highlight *their* misunderstanding here. According to such reasoning, it is assumed that Jesus' teachings about the "end of the world" are clear enough, but it was his community of disciples who mistakenly thought it referred to first-century events. By assuming a misunderstanding of those near to

---

115. Commenting on a near-end expectation in Matthew 10:23, 16:28, and 24:34, David Sim writes, "These texts thus set a general (not precise) time for the arrival of the end. The Parousia will occur before the present generation dies out. Those scholars who deny an imminent end expectation in Matthew approach these texts . . . in one of two ways. The first is to deny any significance to this material by claiming that Matthew has merely copied these texts from sources. For the reasons provided . . . this is not a legitimate response since we must take seriously those texts which Matthew chose to retain intact from his source material. The second approach is to argue that, despite appearances, these passages do not in the context of Matthew carry the meaning of a near end expectation" (Sim, *Apocalyptic Eschatology*, 155-6). According to Sim, many modern scholars who commit to the second approach attempt to separate Matthew 23 from Matthew 24-25 by claiming that chapter 23 ends Jesus' *imminent* eschatological remarks about the temple, whereas chapters 24-25 are almost entirely about *non*-imminent eschatological events. Supposedly "Matthew has structured and edited his sources in order to separate 24:2, the climax of Jesus' visit to the temple, from 24:3, the introduction to the apocalyptic discourse" (Sim, *Apocalyptic Eschatology*, 159). After covering the evidence in favor of such claims, Sim asks an obvious question: "If his [Matthew's] intention was to separate the prophecy of the temple's destruction from the apocalyptic discourse, then why did he not adopt the easiest solution and simply omit altogether the problematic first question and write only the second?" (Sim, *Apocalyptic Eschatology*, 159). I think that is an excellent question!

Jesus, it is purported that such misunderstandings still remain useful to Christians of all future generations; if tradition maintains that Jesus actually referred to his "coming" at the end of "history," as long as Jesus' "coming" in Matthew's Gospel remains in *our* future, the OD informs us how to prepare for that.

There is, I think, a more reasonable alternative to such speculations. The final version of Matthew's Gospel could be viewed according to its own literary design. Statements about first-century events were actually referring to first-century events. Such clearly meaningful statements *would even remain true and useful* if Matthew's OD was *vaticinium ex eventu.*[116] That is to say, even if Matthew's Gospel

---

116. *Vaticinium ex eventu* refers to "prophecy after the events" have taken place. Most critical scholars take this approach. For example, Grant Macaskill says without any hesitation that, "Regarding the date, it is generally held that Matthew is dependent upon Mark (c. 65) and must, therefore have been written some time after this. In addition, some parts of the gospel (22:7; 23:38; parts of chapter 24) are understood as detailed *ex eventu* references to the fall of Jerusalem in 70 C.E." (Macaskill, *Revealed Wisdom,* 116). F.F. Bruce also shows his commitment to *vaticinium ex eventu* while commenting on the disciples' question in the OD. He writes, "In the Markan form of the question they apparently belong to the same temporal complex as the destruction of the Temple. But in Matthew the question is re-worded so that the destruction of the Temple is separated from the events of the end-time: 'Tell us, when will this be [the destruction of the Temple], and what will be the sign of your coming and of the close of the age?' (Matt. 24:3). For, *when Matthew's Gospel was written, the destruction of the Temple had taken place, but the parousia and the 'close of the age' were still future.* A distinction which was patent after A.D. 70 was not so obvious at an earlier stage, and it is such an earlier stage that is implied in Mark's wording." F.F. Bruce, "The Date and Character of Mark" in *Jesus and the Politics of His Day,* ed. Ernst Bammel and C.F.D. Moule (New York: Cambridge University Press, 1984), 81. Italics added.

As far as I am concerned, when Bruce made these remarks, he still had to *assume* what Matthew intended. In this case, Bruce assumed that Matthew intended something *other than* first-century events fulfilled in the past. Even with *vaticinium ex eventu* taken for granted, Bruce could have assumed that Matthew intended to confirm *complete fulfillment in the past,* as promised; but Bruce chose not to. A nearly identical argument as Bruce was also made by Alan Hugh McNeile, *The Gospel According to St. Matthew: The Greek Text with Introduction,*

was composed decades or even a full century after 70 CE, his presentations of first-century events *would still be* referring to first-century events fulfilled by 70 CE.[117] What *cannot* be disputed is that some

Notes, and Indices (1915, repr., Thornapple Commentaries; Grand Rapids, MI: Baker Book House, 1980), 344.

117. As far as I can tell, no modern critical scholars take this into account while attempting to decipher Matthew's life-setting. For example, Donald Hagner's presuppositional commitments are clear from the outset. He views Matthew's *Sitz im Leben* as "between the times" of 70 CE and an "imminent" end-of-the-world expectation of "judgment." Hagner's obliviousness to complete 70 CE fulfillment as Matthew's *intended* reference-point is an unmistakable hole in his paradigm. On this, see Donald A. Hagner, "The *Sitz im Leben* of the Gospel of Matthew" in *Treasures New and Old: Contributions to Matthean Studies*, SBL Symposium Series, no. 1, ed. David R. Bauer and Mark Allan Powell (Atlanta, GA: Scholars Press, 1996), 27-68, and especially 59 with point eight of his outline. Whether Matthew's Gospel was composed after 70 CE or not (and Hagner certainly seems to have assumed a post-70 CE *sitz im leben* in this later essay of his), that does not affect Matthew's literary intentionality. Matthew could have conveyed an eschatological message of first-century, 70 CE fulfillment regardless of what *sitz im leben* can be tentatively postulated by later biblical scholars. Such postulations about Matthew's life-setting are admittedly "among the most challenging tasks that face the New Testament interpreter" (Hagner, "*Sitz im Leben,*" 27).

Russell Pregeant presupposes similarly to Hagner. While describing the reader's response to Matthew's OD, Pregeant says that "Thinking now about the destruction of the temple in light of the eschatological future, the reader hears the disciples voice the pertinent question (24:3): 'when will this be, and what will be the sign of your coming and of the end of the age?' One effect of Jesus' reply, however, is to *disconnect the coming destruction of Jerusalem from the actual end of the age* (24:6): 'for this must take place, but the end is not yet.' From that point Jesus proceeds to outline the eschatological events in such a way as to prepare his followers for the turbulent times to come and encourage faithfulness *in the interim period*" (Russell Pregeant, "*The Wisdom Passages in Matthew's Story*" in *Treasures New and Old: Contributions to Matthean Studies*, SBL Symposium Series, no. 1, ed. David R. Bauer and Mark Allan Powell [Atlanta, GA: Scholars Press, 1996], 223. Italics added). Pregeant, like Hagner and his associates, does not realize that there is an obvious alternative to Matthew's literary intentionality, even if one assumes the legitimacy of a post-70 CE *Sitz im Leben*. In light of this *unexamined* alternative I have proposed, namely, that Matthew intended

remarks, like those discussed above, entail expectation of fulfillment within the first century. What remains disputed, because of a multiplicity of hidden assumptions, is *where* promises about first-century fulfillment are *separable* from those beyond first-century fulfillment. As we have seen, Matthew's version of the OD has remained a critical source for such speculation, but it also presents consistent literary features that challenge such assumptions.

By misunderstanding the nearness of all the events taught by Jesus (as recorded by Matthew), Christian tradition seems to have overlooked some obvious literary designs offered by this essential Gospel. The primary, erroneous oversight is that Jesus did *not* answer the first question of his disciples first in the OD. Matthew has clearly framed his fifth discourse so that Jesus answers the third question about the "end" of the "age" *first*, even though various Christian fathers imagined Jesus' first answer to be fulfilled largely in first-century events.

The significance of this misunderstanding cannot be overstated. Over the centuries, ever since there was a final version of Matthew's Gospel to be studied carefully, both Christian and non-Christian scholars have recognized clear, first-century fulfillment with regard to Jesus' first answer (somewhere between Matt. 24:4 and 24:35). But as we have seen, Jesus did not direct any response within Matthew 24:4-35 to the specific question, "When will these things be?" Matthew 24:4-35 is Jesus' direct response to their question(s) about "the end of the age" and Parousia. Many scholars assume that those verses (24:4-35) refer to first-century fulfillment, yet they also insist that the "end" is conceptually unified with Christ's *Parousia*. In order for Christian tradition to be taken seriously, at least as it pertains to the Matthew's message about "the end of the age," the critics' admission of first-century fulfillment must be taken into account as well.

---

to focus on parousia-fulfillment in the destruction of Jerusalem's temple, these scholars would do well by applying Hagner's own advice about "unavoidable circularity in discerning the life-setting from text" (Hagner, "*Sitz im Leben,*" 27).

As we have seen above, the "end" is conceptually unified with Christ's *Parousia*. However, it is *not* Matthew 24:4–35, but rather, 24:36–25:30 that is actually Jesus' response to the question, "When will these things be?" Perhaps this misalignment of question-and-answer has perpetuated a scholarly misunderstanding of Matthew's OD because interpreters continue to adopt a mistaken assumption that Jesus was prophesying two very different cataclysmic events distanced millennia apart from each other in history.

With all of this in mind, there remains only one more scene within Matthew's OD that has the potential to evoke any end-of-the-world imagery and thereby justify some "time-transcendent" or far-removed, futuristic fulfillment within it. This "final judgment" scene of the OD is what will be discussed next.

2.1.3 THE 'FINAL JUDGMENT' SCENE

As the literary structure above has illustrated, the scene of final judgment in Matthew's OD (25:31–46) is distinctive. Most scholars acknowledge this as well, even though its interpretation and its independence as a unit has been debated.[118] As I have also shown, this scene parallels the introductory remarks of this final discourse (section *A*, 23:1–12), in which Jesus teaches his disciples to observe and submit to the authority of the scribes and Pharisees,[119] for they "sit upon Mo-

---

118. See Sherman W. Gray, *The Least of My Brothers, Matthew 25:31-46, A History of Interpretation* (Atlanta, GA: Scholars Press, 1989), 7.

119. According to R.T. France, "Matthew's most distinctive contribution is the singling out of 'the scribes and the pharisees' to be the butt of Jesus' invective in chapter 23, and many of the points made in that chapter relate especially to the halakhic debates and practices of those groups, but by the end of the chapter they seem to have become a symbol for the failure of the leadership as a whole, with the destruction of the temple (the power base primarily of the priests rather than the scribes) as its inevitable outcome" (R.T. France, "Matthew and Jerusalem" in *Built Upon The Rock*, ed. Gurtner and Nolland, 118). Regarding the unfortunate modern-day caricature of first-century "Pharisaism" to which Matthew 23

ses' seat" (23:2) in the place of judgment. In section A', Jesus is the one who will "sit" in the place of judgment (25:31).[120]

In section A, Jesus tells his disciples *not* to do the "works" of those in authority, because their hypocritical and self-aggrandizing ethics

---

has contributed, John Nolland's admonition is also important to keep in mind. He writes, "There is all the difference in the world between viewing Matt. 23 as something which is addressed *to a group of people* or is comment about a group of people addressed *to those who know these people well*, and reading it as providing a description *of a group of people for those who have no other link to these people.* Criticism of some of the Pharisees some of the time, or even of aspects of the pharisaic movement in general, is easily turned into a general portrait of all of the Pharisees all of the time. And whereas those who listened to the historical Jesus criticizing the Pharisees and even, at least to a considerable degree, those who read Matthew as its original readers could interpret Jesus' criticism of the Pharisees in relation to a reality that they had their own experience of, independent of what Jesus was saying, we are not in that position" (John Nolland, "The Gospel of Matthew and Anti-Semitism" in *Built Upon The Rock,* ed. Gurtner and Nolland, 157). Peter Leithart, *Delivered from the Elements,* 117-8, offers a great summary for why Jesus singles out the Pharisees in the first century. He writes, "Israel was chosen to bring blessing to the nations, but Israel turned the law into a symbol of national privilege and boasting in the flesh. Levitical purity offered rules of controlled *access,* and were rules of exclusion only because all flesh was *already* excluded. As we have seen, Torah's purity rules were rules of access and welcome. Over time, Israel turned the good laws of purity into instruments to bar the way not only to Gentiles but also to other Jews. Jews come to regard impurity as even more virulently contagious than Torah says it is, and those who fail to follow the extended purity system of clean Jews are treated as outcasts. Purity laws, designed to provide access to God for people in the flesh, designed to regulate social connections within Israel, designed to prepare Israel for her mission to the nations, became instruments of exclusion and brute marginalization. At its worst, Pharisaical oral tradition is the law turned to flesh—turned into a means for reinforcing fleshly distinctions, restrictions and enhancing fleshly boasting—which is why Jesus so ferociously attacks the Pharisees."

120. According to Nils Lund, within large chiastic literary structures, distinctive units predictably provide an introduction and conclusion, and within such units there are recognizable "frame-passages" like that which is found here (i.e., "sitting" in a place of authority). On that, see Nils Wilhelm Lund, *Chiasmus in the New Testament: A Study in the Form and Function of Chiastic Structures* (Peabody, MA: Hendrickson Publishers, 1992), 41.

are evident (23:3-7). Instead of sharing a resemblance with the hypocritical rulers of that generation, Jesus wanted his disciples to share a family resemblance with their Father in heaven and to receive and do the instructions of *one* instructor, his Son (23:9-10). As they had learned from God himself, the greatest among them ought to be the most evident servants among them. For "whoever exalts himself will be humbled, and whoever humbles himself will be exalted" (23:11-12).

Another important theme of section *A* (23:1–12) is the *repeated contrast* between Jesus' disciples and the disciples of first-century hypocrites. Notice how frequently "they" and "you" are mentioned in contrast with each other:

> Then Jesus said to the crowds and to his disciples, "The scribes and the Pharisees sit on Moses' seat, so do and observe whatever *they* tell *you*, but not the works *they* do. For *they* preach, but do not practice. *They* tie up heavy burdens, hard to bear, and lay them on people's shoulders, but *they* themselves are not willing to move them with *their* finger. *They* do all their deeds to be seen by others. For *they* make *their* phylacteries broad and *their* fringes long, and *they* love the place of honor at feasts and the best seats in the synagogues and greetings in the marketplaces and being called rabbi by others.
>
> "But *you* are not to be called rabbi, for *you* have one teacher, and *you* are all brothers. And call no man *your* father on earth, for *you* have one Father, who is in heaven. Neither be called instructors, for *you* have one instructor, the Christ. The greatest among *you* shall be *your* servant. *Whoever* exalts himself will be humbled, and *whoever* humbles himself will be exalted."

This introductory theme of contrasting servants is also echoed in the way Matthew frames the so-called "final judgment" scene. Not only are they—*whoever* they are (cf. 23:12)—contrasted by the *works* they do, but Christ himself is the one who *separates* them into two

125

groups while sitting on a throne as their authoritative judge.[121] Section *A'* (Matt. 25:31-46) reads as follows:

> And when the Son of Man comes in his glory, and all the angels with him, then he will sit on his glorious throne, and all the nations will be gathered together before him, and *he will separate them one from another* as a shepherd separates the sheep from the goats, and he will place the sheep on his right, but the goats on the left. Then the King will say *to those on his right*, "Come, you who are blessed by my Father, inherit the kingdom prepared for you from the foundation of the world. For I was hungry and *you* gave me food, I was thirsty and *you* gave me drink, I was a stranger and *you* welcomed me, I was naked and *you* clothed me, I was sick and *you* visited me, I was in prison and *you* came to me." Then the righteous will answer him, saying, "Lord, when did we see you hungry and feed you, or thirsty and give you drink? And when did we see you a stranger and welcome you, or naked and clothe you? And when did we see you sick or in prison and visit you?" And the King will answer them, "Truly, I say to you, *as you did it* to one of the least[122] of these my brothers, *you did it to me.*"
>
> Then he will say *to those on his left*, "Depart from me, you cursed, into the eternal fire prepared for the devil and his angels. For I was hungry and *you* gave me *no* food, I was thirsty and *you* gave me *no* drink, I was a stranger and

---

121. Leslie Walck notes that "God's throne is referred to at 5:34, 23:22 and the throne of David in Lk. 1:32. Thus Matthew is unique in the Gospels in picturing the Son of Man on a throne." Leslie W. Walck, *The Son of Man in the Parables of Enoch and in Matthew*, JCTS, vol. 9 (New York: Bloomsbury T & T Clark, 2011), 206.

122. Butler, *The Originality of St Matthew*, 97, connects the superlative use of "least ones" here with the "little ones" in Matthew 10:42. For added connections with this theme in chapter ten, see **Appendix B**.

you did not welcome me, naked and *you did not* clothe me, sick and in prison and *you did not* visit me." Then they also will answer, saying, "Lord, when did we see you hungry or thirsty or a stranger or naked or sick or in prison, and did not minister to you?" Then he will answer them, saying, "Truly, I say to you, *as you did not do it* to one of the least of these, *you did not do it to me*." And these will go away into eternal punishment, but the righteous into eternal life.

As with all the other parallel sections in this fifth discourse, Matthew seems to have the same objects in mind. Among those who appear to be servants of God in Israel, some are hypocrites and others are not. Some are sheep and others are goats. Some preach and practice what they preach. Others preach and do not practice, for they do not do as their instructor instructs, and do not share a family resemblance with their heavenly Father. Even though they sit in Moses' seat, they will go away into eternal punishment; whereas those on the left do as their Christ instructed, and they will enter into eternal life.

Since the message of this scene is fairly clear, it is worth noting that there is nothing intrinsic about this scene which necessitates its occurrence at the end of human history or even some cataclysmic end-of-the-physical-cosmos scenario. It is simply a scene with Christ *finally* enthroned and *prepared* to judge. Because Christ is seated on his "glorious throne," an obvious implication is the action of this scene taking place in the *heavenly* realm.[123] If one assumes that this scene of

---

123. David L. Turner's insights here are helpful. He writes, "Matthew speaks of the glorious throne twice (19:28; 25:31), both times introducing scenes of final judgment by the Son of Man who is seated ἐπὶ θρόνου δόξης αὐτοῦ. The semantic range of θρόνος involves various nuances of a seat or chair occupied by human or divine figures. Frequently the term is a metonym for power or authority, most commonly that of God in present providential rule from heaven." David L. Turner, "His Glorious Throne: Israel and the Gentiles in Mission and Judgment in the Gospel of Matthew" in *Matthew Within Judaism,* ed. Runesson and Gurtner, 137.

judgment in the heavenly realm is *transcendent* of nature, which could also theoretically involve a transcendence of earthly time and space, that will certainly effect our interpretation of this scene.[124] Regardless of whether we imagine time to be transcended within this final scene of heavenly judgment, the notion of transcending *space* would certainly be difficult to make sense of, since it entails a gathering people from every nation (25:32).

With the action taking place in the heavenly realm, this scene contours both vertical and horizontal dimensions. The angels of God in heaven are described as gathering people "before him," which implies a dimension from below. With that vertical dimension in place, a horizontal dimension of gathering across "all the nations" also makes sense if its point of reference is to those same people below.[125]

Given the preponderance of evidence throughout the literature of Second-Temple Judaism and early Semitic-Christian pseudepigrapha regarding a great "day of judgment" for those waiting in Sheol/Hades below, we may safely presume along with them that this "final judgment" scene in Matthew imagined deliverance out of Sheol/Ha-

---

124. I mention this interpretation based on conversations I have had with students of the local Catholic university and seminary in southeastern Wisconsin. And if I recall correctly, this idea arose in conversation with a student who toyed around with Aquinas' metaphysical views surrounding the final or general judgment.

125. Alongside many controversial interpretations surrounding the identity of "all the nations," Runesson, *Divine Wrath and Salvation*, 417, suggests that Matthew believed in "two separate judgments: one for the Jewish people and one for the nations," and that the identity of the judged in this scene (resulting from Matthew's personal belief?) pertained to "all non-Jewish nations" in relation to "'the least' (Jesus's followers)." I remain unconvinced by Runesson's conjecture here. As far as I can tell, even though bifurcation of some sort is clearly presented in this final judgment scene, two *separate* judgments are not even hinted at. Therefore, it seems even more unlikely that Matthew imagined *separating* one judgment just for "Jewish people."

des for all those who had died up to that point in history.[126] Likewise,

---

126. The vision of 1 Enoch 22:1-14 describes the disembodied-dead as they wait "until the great day of judgment" (22:4), and 24:1-27:5 envisions the final judgment itself (25:3-7); cf. 1 Enoch 25:2-7. In 1 Enoch 62-63, the "Son of Man" is portrayed as dispatching his angels to gather the wicked for their destruction in the great judgment. In *The Testament of Abraham*, the saints are raised and the wicked destroyed at the final judgment, which takes place when everyone who previously died is "judged by the twelve tribes of Israel." Jan A. Sigvartsen, *Afterlife and Resurrection Beliefs in the Pseudepigrapha*, T&T Clark JCT Series, vol. 30 (New York: Bloomsbury T & T Clark, 2019), 38. Those remarks clearly allude to Matthew 19:28, where the apostles are promised they will judge over the twelve tribes of Israel "in the resurrection." In the *Testament of Asher*, angels lead the righteous-dead to an eternal life yet to come, while the wicked are led into definitive punishment. On this, see George W. E. Nickelsburg, *Resurrection, Immortality, and Eternal Life in Intertestamental Judaism and Early Christianity*, HTS, 57, exp. ed. (Cambridge, MA: Harvard University Press, 2006), 199. In the *Assumption of Moses* and *Jubilees*, the eschaton is linked with a great final judgment at the end of *Israel's* history, and in the former, righteous saints anticipate being raised up at the end of the age in which Israel's Messiah appeared. On that, see R.H. Charles, *A Critical History of the Doctrine of a Future Life in Israel, in Judaism, and in Christianity* (London: Adam and Charles Black, 1913), 301-3. In *The Testament of Benjamin* 10:4-10, Israel's restoration is even said to take place when God "sends forth his salvation through the ministration of the unique prophet." After that "unique prophet" arrives and his ministry to the people of Israel is complete, the Lord's salvation will be revealed to all nations (10:5). And when all the righteous saints of old are gathered together, they are "raised up at the right hand in great joy" (10:6). Following this ascension into the presence of Israel's God, the eternal destinies of those who had died and been raised up to face Him are said to receive the everlasting eschatological judgment into either "glory" or "dishonor." On that, see Sigvartsen, *Pseudepigrapha*, 25-7. In *The Psalms of Solomon* (a first-century collection that is sometimes referred to pejoratively as the *Psalms of the Pharisees*), psalms 9, 13, 14, and 15 allude to being raised and judged in the near future (i.e., the first century), with repeated references to a day of life or destruction yet to come. In those same *Psalms of Solomon,* the righteous await their inheritance of a life they have not yet received. At that time, *when God personally visits the land of Israel,* they will be subsequently raised into His blessed presence while the wicked are destroyed eternally as the consequence of His judgment. In 4 Ezra 7 a great judgment upon the "land" of Israel takes place, and the dead are gathered and raised for judgment when God takes the seat of judgment (7:33-34). This great judgment is intriguing because

just as the eschatological expectations of surrounding Semitic-Christian literature do not state exactly when the final judgment takes place, Matthew's judgment scene also does not explicitly state when; it simply takes place when the Son of Man is finally seated, presumably immediately after the time "when the Son of Man comes in glory, and all the angels with him" (25:31).

Since an expectation of fulfillment in the first century *could* have been in view in some of the Second-Temple texts, and first-cen-

---

it correlates with visions of later chapters, among which chapter 11 is believed by most scholars to be *vaticinium ex eventu* pertaining to the destruction of Jerusalem in 70 CE. *The Messianic Apocalypse* of Qumran (4Q521) describes a "Messiah" whose credentials are very similar to those of Jesus in the gospels. There we learn that saints anticipated the fulfillment of resurrection, to be raised up to eternal life at the same time as when their Messiah's enemies are judged; at that time the captives are promised to be set free, and life given to the dead who have waited for their Messiah's "coming." On that, see James Charlesworth, "The Dead Sea Scrolls and the New Testament" in *Resurrection: The Origin and Future of a Biblical Doctrine*, ed. James Charlseworth (New York: T&T Clark, 2006), 151. In Qumran literature more generally, Nickelsburg, *Resurrection*, 179-206, says that the allusions to resurrection in their "two-ways tradition" presupposes death and a place for the dead in order for them to be raised up on the day of judgment. Nickelsburg also points out that from their perspective the destruction of evil-ones and the time of creation's renewal was also *very near* to them. James Charlesworth, *Origin and Future*, 150, also notes that in the *Thanksgiving Hymns* of Qumran the community did not consider the future "end days" to be far off. Commenting on the influence of Isaiah 26:19 for Matthew's Gospel, Foster argues that, "Given the wider context of this passage in the so-called 'Great Apocalypse' of Isaiah 24-27, where the declaration of an eschatological banquet for all peoples (Isa 25:6) is coupled with a promise that God 'will swallow up death for all time' (Isa 25:8), it may be inferred that this post-exilic prophetic vision contemplates the bodily resurrection of faithful martyrs in the eschatological consummation of the ages. Although not tied explicitly to resurrection, Matthew envisages an eschatological banquet for people from the east and the west who join with the patriarchs, but the sons of the kingdom are cast into outer darkness (Matt. 8:11-12)." P. Foster, "The Hebrew Bible / LXX and the Development of Ideas on Afterlife in Matthew," in *Life Beyond Death in Matthew's Gospel: Religious Metaphor or Bodily Reality?*, BTS, vol. 13, ed. Wim Weren, Huub van de Sandt, Joseph Verheyden (Leuven: Peeters, 2011), 8-9.

tury fulfillment definitely makes sense of some prophecies contained in post-70 CE apocalyptic literature,[127] first-century fulfillment with regard to the "dead-ones" in Sheol/Hades cannot be entirely discounted in our interpretation of Matthew 25:31-46 if there is some continuity between Jesus or Matthew and the general expectation for gathering the dead that was prevalent around Jewish communities in the first century.[128]

Ultimately, a heavenly throne-room scenario does not easily prevent this particular scene of judgment from taking place within the first century, and there do not seem to be any internal indicators of this judgment (as it is described) taking place in *our* future.[129] Everything else in the discourse could be interpreted in reference to Jerusalem's destruction in 70 CE when "the end" came upon that generation. As Ulrich Luz points out succinctly, the overall point of this

---

127. For a lengthy list of texts involving ascension from Sheol/Hades alongside themes of final judgment, see Jan A. Sigvartsen, *Afterlife and Resurrection Beliefs in the Apocrypha and Apocalyptic Literature*, T&T Clark JCT Series, vol. 29 (New York: Bloomsbury T & T Clark, 2019), 214-47.

128. For many parallels between 1 Enoch and Matthew's "final judgment" pericope, see Daniel Assefa, "Matthew's Day of Judgment in Light of 1 Enoch," in *Enoch and the Synoptic Gospels: Reminiscences, Allusions, Intertextuality*, ed. Loren T. Stuckenbruck and Gabriele Boccaccini (Atlanta, GA: SBL Press, 2016), 199-213. Also, McNicol highlights the opening statement of this pericope, "Whenever the Son of Man comes in his glory and all the angels with him, then he will sit upon his throne of glory," and shows its relation to Matthew 19:28, which is a unique construction of terminology embedded within Matthew's gospel (McNicol, *Jesus' Directions*, 111). There, in 19:28, Jesus also tells his apostles that those who had followed him in the first century would "also sit on twelve thrones, judging the twelve tribes of Israel." Such a remark alongside Jesus being "seated on his glorious throne"—which only occurs in these two locations within all the gospels—seems to imply a gathering of the righteous dead out of Hades/Sheol and into his heavenly presence.

129. Commenting on Matthew 24 alongside other NT passages (Mark 13, Luke 21; 1 John 2:17-18; 1 Pet. 4:7; Jas. 5:8-9; Heb. 10:25; Rev. 1:3; 22:20), Peter Leithart says, "There is a final judgment yet to come, but the emphasis of the New Testament is on *imminent* judgment" (*Delivered from the Elements*, 133).

peculiar pericope is straight-forward: "The time of warnings is now past. The final judgment is now here. The heavenly judge has spoken. Nothing can be changed at this point."[130] If Matthew intended to situate this pericope of unprecedented judgment as taking place within the first-century generation Jesus addressed, Christians throughout the centuries have largely misunderstood the way Matthew has framed this final judgment,[131] or at least its historical reference for implementation.[132] For our purposes here, it is sufficient to point out

130. Ulrich Luz, "The Final Judgment (Matt. 25:31-46): An Exercise in 'History of Influence' Exegesis" in *Treasures New and Old: Contributions to Matthean Studies*, SBL Symposium Series, no. 1, ed. David R. Bauer and Mark Allan Powell, trans. Dorothy Jean Weaver (Atlanta, GA: Scholars Press, 1996), 307. Although this should go without saying, I am taking Luz's assertions about the point of this final judgment scene and applying it with a different assumption than his own, namely, that first-century fulfillment was also part of "Matthew's" point. Luz assumes that Matthew imagined this "final judgment" scene to eventually take place at the "end of time."

131. For a highly detailed, historical survey of interpretations pertaining to this "final judgment" scene, spanning from the patristic period and into the modern era, see Gray, *The Least of My Brothers*, 11-272. In my opinion, the greatest contribution of Gray's work is his detailed list of every seemingly possible interpretation within the twentieth century, in which he shows that "The overwhelming number of twentieth-century scholars (562 out of a total of 602) understand the final judgment as the subject matter of Matt 25:31-46" (Gray, *Least of My Brothers*, 257).

132. Although the idea of implementing definitive, unprecedented, and eternally weighty judgment upon "the dead-ones" within the first-century is never endorsed by N.T. Wright in any of his writings (at least, not that I am aware of), I agree with his suggestion that "An eschatological reading of Jesus demands, I believe, that we get used to thinking in terms of the dialectic between achievement and *implementation*" (Wright, "*In Grateful Dialogue*," 272). I discuss a little more about this (although, still, merely as a cursory suggestion) in my **Conclusion**. As I understand the slippery development of doctrine over the last two millennia and the multiplicity of indecisive voices across those conversations, there remains some conjectural room for interpreting Matthew's "final judgment" pericope in terms of final *implementation* of definitive judgment and not the only *time* in which definitive judgment takes place. That is to say, more time remains to have scholarly discussions about this, thereby allowing Wright's idea

132

that Matthew has framed the entire discourse clearly and succinctly with sections A and A' designed to be mutually interpretive.

2.2 CONCLUSION

Matthew's OD shows no clear *literary* intentionality of transitioning from first-century events to end-of-the-world events. It begins with first-century disciples of Christ not doing the works of their hypocritical, self-aggrandizing authorities.[133] That is followed by eight woes against first-century hypocrites,[134] along with clear prophetic remarks

---

of implementation to permeate theological systematics and our understanding of an "end" to redemptive history.

133. Kampen points out that many charges brought against Israel's sectarian influencers in Matthew 23 are directly related to the "hypocrites" in Jesus' "Sermon on the Mount": "Matt 23:5-7 . . . constitutes a related set of charges already leveled in 6:2-6 concerning the desire for public recognition and accolades as the primary motivation of these Jewish Leaders. . . . The Matthean references do emerge as important both for their prominence and for the connection between the Sermon on the Mount and this diatribe. The charges against the scribes and Pharisees in Matt 23:2-11, the same people referred to as hypocrites in the following list of woes, bear a remarkable similarity to the portrayal of the hypocrites in Matthew 5:2, 5, and 16 with regard to prayer and fasting. . . . Here in Matt 23 the case is made in a much more vigorous manner. The legitimacy and authority of the scribes and Pharisees are totally undercut in this diatribe on the charge of hypocrisy" (Kampen, *Sectarian Judaism*, 162-3); "In Matt 5:3 the kingdom of heaven belongs to the poor in spirit; in 23:13 the scribes and Pharisees lock people out of the kingdom of heaven. . . . The 'children of hell' in Matt 23:15, who result from the proselytization efforts of the scribes and Pharisees, are the polar contrast to those who 'will be called children of God' in Matt 5:9. . . . Matthew 5:33-36 forbids the swearing of all oaths. The similarity in language of the references 'whoever swears by heaven swears by the throne of God' (23:22) and 'Do not swear at all, either by heaven, for it is the throne of God' (5:34) is striking" (Kampen, 164-5).

134. Akiva Cohen's observation is succinct: "Matthew devotes the entirety of chapter 23 to Jesus' sweeping denunciation of the scribes and Pharisees, which climaxes with his prophetic warning that *their* house will be left ἔρημος ('desolate') and that his presence will be hidden from Israel until its national confession

about their temple being left desolate and destroyed according to their

of his Messianic identity" (Cohen, *Matthew and the Temple*, 95). Commenting on a thematic connection between Matthew's first and fifth discourses, Nathan Eubank offers some helpful insights about the scribes and Pharisees "filling up the measure of their fathers." He writes, "In chapter 23 Jesus denounces the scribes and Pharisees at length, claiming that eschatological judgment is about to come on them. At one point Jesus ironically tells them to 'fill up the measure of your fathers' . . . . Scholars agree that the words ὑμεῖς πληρώσατε τὸ μέτρον τῶν πατέρων ὑμῶν envision a preordained amount of evil that will be tolerated before God steps in to punish the offenders. The guilt for all the blood which has been shed since Abel will come on this generation because the scribes and Pharisees finally 'fill up' the measure that has been filling throughout the history of the world. The guilt reaches a certain tipping point and so God will step in and punish them. . . . In 7:1-2 Jesus says Μὴ κρίνετε, ἵνα μὴ κριθῆτε· ἐν ᾧ γὰρ κρίματι κρίνετε κριθήσεσθε, καὶ ἐν ᾧ μέτρῳ μετρεῖτε μετρηθήσεται ὑμῖν. . . . The best way to ensure that someone pays exactly what is owed is to require him to repay his debt with the same measure that he used to measure out the loan in the first place. Something similar appears to be imagined in Matthew 7:2. When assessing the debt of someone else's sin, the sort of measure one uses makes all the difference. . . . I would suggest that the measure in 23:32 is, like the measure in 7:2, a measure that records the amount owed. Jesus describes the scribes and Pharisees as the sons of those who murdered the prophets. Guilt has been piling up for centuries but the breaking point is near. When Jesus tells them to 'fill up the measure of your fathers,' he would be ironically telling them to bring the debt of their fathers to its limit, the point at which the creditor can tolerate it no more and steps in to collect what is due. The underlying conception of sin as debt is identical to 7:2. The difference is that 7:2 is a warning to be generous when measuring the debts of others, whereas 23:32 is a prophetic declaration that the debt is about to reach its full measure, the time when the creditor comes to settle accounts." Nathan Eubank, *Wages of Cross-Bearing and Debt of Sin: The Economy of Heaven in Matthew's Gospel*, BZNW, vol. 196 (Berlin, Germany: De Gruyter, 2013), 63-7.

Andrew Simmonds adds to these insights offered by Eubank, noting that the final "woe" of Matthew 23 is significant. Simmonds says that Jesus "treats the scribes and Pharisees as though they were foreign despots (which of course they were not). 'Fill up the measure' (23:32) typically refers (e.g., Gen 15:16; 1 Macc. 6:14) to a foreign conqueror and explains that God allows foreign domination to continue until it has reached the tipping point when He will destroy the foreign conqueror and liberate His chosen people (an event associated with the Messiah). In this context the reference to 'this generation' does not extend to the entire populace; it means an 'imminent' or 'immediate' generation. The sentence

134

own evils by God's divinely appointed decision.[135] Following that, the disciples of Jesus ask him three questions, which he answers sequentially but in the *reverse* order. Various Christians throughout the centuries have assumed otherwise. Their inversion of the actual order

---

'Fill up the measure of the guilt of your fathers' is therefore not a command to do it. It is an ironic statement, for if they go ahead and follow in the footsteps of their ancestors by killing prophets, they will suffer the consequences." Andrew R. Simmonds, "'Woe to you …Hypocrites!' Re-reading Matthew 23:13-36" in *BS, 166* (2009), 345.

In light of some unsettling epithets and insults aimed at scribes and Pharisees throughout Matthew 23, Adela Yarbro Collins attempts to offset Jesus' apparent harshness with her own opinion that such "reproof speech of Matthew 23 was most likely composed by Matthew." Her justification for thinking so is because "the other insults are lacking" in Luke's parallel accounts (Luke 11:37-52; Yarbro Collins, *"Polemic,"* 168). Sadly, Yarbro Collins then suggests that even if most of the blame does *not* actually fall on Matthew, and such epithets and insults *do* actually go back to Jesus' authentic sayings, "we can still critique it" because (1) the humanity of Jesus was as influenced by his own culture as humanity in general remains influenced by their own cultures to this day, and (2) Jesus appears to critique himself "in light of the higher standard of the Sermon on the Mount" (Yarbro Collins, *"Polemic,"* 169). In other words, Yarbro Collins is comfortable placing herself in authority over Jesus (at least momentarily and theoretically), in order to selectively critique Jesus' harshness with the "higher standard" of his very own words found elsewhere. This curious approach of Yarbro Collins brings to mind Matthew 7:3-5. It also leaves me wondering if she would select statements within the Sermon on the Mount to critique Jesus' "harshness" contained therein as well. After all, according to her rationale, even Jesus' expressions within the Sermon on the Mount were subject to cultural influences of his own generation, and therefore are subject to her criticism.

135. R. T. France, *Matthew and Jerusalem*, 122, also points out that the people's public statement in Matthew 27:24-25 "stands alongside the sustained polemic against the temple as a marker of the fundamental shift in the divine economy which came about with Jerusalem's rejection of Jesus and which is explained in the discourse of chapters 24-25. The kingdom of heaven is no longer to be focused in the λαὸς, the city and the temple, but in the vindicated and enthroned Son of Man who, after the temple is destroyed, will gather his chosen people from all the corners of the earth (24:29-31). All this will happen within this generation."

leads them to locate fulfillment in the first century and transition aspects of that fulfillment into an unspecified future.

In Matthew's version of the OD, Jesus addresses "the end" with proclamations about first-century events, which various church fathers and biblical scholars throughout the centuries have recognized.[136] Matthew then presents Jesus' "coming" and all the events leading up to it as occurring in connection with that generation. He then offers parables in response to their question about how they could prepare for "when" the temple's destruction and all the woes pronounced against Israel's hypocritical rulers would take place. Following that response to the "when" question, Jesus teaches that he will send his angels to gather up all those awaiting his reign to attain life-eternal with him as promised. At that time, when he is finally seated as the ruler and judge of all creation, he will also separate the righteous from the hypocrites and judge between them according to the works they have done.[137]

If Matthew intended to supply a transition from first-century events to unknowable, futuristic end-of-*our*-world events, such intentions are not perspicuous at all. As it stands, there is no transitional verse inserting a gap of time beyond that generation. There doesn't even seem to be a transitional pericope for the great judgment of

---

136. Kampen, *Sectarian Judaism*, 172, writes, "The survival of Israel, or perhaps more adequately stated, the nature of Israel that will survive the destruction, is what is at stake in this discussion. In the ambiguity of the two centuries of Jewish existence since the Maccabean revolt and the composition of the latter portions of Daniel, the Jewish experience had become much more complicated. That certainly will have been true at the end of the first century CE. At least this is the picture which emerges in the literary evidence, particularly Josephus and certain apocalyptic writings such as the Testament of Abraham, 2 Baruch, and 4 Ezra. Hence, the injunctions to watchfulness in Matt 24:36-44 and the two parables of 24:45-51 and 25:1-13. According to this apocalyptic scenario, only those who accept the wisdom of Jesus and understand his appointment as Son of Man will survive the outcome of the events that are being unleashed in human history."

137. Alternatively, this definitive, historical event of separation could also be understood as implementing the process of separation and final judgment for all who die thereafter.

Matthew 25:31-46, given its literary parallels with Matthew 23:1-12. Understanding all of this, we must now examine how the following millennium of scholarship attempted to sort out this dilemma.

CHAPTER 3

Settled Dogma or Parroted Conjecture?

3.1 PRE-MODERN VARIETIES OF EXPLICATION

First-century fulfillment within the OD was rooted so deeply across the first millennium of exegesis that it became difficult for future generations to closely examine Matthew's OD and uproot the seemingly unfruitful toils of previous generations without risking damage to Jesus' prophetic integrity within the well-tended garden of Christian faith. Before we arrive in the modern period of biblical exegesis (explored in chapter four) and its attempts to produce many new and striking theories about the reliability of Jesus' predictions, we must cover the second millennium of Christian scholarship between the so-called late-Middle Ages and the late-modern era. The purpose of presenting selections from this wide span of history is to highlight the lingering influence of traditional assumptions and questionable methodologies proposed in chapter one and corrected in chapter two.

139

By accentuating these details amidst the wide variety of biblical interpretation that developed over the next millennium, we become able to identify and confirm at least three trends pertaining to the exegesis of Jesus' OD.

As we shall see, the first tendency of this era was to validate the widespread reception of first-century fulfillment somewhere within the range of Matthew 24:4-29 as a response to the first question of Jesus' disciples, i.e., *When will these things be?* The second penchant was to validate patristic sources (e.g., Hilary, Jerome, Chrysostom, *Opus imperfectum*, and other later church fathers)[1] and the sources they commonly utilized (Josephus, Tacitus, Eusebius of Caesarea, etc.) by means of acknowledgement or interaction with them. Third, scholars of this lengthy period maintained a predilection for transition into futuristic, end-of-the-world events somewhere after Matthew 24:22. A presumption is maintained that Jesus could not have actually focused exclusively on first-century events throughout the OD. Some other explanation must be deciphered *from the text*.

Looking back and across this broad and dense period of Christian scholarship, we are left with a curious account of Christian tradition that prioritized and passed on one mistaken assumption after another. It is to that assiduously dense period of Christian exegesis which we now turn, the eloquent rhetoric and conjecture of which would betoken a future need for scholars in our modern era to challenge its seemingly erratic dogmas.

---

1. Madigan, *Olivi and the Interpretation of Matthew*, 29, affirms that by the mid-twelfth century, "scores of Greek and Latin thinkers had produced hundreds of commentaries on the gospels and the Apocalypse. Among those who had written on these biblical texts were the most illustrious figures in patristic exegesis—thinkers like Origen, Chrysostom, Bede, Jerome, Ambrose, Gregory, and Augustine. No exegete writing in the twelfth century, no matter how isolated, could have been unaware of some, at least, of the exegetical writings of these patristic giants, and none, however inventive, could have remained immune to their influence."

3.1.1 THOMAS AQUINAS (1225—1274)

As noted throughout chapter one, Thomas Aquinas's *Catena Aurea* showed great familiarity with the methodology proposed by earlier church fathers. That is why, in his opening remarks about Matthew's OD, Aquinas could confidently assert that the disciples' *first* question pertained to the "consummation" of Jesus' "threats" against Jerusalem:

> He had said that the temple was to be destroyed, so they ask three things: first, about the temple; second, about the coming; third, about the end of the age. Hence, they say, *tell us when these things will be,* namely the consummation of your threats; and about your coming: *and what will be the sign of your coming*; likewise, about the end of the age, *and of the consummation of the world.*[2]

Aquinas' exposition of Matthew's OD is very clear in its methodology. He interprets first-century fulfillment in verses 4 through 22 with an unmistakable transition into futuristic fulfillment at verse 23. Even though Aquinas is crystal clear about verses 4 through 22 referring primarily to first-century circumstances, he nonetheless introduces spiritual interpretations and rival views of early church fathers into the mix. According to Aquinas, the disciples ask about "the coming, and this is twofold." From these few introductory remarks, Aquinas proposes multiple senses in which Christ's "coming" could be legitimately understood, and even lists some disagreements in meaning among renowned saints of old.[3] On this he writes:

---

2. Aquinas, *Commentary*, 287. All italics cited throughout this entire chapter (not just **3.1.1**) are original to the English publication from which they were taken, unless noted otherwise.

3. This approach is interesting in light of Aquinas' definitive commitment to some first-century fulfillment. Paul O'Callaghan observes that "On the whole [Aquinas] is quite sceptical about the reality and nature of end-time signs, since

141

There is a last coming, which is for the sake of judging, and this will happen at the consummation of the age. . . . The other is his coming as the one who comforts the minds of men, to whom he comes spiritually. Below, *they will see the Son of man coming in the clouds* (Matt. 24:30), i.e., in the preachers, for God comes into the minds of men through preachers. Hence it is uncertain to what it should be referred. Augustine says that the whole thing should be referred to the spiritual coming. But some say it should be referred to the second coming, and some explain it as about the destruction of Jerusalem, and the last coming.

First, therefore, he responds as regards the destruction; second, as regards the second coming, at *for as lightning comes out of the east* (Matt. 24:27).

Concerning the first, two things: first, he foretells those things which come before the destruction; second, the destruction itself, at *when therefore you will see "the abomination of desolation"* (Matt. 24:15).[4]

Aquinas was no fool. Trained in the medieval scholastic tradition, he understood history, human psychology, canon law, and political theories very well. As a philosopher and theologian, he understood eschatological disagreements and the power of rhetoric even better. That is why it seems Aquinas had no problem openly agreeing or disagreeing with commentators of the past while presenting a plethora of satisfactory explanations to his interlocutors in the present. With regard to Jesus' response to his disciples' first question, Aquinas

---

they could easily be confused with other events such as the destruction of Jerusalem and the continuous active presence of Christ to his Church (Suppl., 73.1)." Paul O'Callaghan, "Reception of Thomas Aquinas in the Area of Eschatology" in *The Oxford Handbook of The Reception of Aquinas*, ed. Matthew Levering and Marcus Plested (Oxford, UK: Oxford University Press, 2021), 708.

4. Aquinas, *Commentary*, 287-8.

delivers an impressive array of insights that clearly influenced many generations to come:

> He says, then, *take heed that no man seduces you . . . you will hear of wars.* And this immediately after the passion. For immediately, tyrants were sent into Judea by the emperor, who wondrously oppressed them, such that they were as though unable to bear it. Hence, *and you shall hear of wars and rumors of wars* because in wars rumors are powerful. . . . But someone could say: *you say that wars will be heard of, while there have always been wars.* He responds: *you have never seen such wars. For nation shall rise against nation,* namely the Roman nation against the Jewish nation, *and kingdom,* namely the Romans', *against kingdom,* namely the Jews'. *And there will be pestilences . . . and famines, and earthquakes in places.* And all these things happened before the destruction of Jerusalem.[5]
>
>   . . .
>
> *Then they will deliver you up to be afflicted.* Then he sets out certain things which were to happen in the Church beforehand. . . . And he touches on three dangers: affliction, killing, and hatred. They could say: It is true that this world will suffer, but what is that to us? On the contrary, he says. And so he says, *you,* as though to say, *you will not be immune, but you will be afflicted,* literally; *in the tribulation, in necessities* (2 Cor. 6:4). Likewise, they *will put you to death,* as it was clear that they killed Stephen and James. . . . Origen says that it should be referred to the second coming, because there will be such universal persecution that evil men will persecute the good; and this is why he says, *then.* For it was customary that when bad things happened, they said it was owing to the sin

---

5. Aquinas, *Commentary*, 289.

of Christians. So they rose up against them; hence, *then will they deliver you up to be afflicted.*[6]

. . .

And will betray one another. Above, *the brother also will deliver up the brother to death* (Matt. 10:21). And not only bodily, but even spiritually, for some are the beginning of error, and from this it follows that they *will hate one another.* Such are those who seduce many in the Church; *but there were also false prophets among the people* (2 Pet. 2:1). Likewise, *there are become many antichrists...they went out from us, but they were not of us* (1 John 2:18-19). . . . they will *seduce many.* . . . So it will be that way in many, but not in all, because *he that will persevere to the end,* namely of the present life, *he will be saved.* The same thing is said above (Matt. 10:22).[7]

. . .

And this gospel of the kingdom, will be preached in the whole world. . . . Chrysostom says that this was fulfilled before the destruction of the city Jerusalem, and he proves this through the Apostle, where the Apostle says, *yes, verily, their sound has gone forth into all the earth* (Rom. 10:18). . . . Likewise, through another authority which is found in Colossians: *the gospel, which is come unto you, as also it is in the whole world, and brings forth fruit* (Col. 1:5-6).[8]

. . .

And then, namely when all nations believe, *will the consummation come,* i.e., the destruction of Jerusalem. . . . Augustine would have it that it should not be referred to the consummation of Jerusalem, but of the world. . . . And a distinction can be made in this way, that the diffusion of the gospel can

---

6. Aquinas, *Commentary,* 290-1.

7. Aquinas, *Commentary,* 291.

8. Aquinas, *Commentary,* 291-2.

be understood in two ways: either with regard to report only, and in this way it was completed before the destruction of the city, for although some had not received it, nevertheless there was no nation to which the report had not come; but if diffusion is understood with the effect, then what Augustine says is true, that it had not yet come to all the nations.[9]

. . .

He spoke thus: *the consummation will come. When therefore you will see the "abomination of desolation."* What is this thing he calls *'the abomination'*? It can be said that the Roman army is called the abomination . . . Or by abominations are understood idols . . . It is written that Pilate brought an eagle into the temple, which was the sign of the Romans, which the Jews called an "abomination". . . . Or . . . by Titus and Vespasian, and at that time the temple was burned, and some were still left in them.[10]

. . .

He says, *then those who are in Judea, let them flee to the mountains. Then*, namely in the time of Vespasian. At that time a certain man named Agrippa ruled in the mountains, and this man was obedient to the Romans, and did not rebel against them. So, while the other nations were having conflict, he and his nation were in peace. Hence by God's providence the faithful who were in Judea were warned that they should withdraw and go to the kingdom of this man, Agrippa, and so they did. Hence, *then those who are in Judea*, namely the faithful, *let them flee to the mountains.*[11]

. . .

---

9. Aquinas, *Commentary*, 292.

10. Aquinas, *Commentary*, 293-4.

11. Aquinas, *Commentary*, 294.

Where did this necessity of fleeing come from? From the greatness of the afflictions. So, first he sets out the affliction and the greatness of the affliction; second, he sets out the cause, *and unless those days had been shortened. For there will be great tribulation then, such as has not been from the beginning of the world.* And this can be judged well enough by anyone who reads the history of Josephus, for many died by famine. Likewise, there were riots in the city, such that they were killing one another: hence when Titus, who was most meek, wished to spare them, they did not want it. Likewise, there were robbers among them who killed many. And a certain woman ate her own child. So, there was such affliction as had never been seen. And Luke says this: *there will be great distress . . . and they will fall by the edge of the sword* (Luke 21:23).[12]

. . .

Hence if that time had lasted, all would have been killed, for no one would have remained. And why? Because the Romans ruled the whole world, and the Jews were already scattered over the whole world, so if that time had lasted, they would have been killed everywhere on the earth. . . . Then Chrysostom sets out two considerations as to why this is said, for some disciples were there, and likewise John was alive afterwards. So, he says that John does not mention this in his gospel because he wrote after it happened . . . but Matthew and Luke, who wrote beforehand, mention it, because at that time it was yet to happen. So, he says that the miracle became manifest when the Romans fought the Jews, and almost the whole Jewish nation suffered the destruction, the miracle being that so few Jews were able to go through the whole world

---

12. Aquinas, *Commentary*, 295.

146

to convert almost the whole world, and this was the marvelous strength of Christ.[13]

Matthew 24:23 is where Aquinas officially proposes that Jesus intentionally transitions into predictions about the end of the world and the sense in which Christ "comes" at last to consummate all things in history. On this verse Aquinas begins by saying, "After the Lord responded to the disciples' questions about the destruction of the city, here he begins to respond to those which pertain to the second coming."[14] As we shall see throughout this chapter, the power of Aquinas' rhetoric, the breadth of his logic, the simplicity of his historical insights, and his encyclopedic appreciation of patristics would enshrine both his methodology and Jesus' "transitional" verse in ecclesiastical memory in perpetuity.

3.1.2 ST BONAVENTURE (1221–1274)

The contemporary of Aquinas and famous Franciscan "Seraphic Doctor" of the Catholic Church, St. Bonaventure, wrote an equally detailed exposition of Jesus' OD from Luke's Gospel. In it we find a similar reception of patristic tradition and early Jewish history to interpret the meaning of Jesus' predictions. Bonaventure even prefaces his commentary with a note about the literary structure of Luke 21:5–38, which parallels Matthew 24:4-35. On that he surmised:

> Now this section is divided into four parts. In the first he predicts what is to come about *in general terms.* In the second he predicts what is to come about with regard to *the persecution of the Church* where verse 8 reads: *Take care that you be not led astray, etc.* In the third he predicts what is to come

13. Aquinas, *Commentary*, 296.
14. Aquinas, *Commentary*, 299.

about with respect to *the destruction of Jerusalem* where verse 20 has: *And when you see Jerusalem being surrounded, etc.* In the fourth he predicts what is to come about with regard to the final judgment where verse 25 says: *And there will be signs in the sun and moon.*[15]

According to Madigan's assessment of this structure, Bonaventure's most notable arrangement is his "belief that the discourse involves a grand chronological vault from about 70 C.E. to the end of time."[16] Bonaventure begins his lengthy exposition with a defense of the historical context underlying the OD. In offering as much, he not only shows familiarity with the history of the *Jewish Wars* recorded by Josephus, but also that such historical accounts were seriously considered by earlier fathers of Christian tradition. For Bonaventure, the works of St. Bede are of special import.[17] He prefaces the OD this way:

. . . concerning the prediction uttered on this occasion the text continues: *As for these things that you are seeing, the days will come on which there will not be left a stone upon another that will not be destroyed.* Indeed, this is said in general terms and is also true for *the time of the final judgment* when all things will be destroyed, according to what Matthew 24:35 has: "Heaven and earth will pass away," etc. And Revelation 21:1 reads: "The first heaven and the first earth passed away, and the sea is no more," so that what the Psalm says is verified: "They will perish, but you will remain." It is also true

---

15. St. Bonaventure, *Commentary on the Gospel of Luke: Chapters 17-24*, BTTS, vol. 8, pt. 3., ed. and trans. Robert J. Karris (St. Bonaventure, NY: Franciscan Institute Publications, 2003), Ebook, 1969.

16. Madigan, *Olivi and the Interpretation of Matthew*, 119.

17. Footnote 26 of Robert J. Karris' translation makes it very clear that Bonaventure's repeated references to an authoritative, Catholic "Glossa" refer to the *Glossa Ordinaria* from the Venerable Bede.

and in a special way for *the destruction of Jerusalem*, which was effected by Titus and Vespasian during the forty-second year after the passion of the Lord. . . . Therefore, Gregory says that Jerusalem with its temple was totally destroyed . . . . Now the reason why the Lord tarried for forty-two years was that he might wait for them to repent, as it is said in 2 Peter 3:9: "For your sake he is longsuffering, not willing that any should perish." And the reason why he tarried no longer was due to the stubborn perfidy of the Jews, who condemned the truth for the sake of a veil and a shadow. So, the Glossa notes: "God took care to overturn the city and the temple and all its figures, lest anyone after the coming of Christ revert to those things."[18]

According to Bonaventure, Luke has structured Jesus' OD so that Jesus begins by answering his disciples' first question, *"When will these things be?"*, with general predictions. Those general predictions were followed by more yet-to-be fulfilled in the life and struggles of the historically Catholic Church. Commenting on Luke 21:8-9 (which parallels Matt. 24:4-6), Bonaventure elaborates on three things "that arose at the beginning of the Church": "the multiplication of heresy, the severity of wars, and onslaught of pestilences."[19] Among the examples of the "beginning of the Church," he notes what the *Glossa* of St. Bede says:

Wherefore, the Glossa observes: "As Jerusalem's demise was imminent, there were many leaders who said that they were Christ and that the time of liberation had arrived. Also, at the time of the Apostles many heresiarchs went forth." So 1 John 4:1 reads: "Many false prophets have gone forth into

---

18. Bonaventure, *Commentary,* 1971-2.
19. Bonaventure, *Commentary,* 1974.

the world." Among these the first was Simon Magus, who, as Jerome testifies, proclaimed and left these words in his books: "I am the beautiful. I am the paraclete. I am the almighty. I am the word of God." So Acts 8:9-10 says: "There was a certain man by the name of Simon . . . who said that he was somebody great. All from the least to the greatest listened to him and said: This man is the power of God which is called great." Josephus also refers to a Simon the Essene, who was in the camps of Israel and proclaimed that he was the Christ. It is also read that when the sons of Herod were in Rome and were disputing about the kingdom, there were four people in Judea, each of whom proclaimed that he was the Christ.[20]

Bonaventure was not just familiar with the writings of Bede. His commentary also shows intimate familiarity with the commentaries by Jerome, Chrysostom, and the anonymous *Opus imperfectum,* thereby showing that he utilized at least three early patristic sources who shared the questionable methodology proposed in chapter one. Commenting on Luke 21:9, Bonaventure also cites extensively from St. Chrysostom's commentary on *Matthew's* OD and the *Opus imperfectum,*[21] and even blends the phrases of theirs together at times.

Among Bonaventure's own peculiar pontifications about predictions fulfilled after the destruction of the temple, he includes Manichee (the founder of the Manichees) and Mohammed (of Islam) as examples of "multiplications of heresy." Most notably, however, is Bonaventure's vivid portrayal of historical parallels between Luke's version of the OD and certain first-century types and figures *in the book of Acts,* which was also authored by Luke. Strangely, Bonaventure persists in interpreting specific details of the OD in terms of first-century biblical accounts that are supported by extra-biblical accounts

20. Bonaventure, *Commentary,* 1975-6.
21. Bonaventure, *Commentary,* 1977, 1978n44-45.

(like Josephus), while at the same time also referring them to a theoretical and *general* future persecution of Christians "until the end of the Church."

Commenting on Luke 21:10-11 (which parallels Matt. 24:7-8), Bonaventure references the works of Josephus more explicitly:

> And there will be great signs, not only because there will be many, but also because they will be unusual. —Now great and many signs of this kind preceded the destruction of Jerusalem according to the account of Josephus, who said: "A star similar to a sword hung over Jerusalem for a year, both chariots and armed horsemen did battle in the air for forty days, and a bull gave birth to a lamb when it was in the hands of its slaughterers."[22]

Commenting on Luke 21:12-19 (which parallels Matt. 24:9-14), Bonaventure cites the *book of Acts* extensively:

> *But before all these things they will arrest you,* etc. After he has described the persecution of the Church generally with regard to all, here he gives *special attention to the perfect.* Now here he depicts a twofold persecution, against the Apostles and apostolic men. The first is public, the second is private where verse 16 reads: *You will be delivered up by your parents,* etc. Concerning *the public persecution of holy men,* namely Apostles and their imitators, the evangelist raises three considerations, namely, *the battle* of persecution, *the reason* for persecution, and *the clear victory* of those in tribulation.... Therefore, the text states: *they will seize you.* Acts 5:17-18 reads: "The high priest and all those who were with him rose up, that is, the party of the Sadducees. They were filled with

---

22. Bonaventure, *Commentary,* 1979.

151

jealousy and seized the apostles and put them into the public prison." —There will be injury along with the violence. And so the text adds: And persecute you, delivering you up to the synagogues and prisons. Acts 6:12 states: "They stirred up the people and the elders and the scribes. And running together, they seized Stephen and brought him to the Sanhedrin." —Together with this there will also be simulated justice. For this reason the text adds: Dragging you to kings and rulers for my name's sake, as if it were a wicked deed to preach the Crucified. Acts 5:27-28 says: "When they had bought the apostles, the set them before the Sanhedrin. And the high priest questioned them, saying: "We strictly charged you not to teach in this name, and behold, you have filled Jerusalem with your teaching and want to bring this man's blood upon us." And Acts 17:5-7 reads: "The Jews, moved by jealousy, took certain base loafers, and forming a mob, set the city in an uproar [...] And they dragged Jason and certain brethren before the magistrates of the city, shouting: These men who are setting the world in an uproar have come here too...And they are all acting contrary to the decrees of Caesar, saying that there is another king, Jesus." Now adversaries of the name of Christ waged a savage persecution against the apostles and also against their followers. 2 Timothy 3:10-12 has: "But you have closely followed my doctrine, conduct, purpose, faith [...] my persecutions, afflictions, such as befell me at Antioch, Iconium, and Lystra [...], and out of them all the Lord delivered me."[23]

---

23. Bonaventure, *Commentary,* 1981-3. Since the Sadducees are not frequently mentioned throughout the gospels and Acts of the Apostles, Bonaventure's acknowledgment of the Sadducees as representatives within the Sanhedrin is particularly noteworthy. For a survey of scholarly perspectives about why the Sadducees are infrequently mentioned throughout the NT, and why their mention is important, see Henry Pattarumadathil, "Pharisees and Sadducees Together in Matthew" in *The Pharisees,* ed. Sievers & Levine, 136-47.

Commenting specifically on the heavenly protection described in Luke 21:18, Bonaventure elaborates further by drawing upon the insights of St. Chrysostom:

> . . . in this is manifest God's wondrous protection of the just. So Chrysostom comments: "Note the wonderful power of Christ and the fortitude of the apostles. By the Gentiles they were hated as Jews. By Caesar they were expelled as sedition. By the Jews they were stoned as enemies of the Law. Against apostles everyone fought: ruler, governor, the unlearned, and the people. Then the Romans seized numberless thousands of Jews, but did not overcome twelve unarmed men."[24]

As outlined in Bonaventure's preface, Jesus' predictions shift in verse 20 "with respect to the destruction of Jerusalem." Commenting on Luke 21:20-24 (which parallels Matt. 24:15-28), Bonaventure offers a classical series of interpretations based on the quadriga,[25] but nevertheless remains very clear that the foundational, *historical* sense in which these predictions were fulfilled remain primarily in the first century. Although he says that Jesus "here paints a picture *of what will eventuate about the destruction of Jerusalem,*"[26] he goes on to note that the "destruction" mentioned here can be understood in a spiritual sense "as the tribulation that the Church will suffer at the time of the antichrist."[27] Commenting on Luke 21:20-24 he also says:

---

24. Bonaventure, *Commentary*, 1990-1.

25. "The quadriga, or four senses of Scripture, grew out of the exegetical legacy of Paul's dichotomy of letter and spirit (2 Cor. 3:6), as well as church fathers like Origen (c. 185-254), Jerome (c. 347-420), and Augustine (c. 354-430)." Jason K. Lee and William M. Marsh, ed., *Matthew*, RCSNT, vol. 1 (Downers Grove, IL: IVP Academic, 2021), 456.

26. Bonaventure, *Commentary*, 1993.

27. Bonaventure also says, "Now the spiritual understanding is this. *By the army surrounding Jerusalem* is understood the insurrection of the perverse against ecclesiastical peace, and insurrection procured by the antichrist and his ministers"

(Verse 21). Second, concerning *the remedy of flight* the text continues: *Then let those who are in Judea flee to the mountains, lest they be found. And let those who are in her midst go out*, lest they be trapped inside. *And let those who are in the country not enter her*, lest they be captured there. For the Roman army first devastated many cities throughout Judea before coming to Jerusalem. And almost all Jews entered it, as Josephus says, on account of its esteem and for safety. So all were seized through the just judgment of God . . . . So the Glossa from Bede observes: "The Ecclesiastical History narrates that the Christians, who were in Judea, had been warned by an angel when the disaster was imminent and lived beyond the Jordan in the city of Pella until the desolation of Judea was fulfilled."[28]

. . .

(Verse 22). . . . *For these are the days of vengeance, that all things that are written may be fulfilled.* Now the Lord decreed to destroy Jerusalem in punishment for the blood of Jesus Christ and of his prophets. For Matthew 23:35-36 states: "So that upon you may come all the just blood that has been shed on the earth, from the blood of Abel the just unto the blood of Zachariah. [...] Amen, I say to you: All these things will come upon this generation." For so great a crime must in no way remain unpunished.[29]

. . .

(Bonaventure, *Commentary*, 1994). Without recognizing his use of the quadriga and its multiple senses, it might seem unclear to modern interpreters as to whether there is any difference between a first-century antichrist and a futuristic, end-of-the-world antichrist.

28. Bonaventure, *Commentary,* 1994-5.

29. Bonaventure, *Commentary,* 1996. Bonaventure then offers another spiritual sense: "Now *the spiritual understanding* is this. This vengeance of divine wrath is against sins of *ecclesiastical persons,* both secular and religious" (1996–7).

(Verse 23). *But woe to those who are with child and have infants at the breast*, etc. After describing the way that takes place first, he here depicts in a second point the subsequent annihilation. In this description three things are suggested, namely, *the oppression of the occupied city, the destruction of the oppressed city*, and *the devastation of the city that has been destroyed.*[30]

. . .

(Verse 24). . . . *And they will fall by the edge of the sword and will be led away as captives to all the nations.* We see that this was fulfilled *in the literal sense* among the Jews, about whose horrendous slaughter Josephus writes, and we see the astounding dispersion of the survivors.[31]

Luke 21:25 (which parallels Matt. 24:29ff) is where Bonaventure completely transitions from any sense of first-century fulfillment to entirely futuristic territory:

(Verse 25). *And there will be signs in the sun*, etc. After he had predicted what was to happen in general terms, and about persecution, and about the destruction of Jerusalem, here in a fourth point he predicts w*hat will take place concerning the final judgment.*[32]

In summary, Bonaventure is very familiar with the predictions that parallel Matthew 24:4-28 in Luke's version of the OD, and he not only imagined that Jesus *began* by answering his disciples' first question first, but the sources he utilized to formulate his own methodology pertaining to first-century fulfillment were from St. Jerome,

---

30. Bonaventure, *Commentary,* 1997–8.

31. Bonaventure, *Commentary,* 2000.

32. Bonaventure, *Commentary,* 2002.

St. Chrysostom, Pseudo-Chrysostom, St. Bede, and the first-century Jewish historian, Flavius Josephus.

3.1.3 PETER OLIVI (1248–1298)

According to the historian Bernard McGinn, Olivi was "a Provençal student of Bonaventure who was a remarkable combination of Scholastic theologian, apocalyptic propagandist, and charismatic leader."[33] He was also a highly controversial figure with works widely disseminated among monastic communities for decades. In addition to branding him as a "falsifier of the Catholic faith" and both confiscating and interdicting his writings in 1283 by commission of the Catholic Church, in 1326 his commentaries on the book of Revelation and the Gospel of Matthew were also emphatically condemned by Pope John XXII.[34]

In his commentary on Matthew's Gospel, which borrowed ideas from Aquinas's *Catena Aurea* more "liberally" than any other exegetical writing of his era,[35] Olivi proposes that although Jesus' predictions can

---

33. Bernard McGinn, *Antichrist: Two Thousand Years of the Human Fascination with Evil* (New York: HarperCollins Publishers, 1994), 159.

34. Madigan, *Olivi and the Interpretation of Matthew*, 1; see also pp. 67-72 for a more detailed chronological account.

35. Madigan, *Olivi and the Interpretation of Matthew*, 2. Madigan explains more of this in a later chapter, saying: "While his [Olivi's] spiritual readings of the gospels are in many cases strikingly original, many of his literal readings are quite derivative. Olivi himself usually acknowledges their paternity. But in what form did he find them? The greater part of the gospel commentaries are made up of literal interpretation of the gospel in which Olivi offers to his auditors standard readings of the text which he usually explicitly assigns to one of his Greek or Latin predecessors. The most frequently quoted authors are Jerome, Chrysostom, and Augustine. Others, including Origen, Hilary of Poitiers, Bede, Rabanus, and Regimus, are also cited frequently. The question thus arises, did Olivi read and cite from the complete commentaries of these exegetes or did he have available some sort of *florigelium* of patristic authorities? The answer is that he had a chain of excerpts provided him by Thomas Aquinas's *Expositio continua* on the

156

refer to church history beyond the first century, "specific elements can be expected to pertain to one period more than another."[36] Olivi wrote:

> Just as what the prophets said about the Babylonian captivity referred as well to three other captivities pertaining to the time of Christ, and what they said about the liberations of God's people from the Babylonian captivity referred to the three liberations to be completed in the times of grace and then eternal glory, so Christ, in speaking of the captivity under the Romans which would occur around his own time, also included two other captivities in prophetic manner.[37]

When referencing Jesus' initial response to his disciples' first question, he comments on Matthew 24:4-14 in its mystical and "double sense"[38] as pertaining to both "the destruction of Jerusalem and the day of judgment." This exegetical approach is strikingly similar to some of the church fathers discussed in chapter one, but especially Jerome.[39] In describing prophetic fulfillment "literally and openly,"

---

four gospels, better known as the *Catena Aurea*. Olivi's dependence on the *Catena*, especially in the Matthew and John commentaries, is extensive." Madigan, *Olivi and the Interpretation of Matthew*, 76. Italics are original.

36. David Burr, "Olivi, Christ's Three Advents, and the Double Antichrist" in *FS*, vol. 74 (St Bonaventure, NY: St. Bonaventure University Franciscan Institute Publications, 2016), 25.

37. Cited in Burr, "Christ's Three Advents," 24-5.

38. This "double sense" is a frequent feature of his interpretation, which filters all Scriptures through the standard four senses (i.e., the quadriga). In addition to applying the quadriga, he also classifies texts of Scripture into four parts: the historical, legal, sapiential, and prophetic. By means of this system, any historical text would have its literal sense, but it also might have a double sense, too, which could blend historical with other *parts* or *senses*. On this, see Ian Christopher Levy, *Introducing Medieval Biblical Interpretation: The Senses of Scripture in Premodern Exegesis* (Grand Rapids, MI: Baker Academic, 2018), 216.

39. Madigan notes: "Olivi's interpretation of this chapter [Matt. 24] is quite interesting in its own right, both for its reliance on, and independence of, es-

Olivi says that these verses can be understood as that which is "seen in Simon Magus, who claimed to be the son of God, and in Nero, who first persecuted the martyrs, as the Apostle implies in hidden fashion in 2 Thessalonians 2 [:3-12]."[40] Olivi continues this train of thought, saying, ". . . 'many will come in my name,' that is, usurping my name and authority for themselves, saying, 'I am Christ.' According to Jerome, one of these was Simon Magus."[41] Commenting on the "abomination of desolation" mentioned in Matthew 24:15, Olivi raises awareness of differing interpretations among the early Church fathers:

> According to Chrysostom this abomination was the Roman army by which the city was destroyed. But according to Jerome it was Caesar's image, which Pilate placed in the tem-

---

tablished exegetical tradition, as well as its relation to Olivi's well-developed understanding of prophetic texts in general, of which, of course, this chapter in Matthew is one. In part, Olivi seems to be relying for his view of the whole chapter on traditions of interpretation which reach back at least to Jerome, who in his *Matthew Commentary* saw the discourse as a threefold prophecy of the destruction of Jerusalem, the coming of Christ in glory, and the destruction of the world. Through Thomas Aquinas's *Catena Aurea,* Olivi was aware of this view of the chapter and, as a matter of fact, he cites it explicitly and assigns it to Jerome in one of his first comments in the chapter." Madigan, *Olivi and the Interpretation of Matthew*, 116.

40. Cited in Burr, "Christ's Three Advents," 34. Some remarks by Michael Bird and N.T. Wright in this regard are also insightful. They write, "A comparison of 2 Thessalonians with the synoptic Olivet Discourses (Mk. 13; Mt. 24–25; Lk. 21) and the revelation of John demonstrates that belief that certain signs will precede the end is fully compatible with an expectation of the imminence of the end (whatever that 'end' might be). Furthermore, Paul himself seems to have oscillated in his expectation of precisely how near the end was: somewhere between imminent (1 Thess. 5.2; 1 Cor. 1.7; 7:29; 15.23, 51-52; Phil. 3.20-21; Rom. 13.11; 16.20) to impending (2 Cor 5.1-10; Gal. 5.5; Col. 3.4), to perhaps delayed until at least after his own death (Phil. 1.20-25; 2 Tim. 4.6; perhaps 1 Cor. 6.14)." N.T. Wright and Michael F. Bird, *The New Testament in Its World: An Introduction to the History, Literature, and Theology of the First Century Christians* (Grand Rapids, MI: Zondervan, 2019), 420.

41. Cited in Burr, "Christ's Three Advents," 34.

ple, or the equestrian statue of Hadrian which, as he says, "stood there until the present day." For in the Old Testament an idol is called an abomination. "Desolation" is added because the idol was placed in the destroyed and deserted temple. . . . the literal interpretation of Daniel's words, if we consider the meaning of those sixty-two weeks mentioned there [Dan. 9:25-27], seems to refer . . . to their captivity effected by Titus.[42]

Here, again, it is important to notice Olivi's sources for first-century fulfillment between Matthew 24:4 and the passages referring to the events surrounding the abomination of desolation in verses 15 and following. Chrysostom and Jerome are both explicitly appealed to, as well as the book of Acts and 2 Thessalonians. By implication, Olivi was also aware of the works of Josephus. It is only after the section pertaining to the abomination of desolation (Matt. 24:15-28) that Olivi moves on to fixate on Christ's second advent. David Burr summarizes Olivi's exegetical methodology this way: "By the end of chapter 24 [of Matthew] all of these contrasts have taken shape in Olivi's mind in his portrayal of the first advent and they are beginning to do so in relation to the second advent . . . . Thus Matthew 24 is not the end of the story."[43]

3.1.4 JOHN WYCLIFF (1331—1384)

In the next generation we also find familiarity with first-century fulfillment surrounding the OD in the sermons of John Wycliff, the infamous "morning star" of the Protestant "Reformation" who reacted vehemently against the medieval Papacy, both politically and in his exposition of the Scriptures. Although Wycliff's methodology for in-

---

42. Cited in Burr, "Christ's Three Advents," 35.
43. Cited in Burr, "Christ's Three Advents," 39.

terpreting the OD was almost entirely futuristic and predicated on the Pope being the "Anti-Christ" prophesied therein,[44] he still, nonetheless, consistently raised awareness of the first-century context of fulfillment in which Jesus' disciples expected their questions to be answered on the Mount of Olives.

In *Sermon LXXIII*, for the feast of "Many Martyrs," Wycliff commented on Matthew 24:1ff saying:

> This gospel tells, as others before, how men should live in this world, and suffer persecution that must needs happen here. The story says, that Jesus went out of the temple, and his disciples came after him, to show him the structure of the temple; for it was referring to his word that he had said before to the people, to wit, what Christ felt about this structure of the temple. But Christ answered and said to them: See all

---

44. Stephen Vicchio points out that although the origins of the "papal antichrist" theory might stretch as far back as the late twelfth century, Wycliff still played a decisive role in the development of attitudes toward the antichrist because he was the first theologian to publicly and openly identify the antichrist with the papacy. On this, see Stephen J. Vicchio, *The Legend of The Anti-Christ: A History* (Eugene, OR: Wipf & Stock, 2009), 170-9. McGinn also writes, "It was only after the condemnation of some of his views by Pope Gregory XI in 1377 that the prolific English theologian John Wycliffe began his major use of Antichrist rhetoric as a weapon to belabor the papacy. Many were doing so at the time, as we have seen, but Wycliffe's use of Antichrist language was distinctive. . . . Wycliffe's incessant rhetoric was to see the papacy itself, not just any individual pope, as the culmination of the power of the Son of Perdition. This teaching is pervasive in his late works, especially *On Apostasy, On the Pope's Power*, and the commentary on the apocalyptic discourse of Matthew 23-25, which he incorporated as books 3 and 4 of his unfinished *Evangelical Work*" (McGinn, *Antichrist*, 181-2). This peculiar infatuation with the papacy-in-prophecy turns out to be deeply ironic in light of Levy's assessment of Wycliff's fundamental hermeneutic. According to Levy, *Medieval Biblical Interpretation*, 247, Wycliff insisted that "the many terms and propositions within Scripture maintain their logical veracity so long as they are read as originally intended by their divine author, for the literal sense is coterminous with the author's intention."

this? Truly you will see that here there shall not be a stone left upon another that is not destroyed. And this thing was fulfilled, within fifty years after, for in the forty-second year after Christ had ascended to heaven there came two princes of Rome, Titus and Vespasian, and encircled the city, when it was full of men at the feast of Pascha, as Christ told before by Luke.[45]

In *Sermon X*, on "The Tenth Sunday after Trinity," Wycliff commented on what Christ "told before by Luke," saying, "All these words were shown in deed, as Josephus makes mention of them, how Titus and Vespasian, in the forty-second year after that, Christ ascended to heaven, came on the solemnity of Pascha, and encircled Jerusalem, and utterly destroyed the men and walls that were found there."[46] In *Sermon LXXV*, another feast of "Many Martyrs," Wycliff preached on Mark's version of the OD, mentioning the sad state of affairs that would come upon that generation:

But yet, men doubted whether they should fight in this cause against her enemies—especially since Christ moved two princes of Rome for the fight, Titus and Vespasian, that destroyed Jerusalem.[47]

In Sermon XCI, on the feast of "Saint Stephens Day," Wycliff commented on Jesus' promise in Matthew 23:34 that "all these things shall come upon this generation," a phrase that is echoed closely in Matthew 24:34. He preached this way:

45. John Wycliffe, *Select English Works of John Wyclif*, vol. 1, ed. T. Arnold (Oxford: Clarendon Press,1869), 235. The translation from the Middle-English into modern English is mine.

46. Wycliffe, *Select English Works*, 24.

47. Wycliffe, *Select English Works*, 246.

Lo, I send to you prophets, and wise men, and scribes; and all this is for your good, to teach you God's law: and of them shall you kill, and do so upon the cross, and of them shall you torment in your synagogues. Here, also, we can see the malice of this generation, for a synagogue is a holy place, as those seen [at that time]; and therein they torment righteous men. And their sin increased more, and their blindness of wit also, for they went forward to succeed in this. And so, they pursued Christian men from city to city, that vengeance should come on them at the day of judgment. And thus, they accomplished their father's [i.e., the Devil's] work, slaying martyrs by their time [i.e., in the first century], that *all righteous blood* came on them, [all] that is *shed on the earth, from the blood of righteous Abel to the blood of Zachariah that was Barachiah's son, slain of them between the temple and the altar.* Such is a blessed end ordained by God's Law, for no sin may be done and not be given justice with it. And so, this justice [of God] makes the world more fair than such sin might make the world more foul.

. . . Christ said to these people: —*Truly, I say to you, all these things shall come upon this generation.* These Jews were part of that [cause for just judgment]; and so, *this generation* was there, and heard those words of Christ, for a part of them heard those. Afterward, Christ declared that this malice [deserving justice] was only in those [who heard and were there]; for God was of good will to do good to his people; but some of them would not take this goodness of God. And Christ said this: —*Jerusalem, Jerusalem, how often would you gather your children as a hen gathers her chicks under her wings, and you would not,* but received God's grace in vain.

Yet here, men doubt together how God's will was reversed, as the Psalm says: All that God desired to do, he did so in heaven and in earth (Psalm 135:6). But here it seems that . . . as often as Christ desired to gather children of Jerusalem,

162

as often they also remained gathered under his protection. But when he would not gather them, her sin was the cause, and by the just witness of God, they must receive punishment; and so, God's will was fulfilled in punishing them.[48] . . . And afterward, Christ mentioned the vengeance that shall be received for this sin: *Lo, your house shall be left to you deserted*, lacking in people who dwell there. And this thing came afterward in deed, shortly after Christ ascended to heaven. And so, Christ said to that generation, Truly, I say to you, you shall not see me as a result, until you say, blessed is he that is coming in the Lord's name.[49]

In Wycliff's treatise, "Exposition of Matthew 24: Of Ministries in the Church," he describes the entirety of the discourse in terms that pertain to the *general* generation of the church, *beginning* with prophetic perils in the first century:

It has been frequently said before, how Christ left [the temple] to specify the coming of the day of doom. But he spoke of perils beforehand; and therefore, steadfast men in Christ should be satisfied with their ignorance [i.e., of those Jesus spoke to], and be satisfied knowing of the perils that should occur before the end of the world. For both this information and this ignorance was profitable to men, and Christ had ordained them to be that way for our good. Who then should complain? It is said over this, that of the fifteen perils which Christ mentions here, many of which have passed now, and many should continue hereafter. And we suppose that Anti-

---

48. Wycliffe, *Select English Works*, 322-3.
49. Wycliffe, *Select English Works*, 324.

christ, head of all these evil men, shall be the pope of Rome, and it is him that Christ speaks of here.[50]

Although Wycliff's methodology does not comport with the multiple senses espoused by Aquinas, Bonaventure, or Olivi, the historical predicament inciting the questions of Jesus' disciples in the OD is clearly related to first-century events that culminated in the destruction of Jerusalem. Wycliff also shows an acute awareness of Christ's promise of soon-coming "justice" in the form of judgment upon Jerusalem and the wicked people of Israel in that generation. He even shows familiarity with Josephus as a historically reliable source for the fulfillment of Jesus' promises about Jerusalem's destruction. According to Wycliff, God's just judgment was brought about by Titus and Vespasian to destroy Israel's temple.

Unfortunately, due to the nature of Wycliff's commentary in the form of topical sermons, he never offered any detailed exegesis of the OD, as did Aquinas and Bonaventure before him. Instead, Wycliff preached as though the text of OD addressed his own audience and the general age of the church, beginning in the first century with events surrounding the destruction of Jerusalem and moving onward into his own generation, while focusing primarily on the evils of the papacy and how Christ's words warned against "that Antichrist."

3.1.5 CARDINAL CAJETAN (1469–1534)

Although Thomas de Vio Cajetan is best known for his negotiations with Martin Luther on behalf of the pope during the Diet of Augsburg,[51] he was also an exceptional philosopher, erudite theologian,

---

50. Wycliffe, *Select English Works*, 394.

51. This history is well-summarized in Tommaso de Vio Cajetan, *Cajetan Responds: A Reader in Reformation Controversy*, ed. and trans. Jared Wicks (1978, repr., Eugene, OR: Wipf & Stock Publishers, 2011), 12–31. Typically, Luther's encounter with Cajetan is presented in an oversimplified fashion that exalts Lu-

and industrious biblical exegete. One modern historian even describes Cajetan as a representative of "the best Catholic thinking to come out of the Reformation era."[52] Across his career, Cajetan wrote over 150 books and treatises, including commentaries on Aristotle's *De anima* and the *Sentences* of Peter Lombard. Cajetan also composed an extremely influential commentary on the *Summa* of Thomas Aquinas, which received "semi-official status" among Catholic authorities when two popes ordered it to be published alongside authorized editions of the *Summa*.[53]

---

ther's faith while portraying Cajetan as demanding, myopic, unteachable, scripturally inept, and blindly subservient to papal authority. Aspects of this tendency can be seen in the brief account offered by Timothy George, *Reading Scripture with the Reformers* (Downers Grove, IL: IVP Academic, 2011), 111-2. For example, George writes, "In October 1518, Luther was summoned to Augsburg, where he met yet another Dominican theologian, Thomas de Vio, better known to history as Cardinal Cajetan. Speaking in the name of the pope, he demanded that Luther recant. Luther later remembered this meeting as a turning point that led to his final break with Rome. If Cajetan had heard him out, he later recalled, had he been willing to consider scriptural proof rather than simply demanding blind obedience to papal fiat, things might have turned out differently. But at Augsburg, Luther could not bring himself to say those six letters, *revoco*, 'I recant.' Everyone expected Luther to be arrested following his interview with Cajetan. But Luther was ever the reformer of narrow escapes. Under cover of night, with stars for his canopy, he was whisked out of town on an unsaddled horse." Much of this portrayal by Timothy George is mythical, as is demonstrated convincingly in the biographical essay of Cajetan by Jared Wicks in Cajetan, *Cajetan Responds,* 1-46. Regarding Cajetan's diplomatic personality, wide-ranging Christian vision, personal humility, scriptural erudition, and philosophical prowess, see Allan K. Jenkins and Patrick Preston, *Biblical Scholarship and the Church: A Sixteenth-Century Crisis of Authority*, ANCT (Burlington, VT: Ashgate Publishing Company, 2007), 149-233, 244-7, 267-80; the translated works of Cajetan in *Cajetan Responds*, 47-244; see also, Michael O'Connor, *Cajetan's Biblical Commentaries: Motive and Method*, SASRH (Leiden: Brill, 2017), 11-60.

52. William A. Herr, *Catholic Thinkers in the Clear: Giants of Catholic Thought from Augustine to Rahner*, Basics of Christian Thought, vol. 2; (Chicago, IL: The Thomas More Press, 1985), 161.

53. Herr, *Catholic Thinkers*, 155.

In addition to his famous association with Luther and the influence of his philosophical commentaries, Cajetan also played a significant role in the international politics of his time,[54] and subsequently became "well known for his part in the growing accentuation of the papacy in the Catholic ecclesiology dominant [...] from the decline of conciliarism (ca. 1440) to the eve of Vatican II."[55] According to Jared Wicks, "Cajetan ranks [...] as a leading exponent of the papal plentitude of power in the church, a fact acknowledged at Vatican I."[56]

In spite of all this success, Cajetan also became a controversial figure within the Catholic Church. Not only was he "engaged in constant theological and political controversy" for sixteen years during his positions as vicar-general and master-general of the Dominican order,[57] but after his elevation to bishop of Gaeta and cardinal, he remained a passionate advocate of reform within the Catholic Church.[58]

---

54. Herr, *Catholic Thinkers*, 154.

55. Cajetan, *Cajetan Responds,* 9.

56. Cajetan, *Cajetan Responds*, 9-10.

57. Herr, *Catholic Thinkers*, 154. For controversies prior to Cajetan's ecclesiastical elevation, see, O'Connor, *Cajetan's Biblical Commentaries*, 13-5.

58. O'Connor writes: "In the course of his verse-by-verse commentary, he identifies specific ills besetting the Church and the world. These are consistent with the reform needs he had listed earlier. For example, in his discourse to the Fifth Lateran Council (1512), he called for the reform of the Church, the restitution of declining morals, the crushing of schism, the conversion of infidels, the calling back of heretics, the rewarding of virtue, the punishment of vice, and the strengthening of appropriate laws and sanctions. He strongly urged that positions of rank in the Church be given only to those who deserve them. As Dominican Master General (in letters of 1513 and 1515), he called for his confreres to observe faithfully the rule and constitutions and to study sacred letters. When challenged by Martin Luther (1518), he sought to improve legislation on indulgences. Writing to the newly-elected Adrian VI (1522), Cajetan identified the problems facing the new pope: moral degradation, spiritual destitution, ignorance, new heresies, war among Christians and the Turkish threat." O'Connor, *Cajetan's Biblical Commentaries*, 63.

In the last decade of his life, Cajetan devoted the majority of his time writing biblical commentaries, mostly due to his love for Holy Scriptures, but also, partly, because of his pastoral conviction that Lutherans and other Protestant reformers needed convincing arguments from Scripture above all other arguments.[59] In 1524 Cajetan published his first work in the field of biblical studies, *Ientacula Novi Testamenti, literalis expositio*, a collection of sixty-four independent articles that "nibbled" on problematic passages within the New Testament (*Ientacula* are "snacks"!).[60] In April, 1527 Cajetan published his commentary on the Psalter. That was followed immediately by commentaries on all four gospels (1527-1528). His commentary on the Gospel of Matthew was completed first, in November 1527.[61] Between 1528 and his death in 1534, he would also publish commentaries on the Pauline epistles, the book of Acts, the catholic epistles, the Pentateuch, Job, Proverbs, Ecclesiastes, and the first three chapters of Isaiah.[62]

---

59. Cajetan, *Cajetan Responds*, 31. Although it is commonly purported among historians that Cajetan's interest in biblical scholarship was motivated by Luther and the Protestant Reformation, or that Cajetan spent the last decade of his life writing biblical commentaries for the primary purpose of aiding the Catholic counter-reformation, O'Connor's assessment dissolves these myths. Alternatively, O'Connor shows that Cajetan's motive was primarily "diffuse and inclusive," to "make use of the textual critical tools provided by humanist scholars to contribute to a widespread renewal of Christian living. . . . Throughout a long and active career as professor, papal courtier, cardinal, and diplomat, he remained a scholar and a friar: studying and teaching the sacred page in the tradition of his own Dominican order. Even before he met Luther in 1518, Cajetan was clear that scripture should serve as the chief inspiration of Christian intellectual life and mission. When he set out on his programme of biblical exegesis in 1523, he may have gathered some brand new tools, but his basic aim had already been adumbrated in previous decades." O'Connor, *Cajetan's Biblical Commentaries*, 4.

60. O'Connor, *Cajetan's Biblical Commentaries*, 55-6; see also, Jenkins and Preston, *Biblical scholarship*, 152.

61. Hieromonk Gregory Hrynkiw, *Cajetan on Sacred Doctrine* (Washington, DC: The Catholic University of America Press, 2020), 263.

62. Cajetan, *Cajetan Responds*, 34.

His biblical commentaries incited much controversy, as he expected.[63] According to Allan Jenkins, "Doubts about the orthodoxy of some of the opinions about the scriptures that Cajetan advanced in his *Commentaries* began to be expressed soon after the first volumes appeared."[64] In 1532, five masters of the Paris faculty of theology were charged with "extracting erroneous propositions from Cajetan's commentaries."[65] Such propositions were considered erroneous because they were allegedly favorable to Protestantism.[66] In a similar manner to his own examination of Luther, Cajetan was subsequently summoned by ecclesiastical authorities to justify his published views and recant those determined to be erroneous. Although Cajetan would successfully defend his positions on such matters, and the Domini-

---

63. Jenkins and Preston, *Biblical scholarship*, 155.

64. Jenkins and Preston, *Biblical scholarship*, 156.

65. Jenkins and Preston, *Biblical scholarship*, 158.

66. According to a list of errors to be condemned, twenty-four propositions were taken from Cajetan's commentaries on the Psalms and the New Testament. Jenkins and Preston, *Biblical scholarship*, 159, lists them all: "The first four propositions are on marriage as this question is treated in Matthew 19, Mark 10, and 1 Corinthians 7. There are five other propositions that bear more or less on the same subject, since they deal with adultery (though the problem here is also to do with the authenticity of the gospel text), divorce, the suggestion that Paul was married, and the marriage of priests (two propositions). Seven propositions deal with texts that may or may not be authentic, and therefore raise the question of canonicity. Six of the remaining propositions deal with auricular confession, extreme unction, the language in which the Gospel of St. Matthew was written, public prayer in the vernacular rather than in Latin, the Vulgate translation of the Bible, and the authorship of the writings attributed to Dionysius the Areopagite. The other two propositions concern the translation of the Psalms." For a translation of Cajetan's impressive defense in the face of these charges, see Jenkins and Preston, *Biblical scholarship*, 158-225. Shockingly, charges against Cajetan did not include his views about indulgences or simony. According to O'Connor, *Cajetan's Biblical Commentaries*, 81-5, Cajetan's longest and most damning biblical arguments against the clerical immorality of his day pertained to the monopoly of indulgences (made notorious by Johann Tetzel) and the active acceptance or passive acquiescence of simony, i.e., the buying or selling of ecclesiastical offices and privileges.

can order would protect the public reputation of his commentaries, attacks upon his Christian reputation from within Catholic ranks would endure for over a century after his death.[67]

Even though Cajetan relies implicitly on interpretive principles established by Aquinas (e.g., the literal sense being foundational for applying other senses of interpretation)[68] and explicitly on his *Catena Aurea*,[69] Cajetan's literal interpretation of Matthew's OD shows little interest in utilizing the exegetical insights of Aquinas, at least insofar as first-century fulfillment is concerned.[70] For our purposes here, it is worth noting that throughout his biblical commentaries, Cajetan appeals to the works of Theophylact, Ambrose, and Augustine on occasion.[71] Most intriguingly, however, is Cajetan's frequent use of Jerome and Josephus, which O'Connor highlights:

> The two most frequently cited authors, by far, are Jerome and Josephus. Jerome is referred to more than thirty times, not only on matters of textual variation, canonicity, and authorship, but also on etymology, geography, and genealogy. Josephus is referred to more than fifty times, on matters of

---

67. Jenkins and Preston, *Biblical scholarship*, 213-4.

68. Hrynkiw, *Cajetan on Sacred Doctrine,* 220-8, details the relationship between Cajetan's quest for the literal sense of Holy Scripture and his commentary on Aquinas' *Summa*. For more details about Cajetan's reception of Aquinas, see Cajetan Cuddy, OP, "Sixteenth-Century Reception of Aquinas by Cajetan" in *Reception of Aquinas*, ed. Levering and Plested, 144-158; see also Efrem Jindráček, "The Western Reception of Aquinas in the Fifteenth Century" in *Reception of Aquinas*, ed. Levering and Plested, 96.

69. O'Connor, *Cajetan's Biblical Commentaries*, 167-9, 180.

70. This shift within Matthew's OD is interesting in light of O'Callaghan's assessment. O'Callaghan notes that the eschatology of Aquinas was "followed substantially" by Cajetan and others. On that, see O'Callaghan, "*Reception...in the Area of Eschatology,*" 705-6.

71. O'Connor, *Cajetan's Biblical Commentaries*, 164.

genealogy, geography, biblical chronology, Jewish customs, and biography.[72]

Since Cajetan shows familiarity with Josephus, Jerome, and other patristic authorities, it is interesting to discover that his commentaries are intentionally unlike those composed by his predecessors or contemporaries. Even with his frequent use of Jerome and Josephus, Cajetan's commentaries are unique insofar as he refuses to exalt or prioritize the interpretations of others above the authority of Holy Scriptures themselves.[73] Cajetan's wholesale adoption of any patristic interpretation of a singular verse or set of verses is rare when compared with his personal deductions from Scripture's literal sense. Consequently, Cajetan's exposition of the OD is *sui generis* among his contemporaries;

---

72. O'Connor, *Cajetan's Biblical Commentaries*, 164. On one occasion, Cajetan even explicitly mentions the candelabra used in the Most Holy Place of the temple, and it being taken to Rome after the fall of Jerusalem in 70 CE, as can be seen sculpted on the Arch of Titus in Rome. O'Connor, *Cajetan's Biblical Commentaries*, 165. For Cajetan's dependence upon Jerome, see also Jenkins and Preston, *Biblical scholarship*, 154-5.

73. This exegetical approach is, in principle, deeply ironic in light of his condemnation of Luther's interpretive principles. This tendency is also noted by Jenkins and Preston, *Biblical scholarship*, 154-5, who highlight Cajetan's exegetical principles in detail, saying, ". . . since the emphasis on literal interpretation and the search for new meanings 'compatible with the text and not incompatible with the sacred scripture and the doctrine of the church' is in fact a pervasive feature of Cajetan's exegetical work . . . These principles are very controversial. . . . Cajetan's declared readiness to prefer, if necessary, his own judgement to that of the Holy Doctors of the church—is startling indeed. His argument for this is that God did not bind the exposition of the sacred scriptures to the senses of the early doctors. To behave as though he did would take away from us and from posterity the hope of expounding sacred scripture except, 'as they say, by transferring it from one book to another'. He rejects in advance the charge of being motivated by the desire for novelty: he is old and truth is his only concern. Cajetan's appeal to the impartiality of the reader suggests that he anticipated a hostile reaction from his first readers. But at the end he acknowledges his readiness to submit to the judgement of the catholic church, and this establishes that novelty for him is not the first step to heresy."

170

it is also almost entirely futuristic, even though his initial comments appear promising with regard to acknowledging some first-century fulfillment:

> *And Jesus went out of the temple, and his disciples came up to him to show him the buildings of the Temple.* Because they had heard, Behold, the house shall be left desolate, they want to show Jesus the structure of the Temple, to provoke him to pity, or so that they may clearly understand if this desertion will be accompanied by the destruction of the temple.
>
> *But He himself answering* - for "But Jesus . . ." The word "answering" is extra. "*He said to them, Do you see . . . ?*" The word "nonne" (Do you not see . . . ?) is left out. One ought to read, Do you *not* see all these things?
>
> *Truly I say to you, there shall not be left here one stone upon another stone that shall not be thrown down.* The total destruction of the temple is clearly predicted. *But while he was sitting on the Mount of Olives, his disciples came up to him in secret*—meaning, separately—*saying, Tell us*—three marks are sought—*when will these things be?* Meaning, the things that you have said concerning the city and temple. They are asking for the time of the destruction of Jerusalem and the temple to be told to them.
>
> *And what is the sign of your coming*—Behold the second, by which they seek to know the sign of the coming of Christ for judgment. *And of the end of the age?* The third thing which they seek to be told them is the sign of the consummation of this world.
>
> *And Jesus, answering*—one by one to each of the things asked—*said to them, See*—he begins by responding to the

third thing asked, sc. about the sign of the consummation of the world.[74]

In these opening remarks, Cajetan shows familiarity with the first-century historical context of the OD. As Jesus leaves the temple, his disciples engage in conversation with him "so that they may clearly understand if this desertion will be accompanied by the destruction of the temple." According to Cajetan, Jesus then affirms their suspicions: "The total destruction of the temple is clearly predicted."

Afterward, the disciples ask Jesus *three* questions, and Jesus responds to each "one by one," thereby indicating that Cajetan assumes some kind of chronological progression built into Jesus' responses. Intriguingly, Cajetan points out that Jesus "*begins* by responding to *the third thing asked*, sc. about the sign of the consummation of the world." This seems, at least at first glance, to imply that Jesus would end this discourse in response to their first question. However, as we will see, such progression from last-to-first is not the methodology Cajetan presents in his exegesis of this discourse. Cajetan does, however, interpret 24:6-14 in relation to the consummation of the cosmos:

> *For you will hear of wars and reports of battles, for "wars and rumors of wars."* The sequence is reversed, for the sentence begins there.

---

74. Thomas de Vio Cajetan, *Evangelia cum Commentariis* (Paris: Roigny, 1532), 67 recto. As noted in my **Acknowledgements**, Cajetan's commentary is only available in Latin (as it was originally published), and I am relying on the English translation by Matthew Colvin in the citations that follow. As noted on Colvin's blog (www.colvinism.wordpress.com), he holds a PhD in Latin and Greek literature from Cornell University, and has taught classical languages and literature for twenty years. He has published articles on Greek Philosophy (Heraclitus, Plato, and the Stoics) in *Oxford Studies in Ancient Philosophy* and *The Classical Quarterly*. In addition to those works, he has translated the *1550 Magdeburg* Confession of Nicholaus von Amsdorff into English, and is the author of *The Lost Supper: Revisiting Passover and the Origins of the Eucharist* (Lanham, MD; London, UK: Fortress Academic, 2019).

See that you be not disturbed. And there is another thing they must beware of, watching for the emotional part of humankind. And he warns that they should take care not to be disturbed by fear in the hearing of battles which are being engaged in, and rumors of battles that will take place.

For these things must happen. It is necessary for all these things to take place. Of necessity from the appetites of men.

But the end is not yet. These things are not signs of the consummation of the world.[75]

According to Cajetan, Matthew 24:4-14 describes general events yet-to-occur before the consummation of the cosmos. Verse 15 begins a new section within the discourse, and its reference to the "abomination of desolation" is the first place where Cajetan officially begins highlighting exclusive first-century fulfillment, mentioning that "many people of that age lived right up to the time of the desolation, and they were able to see these things." His commentary on 24:15-20 is as follows:

And then—when all these foretold things have been fulfilled, and not before—*the consummation will come.* He does not say the consummation of this or that, but "the consummation," without qualification: since he is speaking of the consummation of this world, directly concluding his response to the disciples' inquiry, *Tell us what is the sign of the consummation of the age.* If you gather together all these sayings of the Lord: you will derive that the Lord has depicted that the time right up to the consummation of the world will have the common evils of battles, etc., as the beginnings of eternal evil, not as signs of the consummation: but proper evils on account of his name, for the merits of eternal salvation: and many

---

75. Cajetan, *Evangelia cum Commentariis,* 67 recto.

Antichrists, many false prophets, the leading-astray of many, the stumbling block, the charity growing cold, the hatred of Christians for the merits of eternal evil; but the preaching of the gospel among all nations, for an infallible sign of the consummation of the world by divine definition. [He speaks] this way, so that the disciples might learn the signs that of necessity precede the consummation of the age; and not signs pointing to the consummation of the world as though it were at the doors, or [pointing] to a certain time after these signs.

When therefore. Since he is replying to the chief question about the time of the destruction of Jerusalem and the temple, therefore he does not use marks of inference, by which the things that must be said are not inferred from the things said, but he proceeds to responding to what was chiefly asked, sc. when will these things be?

You will see. For many people of that age lived right up to the time of the desolation, and they were able to see these things.

The abomination of desolation which was spoken of by the prophet Daniel. Daniel 9 writes, And the abomination of desolation will be in the temple; and the desolation will continue right up to the consummation and the end. Wise reader, note that Jesus, in adducing this prophecy of Daniel, has added, *Let him who reads understand*: no doubt to make us careful, lest we be deceived in the meaning of this prophecy, and consequently in the words of Jesus Himself. He saw indeed that many understood or would understand by the word abomination either some statue that would be in the temple, just as had been in the time of Antiochus, as it says in 1 Maccabees 1 that the author of that book interpreted it as an idol of desolation, applying the prophecy of Daniel to it.[76]

---

76. Cajetan, *Evangelia cum Commentariis,* 67 verso–68 recto.

. . .

And anticipating, he urges him who reads to understand. There is no better interpreter than Luke the Evangelist.
He taught that the army of the Romans should be understood by the name "abomination of desolation." And truly,
the very words of Daniel indicate this, for he does not say
that the abomination will be in the temple, but he specified
the abomination by adding "of desolation." It is as though
he were openly saying, "I do not say there will be an abomination," that is, an abominable statue, but "there will be an
abomination of desolation"—indicating that the destruction
of the temple will be not by an earthquake, not by a flood,
not by fire from heaven, but from abominable idolatries, as
the outcome proved. But it is apparent that the evangelist
Luke (ch. 21) taught this meaning, from the fact that the
appended words here and there (that is, let those who are
in Judea flee to the hills, etc.) are pointers to these words in
Matthew about the abomination of desolation, and are understood literally about the destruction of Jerusalem.[77]

. . .

Then—when the abomination of an army around the
holy city draws near to the city of Jerusalem. *Those who in
Judea*—in the allotted territory of the tribe of Judah, for that
part around Jerusalem will be afflicted. *are, let them flee to
the hills. And he who is on the roof, let him not go down to
fetch anything from his house.* He does not say, let him not go
down, but let him not go down for fetching his own household goods, but for fleeing, with all things cast away. *And he
who is in the field, let him not return to take up his tunic* (for
"clothing," or "his cloak"). *But woe to pregnant women*—those
who are not strong enough to flee on account of the burden

---

77. Cajetan, *Evangelia cum Commentariis,* 68 recto.

175

of their womb. *and nursing mothers*—for "lactating women," who are not able to cast aside their babies and hasten to flee. For moreover he said woe to both pregnant women as well as lactating ones, since they cannot hasten to flee like those busy on the roof or in the field, who can abandon their household goods and clothing. *In those days. But pray . . .* He warned that all hindrances of property should be abandoned, and predicted that the hindrances of children must be born with. By this speech he teaches that the hindrances of the times must be removed. . . . *that your flight may not take place in winter*— unsuitable for the journey of escape. *or on the sabbath*—on which it is not permitted to make a long journey.[78]

Beginning at verse 21, Cajetan shifts subjects again, only this time it is both abrupt and awkwardly dogmatic, without any easement out of the first-century historical context. During this process he also admits to his belief that the disciples' *first* question is addressed and fulfilled back in verses 15-20, and that his understanding of Matthew's methodology here (in 24:21ff) is to complete the "interposition" of "signs" about Jerusalem's destruction.[79] Because the first question has been completely interposed at 24:15-20, Jesus can continue where he left off in verse 14, taking about end-of-the-world predictions. Commenting on the "great tribulation" predicted in verse 21, Cajetan writes:

> *For there will be*—This bit is not part of the response to *the first question about the time of the destruction of the temple*, but is the beginning of a response to *the second question*, namely, what is the sign of your coming. *And it is joined with things said in response to the question about the consummation of the age.* Thus, the combination of these things gives an account,

78. Cajetan, *Evangelia cum Commentariis*, 68 recto.
79. I also highlighted these same "signs" in **2.1.2 (a).**

not of the things said about the destruction of Jerusalem and the temple, but of the things said about the consummation of the world and the glorious coming of Jesus. And Matthew should be understood through the method of interposition, interposing the signs of the destruction of the temple in between those which were signs of the consummation of the age and those which are of the glorious coming of Jesus in such a way that it is contained by the *completed interposition*.

That this passage is not dealing with the tribulation of Jerusalem is apparent as well from the fact that it is by no means clear that the tribulation of Jerusalem was greater than all past ones since the beginning of the world; or, speaking more precisely, that it was not such as there has not been since the beginning of the world, etc.; for the text does not say that there was not one so great (*quanta*), but that there was not one like it (*qualis*). It is also not clear from that that there will be no such tribulation after. But this is the problem: that the Latin translator has translated "nor will there be," but the Greek text has "nor would there be."[80] Thus the quality [of the tribulation] gives the same meaning as what is said in the optative mood of the abomination, that such a tribulation *would* not happen thereafter. And so, the discourse is about the future tribulation in the time of the Antichrist.

For we believe that that [tribulation] will be greater in quantity and quality than the Jerusalem one was. It is also evident that the text clearly speaks about the salvation of all

---

80. In personal communications with me, Colvin notes that "Cajetan is mistaken about this claim. The Greek οὐ μὴ γένηται is a use of the subjunctive for emphatic future assertion, even though it does not use the future tense. To make things more confusing for Cajetan, Greek has a distinct optative mood, not used in this verse, but Latin uses the subjunctive, e.g., 'fiat' here to express wishes ('optative subjunctive') as well as potential and less vivid future conditions. Cajetan has mistaken a strong negative assertion in Greek for one of these constructions in Latin."

flesh, and not of *some* flesh existing in Jerusalem. And this reason is compelling to my mind. Then, too, the text says that those days are to be shortened on account of the elect, simply and absolutely, and does not say "on account of these or those elect" or "in such a place," to wit "in Jerusalem." Since he adds later, with no other tribulation being described, "immediately after the tribulation of those days the sun will be darkened," since the rest clearly is looking to the glorious coming of Christ, we may understand that the tribulation which is here described is the one after which the sun will immediately be darkened, etc.

And so from these things it is apparent that the literal sense of this passage is dealing with the future tribulation before the coming of Christ for judgment; *and that Matthew was silent about the great tribulation of Jerusalem which Luke explained.*[81]

Cajetan's sudden desire *not* to harmonize Matthew's OD with Luke's account is telling.[82] He claims that "Matthew was silent about the great tribulation of Jerusalem which Luke explained." Curiously, Thomas Aquinas—whose works Cajetan was familiar with—unequivocally interpreted Matthew 24:21 with reference to Jerusalem's destruction in 70 CE (see **3.1.1** above).[83] Many more theologians after Aquinas

---

81. Cajetan, *Evangelia cum Commentariis,* 68 recto–68 verso. Italics added, except in Bible citations.

82. I am grateful to Matt Colvin for pointing this out to me within the notes attached to his translation.

83. Aquinas, *Commentary,* 295, says, "Where did this necessity of fleeing come from? From the greatness of the afflictions. So first he sets out the affliction and the greatness of the affliction; second, he sets out the cause, *and unless those days had been shortened. For there will be great tribulation then, such as has not been from the beginning of the world.* And this can be judged well enough by anyone who reads the history of Josephus, for many died by famine. Likewise, there were riots in the city, such that they were killing one another: hence when Titus, who

would do the same, as we shall see throughout this chapter. Aquinas even harmonizes this verse with Luke 21:23, saying that "this can be judged well enough by anyone who reads the history of Josephus." Also, Bonaventure interpreted Luke 21:23 with clear reference to 70 CE, saying "this was fulfilled *in the literal sense* among the Jews, about whose horrendous slaughter Josephus writes, and we see the astounding dispersion of the survivors."[84] Cajetan's literal interpretation, however, seems fixated on convincing his audience that *Jesus* has suddenly shifted in his own emphasis, and that Jerusalem's destruction is of minimal importance for understanding his larger and more important predictions about the end of the cosmos.

It is also worth highlighting Cajetan's inconsistencies pertaining to Matthew's *methodology*. Above, Cajetan begins his commentary with a clear methodology in mind, saying that Jesus answers "one by one to each of the things asked."[85] In verses 4-14, Cajetan argues that Jesus begins by answering the *third* question *first*, which is allegedly about the end of the world. Here, Cajetan says that "*the signs* of the destruction of the temple" are sandwiched between "signs of the consummation of the age and those which are of the glorious coming of Jesus." Put succinctly, Jesus is asked three questions; the first is about Jerusalem's destruction; the second and third are about the end of the cosmos and the glorious "coming" of Jesus. Jesus then answers "one by one to each of the things asked" by sandwiching his answer to the *first* question *between* his answers to the second and third questions. But of course, even though Jesus began all of his answers (in vv. 4-14) in response to his disciples' *third* question, verse 21 picks up where he left off in verse 14 by responding to his disciples' *second* question;

---

was most meek, wished to spare them, they did not want it. Likewise, there were robbers among them who killed many. And a certain woman ate her own child. So there was such affliction as had never been seen. And Luke says this: *there will be great distress…and they will fall by the edge of the sword* (Luke 21:23)."

84. Bonaventure, *Commentary,* 2000.

85. Cajetan, *Evangelia cum Commentariis,* 67 recto.

then, that second question is subsequently "joined with things said in response to the question about the consummation of the age." In other words, Jesus does not simply begin by responding to the third question first; he begins with the third question first, then shifts to the first question second, and then transitions to the second and third questions together *last*.

Given this glaring inconsistency, Cajetan plows forward with complete end-of-the-world fulfillment for the remainder of the discourse. By maintaining this course, he also forces himself into an awkward position in which two clear references to *near*-fulfillment (the fig-tree parable and the reference to "this generation") must be interpreted as *very far away* from the first-century generation in which Jesus uttered such promises. Commenting on 24:32-35, Cajetan writes:

> *From the fig tree, learn the parable*—for "similitude"—*When its branch is tender and leaves have budded, you know that summer is near.* From the signs of his coming which were just now predicted, he declares the relation of the signs to his coming, both according to its nature [*res*] and according to its effect on men. And he declares that the relation of the signs preceding his glorious coming are, as touching their nature, like [the relation] of budding trees, the fig and similar trees, to summer. This is the relation of nearness. For the text clearly explains this relation.
>
> *So also you, when you see these things happening, know that it is near, at the doors.* Supply [as subject] the kingdom of God, or the glorious coming of Christ. *Truly I say to you, that this generation will not pass away*—[generation] of the elect, of humans. The generation of the elect would pass away before those signs, if when the number of the elect was completed, the signs were still postponed, and the coming of Christ

would still be postponed while only the generation of the reprobate was remaining.[86]

According to Cajetan's methodology, the "nearness" taught by the "similitude" of "budding trees" is related to a futuristic "coming" at the consummation of the cosmos. "For," he says, "the text clearly explains this relation." "This generation" is then related to "the elect" who "would pass away before those signs" are completed. The "signs" *preceding* the coming of Christ and the coming itself are both "postponed" until the end of the world finally draws *very* near. The elect generation will "pass away before those signs," leaving "only the generation of the reprobate" to remain and endure the Lord's "glorious coming."

3.1.6 MARTIN LUTHER (1483–1546)

Martin Luther's expositions of the OD blend aspects of Wycliff and Aquinas. On the one hand Luther's interpretations are offered mainly in the form of sermons, as were Wycliff's before him. Also, similar to Wycliff's style, Luther's preaching focused mainly on how to interpret the message of the text in a manner that applied to his own audience in his own generation. Unsurprisingly, then, Luther's application came in the form of polemics, most of which pertained to eccentricities among the papacy and their devoted disciples. To balance these excesses of contemporaneous concern, Luther was not afraid to preach verse-by-verse in order to clarify what he considered to be common misunderstandings of prophetic fulfillment. Such verse-by-verse expositions were common among his predecessors Bonaventure, Aquinas, and Olivi, leaving him in the position of trying to make sense of references to both first-century and end-of-the-world fulfillment within Matthew's OD. For example, in his forty-seventh sermon, which elaborated on Matthew 24:8-14, Luther commented this way:

---

86. Cajetan, *Evangelia cum Commentariis,* 69 recto–69 verso.

181

Recently we heard how the Lord began to answer the two questions of the apostles: first, if Jerusalem and the temple would be destroyed in such a way that not one stone would be left upon another; second, what would signal the end of the world and the Lord Christ's last coming. He answered this by prefacing that many sectarian spirits would arise and that there would be many wars [Matt. 24:5–6]. They had to know this for certain to avoid thinking that Christ would establish the kind of kingdom in which the devil would no longer afflict the world with lies, rebellion, murder, and bloodshed. . . . Do not think, however, that these will cease; instead, they will remain until the end of the world.[87]

Commenting on the "wars" mentioned in Matthew 24:8, Luther clearly shows an awareness of first-century fulfillment "in the history books," yet still cannot help but speculate that these predictions of Jesus were intended to be more *general* signs that accompany the church until the "end of the world." In his previous sermon he said that:

Great wars will not be the end, the Last Day. This is how it has to be. Do not be shocked by this. From time to time there will be wars, as well as famines and plagues. All of this is said, however, so that the disciples are not shocked by these things. We read in the history books of the terrible wars, plagues, and earthquakes that took place after the Lord Christ died [Matt. 28:2], in the first church of the New Testament, and yet it still was not the end.[88]

---

87. Martin Luther, *Sermons on the Gospel of St. Matthew: Chapters 19–24*, LW, vol. 68, ed. B. T. G. Mayes and C. B. Brown (Saint Louis, MO: Concordia Publishing House, 2014), 271.

88. Luther, *Sermons*, 267.

Luther here appears confident in his interpretation of "the end" mentioned by Jesus in Matthew 24:13. This is evident in the translation, "But the one who endures to the end *of the world* will be saved," which conspicuously inserts the words "of the world" into the text as though they were original.[89]

Even though Luther clearly had futuristic interpretations in mind, he could not help but try to make sense of its first-century context. In light of that, Luther portrayed Jesus' (and Matthew's) methodology as answering his disciples' questions *in a linear sequence*, from first to last. He said that Jesus "started to answer the first question of His disciples concerning the destruction of Jerusalem" in Matthew 24:4, but that start only offered general details pertaining to Christ's Church, beginning in the first century. The reason why Jesus "prefaced his answer with a long sermon" was allegedly "to keep them from thinking that His kingdom was supposed to be a worldly kingdom here on earth."

After delivering general principles in verses 4 through 14, Luther imagines that Jesus finally starts delivering *specific* details concerning the destruction of Jerusalem in verses 15 through 22. Luther's awareness of first-century details is most vivid in this section:

15. *"So when you see the abomination of desolation,"* etc.
He also says that the days will be cut short for the sake of the elect [Matt. 24:22]. Now the glorious city and the entire kingdom, even the priesthood, which God Himself instituted, must go to ruin. The words are not entirely clear though. Matthew and Mark mention the tribulation before the end of the world along with the impending destruction of Jerusalem, while also giving indication here and there about the destruction of the world, in such a way that He mixes and mingles both together. It is also usual for the Holy Spirit

---

89. Luther, *Sermons*, 276.

183

to speak this way in Holy Scripture. . . . Thus, Matthew also uses some words here in the same way to shed light on the world's final calamity, which is signified by the fall and destruction of Jerusalem—for the Church's tribulation will be just like this. He says, "If those days had not been cut short, no human being would be saved," etc. [Matt. 24:22]. So this is what Matthew is doing. Now we want to distinguish what will happen at what time.

Luke gives a clear description, without using any words other than those actually belonging to the historical account. After this preface Luke says, "When you see Jerusalem surrounded by armies" [Luke 21:20]. He gets right to the point, as if to say, "The glorious temple is standing now, but it will be made entirely desolate." When? "When Jerusalem is surrounded by armies, when we have perished, then know that this tribulation is at hand. The city will be surrounded by none other than the army, which will utterly destroy it, so that not one stone remains upon another, neither will any stick be left upon another." He also mentions other signs that will take place before the destruction of Jerusalem, signs that are plenty menacing and terrifying, about which we usually preach once a year. This, however, is a certain sign that the Romans will come. Since the Jews opposed the Romans, did not want to pay them tax, and kept inciting revolts, Emperor Vespasian came with a great army, seized all of Judea, and then marched to Jerusalem. This time Jerusalem was not only conquered and captured, as had happened before, but also was totally and utterly destroyed and leveled, so that even to this day it is lying in the ashes. Although Emperor Julian had given permission to rebuild Jerusalem, this did not come to pass, since an angel came and destroyed the lime and stone, making it impossible for them to progress with the building. The prophecy of Christ must remain true. This is the sign Christ gives here: "When this takes place, know that Jerusalem shall be destroyed so as never again to be rebuilt. Therefore, flee, and do not think that you will have peace."[90]

. . .

17. *"And let him who is on the housetop not go down to take anything from his house."*

In the history books we read that when the apostles and other Christians noticed that the Roman army was coming, they were mindful of this prophecy of the Lord Christ and fled from Jerusalem to Herod's region. And when the grain had been threshed out and nothing but chaff was left, as John the Baptist had prophesied [cf. Matt. 3:12], and all the Christians had fled with the apostles, abandoning their homes and possessions, the Lord God set the chaff ablaze, and the Romans captured Jerusalem and set fire to the city and temple, so that not one stone was left upon another. That is why He wants those who have a house in the city to take their wife and children out and flee from there, instead of thinking that our Lord God would still spare the temple or Jerusalem.

Many of them highly praised and loved this city, and so Christ's words hit the apostles hard. Surely they must have cried upon hearing that the city would go to rack and ruin, for it was their fatherland. St. Paul bitterly laments this, and as St. John the evangelist lived at this very time and had to see and experience the destruction of this city, it must have made his heart ache. Yet God had given the Jews about forty years to repent. He also sent them preachers, but the more preaching they heard, the more hardened and obdurate they became.[91]

. . .

---

90. Luther, *Sermons*, 277–9.

91. Luther, *Sermons*, 279–80.

21. *"And there will be [great] tribulation, such as has not been from the beginning of the world until now, and never will be."*

[He says] the situation in the city and the countryside of Judea will be dire, and, in fact, there was such slaughtering and killing that it is dreadful and terrible to hear. The city was struck all at once by famine, pestilence, sword, and wild animals; they also wiped out one another. Consequently, the history books have nothing more dreadful to read about than the destruction of Jerusalem. One affliction would have been severe enough; nonetheless, they had to bear all four afflictions. Then, on top of the pestilence, famine, and enemy's sword, they themselves caused a riot in the city and were so raving mad that they killed one another. The wrath of God against the Jews was great, and they were dreadfully punished. The punishment still hangs over them, as they are scattered throughout the whole world. Yet we pay no heed to this miserable example of the Jews. Instead, we act as if we would also like to see such a calamity some day, for we also kill those who fear God. Matthew writes that such tribulation will also come before the Last Day, namely, the Turk and pope and all the godless princes will unite and want to have us all dead.[92] [...] Therefore, the Lord Christ says, "The time will come when they will set an image in the temple," as happened in the time of Caligula. He had an image made and had people call out that he is the true God. He had his image set up everywhere for offering incense and worshiping, and had such an image sent to Jerusalem as well. This is the sign: an idol, which Daniel calls "the abomination of desolation," will stand in the temple. That is, it will be a sign that this city and temple will be made desolate. When a false god is set up, that is an image of the destruction; such an image should

---

92. Luther, *Sermons*, 280–1.

be a sign for Christians, by which they recognize that the desolation and destruction is at hand. "Therefore, when you see this in a holy place," that is, when such an abomination is standing in the temple, "let the reader understand" [Matt. 24:15]. With these words He clearly points to what kind of desolation the abomination will inflict when it stands there.

These apostles and good hearts do not understand that this city and temple will be completely desolated. Some say that an angel warned the saints when the Roman army was coming, so that they could escape from Jerusalem. Therefore, the Lord means to say, "Bear this in mind. Read this, if you can. Daniel speaks of this and surely means it." Nonetheless, He is simultaneously pointing to our destruction and the desolation of the whole world, which the Turk is now beginning.[93]

Although Luther is convinced that "the history books have *nothing more dreadful to read about* than the destruction of Jerusalem" in 70 CE, he seems unable to retain that contextual train of thought for long. Only a few short breaths afterward, Luther leaps outside of that "most dreadful" first-century context, and even *beyond* the general signs accompanying the first millennium of Church history, by interpreting the "tribulation" of verse 21 as the time "before the Last Day." Luther even goes so far as to imagine, both unnecessarily and disturbingly, that those who will bring such "tribulation" upon the world are "the Turk and pope and all the godless princes." Supposedly, they "will unite and want to have us all dead."

Luther proposes yet another conceptual shift in verses 23 through 26, where he claims that Jesus "is moving" on from the topic of Jerusalem's destruction to the end of the world because he "is more concerned" about the latter than the former:

---

93. Luther, *Sermons*, 283.

> 23. *"Then if anyone says to you, 'Look, here is Christ!'" etc.*
> The false prophets did not say that they were Christ. Therefore, He is moving from this to the [topic of the] final destruction. He stays with this and is more concerned with the question of when the world will be destroyed than when Jerusalem will perish. We will hear about this next Sunday.[94]

Although it is entirely unclear how Luther arrived at this quasi-dualistic interpretation of verses 23-26, he nevertheless insisted in his sermon the following Sunday that the destruction of Jerusalem is only the *beginning* of such prophetic fulfillment. In these verses Jesus "distinguishes between the false christs and false prophets who are to come soon after the destruction of Jerusalem and those who are to come later, at the end of the world, by means of the pope and his followers."[95] After this lengthy "preface" involving first-century fulfillment within verses 4 to 26, Luther finally begins to segue into entirely futuristic pontifications:

> 27. *"As the lightning comes from the east."* With this the Lord concludes His answer to the disciples' question about when Jerusalem would be destroyed. He unfolds this broadly to cover not only Jerusalem but also down to the Last Day, and prophesies what will happen to the whole world and Christendom.[96] . . . Now He takes up and answers the second question, concerning the end of the world and the Last Day. The first part has happened: Jerusalem has been torn apart and destroyed, lying in the ashes for about 1,500 years, while we

---

94. Luther, *Sermons*, 285.

95. Luther, *Sermons*, 292–3.

96. Luther, *Sermons*, 319.

have been miserably plagued with spiritual persecution, and many kings are still caught in this.[97]

Because Luther's exposition remained methodologically similar to his scholastic predecessors by presupposing that Jesus answered his disciples' first question first, Luther finds himself having to interpret Jesus' promise about "this generation" in verse 34 as *future* Jews in the "generation" nearest to the end of the world. He writes:

> 34. *"This generation will not pass away until all these things take place."* Various interpretations have been given to the words "this generation" and "all these things take place." One group understands it as meaning that the Jews who were born when Christ lived and who had seen Christ in the flesh would not die. I think, however, that it means the Jews will remain until the end of the world, and so long as they do not cease to exist, the Last Day will not be far off. This meaning is good and not false.[98]

In summary, Luther begins his series of homilies with an understanding that Jesus' disciples asked two questions pertaining to events that anticipated first-century fulfillment. Jesus then answered their first question first. In response to their first question, he offers general principles and predictions pertaining to the church which began in the first century. Then, Jesus gradually shifted his focus upon events surrounding the destruction of Jerusalem and the wars preceding that cataclysmic event. In verse 23 Jesus adjusted his focus again to subtly overlap and move beyond 70 CE. By the time Luther arrives at verse 27, Jesus "unfolds" his answers "broadly" to cover "events down to the Last Day" of judgment upon the entire world. Thereafter, Jesus

---

97. Luther, *Sermons*, 326.
98. Luther, *Sermons*, 340.

officially transitions into predictions that respond to his disciples' second question.

3.1.7 MARTIN BUCER (1491—1551)

Martin Bucer became a key figure in the reformation of Germany, and an ecumenical leader among various "Reformed" movements in France, Switzerland, and England. At age sixteen he joined the Dominican order, and he became an ordained priest within the following decade. Shortly after being ordained, Bucer met Martin Luther at a public theological disputation, which introduced him to many distinctively controversial views proposed by Luther and similar-minded reformers. Within a decade of meeting Luther, his studies would increase and his public views about Christian theology would expand to the point of excommunication from the Catholic Church. Instead of his excommunication drawing him further away from Christian tradition and closer to sectarianism within "Reformed" circles, Bucer's love for Christian ecumenism remained an essential attribute of his great and lasting legacy.[99] According to the historian Wilhelm Pauck, Bucer presented his ecumenical convictions across a wide variety of platforms,

---

99. Wilhelm Pauck writes, "Because of his accomplishments in Strassburg, he became an organizer of Protestant churches in many places, e.g., in Hesse and in such important cities as Ulm, Augsburg, and Constance. He spent much time and energy in order to obtain unity in the ranks of the Reformers through the reconciliation of Luther and Zwingli. Indeed, he hoped to unite the German and the Swiss movements of the Reformation. At the same time, he was ready to negotiate with Roman Catholic churchmen in order to bring about a reunion between Protestantism and the Roman Catholic Church. He spared no effort in order to overcome differences. He held innumerable 'conversations' and was involved in arguments with defenders of all kinds of religious and ecclesiastical causes—Anabaptists and Spiritualists, trained and untrained theologians, clergymen and laymen, political leaders as well as the common people." Wilhelm Pauck, ed., *Melancthon and Bucer*, LCC, Ichthus Edition (Philadelphia, PA: The Westminster Press, 1969), 155.

. . . not only in numerous memoranda, proposals, and letters addressed to princes and magistrates as well as to clergymen and private persons in Strassburg and elsewhere, but also in theological works of a scholarly character. Most of these were Biblical commentaries (e.g., on The Psalms; the Synoptic Gospels; the letter to the Romans; etc.). Others were in the form of theological treatises, chiefly on ecclesiastical themes (e.g., "Of the True Cure of Souls," "Dialogues on the Christian Magistrate," etc.). These works, which were written (or dictated) in the midst of a very active and greatly varied career of practical church leadership, display broad learning as well as original scholarship. They entitle Bucer to a place of honor next to the technical scholars of the Reformation, especially Melanchthon and Calvin.[100]

Pauck's description of "broad learning" and "original scholarship" is evident in Bucer's commentary *On the Holy Four Gospels*.[101] In it, Bucer writes extensively on the OD, focusing primarily on Matthew's version while also attempting to parallel and harmonize details across the remainder of the New Testament. Additionally, as can be seen among the commentaries of Luther, Bonaventure, and Aquinas, the insights of Josephus and early Church fathers contribute significantly to Bucer's interpretation of the OD.[102]

---

100. Pauck, *Melanchthon and Bucer*, 157.

101. Martin Bucer, *In Sacra Quatuor Evangelia, Enarrationes Perpetuae* (Geneva: Oliva Roberti Stephani, 1553). As noted in my **Acknowledgements** and above in **3.1.5**, Bucer's commentary is only available in Latin (as it was originally published), and I am relying on the English translation by Matthew Colvin in the citations that follow.

102. Although Bucer's familiarity with the works of Josephus is extensive, it is also worth noting Bucer's extensive familiarity with the works of Thomas Aquinas. On this, David Sytsma observes, "Among the first-generation Reformers active in the 1520's, Martin Bucer excelled in knowledge of Thomas. He entered the Dominican Order in 1507, and was in the process of attaining a *baccalaureus*

In his commentary on Matthew 24:1-2, Bucer begins by establishing a well-grounded, first-century historical context for understanding Jesus' prophetic remarks:

> *And going out, Jesus departed from the temple; and his disciples came up [to him] to point out to him the edifices of the temple. But Jesus said to them, Do you not see all these things? Truly I say to you, there shall not be left here one stone upon another, that shall not be torn down.*
>
> *And going out Jesus departed from the temple.* [Mark 13:1a; Luke 21:5a.] Now the Lord had already predicted that Jerusalem was to be sacked: as likewise earlier, when he had approached it sitting on a donkey, as was cited above from Luke 21: the disciples (as was fitting) marveled very greatly: and for that reason, it is likely that they pointed out the magnificent edifices of the Temple, as though commiserating with the Lord, and for that reason some one of them, as Mark writes, said to Him, "Teacher, see what great stones, and what great foundations." The Lord responded to them, "Do you

---

biblicus in the *via antiquita* at Heidelberg (1517-19), when he met Luther in 1518. Bucer's library catalogue of 1518 demonstrates profound interest in Aristotle's philosophy and Aquinas' theology. He owned not only Aristotle's works, but editions of *De anima* and *Metaphysica* with Thomas's annotations . . . . He also owned many of Aquinas' works and other Thomist literature, including Cajetan's commentary on the *Summa theologiae* . . . . While roughly half of Bucer's early library consisted of Thomist philosophical and theological literature, the other half consisted of humanist works (rhetoric, history, grammar, and poetry) . . . . Although Bucer distanced himself from Aquinas in his early writings between 1523 and 1528, 'this farewell to Thomas was not final' (Spijker 2001b: 302-3). Beginning in 1529, he adopted a less polemical tone and emphasized continuity with church fathers, canon law, and Thomas . . . . Many of Bucer's subsequent works, including his commentaries on Psalms . . . and Romans . . . , are sprinkled with citations of Thomas, sometimes negative, but often positive." David S. Sytsma, "Sixteenth-Century Reformed Reception of Aquinas" in *Reception of Aquinas*, ed., Levering and Plested, 124-5.

see these foundations and all these things? Truly I say to you, there shall not be left here one stone upon another, which shall not be torn down." For while the impiety of the Jews was coming to an end, God wanted to declare by this sort of destruction of this people and city and temple that He had rejected them and their worship, so that there had never been seen anything equally horrible, nor would there be.[103]

As Bucer proceeds to comment on Matthew 24:3, two details from it are worth highlighting. First, Bucer imagines that the disciples mistakenly conflate the destruction of Jerusalem with "business" about "the end of the world". Second, he clearly assigns the destruction of the temple to the disciples' *first* question, and their remaining questions to a futuristic "end" beyond 70 CE. By doing so, he sets up a scenario in which Jesus responds to the disciples' questions in the order they were asked. Bucer writes:

> *3. But while he was sitting on the Mount of Olives, his disciples came up to him privately, saying, Tell us, when will these things be? And what is the sign of your coming, and of the consummation of the age?*
>
> *But while he was sitting on the Mount of Olives, they came up to him.* [Mark 13:1a; Luke 21:5a.] It was said above, that in these days the Lord had been accustomed to go out towards evening from Jerusalem to the Mount of Olives . . . . Therefore when the disciples now again heard that Jerusalem and the Temple were to be destroyed, since they thought that the end of all things and the full kingdom of Christ would happen along with this, they ask him, and certain foremost of them (to whom he had also revealed other mysteries), Peter, James, John, and Andrew (as Mark has it) also ask him in

---

103. Bucer, *In Sacra Quatuor Evangelia,* 170 verso.

secret, hoping perhaps that he would disclose this to them alone, as he had most other things, *when these things which he had already predicted would be, and what was the sign of his coming, and of the consummation of the age.* For they thought that all these things would happen at the same time, that Jerusalem would be destroyed, that He himself would come in glory *and that this world would receive its end*, and indeed, in short, they were equally hoping that they would attain to a share in the glory of Christ and in blessedness. But since it was not their business to know about the end of the world and about any sure sign of his kingdom, the Lord answered nothing about these things, nor the details concerning the time of the destruction of the holy city.

But he answered and warned about—*things which were more nearly pertinent to their salvation*—first that there would be many deceivers, so that they might be on their guard against them; and then, about the rumors of wars and other calamities, with which the Jews were going to be afflicted before their destruction, so that [his disciples] might not be badly disturbed thereby. Then [he warned] about the persecution impending over them, and about various trials, which they were going to experience both from apostate brothers as well as from false prophets, so that they might be filled with courage to endure it. *At length he spoke about the horror and cruelty of the destruction of the city and of the Jewish nation, so that thereby the survivors might flee in time, and that all might fear God so much the more, and loathe impiety.*

But after this, he again predicts that there will be false Christs and false prophets, and warns that they must be guarded against these. Soon he spoke about the end of the age, but not when, only how horrible and with what great disturbance of things it will be, and how unexpected by the men of that age. From this, then, let us learn to always inquire into and learn those things which are of more immediate benefit, that we

194

should trust in God more firmly, and with more holiness, and that we should live with more dutiful love towards our neighbors. For these things alone pertain properly to us. Would that more men were persuaded of this! Then we would have much less of superstition and contention, and far more of solid and upbuilding knowledge in the Scripture.[104]

From these introductory comments, Bucer seems to imagine the following scenario: Jesus is asked a question about "when these things which he had already predicted would be." That is followed by questions about "the sign of his coming, and of the consummation of the age." By asking this series of questions, Jesus' disciples mistakenly think "that all these things would happen at the same time, that Jerusalem would be destroyed, that He himself would come in glory and that this world would receive its end." The responses from Jesus are also imagined to proceed in chronological order, from the first question to the last, beginning with "things which were more nearly pertinent to their salvation," such as "the persecution impending over them" prior to Jerusalem's destruction.

As we will see below, verses 4-22 are interpreted as *already* fulfilled in that "impending" persecution. It is only "after this" (as he says above), beginning at verse 23, that Jesus subtly shifts into predictions about "false Christs and false prophets" that are not yet fulfilled. In verse 23, Jesus is poised to transition within a few short verses. At verse 29, Jesus officially transitions into specific predictions about "the end of the age."

Across verses 4-22, the works of Josephus permeate Bucer's interpretation. Understandably, Bucer warns his readers to prepare for this extra-biblical approach, which indicates that some of his readers might not appreciate his extensive use of Josephus as a source for interpreting prophecy. Beginning at verse 4, Bucer openly appeals to his

---

104. Bucer, *In Sacra Quatuor Evangelia,* 170 verso. Italics added.

195

audience, requesting that they do not reject his interpretation outright but rather compare and ponder the words of the Lord "with those things that actually happened":

> *4. And answering, Jesus said to them: see that no one leads you astray. For many will come in my name, saying, I am the Christ, and will lead many astray.*
>
> *See that no one leads you astray, for many will come .* . . [Mark 13:5a; Luke 21:8b.] From the beginning I have undertaken to follow only the word of God in these comments, by which it will be granted to attain to it simply and purely, and I will put forth my effort in the present passage, with judgment left for those who are spiritual. *Therefore, if I say anything besides the opinion of others, let no one reject it just because he sees that it differs from men, but let him compare rather the words of the Lord, both among themselves, and with those things that actually happened,* and let him ponder each one, and then embrace that which seems more to fit the Lord's meaning.
>
> Therefore, what the Lord says here, I therefore receive as if he had said, "Cease to inquire about my coming and the end of the age, and especially about when these things will be. First, therefore, know ye that after my departure there will be many in my name who will say about themselves, *I am the Christ,* and will lead no few people astray. Beware of these men, therefore, lest any of them lead you astray, so that, as though you have divorced me, you follow him in my name.
>
> "This is the very thing that will happen to those haughty Jews, just as I have predicted to them. For they were not willing to receive me, who came in the name of my Father; therefore, they have deserved to fall into that blindness, so that they receive another who will come in his own name, that is, by his own will, and will smuggle himself in as a false savior—though he will put forth my name and the ambas-

sadorship of the Father as a pretext." For thus it has been arranged by the divine will, that he who has rejected the truth of God, afterwards gives credence to a lie, as is clear enough from [Lev. 26:15; Deut. 28:15; Josh. 8; Josh 29:11; 2 Thess. 2:11], and nearly countless other passages of Scripture.

But since it is Christ's title and job to free the people from the tyranny of the wicked and to govern them prosperously, as many as promised that they would be liberators and saviors of the people inveigled themselves among the Jews by Christ's title. Certainly, they had many of these before the destruction [of Jerusalem], who, though they did not persuade the entire people that they were it [sc. the Christ], nonetheless led many astray, as Christ predicted here. For Josephus in *Antiquities* 20.4 recalls a certain sorcerer, Theudas, who, when Cuspius Fadus was governing the Jews' affairs, had persuaded the people to take up their possessions and go out to the Jordan River, which he promised them he would divide by a spoken command. At length he was captured by Fadus, and was punished by beheading, and at the same time many who had been with him were destroyed, and some taken captive. There is no doubt that this Theudas is the one whom Gamaliel mentions in Acts 5:36. For even though he says there, "After this one there rose up Judas of Galilee, who turned aside the people in the days of the registration," that is, when Cyrenius carried out the first census among the Jews, when Christ also was born, which Josephus also mentions in Antiquities 1.18; nonetheless, he did not mean to indicate by this that he led the people astray after Theudas in time. Rather, the words "after this one" are to be taken as referring to the sequence of narration, as though he had said, "Besides this one there was also Judas at an earlier time, etc." For Gamaliel also says there, speaking about Theudas, "Before these days"—by which he indicated, as it were, that he had been a little time before that. But he specifies the time of Judas,

197

reporting that it was in the days of the registration, that is, when the census was conducted. But moreover, in *Antiquities* 20.11, Josephus writes that the province was filled with a crowd of brigands and sorcerers leading the people astray. But by "sorcerers" he means those who wound their way in under the name of prophets. Again, in ch. 12, he makes mention of a certain Egyptian false prophet. He writes of him in *Jewish War* 2.12 that appropriating to himself the reputation of a prophet, he gathered nearly thirty thousand men, whom he led from the wilderness to the Mount of Olives and threatened to take Jerusalem, but they were overwhelmed by Felix who was then the [provincial] governor. When Paul was arrested in Jerusalem, this Egyptian had not yet been put down, as the tribune asked Paul whether he was that Egyptian who before those days had stirred up a tumult when four thousand assassins had been led out into the desert, [Acts 21:38].

Again, Josephus writes about another man, ch. 14, who was promising the people salvation and a respite from their evils, if they followed him into the desert. The people of the Jews were deluded by many such people, all of whom, insofar as they had promised the people liberty and salvation, had so far asserted that they were Christs, although they falsely advertised themselves by this name, which in truth and in the Scriptures is the promised Messiah. Simon Magus was also of this sort, who had persuaded the Samaritans that he was the power of God which is called Great, [Acts 8:38]. Since these men led many astray, it was not off the mark that Christ warned his disciples against them, that they should not be taken captive by those impostors.[105]

---

105. Bucer, *In Sacra Quatuor Evangelia,* 170 verso–171 recto. Italics added.

As Bucer continues to link details from Josephus' works with Jesus' response to the question "When will these things be?", one quickly gets a sense that Bucer is thoroughly convinced of first-century fulfillment as being part and parcel of longstanding Christian tradition. One might even suspect that Bucer becomes convinced of this through familiarity with the lengthiest and most detailed commentaries that preceded his generation, such as those produced by Chrysostom, Bede, and Aquinas (including his *Catena Aurea*).

As we will see throughout the remainder of this chapter, Bucer was not the only Christian exegete to notice and appreciate the relevance of first-century history for interpreting Jesus' OD. Nevertheless, because Bucer is among the first theologians to *substantially* link first-century details with Jesus' initial response, his detailed interpretation of Matthew's OD is of paramount importance for our purposes here. By closely examining Bucer's comprehension of even the smallest historical details, his methodology and its influence upon countless others becomes unmistakable across future generations. He continues:

> 6. *You will hear of wars and rumors* . . . [Mark 13:7; Luke 21:9]. He first warned them to beware of false prophets and false messiahs, seeing that he also repeated further warning against this: for as soon as the sheep listen to someone else other than the one Christ their shepherd, they perish. Now, lest they be excessively disturbed on account of the very many horrible warlike tumults and rebellions by which the nation of the Jews was to be convulsed before it was utterly cut off, he warns them about those things and bids them not to be frightened by them—doubtless because he wanted to save those who trust in him, so they should not be harmed. But those rumors of wars and wars, that is, disturbances, rebellions, and massacres, began chiefly under the governor Cumanus, who had succeeded Tiberius Alexander. For when, on account of the impudence of a certain soldier, who had mocked the Jews during the festival of unleavened

199

bread by exposing his genitals, an uproar had arisen, then a massacre was permitted, with the result that the slaughtered numbered in the thousands. You may read about this riot in Josephus, *Antiquities* 20.6, and *Jewish War* 2.11.

There soon followed another tumult between the Jews and Samaritans with a great massacre of people and devastation of places. But the order of *sicarii* ["dagger-men"] came forth, who, wielding daggers concealed under the clothing, passed here and there in the crowd and bustle of the people, and were not recognized, so that all things were filled with amazing terrors. Soon a third tumult followed in Caesarea. But when P. Festus had replaced Felix (about which succession, see Acts 24:28), he tried indeed to free the province from bandits, but though he urged the vengeance of God, he was not able. For as these two, but most especially Florus, left nothing lacking for the cruelest tyranny, blatant violence, and plunder, so in equal measure the boldness for rebellions among the Jews increased day by day; hence uprisings, banditries, plunderings, and slaughters were brought forth in various places, and the people were exterminated by daily unspeakable evils and calamities, until they were, as it were, compelled to righteous rebellion. With such unheard-of violence and cruelty did Florus rage against them. King Agrippa indeed tried in many ways to dissuade the Jews from rebelling, but all in vain.

At length therefore, when those who were eager for revolution had prevailed, they attacked the Roman garrison and that of king Agrippa in Jerusalem with open war; and when the garrison had been forced to surrender, after they had pledged their right hands and promised them life with an oath, the slaughtered everyone except one of their prefects, Mutilius. On that day, every hour the Caesarians butchered the Jews who were living among them, twenty thousand in number. A little later, the Scythopolitans, following the example of the Caesarians, slew thirteen thousand Jews. Soon the Ascalonites [killed] two thousand five hundred, Ptolemais killed two thousand, the Alexandrians fifty thousand. From that point, Cestius, the prefect of Syria approached them in just war. But when the siege of Jerusalem was broken, and escape had diminished the power of the Jews, the instigators of the rebellion were made bolder, having got hold of all power, they brought upon themselves and their people an untellable Iliad of evils, and they were clean exterminated by Titus. Josephus writes at length about all these things in his *Wars of the Jews* 11.2, up to the end of the seventh book, that is, of the entire work.

And so the prelude, as it were, of these evils, the rebellions of the people, and unrest throughout all of Syria, which were stirred up under Florus, gave forth those rumors of wars and wars, about which the Lord predicted here, when he said, "You will hear of wars and rumors of wars; see to it that you are not disturbed; for all these things must happen, but the end is not yet [*sed nondum est finis*]," *not only of the age, but not even of the people and city of the Jews.* But this word "must"[106] has an uncommon comfort in it. For what wise man shall be afflicted for a thing which he is not able to have otherwise? But what man faithful to God will be disturbed when that which "must" happen, by the ordaining of God, comes to pass—namely, that which is necessary is best and always beneficial for the saints?

From the things predicted, it is obvious that also there was fulfilled at the same time, "Nation shall rise against nation, and kingdom against kingdom." For that appeared all too true in Caesarea, Scythopolis, Ascalon, Ptolomais, Alexandria, and later Damascus, where ten-thousand Jews were

---

106. Colvin notes that the Latin term used here is *oportet.*

slaughtered; and finally, when the kingdom of Agrippa was removed, and in all of Syria and the neighboring kingdoms. But about plagues and earthquakes, Josephus records nothing in particular. I think that he considered these things but light evils when compared with rebellions and wars. But he narrates at length about terrors and great signs, in *Jewish War* book 7, ch. 12. For throughout the year before the siege, they saw a constellation above the city like a sword. A night-time light surpassing the day, it flashed on the temple at the ninth hour and lasted for half an hour. A cow about to be sacrificed, gave birth to a lamb in the temple. The bronze gate of the temple was laid wide open. In the air gathered-armies were seen. A voice was heard in the temple, "Let us remove hence." A monstrous murmuring was heard by Joshua son of Ananias for seven years and five months; read the passage cited.

But Josephus does make mention of the famine which raged in Jerusalem, so that many were consumed by need. In these straits, Helena the queen of the Adiabenians with her son Iazates came to their aid magnificently, as Josephus tells in *Antiquities* 20 ch. 2. Also, in Acts 11:28, we read of a great famine predicted by Agabus over the entire world, which happened under Claudius Caesar. *But here, the word "world" ought to be taken to mean "all the region of the Jews."* Whence Luke writes in the same passage that the disciples set by [money] as each one had abundance, and then sent it to the aid of the brothers dwelling in Judea, which they also did, sending it to the elders by the hand of Barnabas and Saul. And from this anyone may see that Judea alone, or at least especially, was afflicted by this famine. Otherwise, it ought to have been sent to brothers dwelling elsewhere as well.

Thus, also the other evils, wars, pestilences, and earthquakes, terrors, and great signs in the heavens ought to be understood to have come down upon this region especially, since the Lord here wanted especially to make predictions about the future calamities of this people, and thus to declare how vengeance for all the righteous blood was going to be exacted from them . . . .[107] Thus, indeed Chrysostom also plainly gathers firmly. Therefore, what the Lord added, "but the end is not yet" and "but all these things are the beginnings of [birth]pains" have this meaning: You will hear rumors of wars, and wars arising in many places. Do not be afraid from this, nor hold my word with any less courage yourselves, and commend it to others. Each of these things will have to happen, and my kingdom must increase, and this nation must be extirpated by unspeakable evils.[108]

At this juncture, it is important to notice that only one single reference has been made to futuristic, end-of-our-word fulfillment. Bucer mentions in passing that "'You will hear of wars and rumors of wars . . . but the end is not yet,' *not only of the age, but not even of the people and city of the Jews.*" Here in 24:6, Bucer subtly interprets "the end" (τέλος) as extending beyond the first century.[109]

---

107. Bucer, *In Sacra Quatuor Evangelia,* 171 recto-171 verso.

108. Bucer, *In Sacra Quatuor Evangelia,* 171 verso-172 recto. Italics added.

109. As can be seen below, Bucer will oscillate slightly in his interpretation of this τέλος. I suspect that this inconsistency might be due to the Latin text he utilized alongside the Greek New Testament. The Latin text translates τέλος into *finis* at verses 6 (sed nondum est *finis*, "but the *end* is not yet") and 13 (qui autem perseveraverit usque *ad finem*, "he who endures *to the end*"), whereas verse 14 translates τὸ τέλος ("the end") as *consummatio* ("consummation"). The Greek text of 24:14 has καὶ τότε ἥξει τὸ τέλος ("and then the end will come"), whereas the Latin text in Bucer's commentary has *&* [et] *tunc veniet consummatio* ("and then the consummation will come"). The last time this "consummation" occurs in the Latin text used by Bucer [170 verso] is in the questions asked by Jesus' disciples in 24:3, ...*& [et] et consummationis seculi?* ("...and of the consummation of the age?"). Intriguingly, Bucer interpreted this "consummation" in verse 3 as the end of "this world," but his comments about verse 14 will state explicitly a few times that the "consummation" there refers to the destruction of Jerusalem in 70 CE. See his commentary below.

203

Also, at no point thus far has Bucer offered a detailed blend of past and future fulfillment, or even an interpretation of *generalized* historical fulfillment—as Luther and others before him attempted—from the past into the church of his present generation. Bucer seems to be utterly convinced that Jesus' initial response to his disciple's first question is *already* fulfilled.

This conviction of Bucer's becomes even more evident across his interpretation of Matthew 24:9-22, which is where most exegetes expound upon first-century fulfillment (especially in verses 15-22). Because Bucer's comments that follow are remarkably detailed and protracted beyond what is necessary for our purposes here, I will limit the majority of selections to remarks connected explicitly with other New Testament passages, instead of his continuous connections with Josephus (among others[110]):

> 9. *Then they will hand you over etc.* Mark 13:9, Luke 21:12. This is the third thing which he predicts in reply to the disciples, when they had asked about other things. They had asked about the kingdom and glory, and it is foretold to them that after the dangers of false prophets, after the common disasters of the Jewish people, by which they themselves [the disciples], though not harmed, nonetheless must be trained and disciplined, there will come persecution, the cross, ill repute, and furthermore severe stumbling-blocks that will make many fall away from the truth they have received, and at last, dangers of both false apostles and false prophets. Since he predicts that they are to be betrayed into affliction, are

---

110. In addition to multiples references to Josephus' works, Bucer's interpretation of these verses incorporates teaching from Irenaeus, Tertullian, Chrysostom, Jerome (who cites Sextus Julius Africanus), Eusebius of Caesarea, as well as Petrus Galatinus (a Catholic philosopher and contemporary of Bucer). Additionally, Bucer offers an extensive paraphrase and interpretation of Daniel's prophecy in relation to first-century fulfillment in Matthew 24:15, which is grounded in further sources.

to be killed, and will be an object of hatred to all people on account of his name, and that they will clearly pass through the things predicted to them which Matthew made mention of above in ch. 10, and of which Mark and Luke mention even more here.

Moreover, they are listed expressly by him above in ch. 10, from "Behold I send you out as sheep . . ." up to ". . . a disciple is not above his teacher." They soon felt persecution of this sort, from the killing of Stephen, by which all were scattered through the regions of Judea and Samaria, except the apostles. Paul also advanced this in Acts 8:1. "Afterwards, king Herod also stretched forth his hands to afflict some from the Church, and he killed James, and threw Peter into chains. But Paul testifies that he experienced persecution from Jews as well as Gentiles, both in the *Acts of the Apostles*, as well as in his own letters. Clearly Christ here predicted nothing that they did not experience.

10. *And then many will suffer offence . . .* The disciples were also to be trained by this notice, which often works more harm than persecution itself. Certainly, this has always afflicted the saints more than any persecution. Accordingly, it is also a far heavier thing to fall away from the gospel once received than it is never to have received it. But since never does a good part of the gospel seed not fall upon rocky ground, that is, hearts not changed to piety by the Spirit of God, it is always necessary that there will be those whom the storm of persecution turns away from the kingdom of Christ. If it could happen to the famous colleague of Paul, Demas, that embraced this present world (2 Tim. 4:10), then certainly it is not surprising if it should also turn out this way for very many others, although it is not possible for it to happen to

any of the elect. They are the good soil, on which, when the seed of God's word falls, it brings forth sure fruit.[111]

. . .

Paul also experienced this very thing, as he complains in 2 Timothy 2:19, and further in 2:21. Furthermore, they were going to suffer many false prophets and false apostles, nay, even apostles of Satan. Against these Paul always had a great struggle and complaint. These were those servants of their belly, not of Jesus Christ (Rom. 16:18), apostles of Satan (2 Cor. 11:13), striving to be emulated by the Galatians, and attempting to undermine them (Gal. 4:18), dogs, evil-workers, the mutilation, enemies of the cross of Christ, whose god is their belly, etc. (Phil. 3:18), deceivers through philosophy and empty deceit, having the appearance of wisdom in name only, etc. (Col. 2:8).

But why do I list many passages, when there is almost nowhere that Paul does not make mention of them, as also do Peter and John? Iniquity was so widespread, that is, that corrupt of nation by which men are only eager for themselves, being estranged from all kindness toward others; and since this was abounding, it was, as it were, necessary that love[112] grew cold. Paul also indicates that it was no secret that it had grown cold in his own day. Clearly it was a mark of abundant iniquity, and of love growing cold, or rather already cold, that all in Asia had turned away from him (2 Tim. 1:15). Therefore, thus the disciples were to suffer many grim adversities both within and without; but as many as persevered to the end [*in finem usque perseverassent*] with a firm faith in the Lord would overcome them all. Whence he added to all these

---

111. Bucer, *In Sacra Quatuor Evangelia,* 172 recto.

112. Colvin notes that the Latin term used here is *charitas.*

things, "But he who perseveres to the end [*qui autem persever-averit usque in finem*[113]], he shall be saved."[114]

. . .

14. *And this gospel shall be preached . . .* [Mark 13:14]. This is the fourth thing which Christ predicted to his people, doing so for their comfort. *Mark has, "And the gospel must be preached among all nations." This was also completed in the time of the apostles, before Jerusalem was destroyed. Just as the Lord predicted here, saying, "Then" (doubtless after the gospel shall have been preached everywhere for a testimony to the Gentiles) "the consummation will come"—to wit, of the temple, the worship, the city, and the people of the Jews.* Certainly, when Paul wrote (Col. 1:6) that the Gospel had then born fruit in the entire world, it had also been preached to all the Gentiles, that is, to a good part of the Gentiles. Indeed, just how widely even Paul by himself had sown it, he himself bears witness about himself (Rom. 15:19): namely "from Jerusalem and the surrounding regions, as far as Illyricum." Synecdoche is a known figure of speech, and very common in the Scriptures.[115]

. . .

But this prophecy holds in itself a small consolation. For indeed, though they were open enemies about to oppose the kingdom of Christ, and about to betray their brethren, falling away, or false prophets about to begin their schemes, or tottering hypocrites and workers of iniquity, among whom love has grown cold, nonetheless the Gospel had to be

---

113. Technically, according to the Latin text outlined by Bucer on 172 verso, Matthew 24:13 says qui autem perseveraverit usque *ad finem* (not *in finem*, as he writes here in Latin).

114. Bucer, *In Sacra Quatuor Evangelia,* 172 recto-172 verso.

115. Bucer, *In Sacra Quatuor Evangelia,* 172 verso. Italics added.

preached everywhere. Certainly, it was necessary at the time that the Lord preserve his preachers from all these evil men. And plainly, by the very act of predicting these things, he promised that to them.

But when I interpret these things in this way, along with Chrysostom on this passage, and Eusebius of Caesarea in *Ecclesiastical History* book 3 ch. 7, and I understand the "consummation" which Christ here predicts before the gospel being preached everywhere—*when I understand this consummation as being the destruction and consummation of Jerusalem,* the prophecy of Daniel speaking about this does this too, and the history of Luke. In it, in place of those which our author has here, 'When therefore you see the abomination of desolation, etc. . . . then let those who are in Judea flee, etc.", we read thus: "But when you see Jerusalem surrounded by armies, then know that its desolation is at hand. Then let those who are in Judea flee, etc." Therefore, the abomination of desolation spoken of by Daniel, standing in the holy place, about which we read in Matthew, was the siege, abominable to the Jews, which they suffered from the army of the Romans when they were shut up in Jerusalem. . . . *Therefore, let Christians weigh the words of Christ, here and in Luke. Then let them compare the prophecy of Daniel that is here cited, and they will see that I have followed no uncertain things after Chrysostom, Eusebius, and other ancient writers as well.*[116]

. . .

And so, since Christ refers back to the present prophecy of Daniel in this place, and it is sufficiently established already from his words, that nothing was predicted about the reign of Antichrist, but about the destruction of Jerusalem, then it will not be able to be denied that this same thing is the

---

116. Bucer, *In Sacra Quatuor Evangelia,* 172 verso-173 recto. Italics added.

abomination of desolation, which was inflicted upon Jerusalem on the wing of the abominable ones, whether demons or the Romans. About this, he warned in advance in the present, saying, "When you see the abomination of desolation, which was spoken of by Daniel, standing in the holy place—let the reader understand—then let those who are in Judea flee to the hills, etc." But since the evils that are predicted to them come upon the impious more quickly than they believe will come upon them, therefore he urges that the one who reads this prophecy of Daniel should understand, that is, that he should diligently apply himself to perceive and believe the things that were predicted in it. But in it, he orders that when they see this abomination of desolation, which he shows will be most horrible, standing in the holy place, that is, already threatening the holy city, when it has been surrounded by the army of the Romans (as it read in Luke in so many words), then let those who are left in Judea flee as quickly as may be, not into any cities, but into the nearby mountains and deserted places, and indeed with such haste that if anyone is on the roof of his house (for in that region they have flat roofs on which they spend time and are accustomed to do many things), let him not go back down into his house to take anything with him from there.

And if he is caught in the field, [he orders] that he should flee straight to the hills, and not return to his house even to take clothes suitable for flight. And since only flight is then able to accomplish anything for safety, he adds, "Woe to pregnant women and nursing mothers," doubtless because they are not able to flee when they are weighed down with the burden of infants. And to indicate the need for escape all the more, he moreover adds, "But pray that your flight may not take place in winter," when flight is excessively difficult; "nor on the sabbath," when religion forbade making a journey beyond a mile. *With all these things, the Lord wanted to emphasize the atrocity of the evils which were about to strangle the Jews, and to urge what he soon adds in plain words, that that affliction would be so great, that its equal had not been since the beginning of the world up to that time, nor would be ever.*

Whoever reads the history of Josephus will easily acknowledge that this is true. For besides the signal evils which the besieged endured, with countless people dying, in part from mutual slaughter, in part from hunger, which raged so powerfully that besides food of all abominable kinds, a certain woman cooked her own son for herself—[besides all this], the captured in the entire time of the war were ninety-seven thousand, and the dead through all the time of the siege, ten times a hundred-thousand, as Josephus writes in *The Jewish War* book 7 ch. 18. Whence there is no doubt that if those days had not been cut short, there would not have escaped safe all flesh of the Jews—about whom alone (as has been said often), the Lord prophesied here.

Therefore, we read in Luke, "For there will be a great affliction upon the land, and wrath upon this people. And they shall fall by the edge of the sword, and be led captive to all nations." But since he still had, and would still have, some elect from this nation, the Lord shortened these days, lest the entire race of the Jews be snuffed out. Nonetheless, Jerusalem (as the Lord predicted in Luke) will need to be trampled by the Gentiles until the times of the Gentiles are fulfilled. I take this as that verse in Romans 11:25, "Blindness has befallen Israel in part, until the fulness of the Gentiles comes, and thus all Israel shall be saved." But as the Lord here orders his people to flee when these evils are starting, Eusebius writes that when that siege was impending, the Christians remaining in Jerusalem were so warned by the divine answer that they fled across the Jordan to a certain town called Pella, so that this calamity might not catch them in Judea (*Ecclesiastical History* book 3, ch. 4).

210

Thus far, we are going through the things which Christ predicted to his people, both about the things which were going to happen before the destruction of the inhabitants of Jerusalem, and things which were especially of concern to them, as well as about the destruction itself, whose atrocity he adequately declared . . . .[117]

Although verse 29 is where Bucer officially and fully transitions into futuristic territory, Matthew 24:23 is where he finally begins to *hint* toward a transition into Jesus' response to his disciples' questions about "the sign of his coming, and of the consummation of the age." For Bucer, various interpretations could apply to Jesus' promise about false-Christs and false-prophets arising and leading others into error. At this point, Bucer seems to have forgotten that earlier in this discourse, he interpreted verses 4-5 as predictions against "false prophets" in an *exclusively* first-century manner, with multiple historical references from Josephus to validate his remarks. Here, Bucer offers no noticeable connection with his own remarks back 24:4-5, but rather suggests that 24:23-24 predicts imposters like Bar Kochba (under Hadrian's reign)[118] along with "the Romanists and Mohammedans,"[119] who are noticeable figures after 70 CE. Bucer's decided rationale for this mixed interpretation is that *no generation* is lacking in fulfillment of this promise. Bucer says:

But as deception always has its signs and wonders, by which men who did not want to believe the truth might be led astray to believe a lie, and no age is lacking its false prophets; and as every superstition has its origin from the flesh, and attunes itself to the convenience of the flesh; so there is

---

117. Bucer, *In Sacra Quatuor Evangelia,* 175 recto. Italics added.

118. Bucer, *In Sacra Quatuor Evangelia,* 175 verso.

119. Bucer, *In Sacra Quatuor Evangelia,* 176 recto.

> nothing of these things which the Lord predicted here which is not happening also to us in its own way. Therefore, those forewarnings of the Lord should be carefully weighed by all men, and hidden away in their mind.[120]

As I mentioned above, Bucer's interpretation of Matthew 24:29 is where a definitive transition takes place; he no longer mentions Josephus or any first-century history thereafter. Instead, Bucer considers the expression of verse 29, "But immediately," to be "about the last day and the end of the age, the judgment of the world, and his glorious coming."[121] Because of this, Jesus' language about the sun and moon are interpreted somewhat literally, as a way of describing a visibly cataclysmic activity among celestial bodies. The stars falling from heaven are a figurative exception, taken "to mean that they will lose their light."[122] Bucer also speculates about what the "sign of the Son of Man" will be literally (e.g., Will it be the sign of *the cross*?), but he does not adhere to anything specific.[123] He interprets the trumpet call of 24:31 as "the resounding and stentorious trumpet by which the elect shall be called together from everywhere."[124] Astonishingly, Bucer deflects attention away from this futuristic commitment when expositing the parable that follows. There, he understands Jesus' lesson of the fig tree (24:32-33) as having this meaning: "I have predicted many terrible things to you plainly. You yourselves will also experience the majority of them, nay, rather, all of them *except the last day*."[125]

Although such an exception is noticeably inconsistent, it is also predictable considering the history of traditional assumptions and

---

120. Bucer, *In Sacra Quatuor Evangelia,* 176 recto-176 verso.

121. Bucer, *In Sacra Quatuor Evangelia,* 176 verso.

122. Bucer, *In Sacra Quatuor Evangelia,* 176 verso.

123. Bucer, *In Sacra Quatuor Evangelia,* 177 recto.

124. Bucer, *In Sacra Quatuor Evangelia,* 177 recto.

125. Bucer, *In Sacra Quatuor Evangelia,* 177 verso.

questionable methodologies underlying Matthew's OD. Neverthe-less, because Bucer officially transitions into futuristic territory before Jesus promises that all these things will take place in "this genera-tion," he takes advantage of this "exception" at 24:34 and applies it in all the verses that follow. According to him, Jesus' predictions about "this generation" apply to everything *except* the "last day." On this, Bucer writes:

> Γένεα ["generation"] is indeed usually translated as a genera-tion, but more meaningfully (as Erasmus says here) it is trans-lated as a lifetime, an age . . . . Therefore, whatever things Christ predicted here, *except only the last day* (about which he soon adds that it is known to the Father alone), he rightly said that they would come to pass within that age, that is, the hundred years which were then flowing past; and that that age in which he was speaking would not pass away until all those things came to pass. . . . Thus, it is not established that by the words "this generation," we ought to understand the Jewish people, which is to endure until all these things are fulfilled. For even though "generation" is sometimes taken in place of "people," nonetheless an account of time is almost included, so that you should understand it as "a people ex-isting in one time or age." . . . And indeed, whoever ponders each word here will not be in any darkness about the fact that here the Lord has indeed taken τὴν γένεαν as an account of time, doubtless wanting to indicate that whatever things he had predicted would take place shortly, *except the last day*.[126]

To summarize all that has been offered above, Bucer shows himself to be, as Pauck described, a man of "broad learning" and "original scholarship." His detailed investigation into first-century history is

---

126. Bucer, *In Sacra Quatuor Evangelia,* 177 verso.

categorically undeniable. Bucer was also absolutely convinced that Jesus was asked one question that pertained exclusively to first-century fulfillment. Jesus answered that question across Matthew 24:4-22, and copious notes from the works of Josephus and the New Testament bear witness to the credibility and fulfillment of Jesus' predictions. Bucer's remarks in this regard are worth repeating:

> With all these things, the Lord wanted to emphasize the atrocity of the evils which were about to strangle the Jews, and to urge what he soon adds in plain words, that that affliction would be so great, that its equal had not been since the beginning of the world up to that time, nor would be ever. Whoever reads the history of Josephus will easily acknowledge that this is true.[127]
>
> . . .
>
> Therefore, let Christians weigh the words of Christ, here and in Luke. Then let them compare the prophecy of Daniel that is here cited, and they will see that I have followed no uncertain things after Chrysostom, Eusebius, and other ancient writers as well.[128]

However, starting at verse 23, Bucer selects some conveniently slippery language that could *potentially* describe false messiahs and prophets of *any* generation. Bucer then uses that potentiality to slide into absolutely futuristic territory shortly thereafter. Even though Jesus continues to promise that "all these things" will take place in "this generation," and the example of a fig tree (24:32-33) is used to illustrate the predictability and assurance of such near-fulfillment, Matt. 24:29 is where Jesus supposedly transitions. Every seemingly first-cen-

---

127. Bucer, *In Sacra Quatuor Evangelia,* 175 recto.

128. Bucer, *In Sacra Quatuor Evangelia,* 173 recto.

tury referent thereafter contains one—and only one—exception for awaited fulfillment: the "last day" at the end of the world.

3.1.8 JUAN DE VALDES (1490–1541)

The Spanish Catholic theologian, Juan de Valdes, was a critic of the Lutheran schism and a revivalist in his own tradition, being forced to flee from the Spanish Inquisition due to some of his published views, the chief of which involved criticisms of papal policy and corruption within the Latin Catholic Church. In addition to his doctrinal treatises, his influential writings included biblical commentaries and a memorable translation of the Hebrew Psalter.

Valdes's commentary on the Gospel of Matthew was unique insofar as it remained the first biblical commentary of his era to openly express suspicion and confusion about its mixture of past and futuristic fulfillment. Being extremely cautious in his orthodox exposition of the OD, Valdes seemed to be unable to reconcile three things: (1) what theologians before him had offered by way of interpretation, (2) what the historical context of Matthew's gospel clearly implies, and (3) what he had been trained to confess doctrinally about the "Second Coming." In his introduction to Matthew's OD, he writes:

> *I find more difficulty in understanding this chapter than any other of the New Testament*; I will state what I do understand of it up to this present time: remitting myself to a better and more certain apprehension. As to the first, I understand that the disciples pointed out to Christ the temple as a magnificent structure, and that Christ took occasion from that to prophesy to them the destruction of the temple, saying, "There shall not be left here one stone," &c., intimating that the destruction would be, in the highest degree, terrible. And I understand that the disciples, having heard this prophecy, desired to know the precise time in which it was to be ful-

215

filled; and that they, imagining to themselves that the fulfill-ment of that prophecy was to be at Christ's second advent, at the end of the world, came to Christ to ask Him every detail, respecting two things; of the destruction of Jerusalem, and of His coming to Judgment at the end of the world.

And I understand that Christ answered on both sub-jects *so blending the one with the other*, that the disciples might confirm themselves in their thought, that they both should be accomplished at the same time. The reason why Christ thus answered them I do not know; I do indeed think that the disciples were mainly led, by this reply, to think that the world would come to its end in their time.[129]

Regarding the interpretation of Matthew's OD, Valdes' methodolo-gy still operated within the familiar framework proposed by Hilary, Jerome, Chrysostom, and others popular sources offered in previous generations. He begins by offering a general pastoral interpretation of the predictions of Matthew 24:4-14, similar to the style of Luther and others before him. As can be seen below, verses 15 through 22, which pertain to events surrounding the abomination of desolation, are then explicitly stated as being in response to the disciples' *first* question, "When will these things be?"

After proposing as much, Valdes then admits he is *not* satisfied with first-century fulfillment, even though it is seemingly impossi-ble to avoid its cogency in Matthew's literary context. Then, while interpreting verses 23–36 which follow, he admits again that verse 34 is an undeniable reference to first-century events, and he cannot explain how it could be otherwise. Commenting on verses 15-22, Valdes writes:

---

129. Juan de Valdes, *Commentary upon the Gospel of St. Matthew: Now for the first time translated from the Spanish, and never before published in English*, trans. John T. Betts (London: Turner & Co., 1882), 418. Italics added.

It appears that *these words affect the first question* which the disciples made concerning the destruction of Jerusalem . . . . And it appears that because Daniel's words are obscure, Christ added, "He that readeth, let him understand;" *I however do not understand them . . . .* I do indeed understand, that Christ, desiring to express a terrible and fearful ruin and persecution, adduces those things that occur when a city is taken by assault, and when it is made a scene of massacre, for that its inhabitants, having lost the hope of saving their property, only care to save their lives, fleeing to the mountains, hiding themselves on their house-tops, and not even caring to take their clothes; and for that it goes hard with pregnant women, because they cannot flee; and with those who give suck, because natural affection forbids them to desert their offspring. . . . And setting forth the reason for these admonitions, He says, "For then shall be great tribulation," &c. ; and when He adds, "And if those days," &c., it may be understood, that if God had not shortened the tribulation of that time, not permitting that the persecution should extend further, not one Jew would have survived; and in adding, "But for the elect's sake," &c., it may be understood, that God would stop the fury of that persecution, in order that the Jews, whom He had elected to bring to Christ and to give them eternal life with Christ, should not perish in it.[130]

Valdes' contribution is unique insofar as it openly admits that although first-century fulfillment seems obvious in context, he remains dissatisfied with that result. He writes next:

I remain dissatisfied with all this interpretation, for it appears to me, that these last words at least would have harmonized

---

130. Valdes, *Commentary*, 423-2. Italics added.

217

better with the day of judgment, as well because I do not understand that the destruction of Jerusalem has been greater than was that of the deluge, nor than will be that of the day of judgment; and I do understand, that the judgment will be greater than that of Jerusalem, and than that of the deluge.[131]

After commenting on verses 23-36 in detail as though it only referred to the end of the world at the end of time, Valdes suddenly admits, again, that Jesus' remarks about "this generation" in verse 34 make obvious contextual sense in reference to the destruction of Jerusalem, for

---

131. Valdes, *Commentary*, 424. Valdes' puzzlement is understandable insofar as he unnecessarily conflates the "tribulation" ($\theta\lambda\tilde{\imath}\psi\iota\varsigma$) of Matthew 24:21 with the cataclysmic *event* of the "end" itself. "Tribulation" ($\theta\lambda\tilde{\imath}\psi\iota\varsigma$) is just the ordinary term for "distress," "anguish," or burdensome, psychological "suffering." Outside of Matthew's fifth discourse $\theta\lambda\tilde{\imath}\psi\iota\varsigma$ is only used in Jesus' Parable of the Sower (Matt. 13:21), where it describes the same common ideas. Matthew 24:21 should be treated no different. The great "tribulation" mentioned in 24:21 does *not* refer to the greatest destructive event ever to occur in history, as Valdes seems to imagine. Adding to that simple conceptual blunder, Valdes was not comfortable with Jesus' evocative rhetoric remaining localized in its focus. Therefore, according to Valdes, Jesus was not forecasting a "great distress" upon Judeans that *endures up to* the temple's destruction and will never be repeated again. Yet we can see today, millennia after 70 CE, that Jesus' remarks remain accurate insofar as his focus remain on first-century events—and only first-century events—throughout the entire OD. The siege of Jerusalem and the destruction of its temple became the longest and most destructive provincial war in the first century (Jacobson, *Agrippa II*, 119). It even stretched out twelve months longer than the Babylonian siege of Jerusalem with the destruction of Israel's *first* temple. The seemingly endless exhaustion, fretfulness, hostility, starvation, desperation, brutality, bloodshed, and psychological strain to come upon the people of Jerusalem would have been unimaginable during Jesus' lifetime. For those who have studied the siege of Jerusalem, an exact replica of such tribulation still seems unimaginable today. On the agonizing subjugations leading up to the temple's destruction, along with descriptions of gruesome punishments for captives prior to and immediately after Jerusalem's destruction, see Jacobson, *Agrippa II*, 86-120.

he knows of "no other expedient whereby to get out of this difficulty." Commenting on Matthew 24:32-36, Valdes writes:

> There are four things in these words. First, the comparison of the fig-tree, wherein Christ's meaning is, that just as we know the coming of summer by the fig-tree, so by the fulfillment of all these tokens, of which He has spoken, shall we know of His coming to judgment. Second, that the ruin of Jerusalem should come, before that generation of men, who were then living, should pass away, as, in point of fact, it came. *And although it appears strange to refer to these words to the ruin of Jerusalem, I know of no other expedient whereby to get out of this difficulty*. . . . The third thing that there is in these words is the stability and firmness of Christ's words, which are more stable and more firm than heaven and earth. The fourth thing is the profound mystery that God maintains His own purposes, since He has not even revealed to His angels, the day when the final judgment shall take place.[132]

It is clear that Valdes shows familiarity with the methodology of his predecessors, which involved some sense of first-century fulfillment between Matthew 24:4 and 24:34. The remainder of his exposition remains entirely focused on the future, thereby marking a clear transition into end-of-the-world fulfillment.

3.1.9 HEINRICH BULLINGER (1504—1575)

Bullinger was a monumental figure of the Protestant reformations expanding across Europe in the sixteenth century. In addition to becoming the head of the church of Zurich, he also worked alongside Martin Luther, Martin Bucer, John Calvin, and other prodigious reformers at

---

132. Valdes, *Commentary*, 428-9.

219

various stages of his life. Bullinger is most famous for drafting the first and second *Helvetic Confessions*, the latter of which was quickly adopted in the Reformed churches of Switzerland, Scotland, and Hungary, and eventually became the theological standard among Protestant parishes in Bohemia, Poland, and France as well. Bullinger's *Second Helvetic Confession* remains to this day as one of the most popular confessional standards among Reformed churches throughout the world.

In August of 1542, Bullinger published his commentary on Matthew's Gospel, *In Sacrosanctum Iesu Chrisi Domini Nostri Evangelium Secundum Matthaeum Commentariorum Libri XII*. In it we discover many interesting traits that are relevant to this study. First, Bullinger shows great familiarity with early Jewish and patristic materials, frequently referencing the writings and insights offered by Josephus, Eusebius of Caesarea, Jerome, Chrysostom, and Augustine. Second, Bullinger shows familiarity with the works and controversies among Dominicans and Franciscans like Thomas Aquinas, Bonaventure, and Olivi. Third, Bullinger's awareness of first-century fulfillment mixed with futuristic, end-of-the-world fulfillment is glaringly obvious, as his introductory remarks to Matthew 24 illustrate:

> Up to this point, our lord has made mention, in passing *but very frequently, of the destruction of the Jewish people and of the city of Jerusalem*; in this, he includes the rejection of the Jews from fellowship with God, and the profanation of the temple, all its sacrificial system, and its worship. Since these things seemed amazing and unbelievable, sc. that God would profane that people born from holy parents, and likewise that holy place and worship and sacrificial system, *he explains to his inquiring disciples more fully the judgment or fate hanging over the people and the city, graphically describing what marvels and portents, what chaos and disasters and miseries would precede that destruction, and how cruel, horrible, and terrible the devastation would be. Soon on the occasion of the destruction of the city, he treats also of the destruction of the world or of the*

220

consummation of the age, and of that glorious arrival of the Son of Man for judgment: urging all men to sober and diligent watchfulness, setting forth rewards for those who watch, and threatening punishment for those who are slack and snoring. He illustrates these things straightaway with very lovely and full parables, tracing out the lots of those who stay awake and those who slumber. In the end, Matthew adds a description and, as it were, a sort of picture of the coming Judge and that final judgment, in which the last verdict is pronounced by the judge against the whole race of mortals, pleasant things indeed for the good, but very grim things for the wicked. For thus this business is brought to a close, and the latter shall go into eternal punishment, but the righteous into eternal life.[133]

When Jesus declares that not one stone of the temple would be left standing after its destruction, Bullinger's approach is similar to many of his predecessors, appealing to ancient historical sources and their records of Jerusalem's destruction:

The hearts of the disciples ought to have been powerfully affected by this discourse, but since these things are not so greatly considered by them, they are admiring and are affected more by the buildings of the Temple. You have the fullest description of the very solemn Temple in Josephus, *Bellum* 6, ch. 6. This had not been built by the fathers returning from Babylon, of whom mention is made in Ezra 5, but by king Herod, in the manner excellently described

---

133. Bullinger, *In Sacrosanctum Iesu Chrisi Domini Nostri Evangelium Secundum Matthaeum Commentariorum Libri XII* (Zurich, Switzerland: Tiguri: Apud Froschouerum, 1542), 208 verso. Italics added. As noted in my *Acknowledgements* and above in **3.1.5**, Bullinger's commentary is only available in Latin (as it was originally published), and I am relying on the English translation by Matthew Colvin in the citations that follow.

by Josephus, *Antiquities* 15.14. Among other things, he says that, when the old foundations had been destroyed, he laid new ones, and erected the temple on top of them, a hundred cubits in length, a hundred cubits in width, and a hundred and twenty in height. The temple was, moreover, built from white and very close-fitted stones, whose size was 25 cubits in length, 8 in height, and twelve in width. The work had been worthy to be told to all who are under the Sun. There labored in building it ten thousand of the most skilled workmen, and what is more, for eight entire years. Therefore, it is not rashly that the disciples say to the Lord in Mark, "See what big stones and what foundations."

The very ancient historian Hegesippus makes mention of this temple in LI *On the Destruction of Jerusalem,* the first chapter, [section] 35. Our Vadianus also [mentions it] in his *Epitome.* This is the scope of his [sc. Jesus'] discussion: The Temple will be destroyed along with the city. Although it is rather brief, he nonetheless preferred to set forth the same opinion more fully and adorned with figures. For answering to his disciples' gesturing, and himself pointing out the temple to them with his own finger, he says, "Do you not see all these things? This is very vehement—not so much a question as an assertion and a sort of confirmation. As though he were to say, "We marvel very much if a temple so sacred ought to be torn down to its foundations, and you show me its buildings, thinking that it is not fitting that so elegant a building should be destroyed. But I point out to you in turn this very temple with all its majesty, and I add that this very temple, with all its splendor, with all its elegance, is going to be torn down, root and branch."[134]

---

134. Bullinger, *Matthaeum Commentariorum,* 208 verso–209 recto.

222

Commenting on the questions asked by Jesus' disciples, Bullinger also clearly establishes a methodology for his readers to follow. As we shall see below, he begins by asserting that there are only two questions asked by the disciples. The first question, as he visualizes it, is about the city and temple about to be destroyed; the second is about when the world itself "in the end" would be brought to its consummation. Intriguingly, Bullinger also explicates the scope of the first question not only to include "*when*" Jerusalem's destruction will occur, but also "what *signs* will go before" it. Bullinger is comfortable with Jesus mixing responses to the "when" question with added descriptions of "signs" because, allegedly, "The signs and warnings run, as it were, in between" these two great cataclysmic events in history, and therefore "can be applied to both these things." By frontloading his commentary this way, Bullinger attempts to apply *dual* meanings up to a certain point, before transitioning into entirely futuristic territory.

His interpretation of verse 3 is worth noting carefully, for alongside his description of Jesus' "tangled" predictions, Bullinger also remains open to "anyone" who can offer better explanations:

> But while he was sitting on the Mount of Olives, his disciples came up to him privately, saying, "Tell us, when will these things be? And what is the sign of your coming, and of the consummation of the age?"
>
> They now sufficiently understood that the royal city and the sacred temple were to be torn up from the roots together with the holy people, and so the disciples seem to ask further about these things, *When or at what time will the destruction be? What signs will go before the future disaster? When, in the end, is the world to be brought to its conclusion?* And the disciples set these questions to the Lord in secret, that is, privately and with the crowd removed. The Lord answers them, not in order to satisfy human curiosity, but to set forth the judgments of God and to forewarn the pious,

223

and to teach them how they ought to conduct themselves in these disturbances. For he everywhere sprinkles comforts and instructions for the use of the saints. *But he replies to the two questions most frankly, to be sure, When are the city and temple to be destroyed, and when is the world to be brought to its consummation.* The signs and warnings which run, as it were, in between, can be applied to both these things, but sometimes so that some of them fit more properly with one than the other. Certainly, since Jerusalem is a sort of mirror and type of the world, *individual things that are properly said only of Jerusalem can be applied to all the times and kingdoms of the world by way of a kind of Catagogy.*[135] *The passage is tangled in much difficulty, so I bear no grudge against anyone if he himself brings forth better [explanations].* These things which I bring forth, I set before the pious Reader to be judged, just as I do my other [writings].[136]

Bullinger's caveat that "individual things" speaking "*only* of Jerusalem" can be applied to "*all* the times and kingdoms of the world by way of a kind of Catagogy" seems to be an attempt on his part to *untangle* Jesus' mixture of two very different historical events and their fulfillment. Of course, Bullinger will show himself not to be entirely consistent in his application of this principle, for we shall see later on in Matthew 24:36 that he finds a clear point of futuristic transition into the end of the world and its final judgment. Nevertheless, before we arrive at his official transitional verse, it is interesting to see the ways in which Bullinger attempts to untangle Jesus' seemingly knotty answers. Bullinger begins by setting up verse four as though Jesus' *urgent* warnings were intended to apply to both the destruction of Jerusalem and the consummation of the world:

---

135. Colvin notes that "Catagogy" is the opposite of "Anagogy" —i.e., not leading up to heaven, but leading downward to the temporal world.

136. Bullinger, *Matthaeum Commentariorum*, 209 recto. Italics added.

And Jesus, answering, said to them, Watch out that no one leads you astray. For many shall come in my name, saying, I am the Messiah, and shall lead many astray.

The destruction of the city *or* the consummation of the world will not, he says, come about immediately. Many disasters will arise before that, which will go before the destruction and will afflict the good as well as the evil—therefore all the saints must keep watch, lest anyone be led away from true piety and religion into the pitfalls of error and impiety. . . . The histories after the ascension of the Lord into heaven, *and before the destruction of the city,* relate that not a few Jews had come, who billed themselves as the trusted Messiah and liberator. *The wretched people became followers of these men, and thereby were slaughtered by the Roman garrisons. Indeed, it was fitting that those who had been unwilling to receive the true Messiah, the author of life, received false Messiahs, the authors of slaughter and all miseries. Josephus certainly relates that among the people of the Jews, not just one false Christ came forth, and another, but crowds also of magi and false prophets arose, who promised liberation to the simple-minded common people, and so moved them that, following impostors, they soon felt the weapons of the Romans, for Felix and Festus had put down some thousands.* The same historian repeats these things and adds certain things of this sort in his book *On the Jewish War* 2, ch. 12 and 17.

But it was not the Jews alone who felt this evil. The church of Christ also has never been lacking in impostors of this sort. Simon Magus wanted to be hailed as the Power of God. Very many heretics followed after him, who promised salvation and liberation to their worshippers. The blasphemies of Mohammed are obvious. Nor can any of us today be ignorant of what the Pope preaches about himself, and wants others also to preach and be believed about him.[137]

It is worth pointing out that the majority of Bullinger's remarks involve first-century events. It is only after describing a lengthy application for those living in the first century that he begins to apply a tiny smattering of fulfillment to "the church of Christ" after 70 CE, as though very clear New Testament figures, such as Simon Magus, were as equally the *objects* of Jesus' prophetic remarks as Mohammed and the sixteenth century popes of Rome.

Bullinger's comments about Matthew 24:6-8 also continue to place an unusually large emphasis upon first-century events, followed by very brief excursions into futuristic, post-70 CE territory:

For you will hear of wars and rumors of wars. See that you are not disturbed. For all these things must happen, but the end is not yet. For nation will rise against nation and kingdom against kingdom, and there will be plagues and famines and earthquakes in various places. But all these things are the beginning of [birth-]pains.

Since, he says, there shall arise many false messiahs, kings, or liberators, to whom rebellious men will pledge allegiance, therefore wars shall arise, through which those who are eager for revolution will be suppressed; likewise rumors and threats of wars shall be heard. *For the garrisons of the Romans would not have threatened the people with destruction once, if they had not ceased to maintain public peace and tranquility. There were, moreover, wars outside Judea and serious disturbances in other kingdoms as well. Let the history books be consulted as to what wars arose under Claudius, Nero, Galba, Otho, and Vitellius, and were waged now and again by the*

---

137. Bullinger, *Matthaeum Commentariorum*, 209 recto–verso. Italics added.

Romans among themselves and against other nations. For this is why it is shortly added by the Lord Himself, "For nation shall rise against nation, and kingdom against kingdom." *And the preaching of the gospel as well, through the apostles and apostolic men, seemed at that time to have been spread through the world so that there might thereby be more disturbances. For this reason St. Paul was transferred to Rome in chains from Festus to the Emperor Nero as a disturber of the public peace.* Therefore, the Lord, comforting his own, says, "See to it that you are not disturbed." To be sure, a good man is disturbed when so many great calamities appear, but the Lord did not want his people to be so disturbed that they might accomplish the work of the Lord more coldly or sluggishly, or that they should continue in the business of religion more slowly.

All these things had to happen in the Jewish people. For they were rebellious and most impatient with the yoke of the Romans. They had denied their king and liberator, but they had acknowledged and demanded that Caesar hold sway over them; therefore, it was necessary for them to be killed and destroyed most disastrously by Caesar. *But the end, he says, is not yet. The wars and those tumults were not signs of a destruction that was soon to follow,* but it shall go before them slowly, and there will be uproars, disturbances, and revolts of long duration. *For there was unrest by the Jews for thirty-eight and more years before they were cut off at the root by the last and final war.*

If you recall the wars precisely[138] that have existed in the world from when the city was sacked up to the present day, you will find slaughters, massacres, riots, and calamities, most deadly, cruel, and without number. The German and Persian wars were very severe. Gothic and Vandal camps were a greater scourge to our Europe than any military courage ever

---

138. Colvin notes that the literal phrase Bullinger uses is "to the pebble."

was. The Saracens followed on these. Together with the Saracens, the Alemanni, Lombards, and Franks did great harm and waged huge wars. In later times perhaps the most powerful storm burst upon the scene: the Tartars and Turks, who today have ground down and beaten small the entire globe.

. . .

Concerning the famine which occurred under Claudius, Luke writes in Acts 11 and Josephus, *Antiquities* 20 ch. 2, and Suetonius also in his life of Claudius. This Claudius was a man of stupid mind, quite given over to luxury, wine-drinking, and lusts. He had pleasure in servants similar to himself. Through luxury therefore the gifts of God were most foully squandered. *Moreover, the Jews persecuted the worshippers of Christ, cast them out of their cities, drove them into exile, deprived them of all their property, and forced them to be impoverished and without clothing, and to be in equal want of all things. The Pauline epistles bear witness to this, especially those which were written to the Corinthians, Thessalonians, and Hebrews.* Straightaway, by a just judgment of God they were paid back. Similar reasons are also bringing a famine upon us as brought [famine] upon our ancestors also. When Justinian was emperor there was so great a famine throughout Italy that many men consumed their own limbs. Suetonius relates that under Nero some cities were razed by an earthquake. *And there is no doubt but that terrible earthquakes afflicted the Jews before the destruction of their city.* Nay, anyone may read of the apparitions and omens by which they were troubled and warned from the heaven and earth, in Eusebius' *Ecclesiastical History* book 3, ch. 8, and preceding. He adds, 'But these are the beginning of pains." As though to say, Let no one hope that the divine wrath and vengeance has been satisfied by these afflictions, be they ne'er so severe. For although they are horrible and astonishing, they will nevertheless seem light and bearable if they be compared with those which shall follow.[139]

Picking up at verse 9 and continuing through verse 14, Bullinger starts by highlighting the thematic connection of first-century persecution with chapter ten of Matthew's Gospel. Matthew 10 contains Jesus' second discourse in which he declared, similarly to Matthew 24:34, that his "coming" in judgment would occur within the first-century generation of disciples.[140] After these cursory observations, Bullinger continues to oscillate between first-century events and more generalized, futuristic applications:

> Then they will hand you over to torture and shall kill you, and you will be hated by all nations on account of my name. And then many shall suffer offense, and one shall betray another, and they shall have hatred toward each other.
>
> However much he discourses in ch. 10 about persecutions, so he also discourses about them here. *By them the Jews troubled the apostles and apostolic men, and the Gentiles as well.* For you will, he says, be hated by all peoples, not on account of robberies, rebellions, thefts, and frauds, but on account of my name, *because you are preaching repentance and the remission of sins in my name, because you are denigrating the Jewish ceremonies, the Pharisaic traditions, and the Gentiles' idolatry and impiety. The Acts of the Apostles can most abundantly bear witness of this.*
>
> But that same persecution has also lasted among Christians after the city was captured and the Jews were slaughtered, up to the present day. For the emperors of the Romans persecuted the ministers of Christ. For St. Augustine

---

139. Bullinger, *Matthaeum Commentariorum*, 209 verso–210 recto. Italics added.

140. For more on this, see **Appendix B**.

229

in *The City of God* lists ten very severe persecutions. Nor were the Goths and Vandals more merciful than the Romans. The Saracens also persecuted his ministers, and since then, the Pope with his bishops, parsons, and monks; the Turk also, a most gigantic enemy of the truth, has to this day spared no Christian, so far is he from showing favor to the evangelical overseers of our religion. But at that time, when those who are eager for the name of Christian shall be so mercilessly and cruelly torn to pieces, many, having been made to stumble, and overcome by the evil punishments, shall fall away from the profession of the name of Christian.

We see that this is what happened, not only before the city was destroyed, but also afterwards, and that it is happening right up to the present day. Church histories and daily experience furnish examples. Moreover, no possession of anyone will be secure. All things will be done by deceits and betrayals, and corruption will flourish so much that one man will betray another, brother will betray brother, friend will betray friend, and they will persecute each other with mutual hatreds, so that nothing else may appear than riots, seditions, conspiracies, and impending destruction. *Josephus records for us in his books on The Jewish War what things went before the destruction of the city: the factional strife of all classes, hatreds and betrayals. Those books are, as it were, a commentary on the present sermon of Christ. The Lord set forth similar things to his disciples in the 10th chapter of this history.*

And many false prophets shall arise, and deceive many. And because iniquity will abound, the love of most will grow cold. But he who perseveres to the end, he shall be saved.

He predicts another great evil and future danger: that false teachers shall arise, and erroneous doctrines, by which many shall be led astray. *But we read that very many of the Jews received the preaching of the gospel, but mixed the things of the Law with it, and conceived a corrupt teaching and faith, and taught it to many. The apostle contends against teaching of this sort in nearly all his letters, but especially in the epistles to the Galatians, to the Philippians, in his second letter to the Corinthians, and in his epistle to the Romans and to the Hebrews. On account of these men, the Jerusalem synod was held, just as Luke sets forth in Acts 15.*

The apostle John also makes mention of false prophets and antichrists in his canonical books. For it is established that Cerinthus and Ebion and other monsters like them, teachers of errors and impiety, emerged in the times of the apostles and led many astray. Eusebius is a witness of this in *Eccl. Hist.* book 4 ch. 22, and Jerome in his *Famous Men.* St. Peter also predicted in his later letter [sc. 2 Peter] that in times to come a great multitude of false prophets would arise, until the end of the age. Of these were especially Praxeas, Valeninus, Novatus, Arrius, Macedonius, Manichaeus, Donatus, Nestorius, Pelagius, Eutyches, and those who gave us the seduction of Mohammed and the Popish corruption. And it is well known that not a few have joined these heresies, so that the Lord did not speak in vain when he said, "And they shall lead many astray." And Peter, "And many shall follow their destructions." I have spoken more than once about false prophets in my *Apostolic Commentaries* and in the 7th chapter of this history. Moses wrote about these men most carefully in Deut. 13, and Jeremiah in ch. 23.[141]

And this gospel of the kingdom shall be preached in all the world, as a testimony to all nations, and then the consummation will come.

. . .

And it is significant that he says "to the Nations." For by his resurrection and sending of the Holy Spirit upon the apos-

---

141. Bullinger, *Matthaeum Commentariorum*, 210 recto–210 verso. Italics added.

tles, they are sent off to the nations throughout the entire globe. *But before the city was taken, and the Jewish people were dispersed, the apostles of Christ carried the gospel and announced it throughout the entire globe. For Paul says to the Romans, "I have filled up the gospel of Christ from Jerusalem and in the adjoining regions, as far as Illyricum." To the Colossians, he says that the gospel has been preached to every creature under heaven. To Timothy also, he says, God has been manifested in the flesh, has been justified in the spirit, has been seen by angels, has been preached among the nation, faith in him has been had throughout the world, and he was received up in glory.*

Certainly, most of the apostles of the Lord went to the Lord before the city was captured and sacked. Peter and Paul were first crowned with martyrdom in the 14th year of Nero. But around those same times, the emperor Nero transferred Vespasian as the master of his forces against the Jews. The fourteenth year of Nero began in the 70th year from the birth of Christ, as Eusebius reckons it. *But the holy city and the peculiar people of the Lord were preserved by the marvelous providence of God until the gospel of Christ was preached throughout the world, doubtless so that the Jewish people might be judged through the Gentiles, and might be a spectacle of all the Gentile churches and subsequent ages.*[142]

Verse 15 is Bullinger's lengthiest and most detailed exegesis respecting first-century fulfillment. Verse 15 is allegedly where Jesus "fully and openly gives an answer to the question" about Jerusalem's destruction. Apparently, verse 15 is also where Bullinger becomes comfortable breaking his own rule about applying an "individual" reference to Jerusalem to *all* the times and kingdoms of the world. In light of this, Bullinger's intense first-century emphasis is worth citing at length:

---

142. Bullinger, *Matthaeum Commentariorum*, 211 recto. Italics added.

When therefore you see the abomination of desolation, which was spoken of by the prophet Daniel, standing in the holy place, let him who reads understand.

At length, after various warnings, he fully and openly gives an answer to the question of the inquiring disciples, When shall these things be? That is, when will the temple be destroyed along with the city? At that time, he says, when the gospel shall have been preached throughout the world, and the armies of the Romans have surrounded Jerusalem with a severe and persistent siege. For then the city will be taken and laid waste and torn down, and the holy temple of God will be burned. St. Mark has reported the words of the savior thus: When you see the abomination of desolation, which was spoken of by the prophet Daniel, standing where it ought not, let him who reads understand. He said "standing where it ought not" where Matthew put "standing in the holy place." For it was a new and unexpected thing for the Jews, that they were forced to see the Gentiles surrounding their sacred walls, and threatening the temple of the Lord, and the people of God, *Vermeintend das sölte nit sin und Gott sölte es nit zulassen.*[143]

Luke, openly echoing the words of the Savior, says, "When you see Jerusalem surrounded by armies, then know that its desolation is at hand." As for that which Matthew and Mark said, "When you see the abomination of desolation standing in the holy place" and "where it ought not to," Luke replaces them with, "When you see Jerusalem surrounded by armies etc." By "the abomination of desolation" the Lord understood, according to the idiom of Hebrew speech, the abhorrent and astonishing wrath of God himself and the desolation by which he abandoned his people, as well as horrible

---

143. Colvin keeps the original German text in the body of Bullinger's Latin commentary and adds this translational note: "Which should not be supposed, and God should not allow it to happen."

233

devastation of the land and the most severe siege of the city. For it was an astonishing and abominable thing that the Lord had loved that people as passionately as possible hitherto, but now had handed them over into the hand of the Gentiles to be trampled down. For these first devastated Galilee and Samaria in a most cruel manner, and then they led their legions and their eagles to the walls of the holy city.

Here the Roman soldier stood for some time, that is, his gentile courage gloated as a conqueror, and stood intrepid in his camp, threatening destruction to the city. At length, he took the city itself, and sacking it, filled it with blood and corpses, and soon also burst into the temple itself, which in the end, with raging mind, he set on fire together with the city, and razed to its foundations. For Josephus (*Jewish War* 7.18) says, since the army did not have anyone further to kill and rape, because their angry minds were lacking all things (for they would not have held back by sparing anyone if there was anything they might do), Caesar orders them now to raze the entire city and temple to their foundations — albeit the towers that loomed over the rest, Phaselus and Hippicus and Mariamne, were left standing, and as much of the walls as surrounded the city on the western side. These were left so that they might serve as a camp for those who were to be left behind as a garrison, but the towers were left so that they might be a token for future generations of how great a city, and how strongly fortified, the courage of the Romans had taken. They so demolished and razed the entire surrounding area of the city that anyone who drew near to it would scarcely believe that it had ever been inhabited.

Accordingly, the meaning of our Lord's words here will be, When you see the land of Galilee and Samaria a smoking ruin, and that the war has now come to the very walls of the holy city, and when you see that God allows the gentiles to do such great things against the people and the holy city that they erect their eagle standards even there, and without fear and confident they are restrained by no reverence for the place, but continually threaten both the city and temple with destruction, then know ye that God has abandoned this place and his people, and that nothing else now remains but that abhorrent devastation which the prophet Daniel predicted would happen. For the Lord cites this prophet so that thereby his prophecy may have more force, and he refers the readers to the reading of Daniel, so that they may be more fully established from it. For, he says, Let the reader understand. That is, let him so read that he may understand, sc. diligently.

In other words, all things will be done by the Romans against the Jews in such conformity with the divine prediction of the prophet, that there will be no reader who does not understand the prophet's meaning. There is a passage in Daniel 9 that has also been expounded to us in our comments on 1 Peter 1, from which we repeat a few words for the needs of this passage: And after 62 weeks, says Daniel, the Christ will be cut off, and he [will have] nothing. And the princely people that are coming shall destroy the city and the sanctuary (or temple); and his end will be as it were a flood, and right up to the end there will be the desolation of war. In these words, he sets forth the death of the son of God as the most powerful cause of the destruction of both the city and the people. They will kill, he says, their own Messiah, and do no harm to him, [...]. None of their fault and crime will be able to strike against him, since even the Roman judge Pilate testifies, I find no basis for a criminal charge in this man. Therefore, the imperial people, that is the highly trained soldiers of the Roman empire, crossing over from Italy, just as Balaam had once predicted [Num 24], will be sent by God to avenge the harmless blood [i.e., that Jesus was killed, but raised from the dead]. These will overthrow both the holy city itself and the temple, with God approving and ordering them to do it.

235

This overthrow will be like the deluge which once swept away all things by its great onrush, and left nothing behind. For we have heard that both the city with its temple and Galilee with Samaria and Judea were cut down to their foundations. There is added, "And desolation is decreed" right up to the end of the war. That is, when the Messiah has been cut off, the war will be continuous, and in it the Lord will abandon his people and hand them over into the hands of the Romans to be harassed and slaughtered most cruelly. For after the Lord has ascended into heaven, immediately the seeds were cast by Pilate, and soon by other prefects, from which revolts hatched, yea, new disturbances arose every day and moment, new calamities and insurrections, until at length the foundations were town away by war proper.[144]

Bullinger's fiery first-century elucidation does not stop at verse 15. He continues the same through verse 22, barely offering any hints of applicability to *all* times and kingdoms. It is only at verse 22 where he begins to tame his emphasis. According to Bullinger, the primacy of first-century fulfillment at this point in the discourse is part of Jesus' *logical* reasoning, because the events leading up to 70 CE are "ranked ahead of all other calamities and miseries in the world":

Then let those who are in Judea flee to the hills; he who is on the roof, let him not go down to get anything from his house; and he who is in the field, let him not go back to get his clothes.

He further instructs the saints who do not reject sound advice how they should conduct themselves when the destruction is already looming. He orders, moreover, that they should decide upon escape for themselves ahead of all other

---

144. Bullinger, *Matthaeum Commentariorum*, 211 recto–212 recto. Italics added.

things, abandoning even precious and necessary things. For it is more bearable to roll the dice with one's fortune than one's life. And he uses proverbial illustrations in the present case. For to "flee to the hills" is to take refuge in safety. And all sorts of greatest dangers, the people not uncommonly decided upon escape to the hills, as in the time of the Maccabees and often on other occasions. But the words can also be understood literally, so to speak. For the mountains of Arabia and Mt. Libanus are the boundaries of the Jewish land. By indicating the boundaries or limits, therefore, *he urges that those who want to take measures to save their own lives should retreat from Judea. For no other solution remains since the city and the kingdom must be entirely overthrown.*

Now Eusebius says (Eccl. Hist. 3.5), The Church which had been gathered in the city of Jerusalem, when an answer was received from God, is ordered to leave and cross over to a certain town named Pella, across the Jordan. When the saints and righteous men had been taken away from the city to this place, there will be an occasion for exacting heavenly punishment from the sacrilegious city as well as from the impious people, through the destruction and overthrow of their country. Thus Eusebius. Pella, however, was located beyond the river Jabbok, not so far from Philaedlphia. The mountains of the region of Traconitis, and Gilhad, etc. are not far from there. The ones "on the roof" are those who are in a safe place and not exposed to harm or storms of heaven. In German we say *Wer under dem tach ist // lasse sich nit ans watter* ['Those who are under the roof do not let themselves be touched by water']. Let him not mix himself up in danger who has, as it were, escaped danger. The ones "in the field" are those who are not shut in by the enclosures or walls of the cities, and are therefore free, sc. beyond all the risk of war.

. . .

237

But woe to pregnant women and nursing mothers in those days. Pray that your flight may not take place in winter, nor on the sabbath. For then there will be great affliction, such as has not been from the beginning of the world up to this time, nor shall be. And unless those days had been cut short, all flesh would not be saved; but on account of the elect, those days shall be cut short.

The Lord discloses in outline how great and how horrible the disaster will be. Up to this point, he has urged that, jettisoning all their possessions, they should determine to flee for their lives. To these things now he adds by way of exclamation, with astonishing emotion, Woe to pregnant women or nursing mothers in those days. For these are not at all girded for flight, because they love their dear relations more tenderly than their own life; nor are they able to cast off those other things as impediments and, leaving all else behind, pour themselves out in flight. *Here those things also seem to apply, which are composed about the unbelievable and staggering famine in the pages of Josephus, Eusebius, and Hegesippus.* Eusebius has collected a summary of all in Eccl. Hist. book 3 ch. 6. Josephus enumerates them one by one at more length in *On the Jewish War,* book 6, and Hegesippus in his 5th book. Now he increases the atrocity of the evil by the addition of this serious injunction: See that your escape does not happen in winter nor on the sabbath. For by these is signified that the evil will be sudden and huge, such as will scarcely allow anyone to rescue himself.

Moreover, the sentence contains a certain puzzle and enfolding. This is the meaning: Pray that your flight be unencumbered, hindered by no delay or temptation or religion. For an inconvenient time is signified by winter. For winter is inconvenient for making a journey, as much on account of the harshness of the cold as on account of the brevity of the daylight. By the Sabbath, however, religion seems to be meant. And it was an impiety[145] among the Jews to make a journey on the Sabbath except for a few stades. But religion too not infrequently hinders flight. There is now added the reason why they ought to pray this way, and the disaster is magnified by comparison: For then there will be, he says, great affliction, such as has not been from the beginning, etc. *This Jerusalemite destruction and war is ranked ahead of all other calamities and miseries in the world. From these words, he also goes on: And unless those days had been cut short, etc. If the calamity, he says, should be as perpetual as it will be fierce, if it were permitted for the enemies to rage as much and as long as they liked, no one out of all that people would escape it. No one can fail to see how plainly horrible this saying it. But on account of the elect and some few faithful people, the day of the calamity will be cut short.*[146]

In an interesting reversal of contextual meaning, verse 23 is where Bullinger imagines Jesus "joining" first-century references back to futuristic ones again:

Then if someone says to you, Behold, here is the Christ, or There, do not believe it. For false Christs and false prophets shall arise and shall give great signs and wonders such as to lead into error, if it could happen, even the elect. Behold I have told you in advance. Therefore, if they say to you, Behold, he is in the desert, do not go out. Or, Behold, he is in the inner chambers, do not believe it. For just as lightning goes out from the east and appears as far as into the west, so shall the coming of the son of man be. For wherever there is a dead body, there the eagles shall gather.

---

145. Colvin adds a note that the Latin, *nefas*, used here means an "impious crime."
146. Bullinger, *Matthaeum Commentariorum*, 212 recto–verso. Italics added.

He now joins to the destruction of the city the consummation of the age. For the things which he mentions apply to Jewish circumstances, but at the same time they come to be applied to later times as well. Worthless men and impostors shall mix themselves in those Jewish crowds, and they will promise salvation, victory, and liberation to their followers. Some of these shall lead crowds after them into the desert, as though to rush upon the enemy from there. Others shall hide themselves in fortified places so that they may be safe against the might of the Romans. But if you listen to me, you will not go out to them, but will not trust them at all; even though they may garner authority for themselves by their signs and wonders. For they will perform imposing signs by their magic arts, by which even some faithful men would be driven mad, if the divine goodness and justice were not preventing it. Certainly, by this sort of language, such as to lead into error, if it were possible to happen, even the elect, he means nothing else than that astounding and impressive signs were going to be wrought, such as would be able to deceive even the wisest and best men. *Josephus has a fuller account of these sorcerers.* But the very sequence of the things and their connection with each other shows that the things themselves pertain also to the last times.[147]

. . .

For the saints expect his glorious and bodily coming for judgment. Whence St. Jerome said, on this passage, "This also must be said, that the second coming of the Savior, must be manifested not in humility as before, but in glory. And so, it is stupid to seek in a small place or a hidden one him who is the light of the entire world." Thus Jerome. But Paul in his letter to the Hebrews says, Christ, once his one sacrifice had

---

147. Bullinger, *Matthaeum Commentariorum*, 213 recto. Italics added.

240

been offered for sins, sits forever at the right hand of God, what is more, awaiting until his enemies shall be made a footstool for his feet. For by his one offering he has made perfect forever those who are being sanctified. And again, Christ has appeared once before the consummation of the ages for the destruction of sin through the sacrifice of His own self. And thus far it remains for all men to die once, but after this, the judgment. Thus, also Christ having offered once to take away the sins of many, will appear a second time without sin to these who wait for him for salvation. But he compares his coming for judgment to lightning. Nothing is swifter than this, nothing more brilliant. Thus, also the coming of the Lord will be by far the swiftest and most brilliant, just as also other passages of scripture teach. Suddenly, I say, and when no one as yet has thought of it, that fatal day will rush upon them, and in the blink of an eye he shall appear to all men who are busy on the earth, just as also lighting appears suddenly through every direction of the sky.[148]

. . .

In Luke 17 after many dangers have been listed, the disciples ask the Lord, Where, Lord? But the omission from this question seems to need to be filled in thus: Where, Lord, in the meanwhile, among such mobs, impostors, and revolts, shall your people abide? He answers, Wherever there is a body, thither shall the eagles also be gathered together. *That is, there will not be any danger that my people will pass away or perish in those mobs and errors.* For to the same degree that the impious cling to the things by which they are delighted, foul and abhorrent, or crows and vultures cling to dead bodies, to that degree will the pious cling to me, and to holy and good things. And so in the judgment the impious will be gathered together with the

---

148. Bullinger, *Matthaeum Commentariorum*, 213 verso.

devil, to the same degree that the pious are gathered together with Christ. *But see how skillfully our Lord has slipped from the question about the destruction of the city to the question about the future judgment and the consummation of the age. For he arrives here by a certain most convenient transition*, while he has interposed things which are in common to both questions.

But from this passage of the holy gospel all those who are eager for piety learn who are really false Christs, false prophets, heretics and schismatics. These words arise from division and choice. For he who chooses for himself outside the Scriptures, or also from the Scriptures themselves, but distorted and corrupted by human wickedness, a teaching or a meaning contrary to the catholic faith, which he stubbornly holds; and he likewise who points to salvation in many things at the same time, divides Christ and the church and the hearts of the faithful, not the doctrine of unity which supplies all perfection to us in the one God through Christ alone—such a person is a heretic and a schismatic. For the Lord says, There shall arise false prophets and they shall say, Christ is here, and there. He is orthodox and catholic who points to, teaches, and holds to one head, one shepherd, one sheepfold, one righteousness, one sacrifice, one satisfaction, one way, one life in Christ. St. Paul says, I hear that there are divisions among you. For this one says I am of Cephas, I am of Paul, etc. (1 Cor. 1) If any are worthy of the name of schismatics, they are most worthy of it who say, I am of Benedict, or I am of Bruno, or I am of Dominic, and I am of Francis. These people teach that Christ is found in the desert and the inner rooms. But more about these elsewhere.[149]

---

149. Bullinger, *Matthaeum Commentariorum*, 214 recto. Italics added.

242

According to Bullinger, Jesus has just "skillfully slipped" from the first question into the second "by a certain most convenient transition." Ironically, this is not the last place Bullinger will imagine Jesus needing to skillfully slip in and out of historical contexts in order to answer his disciples' questions. Jesus' "convenient transition" only lasts a few more verses before shifting back into first-century fulfillment. Although Bullinger imagines that Jesus "elaborates *more fully* about the consummation of the age and the last judgment" in the verses that follow (vv. 29-31),[150] in verses 32-35 Jesus allegedly swings back to exclusive first-century fulfillment, because "these things seem to relate most strongly to the Jews":

> But from the fig tree, learn a similitude: when its branch is already tender and its leaves have shot forth, you know that the time is near. Thus, also you, when you see all these things, know that it is near, at the door. Truly I say unto you, this age will not pass away until all those things take place. Heaven and earth will pass away, but my words will not pass away.
>
> The parable stirred up the Jewish nation very greatly (*for these things seem to relate most strongly to the Jews*) to watching for these things of which he has made mention so far, that they might not be dull and blind. From the budding of the fig tree, he says, when from the branch, already growing tender, it sends forth buds and gives birth, as it were, to leaves, you gather as it were from the most sure indications that the time is not far off. *From there, when you see that uproars, calamities, plagues, famines, rebellions, wrong doctrines, and deceivers are rising up and rushing upon you like a marching army; furthermore, when you see the Roman army being transported into Syria, and occupying the holy land, now know ye that destruction is at the door.* But "is present at the door" is said

---

150. Bullinger, *Matthaeum Commentariorum*, 214 recto. Italics added.

243

by way of a proverbial allegory, concerning that which is imminent and now at hand. But lest anyone have even the least doubt about such great things, or think that they ought to be despised as though they were empty and puffed-up threats, he says, in the prophetic manner of swearing, confirming all the earlier things about future calamities and the destruction of the city, Amen, I say to you, the age will not pass away, etc. *For within 43 years, the holy city was cut off, along with its temple and the entire people.* To these things, he adds a general pronouncement about the certainty and firmness of the word of God, saying, Heaven and earth will pass away, etc. He brings forward, moreover, the most firm elements, so that by way of an implied comparison he may indicate the certainty and unchangeableness of the word of God.[151]

. . .

Therefore, if the word of God stands more firmly than heaven and earth, it must be the most stable thing in the world of all immovable things. Heaven and earth will not pass away, however, by being abolished, as St. Jerome says, but by being changed. Whence this way of speaking must have a latent comparison, which Chrysostom, expounding it in more open words, says, these firm and changeable things will be destroyed more easily than my words can fail. It seems we ought to add to this: But those things will not be destroyed; thus nothing from the word of God will fail in any way. This is certainly the greatest praise of the word of God, commending it to us in all ways, and setting it ahead of all plans and decrees of the fathers by a long way.[152]

---

151. Bullinger, *Matthaeum Commentariorum*, 214 verso-215 recto. Italics added.

152. Bullinger, *Matthaeum Commentariorum*, 215 recto. Colvin adds a note about the final words of this paragraph, "by a long way," saying, "literally, 'by many parasangs,' a unit of measure by use of chains, used in the Persian empire."

Verse 36 is where Bullinger fully transitions into futuristic interpretation:

But about that day and hour, no one knows, not even the angels of heaven, except my Father alone. But just as the day of Noah was, thus will also be the coming of the son of man. For just as they were in the days which came before the Flood, eating and drinking, marrying and giving in marriage, right up to the day when Noah entered into the ark; and they did not know until the flood came and took them all away. So shall the coming of the Son of Man be.

He spoke about the signs coming shortly before the destruction of Jerusalem, and as it were, about the moment of the destruction. *It was expected that he would thereupon indicate the moment of the consummation of the age by certain signs as well.* Therefore, he adds, 'But about that day and hour, no one knows,' etc. *The moment of time was known, I say, to God alone,* nor is there anyone so excellent either in heaven or on earth to whom he has revealed the moment of that day. *And so, our job is to lay all curiosity aside and not try to find anything our or make inquiry about the point or moment of the last day.* It will have been enough for the saints to know and believe that the Lord will come for judgment, and likewise that it is necessary for us to prepare ourselves for his coming by sobriety, faith, and prayers. Commentators on many manuscripts warn us that these words of the Lord ought to be read thus: About that day and hour no one knows, not even the angels of heaven, nor the Son, except my Father only. But St. Jerome testifies that these words, 'Nor the Son,' are not included in the Greek, neither in the Adamantian and Pierian manuscripts. But John Chrysostom reads and expounds them.[153]

---

153. Bullinger, *Matthaeum Commentariorum*, 215 recto.

From all of this it is evident that Bullinger's methodology is clear enough to decipher. Matthew 24:4-14 is tangled in its intended fulfillments, but its foundational references pertained to first-century events. Matthew 24:15-22 is exclusively fulfilled in first-century events. In Matthew 24:23-28 Jesus rejoins and re-tangles the two catastrophic events together, "skillfully slipping in" end-of-the-world descriptions along the way. In Matthew 24:29-31 Jesus elaborates "more fully" about the end of the world. Then, in Matthew 24:32-35, Jesus swerves back to first-century fulfillment for another few moments. Finally, in Matthew 24:36 the permanent transition takes place into descriptions and applications for the church's future. Although Bullinger's methodology fluctuates a bit, the overwhelming majority of Matthew 24:4-35 retains a foundation of first-century fulfillment.

3.1.10 JOHN CALVIN (1509–1564)

The famous French Reformer John Calvin, is another theologian of this era who seems familiar with the methodology of his predecessors. In his *Harmony of the Evangelists*, he even shows an intimate familiarity with the writings of first-century historians such as Josephus. However, in his attempts to make sense of the OD's clear references to first-century fulfillment, Calvin commandeers and accommodates futuristic interpretations of Christian tradition by insisting that it is *the Apostles* who were the erroneous ones with "foolish imaginations." According to Calvin's assessment, later fathers of the church were less erroneous in this regard because they, unlike the apostles, did *not* make the mistake of confusing and conflating the destruction of the temple with the "end of the world." It is to this basic misunderstanding of Jesus' apostles that a response about the "end of the world" was imagined to be necessary. On this he writes:

> Matthew tells us that they inquired about the time *of Christ's coming, and of the end of the world.* But it must be observed

that, having believed from their infancy that the temple would stand till the end of time, and having this opinion deeply rooted in their minds, they did not suppose that, while the building *of the world* stood, the *temple* could fall to ruins. Accordingly, as soon as Christ said that *the temple* would be destroyed, their thoughts immediately turned to *the end of the world*; and—as one error leads to another—having been convinced that, as soon as the reign of Christ should commence, they would be in every respect happy, they leave warfare out of the account, and fly all at once to a triumph. They associate *the coming of Christ and the end of the world* as things inseparable from each other; and by *the end of the world* they mean the restoration of all things, so that nothing may be wanting to complete the happiness of the godly. We now perceive that they leap at once to various questions, because they had given way to these foolish imaginations, that *the temple* could not fall without shaking the whole world; that the termination of the shadows of the Law, and of the whole world, would be the same.[154]

Given such blind-spots and presuppositional commitments on Calvin's part, it seems evident for him to treat Christ's predictions in verses 4–14 in general terms, somewhat similar to Luther's approach. For instance, commenting on verses 6 and 8, he writes as though first-century fulfillment was in mind. He even cites Josephus as a source for such historical events. Yet by the time Christ's predictions escalate to verse 11, Calvin imagined that the meaning of Jesus' response somehow pertained to "all ages." And by the time verse 14 is addressed, Calvin sees the need, again, to rebuke the "improper restrictions by some" to first-century fulfillment.

---

154. John Calvin, *Commentary on a Harmony of the Evangelists Matthew, Mark, and Luke*, vol. 3 (Bellingham, WA: Logos Bible Software, 2010), 117.

Excerpts of his commentary on these verses are illuminating, as Calvin can be seen oscillating between past and present senses of meaning without applying the aforementioned quadriga:

> 6. *For you will hear of wars and rumours of wars.* He describes here those commotions only which arose in Judea, for we shall find him soon afterwards saying that the flame will spread much wider. As he had formerly enjoined them to *beware lest any man deceived them*, so now he bids them meet with courage *rumors of wars and wars themselves*; for they would be in danger of giving way when surrounded by calamities, especially if they had promised to themselves ease and pleasure.[155]
>
> . . .
>
> 8. *But all these things are the beginnings of sorrows.* Not that believers, who always have abundant consolations in calamities, should consume themselves with grief, but that they should lay their account with a long exercise of patience. Luke adds likewise *earthquakes, and signs from heaven*, with respect to which, though we have no authentic history of them, yet it is enough that they were predicted by Christ. The reader will find the rest in Josephus (*Wars of the Jews*, VI. v. 3.).[156]
>
> . . .
>
> 11. *And many false prophets will arise.* This warning differs from the former, in which Christ foretold that *many would come in his name.* For there he spoke only of impostors, who, shortly after the commencement of the Gospel, gave out that they were *the Christ*; but now he threatens that in all ages false

---

155. Calvin, *Commentary*, 121.
156. Calvin, *Commentary*, 122.

teachers will arise, to corrupt sound doctrine, as Peter tells us (2 Pet. 2:1) . . . .[157]

. . .

14. *And the gospel of the kingdom will be preached throughout the whole world.* Our Lord, having delivered a discourse which gave no small occasion for sorrow, seasonably adds this consolation, to raise up minds that were cast down, or to uphold those which were falling. . . . *And then will the end come.* This is improperly restricted by some to the destruction of the temple, and the abolition of the service of the Law; for it ought to be understood as referring to *the end* and renovation of the world. Those two things having been blended by the disciples, as if the temple could not be overthrown without the destruction of *the whole world*, Christ, in replying to the whole question which had been put to him, reminded them that a long and melancholy succession of calamities was at hand, and that they must not hasten to seize the prize, before they had passed through many contests and dangers. In this manner, therefore, we ought to explain this latter clause: "The end of the world will not come before I have tried my Church, for a long period, by severe and painful temptations;" for it is contrasted with the false imagination which the apostles had formed in their minds. Hence, too, we ought to learn that no particular time is here fixed, as if the last day were to follow in immediate succession those events which were just now foretold; for the believers long ago experienced the fulfilment of those predictions which we have now examined, and yet Christ did not immediately appear.[158]

---

157. Calvin, *Commentary*, 127.
158. Calvin, *Commentary*, 128–30.

According to Calvin, it is only because the apostles knew the temple was "a thing incredible," and their assumptions about its "end" were *erroneously* and inappropriately "strange," as though they "could not be saved apart from being torn from the nation," that Jesus finally begins in verse 15 to predict events surrounding Jerusalem's destruction:

> Matthew 24:15. *When you shall see the abomination of desolation.* Because the destruction of the temple and city of Jerusalem, together with the overthrow of the whole Jewish government, was (as we have already said) a thing incredible, and because it might be thought strange, that the disciples could not be saved without being torn from that nation, to which had been committed *the adoption and the covenant* (Rom. 9:4) of eternal salvation, Christ confirms both by the testimony of *Daniel.* As if he had said, That you may not be too strongly attached to the temple and to the ceremonies of the Law, God has limited them to a fixed time, and has long ago declared, that when the Redeemer should come, sacrifices would cease; and that it may not give you uneasiness to be cut off from your own nation, God has also forewarned his people, that in due time it would be rejected.[159]
>
> · · ·
>
> 16. *Then let them who are in Judea flee to the mountains.* Having shown by the testimony of the prophet that, when the temple had been profaned, the services of the Law would soon afterwards be abolished, he adds, that fearful and appalling calamities will soon overtake the whole of *Judea,* so that there will be nothing more desirable than to withdraw to a distance from it; and, at the same time, he states that they

---

159. Calvin, *Commentary*, 131–2.

250

will be so sudden, that there will scarcely be time allowed for the most rapid flight.[160]

. . .

21. *For there will then be great tribulation.* Luke says also, that there will be *days of vengeance, and of wrath on that people, that all things which are written may be fulfilled.* For since *the people*, through obstinate malice, had then broken the covenant of God, it was proper that alarming changes should take place, by which the earth itself and the air would be shaken. True, indeed, the most destructive plague inflicted on the Jews was, that the light of heavenly doctrine was extinguished among them, and that they were rejected by God; but they were compelled—as the great hardness of their hearts made it necessary that they should be compelled—to feel the evil of their rejection by sharp and severe chastisements. Now the true cause of such an awful punishment was, that the desperate wickedness of that nation had reached its height. For not only had they haughtily despised, but even disdainfully rejected the medicine which was brought for their diseases; and, what was worse, like persons who were mad or possessed by the devil, they wreaked their cruelty on the Physician himself. Since the Lord executed his vengeance on those men for their inveterate contempt of the Gospel, accompanied by incorrigible rage, let their punishment be always before our eyes; and let us learn from it, that no offense is more heinous in the sight of God, than obstinacy in despising his grace. But though all who in like manner despise the Gospel will receive the same punishment, God determined to make a very extraordinary demonstration in the case of the Jews, that the

---

160. Calvin, *Commentary*, 135.

251

coming of Christ might be regarded by posterity with greater admiration and reverence.[161]

As is made clear in this last comment, the "coming of Christ" conceptualized in *Calvin's* future is mentioned alongside the events surrounding 70 CE as an example for Christians of all future generations until the end of the world. Therefore, Calvin continues to interpret verses 26–27 in light of such futurity, interpreting the coming kingdom in a quasi-first-century sense while maintaining an idea that the rapidity of soon-coming disaster was designed to launch a message of hope for the Gospel to reach every part of the world. As Calvin concludes, the speedy desolation of Judea would not hinder Christ from reigning throughout the ages to come:

> But as this passage has been, through ignorance, tortured in various ways, that the reader may ascertain the true meaning, he must attend to the contrast between a state of concealment and that extension of the kingdom of Christ far and wide, and which would be sudden and unexpected, *as the lightning flashes from the east to the west.* . . . The disciples were thus reminded that they must no longer seek a Redeemer within the small enclosure of Judea, because he will suddenly extend the limits of his kingdom to the uttermost ends of the world. And, indeed, this astonishing rapidity, with which the gospel flew through every part of the world, was a manifest testimony of divine power. For it could not be the result of human industry, that the light of the gospel, as soon as it appeared, darted from one side of the world to the opposite side *like lightning;* and therefore, it is not without reason that Christ introduces this circumstance for demonstrating and magnifying his heavenly glory. Besides, by holding out this

---

161. Calvin, *Commentary*, 136–7.

252

vast extent of his kingdom, he intended to show that the desolation of Judea would not hinder him from reigning.[162]

Fascinatingly, when Calvin arrives at verse 29, he manifests a bold interest in correcting influential scholars of previous generations who, he opines, "improperly interpreted" the "tribulation of those days" as the destruction of Jerusalem and the Jewish wars leading up to it.[163] However, in verse 34, only a few verses later, Calvin awkwardly shifts Jesus' concerns *back* to the days of the apostles, claiming that Christ could not be more clear about "this generation" bearing a meaning of first century—and only first century—fulfillment:

> 34. *This generation shall not pass away.* Though Christ employs a general expression, yet he does not extend the discourses to all the miseries which would befall the Church, but merely informs them, that before a single *generation* shall have been completed, they will learn by experience the truth of what he has said. For within fifty years the city was destroyed and the temple was razed, the whole country was reduced to a hideous desert, and the obstinacy of the world rose up against God. . . . Now though the same evils were perpetrated in uninterrupted succession for many ages afterwards, yet what Christ said was true, that, before the close of a single *generation*, believers would feel in reality, and by undoubted experience, the truth of his prediction . . . The meaning therefore is: "This prophecy does not relate to evils that are distant, and which posterity will see after the lapse of many centuries, but which are now hanging over you, and

---

162. Calvin, *Commentary*, 142–3.
163. Calvin, *Commentary*, 145–6.

ready to fall in one mass, so that there is no part of it which the present *generation* will not experience."[164]

In verse 36 and those which follow, not only does Calvin officially transition from any and all first-century fulfillment to strict, end-of-the-world fulfillment, but he also notes that Matthew 24:40 seems to conflict with Luke's use of parallel passages. According to Calvin, Luke presumably linked Jesus' story about the generations of Noah and Lot's wife (Luke 17:26-32) with a message about the end of the world. Yet the warning of Jesus not to carry household belongings with them "is represented *by Matthew* as belonging to the destruction of Jerusalem."[165] As such, Calvin cannot help but point out that his previous interpretation of that was related to the soon-coming exodus of faithful Judeans in the first century. Nevertheless, after highlighting this apparent discontinuity between Lukan and Matthean discourses, Calvin continues to presume that Jesus' OD was not primarily addressing first-century events soon-to-come. As a result, Calvin conveniently suggests that "it is possible that Christ applied the same words to various subjects,"[166] as though that was a frequent occurrence among the Synoptic Gospels. In hindsight, it seems more likely that Calvin's deflection of blatant contradictions within the OD serve merely to suit some traditional assumptions and questionable methodologies he acquired through rigorous study of earlier church fathers.

Calvin also apparently misunderstands Matthew's literary design and structure. He presumes the end of "the age" refers historically to the end of "the world." Yet, he predicates his harmonious exposition of the OD on the "foolish imaginations" of some apostles and not on some of the methodologies he himself inherited.

---

164. Calvin, *Commentary*, 151–2.
165. Calvin, *Commentary*, 158.
166. Calvin, *Commentary*, 158.

3.1.11 JUAN DE MALDONADO (1533—1583)

The Spanish Catholic biblical scholar and outspoken critic of Protestant schisms, Juan de Maldonado, produced a commentary on the gospels that was "highly valued and important" during the Reformation era.[167] Among his other achievements, he was a professor of philosophy and theology in the University of Paris, which was one of the leading schools in the late middle-ages. He also taught the same subjects at the University of Salamanca in western Spain, which remains the oldest university in the Hispanic world to this day. After being ordained to the priesthood in Rome, he also became widely praised for his appointment by the pope to revise the Septuagint (Greek Old Testament).[168]

In his *Commentary on the Holy Gospels*, Maldonado clearly shows his own awareness of first-century fulfillment as part of the longstanding Catholic tradition, but he remains very hesitant to offer that fulfillment as Jesus' *primary* meaning. Maldonado is even dogmatic about its tertiary status within the scope of the OD. Such evasions are not surprising, considering that he shows intimate familiarity with Origen, Hilary of Poitiers, Jerome, Chrysostom, Augustine, the Venerable Bede, Theophylact of Ohrid, and Flavius Josephus. Maldonado seems to be overly familiar with their methodology, too, and so he conspicuously dodges first-century interpretation wherever possible. This becomes clear right away in his adoption of Hilary and Jerome's methodology, beginning with the meaning of the disciples' three questions:

> When shall these things be, and what shall be the sign of Thy coming, and of the consummation of the world?

---

167. Lee and Marsh, *Matthew*, 444.
168. Lee and Marsh, *Matthew*, 444.

The Apostles ask three things: 1. When the ills Christ had foretold to the city and Temple would come to pass? 2. What sign would precede His coming? 3. What would precede the end of the world?

As S. Hilary, S. Jerome, and Strabus say, what should prevent the Apostles from being clearly taught that the coming of Christ and the end of the world would take place at the same time? They thought, indeed, that the destruction of the Temple would happen at the same time, as shall shortly be explained. It is plain to all that questions on the destruction of the Temple and on the coming of Christ are different ones.[169]

According to Maldonado's exposition of verse 5, only "due discrimination" can enable the readers of the OD "in some degree" to distinguish between what was fulfilled in the first century and what remains to be fulfilled at the end of the world. For the first fourteen verses of Matthew's OD, Maldonado seems to prefer a strategy that *deflects* his readers away from first-century fulfillment, especially as patristic tradition aids his insights. Between verses 4 and 15, verse 5 is the only passage with Maldonado's clear commitment to first-century fulfillment, as though he couldn't avoid its presence within longstanding ecclesiastical interpretation:

Verse 5. *For many will come in My name.* The Apostles undoubtedly thought that the advent of Christ and the end of the world would come soon after the destruction of Jerusalem. But it is doubtful whether He here answered about His coming and the end of the world, or not. . . . *Due discrimination will enable us in some degree to distinguish between what is said of the destruction of Jerusalem and of the end of the world.* What Christ now said appears to apply to either. For before

169. Juan de Maldonado, *A Commentary of the Holy Gospels,* trans. George J. Davie (London: John Hodges, 1888), 270.

the destruction of Jerusalem many false Christs arose, and before the end of the world many others will do so . . . . S. Luke tell us of Theudas (Acts v. 36); and Josephus (*Antiq.*, xx. 4, and *De Bell. Jud.*, ii. 12) also mentions him and other seducers of the people. S. Jerome speaks of the Simon Magus of Acts viii. 10, who came under the fate name of Christ, being called "the great power of God." A multitude of others followed, clearly by the divine judgment, that they who would not believe in Christ as the very Son of God might believe in these seducers, as Christ Himself foretold (S. John v. 43, and 2 Thess. ii. 10,11).[170]

It is noteworthy to point out that his commentary on this single verse is almost entirely about first-century proofs of fulfillment. The historical *evidence* he provides comports with first-century events and the first-century historians who recorded them. He only briefly mentions the possibly of it pertaining to the church in general over time. After these comments, in verses 6 through 22, Maldonado cannot help but offer a mixture of traditional opinions among the church fathers while also emphasizing the prevalence of futuristic possibilities as his own preferred interpretation:

Verse 6. *You shall hear.* . . . Some appear to distinguish between "wars" and "rumors of wars" with too much subtlety. Origen and Euthymius are among them. The former things allegorically that "the wars" were those carried on in Jerusalem; and "the rumors" are of such as would arise in other cities of Judaea. If there be any real difference, it may be thought that "wars" refers to the presented "rumors" to be the future; the meaning being that they should see with their own eyes many present wars, and hear with their own ears of many

---

170. Maldonado, *Commentary*, 270-1. Italics added.

257

that were yet in the distance: war thus arising from war, and evil from evil.

For these things must come to pass, but the end is not yet. Many—*e.g.,* S. Chrysostom and S. Hilary, The Author, Euthymius, Theophylact, and Bede—understand it of the wars which preceded the destruction of Jerusalem, which Josephus has described in his *Antiq.,* xx., and his seven books, *De Bell. Jud.* Others, as S. Jerome, take it of the wars of Antichrist, which shall be before the end of the world. Either is possible: as the former can be established by the facts of history, and the latter from the *Apocalypse.*

But the end is not yet. S. Jerome and Theophylact think this "end" is the end of the world. Euthymius and others, that it refers to the destruction of Jerusalem.

Verse 7. *For nation shall rise against nation.* S. Augustin (*Ep.* lxxx.) refers this both to the destruction of Jerusalem and to the times of Antichrist. His opinion seems preferable to that of those who refer it only to the destruction of Jerusalem, as S. Chrysostom, Euthymius, and Theophylact. Many other examples to the same effect may be found in Josephus (*Antiq.,* lib. xx., caps. vii., viii., xv.; and *De Bell. Jud.,* xi. xii., xiv., xix., xx., xxi., xxv.), and in Hegesippus (lib. ii., caps. xi., xiv., xvi., xvii.).

And there shall be pestilences and famines. From the Acts (xi. 28) and Josephus (Antiq., xx. 2) we learn that there were famines before the taking of Jerusalem.[171]

[...]

Verse 14. *And this gospel of the kingdom shall be preached in the whole world.* S. Jerome and Bede[172] conclude from these

---

171. Maldonado, *Commentary,* 272-3.

172. Technically, Maldonado's appeal to Jerome and Bede is inaccurate. Their interpretations were much more nuanced that what Maldonado offers. Bede actually says that "*this* gospel of the kingdom" (Matt. 24:14) was proclaimed

words that the subject is not the destruction of the city and Temple, but the end of the world; because it is said the Gospel should be first preached in the whole world; which evidently neither was done, nor could have been done, before the taking of Jerusalem. S. Chrysostom and Theophylact, however, persist in their opinion that the reference is only and wholly to the taking of Jerusalem; and many of the moderns have followed them. They say, in support of their opinion, that the

---

throughout the whole world within the first century. Bede even concedes that *"Ecclesiastical historians testify that this was fulfilled,* for they relate that all the Apostles long before the destruction of the province of Judaea were dispersed to preach the Gospel over the whole world, except James the son of Zebedee and James the brother of our Lord, who had before shed their blood in Judaea for the word of the Lord" (See **1.2. 7**). Maldonado seems to be deflecting attention away from what Bede emphasized, by focusing exclusively on what follows in Bede's commentary. Bede merely follows through with a statement about future hope and consolation based on the fruits of the apostles' first-century dispersion: "Since then the Lord knew that the hearts of the disciples would be saddened by the fall and destruction of their nation, He relieves them by this consolation, to let them know that even after the casting away of the Jews, companions in their joy and heavenly kingdom should not be wanting, nay that many more were to be collected out of all mankind than perished in Judaea" (See citation in **1.2.7**). One way to interpret Bede here is to reason this way: It would be by fulfilling this great commission within the first century—as ecclesiastical historians testify—that Jesus' immediate disciples received consolation from these remarks. Their "companions" in ministry would then continue reaching future generations beyond Jerusalem's destruction in 70 CE *as a result of their successful mission.* In other words, Bede can be understood as teaching that Jesus' prediction (here in Matt. 24:9-14) pertained to first-century events, but its fulfillment within the first-century would allow many more generations to spread the gospel of Christ's kingdom thereafter.

Maldonado's appeal to Jerome is similarly misleading, for even Aquinas noticed that Jerome's interpretation here can be understood as being "accomplished before the destruction of Jerusalem, when Christ's disciples had been dispersed over the four quarters of the earth" (See **1.2.9**). Aquinas then notes: "Whence Jerome says, I do not suppose that there remained any nation which knew not the name of Christ; for where preacher had never been, some notion of the faith must have been communicated by neighboring nations" (See citation in **1.2.9**).

259

Gospel had been preached to the whole world before Jerusalem was taken, as S. Paul bears witness (Rom. i. 8).[173]

There are two features of these comments that are worth underlining. One is that Maldonado offers a wide variety of details pertaining to first-century fulfillment; the other is that Maldonado makes a cheeky remark (in verse 14) about the "opinion" of Chrysostom and Theophylact of Ohrid, who both understood the Apostle Paul in Romans 1:8 and verse 14 of Matthew 24 as referring to first-century events. In light of this, we do well to consider what has been offered—other than Maldonado's own private opinion—in support of the claim that the gospel "could" not have been preached worldwide in the first century. It seems peculiarly arbitrary for Maldonado to assert such an impossibility so callously while also offering no more than a subtle ad hominem attack on earlier church fathers for its justification.

In verses 15–19, Maldonado offers more awareness of the tradition of first-century fulfillment:

> Verse 15. *When you see the abomination.* S. Irenaeus, S. Hilary, and The Author refer this also to the end of the world. S. Jerome and Bede cannot oppose this opinion, although they do not wholly approve it; and some of it may apply to the times of Antichrist, as in Dan. xii. II, and as S. Paul signifies to the Thessalonians (2 Thess. ii. 4). But although Christ here looked on perhaps to the time of Antichrist, we cannot doubt that He spoke of the destruction of Jerusalem; and none but Calvin and his followers have ever doubted it. . . . Some think that the term abomination was applied to the Roman army which besieged Jerusalem. Origen says this (Tract. xxix.); and

---

173. Maldonado, *Commentary*, 274.

many moderns, apparently with some reason, have adopted this opinion from what Christ said in this place.[174]

. . .

Verse 16. *Then.* All the authorities understand this word "and," as applying to those, "When you see the abomination of desolation." It may be referable not merely to the words of the verse immediately preceding, but to the entire preceding text from the sixth verse, as if Christ had said, "When you hear of wars and rumors of wars, and see all the other signs of the coming destruction that I have described, then let those that are in Judaea flee to the mountains." In these words, Christ foretells the destruction of the Jews, and He speaks of their fleeing to the mountains as people do when there is any terror upon them, and they betake themselves to the mountains and inaccessible places.[175]

. . .

Verse 19. *And woe to them who are with child, and that give suck in those days.* Origen thinks the meaning of this woe upon these women was that the cruelty of the enemy would be so great that they would have no regard even for pregnant and suckling women. . . . Theophylact thinks that this, which is described by Josephus (vii. 8, *De Bell. Jud.*) as having happened at the siege of Jerusalem, was said to foreshow that nursing mothers would be compelled to eat their children. But S. Hilary, Chrysostom, Jerome, The Author, Bede, and Theophylact himself, elsewhere, that it was said because such women would not be able to fly; as it immediately follows (verse 20): "Pray that your flight be not in winter, nor on the Sabbath day."[176]

---

174. Maldonado, *Commentary*, 276-7.

175. Maldonado, *Commentary*, 279.

176. Maldonado, *Commentary*, 280.

For Maldonado, verse 23 is where Jesus officially transitions into futuristic territories of meaning. His most powerful piece of evidence for justifying such reasoning is that the *conjunction* used in verse 16 for first-century fulfillment allegedly does *not* carry the same meaning as it does in verse 23. He simply appeals to the authority of highly selective church fathers and their favorable opinions as dogma and quickly moves on:

> Verse 23. *Then.* This word "then" has not the same meaning as in verse 16, for it does not signify the immediate time, but that which would pass between the taking of Jerusalem and the end of the world, as S. Chrysostom, S. Jerome, The Author, Theophylact, and Euthymius have observed.[177]

Maldonado's comments about "this generation" in verse 34 are also intriguing in light of the immense volume of valuable scholars he cites throughout his commentary, many of whom interpreted "this generation" with an *obvious* first-century point of reference. Maldonado even incorrectly interprets Origen's name-calling of those with first-century fulfillment as being "simple,"[178] followed by his own metaphorical interpretation of "this generation," to describe future generations of the church. Muldonado writes:

> Verse 34. *This generation.* Many Catholics, as well as teachers of heresy, and *some of the highest antiquity, have explained this of an age, as if the meaning were, that before the age of men then living should be ended Jerusalem would be destroyed.*

---

177. Maldonado, *Commentary*, 281.

178. Origen did not label those who merely affirmed a first-century reference "simple." As noted in the **Introduction**, Origen used that term for Christians who *opposed* his allegorical explanations *and* interpreted the Scriptures "literally." According to Origen, it was impossible to understand everything in Scripture according to a strictly literal sense.

Origen calls them simple. S. Chrysostom, Theophylact, Euthymius, and the Author explain it of the generation of faithful men, as if Christ had said, "Although calamities, so many and so great, are about to happen, yet the Church shall not perish to the end of the world."[179]

3.1.12 CORNELIUS A LAPIDE (1567–1637)

Lapide was a tremendously influential Jesuit Catholic scholar during the Reformation era, publishing many treatises and biblical commentaries in his lifetime that were used in a wide variety of universities for many centuries. Some of his commentaries were even translated into Arabic and subsequently disseminated in Eastern Catholic communities. In what has become known as Lapide's "Great Commentary," his introductory remarks about Jerusalem's destruction in Matthew's OD could not be clearer:

> *And His disciples, &c.* The occasion was because Christ, at the end of the preceding chapter, had predicted the destruction of Jerusalem, and consequently of the Temple. The disciples therefore, being amazed at this desolation of so great a city, show him the wonderful fabric of the Temple, its beauty and magnificence, which seemed worthy of lasting forever, in order that they might move Christ to pity, and to revoke the sentence of destruction. For this temple was the wonder of the world, as Josephus says. . . . See. S. Hilary, "After Christ had threatened the destruction of Jerusalem, they show him the magnificence of its construction, as if He could be moved by the desire of it." So, too, Origen, S. Chrysostom, The-

---

179. Maldonado, *Commentary*, 289. Italics added.

ophylact, Jansen, and others. But none of this magnificence moved Christ to recall His sentence.[180]

. . .

But Jesus said, &c. One Stone shall not be left upon another. Listen to Josephus (l. 7, *Bell.* C. 18), "Titus bid them utterly destroy the city and the Temple. But there was left standing the three towers, Hippicus, Phaselus, and Mariamne, and that part of the wall of the city which defended it on the west. This was done for the sake of the garrison which he left. And the towers were allowed to stand, in order to be a witness to posterity how strongly fortified was the city which the valor of the Romans had captured. But the remainder of the fortifications they so completely leveled with the ground, that persons who approached would scarcely have believed that the city had ever been inhabited."[181]

Lapide is also very clear about his adoption of earlier Church methodologies, and goes one step further by adopting the view that the "tribulations" and "the end" mentioned throughout verses 4-14 referred *primarily* to the wars leading up to the destruction of Jerusalem, with only a few "mingled" messages about the end of the world. Commenting on verses 3–14, he wrote:

Tell us: the Disciples here ask two things; the first, that Christ would tell them when Jerusalem was to be destroyed; the second, when the destruction of the world and the Day of Judgment would be, when He should come to judge all men.[182]

. . .

180. Cornelius A Lapide, *The Great Commentary: S. Matthew's Gospel—Chaps. XXII to XXVIII. S. Mark's Gospel—Complete*, trans. Thomas W. Mossman, vol. 3, 3rd ed. (London: John Hodges, 1891), 58–9.

181. Lapide, *The Great Commentary*, 59.

182. Lapide, *The Great Commentary*, 60.

For many shall come, &c. Such were, 1. that Theudas, of whom in Acts v. 36. 2. That Egyptian impostor, of whom Josephus (l. 2, *Bell, cap.* 12) and Acts xxi. 38. 3. Simon Magus, of whom Acts viii. 10, who, as S. Jerome asserts, was wont to say, "I am the word of God: I am beautiful: I am the Paraclete: I am Almighty: I am all in all." For this Simon, as Irenaeus testifies (*lib.* 1, c. 20), used to say that he had appeared in Judea as the Son, in Samaria as the Father, and had come down among the Gentiles as the Holy Ghost. [...] He it was who, by his magic specters, so deluded Nero and the Romans, that a statue was erected to him at Rome, between two bridges, with this inscription, *To Simon, a great god.*[183]

. . .

When ye shall hear of wars, &c. Rumors: . . . Here is another sign given by Christ, prior to the destruction of the city and the world, viz., tumults, wars, seditions, &c. Josephus shows that such took place before the destruction of Jerusalem (*lib.* 2, *de Bello, cap.* 11). As S. Chrysostom says, "He declares there shall be a twofold war, one by the seducers, the other by the enemies."[184]

. . .

For all those things must be. . . . *But the end is not yet*, the end of Jerusalem and the Temple . . . also of the battles and evils prior to the destruction of both.[185]

In his commentary on verse 7, Lapide reminds his readers that although verses 4 through 14 contain a confused mixture of first-century and futuristic references, verses 15 through 28 are treated "expressly of the destruction of Jerusalem, and the signs which should precede

---

183. Lapide, *The Great Commentary*, 60-1.
184. Lapide, *The Great Commentary*, 61.
185. Lapide, *The Great Commentary*, 61.

it." It is only in verse 29 that he imagines Jesus officially transitioning into predictions leading up to "the end of the world":

> For nations shall rise, &c. For, as S. Jerome and Bede observe, and S. Augustine (*Epist.* 80, *ad Hesych.*), Christ answers His apostles, who were asking in a confused manner about the destruction of the city and the world, mingling the two events together, after the same way that they asked. This He does as far as the 15th verse. . . . From the 15th verse He treats expressly of the destruction of Jerusalem, and the signs which should precede it, up to the 29th verse. After that, up to the end of the chapter, He speaks of the signs which shall precede the end of the world.[186]

3.1.13 GIOVANNI DIODATI (1576—1649)

Diodati was an immensely influential Calvinist scholar among the Protestant reformations of Italy, France, and Switzerland. He was even one of the six theologians of his region specifically selected to draft the official *Canons of Dort*, which remains a broadly utilized confessional standard among Calvinists to this day. In addition to that admirable commission, he became the professor of Hebrew at the university in Geneva upon recommendation from Theodore Beza, and eventually became the successor of Beza as its professor of theology. Among Diodati's many accomplishments, his translation of the Bible into Italian and his *Annotations upon the Holy Bible* remain most memorable. It is in his *Annotations* that we find three noteworthy observations pertaining to Matthew's version of the OD.

First, Diodati clearly shows awareness of first-century fulfillment within verses 4 through 28 of chapter 24. In stating as much in the dense form of annotations, Diodati fits his interpretive work with-

---

186. Lapide, *The Great Commentary*, 62.

266

in the wider Catholic tradition of scholarship, while also establishing a standard for future generations of Protestants to utilize.

Secondarily, Diodati, like John Calvin and other reformers before him, imagined that the apostles on the Mount of Olives were the ones *in error* by assuming that the end of "the world" must coincide with the desolation of Jerusalem's temple. This illustrates, yet again, how a simple misunderstanding about the end of *the age* as the end *of the physical cosmos* becomes deeply entrenched in confessionally Protestant views of biblical critics and commentators in the mid-to-late 1800s. Diodati's translation and interpretations of the Bible would remain a standard for Italian protestants over the next hundred years.

Third, Diodati imagined that Jesus proceeded *chronologically* in response to his disciples' *first* question. Jesus only officially transitioned into futuristic prophetic fulfillment beyond the first century in verse 34, in response to his apostles' second question. A small handful of his annotations will suffice to illustrate as much:

> Vers. 1. *To show him.* It seems that the occasion of this discourse came from that which the Lord had spoken, Mat. 23.38. concerning the desolation of the Temple, whose greatness and sounds of building seemed to make his prediction to be very incredible.
>
> . . .
>
> V. 2. *Not be left.* Christ foretelleth the destruction of Jerusalem, and the condition of the people under Vespasian.
>
> . . .
>
> V. 3. *Of thy coming.* Whereof he has spoken in the end of the precedent chapter. Now it should seem that the Apostles understood that coming of the manifestation of Jesus Christ's temporal kingdom, which they imagined to themselves, and that they believed that the desolation of the Temple and the nation should not happen until the end of the world.
>
> . . .

V. 14. *Of the kingdom.* . . . The meaning is, you ask me concerning the end of the world, and of the Temple together, as if the one could not happen without the other. But I tell you, that the ruin of the Temple shall happen first; and after that my Gospel shall be preached all the world over.

. . .

V. 15. *When ye.* He gives an answer to the Apostles' question concerning the time of the desolation of the Temple. Now by this abomination, it should seem must be meant the military Roman ensigns . . . and wheresoever they came, they brought desolation along with them, especially to the Jews.

. . .

V. 16. *Then let them.* After the City is taken, and the Temple profaned, then shall the desolation of the whole nation come, therefore let him that can, save himself.

. . .

V. 20. *On the Sabbath day.* . . . Now Christ in the Apostle's persons, speaks to all of them who in those days should dwell in Judea, where the Jewish ceremonies should still be observed.

. . .

V. 22. *Those days.* That is, if the Jews' persecution under the Romans were not moderated by God's providence, and limited within the compass of a very short time, the whole nation would perish.[187]

Verse 29 is where Diodati offers his first subtle transition into some kind of futuristic prophetic fulfillment beyond the first century. And in verse 34 he makes it even more official, by marking "this gener-

---

187. John Diodati, *Pious and Learned Annotations upon the Holy Bible: Plainly Expounding the most difficult places thereof,* 2nd ed. (London: Miles Flesher, 1648), 34.

ation" as both the beginning of futuristic predictions and Jesus' response to his disciples' question about the end of the world. He writes succinctly:

> V. 29. *Immediately.* viz. With God, to whom a thousand years are but as one day, Ps. 90.4. 2 Pet. 3. 8,9. Or under the aforesaid afflictions of the Jews, we must also comprehend all the afflictions of the Church until Christ's last coming.
>
> · · ·
>
> V. 34. *This generation.* viz. You shall soon see the effects of these my predictions begin.[188]

3.1.14 DAVID DICKSON (1583–1663)

Dickson was the professor of philosophy at the University of Glasgow, Scotland for twenty years, followed by a position as its professor of Divinity. Although he is most famous for his Calvinist expository commentaries on the Bible, his political and ecclesiastical legacy remained highly influential among Scottish reformers for decades as well. He was eventually appointed to be one of the few Divines to draft the *Directory for Public Worship* that accompanied the *Westminster Confession of Faith* and the *Westminster Catechism.* These Westminster documents remained highly influential for centuries, and still remain eminent as critical standards for many Presbyterian and Reformed churches in northern America today.

In Dickson's *Brief Exposition of the Evangel of Jesus Christ According to Matthew,* he commits to a quasi-transitional verse from first-century fulfillment to Christ's "second coming," beginning at Matthew 24:24. That transition slowly develops and continues up through verse 35, where the final break is made between the past and the future in verse 36.

---

188. Diodati, *Annotations*, 35.

Because Dickson imagined a transition of sorts beginning in verse 24, he interpreted verse 34 as a way for Jesus to *remind* his audience about his earlier remarks about Jerusalem's destruction, back in verses 4–23. In verse 24, Dickson imagined that Jesus moves on to expound upon the sureness of his "second coming." His findings are summarized this way:

> Our Lord having told that the Temple shall be destroyed, the disciples ask of the time thereof, and of the signs of his coming, to verse 4. For an answer, He forwarneth them of trial and persecution, wherein all his disciples had need to beware, lest they should be deceived: and showeth the signs of the utter destruction of Jerusalem, to vers. 23, and again teacheth them, that the chief care of his disciples should be, that they be not deceived with false religion, and false Christs, wherein the danger was to be great, even until his second coming, when he should gather all his Elect unto him, vers. 32. As for the time of the destruction of Jerusalem, he telleth, that the forerunners and coming of it should be in their own days, vers. 36. But the time of the day of universal Judgement, and of his second coming was a secret, and should come as the Flood unexpected, vers. 42. and therefore that it was the Disciples' part to watch, that they might be found in peace, following their calling, lest wrath should fall on them.[189]

3.1.15 CAMER AND P. LOFELER VILERIUS (1599)

Among the many Bibles printed and disseminated throughout the sixteenth and seventeenth centuries, Theodore Beza's *New Testament* remained popular. A 1599 edition incorporated some brief commen-

189. David Dickson, *A Brief Exposition of the Evangel of Jesus Christ According to Matthew* (London: 1651), 273.

270

tary on select passages produced by two obscure biblical scholars with the names Camer and Vilerius. Although these two scholars do not offer enough detail to manifest an explicit transitional verse into the future, and the majority of their notes apply to the church generally throughout history, their brief summaries show, nonetheless, an acute awareness of first-century events being fulfilled somewhere between verses 4 and 34 in connection with the disciples' first question.

Commenting on the opening verses of Matthew 24, they note that "The destruction of the city and especially of the Temple is foretold." Commenting on verse 15, they mention that "The Kingdom of Christ shall not be abolished when the city of Jerusalem is utterly destroyed, but shall be stretched out even to the end of the world." In verse 21 they offer an interpretation of "Those things which befell the people of the Jews, in the 34[th verse], when as the whole land was wasted and at length the city of Jerusalem taken, and both it and their Temple destroyed, are mixed with those which shall come before the last coming of our Lord." Finally, in their commentary on verses 22 through 28, attentive students of this New Testament edition learn that Jesus predicted "The whole nation should be utterly destroyed."[190]

No matter what one might deduce from such unrecognized theologians and their very brief comments, one thing is clear: anyone with their edition of Beza's *New Testament* would have been introduced implicitly to a methodology that transitions from Jerusalem's destruction in 70 CE to the "last coming of our Lord." From the time of its publication in 1599, not many biblical exegetes of the 1600s would gloss over, as Camer and Vilerius did, so many details pertaining to first-century fulfillment within the OD. Even with all their attempts to treat Matthew's OD as a pastoral letter to the church

---

190. All the quotations cited above can be found in Theodore Beza, Ioac Camer, and P. Lofeler Vilerius, *The New Testament of our Lord Jesus Christ: Translated out of the Greek by Theod. Beza; with brief summaries and expositions upon the hard places by the said author, Iaoc. Camer., and P. Lofeler Vilerius* (London: Deputies of Christopher Barker, 1599), 13.

generally, the legacy of first-century fulfillment remains intact, and so does a shadow of early patristic methodology.

3.1.16 JOHN LIGHTFOOT (1602—1675)

Among all of the learned scholars of the Protestant Reformation, few were as highly specialized as John Lightfoot in debating the theological decisions bantered among the *Westminster Assembly of Divines.*[191] Lightfoot was one of the founding members of the Westminster Assembly and its most renowned Rabbinic scholar. In addition to this, he served as the Master of St. Catherine's College of Cambridge near the beginning of the Westminster Assembly and was elected as Chief Executor of the University of Cambridge by the time the Assembly was brought to a close.

His most famous publication to this day is the *Horae Hebraicae et Talmudicae,* a commentary on the ancient Jewish *Talmud's* relationship with the New Testament. His volume on the Gospel of Matthew appeared in 1658, shortly after the Westminster Assembly dissolved. No commentary up to his point in history had ever attempted to connect statements within Matthew's version of the OD with rabbinical evidence for its first-century references. Indeed, no commentaries up to his generation had been so clear, as a result of such scholarly research, that *Matthew 24 in its entirety* most likely referred to first-century events, and by implication were *already fulfilled.*

Unfortunately, for our purposes here, due to the limited content of the *Talmud,* Lightfoot's commentary on Matthew 25 does not reflect any historical timeline whatsoever, whether it could be understood as fulfilled in the past or our future. And so, we cannot know for certain if Lightfoot recognized a transitional verse at all within chapter 25. His commentary just shows clear first-century fulfillment through

---

191. On the influence of those gathered in this assembly, see William Maxwell Hetherington, *History of the Westminster Assembly of Divines* (1856; repr., Edmonton, AB: Still Waters Revival Books, 1993).

all of Matthew 24, from its beginning to its end. Some noteworthy remarks from that work are as follows:

> From hence we easily understand the meaning of this question of the disciples:—
> 1. They know and own the present Messiah; and yet they ask, what shall be the signs of his coming?
> 2. But they do not ask the signs of his coming (as we believe of it) at the last day, to judge both the quick and the dead.
>   . . .
>
> Ver. 7: Ἐγερθήσεται γὰρ ἔθνος ἐπὶ ἔθνος· *Nation shall rise against nation*. Besides the seditions of the Jews, made horridly bloody with their mutual slaughter, and other storms of war in the Roman empire from strangers, the commotions of Otho and Vitellius are particularly memorable, and those of Vitellius and Vespasian, whereby not only the whole empire was shaken, and "totius orbis mutatione fortuna imperii transiit" (they are the words of Tacitus), *the fortune of the empire changed with the change of the whole world*, but Rome itself being made the scene of battle, and the prey of the soldiers, and the Capitol itself being reduced to ashes. Such throes the empire suffered, now bringing forth Vespasian to the throne, the scourge and vengeance of God upon the Jews.[192]

---

192. John Lightfoot, *A Commentary on the New Testament from the Talmud and Hebraica, Matthew-1 Corinthians, Matthew-Mark*, vol. 2 (Bellingham, WA: Logos Bible Software, 2010), 311. Such remarks about the "end" to come as a change in "the whole world" are elaborated further in his comments of verse 27 below. Also, in a separate work of his, *The Harmony, Chronicle, and Order of the New Testament... With an Additional Discourse Concerning the Fall of Jerusalem and the Condition of the Jews in That Land Afterward* (London: Simon Miller, 1655), Lightfoot says this about the Temple's demise:
    ". . . this desolation is phrased in Scripture as the desolating of the whole world . . . it will appear no wonder, if we consider that it was the destroying of the old peculiar Covenanted people; of the Lord's own habitation. . . . And a new

273

. . .

Ver. 9: Τότε παραδώσουσιν ὑμᾶς εἰς θλίψιν· *Then shall they deliver you up to be afflicted*. To this relate those words of Peter, 1 Ep. 4:17, "The time is come that judgment must begin at the house of God;" that is, the time foretold by our Savior is now at hand, in which we are to be delivered up to persecution, &c. These words denote that persecution which the Jews, now near their ruin, stirred up almost everywhere against the professors of the gospel.[193]

. . .

Ver. 12: ψυγήσεται ἡ ἀγάπη τῶν πολλῶν· *The love of many shall wax cold*. These words relate to that horrid apostasy which prevailed everywhere in the Jewish churches that had received the gospel. See 2 Thess. 2:3, &c.; Gal. 3:1; 1 Tim. 1:15, &c.

. . .

Ver. 14: Καὶ κηρυχθήσεται τοῦτο τὸ εὐαγγέλιον τῆς βασιλείας ἐν ὅλη τῇ οἰκουμένη· *And this gospel of the kingdom shall be preached in all the world*. Jerusalem was not to be destroyed before the gospel was spread over all the world: God so ordering and designing it that the world, being first a catechumen in the doctrine of Christ, might have at length an eminent and undeniable testimony of Christ presented to it; when all men, as many as ever heard the history of Christ, should understand that dreadful wrath and severe vengeance which was poured out upon that city and nation by which he was crucified.

---

world [as it were] now created, a new people made the Church, a new Economy, and *Old things past, and all things become new*, 2 Cor. 5.17. We are now upon a very remarkable and eminent Period: where should I write an Ecclesiastical History, I should begin, as at the beginning of a new world." Beatrice Groves, *The Destruction of Jerusalem in Early Modern English Literature* (Cambridge, UK: Cambridge University Press, 2015), 1.

193. Lightfoot, *Talmud and Hebraica,* 312.

. . .

Ὁ ἀναγινώσκων νοείτω· *Let him that readeth understand.* This is not spoken so much for the obscurity as for the certainty of the prophecy. . . . Flatter not yourselves, therefore, with vain hopes, either of future victory, or of the retreating of that army, but provide for yourselves; and he that is in Judea, let him fly to the hills and places of most difficult access, not into the city." See how Luke clearly speaks out this sense in the twentieth verse of the one-and-twentieth chapter.[194]

. . .

Ver. 22: Κολοβωθήσονται αἱ ἡμέραι ἐκεῖναι· *Those days shall be shortened.* God lengthened the time for the sake of the elect, before the destruction of the city; and in the destruction, for their sakes he shortened it. Compare with these words before us 2 Pet. 3:9, "The Lord is not slack concerning his promise," &c. It was certainly very hard with the elect that were inhabitants of the city, who underwent all kinds of misery with the besieged, where the plague and sword raged so violently that there were not living enough to bury the dead; and the famine was so great, that a mother ate her son (perhaps the wife of Doeg Ben Joseph, of whom see such a story in *Babyl. Jomaz*). And it was also hard enough with those elect who fled to the mountains, being driven out of house, living in the open air, and wanting necessaries for food: their merciful God and Father, therefore, took care of them, shortening the time of their misery, and cutting off the reprobates with a speedier destruction; lest, if their stroke had been longer continued, the elect should too far have partaken of their misery.[195]

. . .

194. Lightfoot, *Talmud and Hebraica,* 313–4.
195. Lightfoot, *Talmud and Hebraica,* 314.

Ver. 27: Ὥσπερ γὰρ ἡ ἀστραπὴ, &c. *For as the lightning, &c.* To discover clearly the sense of this and the following clauses, those two things must be observed which we have formerly given notice of:—

1. That the destruction of Jerusalem is very frequently expressed in Scripture as if it were the destruction of the whole world, Deut. 32:22; "A fire is kindled in mine anger, and shall burn unto the lowest hell" (the discourse there is about the wrath of God consuming that people; see ver. 20, 21), "and shall consume the earth with her increase, and set on fire the foundations of the mountains." Jer. 4:23; "I beheld the earth, and lo, it was without form and void; and the heavens, and they had no light," &c. The discourse there also is concerning the destruction of that nation, Isa. 65:17; "Behold, I create new heavens and a new earth: and the former shall not be remembered," &c. And more passages of this sort among the prophets. According to this sense, Christ speaks in this place; and Peter speaks in his Second Epistle, third chapter; and John, in the sixth of the Revelation; and Paul, 2 Cor. 5:17, &c.

2. That Christ's taking vengeance of that exceeding wicked nation is called Christ's "coming in glory," and his "coming in the clouds," Dan. 7. It is also called, "the day of the Lord." See Psalm 1:4; Mal. 3:1, 2, &c.; Joel 2:31; Matt. 16:28; Rev. 1:7, &c. See what we have said on chap. 12:30; 19:28.

The meaning, therefore, of the words before us is this: "While they shall falsely say, that Christ is to be seen here or there: 'Behold, he is in the desert,' one shall say; another, 'Behold, he is in the secret chambers:' he himself shall come, like lightning, with sudden and altogether unexpected vengeance: they shall meet him whom they could not find; they shall

276

find him whom they sought, but quite another than what they looked for.[196]

. . .

Ver. 29: Ο ἥλιος σκοτισθήσεται, &c. *The sun shall be darkened, &c.* That is, the Jewish heaven shall perish, and the sun and moon of its glory and happiness shall be darkened, and brought to nothing. The *sun* is the religion of the church; the *moon* is the government of the state; and the *stars* are the judges and doctors of both. Compare Isa. 13:10, and Ezek. 32:7, 8, &c.[197]

. . .

Ver. 30: Καὶ τότε φανήσεται τὸ σημεῖον τοῦ υἱοῦ τοῦ ἀνθρώπου· *And then shall appear the sign of the Son of man.* Then shall *the Son of man* give a proof of himself, whom they would not before acknowledge: a proof, indeed, not in any visible figure, but in vengeance and judgment so visible, that all the tribes of the earth shall be forced to acknowledge him the avenger. The Jews would not know him: now they shall know him, whether they will or no, Isa. 26:11. Many times they asked of him a *sign:* now a *sign* shall appear, that he is the true Messiah, whom they despised, derided, and crucified, namely, his signal vengeance and fury, such as never any nation felt from the first foundations of the world.

. . .

Ver. 31: Καὶα ἀποστελεῖ τοὺς ἀγγέλους αὐτοῦ, &c. *And he shall send his angels, &c.* When Jerusalem shall be reduced to ashes, and that wicked nation cut off and rejected, then shall the Son of man send his ministers with the trumpet of the gospel, and they shall gather together his elect of the several na-

---

196. Lightfoot, *Talmud and Hebraica,* 318–9.
197. Lightfoot, *Talmud and Hebraica,* 319–20.

tions from the four corners of heaven: so that God shall not want a church, although that ancient people of his be rejected and cast off: but, that Jewish church being destroyed, a new church shall be called out of the Gentiles.

. . .

Ver. 34: Οὐ μὴ παρέλθῃ ἡ γενεὰ αὕτη, &c. *This generation shall not pass, &c.* Hence it appears plain enough, that the foregoing verses are not to be understood of the last judgment, but, as we said, of the destruction of Jerusalem. There were some among the disciples (particularly John), who lived to see these things come to pass. With Matt. 16:28, compare John 21:22. And there were some Rabbins alive at the time when Christ spoke these things, that lived till the city was destroyed, viz.b Rabban Simeon, who perished with the city, R. Jochanan Ben Zaccai, who outlived it, R. Zadoch, R. Ismael, and others.[198]

. . .

Ver. 37: Ὥσπερ δὲ αἱ ἡμέραι τοῦ Νῶε, &c. *But as the days of Noe were, &c.* Thus, Peter placeth as parallels, the ruin of the old world, and the ruin of Jerusalem, 1 Pet. 3:19–21; and by such a comparison his words will be best understood. For, see how he skips from the mention of the death of Christ to the times before the flood, in the eighteenth and nineteenth verses, passing over all the time between. Did not the Spirit of Christ preach all along in the times under the law? Why then doth he take an example only from the times before the flood? that he might fit the matter to his case, and shew that the present state of the Jews was like theirs in the times of Noah, and that their ruin should be like also. So, also, in his Second Epistle, chap. 3, ver. 6, 7.[199]

---

198. Lightfoot, *Talmud and Hebraica,* 320.
199. Lightfoot, *Talmud and Hebraica,* 321.

3.1.17 HENRY HAMMOND (1605–1660)

Henry Hammond was a pioneer Anglican theologian and pastor in the mid-1600s. Important aspects of his career involved becoming a trusted chaplain to Charles I and a chief orator of the University in Oxford. Between his service in the royal chaplaincy and his public oration, Hammond published numerous theological treatises and a *Practical Catechism* for the church. Yet none of his works remain as prominent across ecclesiastical memory as his *Paraphrase and Annotations Upon all the Books of the New Testament,* a tediously detailed work published in the final years of his life.

One of the factors that made his *Paraphrase and Annotations* peculiarly memorable over the centuries was his exposition of Matthew's OD, in which he interpreted *all of chapters 24 and 25* as pertaining to first-century events and the assurance of their fulfillment in past history. According to Hammond, only the final judgment scene of Matt. 25:31-46 could possibly be interpreted in relation to a future state for humanity and a future "coming" in judgment; even so, Hammond still interpreted Matthew 25:31-46 in light of its first-century context surrounding the destruction of Jerusalem, which he considered to be the most obvious way in which Jesus' disciples would have understood the entire discourse.

Because Hammond's *Paraphrase* is unique among influential scholars of that generation, only a selection of his interpretations will be necessary to illustrate its key elements. Starting in Matthew 24:3, Hammond's paraphrases are as follows:

> 3. When this destruction of city and nation and temple… shall fall out; and what signs shall there be beforehand of this thy coming in judgment, and of the destruction of the Jewish state?
> 4. To this double question (concerning the time and the signs of this approaching destruction) and first to the last part of

it, what forerunners there should be of this destruction upon the Jews, Jesus gave answer thus, by saying unto them—

5. One sign of the forerunner is this; There shall arise among you many false Christs, Jews taking upon them to be the Messiah expected, and accordingly calling the people to come after them as assertors and vindicators of the liberties of the Jews, and each of them shall have many followers associating themselves to them.

6. And a second sign is great rumors and discourses of wars, which will be apt to fright and discourage you; but these will panic terrors, precursory only to that great and sad ruin that shall follow, but not yet.

7. For there shall be a third change, yet farther preparatory to it, great broils and civil wars and commotions among yourselves (see ver. 9, and note on Luke xxi.) famines and pestilences, &c. through all Judaea.[200]

. . .

15. And therefore to proceed from the signs to the thing itself, from the forerunners to this actual coming of mine in vengeance upon the crucifiers, observe what I now say unto you: As soon as ever ye see the Roman army, which will make such a horrid visitation, that you may resolve it in the ultimate completion of that prophecy of Daniel . . . when, I say, ye shall see this army set down in a siege and begirting the holy city

. . .

16-19. Then is the season for every one that is any part of the region of Judaea to get out of it . . . and to fly to the mountainous parts beyond Judaea, or else he must expect to be

---

200. Henry Hammond, *A Paraphrase and Annotations Upon all the Books of the New Testament, Briefly Explaining all the Difficult Places Thereof* (Oxford: The University Press, 1845), 112.

destroyed in it. For this will be a very sudden vengeance, such as on Sodom, and woeful to them that are not in condition to fly speedily out of it.

. . .

21. For on them that are left in Jerusalem shall fall a more miserable siege, and other consequent pressures, than ever was or shall be heard or read of in the world.[201]

. . .

27. All such deceits may prove ruinous to you; for this judgment and vengeance upon the Jews shall come so as that it cannot be avoided; but it shall at the same time fall upon several parts of the land, or in a moment, like lightning, fly from one corner to another; this day a great slaughter of Jews in this place, tomorrow in another a great way off.[202]

. . .

33. So in like manner resolve ye that these are most certain and infallible signs, by which, when you see them, you may conclude that this coming of the Son of man, for the destruction of the Jews and your rescue and deliverance, is near at hand.

. . .

35. What I say is immutably firm and sure, the whole world shall be destroyed sooner than one word that I have now delivered shall prove otherwise.

36. But of the point of time when this judgment shall come (see note on Heb. x, and 2 Peter iii. 10.) none but God the Father knows that, (see note on Mark xiii.) and that must oblige you to vigilance, and may sustain in your trials (when you begin to faint by reason of persecutions from the Jews,

---

201. Hammond, *Paraphrase*, 113–4.

202. Hammond, *Paraphrase*, 115.

ver. 12, which is to set a period to) by remembering that how far off soever your deliverance seems to be, it may and will come in a moment unexpectedly.

37. But this judgment on the Jews shall be like that on the old world in respect of the unexpectedness of it: see Luke xvii. 20.[203]

Commenting on Matthew 25:1, Hammond continues to interpret these verses as applying to first-century events and people:

Chap. XXV. 1. At that point of time last spoken of, the heavy visitation on this people, the condition of Christians will be fitly resembled by this parable of ten virgins, which took hand-lamps . . . and went out to fetch a bridegroom and the bride, and wait on them to the feast.[204]

Strangely and surprisingly, in Matthew 25:31 Hammond uses language reminiscent of theologians who wish to transition into futuristic dogmas. Long after the place where interpreters commonly transition in Matthew 24, Hammond alludes to a transition in chapter 25. In verses 14 to 30 of Matthew 25, he says that these statements are "put as in a parenthesis" to describe "when Christ comes to judgment."[205]

Without appreciating the first-century context in which Hammond reached such conclusions, one might ordinarily reason that he accidentally skipped over a transitional verse and had now begun pointing out that lost link between first-century judgment and the traditional, futuristic, final judgment upon the whole world. However, that is not what Hammond meant by Christ coming to judgment. That particular parenthetical-like description of judgment still

---

203. Hammond, *Paraphrase*, 116–7.

204. Hammond, *Paraphrase*, 118.

205. Hammond, *Paraphrase*, 122.

referred to the destruction of Jerusalem in 70 CE "to execute vengeance upon this people," i.e., first-century Judeans. By pointing out that such verses are "put as in a parenthesis," he meant that they, too, serve Christians of all generations as an "emblem" of "doom" to each person's "future eternal being."[206] "[T]hen," Hammond says—referring to Christ's coming in judgment upon Israel in 70 CE—"shall his appearance be glorious and full of majesty."[207]

Although there is no strict point of transition within Hammond's understanding of Matthew's OD, his exegesis still illustrates how faithful Christians could retrieve personalized, pastoral insights and meaning from the cataclysmic events fulfilled in the first century. Even though the final judgment scene was understood as occurring in the first century, that great and terrible event was just the beginning of "future eternal being" for Christ's loyal disciples, and certain "doom" for all of God's enemies thereafter.

3.1.18 MATTHEW POOLE (1624—1679)

Matthew Poole was another distinguished pastor, theologian, and author of the mid-1600s. Among his most reputable lifetime achievements was his five-volume *Synopsis Criticorum*, a digest of biblical commentators that included a summary of one hundred and fifty biblical critics and their unique contributions to biblical interpretation. That work was written in Latin and is presently in the process of translation and publication in English.[208] Alongside his *Synopsis Criticorum* is his most famous and voluminous work, titled *Annotations upon the Holy Bible*. Although Poole is credited with completing this entire work, he only completed Genesis through Isaiah, and the remainder

---

206. Hammond, *Paraphrase,* 122.

207. Hammond, *Paraphrase,* 122.

208. See *https://www.fromreformationtoreformation.com/poole-project*

of the commentary attributed to him was completed by friends and colleagues in possession of his lectures, notes, and other treatises.

As can be deduced from Poole's interest in synopses, his published *Annotations* of Matthew's OD offer a wide variety of interpretations. Because of his familiarity with hundreds of Biblical commentators of previous generations, the majority of notes up to Matthew 24:36 allow for first-century fulfillment, although they indicate a few moments in which futuristic, end-of-the-world events appear to be more fitting. The transitional verse into entirely futuristic predictions is explicitly noted at verse 36.

Most importantly, at least for our purposes here, the following *Annotations* indicate a growing awareness among Poole, his friends, and his colleagues that many church fathers and Christian theologians of the past were aware of, and believed in, first-century fulfillment somewhere within the first 36 verses of Matthew's OD. For the sake of brevity (relative to the vast amount of information offered therein), only a select portion need suffice to illustrate as much:

> They seem to propound three questions to him: 1. What should be the sign of the destruction of Jerusalem? 2. Of his coming? 3. Of the end of the world? . . . Some doubt whether the questions propounded were three or two; if but two, the coming of Christ must either be the same with the first, or with the last.[209] . . . He therefore giveth them no such certain signs of these things, as they could from them certainly conclude the particular time; but yet gives them some signs from whence they might conclude, when they saw them, that the time was hastening; which signs, though some have distinguished, appropriating those in the former part of the chapter to the destruction of Jerusalem, and those in the latter part to the day of judgment, yet they rather seem in our

---

209. Matthew Poole, *Annotations upon the Holy Bible*, vol. 3 (New York: Robert Carter and Brothers, 1853), 112.

284

Savior's discourse mixed together; and time, which is the best interpreter of prophecies, must expound them to us.[210]

. . .

For many shall come in my name, saying, I am Christ; and shall deceive many. . . . Our Savior seemeth to have given this as a sign common both to the destruction of Jerusalem and the end of the world, though possibly before the destruction of Jerusalem, while the Jews were in expectation of a Messiah as a temporal prince or deliverer, there were more of them than afterward, for everyone who could get a party together to color his sedition and rebellion, gave out himself to be the Christ. Of this number are said to have been Theudas, and Judas of Galilee, mentioned by Gamaliel, Acts 5:36, 37. Amongst these some also reckon the Egyptian mentioned Acts 21:38, and Simon Magus, who gave out himself to be *some great one*, and the people accounted him *the great power of God.* Such there have been, and probably may be more toward the end of the world. Many were deceived by the impostors: Christ warneth his disciples concerning them.[211]

Commenting on Matthew 24:6–8, it notes:

Interpreters think this prophecy did chiefly respect the destruction of Jerusalem, for the time from our Savior's death to that time was full of seditions and insurrections, both in Judea and elsewhere. The truth of our Savior's words as to this is attested by Josephus largely, from the eleventh chapter of his second book of the Wars of the Jews to the end of the fourth book. Besides that, there were great wars between Otho, and Vitellius, and Vespasian, the Roman emperor who

---

210. Poole, *Annotations*, 112–3.

211. Poole, *Annotations*, 113.

succeeded Nero, we read of one famine, Acts 11:28, which Agabus there prophesied should be in the time of Claudius Cæsar. Of earthquakes in several places mention is made in divers histories. Our Savior tells them that these things should be, but the end should not be presently, which any one that will read Josephus's history of the Wars of the Jews, will see abundantly verified upon the taking of Jerusalem by the Roman armies.[212]

Commenting on Matthew 24:9, Poole's notes say that "the afflictions specified are, a being hated of all nations, delivered up to councils, beating in the synagogues, casting into prisons, and being killed; all which happened to the disciples of Christ before the destruction of Jerusalem."[213] Commenting on verse 14, we also learn that "Some think that *the end* mentioned in the close of this verse refers to the destruction of Jerusalem; others, that it referreth to the day of judgment." Then a variety of options are offered, depending on what one assumes about the meaning of "the end":

If we take *world* (as it is often taken) for the Gentiles in opposition to the Jews, synecdochically, the whole being put for a great part, it is most certain, that before Jerusalem was destroyed, the gospel, which is here called the gospel of the kingdom, either because it shows the way to the kingdom of God, or because it is that sacred instrument by which Christ subdueth men's hearts to himself, was preached to the world, that is, to the Gentiles, and that to a great part of them. Paul alone had carried it from Jerusalem to Illyricum. The Romans' faith was spoken of throughout the world, Rom. 1:8. Paul saith it was *preached to every creature*, Col. 1:23: see also

---

212. Poole, *Annotations*, 113.
213. Poole, *Annotations*, 113.

Rom. 10:18; 15:16; Col. 1:6; 1 Tim. 3:16. But others choose by *the end* here to understand the end of the world.[214]

Commenting on Matthew 24:15–19:

The import of all this is no more than, let every man with as much speed as he can shift for himself, for, as Luke saith, then the desolation of Jerusalem is nigh; *for,* as he addeth, *these are the days of vengeance, that all things which are written may be fulfilled.* Let none of you think the storm will over, for when you see this be assured the time is come when all I have spoken of this city shall be accomplished.[215]

Commenting on Matthew 24:20–22:

Luke speaks more particularly, chap. 21:23, 24. *For there shall be great distress in the land, and wrath upon this people. And they shall fall by the edge of the sword, and shall be led away captive into all nations: and Jerusalem shall be trodden down of the Gentiles, until the times of the Gentiles be fulfilled.* These verses must be understood with reference to the Jewish nation, and whoso shall read in Josephus the history of the wars of the Jews, will easily agree there is nothing in all the foregoing Jewish story which we have recorded in Scripture like unto it; the final destruction of them by Titus was rather an abatement of miseries they suffered by the factions within themselves, than anything else. And thus some think that God shortened those days of their misery by sending the

---

214. Poole, *Annotations*, 114.
215. Poole, *Annotations*, 114.

Roman armies to quiet the seditions and factions amongst themselves, which were more cruel one to another.[216]

Commenting on Matthew 24:23–28:

There is no doubt but that our Savior here hath a special respect to those persons who, about the time of the destruction of Jerusalem, taking advantage of the Jewish expectation of the Messiah as a secular prince, who should restore them to liberty, (an opinion which, as we have often heard, had infected the generality of the Jews, and not a little even the disciples of Christ), made themselves heads of parties, and pretended that they were the Messiah, the Christ, thereby to encourage people to follow them, and to stand up for their liberty; of which kind there were several mentioned both in the history of Josephus, and in the Roman history, respecting those times. . . . The disagreement of interpreters about *the coming of the Son of man*, here spoken of, makes a variety in their interpretation of these verses. Some think the coming of the Son of man here spoken of was his coming to destroy Jerusalem, which, he saith, will be sudden like the lightning, which though the thunder be taken notice of aforehand, as following the lightning, yet is not taken notice of. . . . Some understand by the coming of Christ here, his coming in his spiritual kingdom. The preaching of the gospel shall be like the lightning; you need not listen after those that say, Lo, here is Christ, or, Lo, he is there, for my gospel shall be preached everywhere; and where the carcass is, where my death and resurrection shall be preached, all the elect, my sheep that hear my voice and follow me, shall be gathered together. Others understand it of Christ's coming to judg-

---

216. Poole, *Annotations*, 114–5.

ment, which is compared to lightning for the suddenness and universality of it.[217]

In Matthew 24:29 it is also noted that, "Interpreters are much divided in the sense of these words, whether they should be interpreted, 1. Of Christ's coming to the last judgment, and the signs of that; or, 2. Concerning the destruction of Jerusalem." A variety of interpretive angles are then offered:

> Those who interpret it of the destruction of Jerusalem have the context to guide them, as also the reports of historians, of strange prodigies seen in the air and earth, before the taking of it; likewise, the word *immediately after*, &c. But I am more inclinable to interpret them of the last judgment, and to think that our Savior is now passed to satisfy the disciples about their other question, concerning the end of the world. . . . But without doubt the literal sense is not to be excluded, whether we understand the text of the destruction of Jerusalem, or of his coming to his last judgment; for as historians tell of great prodigies seen before the former, so the apostle confirms us that there will be such things seen before the day of judgment, 2 Pet. 3:10, 12.[218]

A similar series of aberrations are noted with Matthew 24:30–31:

> Interpreters are also divided about these words, as about the former, some understanding them concerning the destruction of Jerusalem, and judging that by the sign of the coming of the Son of man is probably meant some prodigy or some comet seen before that destruction, which should be of that

---

217. Poole, *Annotations*, 115.
218. Poole, *Annotations*, 115.

nature as it should make the Jews (here called *the tribes of the earth*) to mourn. . . . But I cannot agree to this sense, and most interpreters expound these words of the last judgment.[219]

Commenting on verses 32–35, the notes transition back (somewhat confusingly) to only offer an interpretation of first-century fulfillment:

By this similitude of the fig tree (called therefore by Luke *a parable*) our Savior doth not only design to inform them that these things which he had told them should be as certain signs of the approaching of the destruction of Jerusalem, and the coming of his kingdom, as the fig trees and other trees putting forth of leaves is a sign of the approaching summer, as Cant. 2:13; but that as the frosts, and snow, and cold of the winter, doth not hinder the trees from bringing forth fruit in the summer, so these tribulations and troubles should be so far from hindering and destroying Christ's kingdom, that they should prepare the world for it, and promote it: so that as they might know from these tribulations in Judea that the kingdom of grace was at hand, and began; so from the following tribulations upon the world they might know that his kingdom of glory was also hastening. *Verily I say unto you, This generation shall not pass, till all these things be fulfilled.* There are several notions men have of that term, *this generation*, some by it understanding mankind; others, the generation of Christians; others, the whole generation of the Jews: but doubtless our Savior means the set of men that were at that time in the world: those who were at that time living should not all die until all these things shall be fulfilled, all that he had spoken with reference to the destruction of Jerusalem; and indeed the most of those signs which our Savior gave,

---

219. Poole, *Annotations*, 116.

290

were signs common both to the destruction of Jerusalem and the last judgment, abating only Christ's personal coming in the clouds with power and glory. So that, considering that the destruction of Jerusalem was within less than forty years after our Savior's speaking these words, so many as lived to the expiration of that number of years must see the far greater part of these things actually fulfilled, as signs of the destruction of Jerusalem; and fulfilling, as signs of the end of the world.[220]

Finally, after copious amounts of notes have been offered to aid the reader in understanding the meaning of Jesus' discourse, Poole's *Annotations* finally transition to entirely futuristic fulfillment in verse 36. From all of this it can be deduced that scholars within the late-1600s had grown increasingly aware of and influenced by the patristic methodology that grew out of the fifth-century CE.

3.1.19 THE WESTMINSTER ANNOTATIONS (1645)

In the mid-1600s, during the *Westminster Assembly of Divines*, a biblical commentary was commissioned by Parliament and produced by some of the most qualified English Puritans of that decade. The title of that commentary was *Annotations upon all the books of the Old and New Testament: wherein the text is explained, doubts resolved, scriptures paralleled, and various readings observed.* Among its contributing authors we even find a noteworthy array of scholars who were active members of the Westminster Assembly. The commentary's most noteworthy contributors were William Gouge, Thomas Gataker, Daniel Featley, Francis Taylor, and John Ley.

John Ley (1583-1662), a frequent attendee of the Westminster Assembly, was the scholar who prepared notes for the five books of Torah and all four gospels of the New Testament. In his notes we not

---

220. Poole, *Annotations*, 116.

only learn that first-century fulfillment was considered to be the primary reference for Matthew 24:4-22 but also that verse 23 is explicitly stated as Jesus' response to his disciples' *second* question, thereby clearly associating 24:4–22 with Jesus' response to their *first* question. Among the many notes offered, only a small selection is needed to confirm this much:

Vers. 1. *And Jesus went out.* Mark 13:1. Luke 21.5

. . .

V. 3. . . . *Tell us, &c.* Here are three distinct questions propounded: the first, concerning the destruction of Jerusalem and the temple: the second, about Christs coming, not to judgment, but in his Kingdom here, which they expected to be external: the third, concerning the end of the world. The answer to the first, as some conceive, reacheth to verse 23. to the second, from thence to vers. 36. to the third, from that verse to the end of the chapter. Others conceive, they thought the temple would not be destroyed till the world's end, and then Christ would set up his Kingdom. Yet he seems to answer distinctly to two, at least, of them.

. . .

V. 5. *in my Name.* . . . Such were Theudas, and Judas of Galilee, Acts 5.36, 37. and an Egyptian false prophet, Acts 21.38. V. 6. *of wars.* Slaughters committed upon the Jews under Caius, at home and abroad. *and rumors of wars.* Reports, and expectation of further evils from that emperor and others. . . . *the end is not yet.* . . . Jerusalem shall not be destroyed so soon as wars begin: other things must come to pass first, which are foretold before, verse 15.

. . .

V. 13. . . . *in all the world.* Through all that part of the world that is known to the Jews to be inhabited. This was done before Jerusalem's destruction. See Mark 13.9, 10, 11. Rom. 1.8.

and 10.18. Col. 1.23. *for a witness unto all nations.* Of the obstinacy of the Jews. *then shall the end come.* Then the utter ruin of them, and the destruction of Jerusalem shall come.

V. 15. *When ye therefore see the abomination of desolation.* From signs more remote he comes now to a nearer one. When Jerusalem shall be beset with a just army, on every side beleaguered, Luke 21.20. look for destruction, without hope of delivery, as before, when by the Caldeans. He means the Romans besieging Jerusalem, and striving to lay it waste in an abominable manner. Some understand this of a siege a little before, by Sestius Florus, because, when Titus besieged it, it was too late to flee, verse 16.[221]

. . .

V. 22. *those days.* The days of affliction before mentioned. *no flesh be saved.* The whole nations of the Jews should be utterly destroyed. Flesh is by a figure taken for man; and here, for those of that nation, as Jer. 12.12. and 45.5. *for the elects sake.* That some of them may escape, and some others for their sake.

V. 23. *Then.* . . . He proceedeth to answer of the second question propounded, v. 3. concerning his coming, and so to things following the destruction on Jerusalem.[222]

---

221. It is worth pointing out that although the campaign of "Sestius Florus" is mentioned by name, this is most likely a reference to the campaign of Sestius *Gallus*, the legate of Syria, throughout the year 66 CE, which was a campaign responding to the Judean denunciation of their procurator, Gessius Florus, and his barbaric provocations among the people.

222. John Ley, "The Gospel of Matthew," *Annotations upon all the books of the Old and New Testament: wherein the text is explained, doubts resolved, scriptures paralleled, and various readings observed*, ed. John Downame (London: John Legatt & John Raworth, 1645). This document contains no page numbers, but is in the public domain and can be viewed digitally on page 508 at the following link: *https://archive.org/details/annotationsupona00down_0/page/n507/mode/2up*

In summary, it is not a stretch to imagine many notable Westminster Divines and the people whom they instructed becoming increasingly familiar with the methodology proposed around the fifth century. That is what we find in their *Annotations*. Jesus answers his disciples' first question *first* across Matthew 24:4–22, and their last question *second*, beginning in Matthew 24:23. Matthew 24:4–22 is combed through with widely recognizable first-century fulfillment. Matthew 24:23 to the end of the discourse were to become fulfilled near the end of the world.

3.1.20 EDWARD LEIGH (1602–1671)

Edward Leigh was a friend and consultant to many Divines within the Westminster Assembly. He published his own *Annotations upon the New Testament Philologicall and Theologicall: The Gospel according to St Matthew*. In it his methodology is as equally clear as other Westminster Divines before him. Matthew 24:4–22 was believed to have reached fulfillment in the first century, and verses 23 and following were treated as predictions about the coming of Christ to end the world:

> *The buildings of the Temple.* How much that building cost Herod may be gathered by this, that he had ten thousand workmen laboring about it for the space of eight years. The Disciples might well wonder at these stones, for they were goodly and faire, and (as Josephus writeth) fifteen Cubits long, twelve high, and eight broad.
>
> . . .
>
> Vers. 1. *There shall not be left one stone upon another, that shall not be thrown down.* An hyperbole, as if he should say, it shall be utterly overthrown. This was fulfilled forty years after

Christ's Ascension by Vespasian the Emperor, and his Son Titus, say Eusebius and Josephus.[223]

. . .

Vers. 3. When shall these things be. They thought the Temple should stand as long as the world stood; therefore as soon as Christ said the Temple should be destroyed, they presently thought within themselves of the end of the world.

Which question of the Disciples having two parts, when the *Temple shall be destroyed*, and what shall be *the sign of his coming* and of *the end of the world*, receiveth an answer to both: To the former, concerning the destruction of *Jerusalem*, from the 4. ver. to the 23. To the latter, concerning the coming of Christ, and the end of the world, from thence to the 42.[224]

At the end of verses 22–23, Leigh concludes his thoughts about first-century fulfillment in the OD:

Vers. 22. *And except those days should be shortened.* God did not make the days of those troubles shorter than he had decreed, but shorter than the enemy had determined, or than any wise man who judgeth only by the rules of humane policy could have expected.

There should no flesh be saved. That is, with a temporal Salvation from the Roman Sword and devouring calamities which attended that terrible War.[225]

---

223. Edward Leigh, *Annotations upon the New Testament Philologicall and Theologicall: The Gospel according to St Matthew* (London: W.W. and E.G, 1650), 63.

224. Leigh, *Annotations*, 64.

225. Leigh, *Annotations*, 64.

Leigh's transition into futuristic pontifications comes immediately afterward:

> Vers. 24. *For there shall arise false Christ's, and false Prophets, and shall show great signs and wonders, insomuch that (if it were possible) they shall deceive the very elect.* The Fathers teach that this place is to be understood of Antichrist and his Ministers, the Papists confess it.[226]
>
> . . .
>
> Ver. 30. *Then shall appear the sign of the Son of man.* . . . Chrysostom thinketh it to be the Body of Christ itself. Theopylact holdeth the true Cross shall appear whereon Christ died. . . . Some take the words to be a Hebraism, and think Christ himself (the Son of man) is there meant, so Jerome. But it cannot be taken so, (say some) for there is an opposition between these, so that the sign can never be the thing signified, and the words following distinguish him from that sign. *They shall see the Son of man.* Yet other Evangelists have only these words, *then shall the Son of man appear*, which confirms this last exposition. Origen takes it for the miraculous power and virtues of Christ. Chrysostom expounds it of the wounds that be in the hands, feet, and side of Christ.[227]

Notice carefully that in verse 24 Leigh specifically says that "*the Fathers teach* that this place is to be understood of Antichrist and his Ministers." Among all of the patristic resources utilized by Leigh in this section, he highlights Jerome, Chrysostom, Theophylact of Ohrid, and Origen, all of whom were involved in the development and promotion of this seemingly perpetual methodology. Leigh's frequent use of patristic resources indicates, in the very least, that he

---

226. Leigh, *Annotations*, 65.
227. Leigh, *Annotations*, 65-6.

was directly influenced by the methodology propounded among early patristic and medieval commentaries. Considering Leigh's influence among Divines within the Westminster Assembly, it may also be safe to assume that many more theologians unknown to us, yet very well known to him, grew increasingly acquainted with the methodology espoused by himself and other Westminster Divines.

3.1.21 JOHANIS TRAPP (1601–1669)

In 1647, the Oxford graduate, Anglican biblical exegete, and pastor Johanis Trapp published his commentary on the gospels. In that work he offers a unique interpretation of the disciples' question in Matthew 24:3. Instead of linking the second question about the sign of Christ's coming with the third question about the sign of end of the age, Trapp linked the sign of Christ's coming to the disciples' *first* question about the destruction of Jerusalem. His interpretation of the third question was entirely futuristic.

In addition to this unique contribution, which seems to focus the majority of the apostle's questions on first-century events, he only places first-century emphasis of fulfillment on *one single verse* within Matthew's OD, thereby offering one of the most irregular commentaries among his peers. The verse he singled out for first-century fulfillment is Matthew 24:15, which was a verse that most historical scholars interpreted in a first-century setting. According to Trapp, all other verses between 4 and 29 are treated without first-century reference whatsoever and as being entirely fulfilled in ongoing church history up to "the end" of the world.

In other words, Trapp's contribution was unique in two distinct and unconventional ways: (1) it did *not* comport with other English scholars of his time and region (like the Westminster Assembly of Divines), who interpreted most of 24:4–29 as referring to first-century events, and (2) he recognized that Christ's "coming" in verse 3 was believed by Christ's disciples to mean Christ's *judgment upon Jerusa-*

lem's temple. The way in which his hermeneutic played out in verse 30 (with the "sign of the Son of Man *coming* on the clouds of heaven") is glaringly inconsistent. Due to these unique factors which are largely at odds with the methodology presupposed by most theologians of his time, only two brief quotations of his commentary are needed to illustrate this point:

> Verse 3. *Came unto him privately saying.* Because it was dangerous to speak publicly of the destruction of the Temple . . . *The sign of thy coming.* viz. To destroy the Temple. *And of the end of the world.* Which they thought could not possibly out-last the Temple.[228]
>
> . . .
>
> Verse 15. *The abomination of desolation.* That is Antichrist, say some interpreters; and hitherto may fitly be referred that of Baronius; who in his Annals of the year, of desolation standing in God's Temple. Others understand it of the Roman eagles or ensigns. Others of the emperor Caius, his statue, said by some to be set up in the Sanctuary. As others again, of Titus his picture placed there, which haply was that one great sin that so troubled him upon his death-bed. But they do best, that understand the Text of those abominable authors of desolation, the Roman Armies; who laid waste to the pleasant Land, and destroyed the Nation; as, besides what Daniel foretold, is set forth by Josephus, at large in his sixth and seventh book, *De bello Judaico.*[229]

Although there is very little to compare with longstanding patristic, Catholic, and Protestant methodologies of previous generations, it is

---

228. Johanis Trapp, *A Commentary or Exposition upon all the Books of the New Testament* (London: R. W., 1656), 293.

229. Trapp, *Commentary*, 296.

worth noting that Trapp shows himself to be conversant with many popular scholars of his time, as well as with the works of ancient historians like Josephus. That, in the very least, shares *some* resemblance with the methodology proposed by his English peers.

3.1.22 THEODORE HAAK (1605—1690)

Although Haak is best known for producing the first German translation of John Milton's *Paradise Lost*, he also translated into English *The Dutch Annotations Upon the Whole Bible*, which was a work highly commended and frequently utilized by the *Westminster Assembly of Divines*. The *Dutch Annotations* were originally authorized and produced by a committee from the *Synod of Dort* in 1618 during the process of overseeing their translation of the Bible into Dutch. The *Dutch Annotations* and the *Dutch Bible* were first published in 1637. Haak's English translation of the *Dutch Annotations* was published in 1657.

In the *Dutch Annotations* we find interpretations almost identical to the *Westminster Annotations*, with the exception of Matt. 24:29 being the official transitional verse into futuristic predictions beyond the first century. The *Dutch Annotations* also slipped in an interpretation of the period between the destruction of Jerusalem and the end of the world, beginning at verse 23, just as the *Westminster Annotations* concluded. In order to illustrate this transition, a small sampling will suffice:

> 3. *And as he was set on the Mount of Olives, the Disciples went unto him alone, saying, Tell us when shall these things be?* (Namely, which thou hast said here, and at the end of the fore-going chapter, as well of the laying waste of the City, and the Temple of Jerusalem, as of thy last coming to judgment) *and what (shall be) the sign of thy coming, and of the end of the world?*
>
> . . .

6. *And ye shall hear of wars, and rumors of wars, Look to it, be not affrighted: for all (those) things must come to pass, but the end is not yet.* Namely, of all the miseries, and extreamest judgments which should come upon the Jews.

. . .

8. *But all these things (are but) a beginning of pains.* (Gr. *pangs*, like those of women in travel. Of all these wars and miseries, see Josephus, *Antiq.* lib. 20. and *de bello Jud.* lib. 3. &c.)

. . .

14. A*nd this Gospel of the Kingdom shall be preached in the whole world,* (Gr. *the inhabited* (world). See the fulfilling hereof, Rom. 10. verse 18. Col. 1. verse 6.) *for a witness to all people: and then shall the end come.* (namely, of the City Jerusalem, and of the Jewish Government.)

15. *When therefore ye shall see the abomination of desolation,* (that is, the abominable Army of the Romans, as is expounded, Luke 21.20.)

. . .

21. *For then shall be great tribulation, such as was not from the beginning of the world, until now; nor yet ever shall be.* (For as Josephus testifieth, *de bello Jud.* lib. 4. 5,6. and 7. cap. 17. there perished by the sword, famine, and pestilence, within Jerusalem only, *eleven hundred thousand men, and above ninety-seven thousand men were sold for slaves.* The like desolation is not read in any Histories.)

. . .

23. *Then* (Namely, after the desolation of Jerusalem, till the end of the world, of which he begins to speak at the 29th verse) *if any man shall say unto you, Lo here is the Christ, or there,* [Gr. *here*] believe it not.

. . .

29. *And straightway after the tribulation of those days,* (Namely, which the Tyrants and Antichrist shall have brought upon the Church of God) *the sun shall be darkened, and the Moon shall not give her shining, and the stars shall fall from heaven, and the powers of the heavens.*[230]

3.1.23 PASQUIER QUESNEL (1634—1719)

Another important contribution of this era comes from the French Catholic theologian and leader of the Jansenist party[231] in Brussels and Amsterdam, Pasquier Quesnel. Quesnel's commentary is pastoral and

---

230. Theodore Haak, trans., *The Dutch Annotations Upon the Whole Bible: Or, all the Holy Canonical Scriptures of the Old and New Testament, together with, and according to their own Translation of all the Text* (London, 1657). As with the Westminster Annotations, the Dutch Annotations contain no pagination. The volume with annotations on Matthew's Gospel is also *not* in the public domain and is not available digitally. All the references above have been extracted from the two pages within it that pertain to Matthew 24.

231. According to Shaun Blanchard, *The Synod of Pistoia and Vatican II: Jansenism and the Struggle for Catholic Reform*, OSHT (New York, NY: Oxford University Press, 2020), 71, Quesnel was an early Jansenist in the "first phase" of Jansen*ism*. "Jansenism," according to Blanchard, "has meant a variety of things. Originally the appellation was clear: it meant the theology of Cornelius Jansen (1585-1638, bishop of Ypres from 1636), as expounded in his posthumously published book *Augustinus* (1640). Aside from issues of grace and predestination, Jansenism came to denote a Catholic position that maintained combinations of reformist ideas, pastoral tendencies, and theological or even political orientations and aversions" (68). "Jansenists were concerned with defending the teaching of St. Augustine . . . on the depravity of fallen humanity and on the utter inability to follow God's law without grace. They proclaimed a strictly Augustinian form of the doctrine of predestination" (Blanchard, 69-70). By the end of Jansenism's first phase, "its key commitments were firmly in place. Jansenism joined strict views on penance and absolution to a foundation of extreme Augustinianism regarding soteriological matters" [p. 71]. In addition to these commitments, they were also concerned about measures within the church that blocked "the diffusion of vernacular bibles and the needed reform of the liturgy" (Blanchard, 72).

301

highly admirable. He was aware of historical references to first-century events within Matthew's OD. Yet he also clearly preferred, due to the devotional nature of his work, to offer remarks about how the majority of Jesus' predictive statements "belong to all times".[232] Matt. 24:27 is the clearest point of transition wherein all first-century fulfillment drops out of sight within his commentary on the OD:

> 3. "And as he sat upon the mount of Olives, the disciples came unto him privately, saying, Tell us when shall these things be? and what shall be the sign of thy coming, and of the end of the world?" . . . There are three different comings of Jesus Christ, which serve mutually to make known and illustrate one another. One in anger, to punish the Jews, and to put an end to the reign of the law. Another in mercy, to form his church, and to begin the reign of the gospel and of grace. The third is glory, to judge the world, and to consummate the kingdom of God in his saints, and that of his justice in hell. Abundance of people are curious to know the time "of the end of the world;" but very few endeavor to prepare themselves for the end of their own life.[233]
>
> . . .
>
> 5. "For many shall come in my name, saying, I am Christ; and shall deceive many." In this and the following verses, Christ points out unto us several means and occasions of being seduced. The first means proceeds from false Christs. The delivering the Jews up to them was a just punishment for their having rejected the true during his life, for their having

---

232. Pasquier Quesnel, *The Gospels; with Moral Reflections on Each Verse*, vol. 1, (1671; repr., Glasgow: William Collins, 1830), 369.

233. Quesnel, *The Gospels*, 369.

ascribed his miracles to the illusion of the devil, and treated him as a deceiver after his death.[234]

. . .

14. "And this Gospel of the kingdom shall be preached in all the world, for a witness unto all nations; and then shall the end come." The destruction of Jerusalem and of the temple was deferred, till the gospel had been preached everywhere; to the end, that the Jews might see the completion of the prophecies in the vocation of all the Gentiles; that all the Jews dispersed abroad might be called, before the execution of the divine vengeance; and that the church, even from its infancy, might have a kind of universality, and be visible to all the earth, before the shadow of the synagogue disappeared.

. . .

15. "When ye therefore shall see the abomination of desolation, spoken of by Daniel the prophet, stand in the holy place, (whoso readeth, let him understand,)" We are not at all troubled at the dreadful signs of the destruction of Jerusalem, because all that is past.[235]

. . .

21. "For then shall be great tribulation, such as was not since the beginning of the world to this time, no, nor ever shall be. 22. And except those days should be shortened, there should no flesh be saved: but for the elect's sake those days shall be shortened." Everything is disposed and ordered in favor of the elect. The destruction of Jerusalem was hastened, to prevent those among the Jews from falling under such temptations as were above their strength.[236]

. . .

234. Quesnel, *The Gospels*, 370.
235. Quesnel, *The Gospels*, 374.
236. Quesnel, *The Gospels*, 377.

27. "For as the lighting cometh out of the east, and shineth even unto the west; so shall also the coming of the Son of man be." The faith received everywhere in so short a time, not only without any human assistance, but also notwithstanding the greatest opposition from all the powers of the earth, was, as it were, a lightning which shone from east to west, and a miracle from heaven, to confound the incredulity of the sages of the world. The last coming of Christ will be yet more surprising.[237]

3.1.24 MATTHEW HENRY (1662–1714)

Matthew Henry is best known for his *Commentary on the Whole Bible*, of which earlier parts began publication in 1710. Henry's *Commentary* comes across as a blend of Quesnel's devotional style, Diodati's methodology, and Poole's prodigious note-taking about varying traditional interpretations. Because the reception of Henry's *Commentary* has become so widely acclaimed among Protestant scholars and pastors since the early-1700s, his *Commentary* of Matthew 24 is worth citing at length.

From his extensive comments, four things are most noteworthy: **(1)** he shows awareness of many scholarly interpretations from reputable theologians, especially as an interpretation pertained to first-century fulfillment between verses 4 and 28; **(2)** he, like Johanis Trapp before him, preferred to link the destruction of Jerusalem with the disciples' first *and second* questions (although he does not deny the possibility of linking the first question alone to the destruction of Jerusalem); **(3)** beginning at Matthew 24:29 he offers a clear transitional verse into futuristic predictions, which comports with the methodology in development around the fifth century; **(4)** shockingly, he shows himself willing to *correct* and *admonish* the Apostle Paul and

---

237. Quesnel, *The Gospels*, 379.

other Christians like him who "inferred" that the "Day of the Lord" spoken of in 2 Thessalonians 2:2 related with "that day and hour" of Christ's coming in Matthew 24:36. Below are selections of his famous commentary showing as much:

> Now, in this chapter, we have, I. The occasion of this discourse (v. 1–3). II. The discourse itself, in which we have, 1. The prophecy of divers events, especially referring to the destruction of Jerusalem, and the utter ruin of the Jewish church and nation, which were not hastening on, and were completed about forty years after; the prefaces to that destruction, the concomitants and consequences of it; yet looking further, to Christ's coming at the end of time, and the consummation of all things, of which that was a type and figure (v. 4–31). 2. The practical application of this prophecy for the awakening and quickening of his disciples to prepare for these great and awful things (v. 32–51).
>
>   . . .
>
> *When shall these things be; and what shall be the sign of thy coming, and of the end of the world?* Here are three questions.
>
> [1.] Some think, these questions do all point at one and the same thing—the destruction of the temple, and the period of the Jewish church and nation, which Christ had himself spoken of as his coming (ch. 16:28), and which would be the consummation of the age (for so it may be read), the finishing of that dispensation.
>
> [2.] Others think their question, *When shall these things be?* refers to the destruction of Jerusalem, and the other two to the end of the world.
>
>   . . .
>
> The disciples had asked concerning the times, *When shall these things be?* Christ gives them no answer to that, after what number of days and years his prediction should be ac-

complished, for *it is not for us to know the times* (Acts 1:7); but they had asked, *What shall be the sign?* That question he answers fully, for we are concerned to *understand the signs of the times*, ch. 16:3. Now the prophecy primarily respects the events near at hand—the destruction of Jerusalem, the period of the Jewish church and state, the calling of the Gentiles, and the setting up of Christ's kingdom in the world. . . . so this prophecy, under the type of Jerusalem's destruction, looks as far forward as the general judgment.[238]

Commenting on Matthew 24:6, he writes:

. . . the Jews must be punished, ruin must be brought upon them; by this the justice of God and the honor of the Redeemer must be asserted; and therefore *all those things must come to pass;* the word is gone out of God's mouth, and it shall be accomplished in its season. . . . *The end is not yet;* the end of time is not, and, while time lasts, we must expect trouble, and that the end of one affliction will be but the beginning of another; or, "The end of these troubles is not yet; there must be more judgments that one made use of to bring down the Jewish power.[239]

Commenting on verse 14:

It is intimated that the gospel should be, if not heard, yet at least heard of, throughout the then known world, before the destruction of Jerusalem; that the Old-Testament church should not be quite dissolved till the New Testament was pretty well settled, had got considerable footing, and began

---

238. Matthew Henry, *Commentary on the whole Bible: complete and unabridged in one volume* (Peabody: Hendrickson, 1994), 1738.
239. Henry, *Commentary*, 1739.

to make some figure. . . . The persecuting of the saints at Jerusalem helped to disperse them, so that they *went everywhere, preaching the word*, Acts 8:1–4. And when the tidings of the Redeemer are sent over all parts of the world, then shall come the end of the Jewish state. Thus, that which they thought to prevent, by putting Christ to death, they thereby procured; all men *believed on him, and the Romans came, and took away their place and nation*, Jn. 11:48. Paul speaks of the gospel being *come to all the world, and preached to every creature*, Col. 1:6–23.[240]

In Matthew 24:15 he remarks that Jesus "foretells more particularly the ruin that was coming upon the people of the Jews, their city, temple, and nation."[241] In verse 21, Henry expounds even further upon this prediction, saying:

The greatness of the troubles which should immediately ensue (v. 21); *Then shall be great tribulation* . . . Without the city was the Roman army ready to swallow them up, with a particular rage against them, not only as Jews, but as rebellious Jews. War was the only one of the three sore judgments that David excepted against; but that was it by which the Jews were ruined; and there were famine and pestilence in extremity besides. Josephus's *History of the Wars of the Jews*, has in it more tragical passages than perhaps any history whatsoever. . . . It was a desolation unparalleled, such as *was not since the beginning of the world, nor ever shall be*. Many a city and kingdom has been made desolate, but never any with a desolation like this. Let not daring sinners think that God has done his worst, he can heat the furnace seven times and

---

240. Henry, *Commentary*, 1740.
241. Henry, *Commentary*, 1740.

yet seven times hotter, and will, when he sees greater and still greater abominations. The Romans, when they destroyed Jerusalem, were degenerated from the honor and virtue of their ancestors, which had made even their victories easy to the vanquished. And the willfulness and obstinacy of the Jews themselves contributed much to the increase of the tribulation. No wonder that the ruin of Jerusalem was an unparalleled ruin, when the sin of Jerusalem was an unparalleled sin—even their crucifying Christ.[242]

Commenting on Matthew 24:27-28, Henry points out that "Some understand these verses of the coming of the Son of man *to destroy Jerusalem,* Mal. 3:1, 2, 5. So much was there of an extraordinary display of divine power and justice in that event, that it is called the coming of Christ."[243] Commenting on Matthew 24:29-31, he points out a few other controversial claims in his day:

> He foretells his second coming at the *end of time,* v. 29–31. *The sun shall be darkened,* etc.
>
> 1. Some think this is to be understood only of the destruction of Jerusalem and the Jewish nation; the darkening of the sun, moon, and stars, denotes the eclipse of the glory of that state, its convulsions, and the general confusion that attended that desolation. Great slaughter and devastation are in the Old Testament thus set forth (as Isa. 13:10; 34:4; Eze. 32:7; Joel 2:31); or by the sun, moon, and stars, may be meant the temple, Jerusalem, and the cities of Judah, which should all come to ruin. The *sign of the Son of man* (v. 30) means a signal appearance of the power and justice of the Lord Jesus in it, avenging his own blood on them that impre-

---

242. Henry, *Commentary,* 1741–2.
243. Henry, *Commentary,* 1742. Italics added.

cated the guilt of it upon themselves and their children; and the gathering *of his elect* (v. 31) signifies the delivering of a remnant from this sin and ruin.

2. It seems rather to refer to Christ's second coming. The destruction of the particular enemies of the church was typical of the complete conquest of them all; and therefore what will be done really at the great day, may be applied metaphorically to those destructions.[244]

Strangely and abruptly, Henry interprets Matthew 24:32-33 (about the fig tree) as most certainly referring to the "second coming" at the end of history. Yet in verse 34 he says that Jesus is only referring to first-century events leading up to the destruction of Jerusalem in the first century:

> As to *these things*, the wars, seductions, and persecutions, here foretold, and especially the ruin of the Jewish nation; *"This generation shall not pass away, till all these things be fulfilled* (v. 34); there are those now alive, that shall see Jerusalem destroyed, and the Jewish church brought to an end." Because it might seem strange, he backs it with a solemn asseveration; *"Verily, I say unto you.* You may take my word for it, these things are at the door."[245]

After the brief first-century interlude of verse 34, Henry then chides those who, beginning in verse 36, "confound" the day of Jerusalem's destruction with the "day of Christ." In doing so, Henry manifests his full commitment to futuristic interpretation for the remainder of the discourse:

---

244. Henry, *Commentary*, 1742.
245. Henry, *Commentary*, 1744.

But as to *that day and hour* which will put a period to time, *that knoweth no man*, v. 36. Therefore, take heed of confounding these two, as *they* did, who, from the words of Christ and the apostles; letters, inferred that *the day of Christ was at hand*, 2 Th. 2:2. No, it was not; *this generation*, and many another, *shall pass*, before *that day and hour* come.[246]

3.1.25 JOHN WESLEY (1703–1791)

Wesley, like Matthew Henry before him, utilizes a very clear methodology for interpreting Matthew's OD. He imagines Jesus clearly answering the first question first in relation to Matthew 24:4–28. Following that, Jesus answers the second question about Christ's "coming" in verses 29–31. Then Jesus segues back, albeit briefly, to answering the first question again and prophesying more about the destruction of Jerusalem's temple in verses 32–35. But then, in verses 36 and following, Jesus answers the third question last, which is also supposedly about the end of the world. Only one brief comment is needed to summarize his views in this regard. Commenting on verse 3, he wrote:

As he sat on the mount of Olives—Whence they had a full view of the temple. *When shall these things be? And what shall be the sign of thy coming, and of the end of the world?* —The disciples inquire confusedly, 1. Concerning the time of the destruction of the temple; 2. Concerning the signs of Christ's coming, and of the end of the world, as if they imagined these two were the same thing.

Our Lord answers distinctly concerning, 1. The destruction of the temple and city, with the signs preceding, ver. 4, &c, 15, &c. 2. His own coming, and the end of the

---

246. Henry, *Commentary*, 1744.

world, with the signs thereof, ver. 29-31. 3. The time of the destruction of the temple, ver. 32, &c. 4. The time of the end of the world, ver. 36.[247]

3.1.26 THOMAS NEWTON (1704–1782)

As well as being a contemporary of John Wesley, an infamous "universalist" in his soteriology, the Bishop of Bristol, and the Dean of St. Paul's Cathedral in London, Thomas Newton was also a diligent theologian and busy biblical scholar. Among his many works, his *Dissertations on The Prophecies, which have remarkably been fulfilled, and at this time are fulfilling in the world* covers Matthew's OD in great detail.

In that series of dissertations, Newton is the first among all the scholars examined thus far to explicitly argue, as I have shown in chapter two, that Jesus answers *the last question first.* He also teaches that the third question referred to *the destruction of Jerusalem.*

However, unlike what Matthew's OD clearly delineates on its own terms, once Newton arrives at verse 36 of Matthew 24, Jesus is imagined to suddenly shift into a "higher sense" of meaning by describing the end *of the world* and not merely the end of Israel's old covenantal administration. On this, Newton says: "All the subsequent discourse too, we may observe, doth not relate so properly to the destruction of Jerusalem, as to the end of the world and the general judgment. Our Savior loseth sight as it were of his former subject, and adapts his discourse more to the latter."

This discrepancy and adaptation of an otherwise consistent contextual meaning is surprising. Newton is most likely adapting the discourse to suit his audience and the traditional, dogmatic interpretations about the end of the world which they were prone to hearing and trusting. Only a few excerpts of Newton's dense dissertations are

---

247. John Wesley, *Explanatory Notes Upon the New Testament*, 12th ed. (New York: Carlton & Porter, 1754), 78.

needed to illustrate that he, too, had grown familiar with the early patristic, medieval Catholic, and later Protestant methodologies preceding him, and that he, also, was aware of how futuristic prooftexts remained important for dogmatic considerations:

> When we first entered on an explanation of our Savior's prophecies relating to the destruction of Jerusalem, comprised chiefly in this 24th chapter of St. Matthew, it was observed that the disciples in their question propose two things to our Savior; first, when should be the *time* of his coming, or the destruction of Jerusalem; and secondly, what should be the *signs* of it, (Matt. xxiv. 3) "Tell us when shall these things be, and what shall be the sign of thy coming and of the conclusion of the age." The latter part of the question our Savior answereth first, and treateth at large of the *signs* of the destruction of Jerusalem, from the 4th verse of the chapter to the 31st inclusive. He toucheth upon the most material passages and accidents, not only of those which were to forerun this great event, but likewise of those which were to attend, and immediately to follow upon it: and having thus answered the latter part of the question, he proceeds now in verse 32 to answer the former part of the question, as to the *time* of his coming and the destruction of Jerusalem.
>
> He begins with observing that the signs which he had given would be as certain an indication of the time of his coming, as the fig-tree's putting forth its leaves is of the approach of summer, (ver. 32, 33) . . . He proceeds to declare that the time of his coming was at no very great distance; and to show that he hath been speaking all this while of the destruction of Jerusalem, he affirms with his usual affirmation, (ver. 34) "Verily I say unto you, This generation shall not pass, till all these things be fulfilled." It is to me a wonder how any man can refer part of the foregoing discourse to the destruction of Jerusalem, and part to the end of the world, or

any other distant event, when it is said so positively here in the conclusion, All these things shall be fulfilled in this generation. It seemeth as if our Savior had been aware of some such misapplication of his words, by adding yet greater force and emphasis to his affirmation, (ver. 35,) "Heaven and earth shall pass away, but my words shall not pass away." It is a common figure of speech in the oriental languages, to say of two things that the one shall be and the other shall not be, when the meaning is only that the one shall happen sooner or more easily than the other.[248]

According to Newton, the transition into a futuristic "higher sense" of interpretation begins at verse 36. Although he begins by clarifying that the "primary" sense of the entire discourse—including verses 36 and following—relates to the destruction of Jerusalem, that is not the "only" sense in which it must be understood:

Hitherto we have explained this 24th chapter of St. Matthew as relating to the destruction of Jerusalem, and without doubt as relating to the destruction of Jerusalem it is primarily to be understood. But though it is to be understood of this primarily, yet it is not to be understood of this only: for there is no question that our Savior had a farther view and meaning in it. . . . The destruction of a great city is a lively type and image of the end of the world; and we may observe that our Savior no sooner begins to speak of the destruction of Jerusalem, than his figures are raised, his language is swelled, and he expresseth himself in such terms, as in a lower sense indeed are applicable to the destruction of Jerusalem, but describe something higher in their proper and genuine signification. .

---

248. Thomas Newton, *Dissertations on The Prophecies, which have remarkably been fulfilled, and at this time are fulfilling in the world* (London: J. F. Dove, 1825), 377-8.

313

. . the consistence and connexion of the discourse oblige us to understand it as spoken of the time of the destruction of Jerusalem, but in a higher sense it may be true also of the time of the end of the world and the general judgment. All the subsequent discourse too, we may observe, doth not relate so properly to the destruction of Jerusalem, as to the end of the world and the general judgment. Our Savior loseth sight as it were of his former subject, and adapts his discourse more to the latter. And the end of the Jewish state was in a manner the end of the world to many of the Jews. The remaining part of the chapter is so clear and easy as to need no comment or explanation.[249]

3.1.27 JOHN BROWN OF HADDINGTON (1722–1787)

Scottish minister and theologian John Brown is most famous for his *Self-Interpreting Bible*, which was designed to be a commentary for ordinary lay-people and not pastor-theologians like himself. His *Self-Interpreting Bible* contains summaries of commentaries placed in marginal notes, parallel passages of Scripture, a dictionary of biblical terminology, and various illustrations to aid his readers. This was an extraordinary achievement for his day, according to the limited means available to him.

In that work, almost the entire chapter of Matthew 24 is interpreted according to first-century fulfillment. From verse 37 onward there is only futuristic interpretation offered. Yet even those marginal notes are set alongside the destruction of Jerusalem as offering equally weighty meaning and application for basic Christian understanding. Again, only a brief series of excerpts is needed to illustrate as much:

---

249. Newton, *Dissertations*, 380–1.

CHAPTER XXIV. —Before the destruction of Jerusalem many false teachers and pretended Messiahs appeared, ver. 2, 4, 5, 11, 23-26. There were many wars, commotions, famines, pestilences, and earthquakes, ver. 6, 7. Ministers and other Christians were terribly persecuted; and much apostasy from the decay of religion ensued in many places, ver. 9-13. The gospel was preached through the Roman empire and the sanctions adjacent, ver. 14. The Roman army invaded and laid siege to Jerusalem, and the Christians fled with the utmost haste to the mountains around Judea, ver. 15-20. That destruction was terrible, ver. 21; especially to mothers, ver. 19; threatened ruin to the whole Jewish nation, ver. 22; and was universal through the whole country, ver. 27, 28. It was foreboded by signs in the heavens, and quite dissolved the constitution of the Jewish church and state, and it occasioned terrible anguish to the carnal Jews to be thus punished by the Messiah, ver. 27-30. It took place while that very generation among whom Christ taught partly survived, ver. 32-35; and was followed by a remarkable spread of the gospel and conversion of lost sinners to Christ, ver. 30, 31. Many of the wicked Jews were preserved for the sake of children who were in their loins, and who were to descend from them after many generations, ver. 22. Ver. 27, 28 may denote the spread of the gospel among the Gentiles, and the gathering of multitudes to Jesus. . . . the Roman army, beginning at the northeast, would, with fire and sword, desolate the whole country of the Jews, and hunt out and destroy them, be where they would; 29, 30 represent the terrible appearances of Jesus' power, in destroying the Jewish church and state, while his ministers should, by the gospel trumpet, gather multitudes of sinners to him.[250]

---

250. John Brown, *New Self-Interpreting Bible Library with Commentaries, References, Harmony of the Gospels, and the Helps Needed to Understand and Teach*

315

It is in verse 37 of Matthew 24 that Brown offers a transitional verse into the future, beyond the first century. He also subtly blends that transition with a tandem interpretation about the destruction of Jerusalem:

> 37-41. The destruction of Jerusalem, as well as the last judgment, will take place while most men are indulging themselves in sensuality and carnal cares, and are no way provided for it; and of persons in seemingly equal danger, some will be miserably destroyed, and others graciously preserved. 42-51. Since therefore you are so uncertain of the time of this destruction and the last judgment, ye need always to be watching over your hearts and lives that ye may be ready for it.[251]

In context, Brown's passing comment about "this destruction" seems to refer to the destruction of Jerusalem *in contrast with* the "last judgment."

3.1.28 BIELBY PORTEUS (1731—1809)

Even though his influence faded by the mid-1800s, Bielby Porteus was an immensely influential political and ecclesiastical figure in England throughout the mid-to-late-1700s. His public affect began when he was appointed as the Bishop of Chester, in which capacity he served for ten years. After that decade of preaching and teaching and serving within his diocese, he was appointed as the Bishop of London for twenty more years. Additionally, he also served as the domestic chaplain for the Archbishop of Canterbury and King George III, and

---

the Text, Illustrated and Explained, vol. 4 (New York: R.S. Peale and J.A. Hill, 1896), 98-9.

251. Brown, *Self-Interpreting Bible*, 99.

became best known for his work alongside William Wilberforce and other like-minded abolitionists of slavery.

His popularity never grew out of the locally published essays and treatises; instead, he was most vividly remembered for his tremendous preaching abilities and rhetorical insights. After his death, copies of lectures were subsequently published, including those on the Gospel of Matthew delivered in the Anglican Church of St. James in the center of London.

In those lectures we find one of the most eloquent and illuminating expressions of historical exegesis ever presented on Matthew's OD. Instead of preaching and proof-texting in order to offer soundbites of moralisms or to bolster trite theological predispositions, Porteus slowly walked his audience through the reception of Matthew's Gospel over the centuries so they could understand the importance of Jesus' great discourses in their original, first-century, Judean context. Porteus also labored to present a thorough case for why he believed the *entirety* of Matthew 24 pertained to first-century events, and *only* first-century events. This was a very unique approach for his time and a risky endeavor for such a well-known ecclesiastical and political figure. The primary goal of his lectures in 1798-1801 was to inculcate the dozens of parishioners, politicians, and scholars under his care with an appreciation of how certain confusing or erroneous traditions arose in the process of interpreting Matthew's Gospel and how his own audience could profit from Christ's very own words within their original first-century context.

Porteus' lectures on Matthew's OD are most pertinent to this project in three ways: First of all, he considered the *order* of Jesus' answers to his disciples' questions to be of paramount importance. The order he discovered was that Jesus answers the *first* question *last* and the *last* question *first*. It remained most peculiar to Porteus that not many Christian exegetes before him had exposited the text as Matthew has apparently arranged it, with Jesus addressing the "signs" of the third question first and the "when" concern of the first question last.

Secondarily, Porteus understood the terminology used by Jesus (and Matthew) about the "end of the world" to advance into mistaken territories of tradition. Accordingly, the predictions of Jesus would have been most naturally understood by Judeans of the first century as the phrase actually stands in the Greek text—as the "the end of the age," not the "world." He interprets the "end of the age" in its historical context as "*that* age, the end of the Jewish state and polity; the subversion of their city, temple, and government."[252]

Third, he notes that although Matthew 25 is best understood in its enduring relevance as a first-century event that *begins* all subsequent, eternal judgments of Christ thereafter, he remained open to the possibility that Matthew 25 could also be represented properly in Christian systematics as evidence of a "last great day" that awaits all of mankind. These approaches by Porteus accord with what I suggested in chapter two.

Since Porteus' exegesis of Matthew was offered in the form of lectures which are tediously lengthy and detailed, only a select series of his insights will be offered below:

> This course of lectures for the present year will begin with the twenty-fourth chapter of St. Matthew; which contains one of the clearest and most important prophecies that is to be found in the sacred writings. The prophecy is that which our blessed Lord delivered respecting the destruction of Jerusalem, to which, I apprehend, the whole of the chapter, in its *primary* acceptations, relates. At the same time it must be admitted, that the forms of expression, and the images made use of, are for the most part applicable also to the day of judgment; and that an allusion to that great event, as a

---

252. Bielby Porteus, *Lectures on the Gospel of St. Matthew; Delivered in the Parish Church of St. James, Westminster, In the Years 1798, 1799, 1800, and 1801* (Philadelphia: Thomas Kite, 1829), 249.

kind of secondary object, runs through almost every part of the prophecy.[253]

. . .

The evangelist next informs us, that as Jesus sat on the mount of Olives, which was exactly opposite to the hill on which the temple was built, and commanded a very fine view of it from the east, his disciples came unto him privately, saying, "Tell us when shall these things be, and what shall be the sign of thy coming, and of the end of the world." The expressions here made use of, *the sign of thy coming*, and *the end of the world*, at the first view naturally lead our thoughts to the coming of Christ at the day of judgment, and the final dissolution of this earthly globe. But a due attention to the parallel passages in St. Mark and St. Luke, and a critical examination into the real import of those two phrases in various parts of Scripture, will soon convince a careful inquirer, that by *the coming of Christ* is here meant, not his coming to judge the world at the last day, but his coming to execute judgment upon Jerusalem; and that by *the end of the world* is to be understood, not the final consummation of all things here below, but the end of *that age*, the end of the Jewish state and polity; the subversion of their city, temple, and government. . . . The real questions therefore here put to our Lord by the disciples were these two:

1st. At what time the destruction of Jerusalem was to take place: "Tell us, when shall these things be?"

2dly. What the signs were that were to precede it: "What shall be the sign of thy coming?"

Our Lord in his answer begins first with the *signs*, of which he treats from the 4th to the 31st verse, inclusive. The first of these *signs* is specified in the 5th verse, "Many

---

253. Porteus, *Lectures*, 247.

shall come in my name, saying, I am Christ, and shall deceive many."[254]

Commenting on Matthew 24:29 and the predictions which follow, which are usually treated as transitional descriptions about the end of the world, Porteus writes:

> In the three following verses, the language of our divine Master becomes highly figurative and sublime. "Immediately after the tribulation of those days shall the sun be darkened, and the moon shall not give her light, and the stars shall fall from heaven, and the powers of the heavens shall be shaken. And then shall appear the sign of the Son of man in heaven; and then shall all the tribes of the earth mourn, and they shall see the Son of man coming in the clouds of heaven with power and great glory. And he shall send his angels with a great sound of a trumpet, and they shall gather his elect from the four winds, from the one end of heaven to the other."
>
> Few people, I believe, read these verses, without supposing that they refer entirely to the day of judgment, many of these expressions being actually applied to that great event in the very next chapter, and in other parts of scripture; and indeed several eminent men and learned commentators are of that opinion, and imagine that our Lord here makes a transition from the destruction of Jerusalem to the end of the world, conceiving that such very bold figures of speech could not with propriety be applied to the subversion and extinction of any city or state, however great and powerful. But the fact is, that these very same metaphors do frequently in scripture denote the destruction of nations, cities, and kingdoms. Thus Isaiah, speaking of the destruction of Babylon, says, "Behold the day of the Lord cometh, cruel both with wrath

---

254. Porteus, *Lectures*, 249.

320

and fierce anger, to lay the land desolate, and he shall destroy the sinners thereof out of it. For the stars of heaven, and the constellations thereof, shall not give their light; the sun shall be darkened in his going forth, and the moon shall not cause the light to shine." And in almost the same terms he describes the punishment of the Idumaeans, and of Sennacherib and his people. Ezekiel speaks in the same manner of Egypt; and Daniel of the slaughter of the Jews; and, what is still more to the point, the prophet Joel describes this very destruction of Jerusalem in terms very similar to those of Christ. "I will show wonders in the heavens; and in the earth, blood, and fire, and pillars of smoke. The sun shall be turned into darkness, and the moon into blood, before the great and terrible day of the Lord shall come."[255]

Commenting on Matthew 24:32, Porteus points out that Jesus answers the *first* question *last*:

Our Lord then goes on to point out the time when all these things shall take place, and thus answers the other question put to him by his disciples, "Tell us, when shall these things be?" "Now learn," says he, "a parable of the fig-tree; when his branch is yet tender, and putteth forth leaves, ye know that the summer is nigh: so likewise ye, when ye shall see all these things, know that it is near, even at the doors. Verily I say unto you, this generation shall not pass till all these things be fulfilled. Heaven and earth shall pass away, but my words shall not pass away."

The only observation necessary to be made here is, that the time when all these predictions were to be fulfilled is here limited to a certain period. They were to be accomplished

---

255. Porteus, *Lectures*, 257-8.

321

before the generation of men then existing should pass away. And accordingly, all these events did actually take place within forty years after our Savior delivered this prophecy; and this by the way is an unanswerable proof, that everything our Lord had been saying in the preceding part of the chapter related principally, not to the day of judgment, or to any other very remote event, but to the destruction of Jerusalem, which did in reality happen before that generation had passed away.

"But of that day and hour knoweth no man; no, not the angels of heaven, but my Father only;" that is, although the time when Jerusalem is to be destroyed, is, as I have told you, fixed *generally* to this generation, yet the *precise day and hour* of that event is not known either to men or angels, but to God only. This he speaks in his human nature, and in his prophetic capacity. This point was not made known to him by the spirit, nor was he commissioned to reveal it.

It is supposed by several learned commentators, that the words, *that day* and *that hour*, refer to the day of judgment, which is immediately alluded to in the preceding verse, *heaven and earth shall pass away.* This conjecture is an ingenious one, and may be true; but if it be, this verse should be enclosed in parentheses, because what follows most certainly relates to the destruction of Jerusalem, (to which St. Luke in the seventeenth chapter expressly confines it) and cannot, without great violence to the words, be applied to the final advent of Christ. "As the days of Noe were, so shall also the coming of the Son of man be. For as in the days that were before the flood, they were eating and drinking, marrying and giving in marriage, until the day that Noe entered into the ark, and knew not until the flood came, and took them all away; so shall also the coming of the Son of man be. Then shall two be in the field; the one shall be taken, and the other left. Two women shall be grinding at the mill; the one shall be taken, and the other left." That is, when the day of desolation shall come upon the city and temple of Jerusalem, the inhabitants will be as thoughtless and unconcerned, and as unprepared for it, as the antediluvians were for the flood in the days of Noe. But as some (more particularly the Christians) will be more watchful, and in a better state of mind than others, the providence of God will make a distinction between his faithful and his disobedient servants, and will protect and preserve the former, but leave the latter to be taken or destroyed by their enemies; although they may both be in the same situation in life, may be engaged in the same occupations, and may appear to the world to be in every respect in similar circumstances.

Here ends the prophetical part of our Lord's discourse; what follows is altogether exhortatory.[256]

Matthew 25 is where Porteus offers a conjectural transition into the future, based on an assumption that Matthew 24 had reached a definitive conclusion about first-century fulfillment and required no further "particular explanation." Commenting on all of that in a somewhat slippery, yet elegant manner, Porteus progresses upward and onward to suggest that "the last great day" might be envisioned throughout Matthew 25:

With respect to their city, it has remained for the most part in a state of ruin and desolation, from its destruction by the Romans to the present time . . . It is not therefore only in the history of Josephus, and in other ancient writers, that we are to look for the accomplishment of our Lord's predictions; we see them verified at this moment before our eyes,

---

256. Porteus, *Lectures*, 259-60.

in the desolated state of the once celebrated city and temple of Jerusalem.[257]

. . .

I now proceed to the explanation of the next chapter, the 25th of St. Matthew, which begins with presenting to us two parables, that of the ten virgins, and that of the servants of a great Lord entrusted with different talents, of which they are called upon to render an account. As these parables contain nothing that requires a very particular explanation, I shall content myself with observing, that they are designed to carry on the subject with which the preceding chapter concludes; namely, of the last solemn day of retribution; and the object of both is to call our attention to that great event, and to warn us of the necessity of being always prepared for it. . . . After these admonitory parables, and these earnest exhortations to prepare for the last great day, our blessed Lord is naturally led on to a description of the day itself; and it is a description which for dignity and grandeur has not its equal in any writer, sacred or profane. It is as follows: "When the Son of man shall come in his glory, and all the holy angels with him, then shall he sit upon the throne of his glory: and before him shall be gathered all nations; and he shall separate them one from another."[258]

3.1.29 ADAM CLARKE (1762—1832)

Aside from Henry Hammond and John Lightfoot in the 1600s, and Bielby Porteus in the early 1800s, Adam Clarke is, perhaps, the only other Christian exegete to expound in detail a first-century interpretation of Matthew 24 in its entirety. Much like Porteus, his contem-

---

257. Porteus, *Lectures*, 269.
258. Porteus, *Lectures*, 270-1.

porary, Clarke considered that if at any point in Christ's discourse there was a potential place for transitioning into futuristic predictions, Matthew 25 and the "final judgment" scene might be it.

Matthew 25:1 is where Clarke begins to suggest a subtle transition into the future by describing "the kingdom of heaven" within the parable of ten virgins as "The State of Jews and professing Christians—or the state of the visible church at the time of the destruction of Jerusalem, and in the day of judgment." His reasoning behind such a transition is apparently very simple: "[…] for the parable appears to relate to both those periods. And particularly at the time in which Christ shall come to judge the world, it shall appear what kind of reception his Gospel has met with."[259] Clarke's introduction alone is all that is necessary to illustrate his methodology for interpreting Matthew 24:

> Christ foretells the destruction of the temple, 1, 2. His disciples inquire when and what shall be the signs of this destruction, 3. Our Lord answers, and enumerates them—false Christs, 5. Wars, famines, pestilences, and earthquakes, 6–8. Persecution of his followers, 9. Apostasy from the truth, 10–13. General spread of the Gospel. 14. He foretells the investment of the city by the Romans, 15–18. The calamities of those times, 19–22. Warns them against seduction by false prophets, 23–26. The suddenness of these calamities. 27, 28. Total destruction of the Jewish polity, 29–31. The whole illustrated by the parable of the fig-tree, 32, 33. The certainty of the event, though the time is concealed, 34–36. Careless state of the people, 37–41. The necessity of watchfulness and fidelity, illustrated by the parable of the two servants, one faithful, the other wicked, 42–51.

---

259. Adam Clarke, *The Holy Bible with a Commentary and Critical Notes*, vol. 5 (Bellingham, WA: Faithlife Corporation, 2014), 228.

This chapter contains a prediction of the utter destruction of the city and temple of Jerusalem, and the subversion of the whole political constitution of the Jews; and is one of the most valuable portions of the new covenant Scriptures, with respect to the *evidence* which it furnishes of the *truth* of Christianity. Everything which our Lord foretold should come on the temple, city, and people of the Jews, has been fulfilled in the most correct and astonishing manner; and witnessed by a writer who was present during the whole, who was himself a Jew, and is acknowledged to be an historian of indisputable veracity in all those transactions which concern the destruction of Jerusalem. Without having designed it, he has written a commentary on our Lord's words, and shown how every tittle was punctually fulfilled, though he knew *nothing* of the Scripture which contained this remarkable prophecy. His account will be frequently referred to in the course of these notes; as also the admirable work of *Bishop Newton* on the prophecies.[260]

What makes Clarke's commentary unique among all of his contemporaries is not just his conviction about first-century fulfillment throughout the entirety of Matthew 24 (and partially through chapter 25). Even his frequent references to the works of Josephus, the early church fathers, and some respected Divines such as John Lightfoot and Thomas Newton are not the only factors lending credibility to his insights. Clarke's commentary is noticeably sagacious insofar as he manifests a vast, encyclopedic comprehension of ancient Jewish and rabbinical sources, Greco-Roman literature and artifacts, ancient archeological records, and textual insights from Coptic, Sahidic, Armenian, Ethiopic, Slavonic, and Latin manuscripts of Scripture, *in order to support first-century fulfillment in Matthew 24.* All of that in-

---

260. Clarke, *Commentary*, 225.

326

formation was readily available to him through forty years of constant research, which included his membership in the *British and Foreign Bible Society* and the *Royal Irish Academy*, as well as being an associate of the *Geological Society of London*, the *University of Aberdeen*, and the Methodist seminary founded by John Wesley (who, incidentally, became a close acquaintance of his).

3.1.30 GEORGE LEO HAYDOCK (1774–1849)

The *Haydock Bible* was one of the most popular Catholic Bibles with added commentary used by Catholic laymen throughout the 1800s. In it, Haydock composed a wide variety of comments from church fathers and contemporary scholars, as well as his own unique considerations, in order to counter the influence of Protestantism in England. English Catholics were so enthusiastic about his work, that its first printing began in 1811 and sold 1,500 copies, which was a remarkable volume of sales for its time. More than a dozen editions of Haydock's Bible have been published since then.

As a unique nineteenth-century contribution to the education of English Catholics, it is worth highlighting a few things. First, his exegesis clearly involves an awareness of patristic tradition and the history of incorporating first-century fulfillment throughout much of Matthew 24. Second, Haydock was peculiarly alert to the writings of influential Catholic commentaries during the Protestant Reformation era, and he had an enormous respect, in particular, for *Juan de Maldonado's* sixteenth-century commentary. Haydock even offered the same general outline as Maldonado, transitioning from first-century fulfillment within Matthew 24:4-23 to entirely futuristic fulfillment in verses 34 and following. Only a handful of marginal notes are needed to illustrate as much:

> Ver. 2. *Do you see all these things?* Examine again and again all this magnificence, that the sentence of heaven may appear

more striking—*A stone upon a stone.* We need not look on this as an hyperbole. The temple was burnt by the Romans, and afterwards even ploughed up. See. S. Gregory Nad. frat. ii. cont. Julianum, Theodore I. iii. Histor. c. xx. & c. Wi.— Julian the apostate, wishing to falsify the predictions of Daniel and of Jesus Christ, attempted to rebuild the temple. For this purpose, he assembled the chief among the Jews, and asking them why they neglected the prescribed sacrifices, was answered, that they could not offer anywhere else but in the temple of Jerusalem.[261]

. . .

Ver. 3. *Tell us, when shall these things be? and what shall be the sign of thy coming, and of the consummation of the world?* We must take good notice with S. Jerome, that three questions are here joined together. 1. Concerning the destruction of Jerusalem; 2. of the coming of Christ; 3. of the end of the world. Christ's answers and predictions in this chapter, are to be expounded with a reference to the three questions. This hath not been considered by those interpreters; who expound everything here spoken by Christ of the destruction of Jerusalem; nor by others, who will have all understood of his coming to judgment, and of the end of the world. . . . It is probable the apostles themselves did not understand that they were asking about two distinct events. Being filled with the idea of a temporal kingdom, they thought that Christ's second coming would take place soon; and that Jerusalem, once destroyed, the Messiah would begin his reign on earth.[262]

. . .

---

261. George Leo Haydock, *The Holy Bible, Translated from the Latin Vulgate with Useful Notes, Critical, Historical, Controversial, and Explanatory* (New York: Edward Dunigan and Brother, 1852), 1299.

262. Haydock, *The Holy Bible with Notes*, 1299.

Ver. 14. *This gospel . . . shall be preached in the whole world*, to serve as a testimony to all nations, of the solicitude of heaven in having the doctrine of salvation announced to them. This then is a fifth sign, and not till then shall the consummation come. *—And then shall the consummation come.* The end of the world, says S. Jerome. The destruction of Jerusalem, says S. Chrys. and others. . . . If the final destruction of Jerusalem be here meant, the gospel had been preached throughout the major part of the world, there is the greatest probability that the true faith will have been announced to every part of the globe, before that period.[263]

. . .

Ver. 15. . . . *The abomination of desolation*, or the abominable desolation. Instead of these words, we read in S. Luke, (xxi. 20) *When you shall see Jerusalem surrounded by an army.* Christ said both the one and the other. But the words in S. Luke, seem rather to give us a sign of the ruin of Jerusalem, than of the end of the world. *—Spoken of by Daniel, the prophet.* ... Some expound it of the heathen Roman army, approaching and investing Jerusalem, called the *holy city*. Others understand the profanation of the temple, made by the Jews themselves, a little before the siege under Vespasian.

. . .

Ver. 22. *No flesh:* a Hebraism for no person; denoting that no one would have escaped death, had the war continued. . . . All the Jews would have been destroyed by the Romans, or all the Christians by Antichrist. Maldonatus—From this place, Jesus Christ foretells the coming of Antichrist, and forewarns Christians of latter ages, to guard all they can against seduction.

. . .

---

263. Haydock, *The Holy Bible with Notes*, 1300.

Ver. 26. *Behold, he is in the desert.* This prediction of false Christs, may be understood before the destruction of Jerusalem, but chiefly before the end of the world.

. . .

Ver. 34. *This generation*; i.e. the nation of the Jews shall not cease to exist until all these things shall be accomplished: thus we see the nation of the Jews still continue, and will certainly continue to the end of the world. . . . This race, I tell you in very truth, shall not pass away till all this be finally accomplished in the ruin of Jerusalem, the most express figure of the destruction and end of the world. . . . By *generation*, our Savior does not mean the people that were in existence at that time, but the faithful of his Church.[264]

For our purposes here, it is important to keep in mind that although Haydock intended to "obviate the misinterpretations of the many heretical works which disgrace the Scripture," as he states in the preface of his Bible, and the majority of sources he consulted "dwelt upon the works of Catholic authors, both with greater pleasure and advantage," the *methodology* he ultimately adopted was not considerably different than the many "heretical" Protestant commentators he denounces throughout his commentary. Needless to say, if there were any "heretical" differences between the majority of Catholic and Protestant interpretations preceding Haydock's Bible, none of them precluded a *transition* from Jesus' promise of first-century fulfillment to futuristic fulfillment in the "end of the age."

3.1.31 RICHARD WATSON (1781—1833)

Richard Watson was a contemporary of Adam Clarke and also a vocal critic of him in some ways. As a fellow Methodist minister and

---

264. Haydock, *The Holy Bible with Notes*, 1301.

theologian working alongside Clarke and Wesley, the works of both were immensely formative for Watson's roles of leadership within the Methodist movement in the early 1800s. Among Watson's many influential writings, which included a *Biblical and Theological Dictionary* and a standard systematic theology textbook used by Wesleyan Methodists, his only official biblical commentary was on the Gospels of Matthew and Mark together.

In that commentary, Watson's unique contribution to understanding Matthew's OD consists mainly in its complete first-century fulfillment up to Matthew 24:29, after which he begins a very lengthy transition into futuristic speculations by *merging* first-century fulfillment with the end of the world well into Matthew 25. According to Watson's interpretation of the OD, Matthew 24:29 begins to function as a *type* of "great judgment" preceding its great antitype, the end of the world. This slow and steady transition of his ends only slightly prior to the final judgment scene of Matthew 25, after which Watson officially drops the typology altogether and transitions to entirely futuristic fulfillment. His comments most relevant to this study are as follows:

> *When shall these things be?* —The total destruction of the temple just spoken of was doubtless first intended in the things respecting which they inquired; but they properly associated, with so great a calamity, many other events they knew must be necessarily concomitant.
>
> *The sign of thy coming.* —It is difficult to say what idea the disciples attached to the coming of Christ. . . . But when our Lord speaks of his coming, it is to be remembered, that he uses the phrase in three views. 1. A spiritual manifestation either to his disciples, or to the world by his gospel. 2. His invisible agency as Judge in bringing total destruction upon the impenitent nation of the Jews, through the instrumentality of the Roman armies. 3. His final visible and glorious second advent to judge the world of wicked men; of which,

almost throughout the following prophecies, he makes the destruction of the Jews a type and prophecy.

And of the end of the world. —The phrase συντελείας τοῦ αἰῶνος, *the end of the age*, refers in the language of the Jews both to the coming of Messiah, and to the end of time, and is used in both senses in the New Testament. Here the disciples appear to employ it for that glorious manifestation of their Master which they anticipated; one of honor and glory to them, and destruction to his enemies. This question appears therefore of nearly the same import as the preceding. They, as above observed, had yet no very definite ideas on this subject; but our Lord replies to the question, by speaking of his coming to take vengeance on the Jews, but expresses this in terms which carry us above that event to the general judgment.[265]

According to Watson, Matthew 24:29 begins a series of prophecies that pertain to first-century events and God's judgment at the end of the world. Watson writes:

Verse 29. Immediately after the tribulation of those days, &c. —From this verse to the thirty-first, another instance occurs of prophecy with a double reference, as of the elevation of the style itself intimates; for this coming of our Lord to judge the Jewish nation is described in the strongest and sublimest language of the Old Testament.[266]

Intriguingly, Watson does not stop this blend of first-century and end-of-the-world prophecy at Matthew 24:31. He actually maintains this interpretation into the early parts of Matthew 25, saying with

---

265. Richard Watson, *An Exposition of the Gospels of St. Matthew and St. Mark, and of some other detached parts of Holy Scripture* (London: John Mason,1833), 340.

266. Watson, *An Exposition*, 349.

regard to the parable of the virgins, that "In an inferior sense" this parable may also apply to "the coming of Christ to judge the Jewish nation." But the "ultimate reference is admitted" to the "day of judgment" at the end of the world.[267] It is only when the parable of the coming Master and his servants in Matt. 25:14 is reached that Watson finally relinquishes all noticeable adherence to a blend of first-century and futuristic fulfillment, and focuses entirely on end-of-the-world scenarios until the end of Jesus' discourse.

3.1.32 JOHN BIRD SUMNER (1780–1862)

When John Sumner was appointed as the Archbishop of Canterbury in 1848, he was subsequently elected into the *Fellowship of the Royal Society* alongside such highly influential figures as Isaac Newton, Michael Faraday, and Charles Darwin. As a fellow of the Royal Society— one of the most prestigious scientific academies of England—recognition of Sumner's achievements increased all the more. Among his many accomplishments prior to 1848 that only became acclaimed after his elevation to the most honorable episcopal chair in the Church of England, is a series of lectures on the Gospels of Matthew and Mark, published in 1831. In that publication, titled *A Practical Exposition of the Gospels of St. Matthew and St. Mark*, Sumner continued to advance the methodology proposed by his predecessors in the faith. Specifically, he taught that Matthew 24:4–35 contained clear references of first-century fulfillment surrounding the destruction of Jerusalem, and that an official transition into the future was established in verse 36 of that same chapter.

> Verily I say unto you, there shall not be left here one stone upon another, that shall not be thrown down. Forty years after these words were spoken, a stranger visiting the spot on

---

267. Watson, *An Exposition*, 357.

333

which Jerusalem was now standing, would have been unable to discover the site of the temple which "was adorned with goodly stones and gifts," and had been "fifty years in building." The foundation was dug up, and the surface ploughed. Because it "knew not the time of its visitation."[268]

. . .

In answer to the question, *Tell us when these things shall be*: our Lord reveals many events relating to the country, and many relating to the apostles themselves. There should be an interval; a dangerous and fearful interval; and many presages of the gathering storm. . . . It has pleased God, for the confirmation of our faith, that the history of the destruction of Jerusalem should be related not by a Christian, but a Jewish author, Josephus, who was himself concerned in all the affairs of that awful period. And he fully acquaints us how all these things happened as they are here foretold.[269]

Commenting on the verses leading up to Matthew 24:14, Sumner summarizes his thoughts about first-century fulfillment this way:

Such were to be the trials of the infant church, before *the end came*; before the event took place which would prove the truth of Christ's words, and signally confound the most determined enemies of his faith.[270]

Although the destruction of Jerusalem in 70 CE is, likewise, his explicit interpretation of Matthew 24:15 through 28,[271] verse 29 is where

---

268. John Bird Sumner, *A Practical Exposition of the Gospels of St. Matthew and St. Mark in the form of Lectures, intended to assist the practice of domestic instruction and devotion* (London: J. Hatchard and Son, 1831), 318.

269. Sumner, *A Practical Exposition*, 319.

270. Sumner, *A Practical Exposition*, 321.

271. Sumner, *A Practical Exposition*, 323-7.

Sumner begins *blending* the fulfillment of first-century events with the end of the world, as others before him had suggested. On this he said:

> The preceding verses had described the tribulation which should attend the siege of Jerusalem. The utter destruction of the city follows. . . . Still, there would be many circumstances in common, between the destruction of Jerusalem and the end of the world, which render the like description applicable to both. Especially its suddenness: the unprepared state in which the great mass of the people should be found. Its certainty must be taken on trust: the exact period would never be revealed.[272]

Verse 36 is where Sumner indelibly transitions into futuristic fulfillment:

> Our Lord continues to enforce this in words, which are meant to carry on our thoughts from his first coming, when Jerusalem should fall, to his second coming, when heaven and earth shall pass away, and make room for "new heaven and a new earth, wherein dwelleth righteousness."[273]

3.2 CONCLUSION

In Matthew's version of the OD, Jesus submitted a question to his disciples in response to their first question about *when* his "coming" in judgment would be: "*Who then is the faithful and wise servant, whom his master has set over his household, to give them their food at the proper time?*" (Matt. 24:45, ESV). Jesus foreknew that some of his servants would not prepare themselves or their families and friends for the

---

272. Sumner, *A Practical Exposition*, 329.

273. Sumner, *A Practical Exposition*, 331.

tribulations drawing near to them; He deemed them wicked, not only for not remaining vigilant, but also for acting cruelly toward others in the house of God. Only the servants who responded in faithful preparation and dutiful service are declared "blessed" by Jesus. Only they could rest assured that their labors would not be in vain. Each would receive their just reward for loyalty or lack thereof, as each awaited his "coming." And his "coming" was most assuredly in *that* generation.

All of those remarks by Jesus made *complete* sense within the context of Matthew's Gospel, as well as within the broader New Testament message of soon-coming judgment upon Israel, Jerusalem, and its temple. Ancient historians like Josephus and Tacitus added their own testimonies, thereby confirming the Apostolic message of first-century judgment upon Israel, their city, and their temple as the most memorably cataclysmic event at that time.

As the survey of Christian scholars, pastors, and theologians above testify, all sorts of loyal, dutiful, and vigilant Christians between the late Middle Ages and the late modern era were intelligent enough to notice the apostolic emphasis of first-century fulfillment as well. Yet their adherence to traditional assumptions and questionable methodologies goaded or encouraged most of them to rationalize the primacy of *disjointed* tradition over first-century apostolic witnesses—no matter how opaque or inconsistent the meaning of traditional details remained—teaching such things as those wicked servants in the first century, saying *"My master is delayed"* (Matt. 24:48).

Fortunately, in God's good providence, the majority of those theologians, pastors, scholars, and authors did not have to worry about Jesus actually coming *as promised* to destroy their great cities, monasteries, or cathedrals. According to Matthew's Gospel, Jesus and his apostles knew he was coming in the first century, and his question about the wise and faithful servant did *not* involve a general prediction of soon-coming judgment upon unprepared Dominicans, Franciscans, Wycliffites, Lutherans, Calvinists, Spanish Catholics, French Jansenists, English Methodists, Westminster Divines, or Archbishops of Canterbury. The way Matthew framed his fifth discourse clarifies

336

virtually all of their misunderstandings: Jesus was answering his disciples' first question *last*, and their last question *first*. He also was not answering their question about the "end of the age" to describe the "end of the world" millennia beyond that first-century generation. He was coming to end *that* age and judge *that* generation, when *they* could see "all these things" come upon *them* (Matt. 24:33), as Josephus and other ancient historians reported.

Does this mean that a venerable cloud of Christian witnesses across past centuries have prepared in vain for their own personal day of the Lord? Certainly not. Does their misunderstanding of Matthew's OD mean that they *encouraged* wickedness, laziness, or indifference by waiting for Jesus to return and destroy the whole world and magically make all things new? Absolutely not. But their questionable methodology *has* perpetuated much unnecessary strife and discord among brethren; it has stirred up many thousands of unnecessary controversies and cartoonish speculations; it has misled millions into questioning Jesus' prophetic authority and the cogency of the New Testament witness with its apostolic gospel.

In light of this, Ulrich Luz offers some important insights concerning the history of ancient biblical texts and their influence upon all exegetes. He writes:

> . . . to become aware of the history of influence of a text means to become aware of how we ourselves have been shaped by the text. This means at the same time that we must become aware of our own position vis-à-vis the text, a position which is never simply a neutral one. . . . Every critical interpretation of a biblical text which is not simply historically blind or dogmatically rigid must take into consideration the historical influences created by this text up to the present time, just as it

takes into consideration the other critical criteria which guide present-day biblical scholarship.[274]

Given the lengthy and disjointed tradition of interpreting the OD, it should not surprise us to discover new schools of highly influential, systematized theories rising to prominence, beginning in the mid-1800s. As a result of centuries filled with traditional assumptions and questionable methodologies, many interpreters responded in kind to the curiously incomplete and incompatible traditions they inherited and learned to doubt. Among them, some would wonder if Jesus really meant what he said, but was truly mistaken, and not really a prophet of God. Others would speculate that Jesus' disciples were most likely unreliable in their comprehension of his teaching, and the gospels they produced were really just pieced together from lost, disjointed, apocalyptic sayings of his. Still, others would imagine that Matthew (or whoever composed his Gospel) crafted an apocalyptic Jesus whose teachings on the subject never really existed outside of later "Matthean communities" and their own imaginary concerns about the end of the physical cosmos. It is even asserted that although many traditions of our forefathers were correct about some things, they were demonstrably wrong about the historical integrity of Matthew's OD and some of the apocalyptic sayings of Jesus.[275]

---

274. Luz, "The Final Judgment", 271.

275. Modern scholarship frequently inserts reminders about the lack of integrity among NT Gospel accounts. Gärtner mentions in passing that, "It must of course be remembered that the gospel texts do not give us a wholly authentic account of the Jesus traditions, since they lived and were formed in the early Church." Bertil Gärtner, *The Temple and the Community in Qumran and the New Testament: A Comparative Study in the Temple Symbolism of the Qumran Texts and the New Testament*, SNTS Monograph Series 1 (1965; repr., Cambridge, UK: Cambridge University Press, 2005), 105. Steve Mason and Tom Robinson also contribute to this contemporary cause, saying, "Because these texts tell the story of Jesus' life and the church's first generation, and the NT places them first in its arrangement, it takes a great deal of mental discipline to remember that they are

Intriguingly, among all of the novel theories which began to rise in popularity in the mid-nineteenth century, some traditional assumptions and questionable methodologies remained virtually unchecked. It is to that time period which we now turn.

---

actually products of the second and third generations of Jesus' followers (say, 65 to 120 C.E.)." Mason & Robinson, *Early Christian Reader*, 243.

CHAPTER 4

Who Then is the Faithful and Wise Servant?

4.1 MODERN VARIETIES OF EXPLICATION

Biblical scholarship from the nineteenth-century onward is so vast and speculative that little agreement remains in how to interpret the OD consistently across the Synoptic Gospels.[1] Minimally, at least three

---

1. According to my own estimation, this is largely due to constant shape-shifting postulations about the "sources" underlying the composition of pericopes within each Gospel. In a recent research project by Michael J. Kok (*Tax Collector to Gospel Writer: Patristic Traditions about the Evangelist Matthew* [Minneapolis, MN: Fortress Press, 2023], 12), he suggests that "The evangelists were either copying each other or common sources for their shared material." For lack of a better alternative, this suggestion seems fair and reasonable. However, one large problem looming over such suggestions is that "An academic consensus over the question of who was copying who remains as elusive as ever" (12). Around the dawn of the 20th century, a source labeled "Q" was hypothesized, and that hypothesis remains popular to this day among Synoptic scholars. "Q" refers to the "sayings" of Jesus that are common between Matthew and Luke, but not contained in Mark at all. (Some scholars imagine "Q" to be a single source, whereas

general schools of thought continue to this day.[2] Despite their exten-

---

others speculate that it developed over time and consisted of multiple sources compiled together.) By means of postulating "Q's" existence, it is also frequently maintained that Matthew and Luke compiled their Gospels independently, and in order to do so they each utilized "Q" along with Mark's Gospel. "The primary reason for postulating its existence," Eric Franklin writes, "is a belief that Luke could not have taken at least the bulk of the material that is common to him and Matthew out of Matthew to produce what we now have in his Gospel. It would have entailed too great a re-ordering of Matthew's material: it would have meant too great a revision of both his incidents and his sayings. It would have served to produce something which seems in large parts at any rate inferior to the original. So Q is regarded as necessary" (Eric Franklin, *Luke: Interpreter of Paul, Critic of Matthew*, JSNTSS, no. 92 [Sheffield, England: Sheffield Academic Press, 1994], 280). Beyond the well-known conservative criticism about "Q's" vagaries, as well as the subjectivity and arbitrariness in its reconstruction (Franklin, *Luke*, 280), one problem remains constant. Franklin describes this problem succinctly: "The material that is common to Matthew and Luke and out of which Q is culled is, in fact, not all that 'common.' If there are passages such as Mt. 7.7-11/Lk. 11.9-13, Mt. 11.25-27/Lk. 10.21-24 and Mt. 23.37-39/Lk. 13.34-35 where the identity of wording is such as to suggest a direct use of some common source, at other times the relationship appears far less obvious. . . . Belief in the existence of Q requires an assumption that the evangelists are primarily compilers, perhaps collectors, often tidiers-up, pickers and choosers of material through which their own ideas can be expressed, rather than radical revisers using material before them as springboards to be refashioned so that they, and more importantly their readers, can land where the evangelist wants himself and them to be. By its very nature, belief in Q must reduce the activity of the evangelist to a minimum" (Franklin, *Luke*, 280-1).

2. Milton Terry summarizes the state of scholarship up to the late nineteenth-century, saying: "There are at least three different hypotheses which have been employed to explain this scripture. There is, first, (1) That which regards the discourse in its present form as a composition of incongruous materials. The writers who penned our synoptic gospels are supposed to have misapprehended much of what the Lord said, and to have united in one address various statements which were originally uttered on different occasions. (2) Another class of interpreters find in these words of Jesus teachings concerning two entirely different events, widely separated in time, namely, the destruction of Jerusalem and the end of the world. (3) A third method of interpretation maintains that the entire prophecy may be most simply explained as finding its fulfillment in the overthrow of the temple and the introduction of Christianity into the world."

342

sive differences, some new assumptions have developed which complicate previous interpretations and methodologies.[3] One assumption is the likelihood of Markan priority, which is imagined to be a primary *source* in the formation of other Synoptic Gospels. Lukan priority has also been debated as a possibility among such source critics.[4] These operating assumptions have developed to the point where Matthean priority is rarely offered anymore.[5] Another assumption is that Matthew's Gospel was surely *composed after 70 CE,* which is a natural byprod-

---

(Milton S. Terry, *Biblical Apocalyptics: A Study of the Most Notable Revelations of God and of Christ in the Canonical Scriptures* [New York, NY: Eaton & Mains, 1898], 213-4). For Terry's critique of hypotheses (1) and (2) and his defense of hypothesis (3) above, see Terry, *Biblical Apocalyptics*, 213-52.

Grant Macaskill, *Revealed Wisdom*, 163, outlines various historical interpretations of Matthew 24 (specifically 24:4-44) up to the present day, and categorizes them into four main groups: "1. Matthew 24:4-44 refers exclusively to the fall of the temple in a non-eschatological sense, that is, it does not speak of the end of the present cosmos. 2. Matthew 24:4-44 refers exclusively to the *eschaton* and does not refer to the temple at all. 3. Matthew 24:4-44 refers to the fall of the temple as part of an eschatological scenario, the details of which are impossible to separate from one another. 4. Matthew 24:4-44 refers, in part, to the fall of the temple, but this event is deliberately separated in Matthew's redaction from future/final elements of the eschatological scenario."

3. In the pages that follow, I will not be discussing the novel development of communitarian hermeneutics such as "Feminist" or "Liberation" readings of Gospel texts. Although such hermeneutics and their assumptions (faulty or not) are relevant for understanding how complicated Matthean studies have become since the 1990s, I have not discovered one commentary among the few that are available whose insights propose a noteworthy challenge to my overall thesis. For more about such communitarian hermeneutics and their influence, see Sandra M. Schneiders, "The Gospels and the reader," *The Cambridge Companion to the Gospels*, ed. Stephen C. Barton (New York, NY: Cambridge University Press, 2006), 97-118. Additionally, see Brown & Roberts, *Matthew*, 405-59.

4. For a helpful survey of source criticism in the New Testament, see Amy Balogh, Dan Cole, and Wendy Widder, "Source Criticism," *Social & Historical Approaches to the Bible*, ed. Douglas Mangum and Amy Balogh, LMS, vol. 3 (Bellingham, WA: Lexham Press, 2017), 85-97.

5. See Peabody, Cope and McNicol, *One Gospel from Two*; see also Stoldt, *History and Criticism.*

uct of trends committed to Markan or Lukan priority. Accordingly, Matthew's OD has become a prophecy crafted with an understanding that Jerusalem had already been destroyed. The technical term for this prophetic literary genre is *vaticinium ex eventu*. I touched upon *ex eventu* assumptions briefly in chapter two, pointing out that *after-the-fact predictions* still do not change "Matthew's" literary structure or his intentionality with regard to first-century fulfillment.[6] Although the shifting theological climate of modern scholarship continues to disagree with Matthean priority, most interpretations still assume that Jesus answered his disciples' *first* question *first*.

In addition to source critics, there are also many biblical form and redaction critics across modern scholarship.[7] Among these

---

6. The same could be said about a lot of Old Testament critical scholarship regarding oracles by OT prophets. As Matthew Neujhar has pointed out, "Prophetic oracles may have been composed and delivered by prophetic figures, but prophetic *texts* are the work of scribes." Matthew Neujhar, *Predicting the Past in the Ancient Near East: Mantic Historiography in Ancient Mesopotamia, Judah, and the Mediterranean World* (Providence, RI: Brown Judaic Studies, 2012), 4.

7. Neujhar aptly summarizes two essential aspects of biblical form criticism: "First, form criticism deals almost uniformly in small units, and—with the exception of individual psalms—generally does not deal with literary works in their entirety. Form critics tend to deal with the individual components of a biblical book as independent compositions, and seldom make genre claims based on the received form of a book as a whole. Second, biblical form criticism has never been entirely literary—by which I mean aesthetic—in its practice" (Neujhar, *Predicting the Past*, 77). Mason and Robinson also mention that the "form critics' most controversial proposal, and the one with which the label 'form criticism' is often associated," is that "any pericope that presupposes conditions that only existed in the church's life must have come into being within the first-generation church and not in Jesus' lifetime. All of the gospel material has been shaped by its use in the church, they said, but some pericopes actually show signs of having *originated* in the church's preaching." Mason and Robinson, *Early Christian Reader*, 264; italics original. For a helpful survey of form criticism in the New Testament, see Gretchen Ellis, "Form Criticism" in Mangum and Balogh, *Social & Historical Approaches to the Bible*, 115-9, 128-30.
   "Redaction criticism," according to Donald Hagner and Stephen Young, "is concerned with the final stage of the formation of the Gospels, and focuses

schools of criticism, many insist that the Synoptic Gospels contain the remnants of a "little apocalypse,"[8] a residual group of "sayings"[9] originating independently outside of the gospels yet largely contained within Mark's version of the OD.[10] This alleged group of "sayings" is assumed to be at least one source incorporated into Matthew's version of the OD.[11] Even when patristic interpretations of Matthew's OD re-emerged in popularity throughout the late twentieth-century and

on the evangelists' editorial work in using their sources. The aim of redaction criticism is 'the detection of the evangelists' creative contribution.'" Donald A, Hagner and Stephen E. Young, "The Historical-Critical Method and the Gospel of Matthew," *Methods for Matthew*, MBI, ed. Mark Allan Powell (New York, NY: Cambridge University Press, 2009), 27.

8. Grant Macaskill argues convincingly that Mark 13 and its OD parallels in Matthew and Luke cannot adequately be described as an "apocalypse." On this, see Macaskill, *Revealed Wisdom*, 161-3.

9. As summarized succinctly by Werner Kahl, the distinctive idea about "sayings" that were collected and attributed to Jesus began with Friedrich Schleiermacher in 1832. He theorized this from a quotation by Eusebius, who in turn cited Papias. On this, see Werner Kahl, "The Gospel of Luke as Narratological Improvement of Synoptic Pre-Texts: The Narrative Introduction to the Jesus Story (Mark 1.1 - 8 Parr.)," *Gospel Interpretation and the Q-Hypothesis*, LNTS, vol. 573, ed. Mogens, Muller, and Heike Omerzu (New York, NY: T&T Clark, 2020), 223.

10. W. F. Albright and C. S. Mann, *Matthew: A New Translation with Introduction and Commentary*, AYB, vol. 26 (1971; repr., New Haven: Yale University Press, 2011), 288, say that "The history of NT study of the apocalyptic material can be simply stated. From the second half of the nineteenth century onwards it has been generally agreed that the material is composite, gathered from various occasions and contexts. G. R. Beasley-Murray . . . sums up the accepted theory that the whole discourse in Mark (and therefore, on the usual premises, in Matthew also) is based on a 'little apocalypse' of Jewish origin."

11. According to Ellis, "as in OT studies, form criticism came swiftly on the heels of source criticism, which was applied to the NT in order to assess and delineate the sources lying behind the Synoptic Gospels." Ellis, *"Form Criticism,"* 116. For a brief critique of form criticism and the negative influence upon synoptic studies by some of their most notable adherents, see N.T. Wright, *The New Testament and the People of God*, COQG, vol. 1 (Minneapolis, MN: Fortress Press, 1992), 418-43. For additional insights about form criticism and its generally accepted, yet skeptical, criteria, see Craig S. Keener, *The Historical Jesus*

early twenty-first century, many of those works also became revised according to modern assumptions. Therefore, any interaction with modern scholarship must address these common assumptions and interact with them, because they are prevalent and influential, regardless of how varied or speculative modern interpretations may seem.[12]

Since this project is ultimately about the questionable methodology and assumptions of longstanding Christian tradition, it will be helpful to operate favorably with the common assumptions of modern scholarship in order to determine whether or not these scholars, too, have shared in similarly questionable methodologies. My purpose in this chapter is not primarily a defense or argument against the many views presented, but rather to illuminate a long and wide

---

of the Gospels (Grand Rapids, MI: William B. Eerdmans Publishing Company, 2009), 153-61.

12. As with all interpretations, underlying assumptions are critical. One relatively recent assumption underlying synoptic scholarship has grown in influence over the last few decades, and is represented well in Douglas Hare's monograph. Hare imagined that "Matthew," writing many decades after 70 CE, exaggerated the persecution of Christians before 70 CE. According to Hare's thesis, the Pharisees are portrayed by Matthew to *appear* to be chief instigators of Christian persecution before 70 CE, even though they probably were not. Hare also considers the majority of pre-70 CE evidence to be inadequate to determine if Christians were persecuted by Jews for certain; if they were, it was relatively minor (so he argues). Hare even goes so far as to claim that "non-acceptance, not persecution, was the normal response of the Jewish communities in Palestine" before 70 CE, and that it was only after the "gradual consolidation of Pharisaic power in the post-war years" that "Christians in Palestine found themselves strongly opposed in the synagogues." Douglas R. A. Hare, *The Theme of Jewish Persecution of Christians in the Gospel According to St. Matthew*, SNTS Monograph Series, vol. 6 (London: Cambridge University Press, 1967), 168. His arguments from cover-to-cover assume that Matthew's post-70 CE community was imposing *contemporary* Pharisaic persecutions upon pre-70 CE events in order to advance a more-or-less exclusivist ideology of mission to Gentiles, not Jews. Hare's arguments stem from a clear presuppositional commitment about Matthew's intentions, imagining that he "looks back at the era of persecution, surveying both its pre-war and post-war phases from a vantage point outside the synagogue community." Hare, *The Theme of Jewish Persecution*, 127.

path traveled in response to the traditional Christian methodology, as illustrated in chapter one. Along the way I will certainly point out oddities of scholarly interpretation in relation to the conclusions of the second chapter.

My investigation focuses on interpretations of the OD that refer to first-century fulfillment in clear distinction from futuristic fulfillment at the end of the world. A wide variety of scholarly conjecture spans from the nineteenth-century into our own day. However, this survey will not necessitate much interaction with the development of scholarly conjecture underlying such evaluations or even how each scholar built upon or reacted to the theories of others within their own academic circles. Such historical studies have been documented and summarized elsewhere.[13] There is also no need to parse through the historical development underlying the so-called "delayed Parousia,"[14]

---

13. George R. Beasley-Murray, *Jesus and the Last Days: The Interpretation of the Olivet Discourse* (Peabody, MA: Hendrickson Publishers, 1993); *Jesus and the Future: An Examination of the Criticism of The Eschatological Discourse, Mark 13 with Special Reference to the Little Apocalypse Theory* (London: Macmillan & Co LTD, 1954); N.T. Wright, *History and Eschatology: Jesus and the Promise of Natural Theology* (Waco, TX: Baylor University Press, 2019)**,** 41-69 and 165-88; *Jesus and the Victory of God,* 3-124. Due to the superabundance of scholars presented throughout Beasley-Murray's work, I will be using his studies as guides for selecting critical scholars of the nineteenth and early twentieth centuries.

14. For a detailed history of how the "delayed parousia" came to be and evolved over time, see James Carleton Paget, "Some Observations on the Problem of the Delay of the Parousia in the Historiography of Its Discussion" in *The "Delay of the Parousia,"* EC, vol. 9 (Tubingen, Germany: Mohr Siebeck, 2018), 9-36. For a helpful critique of this "delay" offered by Paget and others, see N.T. Wright's essay in the same volume, "Hope Deferred? Against the Dogma of Delay," 37-82. For arguments attempting to justify this "delay," see Richard Bauckham, *The Jewish World Around the New Testament: Collected Essays 1,* WUNT, vol. 233 (Tubingen, Germany: Mohr Siebeck, 2008), 65-88; Stephen S. Smalley, "The Delay of the Parousia," *JBL,* vol. LXXXIII (Philadelphia, PA: Society of Biblical Literature, March 1964), 41-54; Vicky Balabanski, *Eschatology in the Making: Mark, Matthew, and the Didache* (New York, NY: Cambridge University Press, 1997), 4-23; David E. Aune, "The Significance of the Delay of the Parousia for Early Christianity," *Current Issues in Biblical and Patristic Interpretation: Studies*

although that conviction, which is alive and well today, remains important for appreciating the findings of this chapter.[15]

I will attempt to show that most arguments in favor of such assumptions are predicated, at least in part, on either the questionable methodology or traditional assumptions (and sometimes both together) proposed by the church fathers. Modern interpreters appear to be aware of this patristic methodology, for they seem to either question some futuristic interpretations about the end of the world while accepting an original first-century fulfillment for part of the discourse, or they *react* vigorously to futuristic (post-70 CE) interpretations. The former approach tends to theorize within boundaries of orthodoxy, whereas the latter is evinced in callous disregard for Jesus as a prophet, due to either his own or his apostles' alleged misunderstandings. In order to reach such conclusions, there must be an awareness of deeply rooted Christian tradition.

Ultimately, once it is clear that modern critical scholarship has adopted an awareness of methodologies proposed by patristic, medieval, and Reformation-era theologians, the following question needs to

---

in Honor of Merrill C. Tenney Presented by His Former Students, ed. Gerald F. Hawthorne (Grand Rapids, MI: William B. Eerdmans Publishing Company, 1975), 87-109. For a brief and important (yet ultimately unconvincing) summary of the most important theological problems involving the concept of the Parousia, see W. Harold Mare, "A Study of the New Testament Concept of the Parousia" in Hawthorne, *Current Issues,* 341-5. For an alternative approach to this "delayed" parousia, along with a surprising twist of philosophical conjecture that purports to be faithful to "Christian tradition," see Christopher M. Hays in collaboration with Brandon Gallaher, Julia S. Konstantinovsky, Richard J. Ounsworth, OP, and C.A. Strine, *When the Son of Man Didn't Come: A Constructive Proposal on the Delay of the Parousia,* (Minneapolis, MN: Fortress Press; 2016). This chapter will close with a summary and assessment of this proposal by Hays and his colleagues.

15. Balabanski notes that "In modern scholarship the delay of Christ's return and the presumed disappointment it engendered has been seen as a primary factor, and in some cases as *the* primary factor, in the development of Christian eschatology." Balabanski, *Eschatology in the Making*, 4. Italics are original.

be addressed: Have modern scholars also assumed too much in their explications of the OD?

4.1.1 STRAUSS, HASE, AND H. A. W. MEYER (CIRCA 1850)

In his massively influential three-volume quest *The Life of Jesus*, first published in 1835-1836, David Strauss comments on Matthew 24:4-35 and the vulnerability of orthodox Christian interpretations who attribute futuristic, "end of the world" predictions to Jesus. Strauss notes that Jesus "at first" speaks of the destruction of Jerusalem. That comment is followed by Strauss's own assumption that the remainder of the OD refers to "his return at the end of all things":

> It is impossible to evade the acknowledgement that in this discourse, if we do not mutilate it to suit our own views, *Jesus at first speaks of the destruction of Jerusalem* and further on, and until the close, of his return at the end of all things, and that he places the two events in an immediate connexion.[16]

This methodology did not probe deep enough into the real and obvious problem of historical Christian exegesis. For Strauss, Jesus' predictions about the "end of all things" were *wrong*, thus illustrating a fallible Savior.[17] The rationalizations of historic Christianity simply will not suffice insofar as arguments about cataclysmic nearness ultimately deliver a message for all ages to prepare for his return some day:

> As it will soon be eighteen centuries since the destruction of Jerusalem, and an equally long period since the generation contemporary with Jesus disappeared from the earth, while

---

16. Strauss, *Life of Jesus* (ET London, 1846) 3:95., as cited in Beasley-Murray, *The Last Days*, 3. Italics added.

17. Beasley-Murray, *The Future*, 3.

his visible return and the end of the world which he associated with it, have not taken place, *the announcement of Jesus appears so far to have been erroneous.*[18]

. . .

One whose mind is in a healthy state conceives the possible to be *possible*, the probable as *probable*; and if he wishes to abide by the truth, he so exhibits them to others; the man, on the contrary, by whom the merely possible or probable is conceived as the *real*, is mistaken; and he who, without so regarding it himself, yet for a moral or religious reason so represents it to the others, permits himself to use a pious fraud.[19]

According to Strauss, the only *alternative* to Jesus being "flagrantly false" is to suggest "premeditated deception" on the part of his disciples and the gospels they produce.[20] However, most likely, Jesus is simply a false prophet with a grossly mistaken following.

Karl Hase, the great-grandfather of Dietrich Bonhoeffer and distinguished professor of historical theology in Jena, composed his own historical account of Jesus' life as an attempt to explain how Jesus' self-understanding evolved. In the first edition of his commentary on the OD, he summarizes his own futuristic interpretation this way:

As He now sat on the Mount of Olives and looked down on the Holy City, his view of the future, proceeding from a very clear comprehension of the history of the world and from the deepest understanding of the kingdom of God, disclosed itself to the apostles in prophetic pictures . . . (viz. concerning) the destruction of Jerusalem, the ruin of the Roman Empire through the migration of the nations and the

---

18. Beasley-Murray, *The Future*, 3. Italics original.

19. Beasley-Murray, *The Future*, 3-4. Italics original.

20. Beasley-Murray, *The Future*, 4.

victory of Christianity . . . [He] takes in at a glance the coming centuries according to his spirit and comprehends them with his plan.[21]

According to both Strauss and Hase, the OD describes distinctive events in connection and succession: First, Jerusalem's destruction and next, the "end" of all things in the ensuing centuries. For all editions of Strauss' work, Jesus' predictions about the "end of the world" are a pious fraud; for Hase's initial publication, Jesus *symbolically* describes the triumph of his kingdom at the end of the world by means of predictions surrounding Jerusalem's demise in the first century. In the early stages of forming an explanation, Hase imagines events surrounding 70 CE to be precursors and types of a great antitype: the destruction of the world. For later editions of Hase's same publication, it becomes evident that Strauss' reasoning influenced and changed his methodology completely. He eventually sides with Strauss insofar as a futuristic "second coming" at the "end of the world" is concerned.[22]

H. A. W. Meyer speculates in a curiously disparate manner, but concludes with familiar results. In his commentary on Matthew's Gospel, he argues that Jesus' references to his own *Parousia* are spoken in prophetic language that mixes the "real" sense with the "ideal" sense among his apostles. When Jesus describes signs and wonders in prophetic language, he utilizes these senses. "Matthew" then records it all in an orderly fashion. Jesus speaks of the events leading up to the destruction of Jerusalem in Matthew 24:4-28, but the rest of his speech alludes to various senses of Christ's *Parousia* in 24:29–25:46. By utilizing multiple senses his objective is to preserve a message about the "real" kingdom to come, in which a literal sense of bodily resurrection, judgment, and the final setting up of his kingdom will take place at the "end." Jesus' presentation is multi-faceted because he

---

21. Hase, *Leben Jesu* (Leipzig, 1835), 224, as cited in Beasley-Murray, *The Last Days,* 5.

22. Beasley-Murray, *The Future*, 6.

knows in advance that his apostles might mistakenly apply an "ideal kingdom" and "ideal Parousia" of their own imagination to real events within the first century.

By anticipating their confusion of the *ideal* with the *real*, Jesus hopes the ideal would inevitably fade away once Jerusalem is destroyed without the real *Parousia* occurring at that time. Jesus only intends the *real* to remain "the object of expectation." Commenting on the OD, Meyer writes:

> Jesus had most definitely set the destruction of Jerusalem in the lifetime of that generation; and at the same time had seen and proclaimed in prophetic symbol what could not be hidden from him, the connection in which the victory of his ideal kingdom would stand to this catastrophe; nothing more natural therefore than that the further the time of the generation declined to its expiration, the more surely was the parousia awaited as occurring immediately after the destruction of Jerusalem. . . . Inevitably the form of the expectation reflected on the form of the promise; the ideal parousia and founding of the kingdom were identified with the real, so that the former was obliterated in the tradition and only the latter remained the object of expectation.[23]

We can see that Meyer, along with Strauss and Hase, imagines that Jesus' OD in Matthew's Gospel refers to two distinctive events. For Meyer, the first is a proclamation of prophetic symbols that could be confused with events leading up to the destruction of Jerusalem, delineated in Matthew 24:4-28. But such is *only a foil* used by Jesus, for he knows his apostles might mistake his real *Parousia*, also mentioned therein (vv. 29ff), with their "ideal kingdom." Matthew paints Jesus

---

23. Meyer, *Kritisch Exegetisches Handbuch über das Evangelium des Mathaus*, 3rd ed. (Gottingen, 1855), 409ff., cited in Beasley-Murray, *The Last Days*, 9-10.

as subtly and intimately connecting the two in order that Christian tradition will later focus upon the "real" sense.

4.1.2 PFLEIDERER, WENDT, AND GESS (CIRCA 1880)

Otto Pfleiderer was a nineteenth-century scholar who sought coherence in Mark's version of the OD in order to establish a foundation for understanding Matthew and Luke's versions. In his venture to understand the OD's message he subdivides it into multiple sections. Instead of hazarding to identify transitional verses between first-century fulfillment and end-of-the-world fulfillment, he strives to distinguish between *authentic* and *inauthentic* sayings.

Mark 13:7-8, 14-20, and 24-27 are his first excisions. Each of them is comprised of "apocalyptic" sayings attributed to Jesus. Such sayings, however, are not necessarily authentic and should be classified as separate from the rest of the discourse. Pfleiderer applies these "apocalyptic" sayings to "world events that affect the nations and natural life."[24] Because the central "saying" (vv. 14-20) is clearest in its reference to the first-century "Jewish catastrophe," and there is an "impatient expectation of an immediately impending parousia" derived from it,[25] Pfleiderer surmises that Mark needed to temper such first-century "apocalyptic" compositions. Therefore, the non-apocalyptic sayings of Mark 13:9-13, 21-23, and 28-32 (which correspond with Matthew 24:9-14, 23-26, and 32-35) were inserted alongside "apocalyptic" sayings. These non-apocalyptic divisions likely constituted the genuine eschatological sayings of Jesus intended to warn Christian believers of "threatening dangers" while exhorting them to faithfulness.[26]

---

24. Beasley-Murray, *The Last Days*, 35.

25. Beasley-Murray, *The Last Days*, 36.

26. Beasley-Murray, *The Last Days*, 35.

The closing section of Mark's OD (13:33-37) supplies "a cosmic background for the initiation of the sovereignty of Christ with his elect,"[27] which does not necessarily entail an *authentic* prediction about the end of the world or events within the first century. Rather, it merely illustrates the *hope* of the Lord's "coming" within the lifetime of the present generation.[28]

This approach allegedly settles the problems arising from discrepancies between the disciples' questions and the answers attributed to Jesus. To summarize, the disciples ask Jesus two questions related to events they expect to occur in that generation. But Mark possesses a combination of sources with responses attributed to Jesus, some of which only nineteenth-century scholars discover to be "inauthentic." Mark recognizes that at least one "apocalyptic" saying alludes to Jerusalem's impending destruction. In light of this, the entire discourse necessitates some tempering because of the people's general impatience. Mark then incorporates some sayings that are general warnings for Christian believers. Mark's final composition of the OD intends to exhort Christians to hope for the Lord's "coming" within their own generation, even though no one—not even Jesus—actually knows that specific day or hour.

Hans H. Wendt follows a similar path as Pfleiderer by dividing Mark's OD into authentic and inauthentic sayings. Wendt differs from Pfleiderer insofar as he distinguishes Mark 13:7-9a, 14-20, 24-27, and 30-31 as "apocalyptical" insertions of an otherwise authentic discourse from the lips of Jesus. He considers the authentic sayings to be verses 1-6, 9b-13, 21-23, 28-29, and 32-37. Wendt also proposes that verses 21-23 properly belong prior to verses 9b-13, which allegedly improves Mark's purposes.[29] By identifying these authentic

---

27. Beasley-Murray, *The Last Days*, 35-6.

28. Beasley-Murray, *The Last Days*, 37.

29. Beasley-Murray, *The Last Days*, 42-3. Wendt viewed Mark 13 as consisting of two authentic discourses. One discourse pertained to persecuted disciples, and another pertained to "Jews facing the tribulation of Judea." Beasley-Murray,

"sayings," Jesus can be viewed as having no *special* knowledge of future events and no ability to prophesy about any *specific signs or portents*. Christian tradition believes Jesus had special knowledge about specific future events mainly because other evangelists relied upon Mark's version with its inauthentic, apocalyptic "sayings."

When asked how the authentic group of "sayings" relates to the questions asked by Jesus' disciples, Wendt's response is that those questions are related to events in the first century. Modern investigations into these "sayings" are necessary because Jesus' response to his disciples' question relates to first-century events with first-century fulfillment. Highlighting *inauthentic* "sayings" helps eliminate most of the confusion across all three Synoptic Gospels insofar as the fulfillment of predictive prophecy is concerned. By determining authentic sayings in Mark's version (which is the primary source for Matthew and Luke's versions), Jesus can be trusted as one who only offers non-specific expectations of soon-coming persecutions.

Wendt's commitment to first-century fulfillment, tendentious as it appears, is ironic because his entire study was predicated on the OD containing inauthentic "apocalyptic" sayings that were distinguishable from authentic sayings. In doing so he adopts many common assumptions that *had already formed the major basis of scholarly objection to the OD's authenticity.*[30] The OD clearly pertains to a first-century audience with first-century expectations; other parts are assumed to be "apocalyptic" and futuristic. Therefore, Wendt's scholarly response to this "Synoptic problem" assumes just enough to be compatible with a consistent, contextual reading of first-century fulfillment in the OD, but he adopts far too much scholarly conjecture in the process of proving his point.

W. F. Gess attempts to solve these and other perceived problems between first-century fulfillment and end-of-the-world events by

---

The Last Days, 58. Both still originated around the first century and therefore pertained to first-century expectations.

30. Beasley-Murray, *The Last Days,* 44.

arguing that "Jesus anticipated a period *between* Jerusalem's fall and his Parousia."[31] Supposedly, "Jesus could not possibly have placed his parousia immediately after the events of AD 70."[32] Instead of focusing on Mark's OD, Luke's version contains the key source-material requiring rearrangement. According to Beasley-Murray, "Gess would solve the problem . . . by inserting Luke 21:24 at v. 19."[33] By reconfiguring Luke's version of the OD and arguing that its 'sayings' contain authentic source-material for other Gospels, all problems seemed to be resolved. "[A]n intermediate period" can be "set between the fall of Jerusalem and the Parousia," allowing the discourse to run "a straight course through history."[34]

In all these examples of selective rearrangement within the OD, two common assumptions remain. First, the events described in parallel with Matthew 24:4-35 involve some first-century fulfillment that coincides with the *first* question of Jesus' disciples, whereas parallels after verse 35 *only* refer to futuristic events. Second, exhortations surrounding the first-century destruction of Jerusalem are separable from the Parousia.

4.1.3 ZAHN, MERX, AND LAGRANGE (CIRCA 1900–1920)

Forty years after Gess, Theodor Zahn follows another method of selective interpretation. Zahn's rearrangement depends more on the conceptual nature of the OD as a whole, and not so much the modern dissections of its "authentic" parts. For Zahn, the "abomination of desolation," as he understood that reference, could *not* refer to events

---

31. Beasley-Murray, *The Last Days,* 124. Italics added.
32. Beasley-Murray, *The Last Days,* 124.
33. Beasley-Murray, *The Last Days,* 124.
34. Beasley-Murray, *The Last Days,* 124.

fulfilled in the first century.[35] Likewise, Jesus mentions preaching a gospel to *all* of the "world,"[36] which, in Zahn's mind, could only occur *after* the destruction of Jerusalem. Therefore, a conceptual gap must exist between the destruction of Jerusalem and the *Parousia, even though the disciples' questions appear to anticipate first-century fulfillment.* All the verses in Matthew's Gospel pertaining to a first-century catastrophe would occur as Jesus predicted in that generation; whereas all the verses pertaining to the "end" would occur around the *Parousia*.[37]

Syriac scholar Adalbert Merx reacts strongly to the expectations of a future world wherein Jesus' promises to the people of Israel would await fulfillment. As he understands the eschatology of Jesus, disciples in the first century anticipate persecution, wars, and the impending destruction of their temple, which accompanies their preaching of Jesus' gospel. Because Merx thinks much of Mark's OD pertains to first century events, he limits the authentic sayings of Jesus to verses 1–22. Even the verses traditionally assigned to the *Parousia*—like the parable of the fig tree in 13:28-29—are speculated as being falsely produced.[38]

---

35. McNicol, along with a handful of contemporary twentieth-century scholars, argues otherwise: "Matthew appears to have had the presumption that his readers would be able to identify the Horrible Desecration when it occurred. Since it was common knowledge that the temple in previous times had been profaned by Gentiles (Antiochus Epiphanes, Pompey, Gaius's attempt in 40-41 CE to compel the Jews to do obeisance before Roman standards), it would seem natural in the political turmoil of the late 60s that Matthew could conceive of something similar happening again at the instigation of the Romans." McNicol, *Jesus' Directions*, 101-02.

36. In Matthew's version of the OD, Jesus does not say that his gospel would be preached to all the "world" in the global sense which most people would interpret the term "world" today. The Greek term used here (and nowhere else by Matthew) is οἰκουμένη, which repeatedly refers to the Roman "empire" throughout the New Testament. (cf. Luke 2:1; 4:5; Acts 11:28; 17:6; 19:27; 24:5).

37. Beasley-Murray, *The Last Days*, 125-6.

38. Beasley-Murray, *The Last Days*, 82-3.

The Roman Catholic scholar Marie-Joseph Legrange was another critic who reacted to those portions of Mark's OD commonly attributed to the future Parousia of Jesus. To resolve the confusion, he insists that Mark's version actually contains *two* discourses in parallel with each other. Intriguingly, this creates a clever parallel not too far removed from the actual conceptual arrangement of Matthew 24:4-22 alongside 24:23-35.[39]

According to Legrange, verses 6-8 describe a time of distress regarding Jerusalem's destruction, and verses 19-20 describe a time of distress regarding the *Parousia*. Likewise, verses 9-13 describe how his apostles were to behave in light of Jerusalem's impending destruction, and 21-23 describe how they are to behave in light of the *Parousia*. Verses 14-18 refer to the catastrophe of Jerusalem's destruction, while 24-27 refer to the catastrophe of Christ's *Parousia*. Finally, verses 28-31 are parables of Jerusalem's destruction, whereas 32-37 are parables of Christ's *Parousia*. Beasley-Murray has provided a helpful layout of this parallel division:[40]

Discourse on the ruin of the Temple		Discourse on the Coming of the Son of Man
6-8	The time of distress	19-20
9-13	How disciples are to behave	21-23
14-18	The catastrophe	24-27
28-31	The parables	32-37

Regarding all the sayings associated with the *Parousia*, Legrange is hesitant to affirm their authenticity unless they are authentically separate discourses altogether. For those sayings associated with Jerusalem's de-

---

39. On Matthew's conceptual arrangement, see the "*eight* sections of prophetic response" in **2.1.2 (a)**.

40. Beasley-Murray, *The Last Days*, 84. See also Beasley-Murray, *The Future*, 85.

struction alone, there is no room for doubting authenticity. However, because there appear to be two distinctive discourses within Mark's version that *ought* to be considered *entirely separate* from each other, Mark must have "blocked" them off from one another.[41] Legrange thereby raises some doubt as to whether the sayings about Jerusalem's destruction that are commonly associated with a future *Parousia* in other passages of Scripture, can ultimately be attributed to the lips of Jesus. Jesus did not promise to "come" in that generation because Mark 13:24-27 (cf. Matt. 24:29-31) is a separate "block" of discourse from 13:28-31 (cf. Matt. 24:32-35), and the latter block clearly describes the ruin of Jerusalem's city and temple within the first century.

Such highly selective interpretations of what Jesus taught and meant all assume that Jesus' OD, insofar as Matthew's version parallels Mark's version, was not organized clearly or thoughtfully by either evangelist. Separate blocks, false productions, or bewildering chronological gaps of "sayings" are all clumsily compiled together with the best of human intentions, even under divine inspiration. In contrast with this, I attempted to show in chapter two that Matthew arranged and paired each section of his discourse so that Jesus' answers to all of his disciples' questions are clear and consistent.

4.1.4 MANSON AND R.H. LIGHTFOOT (CIRCA 1930)

According to T. W. Manson's research, Mark's version of the OD contains three distinctive sources compiled into one, and each represents a different tradition than the sources used to compile Luke's version.[42] The first source of sayings splits into two sections and pertains to predictions about Jerusalem in the first century (Mark 13:1-4 and 14-20, which parallel Matt. 24:1-3a and 15-22). The second source describes persecutions of Jesus' disciples and is more general in its descriptions

41. Beasley-Murray, *The Future*, 85.
42. Beasley-Murray, *The Last Days,* 94.

(Mark 13:5-13; cf. Matt. 24:4-14). The third source involves the end of the world (Mark 13:24-31; cf. Matt. 24:29-35).[43] For Manson there is no intrinsic solution to the seemingly disparate interpretations of the OD apart from identifying source materials. The OD's interpretation depends on the proper identification of each source.

Contrary to this view, R. H. Lightfoot argues that the chief significance of the OD is not to be found in its sources but in its literary design. In all the Synoptic versions, but especially in Mark's, the OD is "designed by the evangelists as the immediate introduction to the passion narrative."[44] By comparing Mark's OD with the events described in the chapters that follow immediately thereafter (Mark 14-15), Jesus' passion narrative seems to be an eschatological event. The eschatologically-oriented passion event could then *proleptically* anticipate fulfillment in the *Parousia*. According to Lightfoot, Christ's passion "is an eschatological event, participating in the finality of the consummation for which it prepares."[45] As confusing as this interpretation of the OD's literary design might seem, it cleverly deflects attention away from the OD's first-century references without overtly denying their relevance. By shifting attention away from first-century references, a futuristic Parousia can remain assumed, and all first-century references in the OD can become, by each evangelist's design, "subordinated to Christian ends" (i.e., pushed beyond *mere* first-century fulfillment).[46]

With such a view in mind, one must wonder if that conflicts with the evidence presented by Peter Leithart in chapter two (above). Although Leithart showed that Matthew has designed the placement

---

43. Beasley-Murray, *The Last Days*, 93-96. Beasley-Murray notes that Manson is not clear about how verses 32-37 should be analyzed. Nothing is mentioned about Manson's view of verses 21-23.

44. Lightfoot, *The Gospel Message of St. Mark* (Oxford, 1950), 51, as cited in Beasley-Murray, *The Last Days*, 100.

45. Beasley-Murray, *The Last Days*, 101.

46. Beasley-Murray, *The Last Days*, 101.

of his fifth discourse in preparation for the passion, the passion narrative presents a type of Israel's death and resurrection leading into the "great commission" of the Lord's "anointed one." The OD's prophetic pronouncement of soon-coming judgment upon Jerusalem and its temple is a predictable precursor to the Gospel's typological message of *Israel's* death, resurrection, and "great commission." In order to conclude that Matthew's 'passion' and resurrection narrative *participates in the consummation of the world* and its futuristic final judgment, one must assume in advance that the OD necessarily entails a prophetic message about the consummation of the world *as we experience it* and our final judgment at *its* end. Yet as we have seen in chapter two, Matthew neatly structured his Gospel to *avoid such misinterpretations.*

No scholar that I am aware of *denies* that somewhere in Matthew's OD, or in any of its Synoptic parallels, Jesus was asked at least one question about the destruction of the temple in Jerusalem. Also, no one denies that such a cataclysmic event occurred in the first century. Therefore, to reason alongside Manson and Lightfoot, one must first take for granted their unproven assumptions about a futuristic consummation and judgment of the cosmos within Matthew's OD. Even though such assumptions might be valid for interpreting other statements within Scripture, they have not proven helpful for understanding Matthew's version.

4.1.5 LENSKI, E. SCHWEIZER, HENDRIKSEN, AND RATZINGER (CIRCA 1960—1970)

Lenski was an evangelical Lutheran pastor and influential professor whose major works were published decades after his death. In his attempt to adhere to the traditional methodology of the ancient church fathers, he insists that it is "fruitless" for Christians to speculate *how* Jesus' apostles "conceived their questions" on the Mount of Olives.[47]

---

47. R.C.H. Lenski, *The Interpretation of St. Matthew's Gospel* (Columbus, OH: Wartburg Press, 1943), 929.

361

"Far more fruitful," he says, "is the proper understanding of the long reply of Jesus by which he intended to enlighten the Twelve in regard to all they had asked."

Unsurprisingly, Lenski notes that by asking when "all these things" will take place, it is obvious that such a question refers to "the destruction of the temple."[48] But when they ask about his *Parousia*, their conversation enlarges. Supposedly, they already knew about his Parousia, which Lenski described as "Jesus' return to judgment and of the winding up of all the affairs of the world-age" at the end of history as we know it.[49]

Again, in line with the patristic methodology illustrated in chapter one, Lenski offers a lot of evidence in favor of first-century fulfillment regarding Jesus' initial response in Matthew 24:4-28. For Lenski, the transitional verse is somewhere between Matthew 24:27-29. His comments in this regard are worth noting at length:

> We see how exactly Jesus answers the questions addressed to him in v. 3; first, about the destruction of the Temple and, then, about the end of the world and his Parousia. The first sketch (v. 4-14) presents a world survey which brings us to τὸ τέλος, "the end." The second sketch (v. 15-28) presents the overthrow of the Jewish nation and brings us a reference to the true παρουσία which will be like a mighty flash of lightning and will not occur in connection with the Jewish calamity. Now Jesus tells just what "the end" and the Parousia will be, for the two will occur together.[50]

---

48. Lenski, *Interpretation*, 928.

49. Lenski, *Interpretation*, 928.

50. Lenski, *Interpretation*, 946-47.

This, according to Lenski, is the "proper understanding" of Jesus' long reply; it is simply taken for granted that Jesus answered the first question first.

The exposition of Eduard Schweizer, a Swiss Reformed pastor and professor, is not as detailed as Lenski's with regard to first-century events and their fulfillment. Nevertheless, he agrees with Lenski that a transition takes place between verses 27-29.[51] According to Schweizer, Jesus "has already referred to the final coming of Jesus" in Matthew 23:39, only a few verses prior to the disciples' questions. Consequently, Schweizer cannot help but continue to assume that the "coming" of Jesus in the remainder of the discourse *is the same* as in 23:39. He presupposes that Jesus could not be referring to first-century fulfillment *alone within the OD*. Only Jesus' initial responses to his disciples' *first* question could possibly refer to events in the first century. Schweizer's comments in this regard are crystal clear:

> Matthew . . . clearly distinguishes between the judgment upon Israel for rejecting Jesus, which can be seen in the destruction of the Temple in the year 70, and the second coming of the Son of Man, which will inaugurate the Last Judgment.[52]

Hendriksen, a Calvinist minister and professor, decided to break away from the traditional methodology adopted by Lenski and Schweizer, offering in its place a slight-of-hand suggestion that Matthew's OD is actually *not* his fifth discourse (as the literary structure makes clear). Instead, he claims that Matthew's OD is a fifth and sixth discourse *combined*.

Hendriksen argues that "by means of this manipulation," Matthew reduces the discourses to *appear* like five discourses, "comparable

---

51. Eduard Schweizer, *The Good News According to Matthew*, trans. David E. Green (Atlanta, GA: John Knox Press, 1977), 449-54.

52. Schweizer, *The Good News*, 448-9.

to the five books of Moses."[53] However, this manipulation "cannot succeed" in convincing anyone to believe that both describe first-century events, because the truly fifth discourse is delivered in Herod's Temple while the *sixth* discourse takes place on the Mount of Olives.[54]

---

53. William Hendriksen, *The Gospel of Matthew* (Grand Rapids, MI: Baker Book House, 1973), 846.

54. I mentioned this conceptual scheme briefly in **2.1.2**. Supposedly, Matthew 23 must be an entirely *separable* (as opposed to *distinguishable*) discourse from chapters 24–25 due to the *topographical* transition which takes place in Matthew's audience and scenery. However, as Vicky Balabanski has aptly noted (*Eschatology in the Making*, 136), such arguments do not "give sufficient weight to the fact that in the parable discourse of Matt. 13, a similar shift in both audience and scene takes place . . . (13:36)." In other words, Balabanski notices that it is rare to find modern scholars who assert there must be *two separate discourses* within chapter 13. Why then insist, given the same shift in audience and scenery, that there must be two *separate* discourses between Matthew 23-25? Another method used to divide Matthew 24 from 23 is to place chapter 23 into a *previous* literary unit. A contemporary example of this is seen in the research of Brian Carrier, who insists that "Matt 21–23 forms a textual unit." Brian Carrier, *Earthquakes and Eschatology in the Gospel According to Matthew*, WUNT, vol. 534 (Tubingen, Germany: Mohr Siebeck, 2020), 119n48. Carrier's defense of this claim is not very weighty. The reasons he presents are as follows: "in 21:1–12 Jesus comes from the Mount of Olives and enters Jerusalem and the temple; in 24:1–3 Jesus exits the temple (and Jerusalem) by way of the Mount of Olives. In 21:9 Jesus enters amidst praise from Ps 118:26 ("Blessed is the one who comes in the name of the Lord!"); in 23:39 Jesus repeats these very words to Jerusalem before leaving the temple and city. Jerusalem is mentioned in 21:1, 10 (Ἰεροσόλυμα) and 23:37 (Ἰερουσαλήμ). Furthermore, the discourse of Matt 24–25 breaks the narrative flow of Matt 21–23." Carrier, *Earthquakes*, 119n48. Besides failing to notice the balanced chiastic framework of Matthew's entire Gospel, as noted above in **2.1.1** (which illustrated clearly differentiated portions of discourses and narratives), Carrier also fails to notice that the narrative section of Matthew 19–22 is chiastically arranged and *bracketed* with pericopes that match each other in themes and terminology, thereby positioning chapters 19–22 as one continuous narrative section. In both chapters (i.e., 19 and 22) Jesus uses identical terminology, which Matthew utilizes to form a large *inclusio* around this narrative section. He does so with the phrase, "you shall love your neighbor as yourself (19:19; cf. 22:39). In both chapters Jesus also teaches with rhetoric about "the kingdom of heaven" (19:12-15, 23ff.; cf. 22:1-2). Matthew

Therefore, as Hendriksen confidently remarks, "two momentous events are here *intertwined*, namely, *a.* the judgment upon Jerusalem (its fall in the year A.D. 70), and *b.* the final judgment at the close of the world's history."[55] In merging these two discourses, Jesus only predicts Jerusalem's "approaching catastrophe as *a type* of the tribulation at the end [...]".[56]

By intertwining two discourses into one and imagining Jesus' answers according to two corresponding *types*, Matthew portrays Jesus' remarks about the end of world history as "painting in colors borrowed from the destruction of Jerusalem by the Romans."[57]

---

19 also begins with scenery that is *peculiar* to chapter 22, in which we find some pharisees approaching Jesus to test him (19:3; cf. 22:15). They ask Jesus about distinct topics related to *marriage with multiple spouses* and attaining *eternal life*, all the while arguing from the Torah along with Jesus (19:3-12, 16-22; cf. 22:23-40). By beginning Matthew 19 the way chapter 22 ends, Matthew has clearly framed chapter 19 so that it sets the stage of *upcoming confrontation in Jerusalem among its ruling class*. After Jesus had been tested by Pharisees, had argued with those twisting the Torah, and had made claims about the kingdom of heaven within Matthew 19 (thereby mirroring the themes of chapter 22), Matthew follows through with a parable from Jesus about a "master of a house" who owns a "vineyard." Immediately after this parable, Jesus warns his disciples that the "*Son* of man" is about to be killed in Jerusalem (20:1-19). This exact same imagery is mirrored *immediately prior* to chapter 22 where we find another parable about the "master of a house" who owns a "vineyard." In the end of that parable the tenants of the vineyard want to kill the Master's "son" (21:33-44), just as Jesus warned back in 20:18-19. All of this points to a chiastic structure for chapters 19–22, with Jesus' entry into Jerusalem as the very center of one literary *narrative* unit. All of the arguments in chapter 19 take place "as Jesus was going up to Jerusalem" (20:17). By the end of Matthew 22, Jesus has an established "presence" inside Jerusalem, thus solidifying one continuous narrative section before the fifth block of discourse begins. So then, in actuality, Brian Carrier is mistaken: Matthew 23 actually "breaks the narrative flow" of 19-22 (contra his claim that chapter 24 breaks the narrative flow of chs. 21-23), because chapter 23 *begins* the following literary *discourse* unit (chs. 23–25).

55. Hendriksen, *Matthew*, 846.

56. Hendriksen, *Matthew*, 847.

57. Hendriksen, *Matthew*, 847.

As a result of such borrowing and intertwining of two disparate discourses, Hendriksen is unwilling to locate a transitional verse; but he is willing to acknowledge that the "lofty language" of Matthew 24:29-31 and 25:31-46 *appears* to refer to "Jerusalem's destruction in A.D. 70,"[58] which is far more than Lenski and Schweizer are willing to admit. Conveniently, Hendriksen could confidently claim that no "exegete is able completely to untangle what is here intertwined, so as to indicate accurately for each individual passage just how much refers to Jerusalem's fall, and how much to the great tribulation and second coming."[59] For Hendriksen, it is unfortunate that Matthew has not structured his final combination of discourses so that it more clearly differentiates between Jerusalem's destruction and "the end" of the world.

Joseph Ratzinger, who would later be appointed Pope Benedict XVI, chose yet another route in distinction from his confessionally protestant contemporaries. In predictably slippery academese, he suggests that Jesus' message becomes intelligible when two very different predictions are *perceived* as one, in very close relation to each other. According to Ratzinger, "Jesus' message [in the OD] becomes intelligible for us through the echo effect it has created in history."[60] By means of this "echo effect" in which Jesus prophesied two different events in time—which Ratzinger demarcates as "the imminent destruction of Jerusalem and the Parousia"[61]—Christians are given the impression that these two events are designed to be "temporally related,"[62] even though each takes place at different times in world history. According to this supposed echo effect, an "impression persists that

---

58. Hendriksen, *Matthew*, 847.

59. Hendriksen, *Matthew*, 847-8.

60. Joseph Ratzinger, *Eschatology: Death and Eternal Life* (Washington, DC: The Catholic University of America Press, 1988), 41.

61. Ratzinger, *Eschatology*, 39.

62. Ratzinger, *Eschatology*, 39.

the trials and tribulations entailed in the destruction of Jerusalem *are* connected in time with the events of the end of the world."[63]

According to Ratzinger, Matthew 24:15-22, Mark 13:14-20, and Luke 21:20-23 clearly illustrate Jesus' answer to the disciple's *first* question, and all those verses "describe the fall of Jerusalem."[64] Indeed, his "echo effect" paradigm alludes to some kind of literary transition—from Jerusalem's destruction to the future *Parousia*—taking place between Matthew 24:29-31. What is unique about this "temporal relation" is Ratzinger's conclusion. Instead of focusing on the methodology, he insists that, "The fall of Jerusalem is not the end of the world but the start of a new age in salvation history."[65] For

---

63. Ratzinger, *Eschatology*, 40.

64. Ratzinger, *Eschatology*, 38.

65. Ratzinger, *Eschatology*, 39. Steven Smith, a dutiful Roman Catholic theologian, sympathizes with Ratzinger's rhetoric when he writes: "This prophecy of the coming destruction of the Temple by Jesus must have certainly dismayed his disciples. First, on a purely physical level, the beauty and grandeur of Herod's Temple exceeded most of the seven wonders of the ancient world. It was more than twice the size of the Acropolis in Athens. . . . Would not God spare them such a catastrophe? Jesus's prophecy came to fruition just a generation after his death, precisely in 70 AD, when the Romans conquered Jerusalem under Titus, who burned the Temple to the ground. Second, and more deeply, the notion that this could happen in the future was so cataclysmic to the disciples' worldview *that it could only happen as part of the end of the age altogether.*" Steven C. Smith, *The House of the Lord: A Catholic Biblical Theology of God's Temple Presence in the Old and New Testaments* (Steubenville, OH: Franciscan University Press, 2017), 282; italics added.

After presenting a case for the "end of the age" coinciding with the destruction of the temple in Jerusalem in 70 CE, Smith adds the following caveat without providing any reasonable warrant (Scripture or otherwise) for its justification: "A final point may be added about Jesus's words about the coming destruction of the Temple. On the surface of things, *it appears that the explanation given to the disciples conflates the destruction of the Temple with the end of the age as two connected events that would occur together.* This is not simply the case; the Temple's demise and the 'end of the age' were not one in the same event, nor were their fates tied. To be sure, there is an imminence to *both* future events as described in the Gospel. Yet each had its own 'event horizon' as well as dis-

Ratzinger, the "echo effect" places Christian interpretation somewhere *between* the two events, acknowledging the significance of Jerusalem's destruction as the end of the old covenant administration while holding firmly to the expected *Parousia* at the end of this new covenant administration.[66] In this manner, Ratzinger's methodology is similar to Bonaventure's insofar as he envisions a grandiose chronological leap from about 70 C.E. to the end of time.

Here, again, we find a common thread among contemporary scholars. Matthew crafted two thematic discourses together to *appear* as though they were talking about the same first-century events. But since they *presumably* describe two different events millennia apart from each other, they only appear to be temporally related by design. By assuming that Matthew is describing two very different events in history, it is supposedly impossible to untangle them entirely, except somewhere within Jesus' initial response to his disciple's *first* question.

---

tinct characteristics. *The truly immanent event* was the destruction of the Temple, which would be immediately preceded by its own discrete signals and would happen in the next generation. The 'end of the age,' while included in the same discourse, was not tied directly to the Temple." Smith, *The House of the Lord*, 285; italics added.

66. According to Aidan Nichols, *The Theology of Joseph Ratzinger: An Introductory Study* (Edinburgh, Scotland: T&T Clark, 1988), 165, Ratzinger's eschatology attempted to "subvert the assumption that a doctrine of the radical imminence of the Parousia belongs with the *oldest* stratum in the Gospel tradition." That is to say, according to Ratzinger, "the idea of an immediate End to the world may be the result of re-Judaisation: taking place later, not earlier." By focusing on "the Gospel of the Kingdom as a reality at once present and yet to come," and by "gazing on the risen Christ," the church "learned that *a* Parousia had already taken place." Allegedly (at least, according to Nichols' assessment of Ratzinger), "The Church knew no pure theology of hope, but rather a 'now' in which the promise was a presence. But this presence was itself hope—it was understood to bear the future within itself" (Nichols, 166).

368

4.1.6 GUNDRY, CARSON, HAGNER, STINE, DAVIES, AND ALLISON (CIRCA 1980—1990)

According to Gundry's detailed exegesis of Matthew's OD, the possibility of a "double fulfillment" seems appropriate. This is due, in part, to his assumption that the "coming of the son of man" is an event that "did not occur soon after A.D. 70, and has not occurred to this day."[67] At first, Gundry concedes that Jesus' reference to "these things" in Matthew 24:34 most clearly echoes the "these things" of Matthew 24:3, a verse which is naturally "restricted" to "the destruction of the temple."[68] He nonetheless deflects attention away from any singular fulfillment of prophecy by insisting that Matthew's language dwells on "the qualitative rather than chronological sense" of important phrases, such as "this generation," thereby leaving "the chronological extent" to remain open for future fulfillment.[69]

Gundry's assessment shows *numerous parallels* with first-century fulfillment prior to Matthew 24:34, but alongside such parallels he adds *opinions* about the *improbability* of Jesus' intentions being exclusively related to first-century events. Most notably, after verse 35, Gundry clearly transitions from first-century allusions to end-of-the-world events, all the while stressing the qualitative meaning of everything within the remainder of the discourse. This transition seems to be taken for granted, too, based on his assumption that the *Parousia* described in Matthew's OD has not yet occurred in history and remains unfulfilled.

D. A. Carson lists a wide variety of interpretations regarding the OD, and he even admits to the popularity of first-century fulfillment among expositors. However, his ultimate conviction is that Matthew's OD represents a "single complex web of events." Some events involve

---

67. Gundry, *Matthew*, 491.

68. Gundry, *Matthew*, 490.

69. Gundry, *Matthew*, 491.

first-century fulfillment; others, end-of-the-world fulfillment; still, others are a mixture of both. He reaches this conclusion because he envisions "the *disciples" to be thinking of* "Jerusalem's destruction and the eschatological end" as one and the same thing, even though they are actually mistaken about those two things being *chronologically* related.[70] According to Carson, Jesus warns about a "delay *before* the End."[71] As a result, Carson's presuppositional commitments lead him to conclude that Matthew 24:15-21 illustrates "one particularly violent display of judgment in the Fall of Jerusalem," while the remainder of the discourse characterizes "the interadvent period" and the "Second Advent" at the end of history.[72] In this approach, Carson implicitly admits to a transition that takes place somewhere in Jesus' initial response to his disciples' first question.

Hagner agrees largely with Carson's perspective, although he also remains sympathetic to the possibility of "double fulfillment" suggested by Gundry and others,[73] especially in regard to Matthew 24:15-22.[74] Hagner prefers to argue matter-of-factly that two events are described, and the confusion we see in Matthew's version rests entirely upon "the mindset of the disciples" which misleadingly conflates the two. He writes:

> That the two parts of the question are asked in one breath indicates that the disciples could not dissociate the destruction of the temple from the end of the age. The misleading manner in which the questions are juxtaposed thus reflects the mindset of the disciples (including the evangelist, as may be determined by his redaction of Mark). The generalizing

---

70. Carson, *Matthew*, 495.

71. Carson, *Matthew*, 495.

72. Carson, *Matthew*, 495.

73. Hagner, *Matthew 33B*, 699.

74. Hagner, *Matthew 33B*, 697-8.

plural ταῦτα, "these things," apparently includes not only the leveling of the temple but events that had to accompany it, such as the fall of Jerusalem. Remarkably, the first question, concerning "when" (πότε) these things were to occur, is not answered in the discourse. Although Jesus does not answer directly, however, v. 34, insofar as it refers to the destruction of Jerusalem, would intimate that that event was to occur within that generation. The second question concerns τὸ σημεῖον, "the sign," that will point to the eschatological denouement, indicating τῆς σῆς παρουσίας, "your coming," and συντελείας τοῦ αἰῶνος, "the consummation of the age."[75]

Philip Stine, who was influenced by Eduard Schweizer,[76] gets right to the point in his commentary by largely ignoring allegations of confusion on the part of Jesus' disciples. Instead, he clearly demarcates historical events fulfilled in the first century from non-specific events yet to be fulfilled in our future:

> Matthew, even more emphatically than Mark (13.4), divides the response of the disciples into two distinct questions: (1) When will this be, and (2) what will be the sign of your coming and the close of the age? The first of the two questions relates to the destruction of Jerusalem, which is a historical event that may be predicted with relative certainty by the observation of other events. It receives answer in verses 15-28 and 32-35. But the second question concerns a happening that is not one in a series of cause-and-effect events.[77]

---

75. Hagner, *Matthew 33B*, 688.

76. Philip C. Stine and Barclay M. Newman, *A Handbook on The Gospel of Matthew* (New York, NY: United Bible Societies, 1988), 4.

77. Stine and Newman, *Handbook*, 732.

Davies and Allison are among the most rigorous in their assessment of the various interpretations of this discourse. Much like Carson, they cover a lot of historical ground while offering their own reasons for agreement and disagreement. Ultimately, however, Davies and Allison share very different presuppositional commitments than Carson. For example, contrary to Carson's assessment, Davies and Allison think it "seems likely" that there is credibility to the theory about "sayings" of Jesus circulating early in the first century, and a form of "Jesus tradition" composed "shortly before AD 70, under the impact of the trouble in Judaea."[78] Matthean posteriority also plays a decisive role in all of their interpretations. Therefore, their exegesis of Matthew's version can be interpreted from multiple *indecisive* angles while claiming ambiguity for its *intended* fulfillment.[79] The closest references to any *intended* first-century fulfillment are allegedly found scattered across

---

78. Davies & Allison, *Matthew*, 332-3.

79. In a scholarly critique of two works by N.T. Wright, *Jesus and the Victory of God* and *The New Testament and the People of God*—works which have sparked heated debates about first-century fulfillment in the Synoptic Gospels—Allison asserts dogmatically that "most of what Jesus envisioned in his eschatological prophecies cannot be identified with past events." Dale C. Allison Jr., "Jesus & the Victory of Apocalyptic," *Jesus & The Restoration of Israel: A Critical Assessment of N.T. Wright's Jesus and the Victory of God*, ed. Carey C. Newman (Downers Grove, IL: InterVarsity Press, 1999), 141. Allison, of course, is being consistent with how *indecisive* he believes first-century fulfillment ought to be perceived when evaluating eschatological statements such as those contained in the OD. Interestingly, though, his basis for this judgment is partly traditional and partly emotional. Prior to reaching a conclusion about "most of what Jesus envisioned," he anxiously insists: "Christian theology has always held that, when Jesus came at his first advent, *he fulfilled some of the eschatological expectations of Judaism*, but that it will take a second advent to fulfill all of them: much was left undone. *The reason for this commonplace is that the world around us does not seem to be the world of our hopes and dreams, which is precisely what the world of eschatological promise is supposed to be.* The problem of evil has not been solved, and *God's will is not done on earth as it is in heaven. ...Is not eschatology the divinely inspired hope for* a return to Eden, for *a truly perfect world, for utopia?*" Allison, "Jesus & the Victory," 140; italics added. N.T. Wright's incisive response to these remarks by Allison are noted in my **Conclusion** and in **Appendix C.1**.

Matthew 24:15-28 and are described by them as "deliberate literary anachronism descriptive of events surrounding AD 70."[80] Verse 15 is also, allegedly, *the* closest example of Jesus answering the disciples' *first* question.[81]

All these scholars retain one common tendency: to view Jesus' *first* response with some connection to first-century events, and that response is directly addressed to his disciples' *first* question.

4.1.7 GIBBS, BRUNER, AND GARLAND (CIRCA 1990–2000)

In his highly detailed and thoughtfully crafted book, *Jerusalem and Parousia: Jesus' Eschatological Discourse in Matthew's Gospel*, Jeffrey Gibbs contends for a "bipartite structure" to both the disciples' questions *and* the order in which Jesus responds to them. Gibbs *urges* his audience to accept this structure to justify what he believes to be a clear, intentional transition from first-century fulfillment to end-of-the-world events yet to be fulfilled:

> Owing to what I shall argue is the double question of the disciples in 24:3, I will present the evidence for the overall bipartite structure of the ED [Eschatological Discourse], namely, 24:4-35 and 24:36–25:46. As will become evident in my discussion, I regard the first half of the ED as Jesus' response to the disciples' first question in 24:3 and the second half of the ED as Jesus' response to the disciples' second question in 24:3.[82]

---

80. Davies and Allison, *Matthew*, 349.

81. Davies and Allison, *Matthew*, 345.

82. Jeffrey A. Gibbs, *Jerusalem and Parousia: Jesus' Eschatological Discourse in Matthew's Gospel* (St. Louis, MO: Concordia Publishing House, 2000), 167.

Accordingly, Gibbs goes on to teach that the first half of Matthew's OD predicts events already fulfilled in the first century, whereas the second half is yet to be fulfilled in *our* future. Allegedly, Jesus' initial remarks in Matthew 24:4-14 are so clearly delineated that his intended meaning was: "Do not be deceived! Do not juxtapose the destruction of Jerusalem and the Parousia."[83] This "bipartite" structure of Matthew's OD is ostensibly so pronounced that Gibbs claims a serious problem will arise for all interpreters who do *not* break up the discourse in this way. He writes:

> For those who do not break the discourse between 24:35 and 24:36, the opposing themes of "warnings and signs" and "sudden, unexpected event" pose a serious problem. For those, like myself, who do break the discourse between 24:35 and 24:36, the "tension" dissolves.[84]

In order to clear away this alleged tension, Gibbs argues that a very precise and noticeable "hinge" exists between 24:35 and 24:36. This "hinge" is Matthew's use of the words περὶ δὲ ("but concerning"), the conjunction (δὲ) of which allegedly *strengthens* the "resumptive function" of περὶ ("concerning") used by Matthew elsewhere.[85] In defense of this position, he only offers two examples from the Gospel of Matthew: καὶ περὶ ("and concerning") in Matthew 6:28 and περὶ δὲ

---

83. Gibbs, *Jerusalem and Parousia,* 196.

84. Gibbs, *Jerusalem and Parousia,* 171.

85. Gibbs, *Jerusalem and Parousia,* 172-3. "Resumptive function" refers to resuming discussion of a topic already mentioned. In this case, Gibbs is arguing that the περὶ δὲ of Matthew 24:36 is resuming the "second" question asked by Jesus' disciples. Most ironically, by overlooking the fact that Jesus answers the *first* question *last* (beginning at 24:36), Gibbs does not realize that he is *presupposing* that Jesus could only be resuming discussion about the so-called "second" question. Gibbs also presupposes that the disciple's questions are completely unrelated in terms of a timeline of historical fulfillment. This argument of Gibbs will be addressed again in **Appendix C.1.2**.

("but concerning") in 22:31.[86] After these remarks, he dogmatically concludes that,

> These two examples from Matthew's Gospel suggest that περὶ δὲ, heading the opening sentence of the second major section of the ED, reaches back to the beginning of the discourse *and brings into focus the disciples' second question* concerning the Parousia and consummation of the age. . . . Jesus' words in 24:36, "But concerning that day and hour no one knows" are precisely the things that one would expect to find when the ED moves from its first major part to its second major part.[87]

Very few modern scholars are as adamant about the *precise* transitional verse as Gibbs is.[88] And even fewer scholars make arguments that

---

86. Gibbs, *Jerusalem and Parousia,* 172-3. Ironically, these two examples illustrate more about Gibbs' desperation than any amount of stress which Jesus or Matthew are imagined to convey.

87. Gibbs, *Jerusalem and Parousia,* 173-4; italics added.

88. Gibbs says: "I shall argue that in 24:29-31 Jesus utilizes eschatological language in a way that parallels the OT prophets. His purpose is to describe the events of end-time judgment that God will bring upon the nation of Israel through the destruction of Jerusalem. . . . [24:32-35] emphasizes the necessity of rightly perceiving 'all these things' that Jesus has predicted in order to discern the nearness of the events before they occur. Jesus applies a solemn and specific temporal limitation at 24:34: 'Truly I say to you that this generation will certainly not pass away until all these things take place.' With these words, Jesus has answered the first of the disciples' questions in 24:3: '*When* will these things be?' Finally, 24:35 acts as an oath to verify and validate the predictions that Jesus has just made in the first major part of the ED." Gibbs, *Jerusalem and Parousia,* 174-5.
  Another contemporary Protestant scholar, Kenneth Gentry Jr., parrots these arguments from Gibbs as though they are dogmatically air-tight. Gentry even points out that "Gibbs offers two illustrations from Matthew's Gospel," which are the two unhelpful verses Gibbs cited, as shown above. On this, see Kenneth Gentry Jr. *The Olivet Discourse Made Easy* (2010; repr., Chesnee, SC: Victorious Hope Publishing, 2021), 130. As with the logic of Gibbs's overall presentation,

essentially hinge upon a subtle difference between περὶ δὲ and καὶ περὶ, considering that δὲ is *always* postpositive when beginning a new sentence, and the beginning of a new sentence does not, in itself, justify a "transitional" interpretation regarding *chronological* sequence or a *complete change* of historical context. Put simply, the disciples could be asking multiple questions about *related events converging within the same time period.* But Gibbs' rationale does not allow this.

Gentry assumes too much from the outset and imposes his assumptions upon his readers. Two further assertions by Gentry are noteworthy. He says: "In approaching the remainder of the Discourse we must bear in mind that the disciples originally think that Jesus' prophecy of the destruction of the temple (Matt. 24:2) requires the simultaneous conclusion to history," and "They were asking *when* the destruction of the temple was to occur. And because of their false assumption regarding its permanence, they also asked: *what* will be the sign of your coming to effect the end of history." Gentry, *Made Easy*, 127-8; italics original. Notice carefully that Gentry *presupposes* an interpretive "conclusion to history" with regard to the "end of the age" within the apostles' questions. Even the "signs" they inquired about allegedly pertained to "the end of history." Not once does Gentry point out the possibility that Jesus answered their first question *last*, or their last question *first*. In light of this, I have offered a thorough response to thirteen arguments presented by Gentry in defense of a "transitional" verse (or, as he calls it, a "hinge passage"). On that, see **Appendix C**.

Daniel M. Doriani's arguments are as equally embarrassing as Gentry and Gibbs', if not more so, because he not only dogmatically asserts what *Jesus* was thinking (cf. Gentry's assertion above, about what "the *disciples* originally think"), but also that Jesus emphatically did *not* respond to his disciples' *first* question with content pertaining to *timing*, but with content pertaining to "what and how" these things would happen (i.e., *signs*). In doing so, Doriani's exposition offers the exact *inverse* of Matthew's literary design, even though he patently admits what is obvious—that Matthew has not arranged Jesus' initial response to his disciples' "when" question with a "when" answer. On this, Doriani writes, "Whatever the disciples intended, Jesus heard and answered two questions, one at a time. The first part of his reply predicts events that will take place in 'this generation' (24:34), that is, within forty years—The lifetime of the disciples. . . . Notice that the disciples ask questions about *timing*. They want to know, 'When will these things be?' . . . But Jesus does not reply with a *when*—a set of dates . . . —but with a *what* and *how*." Daniel M. Doriani, *Matthew Volume 2: Chapters 14-28*, REC (Phillipsburg, NJ: P&R Publishing, 2008), 350 and 352. Emphasis in italics is original.

376

Gibbs also does not realize that Jesus begins by addressing the last question first. Even if Gibbs' rationale about a "resumptive function" is accepted at face value, περὶ δὲ actually makes more sense if Jesus reaches back *to the very beginning of the questions asked* and brings into focus *the first question which had not yet been answered.* However, Gibbs does not consider this alternative approach, nor does he propose that anyone else should consider it. Therefore, his proposed methodology only appears winsome once one presupposes along with him that Jesus answers the *first* question *first.*

Both David Garland and F. D. Bruner also favor the view of a bi-partite structure[89] and consider Matthew 24:35 to be the most likely place for a transitional verse between past and future fulfillment. Garland writes:

> The key to the structure of this discourse on the Mount of Olives is the disciples' double question in 24:3. (1) the answer to the first half of the question, "When will these things be?" is given in 24:4–35. "These things" refer to Jesus' announcement about God's judgment on the temple and Jerusalem. This interpretation is only one of many ways to treat this much-disputed passage, but it best explains why everything in this section is described in terms of what the disciples are able to witness and experience (24:6, 9, 10, 15, 20, 23, 25, 26, 33) and why it concludes with the affirmation that "all

---

89. Bruner seems to be bothered by the possibility of *three* questions. He insists that a single definite article connects the sign of Christ's *parousia* and the "end," thereby making "these two end-time realities a *single unit.*" Bruner, *Matthew: The Churchbook,* 473. Since Bruner believes that both Jesus and Matthew viewed "the destruction of Jerusalem and the end of the world as being *almost* contemporaneous" (emphasis is Bruner's), a total of three questions would seem to break up that intentional design of closely associating the two. Bruner's hermeneutic requires a bi-partite structure for the sole purpose of justifying future, end-of-*our*-world prophecy.

these things" will be fulfilled before "this generation" passes away (24:34; see 23:36; 27:25).[90]

Bruner's approach to exegesis is much more eclectic than those of Garland and Gibbs. Bruner argues that all the references to first-century fulfillment (i.e., the destruction of Jerusalem and the "signs" leading up to it) are *prototypical* of the reality—the so-called "Second Coming."[91] Therefore, according to Bruner, Matthew has arranged Jesus'

---

90. David E. Garland, *Reading Matthew: A Literary and Theological Commentary* (Macon, GA: Smyth & Helwys, 2001), 240. In Garland's published doctoral dissertation, he also presents a convincing case for relating Matthew 23 with chapters 24-25, especially insofar as Markan priority is presupposed. On that, see David E. Garland, *The Intention of Matthew 23*, SNT, vol. LII (Leiden, Netherlands: E. J. Brill, 1979), 26-9. In Garland, *Intention*, 28-9, he concludes that "Chapter 24, then, should not be viewed as a new discourse. The opening of the discourse must be considered to be 23:1. The fact that there is a change of place and a narrowing of the audience in 24:1 should not lead to the conclusion that a new discourse begins that is totally independent of chapter 23. . . . It should also be noted that the typical Matthean transition sentence which usually closes a discourse (cf. 7:28; 11:1; 13:53; 19:1; and 26:1) is absent. It is included at the conclusion of chap. 25, which suggests that chaps. 23-25 were considered one discourse; and the same themes may be seen running through all three chapters. Again, if chaps. 23 and 24 are viewed as two separate discourses this would also break Matthew's normal pattern whereby narrative material usually precedes a discourse. The conclusion is that there is no reason to consider chap. 24 as unconnected to chap. 23 and every reason to see them as connected."

Unsurprisingly, in spite of Garland's insistence that Matthew has intentionally arranged chapters 23-25 as a single, unified discourse, he also claims (with virtually no evidence other than his opinion) that Matthew has made it "absolutely clear" that two very different events are in mind. He writes, "Chap. 23 explains the judgment which has come to Israel with the fall of Jerusalem; chap. 24 deals with the cosmic judgment at the end of time (συντελεία τοῦ αἰῶνος, 24:3) that is ushered in by the παρουσία of Jesus (both words are without synoptic parallel) and which Christians must face with all mankind. That this is an accurate interpretation of the facts is shown by the major concern in chap. 24, apparently Matthean, to make absolutely clear that the fall of the Temple and the end of time were distinct events." Garland, *Intention*, 29.

91. Bruner, *Matthew: The Churchbook*, 474.

answers chronologically in order to show that the "reality" makes sense in light of its immediate prototype. Because Jesus responds to their questions both chronologically and typologically, the result of this methodology is a lot of flexibility around typological ambiguities, all of which, unsurprisingly, seem to conclude at Matthew 24:34. Once Bruner reaches verse 34, he suddenly shows a lot of certainty about a transition taking place in Matthew's (or Jesus') mind:

> We learned from the previous verse [v. 33] that "all these things" are the *preliminaries* before the end—they are the sermon's vividly described *tribulations*. Exactly a generation after Jesus' words (spoken about AD 30), Jerusalem *was* destroyed and its temple razed (in AD 70). So Jesus' prophecy came true insofar as his sermon answered the disciples' first question about the end of the temple, "When will these things happen [to the temple]?" (v. 3). Answer: "the temple will end with this generation" (v. 34).
>
> But Jesus' prophecy did *not* come true if it is applied to the disciples' *second* question about the Great End, "What will be the sign of your coming and of the end of the world?" (v. 3c).[92]

It is beyond question that these scholarly interpretations share the assumption that **(1)** Jesus answers the first question first, **(2)** that Matthew or Jesus (or both) must have had two distinctive events in mind, which is illustrated by two distinctive questions, and **(3)** the so-called "second" question consists of two parts that are intended to be a single unit. None of them seem to have considered that Jesus answers the *last* "part" of the "second" question *first*; then Jesus makes remarks about his *Parousia*; and finally, Jesus answers the *first* question about the "end" *last*.

---

92. Bruner, *Matthew: The Churchbook,* 518.

As noted already, the case I am presenting really does not depend upon the disciples asking two questions or three questions. Matthew has arranged the teaching of Jesus so that all the "parts" which these scholars clearly believe to contain first-century fulfillment (Matt. 24:4-35) are actually *not* in direct response to the disciples' first question. Moreover, according to Matthew's balanced literary layout, 24:36–25:30 is clearly addressing *one* question: a "when" question.[93] This balance complicates a strict bi-partite proposal, especially once one assumes, as many do, that the Parousia mentioned therein must have its fulfillment *disconnected* from first-century events surrounding Jerusalem's destruction.[94] Nevertheless, after recognizing that the "when" question receives a direct response after verse 35, it seems tragically ironic to find these scholars acknowledging that Jesus answers the "when" question with descriptions of first-century events, all because they assume Jesus answers that question first.

---

93. See **2.1.2 (a)**

94. The term παρουσία is mentioned in four locations of Matthew's OD: (1) Matthew 24:3, which is the second question no matter which interpretive structure is proposed (bi-partite or tri-partite), (2) Matthew 24:27, which addresses the "second" question directly according to the tri-partite structure illustrated in **2.1.2 (a)**, and (3) Matthew 24:37 and 39, which addresses the "when" (i.e., the "first") question directly. According to the strict "bi-partite" proposal, there must be some co-mixture of first-century context and a presumed, futuristic παρουσία prior to an official "transitional" verse at Matthew 24:36. This co-mixture within a "bi-partite" structure unmistakably contributes to a wide variety of inconsistencies, as was shown in **Chapter 3**; whereas, according to Matthew's balanced structure, it is reasonable to mention the παρουσία within Jesus' response to the "when" question because all three questions and Jesus' responses to them are related to Jerusalem's soon-coming destruction and the definitive end of the "old covenant" administration.

380

4.1.8 KEENER, NOLLAND, LUZ, FRANCE, FARLEY, MITCH, SRI, KONRADT, WILSON, AND HAYS (CIRCA 2005–PRESENT[95])

Craig Keener is generous toward many interpretations. Although he concludes that most of the events described in Matthew 24:4-14 "occurred between A.D. 30 and 70,"[96] he sees a variety of viable interpretations for verses 15–28. Jesus could have (1) skipped from first-century events to "the next eschatologically significant event, his return," (2) regarded the entire period between Jerusalem's impending destruction to his return as "an extended tribulation period," (3) blended "the tribulation of 66-70 [CE] with the final one, which it prefigures," (4) initiated the tribulation in 66 CE but postponed it, or (5) intended his "coming" to be interpreted "symbolically for the fall of Jerusalem."[97] In sophisticated academic fashion, Keener opts

---

95. After completing the first draft of this chapter, two commentaries on Matthew's OD came to my attention: James B. Jordan, *Matthew 23-25 A Literary, Historical, and Theological Commentary* (Powder Springs, GA: American Vision, 2022), and Walter T. Wilson, *The Gospel of Matthew*, Eerdmans Critical Commentary, two vols. (Grand Rapids, MI: Wm. B. Eerdmans Publishing Co., 2022). Suffice it to say, after an investigation into both commentaries, neither of them addresses the *precise* concerns of my thesis regarding the order in which Jesus responds to his disciples' questions. In many ways, Wilson's two-volume commentary is similar in outlook to the critical conjectures of Davies and Allison (see **4.1.6** above) and Konradt (see below), allowing only a miniscule portion of first-century fulfillment within Matthew 24, which predictably occurs in response to the disciples' *first* question. Jordan's commentary, however, is exceptionally more interesting, adding many structural, historical, thematic, and typological insights I had never considered, and which in many ways substantiates and corroborates various arguments I have made throughout this book. The outlook of Jordan's commentary differs from mine insofar as he imagines the "Parable of the Talents" beginning at Matthew 25:14 to describe a period of history that begins at either Pentecost *or* 70 CE and extends to the end of history. On that, see Jordan, *Matthew 23-25*, 200-10.

96. Keener, *Matthew*, 569.

97. Keener, *Matthew*, 577-8.

in favor of a blend of multiple options. He accepts options 1 and 2, "with elements of" option 3.[98] Most notably, however, is Keener's observation that a transition takes place in Matthew 24:36. In verse 36 the "day" that will catch most people off-guard "is presumably the day of the Lord,"[99] which is the day of *futuristic* judgment presumably described in Matthew 25 as well.

John Nolland also treks down methodological paths laid by his predecessors. He notes that "the destruction of the temple and the completion of the age are closely connected with each other."[100] Nolland shows many ways in which first-century fulfillment would have been easily understood by Jesus' generation throughout Matthew 24:4-35. He even concludes—contrary to some of his contemporaries—that the phrase "this generation" in verse 34 "is the generation of Jesus' contemporaries."[101] However, because his methodology begins with Jesus answering the disciples' first question first, he transitions into predictions of futuristic fulfillment in verse 36, which merely mentions "that day." He also awkwardly rationalizes the meaning of "all these things" in verse 33 to *exclude* first-century fulfillment, by relating it to the future "coming" of Christ. Regarding verse 33, he says:

> Since the topic is the timing of the coming of the Son of Man, Matthew's actual account of the coming must be excluded from the scope embraced by "all these things" here. He probably wants to exclude the whole of vv. 29-31, with the present language of nearness functioning as an equivalent to the use of "immediately" in v. 29.[102]

---

98. Keener, *Matthew*, 578.
99. Keener, *Matthew*, 590.
100. Nolland, *Matthew*, 963.
101. Nolland, *Matthew*, 989.
102. Nolland, *Matthew*, 987.

According to Ulrich Luz, Jesus *merely* addresses the first question asked by his disciples. Supposedly, Jesus did not *actually answer their first question* throughout Matthew 24:4-28. Nevertheless, beginning in verse 32, a transition somehow takes place. "Of course," Luz says at verse 32, "now the issue is no longer the destruction of Jerusalem but the time of the end" that will occur in our future.[103] By this quick slight-of-hand, all of his previous comments about "chronological progression" and Matthew's readers identifying with "the Jewish War" begin to fade away into obscurity.[104] Interestingly, among the "four possible interpretations" of this discourse that Luz offers, he fails to mention that Jesus answers the *third* question *first*.[105] Furthermore, he seems to take for granted that Jesus addresses the first question first.

In R.T. France's view, Matthew has "deliberately expanded" Mark's version of the disciples' questions "to make it clear that the discourse that follows is not concerned only with the destruction of the temple," but also with the *Parousia*. For France, the Parousia is "the climactic event which will be the theme of the second part of the discourse."[106] Jesus' answer to the question "When will these things happen?" is also "rounded off" in Matthew 24:32–35. There, in verses 32-35, Matthew has "rule[d] out decisively any suggestion that the preceding verses (apart from the anticipatory comment in v. 27) are concerned with some more ultimate 'end' than the destruction of the temple which the disciples had asked about."[107] It is only after verse 35 that a transition into futuristic, end-of-the-world promises occurs.

---

103. Luz, *Matthew 21–28,* 207.

104. Luz, *Matthew 21–28,* 184-95.

105. i.e., the second (or last) "part" of the second question, if one must insist upon there being only two grammatical questions, instead of three conceptual questions.

106. France, *Matthew,* 895.

107. France, *Matthew,* 929. Brown and Roberts, *Matthew,* 214-219, *explicitly* follow the arguments of France about a transitional verse.

The first-century interpretations of two notable Roman Catholic scholars, Curtis Mitch and Edward Sri, are similar to their contemporaries.[108] First, they state what is obvious to everyone with homogenous misunderstandings,[109] that "By all accounts, this final discourse is the most difficult to interpret."[110] They also ask the typical, predictable questions that many interlocutors across Christian tradition have asked: "Is Jesus speaking about the near future and the Roman destruction of Jerusalem and its temple in AD 70? Or is he peering into the distant future and describing events that will herald the end of the world? Or can we maintain that both events are in view?"[111]

Although their comments about a few select verses between 24:4-35 suggest *potential* past and future overlap (vv. 24:23-26 and 24:32-35), first-century fulfillment is offered everywhere except verses 27-31. Furthermore, they demonstrate clearly, along with most others, that Jesus answers the first question first, starting at verse 4, and the last question last, starting at verse 36. "At this point," they write, "Jesus makes a transition" that "narrows" the focus to the "'day' and 'hour' of his coming (vv. 36, 42, 44)."[112] Curiously, they do not notice that such references to *time* most clearly address the disciples' first question (i.e., the "when" question).

The Eastern Orthodox pastor and biblical exegete, Lawrence Farley, interprets Jesus' response to his disciples' questions similarly to Mitch and Sri, except Farley thinks the transitional verse about *our* future officially takes place in verse 29.[113] Immediately prior to

---

108. Curtis Mitch and Edward Sri, *The Gospel of Matthew*, CCSS (Grand Rapids, MI: Baker Academic, 2010), 301-13.

109. See **2.1.2 (a)** and **2.1.2 (b)**.

110. Mitch and Sri, *Matthew*, 301.

111. Mitch and Sri, *Matthew*, 301.

112. Mitch and Sri, *Matthew*, 313.

113. Lawrence R. Farley, *The Gospel of Matthew: Torah for the Church*, OBSCS (Chesterton, IN: Ancient Faith Publishing, 2009), 313-21.

commenting on verse 29, in the conclusion of 24:28, Farley offers an extensive first-century context for fulfillment:

> Thus, Jerusalem will not enjoy any special protection from God, nor any immunity from judgment. Where the corpse is, there the vultures will be gathered to feed on the carrion. In the same way, where Jerusalem's sin is, there will come the judgment of God.
>
> It all happened exactly as the Lord predicted. In the days leading up to AD 70, there were indeed earthquakes and famines, and as Jewish nationalism grew ever more intense, the persecution of Jesus' followers grew more savage. In October 66, the Roman armies under Cestius Gallus marched against Jerusalem and surrounded her. The Christians there remembered the Lord's words and fled to the mountain city of Pella. In 70, the Romans returned under Titus and laid siege to Zion again. The city put up a valiant struggle, even though starvation reduced them to cannibalism. At last the city fell and the Temple was burned to the ground, with not one stone left upon another. (The story of Jerusalem's fall and the Christian's flight is narrated by Eusebius in his Church History, 5.5-8.)[114]

At verse 29 of Matthew 24, Farley changes gears and travels fast toward a destination at the end-of-*our*-world. He says that "The disciples asked the Lord not only about the destruction of the Temple, but also about the final end, and here Christ begins to answer that part of their question. . . . Thus Christ's reference here to the tribulation of those days looks beyond AD 70 to encompass all the upheavals of the present age."[115] Although Farley interprets "this generation" in 24:34

---

114. Farley, *Matthew*, 319-20.

115. Farley, *Matthew*, 321. As an aside, it is worth highlighting that Farley's detailed commentary on Matthew's Gospel is from an Eastern Orthodox per-

as "the adulterous generation then living and resisting him," he insists that the "Second Coming" of Christ is *excluded* from such prophecies because "fulfillment" only *began* in that generation; the final return promised by Jesus remains yet to come.[116]

Matthias Konradt proposes that Jesus' prophecies in Matthew 24-25 are "triggered" by the disciple's "two-part question."[117] The first question undoubtedly "refers back to v. 2, so it is about the time when the temple will be destroyed."[118] Because there appears to be a connection between the first question and the "signs of the parousia" which *"opens up the option of a direct connection* between the destruction of Jerusalem and the final events," Konradt imagines it was "urgent

---

spective, which he contends is "consistent with the presuppositions of the Fathers and therefore consistent with Orthodox Tradition." Farley, *Matthew*, 11. Detailed, extensive commentaries of the entire Gospel of Matthew are comparatively rare and few in number as compared with Catholic and Protestant publications. Moreover, most commentaries (if they can be called that) within the Orthodox tradition are either derived from liturgical sources or homilies by hierarchs and monastics (Gregory Palamas, Philaret of Moscow, et al.), which only cover bits and pieces of the OD. Apart from Farley's commentary, the only extensive "Orthodox" commentary of the Olivet Discourse I have found within the last two-hundred years was composed by Apostolos Makrakis (1831-1905), *Interpretation of the Entire New Testament, Volume One – The Four Gospels, Book One: The Gospel According to St. Matthew* (1949; repr., Sheridan, WY: Eastern Light Publishing, 2020). In it, Makrakis shows familiarity with first-century fulfillment throughout Matthew 24:15-26, but he interprets Matthew 24:4-14 as predicting "the great migration of the nations" that began in "the year 376 AD" (458-61). Makrakis also interprets 24:27 onward as pertaining entirely to our future and "the end of the world." Because of his peculiar "Orthodox" commitment to past and present predictions throughout the OD, the phrase "this generation" in Matthew 24:34 is unsurprisingly interpreted as "the unbelieving race of the Jews" who "will exist upon earth until all the prophecies are fulfilled from the days of Christ until His second appearance and coming to the earth" (467).

116. Farley, *Matthew*, 323.

117. Matthias Konradt, *The Gospel according to Matthew: A Commentary* (2015; repr., Waco, TX: Baylor University Press, 2020), 356.

118. Konradt, *A Commentary*, 356.

that Matthew separate it from the eschatological events."[119] Therefore, according to Matthew's redacted arrangement, "the following discourse will *reject* this option" of connecting the first question with "final events."[120]

According to Konradt, a few things are crucial for interpreting the OD properly: "For the overall understanding of Jesus' answer in vv. 4-31, it is crucial to see that we do not have *one* single chronological sequence pictured, but that, after the introduction in vv. 4-5, two perspectives on the course of events are to be distinguished."[121] Allegedly, verses 6-14 picture "the events of the endtime from a comprehensive perspective that embraces the whole earth," while verses 15-28 "view the events in Judea."[122] The "final view," according to Konradt, is pictured in verses 29-31, which "focuses on the coming of the Son of Man."[123] With this schema in mind, Konradt determines that 24:32–25:30 describes "the unknown time of the end and the admonition to be alert."[124] Predictably, Konradt runs into a dilemma with verse 34, wherein he translates "this generation" as "this kind of people" in order to avoid a direct connection with the Parousia.[125] Because he imagines it to be urgent that Matthew separates these two events, Konradt's comments about verse 34 are telling:

> Verse 34 is difficult to understand. The Greek word rendered "kind of people" in the translation (genea) can also mean "generation," as in 1:17. At first glance, this temporal meaning seems to be appropriate for v. 34. But if here "until

---

119. Konradt, *A Commentary*, 356-7; italics added.

120. Konradt, *A Commentary*, 356; italics added.

121. Konradt, *A Commentary*, 357; italics original.

122. Konradt, *A Commentary*, 357.

123. Konradt, *A Commentary*, 357.

124. Konradt, *A Commentary*, 362.

125. Konradt, *A Commentary*, 362-3.

all these things happen" includes the parousia, the problem emerges that "this generation," if the composition of Matthew is to be dated in the 80s of the first century CE, must span a time of at least fifty years (the parousia has not yet happened!).[126]

Besides Konradt's conspicuous omission that the phrase "this generation" is mentioned elsewhere within this discourse (23:36) and throughout Matthew's Gospel (11:16; 12:41, 42), another of his mistaken assumptions is revealing. Instead of interpreting Matthew's OD as addressing the same first-century events, Konradt redacts "this generation" around an event he *presumes* Matthew did not believe had occurred yet.

Alistair Wilson's contribution to the study of Matthew's OD is extremely significant. While presenting an extensive case in defense of literary and thematic unity between Matthew 21–25,[127] he contends against many of the futuristic, end-of-the-physical-cosmos presuppo-

---

126. Konradt, *A Commentary*, 363.

127. Wilson begins his analysis of Matt. 21–25 by highlighting its *inclusio*: "Ch. 21 begins with the approach to Jerusalem and the events that follow do indeed occur in and around this *theologically* significant city. In the same verse, Matthew brings us to the Mount of Olives, which plays such an important role in understanding biblical eschatology. Can it be pure coincidence that ch. 21 begins here and chapters 24-25 also are set on this mountain (compare 21:1 and 24:3)? A vital piece of evidence regarding chapters 21-25 as a unit, seldom adequately recognized, is the theme of the coming king in 21:1-11 and 25:31-46." Wilson, *When will these things happen?*, 69. Wilson also highlights that ὁ βασιλεύς ("the King") is "an important term for Matthew, found in both 21:5 and 25:34" (69). Although I agree with Wilson's assessment of the literary and thematic unity between Matthew 21–25 with regard to the catastrophe coming upon Jerusalem and its temple, he does not make use of any distinctions between "narrative" sections and the five major discourses of Matthew's Gospel. This, I think, would not only strengthen his case, but also put to rest the arguments of other scholars (such as Brian Carrier, mentioned in footnotes of section **4.1.5** above) who contend that Matthew 21-23 is one literary unit set in contrast with Matthew 24-25 as its own literary unit.

sitions dominating historic biblical exegesis. He also engages extensively with Second Temple literature and its themes related to Matthew's OD, including the "cosmic catastrophe" language that most frequently symbolizes "a mighty reversal of fortunes within history and at a national level."[128] Most notably, however, are his insightful critiques of contemporary Matthean scholars who assume *vaticinium ex eventu* across Matthew's entire composition and thereby presume unnecessarily that a post-70 CE date of composition precludes the

---

128. This quote comes from G.B. Caird, whom Wilson cites (*When will these things happen?*, 129). The quote by Caird encapsulates Wilson's overall portrayal of "cataclysmic catastrophe" language in perceived eschatological discourses. On that entire argument, see Wilson, *When will these things happen?*, 109-32. Later on, Wilson, *When will these things happen?*, 144, makes clear that "Previously we argued that Jewish writers (in the OT, in the intertestamental literature and in early Christian literature) often used language, which might appear to modern western readers to have its primary referent in the end of the physical universe, in a figurative sense in order to refer to the activity of God in history." By this "activity of God in history," Wilson intends to contrast end-of-the-physical-universe interpretations of cosmologically prophetic pronouncements with concretized, historical fulfillment pertaining to empires, nations, and temples of past history.

Wilson's insights about cosmic catastrophe language are nothing new among biblical scholars, systematic theologians, or historians. Paul Fiddes introduces similar insights prior to his study of eschatological influences across mainstream literature. He writes, "When the prophets spoke of 'the day of the Lord', or 'that day' or 'the latter end of times' they had in view a decisive turn of events in history, a day when Yahweh would act to vindicate his faithful people and judge both their oppressors and the unfaithful in the nation itself . . . . The imagery of cosmic disturbance and dissolution which accompanies this expectation is not to be taken literally; it may be the traditional language of theophany, or imagery enlisted from creation myths (protology), or even 'end of the world' imagery applied metaphorically to a historic event. Jeremiah describes such a day as one in which the sky rolls up like a scroll and the stars fall, but we realize as we read on that this picture of cosmic collapse is metaphor for a foreign army coming over the hill and razing Jerusalem to the ground. It was appropriate to use such dramatic imagery, as the Day would be a moment after which nothing would ever be the same again." Paul S. Fiddes, *The Promised End: Eschatology in Theology and Literature* (Oxford, UK: Blackwell Publishers, 2000), 23-4.

possibility of accurately portraying *predictive* prophecy on the lips of Jesus regarding Jerusalem's destruction.[129] In this regard, Wilson's investigation counters many exegetical insights offered among contemporary Matthean scholars. Ultimately, he argues that Matthew 21–25 is *almost* entirely about soon-coming judgment upon Jerusalem and its temple in 70 CE. For Wilson, the break into futuristic end-of-the-world territory occurs definitively at Matt. 24:36.

When Wilson arrives at Matthew 24, he argues for a "recognizable structure" that "will not only allow us to interpret the text in an orderly way but should also give us an insight into the thinking that led Matthew to present his material as he did."[130] He begins with a frequently cited and highly favored literary structure among contemporary scholars, as suggested by Craig Blomberg:

---

129. Wilson's comments are worth citing at length. Wilson, *When will these things happen?*, 136n229, says: "It should not be necessary to treat Jesus' words regarding the fall of the temple as *vaticinia ex eventu* simply on the basis of choosing a post-AD 70 date for the composition of the gospel. If the author of Matthew was indeed able and willing to distinguish the 'past of Jesus' from his own day, then we could expect that he would record Jesus' pre-AD 70 words accurately even if he was writing post-AD 70. . . . I would add that it is not only from a literary point of view that this issue should be viewed. If we are to believe that Matthew intended to portray Jesus with historical credibility then it is acceptable to believe that Matthew would record Jesus' point faithfully whether the temple had been destroyed or not. Thus, Casey's criticism of France to the effect that 'the foundation of France's expectation is a dogmatic belief in the authenticity and accuracy of Jesus' predictions so strong that he expects the Marcan prophecy to read like some pedant's account of the event written after it' (173), apart from revealing clearly Casey's own presuppositions, is not telling. It does not matter when the account was written; what matters is whether it accurately reflects what Jesus prophesied. Keener cites 1QpHab 9.6-7 (which is quite clearly to be dated pre-AD 70) as a contemporary 'prediction' of the raiding of the temple which cannot, by that very fact, be turned into a post-AD 70 document: 'but in the Last Days their riches and plunder alike will be handed over to the army of the Kittim, for they are 'the rest of the peoples.'"

130. Wilson, *When will these things happen?*, 133.

390

1. Signs and Times of the Temple's Destruction and of Christ's Return (24:1-35)

(a) Introduction (24:1-3)

(b) Signs that do not yet herald the end (24:4-14)

(c) Destruction of the temple (24:15-20)

(d) The Great Tribulation (24:21-28)

(e) Christ's second coming (24:29-31)

(f) Concluding implications (24:32-35)

2. Commands to Perpetual Vigilance (24:36-25:46)

(a) Introduction and thesis: No-one but God the Father knows the time of Christ's return (24:36-42)

(b) The Parable of the Householder and thief (24:43-44)

(c) The Parable of the Faithful and Unfaithful Servants (24:45-51)

(d) The Parable of the Ten bridesmaids (25:1-13)

(e) The Parable of the Talents (25:14-30)

(f) The Sheep and the Goats (25:31-46)[131]

Before Wilson moves beyond this literary structure into more consistent alternatives, he highlights the pros and cons of Blomberg's proposal:

> Blomberg admirably recognizes that the language of 24:4-20 refers primarily (to discounting possible secondary references) to the first-century situation. He also recognizes that verse 35 forms a clear pause in the discourse, while verse 36 indicates a new beginning, thus picking up two of the clearest literary signals in the text. He struggles, however, with the language of v. 21 and feels compelled to generalize this verse into a reference to the 'great tribulation' of the 'church age'. This immediately introduces a long-term view into the section which naturally leads Blomberg to regard vv. 29-31 as a

---

131. Wilson, *When will these things happen?*, 133.

description of the Second Coming. However, *this generalization is unnecessary and in fact stands in contradiction to the clear division which Blomberg has recognized in verses 35 and 36. The horrors of the siege of Jerusalem could quite legitimately be described in the dramatic language of v. 21, and then vv. 23-26 return to the discussion of false messiahs begun earlier in v. 5.*[132]

Because of this "unnecessary generalization" and structural "contradiction," Wilson ultimately settles with the alternative literary structure offered by R. T. France:

(i) Jesus foretells the destruction of the temple (24:1-2)
(ii) Warnings against premature expectation (24:3-14)
(iii) The coming crisis in Judea (24:15-28)
(iv) Climax of the crisis within "this generation" (24:29-35)
(v) The unexpected *Parousia* of the Son of Man (24:36-25:13)
(vi) The Parable of the Talents (25:14-30)
(vii) The Last Judgement (25:31-46)[133]

By settling with France's proposed literary structure, Wilson says that there are two significant advantages to this approach:

(a) It allows the discourse to be understood as a coherent and ordered response to *the two-part question of verse 3.* It avoids the complications of *continually switching back and forth between references to the judgement on Jerusalem and references to the Parousia.* This is not to say that we ignore the theological connection between the two events but it allows us to recognize connection without confusion.

---

132. Wilson, *When will these things happen?*, 133-4; italics added.
133. Wilson, *When will these things happen?*, 134.

(b) The understanding of the phrase τὸν υἱὸν τοῦ ἀνθρώπου ἐρχόμενον [the Son of Man coming] in terms of apocalyptic imagery allows us to make sense not only of this passage but of the other similar difficult texts (10:23; 16:28; 26:64) without either impugning the integrity of Jesus by claiming that he was mistaken *or straining the language of the texts beyond what they can bear.* It has the added advantage of retaining the natural sense of Dan. 7:13 which would have been appreciated by the original readers. If we are to truly understand Jesus in the context of his own time and culture then *we have to beware of imposing an interpretation on his words* which, while appearing 'obvious' to us, would not have been the natural meaning for his original audience.[134]

Somewhat unsurprisingly, Wilson offers scant support for his presuppositional commitment to a futuristic transition at 24:36. This seems to be par for the course with all those who deconstruct 24:3 into a "two-part question" in order to squeeze in two separate events spaced *millennia* apart from each other. Wilson's commitment to this transition at the second part of the disciples' question is based on two distinguishable characteristics. First, he says that Matthew 24:36–25:46 "is separated from the earlier portion of Matthew 24 by the transitional verse 36." Second, he posits that this transition is obvious because "it is largely composed of material of quite different form to that found in 24:1-35, namely *meshalim* ["parables"] of one kind or another."[135]

In support of Wilson's claim that 24:36–25:46 contains *meshalim* ["parables"] which are "quite different" in form than Jesus' rhetoric in 24:4-35, he devotes nearly fifty pages to this topic prior to

---

134. Wilson, *When will these things happen?*, 134; italics added.
135. Wilson, *When will these things happen?*, 134-5.

393

his defense of a transitional verse.[136] However, when he is finally prepared to defend the actual transitional verse, the only direct evidence he provides is less than two pages. These two pages are also poorly thought through. In an almost identical format as Gibbs' argument for transition, Wilson insists that Matthew's "use of the disjunctive phrase περὶ δὲ, along with the technical term τῆς ἡμέρας ἐκείνης καὶ ὥρας" is extremely weighty. Allegedly, this grammatical construction "signals the beginning of a new subject."[137] According to Wilson, the phrase "that day and hour" (τῆς ἡμέρας ἐκείνης καὶ ὥρας, Matt. 24:36) is significant because it "is clear that reference is being made to the 'Day of the Lord,'" which he *presumes* could not possibly also refer to a first-century event within the context of Matthew 21–25.[138] Wil-

---

136. Wilson, *When will these things happen?*, 175-224. According to Wilson, the "form" of parables is treated as *prima facie* evidence that Jesus has *already* transitioned into a different historical context pertaining to the end of *our* world, which is why Wilson discusses *meshalim* extensively. Alternatively, I suggest that a rhetorical alteration in "form" evinces no transition *from one historical time-frame in the first-century to another at the end of all centuries.* A transition *out of* first-century fulfillment *and into* end-of-*our*-world fulfillment is the very thing that needs to be demonstrated, not merely assumed and asserted. As I illustrated in **2.1.2 (a)**, this section of parables addresses the "when" question. The transition that takes place at 24:36 is *not* from first-century fulfillment to end-of-*our*-world fulfillment, but from *what* certain signs will occur to *when* certain signs will occur.

137. Wilson, *When will these things happen?*, 224.

138. It is interesting that Wilson interprets "that day and hour" as the "Day of the Lord" in a *definitive*, end-of-*our*-world sense, even though Matthew has arranged the discourse to be clear that Jesus is answering the "when will these things happen" question, which *millennia* of historical scholarship links with first-century fulfillment. Caird's insights about "The Day of the Lord" in biblical prophecy counter this claim by Wilson, thereby exposing many futuristic, end-of-*our*-world interpretations as clear prejudices. Commenting on "The Day of the Lord" mentioned in Isaiah 13:9-11, Caird writes, "On a superficial reading the referent of these verses might appear to be the end of the world, and it is fact one of the passages out of mediaeval theology constructed its gruesome picture of the Dies Irae ["Day of Wrath"]. Yet when we read on it becomes apparent that what the prophet intended to describe, under the symbols of world judg-

son argues that Matthew 24:36 must be describing "a new subject" unrelated to first-century fulfillment because it contains "the first significant occurrence of the singular phrase with the demonstrative pronoun 'that day and hour.'"[139]

At first glance, such confident remarks might appear persuasive. For the unsophisticated reader, rhetoric sugars the pill. However, upon careful examination and reflection, Wilson's conclusion seems reasonable primarily because he does not introduce the reader to any alternatives. As a result, the reader might not recognize that a

---

ment, was the end of Babylon's world, the coming destruction of the Babylonian empire by the invading armies of Cyrus the Mede." G. B. Caird, *The Language and Imagery of the Bible* (Philadelphia, PA: The Westminster Press, 1980), 114. Ironically, earlier in Wilson's thesis he defends this approach by Caird (Wilson, *When will these things happen?*, 117-20), yet his prejudice is apparent when he arrives at Matthew 24:36 by pretending that 24:36–25:46 could not refer, in context, to Jerusalem's destruction, judgment upon the rulers of that age, or the definitive "end" of the Old Covenant administration in that generation. According to Wilson, everything prior to 24:36 is fulfilled in the past; everything afterward is not, but instead will be fulfilled in *our* future. In this instance, Wilson agrees with Caird where it is convenient for his thesis. Wilson warns his audience that: "we must be guided by the literary context of a particular occurrence of a phrase at all times, but Caird's point does remind us that it is possible for language bearing one significance to be misconstrued by another writer who gives it a very different significance." Wilson, *When will these things happen?*, 119. Wilson also attempts to argue alongside Caird (in my estimation, unpersuasively) that "biblical writers *sometimes* used 'end of the world' language to refer to this-worldly events, but never in a way that was detached from the ultimate event of God's judgment." Wilson, *When will these things happen?*, 118. This is what Caird describes as a "short range and a long application" (Caird, *Language and Imagery*, 260). Yet this application involves a misleading assumption on both Wilson and Caird's part insofar as it is applied to Matthew's fifth discourse. Clearly, Isaiah 13:9-11 was intended to be detached from the end of *our* world. I contend that Matthew 23-25 was also intended to be detached in similar fashion. By applying first-century reference to Matthew 21:1-24:35, and then transitioning into futuristic, end-of-*our*-world scenarios in Matthew 24:36–25:46, Wilson is doing the very thing he warns others to be cautious of, namely, misconstruing Jesus' language and giving it a very different significance.

139. Wilson, *When will these things happen?*, 224-5.

395

disjunctive phrase can also describe a new *aspect* of the same subject (like "when" certain signs will occur, instead of "what" certain signs will occur) or introduce subtopics of a main topic.[140] In Matthew's

---

140. This is evident in early Christian writings. For example, Didache 2:7 says: "You will not hate any person; instead, you will reprove some; but concerning [these] others, you should be praying; and some you will love even more than your own life" (οὐ μισήσεις πάντα ἄνθρωπον ἀλλὰ οὓς μὲν ἐλέγξεις περὶ δὲ ὧν προσεύξῃ οὓς δὲ ἀγαπήσεις ὑπὲρ τὴν ψυχήν σου). It would take a huge stretch of imagination to argue that περὶ δὲ transitions away from the main topic of *loving others* and introduces an entirely new or divergent subject (of prayer), simply by inserting disjunctively that they ought to pray for others. The "others" in context are relative to "any person" they might be tempted to hate in the future. Some "others" need reproof; some need to be loved self-sacrificially even more than they deserve. Regardless of whether one needs situational correction or a deluge of affection, all of these "others" will need constant prayer for their well-being. According to this disjunctive construction, an active disposition of prayer for all others remains integral to the Christian self-discipline of *refraining* from hatred in future encounters with all others.

Another example comes from Didache 6:1-3, which says: "See that no one leads you astray from this way of the teaching, for such a person teaches you without regard for God. For *if you are able to bear the whole yoke of the Lord*, you will be perfect. But if you are not able, then do what you can. Now concerning food (Περὶ δὲ τῆς βρώσεως), *bear what you are able*, but in any case, keep strictly away from meat sacrificed to idols, for it involves the worship of dead gods." Again, because there is no contextual reason to view this "new subject" as being completely unrelated to the theme which preceded it, this disjunctive phrase seems to describe one aspect of a much larger concern, which is "bearing the whole yoke of the Lord." On this, see "The Didache," *The Apostolic Fathers: Greek Texts and English Translations*, ed. and trans. Michael W. Holmes, 3rd ed. (Grand Rapids, MI: 2007), 346-9 and 352-5. Additionally, none of the suggestions I proposed above, as I understand them, conflicts with the "redactional layers" underlined by περὶ δὲ across the Didache, as proposed by Alan J. P. Garrow, *The Gospel of Matthew's Dependance on the Didache*, LNTS and JSNTSS, vol. 254 (New York, NY: T&T Clark International, a Continuum imprint, 2004), 93-101.

Ignatius of Antioch's letter to the Ephesian church also illustrates this point. In *Ign. Eph.* 1:3-2:1, we learn that Ignatius is concerned about his reception among the whole congregation, especially as they strive to retain union with their bishop (as Ignatius, himself, is a fellow bishop). He writes: "Since, therefore, I have received in God's name your whole congregation in the person of Onesimus, a man of inexpressible love who is also your earthly bishop, I pray

OD, there certainly seems to be literary intentionality pertaining to a main topic (see the typological structure of the discourse in **2.1.1** and the chiastic balance of sections *B* & *B'* in **2.1.2**). Such literary intentionality focuses on the cataclysmic end of *something* in the first century, and that first-century "thing" can reasonably be perceived as the primary issue or concern that provides cohesion to each question asked in Matthew 24:3. As with Gibbs' arguments, Wilson's proposed methodology only appears well-grounded once one presupposes along with him that **(1)** Jesus answers the *first* question *first and* **(2)** *the "end of the age" is an event completely separate in history from "this generation" in which the destruction of Jerusalem and its temple takes place.*

Adding insult to injury, Wilson finds extra-special significance in the terms "no-one" (οὐδείς) and "only" (μόνος) in Matthew 24:36. Supposedly, when Jesus says, "But concerning that day and hour *no one* knows, not even the angels of heaven, nor the Son, but the Father

---

that you will love him in accordance with the standard set by Jesus Christ and that all of you will be like him. For blessed is he who has graciously allowed you, worthy as you are, to have such a bishop. Now concerning (περὶ δὲ) my fellow servant Burrhus, who is by God's will your deacon, blessed in every respect, *I pray that he might remain with me both for your honor and the bishop's.* And Crocus also, who is worthy of God and of you, whom I received as a living example of your love, has refreshed me in every way; may the Father of Jesus Christ likewise refresh him, together with Onesimus, Burrhus, Euplus, and Fronto, in whom I saw all of you with respect to love." In light of this disjunctive phrase, it would be absurd to contend that by *highlighting* Burrhus, Ignatius was deviating from the main topic. Instead, what we find is that Ignatius remains focused on Christian honor and unity. Ignatius expresses gratitude that he received the whole congregation in the person of their bishop, Onesimus, who visited him on his way to execution. Ignatius then prays that the whole congregation refreshes Onesimus by loving and honoring him in a Christ-like manner. But concerning Burrhus (περὶ δὲ), who also visited Ignatius along with their bishop, Ignatius requests that he (Burrhus) remains with him on his way to execution, even though Burrhus is their deacon. This, Ignatius says, is for *their* honor and *the bishop's* honor. Again, it would be very odd to argue from this context that Ignatius has introduced a "new subject" in order to detach it from the main theme of *honor and unity*. On this, see "The Letters of Ignatius" in Holmes, *The Apostolic Fathers,* 182-5.

only", "the force" of such remarks "is that the day is completely unpredictable."[141] Wilson then concludes all of his seemingly insurmountable arguments with a most ironic, autobiographical remark. He says that in light of "the force" of such strong terminology, such complete unpredictability *"surely places unbearable strain* on Matthew's credibility as a redactor and/or on Jesus' credibility as a teacher to claim that Jesus is referring to the same event in vv. 33-4 and in v. 36."[142] By arguing this way, we learn how Wilson *feels* about those who differ with his interpretation, instead of learning what Matthew or Jesus could have meant in the situational context. Apparently, Wilson never considered that by focusing throughout the discourse on one great catastrophe culminating in "this generation" and pinpointing multiple aspects of its culmination, the credibility of Jesus and his apostles remains entirely bearable, and Matthew's literary intentionality remains extremely clear and consistent.[143] What remains incredible and

---

141. Wilson, *When will these things happen?*, 225.

142. Wilson, *When will these things happen?*, 225; italics added.

143. Caird offers a straightforward solution to Mark's version of the OD that Wilson refuses to accept for Matthew's version. Caird writes: "the disaster to Jerusalem will come within the lifetime of the present generation, and, when it arrives, they are entrusted the judgment of the nations . . . . Jesus knows that the Son of Man will come within a generation, but the day and the hour are known only to God . . . . Literalists are accustomed to explain that Jesus knows roughly the year in which the world will end, but not whether it will be a Tuesday or a Wednesday, not whether it will be at 10 a.m. or 6 p.m.; and against such bathos it is pointless to argue. The paratactical Hebrew mind did not need to be told that the two sayings were at different levels: embodied in the historical event which Jesus predicted, the day would come within a generation; in its full, final, literal reality its time was known only to God." Caird, *Language and Imagery,* 266-7. Wilson even admits this possibility while attempting to evade certain interpretations of Caird and N.T. Wright, who also argue that the OD is best understood as referring throughout to first-century events. On this, Wilson, *When will these things happen?*, 123, says: "While adopting the hermeneutical approach of Caird . . . and in its most nuanced form, Wright, would certainly make several vexed issues of NT interpretation, such as the problem of the delay of the *Parousia*, vanish at a stroke, we cannot accept their view simply because it

398

strained is this: forcing Matthew's recognizable structure to describe two separate events spaced *millennia* apart from each other.[144]

would make our life simpler." Immediately thereafter, Wilson has the audacity to write, as though Caird and Wright together have not written many *thousands* of pages on Second Temple Judaism, that "It [i.e., a sound hermeneutical approach] must reflect the understanding of the Jewish people who read the ancient documents, as far as we can discern that understanding from the ancient texts available to us."

144. While commenting on the Parable of the Talents (Matt. 25:14-30) toward the end of his book, Wilson reverts to the exact same problematic assumptions he criticizes among other contemporary scholars. While criticizing David Sim for imagining that Matthew believed in an imminent Parousia, faced an unexpected delay, but still maintained his imminent expectation despite that delay, Wilson claims that "Sim's argument falls because of the assumption on which he founds it. . . . He does not demonstrate Matthew's view *but extrapolates it from the worldview which,* according to Sim, *he accepts.*" Wilson, *When will these things happen?,* 235; italics added. Then comes Wilson's sleight-of-hand argument against Sim without realizing that he is fallaciously *begging the question* as much as Sim is. Wilson writes: "Matthew has presented Jesus as teaching that disaster would fall upon Jerusalem within a clearly defined period of time. The *Parousia* of Jesus must either be immediately connected to that disaster or not. If it is, then Matthew writing (as is commonly held) around AD 80 must have faced a real problem which does not seem to be resolved by this *mashal* [the Parable of the Talents, 25:14-30]. If the temple has been destroyed for a decade and still there is no *Parousia,* how could Jesus' words concerning 'this generation' be fulfilled (some fifty years after Jesus spoke them) if there may still be 'a long time' to wait. If, on the other hand, Jesus distinguished the events to fall upon Jerusalem from his Parousia (as I believe Matthew indicates in his narrative), then there is no problem to be faced since Jesus explicitly denies the possibility of predicting the time of his *Parousia.*" Wilson, *When will these things happen?,* 236. The glaringly obvious problem with this argument, as I see it, is that Wilson is guilty of the very thing he accuses Sim of doing, namely, *extrapolating from the worldview he personally accepts,* while denying any "worldview" for Matthew or Jesus in which the Parousia is immediately connected with Jerusalem's disaster. Wilson does not "prove" in his book that Jesus answers the first question *first* and the last question *last.* He assumes it. He also assumes that the third question pertains to the end of *our* world. Consequently, Wilson does not "demonstrate Matthew's view" about the so-called "delayed Parousia" any more than Sim does. Instead, Wilson assumes, as Sim does, that Jesus had two completely separate events (in time) in mind as he responded to his disciples' questions.

I find it both peculiar and fascinating to learn, after two hundred and twenty four pages of building up an argument in defense of first-century fulfillment, that Wilson only offers a few brief paragraphs of actual literary evidence in support for a *futuristic,* end-of-*our*-world "transition" at Matthew 24:36. I do not deny that a literary transition of some sort takes place at 24:36, as can clearly be seen in section **2.1.2 (a)**. Verse 36 *begins* Jesus' answer to his disciples' *first* question. But what was their first question about? Was it about the end of *our* world or the destruction of the temple in Jerusalem in their own generation? Certainly, the overwhelming majority of historical support for the answer is to be found in the Jerusalem's destruction. Moreover, none of Wilson's evidence in support of *meshalim* throughout 24:36–25:46 conflicts with my thesis. In fact, in many more ways than Wilson might wish to acknowledge, his evidence about *meshalim* supports my thesis very well, especially with regard to understanding the typological and eschatological remarks of Matthew's third discourse (ch. 13) and "final judgment" scene (Matt. 25:31-46).[145]

Finally, we arrive at Christopher Hays and his colleagues, who have proposed a fascinatingly different paradigm than all of the other scholars mentioned above.[146] Instead of locating a transitional verse that is pitted against first-century fulfillment and end-of-the-world fulfillment, it is simply noted multiple times that the *Parousia* of

---

145. The *mashal* of the sheep and goats is highlighted by both Wilson and Macaskill, using nearly identical arguments (with Macaskill parroting Wilson in many respects). And although they both presuppose that this pericope speaks of universal judgment upon all humanity at the end of the physical world, their insights comport well with my thesis. For example, Macaskill, *Revealed Wisdom*, 178, writes: "while the criterion of judgment is ultimately their attitude to the King, that attitude is exposed by the extent to which they have shown humanitarian concern for 'the least of these brothers of mine' (25:40, 45). Again, a link may be seen with the woes pronounced upon the Jewish leaders. In 23:23-4, they are condemned for neglecting 'the more important matters of the law: justice, mercy and faithfulness.' The condemnation pronounced upon the nations of the world is, therefore, linked to that pronounced upon the Jewish leaders."

146. Hays, *When the Son of Man Didn't Come.*

Christ takes place at the "end," and that "end" is clearly alluded to in Matthew 24:36 along with the verses that follow (as well as their parallels in Mark and Luke).[147] Yet Hays is also abundantly clear about two other important issues: (1) that Jesus *actually* prophesies about first-century events to *first-century* disciples, and (2) all three authors of the Synoptic Gospels *faithfully* record Jesus' predictions about first-century events to them.

According to Hays, an honest reading of the OD does not separate potential fulfillment within the first century. All three of the Synoptic Gospels "imply that Jerusalem's sack and Jesus' return would occur in reasonably quick succession."[148] This interpretation means that all three Gospels seem to honestly communicate predictions within the Olivet Discourse—including predictions about Christ's *Parousia*—that were *intended* to be fulfilled in the first century. Hays does not stop there. He goes one step further by insisting that Jesus' predictions about the end-times of the world are *not* wrong, mistaken, or unclear.[149] Jesus *was*, in fact, referring to first-century events and their *intended* fulfillment. "We do not deny," writes Hays, "that Jesus prophesied his return in glory and wrath within the first century."[150]

However, Hays offers an unexpected twist in response to the biblical evidence. Instead of arguing that Jesus' predictions about *that generation* ought to be set *against* an intended *Parousia* of Christ in *that generation*,[151] thereby portraying Jesus as a *false* prophet, Hays defends the uncomfortable position that "the timing of the consummation of the kingdom of God [at the end] is contingent upon the behavior of mortals." In other words, everything in the OD was *intended* to be fulfilled within the first century, as all the Synoptic versions seem

---

147. Hays, *When the Son of Man Didn't Come,* 80; see also 196 and 277.

148. Hays, *When the Son of Man Didn't Come,* 81.

149. Hays, *When the Son of Man Didn't Come,* 83.

150. Hays, *When the Son of Man Didn't Come,* 87.

151. Hays, *When the Son of Man Didn't Come,* 83.

to indicate, but Jesus' prophecies about the timing of the "end" were *conditional.*

According to Hays' thesis, true prophecy entails *human* contingencies for its fulfillment *in time,* which means that the so-called "transitional verses" regarding the *Parousia* and "final judgment" are actually describing events which have been "delayed as a consequence of human action" and "deferred because of the insufficiency of human repentance."[152] "We do not deny the certainty of that return [of Christ]," Hays writes. "We simply deny the fixity of that timing."[153]

Even more memorable than Hays's unconventional proposition about "fixity" is his *assumption* that the OD itself distinguishes between two separable, cataclysmic events. Hays does not deny that Jerusalem was destroyed in 70 CE according to Jesus' predictions. He and his colleagues just do not see Matthew or any of the other Synoptic OD's *pairing* descriptions of Jerusalem's destruction with the prophetic descriptions of Christ's *Parousia.* For Hays and his colleagues, it does not matter where a so-called "transitional verse" takes place. What matters to them is that Jesus prophesies two events in tandem; one of them, Christ's *Parousia,* has *still* not yet occurred in history. *That part* of Christ's tandem prophecy was conditional.

---

152. Hays, *When the Son of Man Didn't Come,* 86.
153. Hays, *When the Son of Man Didn't Come,* 87.

Conclusion

As we have seen, a peculiar methodology emerges around the dawn of the fifth century. Various church fathers assert that Matthew's Olivet Discourse contains some first-century fulfillment, particularly within Matthew 24:4-29; but then they transition into predictions about the "Second Coming" of Christ at end of the world. **Chapter one** exhibits church fathers before and after the fifth century who adhere to this paradigm of first-century fulfillment in response to the disciples' first question, "*When shall these things be?*"

Chapter two demonstrates multiple examples of Matthew's literary intentionality. His entire Gospel portrays Jesus as the faithful son of God that Israel was not.[1] Leithart's examination of typological

---

1. Brandon D. Crowe, *The Obedient Son: Deuteronomy and Christology in the Gospel of Matthew*, BZNW, vol. 188 (Berlin, Germany: De Gruyter, 2012), 229-30, summarizes this theme of Matthew well, saying, "The covenantal obedience required of God's people was a standard to which they never attained in the OT storyline. Matthew recognizes this and thus articulates the story of Jesus in contrast to Israel, using *Son of God* as a primary means for conveying this asymmetrical correspondence. It was thus necessary for Matthew to demonstrate that Jesus fulfills God's design for Israel, and in so doing is able to mediate his sonship to his disciples and enable their own obedience. Hence Jesus, as the obedient Son of God, is able to grant the privilege of sonship also to his disciples, who are therefore called to follow in his path of filial obedience."

parallels across Matthew's Gospel shows that the Olivet Discourse was not some *haphazardly* collected composition of unrelated "sayings" or sources but rather typologically motivated and carefully crafted. The design conveys a message about covenantal judgment and exile preceding God's covenant-renewal with creation. Jesus guarantees this new covenant by his own death and resurrection.[2] Thereafter, Jesus lays the foundation for his apostles and their disciples and commissions them to start building the kingdom of God according to his promises. Following Jesus' teachings, they await his vindication as a true prophet of God and prepare for the definitive, historical "end" of the old covenant administration in that generation.[3]

Having examined the overall message of Matthew's Gospel, we next concentrate on the literary structure of the fifth discourse. How much of Matthew's message does the ancient patristic methodology of interpretation discover or obscure what we examined? Two common

---

2. N.T. Wright's remarks about this message are on point: "The early church clearly believed that Jesus had been vindicated by the resurrection: 'God has made him [Jesus] both Lord and Messiah' (Acts 2:36). '[Jesus Christ] was declared to be the Son of God [i.e., Messiah] . . . by the resurrection from the dead' (Romans 1:4). Jesus had already been vindicated. The resurrection was more important to them than any other single event; it is truer to say that they saw themselves (and knew and felt themselves) to be living in the first days of God's new world than to say that they saw, knew or felt themselves to be living in the last days of God's old world." N.T. Wright, "In Grateful Dialogue: A Response" in Newman, *Jesus & The Restoration of Israel*, 269.

3. When asked how the early church believed that Jesus would be vindicated in the future, beyond the claims about his resurrection, Wright says: "The early church also continued to tell the story of Jesus' confrontation with the temple and its hierarchy, and to see that story as coming to its denouement in the temple's destruction, which would prove that Jesus had spoken the truth and thus was vindicated as a true prophet. They continued to use 'apocalyptic' language about this forthcoming event, not least presumably because Jesus himself had done so. And they looked outwards to events on a far larger scale: the renewal of heaven and earth, the 'exodus' of the whole creation, God's defeat of death itself. Of such matters only small hints can be found in the sayings of Jesus." Wright, "In Grateful Dialogue," 269-70.

misunderstandings occur when the ancient patristic methodology is used to interpret the Olivet Discourse. The first error suggests that Matthew's version of the Olivet Discourse presents a sequential or chronological series of questions along with a series of answers that follow the same sequence: Jesus is first asked a question about Jerusalem, and next asked questions about the end of the world; Jesus then answers the first question first and the last questions last. *The inverse is actually what we find in Matthew's version:* Jesus answers the last question first and the first question last. The second misunderstanding of Matthew's OD is the unnecessary assumption that Christ's *Parousia* or "coming" in the "end" referred to an event beyond the first century at some imagined "end" of human history or the world.[4] Because

---

4. In a lengthy footnote of section **4.1.6** I highlight Dale Allison's scholarly pseudo-ambivalence, which I consider to be the result of his dogmatic commitment to the *"second misunderstanding"* I proposed in section **2.1.2 (b)**. In the same book in which Allison criticized N.T. Wright, Wright responded to Allison's remarks (among others), and those responses are worth noting at length. Wright argues: "Several still read Mark 13 as though it 'must' really be about an end, a transformation, that has not yet taken place, even though the question with which the chapter opens, and for which the previous chapters have exactly prepared us, is about the fall of Jerusalem and the temple in particular. Perhaps a comment about the nature of the discussion may be allowed at this point. I sense a huge anxiety in many contributors: a fear that, if they concede the point that Mark 13 is basically about events in the first century, something will be irreplaceably lost from their theology. [...] Of course, we are at liberty to invoke a *sensus plenior* reading if we wish. But it is heavily ironic for conservative Protestants to pull that rabbit out of the hat; and those who have pressed me personally to allow for second-level meanings in Mark 13 and its parallels, meanings that make the passage refer not only to first-century events but to events yet to come, seem clearly to be looking for a let-out, a way of focusing not on what the passage refers to but on something else. How can this be loyalty to the text? . . . (By the way, the argument 'the early church said such-and-such, therefore Jesus must have meant such-and-such when he used similar words' is not, shall we say, the most secure piece of logic in the world.)" Wright, "In Grateful Dialogue," 265-6.

Wright concludes his response to Allison (and others) by saying: "An eschatological reading of Jesus demands, I believe, that we get used to thinking in terms of the dialectic between achievement and *implementation*. Jesus did not

of the common allure of this second misunderstanding, I conclude chapter two by discussing the only place in Matthew's fifth discourse where futuristic end-of-the-world fulfillment could be legitimately imagined. Yet even in 25:31-46, I argue for the likeliness that Jesus' descriptions remained localized and pertained to his own disciples in contrast with the disciples of the hypocrites "in Moses' seat." Even though all "the nations" are gathered together for judgment in that scenario, the language and concepts of this literary section comport well with the descriptions of disciples in the beginning of Matthew 23 who would undergo first-century social upheaval and the definitive end of the old covenant administration.

Chapter three explores the intense and dense hermeneutical spiral of late medieval discourse analyses through the Renaissance and Reformation eras and into the late modern period. This lengthy stretch of biblical exposition develops doctrine worldwide, but it does not establish any methodological dogmas definitively. Instead, scholars of this period tip-toe around obvious exegetical dilemmas, make excuses, punt very clear time-related statements into the distant future, and deflect attention away from *obvious* meaning within a very straightforward, contextually consistent discourse. The entire exegetical tradition is noticeably disjointed. Only a handful of vigilant exegetes notice that Jesus answers the first question last, and the last question first. Most others just parrot the same routine methodology, assigning Jesus' first response to his disciples' first question while arguing that both the first question and answer involve some kind of clear first-century fulfillment. Compared with Matthew's fifth discourse, the order of questions-to-answers is noticeably inverted. Theologians

---

come to teach an abstract ethic that the church should just go on teaching. He came . . . to compose the score for others to sing, to provide the medicine for others to administer. To point out tartly, as some no doubt will do, that much of the singing has been out of tune and that many of the patients have not improved is to say nothing whatever about the mindset of Jesus. To use the failure of the church as a lever to rewrite the history of its Lord would pass beyond irony toward blasphemy." Wright, "In Grateful Dialogue," 272.

acknowledge first-century fulfillment in response to the disciple's first question about "when" these things would occur. But according to Matthew's literary structure, Jesus' answers (as they imagine it) are actually in response to their *last* question about a "sign" of the impending "end" in that generation. Also, during the long era surveyed across chapter three, interpretations of futuristic 'end-of-the-world' fulfillment ironically respond to the disciples' question about "when" the temple would be destroyed.

Chapter four surveys the landscape of influential modern scholarship pertaining to the Olivet Discourse. Although many interpretations involve novel and innovative assumptions about Matthew's sources and Jesus' "sayings," every scholarly approach toward resolving time-sensitive tensions within the Olivet Discourse still adopt (either implicitly or explicitly) some of the questionable assumptions and methodologies of previous generations. As a result, even the most unconventional and inventive solutions to the "delayed Parousia" seem to be in need of considerable re-evaluation.

By saying so, I do not wish to imply that all arguments in this study are airtight and immune to serious criticism. I realize that some observers might wish to aim criticism at my dependence upon literary structures, typologies, or unexamined nuances of patristic hermeneutics; others might disregard my thesis as being too heretical to be seriously entertained. Insofar as heresy involves the condemnation of novelty,[5] my approach from the beginning has been to evade inter-

---

5. On this historical distinction, see Jonathan Klawans, *Heresy, Forgery, Novelty: Condemning, Denying, and Asserting Innovation in Ancient Judaism* (Oxford, UK: Oxford University Press, 2019). Although I am raising important and legitimate questions about the interpretation of Matthew's OD within Christian tradition, I have no intention of challenging the very substance of Christian faith. I also recognize, as Marcus Plested has pointed out, that "heresy is a category imposed by the victors," and I agree with him that "The concept of heresy remains essential for distinguishing between an incorrect and a correct (or at least less incorrect) articulation of the faith." Marcus Plested, "Eutychianism: Is Jesus Christ divine and human or a hybrid, a third thing that is neither fully one nor the other?",

pretive novelty by going back to the basics of first-century literary intentionality—many basics of which were defended by theologians of previous eras and remain widely acknowledged to this day among scholars of Second Temple Judaism and early Christianity—rather than attempting to re-invent the wheel myself. With such an approach, I hope to have shown that interpretive novelties *posterior* to first-century literary intentionality are vulnerable to serious scrutiny, even though many novelties have become valorized over time. One frequently overlooked factor derived from my research is that no matter when Matthew's Gospel was originally composed, or even its final form solidified, it remains noticeably designed to correct futuristic, end-of-*our*-world novelties of interpretation. Among the Synoptics, Matthew's Gospel seems unique in this regard.

Another overlooked factor is that the overwhelming majority of theologians and scholars in this study are aware of first-century fulfillment within Jesus' response to his disciple's "first" question. My research not only highlights that tradition and its long-standing importance, but also that such tradition is noticeably essential for understanding Matthew's literary design. As tradition confirms, Jesus *does* begin his response with prophetic remarks about first-century events leading up to Jerusalem's destruction. But that initial response is to his disciples' *last* question, which underlines the location of true novelty across Christian traditions: all subsequent misunderstandings about the order in which Jesus responds necessarily involve novel interpretations.

In light of this, it should also be noted that this study does not attempt to settle any dogmas of the Christian church, especially eschatological ones. I personally profess and believe the Catholic and Orthodox creed of the first council of Nicaea (325 CE), so my research and its results are not designed to restructure the faith affirmed by those 318 church fathers. Moreover, since my focus remains on Mat-

---

Heresies and How to Avoid Them: Why it matters what Christians believe, ed. Ben Quash and Michael Ward (Peabody, MA: Hendrickson Publishers, 2007), 43.

thew's version of the Olivet Discourse, I have not attempted to solve all dilemmas or harmonize all New Testament statements associated with eschatological dogmas. Many more studies need to be produced in order to resolve all tensions across the New Testament.

Matthew's unique final judgment scene is one example of a paradigm ripe for further study. Although not explicitly stated, Christ's "coming in glory" most closely associates with the promised destruction of Jerusalem in 70 CE and the gathering of his saints awaiting vindication and final judgment from their Messiah at that time.[6] Al-

---

6. While arguing against N.T. Wright's position about first-century fulfillment, Allison makes some astoundingly ironic and cartoonish remarks about the final judgment in Mark's version of the OD, which does not contain an actual final judgment scene as Matthew's version does. Allison's unpersuasive argument is as follows: "What is the relationship between Mark 13 and 1 Thessalonians 4:13-18? Wright argues at length that Mark 13 is, from our vantage, not about the future but rather about the past: it came to fulfillment in the events surrounding 70 C.E. Others have previously said the same thing, but they have not won the day. Part of the reason is that *there are so many striking parallels between Mark 13 and Jewish apocalyptic literature that if one associates the latter with the last judgment, as is usually done, then it is natural to associate the former with it too. And the last judgment has not yet come.* . . . Another possible defect appears when Paul is considered. In 1 Thessalonians 4:13-18, the apostle passes on a tradition closely related to Mark 13:24-27. . . . One has great difficulty imagining that Paul was not referring to literal clouds in the atmosphere or that his first readers might have given his words a figurative sense. So an appeal to metaphor when pursuing the meaning of the closely related Mark 13:24-27 (and par.) seems equally out of place. In other words, Paul did not interpret the tradition behind Mark 13:24-27 as does Wright—that is, as a symbolic prophecy of Jerusalem's destruction . . . . Rather, the apostle construed it as have millenarian Christians down through the centuries: Paul expected Jesus to come on the clouds." Allison, *Jesus & Victory*, 134-5; italics added.

One alternative thesis to both Allison and N.T. Wright is the postulation by Charles Quarles that "Paul [in I Thess. 4:15-18] is alluding to a saying of Jesus that has not been preserved in our Gospels and is not to be identified with Matt 24:29-31." Quarles, *Matthew*, 633. "Consequently," Quarles asserts, "no tension exists between Paul's discussion of the second coming and Matt 24:4-31" (633). These concluding remarks by Quarles follow his extensive commentary of Matthew 24:4-31, which he unsurprisingly argues is in response to the disciples'

409

ternatively, it is possible that this scene in Heaven describes an end-of-*our*-world event or a time-transcending event, or even a combination of all three. If that is so, our re-evaluation of the scene makes it reasonable to imagine Jesus enthroned to judge the living and the dead from 70 CE onward, beginning with him gathering the righteous and unrighteous dead among all the nations out from Hades in that definitive end of the old covenant administration. As long as Jesus reigns over all, there remains a certain and final judgment for all.[7]

---

first question, and pertains *exclusively* to first-century fulfillment. On that, see Quarles, *Matthew*, 598-633.

7. An ascension of remaining first-century saints from Sheol/Hades in 70 CE—in distinction from the early Christian tradition about the "harrowing of Hades," which traditionally took place on *Pascha*—may also help clarify Paul's comments in 1 Thessalonians 4:14-16, where he says assuredly that at the *Parousia* Jesus will "bring with him those who have died." He also says, "we who are alive" at that time "who are left until the *Parousia* of the Lord" will not ascend *prior* to those saints who had already died and were waiting ascension. He insists that "The dead in Christ will rise first." One obvious implication of these very plain remarks is the belief that people who had died prior the *Parousia* would ascend as the "first" saints in that generation. Another implication is that all who die "in Christ" *thereafter* would assuredly ascend into the Lord's presence, too. These remarks by Paul make sense if neither he nor any other Christians of that generation *were planning to die* before the *Parousia*—being assured that the Parousia would occur soon—while also fully expecting to be raised up immediately to God *if they died after the promised Parousia of Christ in that generation.*

Not only does this view of post-70 CE ascension into God's presence for either eternal life (for the righteous) or condemnation (for the wicked) make sense of many controversial and seemingly opaque passages in the New Testament, but it also comports well with the unequivocal view of the late first-century apostolic father, Ignatius of Antioch, whose full expectation for Christian disciples after death was to "reach" (ἐπιτυχεῖν) God (cf. *Ign. Eph.* 10:1; 12:2; *Ign. Magn.* 1:2; 14:1; *Ign. Tral.* 12:2; 13:3; *Ign. Rom.* 1:1; 2:1; 4:1; 5:3; 9:2; *Ign. Phil.* 5:1; *Ign. Smyr.* 9:2; 11:1; *Ign. Polycarp* 2:3; 7:1). On that, see "The Letters of Ignatius" in *The Apostolic Fathers: Greek Texts and English Translations*, 182-271. As David Sim has evinced in one of his essays about death and afterlife in connection with the "end of the age," early *Christianity* is not the only place we find this theme. He writes: "We find in both Second Temple Judaism and early Christianity a wide range of schemas that speculated on this theme, and a number of these held

410

Given the consistent and clear emphasis upon first-century expectations of fulfillment, Matthew's version of the Olivet Discourse conveys a message from Jesus that is at odds with some traditional Christian assumptions and methodologies. This is especially noticeable with prophecies perceived to be about our future and its end-of-the-age. I believe one helpful approach to resolving this purported dilemma begins with becoming more conversant in the Scriptures according to its own first-century context, instead of merely parroting anachronistic conjecture of later generations. Furthermore, as Peter Leithart has suggested in his "Theopolitan" vision for the church,[8] Christians must also allow Jesus' gospel to speak on its own terms rather than forcing Scripture to fit in the idioms we are accustomed to hearing or want to hear. By doing so, we accept Jesus as our Lord. As Lord, he has the authority to correct and renew us by his word. Whatever horizons must yet be explored in light of what Jesus taught, Christians need to allow themselves to be confronted and corrected by his teaching.

---

that the dead would experience some form of existence immediately after death." David C. Sim, "Life after Death? The Question of Immediate Life after Death in the Dead Sea Scrolls and in the Gospel of Matthew," *Matthew Within Judaism: Israel and the Nations in the First Gospel*, Early Christianity And Its Literature, no. 27, ed. Anders Runesson and Daniel M. Gurtner (Atlanta, GA: SBL Press, 2020), 319. Intriguingly, Sim interacts extensively with opposing viewpoints and counter-arguments, and in his interpretation of Matthew 22:32, which illustrates a debate about the resurrection of the dead, he concludes that "Jesus is making the point that God is the God of the living insofar as he has the power *at the end of the age* to raise the now-dead patriarchs to eternal life." Sim, "Life after Death?", 341; italics added.

8. Peter J. Leithart, *The Theopolitan Vision* (West Monroe, LA: Theopolis Books, 2019), 55 and 57. Leithart's suggestions about the "immeasurable contributions" of modern scholarship, as well as their "systematic, relentless, centuries-long experiment in quenching the spirit" are also apt descriptions worthy of every Christian's consideration. On that, see Peter J. Leithart, *Theopolitan Reading* (West Monroe, LA: Theopolis Books, 2020), 9-10.

Appendix A

A.1 JESUS AS ISRAEL

As **chapter two** illustrates, Matthew's Gospel is arranged both chiastically and typologically. This is not a new or unusual conceptual arrangement for books of the Bible.[1] Leithart's thesis is, however, a

---

1. For literary structures within the Bible, see David A. Dorsey, *The Literary Structure of the Old Testament: A Commentary on Genesis–Malachi* (Grand Rapids, MI: Baker Academic, 2005); Jeremy T. Walsh, *Style & Structure in Biblical Hebrew Narrative* (Collegeville, MN: The Liturgical Press, 2001); John Breck, *The Shape of Biblical Language: Chiasmus in the Scriptures and Beyond* (Crestwood, NY: St Vladimir's Seminary Press, 2008); James L. Resseguie, *Narrative Criticism of the New Testament: An Introduction* (Grand Rapids, MI: Baker Academic, 2005); Peter F. Ellis, *The Genius of John: A Composition-Critical Commentary on the Fourth Gospel* (Collegeville, MN: The Liturgical Press, 1985); John Paul Heil, *The Death and Resurrection of Jesus: A Narrative-Critical Reading of Matthew 26-28* (1991; repr., Eugene, OR: Wipf & Stock, 2003).

For appreciating the typological themes of biblical narratives, see Ralph Allan Smith, *Hear, My Son: An Examination of the Fatherhood of Yahweh in Deuteronomy* (Monroe, LA: Athanasius Press, 2011); Alastair J. Roberts and Andrew Wilson, *Echoes of Exodus: Tracing Themes of Redemption through Scripture* (Wheaton, IL: Crossway, 2018); James B. Jordan, *Through New Eyes: Developing a Biblical View of the World* (1988; repr., Eugene, OR: Wipf & Stock, 1999); Seth D. Postell, *Adam as Israel: Genesis 1-3 as the Introduction to the Torah and Tanakh* (Eugene, OR: Pickwick Publications, 2011); L. Michael Morales, *The Tabernacle Pre-Figured: Cosmic Mountain Ideology in Genesis and Exodus* (Leuven-Paris-Walpole, MA: Peeters, 2012); L. Michael Morales, ed., *Cult and Cosmos: Tilting Toward a Temple-Centered Theology* (Leuven-Paris-Walpole, MA: Peeters, 2014); Matthew H. Patton, *Hope for a Tender Sprig: Jehoiachin in Biblical Theology*, BBRS, vol. 16 (Winona Lake, IN: Eisenbrauns, 2017); Adam Winn, *Mark and the Elijah-Elisha Narrative: Considering the Practice of Greco-Roman Imitation in the Search for Markan Source Material* (Eugene, OR: Pickwick Publications,

relatively new approach to studying Matthew's Gospel, which is why it is worth exploring further.

I distinctively remember stumbling across Leithart's essay, *Jesus as Israel: The Typological Structure of Matthew's Gospel,* in the Spring of 2011, and initially reserving serious doubts about it. At that time, I preferred the approach of Dale C. Allison Jr.'s rigorous study, *The New Moses: A Matthean Typology.* Although I do not consider their works to be mutually exclusive, after a deep dive into the literary structure of each chapter within Matthew's Gospel, I began to seriously consider the relevance of the typological and thematic structuring evident therein, and hence, gradually accept Leithart's thesis more and more.

2010); Rikki E Watts, *Isaiah's New Exodus in Mark* (1997; repr., Grand Rapids, MI: Baker Academic, 2000); Hans M. Moscicke, *Goat for Yahweh, Goat for Azazel: The Impact of Yom Kippur on the Gospels* (London: Lexington Books/Fortress Press, 2021); Warren Austin Gage, *Typological Poetics: Typology, Symbol, and the Christ* (Ft. Lauderdale, FL: St Andrews House, LLC, 2010); *Essays in Biblical Theology* (Ft. Lauderdale, FL: St Andrews House, LLC, 2010); *The Romance of Redemption: Biblical Types of the Bride of Christ* (Ft. Lauderdale, FL: St Andrews House, LLC, 2014); *There is No Greater Love: How Jesus is Greater Than All Who Came Before Him* (Ft. Lauderdale, FL: St Andrews House, LLC, 2013); Jean Danielou, *From Shadows to Reality: Studies in the Biblical Typology of the Fathers* (1960; repr., Jackson, MI: Ex Fontibus Company, 2018); Richard M. Davidson, *Typology in Scripture: A Study of Hermeneutical* τύπος *Structures*, AUSDDS, vol. 2 (Berrein Springs, MI: Andrews University Press, 1981); Buchanan, *Matthew Vol 1*, 8-18.

For some highly formative studies in both biblical typology and literary structure together, see Warren Austin Gage, *A Literary Guide to the Life of Christ in Matthew, Mark, and Luke-Acts* (Ft. Lauderdale, FL: St Andrews House, LLC, 2014); Warren Austin Gage and Christopher Barber, *The Story of Joseph and Judah*, TMSS, vol. 1, 2nd ed. (Ft. Lauderdale, FL: St Andrews House, LLC, 2010); Kenneth E. Bailey, *Jacob & the Prodigal: How Jesus Retold Israel's Story* (Downers Grove, IL: IVP Academic, 2003). See also Peter J. Leithart, *Deep Exegesis: The Mystery of Reading Scripture* (Waco, TX: Baylor University Press, 2009); *A House For My Name: A Survey of the Old Testament* (Moscow, ID: Canon Press, 2000); *A Son To Me: An Exposition of 1 & 2 Samuel* (Moscow, ID: Canon Press, 2003); *1 & 2 Kings*, BTCB (Grand Rapids, MI: Brazos Press, 2006); *1 & 2 Chronicles*, BTCB (Grand Rapids, MI: Brazos Press, 2019).

Although the typology surrounding the figure of Moses loomed large in my mind at that time, Allison's study did not account for the other perplexing typologies or literary structures proposed within Leithart's investigation.

With over a decade of research invested in one single book of the New Testament, I remain convinced that Matthew has organized his Gospel in an intentionally intricate manner.[2] The purpose of his organization is to highlight Jesus' life as the "interpretive key" to the meaning of Israel's holy Scriptures.[3] In this section I would like to add a few more details I found helpful in my early studies long ago, by offering a typological overview that was left out of chapter two (**2.1.1**). By doing so I hope to show, albeit in abbreviated fashion, why further studies in Matthew's Gospel are greatly needed.

---

2. I greatly appreciate the comments of John Nolland in this regard, who wrote: "It is very likely that a Gospel writer like Matthew worked instinctively or consciously with an awareness that he would communicate to different degrees to different readers. He produces a text in which the large movements of the story could hardly be lost on even the most minimally attentive hearer of an oral performance of the Gospel. But he also produces a text with extremely complex cross-references and allusions to materials from the OT and wider Jewish tradition. He can hardly have assumed that all his intended readers would be able to decipher the complex coding he makes use of. He produces a text in which the large structural blocks and elements of the more detailed structuring are very obvious indeed, but in which, despite the very evident intense investment in structuring, the details of the intended structure evade even the most attentive readers (sometimes the structure markers can be identified more readily than their function)." R. T. France and John Nolland, "Reflections on the Writing of a Commentary on the Gospel of Matthew," *Built Upon The Rock: Studies in the Gospel of Matthew*, ed. Daniel M. Gurtner and John Nolland (Grand Rapids, MI: William B. Eerdmans Publishing Company, 2008), 275.

3. Knowles, *Jeremiah in Matthew's Gospel*, 44, says this while arguing for Matthew's exegesis of OT passages. Here I have expanded that concept to relate to the purpose of Matthew's organizational structure as well.

The charts below extract descriptions found within various studies published by Peter Leithart,[4] but foundationally from his essay, *Jesus as Israel: The Typological Structure of Matthew's Gospel*. I have also adapted my findings in order to simplify its presentation. In each chart, the *narrative sections* mentioned in chapter two (**2.1.1**) are outlined with typological references from the Old Testament. For the sake of brevity, and also for the sake of what seems somewhat obvious at face-value (at least to me), I have chosen *not* to include an overview of literary parallels within Matthew's five *discourses*, or in the *final* narrative section that covers the death, resurrection, and "great commission" of Jesus. What remains is for your own investigation and edification and is designed to be a companion to the literary structure proposed in chapter two above.

A.1.1 MATTHEW 1–7

GOSPEL OF MATTHEW	OLD TESTAMENT
Beginnings, Birth, and Youth of God's Son	**Israel's Genesis – Mount Sinai**
1:1 Book of Beginning/Genesis (βίβλος γενέσεως)	Gen. 2:4; 5:1 (LXX) Book of Beginning/Genesis (βίβλος γενέσεως)
1:1-17 Son of Abraham	Gen. 12-26 Abraham and promised Son
1:18-25 Joseph the dreamer	Gen. 37 Joseph the dreamer
2:1-12 Magi travel from east to west to Jerusalem	Gen. 46:27 Representatives of nations travel from east to west

---

4. Leithart, *Typological Structure; The Four; Matthew Through New Eyes*. See Bibliography.

416

Micah 5:2-5a (LXX) is quoted, referring to Gen. 49:10[5]	Gen. 49:10 (LXX & Syriac) say, *for he is the expectation* of the nations." The MT says "until Shiloh comes," with a variant that says instead: "until He comes to whom it belongs"
2:13-15 Herod kills children	Exod. 1-2 Pharaoh kills children
2:14 Jesus rescued & flees to fulfill Hos. 11:1	Exod. 2 Moses rescued, flees
3:1-12 Announcement of judgment & exodus	Exod. 5-12 Moses announces judgment & exodus

5. Although Genesis 49:10 is a blessing given by the patriarch Jacob, which fits neatly within the typological framework of Leithart's proposal, David Instone-Brewer argues that post-70 CE rabbinic Targums are *better* background-sources for understanding the quotations in Matthew chapter two, especially insofar as later rabbis made typological associations between *Laban* (Jacob's father-in-law) and *Balaam* (the seer of Numbers 22–24). Some of the literary links offered by Instone-Brewer are fascinating (especially that which links the concept of a "Nazarene" to Balaam's prophecy and Laban's plan to kill the ancestor of the Messiah). Nonetheless, I find his overall thesis to be entirely unconvincing due to its immense complexity and (almost complete) dependance upon post-70 CE rabbinic interpretations. On this, see David Instone-Brewer, "Balaam-Laban as the Key to the Old Testament Quotations in Matthew 2," *Built Upon The Rock*, 207–27. Alternatively, it seems (at least to me) that very early rabbinic interpretations would have likely deflected attention away from the typological interpretations of Jesus-as-Israel offered by Matthew's Gospel and similar sources. Many of the literary and conceptual parallels presented by Instone-Brewer are also offered in a brief section of Amy Richter's monograph, *Enoch and the Gospel of Matthew*, PTMS (Eugene, OR: Pickwick Publications, 2012), 161-71. However, contrary to Instone-Brewer's proposal, Richter's thesis is not advocating *Talmudic* sources for the literary background of Matthew 2. Instead, her focus is on the four unique women mentioned in Matthew's opening genealogy, connecting them with 1 Enoch, and ultimately contending that "the birth of Jesus" by the "fifth woman" (i.e., Mary) overturns the effects of the Enochic Watchers' template by using the very elements of that template" to "redress the watcher's transgression" (127).

3:13-17 Jesus passes through waters	Exod. 13:1-15:21 Exodus/Passing through waters
4:1-11 Temptation in "wilderness"	Exod. 15:22-17:16 Temptation in "wilderness"
Verses 7 & 10 are quotes from Deut. 6:16	Exod. 17:7 is referenced in Deut. 6:16
4:18-22 Jesus calls disciples	Exod. 18 Moses appoints rulers
4:2 Fasting 40 days & 40 nights	Exod. 34:27-29; Deut. 9:18 Fasting 40 days & 40 nights
Chapters 5-7 Sermon on the Mount	**Exod. 19 *ff.* Giving the Law at Mt. Sinai**

A.1.2 MATTHEW 8–10

GOSPEL OF MATTHEW	OLD TESTAMENT
Wilderness Wandering	**Wilderness Wandering: (Moses - Joshua)**
8:1 Jesus leaves mountain & crowds follow	Num. 10:11-13 Israel leaves Mount Sinai & cloud follows
8:2-4 Healing of leprosy	Num. 12:1-16 Miriam healed of leprosy

418

Chs. 8-9 Ten miracles[6] bring healing & restoration	Num. 14:22 Ten rebellions[7] of Israel bring judgment and despair
9:34 Pharisees oppose/ discredit Jesus	Num. 16:1-3 Leaders oppose/ discredit Moses

6. France, *Matthew*, 300, notes that these ten miracles were presented as one "collection," and that there also appears to be a unique placement of each miracle into three distinctive groups when compared with the other two synoptic gospels. He writes: "The collection consists of nine separate miracle stories comprising ten individual miracles (since one of the stories, 9:18-26, contains two intertwined miracles of healing), which are arranged in three groups of three (8:1-17; 8:23-9:8; 9:18-34). Between these three groups are two narrative interludes (8:18-22; 9:9-17) each of which focuses on the call to discipleship and the response of a variety of individuals to that call." The result of France's description looks something like this (below):

Miracle #1 - Leper (8:1-5)
Miracle #2 - A Gentile's "son" (8:5-13)
Miracle #3 - Peter's mother-in-law (8:14-17)
Narrative interlude: Two types of disciples (8:18-22)
Miracle #4 - Miracle on the sea with disciples – calms the sea (8:23-27)
Miracle #5 - Miracle across the sea in another city – casts out demonic-oppressors (8:28-34)
Miracle #6 - Miracle back across the sea in his own city – comforts & heals paralytic (9:1-8)
Narrative interlude: Two types of disciples (9:9-17)
Miracles #7 & #8 - Dead daughter & Bleeding woman (9:18-26)
Miracles #9 - Two blind men (9:27-31)
Miracle #10 - Demon-possessed mute man (9:32-34)

7. According to Ulrich Luz, *The Theology of the Gospel of Matthew*, trans. J. B. Robinson (Cambridge: Cambridge University Press, 1995), 63, and Stephanie Black, "How Matthew Tells the Story: A Linguistic Approach to Matthew's Narrative Syntax," *Built Upon The Rock*, 46-52, Matthew 8:1–9:34 is one continuous literary unit with many linguistic cues pertaining to Jesus' conflict with Israel's rebellious leaders. The concept of healing in Matthean typology pairs nicely with the rebellions of Israel in the wilderness, and is much more convincing than the post-70 CE opinions of rabbis as suggested by Knowles. Knowles posits that the "sequence of ten miracles" in Matthew chapters 8-9 possibly recalls "the ten miracles of Moses in Egypt that were celebrated by rabbinic tradition (*m. Ab.* 5.4) and were expected to have their counterpart in the last days (Mic. 7.15)." *Jeremiah in Matthew's Gospel*, 240.

9:36 "Sheep that have no shepherd" describe the people of Israel	Num. 27:17 "Sheep that have no shepherd" describe the people of Israel
10:2,5 Jesus *sends* ($\dot{\alpha}\pi o\sigma\tau\dot{\epsilon}\lambda\lambda\omega$) twelve Apostles ($\dot{\alpha}\pi\dot{o}\sigma\tau o\lambda o\varsigma$) into the land	Josh 2:1 (LXX) Joshua *sends* ($\dot{\alpha}\pi o\sigma\tau\dot{\epsilon}\lambda\lambda\omega$) spies into the land
10:5-7 Twelve apostles ($\dot{\alpha}\pi\dot{o}\sigma\tau o\lambda o\varsigma$) are sent first into land of Israel, and later to be sent throughout the Roman empire (28:16-20)	Num. 13:12 (LXX) The spies sent out ($\dot{\alpha}\pi o\sigma\tau\dot{\epsilon}\lambda\lambda\omega$) first fail under Moses. More spies will be sent out ($\dot{\alpha}\pi o\sigma\tau\dot{\epsilon}\lambda\lambda\omega$) into the promised land under Joshua (Josh. 2:1 LXX)
Chapter 10 Mission of the Twelve: Preparation	**Deuteronomy / Preparation for Conquest**

A.1.3 MATTHEW 11–13

GOSPEL OF MATTHEW	OLD TESTAMENT
Entrance into Land of Rest The Rise of a King	**Entrance into Land, the Rise of a King (Joshua - David)**
11:1-19 "This generation" of Israel fails to respond faithfully to God's "Messenger"	The Exodus generation fails to enter the promised land
11:10 The promised $\dot{\alpha}\gamma\gamma\epsilon\lambda o\varsigma$ (messenger) of Mal. 3:1 LXX echoes the promised $\dot{\alpha}\gamma\gamma\epsilon\lambda o\varsigma$ of Exod. 33:2 LXX who would drive out the enemies within the promised land and lead Israel into their promised rest	Exod. 33:2 An $\dot{\alpha}\gamma\gamma\epsilon\lambda o\varsigma$ (messenger) is promised to lead Israel into the promised land and drive out their enemies (fulfilled under Joshua)
11:25-30 Jesus offers rest to Israel	Joshua 11:23; 21:44; 23:1 YHWH offers rest to Israel
12:7 Compassion, not sacrifice ($\theta v\sigma i\alpha$)	1 Sam 15:22 LXX Obedience, not sacrifice ($\theta v\sigma i\alpha$)

420

12:1-8 David and the "showbread"	I Sam 21 David and the "showbread"
Jesus is persecuted by leaders of Israel	David is persecuted by King Saul and his men
12:14 Pharisees plot to murder & Jesus withdraws	I Sam 27:1-2 Saul plots to murder & David withdraws
12:24-41 Jesus rebukes the Pharisees and their servants for blaspheming the Holy Spirit and seeking after signs	I Sam 28 Yahweh rebukes Saul and his servants for his blasphemy and seeking 'signs' from a Medium of the Dead
12:42-45 Solomon's wisdom is highlighted & "One Greater than Solomon is here" & justice for "this evil generation	I Kings 3-4 Solomon's wisdom is "wiser than all other men" & the "wisdom of God in him to do justice"
Chapter 13 Parables, Proverbs, & Wisdom for the Coming Kingdom	**Parables, Proverbs, & Wisdom of Israel's Kingdom**

A.1.4 MATTHEW 14-18

GOSPEL OF MATTHEW	OLD TESTAMENT
Prophetic Ministry in the North	**Prophetic Ministry in Northern Kingdom (Elijah - Elisha)**
14:1-12 Herod attacks and kills John the prophet & a wife (Herodias) influences the attack	1 Kings 19 Ahab attacks and almost kills Elijah the prophet & a wife (Jezebel) influences attack
14:10 John's departure	2 Kings 2:11 Elijah's departure
Herod v. Jesus	Divided kingdom; Omrides v. YWHW's prophets
15:21-28 Jesus heals a Syro-Phoenician woman & disciples want to keep her away	2 Kings 4:8-37 Elisha heals Shunammite woman's son & Gehazi (Elisha's disciple) wants to keep her away

15:32-39 Jesus' ministry: four thousand are fed	2 Kings 4:38-44 Elisha's ministry: food miracles
16:5-12 Discussion of leftover bread	2 Kings 4:42-44 Discussion of leftover bread
16:13-20 Peter confesses Jesus to be the "anointed" one of God	Elisha is publicly "anointed" as a prophet of God
17:1-13 "Angelic" transfiguration of Jesus. Moses & Elijah appear before Jesus and his disciples	2 Kings 6:15-19 Angels of God appear before Elisha and his servant
17:12 Jesus tells his disciples, "Do not fear"	2 Kings 6:16 Elisha tells his disciple, "Do not fear"
17:14-21 Disciples fail to heal	2 Kings 4:29-31 Gehazi (Elisha's disciple) fails to heal
Chapter 18 Instructions for a divided Kingdom	**Israel's Kingdom is hopelessly divided**

A.1.5 MATTHEW 19–28

GOSPEL OF MATTHEW	OLD TESTAMENT
Prophetic Ministry in the South	**Prophetic Ministry in Southern Kingdom (Jeremiah, *et al.*)**
19:1 Jesus enters Judaea, the southern kingdom	Prophetic ministry in southern kingdom
21:1-11 Jesus' triumphal entry. Procession of the "King" ($\beta\alpha\sigma\iota\lambda\epsilon\acute{\upsilon}\varsigma$) over carpet of garments. Acclamation of "Son of David" by their followers	2 Kings 9:1-13 (LXX) Jehu is anointed by unnamed prophet of Judah. Procession of the King over a carpet of garments. Acclamation of "King" ($\beta\alpha\sigma\iota\lambda\acute{\epsilon}\alpha$) by their followers
21:12-16 Jesus's first action: cleansing Herod's temple & enacting its coming destruction	2 Kings 10 Jehu's first action: destroys temple of Baal in the northern kingdom of Israel & cleanses the house of Ahab

422

Jesus is an apocalyptic prophet in Judah	Apocalyptic prophets in southern kingdom
21:5 The King comes mounted on a donkey	Zech 9:9 The King comes mounted on a donkey
21:13 Jesus in Herod's temple. Described as a "robbers' den" (σπήλαιον λῃστῶν)	Jer. 7:11 (LXX) Jeremiah in temple. Described as a "robbers' den" (σπήλαιον λῃστῶν)
21:18-21 Cursed & withered fig tree	Jer. 8:13 Cursed Israel shall be as a withered fig tree
21:44 Kingdom of God is a heavy "stone" which hurts those who attempt to seize it	Zech 12:3 Jerusalem is a heavy "stone" which hurts those who attempt to seize it
21:33-46 Parable of the Master's vineyard being ruined by tenants (a reference to Jerusalem)	Jer. 12; Isa. 5 The Master's vineyard is ruined by tenants (a reference to Jerusalem)
21:35 The Lord's servant is sent to tenants & the servant is beaten	Jer. 20:2 Jeremiah preaches in Jerusalem, and is the only prophet recorded in OT to be "beaten"
Chapters 23-25 Woes and Prophecy about the House of Israel	**The End of the Judaean Kingdom / Warnings of Temple destruction & Babylonian exile[8]**
Matt. 26-28 Death, Resurrection, and Great Commission of God's Son	**Death & Resurrection of Israel, and the "Great Commission" of the Lord's "Anointed" (Cyrus)**

---

8. Commenting on Matthew 24:2b in connection with "the mounting conflict and climax" of Jerusalem's destruction, Akiva Cohen quotes Mark Goodacre, who once said that reading Matthew here "is like reading Jeremiah. It works because the reader knows that the prophecies of doom turned out to be correct." Cohen, *Matthew and the Temple*, 95-6.

Appendix B

B.1 ADVENTURES IN MISSING THE POINT (MATT. 10)

The second discourse within Matthew's Gospel contains many phrases that are reminiscent of remarks within the Olivet Discourse. For example, in Matthew 10:23 (ESV) Jesus says, "*When they persecute you in one town, flee to the next, for truly, I say to you, you will not have gone through all the towns of Israel before the Son of Man comes.*" A strikingly similar message is repeated in Matthew 24:34: "*Truly, I say to you, this generation will not pass away until all these things take place.*"

As I have argued in **chapter two**, common misunderstandings about Matthew's Gospel as a whole help explain why the meaning of these two statements are frequently distorted, overlooked, or minimized in their importance. Some misunderstandings presuppose all of Jesus' promises about "the end" essentially require futuristic, end-of-*our*-world events. Other misunderstandings result from unfamiliarity with the kind of literary work in hand. Sometimes the text is misunderstood because the underlying Greek text is poorly understood; at other times, it is because the literary structure or typological framework is not brought into one's examination of the passage. There are also times when a student of Scripture is not familiar with first-century history, and so everything Jesus says can be mistakenly interpreted as speaking to all audiences of all generations, instead of weighing how it would have been received in its original, historical context.

Proof-texting has also become a problematic, yet socially acceptable approach to justify soundbites of Christian lifestyles. Matthew 10 is frequently utilized across Christian traditions for such soundbites. Some people will quote Jesus' words, "*Heal the sick, raise the dead, cleanse lepers, cast out demons*" (10:8 ESV). Then they will conclude that this commission from Jesus can be assigned to Christians today. Pentecostal Christians and other charismatic-gift-oriented traditions may defend their practices with a quick glance toward this passage. Other soundbites are equally popular among strands of Christian tradition:

> "If anyone will not receive you or listen to your words, shake off the dust from your feet" (10:14, ESV).
>
> . . . .
>
> "Behold, I am sending you out as sheep in the midst of wolves, so be wise as serpents and innocent as doves" (10:16, ESV).
>
> . . . .
>
> "You will be dragged before governors and kings for my sake, to bear witness before them" (10:18, ESV).
>
> . . . .
>
> "Do not be anxious how you are to speak or what you are to say, for what you are to say will be given to you in that hour. For it is not you who speak, but the Spirit of your Father speaking through you" (10:19, ESV).
>
> . . . .
>
> "You will be hated by all for my name's sake" (10:22, ESV).
>
> . . . .
>
> "Truly I say to you, you will not have gone through all the towns of Israel before the Son of Man comes" (10:23, ESV).
>
> . . . .
>
> "Everyone who acknowledges me before men, I also will acknowledge before my Father who is in heaven, but whoever denies me before men, I also will deny before my Father who is in heaven" (10:32, ESV).
>
> . . . .

426

"A person's enemies will be those of his own household" (10:36, ESV).

One prooftext makes some Christians think they do not need to be equipped with anything but their Bibles in order to witness or evangelize unbelievers. This is because, allegedly, the Holy Spirit will give them the right words to say "in that hour," as Jesus promised. Others want to believe that Jesus equates our own personal enemies with "wolves," and that his message to us is to treat them as such. But is that really what Jesus meant when he said, "*I am sending you out as sheep in the midst of wolves*"?

I have even heard Matthew 10:18 used to teach that faithfulness to Jesus is *not* patriotic enough if one is unwilling to provoke persecution from civil magistrates. Forget about how obnoxious, excessive, or obtuse Christians may appear to be during their expression of faithful patriotic zeal. The *real* important truth, so I have been told, is for faithful Christians to behave so patriotically that they are guaranteed persecution from civil authorities.

Another token virtue of genuine loyalty to Jesus is to have those of your own household become your enemies. This doctrine is even construed as being abundantly clear and impossible to misunderstand. Do not compromise the Christian faith by being friendly, patient, compassionate, or (heaven forbid) *silent* when others of your own household do not believe the truth revealed to you by God's Word. Instead, stick to your guns, stand up for what is "right," and focus all of your attention upon being loyal to Jesus, even if that means those of your own family will become your enemies by hardening their hearts against God's truth. After all, *you* have been commissioned, according to Matthew 10:36, to proclaim truth to their faces.

Instead of piecemealing Jesus' statements to rationalize and justify contemporary trends of applicability, it seems much healthier to understand and respect a gospel's fundamental attributes first, namely its historical context, literary genre, and compositional intentionality. If this second discourse within Matthew's Gospel was intended to be coherent, unified, and meaningful—not just a smattering of eternal truths for people of every generation to apply to themselves whenever it becomes convenient—one would certainly hope that Matthew left us clues to interpret it properly. Thankfully, Matthew has left us many clues. Because Jesus' second discourse has many parallels with his fifth discourse, the excursus below will attempt to illustrate how Matthew has paved a path for understanding Jesus' message, thereby avoiding common pitfalls of interpretation.

B.2 IDENTIFYING THE DISCOURSE AND ITS STRUCTURE

To begin one's exegesis of a specific discourse, the boundaries need to be identified. In this instance, the technical starting point of the second discourse is verse 5. The first four verses of chapter ten are not part of the discourse. Rather, they describe Jesus calling twelve disciples and appointing them as his apostles. This appointment is followed by a list of each apostle by name, which ends in verse 4. Immediately after verse 4, Jesus' official discourse begins, saying: "These twelve Jesus sent out, instructing them, *Go nowhere among the Gentiles and enter no town of the Samaritans, but go to the lost sheep of the house of Israel*" (10:5-6, ESV). Matthew signals the end of this discourse in 11:1, as he does with the other four discourses, by writing, "*When Jesus had finished instructing his twelve disciples.*"

Everything between 10:4 and 11:1 is Jesus' second discourse. After discovering where this discourse begins and ends, its contents can be examined so that a literary structure can be identified within those boundaries. Many modern bibles even contain headers (inserted by the editors) between chapters that describe the contents of various paragraphs. These headers are one way to easily identify literary units within a lengthy discourse. The following arrangement can be deduced from closely examining the second discourse:

A) Instructions to the twelve apostles (10:5-15)
  B) Persecution and family division (10:16-23)
    C) Enemies of the Master's household (10:24-25)
      D) *Consolation of the twelve apostles* (10:26-33)
    C') Enemies of the Master's household (10:34-36)
  B') Persecution and family division (10:37-39)
A') Reception of the twelve apostles (10:40-42)

In each section Matthew has arranged various repeated words, phrases, and themes which confirm this structure. "Sent" is mentioned in two locations (vv. 5 and 40), and "receive" is mentioned multiple times (vv. 14 and 40-42). Both terms are found in sections *A* & *A'*. Parents and children are mentioned twice (vv. 21 and 37) in sections *B* & *B'*. "Household" is mentioned twice (vv. 25 and 36) in sections *C & C'*. In the central section (section "D") there are three negative statements about "fear" and one positive statement: "Do not fear them . . ." (v. 26), "Do not fear those who. . . *but fear Him who can . . .*" (v. 28), and "Do not fear, therefore . . ." (v. 31). It is clear from this positive statement in v. 28 that the central section is structured in three smaller parts (i.e., a triad), with a unique emphasis on the central section of this triad.

Therefore, another way of viewing the literary structure of the second discourse is to split up the central section into its own distinctive triad:

A) Instructions to the twelve apostles (10:5-15)
  B) Persecution and family division (10:16-23)
    C) Enemies of the Master's household (10:24-25)
      D1) "Do not fear them..." (10:26-27)
        D2) "Do not fear those who...
          but Fear Him who can..." (10:28-30)
      D3) "Do not fear, therefore..." (10:31-33)
    C') Enemies of the Master's household (10:34-36)
  B') Persecution and family division (10:37-39)
A') Reception of the twelve apostles (10:40-42)

B.2.1 EXEGESIS OF SECTIONS *A* & *A'*

The first thing worth noting is that Jesus' audience is categorically limited to his twelve apostles. Jesus begins and ends with instructions for twelve apostles. He tells *them,* and only them, to go "to the lost sheep of the house of Israel" (10:6), proclaiming that "the kingdom of heaven is at hand" (10:7). The purpose of their mission is to find out "who is worthy" of the kingdom as they go from town to town, from one Israelite household to another (10:13). It is to be expected that many would not receive them or listen to their message (10:14). These twelve apostles are also commissioned to heal the sick, raise the dead, cleanse lepers, and cast out demons (v. 8). They are not to carry any gold, silver, or copper as they evangelized. Even a staff, bag, sandals, or *two* tunics (a strange specification, to be sure) are unnecessary provisions (vv. 9-10). Although these instructions might seem odd to Christians today, there is one good reason why they were given these instructions as they went door to door: judgment was coming upon that generation very soon. At the end of section *A,* Jesus says, "Truly, I say to you, it will be more bearable on the day of judgment for the land of Sodom and Gomorrah than for *that* town."

This message for an entire town to face God would have given first-century Israelites the impression that soon-coming judgment was approaching them, causing them to face their Maker and give an account before Him much sooner than later. Sodom and Gomorrah were destroyed suddenly because of its great lawlessness and idolatry (Gen. 13:13; 18:20; 19; Deut. 29:23). As a result, "Sodom and Gomorrah" became a proverbial expression of warning upon *any* idolatrous nation (Isa. 1:9; 13:19; Jer. 22:14; 50:40; Amos 4:11). Sodom and Gomorrah faced a swift judgment from God in the days of Abraham, just as the towns of Israel who rejected the apostles would receive God's swift judgment.

Section *A'* corresponds nicely with this message in section *A.* Jesus can confidently tell his twelve apostles that *"Whoever welcomes you welcomes me, and whoever welcomes me welcomes him who sent me"*

(10:40) because judgment is coming soon. Those who would welcome ($\delta \acute{\epsilon} \chi o \mu \alpha \iota$) this message of the twelve apostles ($\dot{\alpha} \pi \acute{o} \sigma \tau o \lambda o \varsigma$), would also welcome Jesus (10:40). And those who welcome Jesus, welcome the Father who sent ($\dot{\alpha} \pi o \sigma \tau \acute{\epsilon} \lambda \lambda \omega$) him (10:40). By welcoming the Father, they welcome the inheritance promised by the Father, namely the kingdom of heaven and eternal life with God the Father and the Son (10:42; cf. 10:39). By welcoming the words of God whom the Father and Son had sent, those towns would receive exactly what each prophet pronounced to them so they could endure faithfully through the coming judgment (10:41). Jesus also says that by welcoming the innocent ($\delta \acute{\iota} \kappa \alpha \iota o \varsigma$) into their home, they would receive rewards for protecting the innocent (10:41). Consequently, by rejecting an innocent man in the name of the Lord, they will receive justice for rejecting Jesus and the Father who sent him.

When an Israelite heard that the kingdom of heaven was in their midst as promised, the people had one of two choices to make: they could either side with Jesus as their promised Messiah and King and heed the message of his apostles, or reject them and accept a false hope. According to this commission, it is evident that the responsibility given to these twelve apostles before Jesus' passion was no laughing matter. Whoever would receive one of Jesus' apostles, supporting them and giving them a cup of cold water after hearing *their* message (v. 42), would not lose their reward. After Jesus' passion, his commission to them became even greater in scope within that generation.

B.2.2 EXEGESIS OF SECTIONS *B* & *B'*

The next two parallel sections are B and B'. They both describe persecution and family division. Jesus took his twelve apostles aside and told them that they did not need to be anxious about how they were to speak or what they were to say (10:19). In the hour of their declaration of his gospel, the Holy Spirit promised to give them what they were to say (10:20). The Son of Man was coming upon that generation in judgment (10:23). They would be hated throughout all of Israel's towns for the sake of Jesus' name, and their only hope was to endure to "the end" and be saved (10:22).

This is the context in which Jesus speaks of either losing or finding "life." Those who would not lose their life for Jesus' sake would be judged according to their complacency (10:39). Those who would not carry their own cross and follow Jesus would not be worthy of receiving Jesus in the end (10:38). The Son of Man was going to come upon that generation in judgment, so the call to make a decision was time-sensitive. All of this was spoken clearly by Jesus: "When they persecute you in one town, flee to the next, for truly, I say to you, *you will not have gone through all the towns of Israel before the Son of Man comes*" (10:23).

This language about the Son of Man coming in judgment is mentioned in multiple places throughout Matthew's Gospel, which should lead us to believe that each passage is talking about the exact same time-frame of events. For example, in Matthew 16:24-28, Jesus tells his disciples that,

> If anyone would come after me, let him deny himself *and take up his cross and follow me. For whoever would save his life will lose it, but whoever loses his life for my sake will find it. . . . For the Son of Man is going to come with his angels in the glory of his Father, and then he will repay each person according to what he has done. Truly, I say to you, there are some standing here who will not taste death until they see the Son of Man coming in his kingdom.*

Jesus' emphasis is upon a very close time-frame in which this "coming" of the Son of Man would take place. It is as though Matthew insisted on repeating Jesus' message over and over again for the sake of abundant *clarity*. Jesus repeats this same message again in Matthew 23:32-39 (ESV), where we find him condemning the ungodly rulers of Israel:

432

Fill up, then, the measure of your Fathers! You serpents! You brood of vipers! How are you to escape being sentenced to hell? Therefore, I send you prophets and wise men and scribes, some of whom you will kill and crucify, and some you will flog in your synagogues and persecute from town to town, so that *on you* may come all the righteous blood shed on earth... Truly, I say to you, *all these things will come upon this generation.* O Jerusalem, Jerusalem, the city that kills the prophets and stones those who are sent to it! How often would I have gathered your children together as a hen gathers her brood under her wings, and you were not willing! See, your house is left to you desolate!

When Jesus sits on the Mount of Olives and his disciples ask about *"the sign of your coming and of the end of the age"* in Matthew 24:3, Jesus begins by answering their question about "the end" in language reminiscent with his *second* discourse:

> . . . they will deliver *you* up to tribulation and put *you* to death, and *you will be hated by all nations for my name's sake.* And then many will fall away and betray one another and hate one another. And many false prophets will arise and lead many astray. And because lawlessness will be increased, the love of many will grow cold. *But the one who endures to the end will be saved.* And the gospel of the kingdom will be proclaimed throughout the whole world as a testimony to all nations, and *then the end will come* (Matt. 24:9-14, ESV).

In Luke's version of the OD, we find Jesus repeating the exact same phrases Matthew recorded in Matthew 10:16-23 (section *B* above). Luke 21:10-24 (ESV) says:

> Then [Jesus] said to them, "Nation will rise against nation, and kingdom against kingdom. There will be great earth-

quakes, and in various places famines and pestilences. And there will be terrors and great signs from heaven. But before all this *they will lay their hands on you and persecute you, delivering you up to the synagogues and prisons, and you will be brought before kings and governors for my name's sake. This will be your opportunity to bear witness. Settle it therefore in your minds not to meditate beforehand how to answer, for I will give you a mouth and wisdom, which none of your adversaries will be able to withstand or contradict. You will be delivered up even by parents and brothers and relatives and friends, and some of you they will put to death. You will be hated by all for my name's sake. But not a hair of your head will perish. By your endurance you will gain your lives.*"

"But when you see Jerusalem surrounded by armies, then know that its desolation has come near. Then let those who are in Judea flee to the mountains, and let those who are inside the city depart, and let not those who are out in the country enter it, for these are the days of vengeance, to fulfill all that is written. Alas for women who are pregnant in those days! For there will be great distress upon the earth and wrath against this people. They will fall by the edge of the sword and be led captive among all nations, and Jerusalem will be trampled underfoot by the Gentiles until the times of the Gentiles are fulfilled."

In Luke's version of the OD, Jesus says they will be persecuted, delivered to synagogues, and brought before governors and kings (cf. Matt. 10:17-18). They will bear witness to Jesus' sufferings (cf. Matt. 10:18). They will be given words of wisdom to speak in that hour (cf. Matt. 10:19-20). Division will arise within one's own household (cf. 10:21), and they will be hated by all of Israel for his name's sake (cf. 10:22).

By comparing the language of Matt. 10 alongside Jesus' Olivet Discourse, it seems obvious that Matthew viewed Jesus as prophesying about the same soon-coming judgment upon the land of Israel. This is especially evident if one assumes (as many scholars do) that Matthew used Luke's Gospel as a source for his own composition. "*These are the days of vengeance*," Jesus said in Luke's OD, "*to fulfill all that is written.*" In Matthew 10:16, Jesus sends his twelve apostles "out as sheep in the midst of wolves" in these days of God's vengeance. For this reason, they are exhorted to "be wise as serpents and innocent as doves" (Matt. 10:16).

B.2.3 EXEGESIS OF SECTIONS C & C′

In Matthew 10:24-25 (section *C*) Jesus illustrates the relationship between a disciple and his teacher, as well as a servant and his master. In doing so, he is preparing his disciples for persecution against those who would accuse them of even worse things than what they had already accused Jesus of being, i.e., "Beelzebul." (Matt. 10:25; cf. 9:32-34). "Baal-Zebul" was a derogatory term associated with a pagan deity whom many Jews believed to be the "Lord" of evil spirits and their "house." Jesus' apostles would need to be prepared for worse accusations than this because Jesus was going to *give them authority over unclean spirits*" (10:1), with a unique and crucial mission within Israel to "*heal the sick, raise the dead, cleanse lepers, and cast out demons*" (10:8). Jesus did not give this authority merely to anyone who wanted it, or everyone capable of possessing it. He was going to give it *to them*, and only for this unique mission until the Son of Man would come in judgment upon that generation.

Jesus did not want his apostles *merely* to think of themselves as ones with the authority of the Messiah. He also wanted them to think of themselves as servants of God's *household*. The twelve apostles would have understood this language about household servants. Jesus is teaching that if God's enemies are not able to touch the Lord of glory himself, they will go after his children. And if they show themselves willing to destroy the Lord of glory himself, they will pursue his children unto death as well. Therefore, Jesus is warning his twelve apostles about this reality and the temptations that come with their responsibility to guard and keep God's household.

Matthew 10:34-36 (section C) corresponds well with this first-century message of responsibility and accountability in the face of unjust persecution. Jesus tells them that he did not come to bring peace to the "earth." In Greek, the word translated here as "earth" is γη, a term used throughout the Greek Old Testament for the promised "land" and territories of Israel. Jesus did not come to bring peace to *the promised land* and territories of Israel, i.e., the land in which the lost sheep of the house of Israel dwelled. Jesus had come to divide the land, dividing its wheat from chaff, sheep from goats, and those who were with him from those who were against him.

Jesus also emphatically says that he did not come to bring peace; he came to bring a sword (10:34). His ministry as the Messiah to the nations would necessarily divide the land of Israel because the leadership of Israel had become idolaters just like the Canaanites long before them. But the rulers of Israel had actually done much worse than the Canaanites. Not only had their leaders been slandering Jesus as a demonic "lord" and false prophet, thereby promoting allegiance to actual rival gods, but they had also repeatedly rejected the living and true God who tabernacled in their midst. Jesus came to bring a sword *against them*. Enemies would even creep up within one's own household (10:36). In light of this corrupt and terminal generation, Jesus came to set a man against his own biological father, and a daughter against her biological mother, and a daughter-in-law against her legal mother-in-law (10:35). The boundaries which defined God's people were being divided in the first century, chopped up with the sword of the Spirit, wielded by the Word of God dwelling in their midst.

Jesus could assure his twelve apostles that enemies would be those of one's own household because he understood that God's family transcends the legal and blood-related households of Israel. God's family is more important than legal family ties and blood-relationships which bind the twelve tribes of Israel together; and in that sense,

436

water really is thicker than blood. The waters of baptism which John the baptizer brought to repentant sheep of the house of Israel would be taken seriously by God, and John the baptizer only baptized *repentant* sheep (Matt. 3:1-12). As noted by Luke 7:30, which stands in very close connection with the narratives surrounding Jesus' second discourse in Matthew's gospel, "the Pharisees and teachers of the Law rejected the purpose of God for themselves, *not having been baptized by John.*" Jesus had come to bring a sword against *those* rulers and *their* disciples, for they were enemies of God's household; they were priests of Baal's *Zebul.*

B.2.4 EXEGESIS OF SECTION *D*

D1) So have no fear (μη ουν φοβηθητε) of them, for nothing is covered that will not be revealed, or hidden that will not be known. What I tell you in the dark, say in the light, and what you hear whispered, proclaim on the housetops.

D2) And do not fear (μη φοβεισθε) those who kill the body but cannot kill the soul. Rather fear (φοβεισθε δε μαλλον) him who can destroy both soul and body in hell. Are not two sparrows sold for a penny? And not one of them will fall to the ground apart from your Father. But even the hairs of your head are all numbered.

D3) Fear not, therefore (μη ουν φοβηθητε); you are of more value than many sparrows. So everyone who acknowledges me before men, I also will acknowledge before my Father who is in heaven, but whoever denies me before men, I also will deny before my Father who is in heaven.

These exhortations reinforce Jesus' encouragement for his twelve apostles to be wise in their mission to the lost sheep of the house of Israel.

They were to trust in God's care and protection. Every bird worth half a penny in the marketplace falls to the ground because of God's will, so it is not difficult to imagine how valuable each human hair of one's head is worth in comparison. Strands of hair fall to the ground every day, and most people think nothing of it; nonetheless, Jesus encouraged his apostles to trust that their heavenly Father values *every* hair that falls. As the twelve apostles traveled from town to town proclaiming the gospel while attempting to prepare disciples for the soon-coming judgment, they needed to remember to fear the living and true God, not man or their rival gods.

B.3 TYPOLOGICAL OVERVIEW OF THE SECOND DISCOURSE

As noted in **chapter two** and **Appendix A**, the typology of Matthew 10 involves Israel during their wandering in the wilderness. It was in the wilderness that they awaited God's instructions concerning their entrance into His promised inheritance. This discourse functions similarly to the book of Deuteronomy, which is a sermon-like discourse given by Moses before the people entered the promised land. Throughout Deuteronomy, the people of Israel receive instructions from Yahweh through their mediator, Moses, *not* to fear the idolaters of the land (Deut. 1:21; 3:2, 22; 20:3; 31:6,8), but rather to fear Yahweh instead (Deut. 4:10; 5:29; 6:2, 13, 24; 8:6; 10:12, 20; 13:4; 14:23; 17:13, 19; 19:20; 28:58; 31:12, 13).

In Matthew 10, the typology between Jesus and Moses is evident. Just as Moses, the mediator between God and Israel, was a type of Christ, so Jesus is a type of Moses, only a *greater* Moses, who instructs twelve "rulers" of Israel in preparation for conquest. But Jesus is not set on the mere conquest of the land of Canaan (or Judaea). Rather, Jesus is set on a conquest which begins in Judaea, then spreads to Samaria, followed by its permeation through the uttermost parts of the world (Acts 1:8; 8:1; 9:31; Col. 1:3-6). Before the promised "end" comes, Jesus sends ($\dot{\alpha}\pi o\sigma\tau\acute{\epsilon}\lambda\lambda\omega$) these twelve men of Israel to spy out

438

the land even as Moses sent (ἀποστέλλω) twelve men of Israel (Num. 13:2, 17 LXX; Deut. 1:22-23 LXX). Like Moses, Jesus knows the same land is filled with idolatry and corruption, just as it was in the land of Canaan long ago. Jesus knows he is sending these men into the midst of giants—giant idolaters and cultural influencers—who despise and prey upon his disciples like wolves because of the God they worship and the gospel of his kingdom which they proclaim. But because the Lord of armies is with them, they can have confidence in the overall success of their mission to proclaim the gospel that the kingdom of heaven *is at hand* and that resistance to this gospel is futile.

Even when the Lord's own people resist Him, the promise of His word remains true. If they choose to reject His gospel, the good land that He swore to give them is rejected as well (Deut. 1:35). This gives a great sense of *urgency* to Jesus' instructions. The twelve apostles were to proclaim to the inhabitants of the land—in this case, the "lost sheep of the house of Israel" (10:6)—that the kingdom of God was at hand, and that any who refused to welcome His good news would need to fend for themselves during God's judgment.

Appendix C

C.1 THE HINGE PASSAGE

In his book *Have We Missed the Second Coming? A Critique of the Hyper-Preterist Error,* Ken Gentry Jr. offers thirteen arguments under the header, "The Hinge Passage."[1] Before listing all thirteen arguments, Gentry supplies an important preface:

> As Jeffrey Gibbs, R. T. France, and others argue, the Olivet Discourse has a two-part structure which corresponds to the disciples' two questions in Matthew 24:3. Their first question asks "when" the destruction of the temple will occur. This is answered in vv. 4–31. Their second question regards "what" will be sign of "Your coming." This is answered in 24:36–25:46.

---

1. Kenneth Gentry Jr., *Have We Missed the Second Coming? A Critique of the Hyper-Preterist Error* (Fountain Inn, SC: Victorious Hope Publishing, 2016), 76. According to his website (www.kennethgentry.com), Kenneth L. Gentry, Jr., Th.D., is a theological researcher and writer, conference speaker, and retired Presbyterian minister with 37 years of experience in pastoral ministry. His academic training includes a degree from Tennessee Temple University (B.A., cum laude, in Biblical Studies), Reformed Theological Seminary (M. Div.), and Whitefield Theological Seminary (Th. M.; Th. D., summa cum laude, in New Testament). He is the author of *Before Jerusalem Fell: Dating the Book of Revelation* (American Vision, 1999) and a contributor to two books in the Zondervan Counterpoints Series of Bible and Theology: *Four Views of the Book of Revelation,* ed. C. Marvin Pate (Zondervan, 2010); *Three Views on the Millennium and Beyond,* ed. Darrell L. Bock (Zondervan, 2010).

But how do we *know* this is the intended structure of the passage? It is one thing to *declare* a two-part structure, it is another to *prove* it. Let us now look at the evidence that Jesus is shifting his attention from the destruction of the temple in AD 70 to his second coming at the end of history. We should keep in mind that AD 70 is theologically linked to the second advent, being a distant picture of it.[2]

In the pages that follow I will attempt to respond to all thirteen arguments offered by Gentry. My purpose in doing so is to help readers notice particular ways in which traditional assumptions and questionable methodologies cloud many scholarly interpretations, especially insofar as they relate to interpreting Matthew's version of the OD.

However, before I begin responding to each argument of Gentry's in detail, it needs to be highlighted again that throughout this book I have not defended or endorsed movements associated with the label "hyper-preterism" or denied the so-called Second Coming of Christ. Gentry's book is *aimed* at hyper-preterists. I am *not* a hyper-preterist. I share many philosophical concerns with Gentry about hyper-preterism, and I am not convinced by (nor have I adopted) the hermeneutical-framework frequently advocated by hyper-preterists.[3] In my opinion there are *many* legitimate alternatives to such idiosyn-

---

2. Gentry, *A Critique*, 76.

3. For a compilation of popular hyper-preterist interpretations covering the entire Protestant canon, see the "clarified" New Testament translation, book-by-book synopsis, and commentary within *The Kingdom Bible* (2016), which is a revised version of Michael Day, ed., *The Fulfilled Covenant Bible* (Anthem, AZ: Bible Prophecy Fulfilled, 2012). For a litany of hyper-preterist errors from one leading "hyper-preterist" who left the hyper-preterist sect, see Samuel M. Frost, *Why I Left Full Preterism* (Powder Springs, GA: American Vision Press, 2012). Richard Hays also offers seven insightful reasons (five of which I wholeheartedly agree with) as to why a "fully realized" eschatology does not offer a satisfactory solution to the New Testament "gospel." On that, see Richard B. Hays, "'Why do you stand looking up toward heaven?' New Testament Eschatology at the Turn of the Millennium," *Theology and Eschatology at the Turn of the Millennium*,

cratic sects and their peculiar systems of interpretation. My efforts in producing this book are, as I see it, primarily designed to facilitate scholarly discussion among Matthean scholars, but also, in part, to encourage credible, scholarly alternatives to hyper-preterism.[4]

---

ed. James Buckley and L. Gregory Jones (Oxford, UK: Blackwell Publishers, 2001), 123-9.

4. Much to my surprise, the Eastern Orthodox scholar, philosopher, and cultural commentator David Bentley Hart recently admitted to "an almost unassailable hermeneutical advantage" of preterists "over all interpreters." The complete context for this remark is worth citing at length in order to highlight the need for more scholars to pursue credible academic alternatives to "hyper-preterism." Speaking of apocalyptic and eschatological language in the Synoptic Gospels, Hart writes, ". . . admittedly, it seems obvious that those who take the so-called preterist view of much of this language—that is, the view that a great deal of the gospels' talk about a coming tribulation and judgment is most properly understood as referring principally to the fall of Jerusalem and the destruction of the Temple, and therefore to events that are (for us) already long past, even though it is all expressed in venerable prophetic tropes of a coming epoch of divine wrath and mercy—enjoy an almost unassailable hermeneutical advantage over all other interpreters. If nothing else, the dominical *logia* recorded in Mark (9:1; 13:30) and Matthew (16:28; 24:34) do clearly promise that the 'final' tribulations and judgment predicted by Christ will come to pass within the lifetimes of some of his contemporaries, and this apparently caused the evangelists no great embarrassment. And it has been noted often enough by attentive readers that a significant number of Christ's prophecies in the synoptic gospels consist quite literally in jeremiads—that is to say, it is Jeremiah in particular, more than any other of the prophets, whose voice seems at times to be resumed and amplified in the voice of Christ. And just as Jeremiah—specifically in chapters 7, 19, and 31 to 32 of his book—invoked the language of divine judgment and of 'the Gehenna' to prophesy the imminent destruction of Jerusalem, followed by its divine restoration and preservation 'unto the Age' (31:40), so also Jesus warns in the gospels of a ruin every bit as imminent and as terrible as the one Jeremiah foresaw, also succeeded by a mysterious restoration. One does not even have to believe, as New Testament scholars tend to do, that the most obviously historically situated of these prophecies—the so-called little apocalypse of Mark 13, Matthew 24, and Luke 21—is a specimen of *vaticinium ex eventu* (that is, prognostication written back into the record retrospectively, after the events supposedly foretold have already come to pass). Jesus may indeed have foreseen and foretold it all. Let us assume he did. Even then, in doing so, he nevertheless seems to have been

From beginning to end, I remain concerned about the internal coherence and intelligibility of *Matthew's* Gospel, which I believe necessitates clearing up unnecessary confusion surrounding an alleged transitional verse (or "hinge passage") within Jesus' OD. In some ways, I consider my efforts to be built upon the scholarly insights and discussions initiated by N. T. Wright, who also does not defend or endorse hyper-preterism. Although Wright's research looms above Mark's Gospel and Pauline epistles more than other New Testament scriptures, my focus remains on Matthew's Gospel and his literary design. Many of Wright's insights have been noted already, but one tucked away (and possibly overlooked) is found in a lengthy footnote and bears repeating again:

> Several still read Mark 13 as though it "must" really be about an end, a transformation, that has not yet taken place, even though the question with which the chapter opens, and for which the previous chapters have exactly prepared us, is about the fall of Jerusalem and the temple in particular. Perhaps a comment about the nature of the discussion may be

---

using the cosmic and apocalyptic imagery of transcendent judgment as symbols of a catastrophe immanent to history." David Bentley Hart, *That All Shall Be Saved: Heaven, Hell, & Universal Salvation* (New Haven and London: Yale University Press, 2019), 110.

I reference Hart's lengthy opinion in order to highlight some tertiary points permeating my thesis: (1) there are credible alternatives to "hyper-preterism" to be found across Christian scholarship, and it would be helpful for biblical scholars and theologians to dialogue about such alternatives more openly and publicly; (2) "preterism" and "hyper-preterism" are not synonymous labels, and need not be treated as such; (3) Hart is only one scholar among many who is clearly and undeniably *not* a "hyper-preterist" (and as far as I can tell, not really even a "preterist" either!), yet still has some way of mapping out first-century eschatological language and future-oriented Christian tradition together. My sincere hope is that many more scholars, like Hart, will increasingly and openly acknowledge the credibility of "preterist" interpretations while pursuing cogent alternatives to "hyper-preterism."

allowed at this point. I sense a huge anxiety in many contributors: a fear that, if they concede the point that Mark 13 is basically about events in the first century, something will be irreplaceably lost from their theology. . . . Of course, we are at liberty to invoke a *sensus plenior* reading if we wish. But it is heavily ironic for conservative Protestants to pull that rabbit out of the hat; and those who have pressed me personally to allow for second-level meanings in Mark 13 and its parallels, meanings that make the passage refer not only to first-century events but to events yet to come, seem clearly to be looking for a let-out, a way of focusing not on what the passage refers to but on something else. How can this be loyalty to the text? . . . (By the way, the argument 'the early church said such-and-such, therefore Jesus must have meant such-and-such when he used similar words' is not, shall we say, the most secure piece of logic in the world.)[5]

If one replaces N. T. Wright's references to "Mark 13" with "Matthew's fifth discourse," that would summarize my approach to Matthew's OD very well. As I see things, Gentry's thirteen arguments illustrate why I believe Wright's approach—which is best understood as "loyalty to the text"—is far more compelling and helpful than any rationalizations I have encountered about a *hinge* passage.

Gentry's arguments in defense of a "hinge passage" are outlined below. Although my numbering configuration varies slightly from Gentry's outline (e.g., **C.1.1**, **C.1.2**, **C.1.3**, etc.) the *order* and *title* of each argument offered by Gentry remains intact.

---

5. Wright, "In Grateful Dialogue," 265-6. This lengthy quotation was cited earlier in the footnotes of my **Conclusion**.

C.1.1 ARGUMENT FROM CONCLUDING STATEMENT

By all appearance, Matthew 24:34 functions as a *concluding* statement; it seems to *end* the preceding prophecy: "Truly I say to you, this generation will not pass away until all these things take place." Why would such a statement be inserted one-fourth of the way through the discourse if it were dealing *in its entirety* with events that were to occur in "this generation"? Such would not make sense. . . . In addition, the Lord's very next statement helps confirm our suspicions: "Heaven and earth will pass away, but My words shall not pass away" (Matt. 24:35). Here he is confirming his *previous* words. He is declaring *their* certainty . . . . Consequently, we must understand Matthew 24:34 as serving to close out one portion of the Discourse. At this point Jesus is announcing that he has answered the disciples' question regarding "when" these things shall be (Matt. 24:3). He still has their next question before him. This then means that the following material relates to events *not* occurring in "*this generation.*"[6]

Even *if* one accepts that "Matt. 24:34 functions as a concluding statement" of some kind (which is a dubious proposition), and verse 35 confirms Jesus' "previous" pronouncements, it still is not necessary to assume that the "prophecy" which preceded it is in response to the disciples' *first* question in 24:3 (regarding "when" these things shall be). Gentry assumes that "their next question" is following a chronological progression of A-B-A'-B'. As I have shown in **2.1.2** and **2.1.2 (a)**, Jesus is asked a series of questions and he begins by responding to the *last* question *first*.

Gentry declares that it "would not make sense" to insert a concluding statement "one-fourth" of the way through the discourse. I

---

6. Gentry, *A Critique*, 76-7. Italics original.

446

agree. That would be a very odd transitional point within a discourse. Such polemics, of course, assume that Gentry has properly identified Matthew's literary structure. As I illustrated in **2.1.2**, Matthew's literary structure follows a chiastic A-B-C-C'-B'-A' pattern. In light of that, it seems *stranger* to argue for a "hinge passage" half-way through section B', as Gentry insists, which is not even remotely close to the typical location of a "hinge" within a chiastically organized discourse. The "hinge" of a chiastic structure—whether the hinge is conceptual or thematic—occurs within its central sections (C & C').[7]

C.1.2 ARGUMENT FROM TRANSITION INDICATOR

In Matthew 24:36 we come upon a subject-matter transition device: "*But of* that day and hour no one knows." The introductory phrase here in the Greek is: *peri de* ("but of, concerning, regarding"). This grammatical structure suggests a transition in the passage involving a change of subject.

We see this phrase frequently marking off new material, as in Matthew 22:31; Acts 21:25; 1 Thessalonians 4:9; and 5:1. Allow me to quickly focus on several very clear subject-transition uses of *peri de* in 1 Corinthians. There we see that the Corinthians had asked him: "Now concerning the things about which you wrote" (I Cor. 7:1). "Now concerning virgins" (7:25). "Now concerning things sacrificed to idols" (8:1). "Now concerning spiritual gifts, brethren" (12:1). In each case he is clearly introducing new subjects that respond to different questions presented to him.[8]

. . .

---

7. Breck, *The Shape of Biblical Language*, 35-55. See also, Lund, *Chiasmus in the New Testament*, 43.

8. Gentry, *A Critique*, 77. Italics are original.

What is more, Gibbs demonstrates that the lone preposition *peri* can in and of itself have a resumptive force. That is, *peri* ("concerning") can pick up on the subject broached earlier in a narrative by serving as a sign that the speaker is returning to that issue once again. Gibbs offers two illustrations from Matthew's Gospel, one from Matthew 6:25 and the other from Matthew 22:23ff.

In Matthew 6:25 Jesus challenges his followers not to be anxious regarding *both* "what you shall eat" (food) *and* "what you shall put on" (clothing). Then in v. 26 he immediately urges them to "look at the birds" to observe that "your heavenly Father feeds them." He intends this to resolve their first anxiety regarding food. Then in v. 28 he returns to his original exhortation in v. 25 and picks up on their second concern, *clothing*: "And why [*kai peri*] are you anxious about clothing?" (6:28). Thus, his instruction in verses 28 and 29 picks up on a portion of his earlier statement in v. 25; it *resumes* his initial concern regarding clothing.

The same function operates in Matthew 22. . . . So now for our purposes: In Matthew 24:36 *peri* reaches back to the disciples *second* question of the two that were raised in v. 3. Having dealt with their *first* question in vv. 4-35, he now returns to consider their second one. By this structuring of the passage we see that v. 36 introduces new material differing from vv. 4-35. At this point he moves away from his AD 70 prophecy and begins speaking of his second advent at the "end of the age," which he will cover in 24:36–25:46.[9]

I have already commented on the use and misuse of *peri de* (περὶ δὲ) in **4.1.7** and **4.1.8**. As I stated in those sections, *peri de* is not limited in function to a complete change in subject; it can also segue into

---

9. Gentry, *A Critique*, 77-8. Italics original.

multiple *aspects* of the *same* subject (like "when" certain signs will occur instead of "what" certain signs will occur) or sub-topics that are related to a broader issue or concern in context. Gentry fails to point this out. Without any obvious contextual reason for insisting upon a complete change in historical situation, *peri de* remains a predictable, grammatical invitation to ponder one perspective among many within a conversation, and without necessarily changing the main topic or concern of that conversation.

Gentry appeals to Paul's first letter to the Corinthians to prove his point. He claims that "In each case he [Paul] is clearly introducing new subjects that respond to different questions presented to him." Two things about this argument immediately stand out: (1) Gentry admits that all of these new subjects are in response to "different questions" presented to Paul, and (2) each question falls under the rubric, "Now concerning (*peri de*) the things about which you wrote" (1 Cor. 7:1).[10]

---

10. Margaret Mitchell's essay, "Concerning περὶ δέ in 1 Corinthians" is commonly cited across commentaries in support of περὶ δέ as an indicator of a change in subject. Mitchell's arguments can be summarized succinctly: She says that περὶ δέ "is simply a topic marker, a shorthand way of introducing the next subject of discussion." Margaret M. Mitchell, "Concerning περὶ δέ in 1 Corinthians," *Novum Testamentum*, vol. 31, no. 3 (Netherlands: Brill, 1989), 234. Although Mitchell's research on the topic is thorough, and I find much of the evidence she presents to be well-founded, her arguments do not contradict my proposals here. Moreover, her research is pinpointed to counter "partition theories" across *Pauline* scholarship. According to Mitchell, "partition theories" contain specific assumptions about how Paul *organized the entirety* of his first letter to the Corinthians. The moving target of Mitchell's essay is made explicit from the outset: she wishes to challenge "the absolute validity" (232) of three common assumptions among interpreters of 1 Corinthians: (1) "the assumption that each περὶ δέ in 7:25; 8:1; 12:1; 16:1, 12 refers back to 7:1, and thus must introduce a topic contained in the Corinthians' letter," (2) "the inverse assumption that Paul would only introduce a topic broached by the Corinthians in their letter to him with περὶ δέ", and (3) "the further assumption that Paul responds with περὶ δέ point by point, in its order, to the Corinthians' letter" (232-3). Not only are these assumptions not my own, but Mitchell offers some evidence in support

Paul is certainly responding to different topics written to him (or questions presented to him). Each example of *peri de* across 1 Corinthians 7 seems to be in response to questions or concerns they addressed to authorities within the Church. Paul, then, seems to be responding to various topics under a general rubric, "the things about which you wrote." Since Paul became aware of their questions or concerns, it is reasonable to expect *peri de* to segue within a conversation as he responds to them. At the same time, Paul uses *peri de* to segue within multiple aspects of a wider ranging concern he wishes to cover succinctly. This is clearly seen in 1 Corinthians 7:25. Paul does not merely say "Now concerning virgins"; he says, "Now concerning virgins, *I have no command from the Lord*, but I give my judgment as one who by the Lord's mercy is trustworthy." This notion of a command "from the Lord" is used like a thread, pulling together pieces of a much broader concern across 1 Corinthians 7:1-24, and specifically echoes verses 10-12 (ESV), which say:

> To the married I give this charge (*not I, but the Lord*): the wife should not separate from her husband (but if she does, she should remain unmarried or else be reconciled to her husband), and the husband should not divorce his wife. To the rest I say (*I, not the Lord*) that if any brother has a wife who

---

of my thesis. For example, Mitchell points out that as a "topic marker," περὶ δέ sometimes functions to proceed across various *sub*-topics related to a larger concern. On this, see her comments about περὶ δέ in Diogenes Laertius' *Lives of Eminent Philosophers* (237). Mitchell also ends her article with an admission that Paul's use of περὶ δέ across 1 Corinthians includes the introduction of topics *within* a lengthy argument, and even within a "sub-argument" (256). Finally, Mitchell comments on the use of περὶ δέ in Mark 13:32 (which mirrors Matt. 24:36), which is helpful for my thesis insofar as she explicitly argues *against* its use as a transitional verse in Mark's OD. She explicitly states that structural arguments about Mark 13:32 transitioning into Jesus' "second answer to the disciples regarding the end of the age" are faulty. According to Mitchell, περὶ δέ in Mark 13:32 could serve the purpose of emphasizing or *re*-emphasizing the present topic within the discourse (252-3).

450

is an unbeliever, and she consents to live with him, he should not divorce her.

So then, even within Gentry's own set of proof-texts for a "hinge passage," Paul illustrates that *peri de* can be used to change subjects *and also* segue into different aspects of a more comprehensive issue, such as one's *calling* as a Christian within a terminal generation.[11]

Gentry also argues alongside Gibbs that "the lone preposition *peri* can in and of itself have a resumptive force." That is to say, *peri* occasionally picks up on a portion of an earlier statement and *resumes* an initial concern within a conversation. Interestingly, Gentry does not realize that this actually makes better sense of the questions asked in Matthew 24:3 and Jesus' *inverted* response to them, beginning with the *last* question *first*. I am not opposed to the argument that *peri* is used with "resumptive force" in Matthew 24:36. That is actually quite helpful, if accurate. Jesus would then be very clear about responding to the *first* question *last* in 24:36–25:46, because he already began by answering the *last* question *first*. Since Jesus begins by answering their *last* question *first*, it makes sense to *resume* their initial concern of "when these things will happen" at verse 36 by responding to their *first* question *last*. Resuming their initial concern about *when these things will happen* makes sense in context and supports my research in **2.1.2 (a)**.

---

11. Technically, the Greek of 1 Corinthians 7:25 says, "Now, concerning *the* virgins" (Περὶ δὲ τῶν παρθένων), which implies a particular life-situation assigned to this group by the Lord (cf. 7:25). A few sentences prior (1 Cor. 7:20), Paul attends to the anxieties of various groups together, advising that "in this situation, each person should remain in the calling in which each was called" (ἕκαστος ἐν τῇ κλήσει ᾗ ἐκλήθη ἐν ταύτῃ μενέτω). By addressing common anxieties among "the called," Paul groups together the circumcised and the uncircumcised, the slave and the free, the believer and unbeliever, the married and unmarried. Many common anxieties of that generation could be anticipated and addressed by Paul because "the form of the world" in that generation was "passing away" (1 Cor. 7:31).

C.1.3 ARGUMENT FROM HUMILIATION LIMITATION

> Focusing once again on Matthew 24:36 we read: "But of that day and hour no one knows, not even the angels of heaven, *nor the Son*, but the Father alone." Here Christ declares that in his state of humiliation . . . he himself has no knowledge as to when "that day and hour" will occur. But of what "day and hour" is he speaking? He must be speaking of his future second advent because, in the preceding section of his Discourse, he informs his disciples of numerous signs, noting that "the end [of the temple] is not yet" (Matt. 24:6). This indicates that he definitely knows when *that* event will occur. He also dogmatically teaches them that these earlier things will certainly happen in "this generation" (24:34).[12]

In argument number two (**C.1.2**), Gentry declared dogmatically that "the end" of the age question referred to Christ's "second advent." But here, in argument number three, Gentry asserts that "the signs" of "the end" inform disciples that "the end of the temple is not yet."[13] In this argument, Gentry underlines the literary fact that "in the preceding section of his Discourse [24:4-35] Jesus informs his disciples of numerous *signs*." With this rationale Gentry is showing clearly, although unwittingly, that Jesus' language about "the end" and the "signs" accompanying it are all addressed in 24:4-35. This is my argument in **2.1.2 (a)**.

Assuming that the well-known textual variant "nor the Son" is authentic (which remains somewhat disputed among textual critics), if one takes for granted that Jesus' *human* limitations are being emphasized by this phrase, this does not logically lead to Gentry's

---

12. Gentry, *A Critique*, 78. Italics and brackets are original.

13. For the sake of simplicity and clarity, here I have removed the brackets from what Gentry wrote.

452

conclusion about two contrasted events in history, separated by thousands of years.

Gentry argues that in Jesus' *human* nature, he "definitely" knows when the destruction of the temple will occur. It will take place in "this generation." Gentry then leaps to the conclusion that there must be a second event in the distant future because Jesus does not know *that* "day and hour." Notice carefully that Gentry's conclusion does not logically follow his premises. Human limitations can definitely include knowledge about an event within a specific generation and yet still not know the exact day and hour the event will occur within it. For example, as a human being I can be dogmatically certain that I will die in *this* generation. As a human being I have limited knowledge, but my knowledge is not so limited as to be uncertain about the generation in which my death will occur; and yet, such certainty does not contradict *another* human limitation of my own, which is not knowing what day and hour I will die.

In light of this, it becomes clear that when Gentry asks, "But of what 'day and hour' is he [Jesus] speaking?", Gentry *assumes* that a particular day and hour could not possibly refer to a day or hour within that generation. It is precisely because of Jesus' *human* limitations (i.e., his "humiliation limitation") that it remains logically possible for Jesus to be *un*certain about the precise "day and hour" of the Father's judgment and also know for certain that it will occur within that same generation.

C.1.4 ARGUMENT FROM TEMPORAL MARKERS

As we continue looking at Matthew 24:36, we also note that it lacks any temporal-transition markers to link it with the preceding events. It is wholly unconnected with the preceding material in terms of temporal progression. This is surprising in that in the preceding material we see a well-connected historical progress with recurring "then" statements (24:9,

14, 16, 21, 23, 30), as well as an "immediately after" (24:29) declaration. But when Christ makes the statement in Matthew 24:36 we hear nothing that links it with the preceding material. We hear absolutely no "then" or "after" nor any other such temporal progress indicator.[14]

As I have shown in **2.1.2 (a)** and **4.1.8**, I do not deny that a literary transition of some sort takes place at 24:36. Verse 36 *begins* Jesus' answer to his disciples' *first* question. But what was their first question about? Was it about the end of *our* world or the destruction of the Temple in Jerusalem in their own generation? Certainly, the overwhelming majority of historical support is found in Jerusalem's destruction. It is only because Gentry assumes a "temporal progression" from a limited first-century context to a seemingly *unlimited* end-of-*our*-world context that his argument from so-called "temporal markers" appears relevant. Based on the research of Alistair Wilson about *meshalim* as elaborated in **4.1.8**, a lack of "temporal progress indicators" after 24:36 is completely and demonstrably irrelevant.

C.1.5 ARGUMENT FROM DEMONSTRATIVE DISTINCTION

. . . Matthew 24:34-36 provides further evidence of a subject transition. Jesus contrasts near and far events:

"Truly I say to you, *this* generation will not pass away until all *these* things take place." (Matt. 24:34)

"But of *that* day and hour no one knows, not even the angels of heaven, nor the Son, but the Father alone." (Matt. 24:36)

In this passage, "this generation" is set in contrast to "that day."

---

14. Gentry, *A Critique*, 79. Italics original.

With these words the Lord looks beyond the signs just given for "*this* [*haute*] generation" (Matt. 24:34) to the event of "that [*ekeinos*] day" (24:36). According to BAGD (740 under *houtos*): the word *haute* is a "demonstrative pron[oun], used as adj[ective] and subst[antive]," and can point to a "person or thing comparatively near at hand in the discourse material, *this, this one* (contrast *ekeinos* referring to someth[ing] comparatively farther away; cp. Lk 18:14; Js 4:15)." Thus, the Lord's attention turns to his distant second advent at the end of history.[15]

Gentry's selective emphasis from BAGD[16] upon a thing "comparatively near" is not as helpful as he imagines. As many theologians between **3.1.1** and **3.1.32** noticed, Matthew 24:4-36 contains clear events that are comparatively closer to the time of Jesus' discourse than the end of the temple's functionality in 70 CE. Wars, rumors of wars, betrayal, persecutions in synagogues, false prophets, famines, and earthquakes will all be the *beginning* of "birth pains"; but "the end" is not yet, Jesus says. The "end" is *beyond* events which are closer in time, *comparatively* speaking. As noted in the literary structure of **2.1.2 (a)**, Jesus begins by answering the last question first, describing signs *preceding* the end and signs *preceding* the Parousia. As such, it is not difficult to imagine why Jesus would use a demonstrative pronoun after answering the last question first, thereby pointing to something *comparatively* father away within that generation.

Thus, Gentry's *declaration* that "the Lord's attention turns to his distant second advent at the end of history" is demonstrably arbitrary. Because Jesus answered the last question first and the first question last, the "when" question addresses a concern that is comparatively

---

15. Gentry, *A Critique*, 79. Italics and brackets are original.

16. BAGD is a common abbreviation for *A Greek-English Lexicon of the New Testament and Other Early Christian Literature* (Chicago, IL: University of Chicago Press) by Bauer, Arndt, Gingrich, and Danker.

farther away insofar as *that* particular "day and hour" is concerned. Again, Gentry assumes what needs to be proven, namely, that Jesus "turns to . . . the end of history."

C.1.6 ARGUMENT FROM OBSERVATIONAL PROSPECTS

Before his statement in Matthew 24:34, Christ mentions numerous events that serve as historical signs, events such as: "wars and rumors of wars" (Matt. 24:6), "famines and earthquakes" (v. 7), "false prophets" (v. 11), and so forth. He specifically mentions a pre-eminent sign: "the sign of the Son of Man."

Furthermore, he personalizes this portion of his Discourse by repeatedly warning the very disciples sitting before him on the Mount of Olives . . . . Thus, he is informing his disciples (who asked him the questions) how *they* might know the time of the coming end of the temple; it is a predictable event. . . . But after Matthew 24:34 Jesus drops all mention of signs and predictability. Instead, he includes statements emphasizing absolute surprise and total unpredictability . . . . This indicates that the following section involves an event that is coming at an altogether unknown and indeterminable time. He is no longer speaking of the destruction of the temple in AD 70, but of his second coming in the distant future.[17]

This is a poorly developed argument. Notice again that Gentry underlines historical *signs* with first-century fulfillment, as though Jesus is addressing the last question (about signs) first. Gentry even emphasizes "a pre-eminent sign," which corresponds nicely with the literary structure I proposed in **2.1.2 (a)**.

---

17. Gentry, *A Critique*, 80-1. Italics original.

Gentry's interpretation of "absolute surprise and total unpredictability" also does not conflict with anything I have proposed. I do not doubt that surprise and unpredictability can be highlighted within Jesus' OD. I merely doubt, for many cogent reasons, that Jesus is suddenly transitioning—completely out of his situational context—to "the distant future" at the end of the world.

According to Josephus (*Jewish Wars,* Bk. 6, ch. 9, sections 3-4), over 200,000 animals were sacrificed in Jerusalem for the Passover as the Roman siege began. If one projects, as Josephus does, that at least ten people belonged to one paschal lamb ("for it is not lawful for them to feast singly by themselves"), we are left with an exponentially larger number of people trapped in the city. Josephus estimated that Jerusalem was crowded with more than two million people as "the Roman army encompassed the city," leaving them all trapped "as in a prison".[18] Even if that number was arbitrarily reduced to a *quarter* of the estimated amount, it still remains reasonable to visualize an entrapment of *over* half-a-million people as appearing "sudden" and "unpredictable." Therefore, when compared with Josephus' estimation, even with exceedingly low figures it still seems reasonable to perceive Jesus speaking in terms of "sudden" and "unpredictable" *first-century* fulfillment, even though the *exact* day and hour was "altogether unknown" within that generation, as Gentry asserts.

C.1.7 ARGUMENT FROM MULTIPLE DAYS

By the very nature of the case, numerous events leading up to the Roman military destruction of the temple in AD 70 will require a number of days. Hence, in the portion of his Discourse prior to Matthew 24:36 Jesus mentions "those *days* [plural]" (vv. 19, 29) and even comforts his disciples by not-

18. The quotations in this paragraph are from William Whiston's translation of Josephus, *The Works of Josephus: Complete and Unabridged* (Peabody, MA: Hendrickson Publishers, 1987), 749.

457

ing that "those *days*" will be "cut short" (v. 22). This mention of the *days* of the tribulation period are set in stark contrast to the singular *day* – indeed, the exact moment—of the second coming. . . . The second advent does not involve a series of historical actions, as is the case with the Roman military operations against the Jews, Jerusalem, and the temple. The second advent is a one-time, catastrophic event conducted by a singular individual, Christ himself.

This, again, is not a compelling argument. If Jesus describes events *preceding* the temple's destruction and the "end" of the temple's significance in 70 CE, as I showed in **2.1.2 (a)**, Gentry's argument amounts to: "*Days* are mentioned alongside a *day* within the same discourse: therefore, the day [singular] can *only* refer to a one-time catastrophic event *at the end of human history*." Such is simply not a compelling argument because it begs the question, "Can a day [singular] among many days *only* refer to an event *at the end of human history*?" I see no reason why a day [singular] among days [plural] could not refer to time within that generation.

Moreover, Gentry's argument insists that days (plural) are "required" by "the very nature" of events (plural) "leading up to" Jerusalem's destruction. Conspicuously, Gentry neglects highlighting Matthew 24:37-39,[19] which mentions "days" alongside the Parousia twice: "For as were the *days* of Noah, so will be the coming (παρουσία) of the Son of Man. For as in those *days* before the flood they were eating and drinking, marrying and giving in marriage, until *the day* when Noah entered the ark, and they were unaware until the flood came and swept them all away. So will be the coming (παρουσία) of the Son of Man." Clearly, in Noah's generation, there were "days" (plural)

---

19. For earlier remarks of mine about the Parousia mentioned in this section, and why this complicates arguments of those who insist upon a strict "bi-partite" structure of the discourse (while *not* complicating the structure I presented in **chapter two**), see the footnotes of section **4.1.8**.

that preceded a soon-coming judgment (i.e., a flood). On "the day" (singular) of that particular historical judgment, the people remained unconcerned until the flood destroyed them. That "day" of the flood preceded "days" of preparation and warning for a *soon-coming* flood in that generation. Jesus says this example of a historical event in the past, preceded by "days," will be just like the "day" of the Parousia in "this generation" (Matt. 24:34). In light of such clear comparative remarks, it remains unclear why Gentry makes an exception. His distinction seems arbitrary. Given Matthew's literary structure, a singular "day" of judgment could refer to a conclusive end in 70 CE.

Also, notice one more assumption by Gentry: He assumes that the functionality of Jerusalem's temple ends *some day* within 70 CE. Gentry does not argue that the temple's significance extends into 71 CE or 72 CE insofar as Jesus' prophetic remarks are concerned. This is because Gentry knows there was a "day" in which Jerusalem's temple ceased having significance within God's plan of redemption. For Gentry, that "day" occurred *sometime* within the year 70 CE.

C.1.8 ARGUMENT FROM DECEPTION FEARS

In the first part of the Discourse Jesus repeatedly warns of the danger of deception by those who would "mislead" (*planao*):

"And Jesus answered and said to them, 'See to it that no one misleads you. For many will come in My name, saying, "I am the Christ," and will mislead many.'" (Matt. 24:4-5)

"And many false prophets will arise, and will mislead many." (24:11)

"For false Christs and false prophets will arise, and will mislead many." (24:24)[20]

. . .

---

20. Gentry, *A Critique*, 81. Italics original.

Indeed, the Lord warns that these are obvious deceivers because when he returns in his second advent, it will be impossible to miss; no deception will be possible: "For just as the lightning comes from the east, and flashes even to the west, so shall the coming of the Son of Man be" (Matt. 24:27).

All of this serves as a significant indicator of a subject shift when we compare this to his teaching after Matthew 24:36. After that point he no longer mentions the danger of deceit: the word *planao* ("mislead") vanishes from the narrative. In fact, the second advent will suddenly overwhelm people in the midst of their daily activities: they will be eating, and drinking and marrying (Matt. 24:38-39). They will be working in the field (v. 40). They will be grinding at the mill (v. 41). They will be surprised as one whose house is broken into without warning (v. 43).

Contrary to this, no one would be surprised at the destruction of Jerusalem of the temple in AD 70. After all, the Romans took five months of relentless siege warfare to get into Jerusalem and destroy the temple after they encircled Jerusalem in April, AD 70. And even this occurs well after the formal engagement of the Jewish War in the Spring of AD 67 and the early military operations in Galilee and elsewhere.[21]

This eighth argument continues to beg many questions. Supposedly, between the spring of 67 CE and 70 CE, Gentry imagines that there was no eating, drinking, marrying, field-working, or mill-grinding that could suddenly become overwhelmed by military invasion. Not only is such an argument unrealistic, but this angle of interpretation also seems to nullify Gentry's previous arguments about fleeing to the mountains (24:16) before *escape from Jerusalem becomes impossible.*

---

21. Gentry, *A Critique*, 81-2. Italics original.

460

Moreover, Gentry's rhetoric is couched in verbiage that implies many months of *encircling Jerusalem* with many months of unsurprised inhabitants.[22] Gentry mentions "five months" taking place for the Romans "*to get into* Jerusalem and destroy the temple after they encircled Jerusalem." As a matter of demonstrable, historical fact, it did *not* take five months to "encircle" Jerusalem; and presumably, Gentry knows this. The actual encircling of Jerusalem was comparatively sudden according to Josephus' account. Therefore, this argument by Gentry is too slippery to be taken seriously. His argument is designed to envision five months *without* surprise at the time of Jerusalem's encirclement, but his descriptions conspicuously avoid the actual time it took to encircle Jerusalem. Gentry's additional appeal to a "formal engagement of the Jewish war" in "Galilee and elsewhere" a few years prior is also misleading because it does not take into account that the majority of people in Jerusalem still lived, worked, and worshipped as possible and necessary alongside the warfare of various regions surrounding Jerusalem.

Furthermore, Gentry's descriptions appear plausible because of the way in which he slips Matthew 24:27 into the argument. According to Gentry, verse 27 is allegedly the *only* verse within 24:4-35 that does *not* involve Jerusalem's inevitable destruction. This is a curious detail within his overall agenda. While presenting this eighth argument, Gentry does not remind his readers of this conveniently inconsistent alteration on his part. Earlier in his book—before Gentry presents arguments for a "hinge passage"—he says in passing that "all things in Matthew 24:4-34 (excluding v. 27)—are to occur *in the very generation of the original disciples*: Truly I say to you, this generation

---

22. Exaggerated statements abound in Gentry's exegesis. The rhetorical design of phrases like "*Contrary* to this," and "*no one* would be surprised," and "*relentless* siege warfare" seems calculated and strategic on Gentry's part. Ironically, Gentry's exaggerated rhetoric is what really seems contrary to Josephus' account of Jerusalem's demise and Jesus' descriptions of the same.

461

will not pass away until all these things take place."[23] Gentry's only explanation for excluding verse 27 from first-century fulfillment is contained in a brief footnote. There, he alleges that verse 27 is "an aside in the Discourse"[24] in which "Jesus states that when he *physically* comes again to the earth, it will be an unmistakable event."[25] Not counting Gentry's presumption about "physicality" in 24:27,[26] surely, if one *includes* verse 27 among the many descriptions to take place in the generation of the original disciples, this argument by Gentry quickly falls apart.

C.1.9 ARGUMENT FROM SOCIAL CONTRASTS

The social circumstances of the early portion of the Olivet Discourse dramatically differ from those of the latter portion. In the first section (up to Matt. 24:36)[27] all is chaotic, dangerous, and confused. . . . Thus, woe upon woe befalls men in the chaotic first portion of the discourse.

But in the second section all of this upheaval and danger disappears. Social activities appear tranquil, allowing business as usual while the mundane activities of life continue. People are marrying and eating and drinking (Matt. 24:38), working in the field (v. 40), and grinding at the mill

---

23. Gentry, *A Critique*, 75. Italics original.

24. Here Gentry seems to borrow the language of R.T. France (*Matthew*, 917), who describes verse 27 as "a sort of aside" from the topic of Jerusalem's destruction that is present everywhere else in 24:4-35.

25. Gentry, *A Critique*, 75. Italics added.

26. Where in Matthew 24:27 is there any description of Jesus "physically" coming "to the earth"? Verse 27 in the ESV says, "For as the lightning comes from the east and shines as far as the west, so will be the coming (*parousia*, "presence") of the Son of Man."

27. Notice that Gentry does not mention the exclusion of 24:27 among this seemingly ubiquitous chaos, danger, and confusion.

(v. 41). The wholesale chaos leading up to AD 70 stands in stark contrast to the peaceable conditions at the time of Christ's second coming.[28]

As I hope to have shown by now, every cumulative "argument" offered by Gentry stretches further and further beyond the limits of credibility. According to Josephus' account of the *Jewish Wars* (Bk. 6, ch. 9, sec. 3), 1.1 million non-combatants *died* within Jerusalem during its siege, and an additional 97,000 combatants were *enslaved*. Many of the casualties among non-combatant Jews were visitors from the diaspora across the Roman empire who came to celebrate the annual Passover. Taking this information into account, Gentry might imagine that 1.1 million Jews were aware of "wholesale chaos" and entered Jerusalem anyway, knowing that all "mundane activities of life" would cease upon entry. Of course, such an imaginary scenario seems ridiculous to me. Even if one adopts Gentry's contrived "stark contrast" between "tranquil" conditions and "wholesale chaos," one could still reasonably conclude that a lot of naïve people entered Jerusalem because many "mundane activities of life" continued until they realized they were trapped.

C.1.10 ARGUMENT FROM FLIGHT OPPORTUNITY

In the first section Christ urges flight from the area, clearly implying there will be time and opportunity to flee: "then let those who are in Judea flee to the mountains" (Matt. 24:16). In fact, one particular sign – the abomination of desolation – will be the cue to leave the area. Because of this opportunity of flight, many lives of God's elect will be saved . . . (24:22).

But upon entering the second section of the Discourse we hear of no commands to escape, no opportunities for

---

28. Gentry, *A Critique*, 82.

flight. Indeed, we witness just the opposite. Once against we can read through the warnings of the unpredictable nature of the second advent (as in #6 above) and realize that by the very nature of the case no opportunity for flight will exist.[29]

This is what apologists describe as an argument *from silence*. Supposedly, because we do not hear "commands to escape" or "opportunities for flight" in the "second section," it must be describing the "unpredictable nature of the second advent (as in #6 above)." However, everything taught within this discourse can pertain to first-century history, especially if the "signs" *preceding* "the end" urge people to get out of Jerusalem before there is no more opportunity for flight.

Since Jesus is addressing the "when" question pertaining to the temple's inevitable destruction, no opportunity or command to escape is mentioned in these *meshalim* because signs and commands have already been mentioned. There is no need to mention them in detail *again*. Instead, one point to be learned from this evidence of Gentry's is that those who would not trust in Jesus' promise regarding the temple's destruction in that generation would suffer the consequences of trusting in the temple's security more than Jesus and the temple of his Body, the church.

C.1.11 ARGUMENT FROM NARRATIVE FUNCTION

Gibbs notes that when we compare the two sections of the Lord's Olivet Discourse we may quickly observe that the first section issues *warnings* regarding deception and danger. . . . The second section of the narrative differs in tone by issuing *exhortations* related to future judgment and reward, calling upon the reader to exercise faithfulness and diligence.[30]

---

29. Gentry, *A Critique*, 82-3.

30. Gentry, *A Critique*, 83. Italics original.

464

. . .

Fearful warnings of imminent danger in the earlier section greatly differ from moral exhortations to long-term faithfulness and preparedness in the latter section. This difference demonstrates what we have seen on the basis of other considerations, that is, that these two sections are fundamentally different.[31]

On the basis of Gentry's other considerations, these two sections only appear to be "fundamentally different" because Gentry *needs them to be so* in order to squeeze in an imaginary transition for an entirely futuristic, end-of-*our*-world scenario. Such is not necessary anywhere else within this discourse. Contrary to Gentry's argument, calling upon the reader to exercise faithfulness and diligence makes complete sense in light of all the warnings Jesus described in 24:4-35.

C.1.12 ARGUMENT FROM ESCHATOLOGICAL CONTRAST

Jesus appears to use key terms that distinguish his metaphorical coming in AD 70 from his literal coming at the second advent. In Matthew 24:4-34 he never uses the word *parousia* ("coming," "presence")—except in v. 27 where he intentionally distinguishes his visible second advent from the first-century (24:34) deceptions which claim Jesus is hidden here or there (24:24-26).

This is significant in that the disciples' original question regarding his "coming" uses the word *parousia* . . . . Yet Jesus studiously avoids the term to describe events occurring in the first section.[32]

---

31. Gentry, *A Critique*, 84.
32. Gentry, *A Critique*, 84. Italics original.

First of all, this is not an argument. Gentry simply declares that Jesus uses "key" terms that "distinguish" between *metaphorical* and *literal* meanings. Gentry does not prove his claim. Allegedly, we are to believe, based purely on Gentry's private interpretation, that *parousia* must be understood "literally" because it is not mentioned in the first-century promises of Matthew 24:4-34, except, of course, in verse 27 where it conveniently *must* mean something literal (i.e., his "*visible* second advent"), not metaphorical. Secondarily, close attention to Matthew's *actual* literary structure easily dismisses the woodenly bipartite structure that Gentry forces upon his readers.

C.1.13 ARGUMENT FROM TEMPORAL DURATION

In the early section of Matthew 24, the time frame is short. The disciples will be facing real dangers that will transpire in "this generation" (Matt. 24:34). They are to be on the lookout for various signs, especially that one that occurs within the then-standing temple (24:15). For then they are to flee the area (24:16). This all fits with Jesus' introductory warning of judgment that will befall the scribes and Pharisees – which will also be in "this generation" (24:34-36).

In the following section from Matthew 24:36 and into chapter 25, the time frame is much longer. No longer do we hear of "this generation," rather Jesus' parables anticipate a distant future.

"But if that evil servant says in his heart, 'My master is *delaying* his coming." (Matt. 24:48)

"But while the bridegroom was *delayed*, they all slumbered and slept." (Matt 25:5)

"After a *long time* the lord of those servants came and settled accounts with them." (Matt. 25:19)[33]

---

33. Gentry, *A Critique*, 84-5. Italics original.

Gentry's selective proof-texting is curious. First, he insists that the early section of Matthew 24 describes a "short" time frame. Even though Matthew 24:22 mentions "short" twice, his defense of a short time frame does not come from appealing to the term "short," but instead comes from the phrase "this generation"; whereas, in the following section Gentry highlights the phrase "a long time" in 25:19 as though that *definitively* settles the time-frame in which these statements reach their intended fulfillment.

Looking closely at Matthew 24:22 (which Gentry does not do), Jesus mentions that days will be "cut *short*" for the sake of the elect, thereby implying that those days would *seem* long to those awaiting his promised judgment upon the temple. In light of this seemingly lengthy period of waiting that would be "cut short" within "this generation"—an interpretation which Gentry assigns to first-century fulfillment (24:4-34, *excluding* v. 27)—Gentry's insistence that the parables following 24:36 "anticipate a distant future" at the end of human history is manifestly contrived.

C.2 CONCLUSION

I remain unpersuaded by all thirteen of Gentry's arguments for a "hinge passage." But I agree with one thing Gentry proposed in his preface. It is one thing to *declare* that the Olivet Discourse describes a distant future at the end of our world, and it is another thing altogether to actually *prove* it.

Bibliography

Albright, W. F. and C. S. Mann. *Matthew: A New Translation with Introduction and Commentary.* Vol. 26 of the Anchor Yale Bible Series. 1971. Reprint, New Haven, CT: Yale University Press, 2011.

Allison, Dale C. Jr. *The New Moses: A Matthean Typology.* 1993. Reprint, Eugene, OR: Wipf & Stock, 2013.

————. "Jesus & the Victory of Apocalyptic." In *Jesus & The Restoration of Israel: A Critical Assessment of N. T. Wright's Jesus and the Victory of God,* edited by Carey C. Newman, 126-141. Downers Grove, IL: InterVarsity Press, 1999.

Ambrose of Milan. *Exposition of the Holy Gospel According to Saint Luke.* Translated by Theodosia Tomkinson. 2nd ed. Etna, CA: Center for Traditionalist Orthodox Studies, 2003.

Aquinas, Thomas. *Catena Aurea: Commentary on the Four Gospels, Collected out of the Works of the Fathers: St. Matthew.* Vol. 1. 1841. Translated by J. H. Newman. Reprint, Oxford: Veritas Splendor Publications, 2012.

————. *Catena Aurea: Commentary on the Four Gospels, Collected out of the Works of the Fathers: St. Mark.* Vol 2. Translated by J. H. Newman. Oxford: John Henry Parker, 1843.

————. *Catena Aurea: Commentary on the Four Gospels, Collected out of the Works of the Fathers: St. Luke.* Vol. 3. Translated by J. H. Newman. Oxford: John Henry Parker, 1843.

————. *Commentary on the Gospel of Matthew, Chapters 13-28.* Vol. 34, Biblical Commentaries (Latin/English Edition of the

Works of St. Thomas Aquinas). Translated by Jeremy Holmes. Lander, WY: The Aquinas Institute for the Study of Sacred Doctrine, 2013.

Assefa, Daniel. "Matthew's Day of Judgment in Light of 1 Enoch." In *Enoch and the Synoptic Gospels: Reminiscences, Allusions, Intertextuality*, edited by Loren T. Stuckenbruck and Gabriele Boccaccini, 199-213. Atlanta, GA: SBL Press, 2016.

Aune, David E. "The Significance of the Delay of the Parousia for Early Christianity." In *Current Issues in Biblical and Patristic Interpretation: Studies in Honor of Merrill C. Tenney Presented by His Former Students*, edited by Gerald F. Hawthorne, 87-109. Grand Rapids, MI: William B. Eerdmans Publishing Company, 1975.

Bailey, Kenneth E. *Jacob & the Prodigal: How Jesus Retold Israel's Story.* Downers Grove, IL: IVP Academic, 2003.

Balabanski, Vicky. *Eschatology in the Making: Mark, Matthew, and the Didache.* New York, NY: Cambridge University Press, 1997.

Balogh, Amy, Dane Cole and Wendy Widder. "Source Criticism." In *Social & Historical Approaches to the Bible.* Vol. 3, Lexham Methods Series, edited by Douglas Mangum and Amy Balogh, 55-98. Bellingham, WA: Lexham Press, 2017.

Bauckham, Richard. *The Jewish World Around the New Testament: Collected Essays 1.* Wissenschaftliche Untersuchungen zum Neuen Testament. Tubingen, Germany: Mohr Siebeck, 2008.

Bauer, David R. *The Gospel of the Son of God: An Introduction to Matthew.* Downers Grove, IL: IVP Academic, 2019.

Beale, G. K. *The Erosion of Inerrancy in Evangelicalism: Responding to New Challenges to Biblical Authority.* Wheaton IL: Crossway Books, 2008.

Beasley, Bob. *Flavius Josephus: The Jewish Wars.* Hartville: OH, Living Stone Books, 2015.

Beasley-Murray, George R. *Jesus and the Future: An Examination of the Criticism of The Eschatological Discourse, Mark 13 with Special Reference to the Little Apocalypse Theory.* London: Macmillan & Co LTD, 1954.

———. *Jesus and the Last Days: The Interpretation of the Olivet Discourse.* Peabody, MA: Hendrickson Publishers, 1993.

Bernier, Jonathan. *Rethinking the Dates of the New Testament: Evidence for Early Composition.* Grand Rapids, MI: Baker Academic, 2022.

Beza, Theodore, Ioac Camer, and P. Lofeler Vilerius. *The New Testament of our Lord Jesus Christ: Translated out of the Greek by Theod. Beza; with brief summaries and expositions upon the hard places by the said author, Ioac Camer, and P. Lofeler Vilerius.* London: Deputies of Christopher Barker, 1599.

Binder, Donald D. *Into the Temple Courts: The Place of the Synagogues in the Second Temple Period.* No. 169, Society of Biblical Literature Dissertation Series. Atlanta, GA: Society of Biblical Literature, 1999.

Black, Stephanie L. "How Matthew Tells the Story: A Linguistic Approach to Matthew's Narrative Syntax." In *Built Upon The Rock: Studies in the Gospel of Matthew,* edited by Daniel M. Gurtner and John Nolland, 24-52. Grand Rapids, MI: William B. Eerdmans Publishing Company, 2008.

Blanchard, Shaun. *The Synod of Pistoia and Vatican II: Jansenism and the Struggle for Catholic Reform. Oxford Studies in Historical Theology.* New York, NY: Oxford University Press, 2020.

Bonaventure. *Commentary on the Gospel of Luke: Chapters 17-24.* Vol. 8, Part 3, Bonaventure Texts in Translation Series. Edited and translated by Robert J. Karris. St. Bonaventure, NY. Franciscan Institute Publications. 2003, Ebook.

Boxall, Ian. *Matthew Through the Centuries.* Wiley Blackwell Bible Commentaries. Hoboken, NJ: Wiley-Blackwell, 2019.

Brandon, S. G. F. *The Fall of Jerusalem and the Christian Church: A Study of the Effects of the Jewish Overthrow of A.D. 70 on Christianity.* 2nd ed. Eugene, OR: Wipf & Stock, 2010.

Brannan, Rick. "1 Apocryphal Apocalypse of John: A New Translation and Introduction." In *New Testament Apocrypha: More Noncanonical Scriptures, Volume 2*, edited by Tony Burke, 378-398. Grand Rapids, MI: William B. Eerdmans Publishing Company, 2020.

Bray, John L. *Matthew 24 Fulfilled.* 5th ed. Powder Springs, GA: American Vision Press, 2008.

Breck, John. *The Shape of Biblical Language: Chiasmus in the Scriptures and Beyond.* Crestwood, NY: St Vladimir's Seminary Press, 2008.

Brown, Jeannine K. and Kyle Roberts. *Matthew.* The Two Horizons New Testament Commentary. Grand Rapids, MI: Wm. B. Eerdmans Publishing Co., 2018.

Brown, John. *New Self-Interpreting Bible Library with Commentaries, References, Harmony of the Gospels, and the Helps Needed to Understand and Teach the Text, Illustrated and Explained.* Vol. 4. New York: R.S. Peale and J.A. Hill, 1896.

Bruce, F. F. "The Date and Character of Mark." In *Jesus and the Politics of His Day*, edited by Ernst Bammel and C.F.D. Moule, 69-89. New York, NY: Cambridge University Press, 1984.

———. *The New Testament Documents: Are They Reliable?* Grand Rapids, MI: William B. Eerdmans Publishing Company, 1981.

Bruner, Frederick Dale. *Matthew: A Commentary, Volume 2: The Churchbook.* Rev. ed. Grand Rapids, MI: William B. Eerdmans Publishing Company, 1990.

Bucer, Martin. *In Sacra Quatuor Evangelia, Enarrationes Perpetuae.* Geneva: Oliva Roberti Stephani, 1553.

Bucer, Martin and Philip Melanchthon. *Melancthon and Bucer.* Edited by Wilhelm Pauck. Library of Christian Classics, Ichthus Edition. Philadelphia, PA: The Westminster Press, 1969.

Buchanan, George Wesley. *The Gospel of Matthew, Volumes 1-2.* The Mellen Biblical Commentary Intertextual New Testament Series. Reprint, Eugene, OR: Wipf & Stock Publishers, 2006.

Buchholz, Dennis. *Your Eyes Will Be Opened: A Study of the Greek (Ethiopic) Apocalypse of Peter.* No. 97, Society of Biblical Literature Dissertation Series. Atlanta, GA: Scholars Press, 1988.

Bullinger, Heinrich. *In Sacrosanctum Iesu Chrisi Domini Nostri Evangelium Secundum Matthaeum Commentariorum Libri XII.* Zurich, Switzerland: Tiguri: Apud Froschouerum, 1542.

Burr, David. "Olivi, Christ's Three Advents, and the Double Antichrist." In *Franciscan Studies:* Vol. 74, 15-40. St Bonaventure, NY: St. Bonaventure University Franciscan Institute Publications 2016.

Butler, B. C. *The Originality of Matthew: A Critique of the Two-Document Hypothesis.* Reprint, Cambridge, UK: Cambridge University Press, 2011.

Caird, G. B. *The Language and Imagery of the Bible.* Philadelphia, PA: The Westminster Press, 1980.

Cajetan, Thomas de Vio. *Cajetan Responds: A Reader in Reformation Controversy.* Edited and translated by Jared Wicks. 1978. Reprint, Eugene, OR: Wipf & Stock Publishers, 2011.

————. *Evangelia cum Commentariis.* Paris: Roigny, 1532.

Calvin, John. *Commentary on a Harmony of the Evangelists Matthew, Mark, and Luke.* Vol. 3. Bellingham, WA: Logos Bible Software, 2010.

Carey, Greg. *Death, The End of History, and Beyond: Eschatology in the Bible.* IRUSC. Louisville, KY: Westminster John Knox Press, 2023.

Carr, David M. *The Formation of the Hebrew Bible: A New Reconstruction.* New York, NY: Oxford University Press, 2011.

Carrier, Brian. *Earthquakes and Eschatology in the Gospel According to Matthew.* Wissenschaftliche Untersuchungen zum Neuen Testament 2. 534. Tubingen: Mohr Siebeck, 2020.

Carson, D. A. *Matthew.* Expositor's Bible Commentary, Volume 8. Grand Rapids, MI: Zondervan Publishing House, 1984.

Case-Winters, Anna. *Matthew.* Belief: A Theological Commentary on the Bible. Louisville, KY: Westminster John Knox Press, 2015.

Charette, Blaine. *The Theme of Recompense in Matthew's Gospel.* Vo. 79, Journal for the Study of New Testament Supplement Series. Sheffield, England: Sheffield Academic Press, 1992.

Charles, R. H. *A Critical History of the Doctrine of a Future Life in Israel, in Judaism, and in Christianity.* London: Adam and Charles Black, 1913.

Charlesworth, James. "The Dead Sea Scrolls and the New Testament." In *Resurrection: The Origin and Future of a Biblical Doctrine,* edited by James Charlseworth, 138-186. New York, NY: T&T Clark, 2006.

Chrysostom, John. *Homilies on the Gospel of St. Matthew.* Vol. 10, Nicene and Post-Nicene Fathers, First Series. Edited by Philip Schaff. Reprint, Peabody, MA: Hendrickson Publishers, Inc., 1999.

Clarke, Adam. *The Holy Bible with a Commentary and Critical Notes.* New Edition, Vol. 5. Bellingham, WA: Faithlife Corporation, 2014.

Cohen, Akiva. "Matthew and the Temple." In *Matthew Within Judaism: Israel and the Nations in the First Gospel.* Early Christianity and Its Literature, no. 27, edited by Anders Runesson and Daniel M. Gurtner, 75-100. Atlanta, GA: SBL Press, 2020.

Contreni, John J. "The Patristic Legacy to c. 1000." In *The New Cambridge History of the Bible, Volume 2: From 600 to 1450*, edited by Richard Marsden and E. Ann Matter, 505-535. Cambridge, UK: Cambridge University Press, 2017.

Coogan, Jeremiah. *Eusebius the Evangelist: Rewriting the Fourfold Gospel in Late Antiquity.* New York, NY: Oxford University Press, 2022.

Crawford, Matthew R. *The Eusebian Canon Tables: Ordering Textual Knowledge in Late Antiquity.* Oxford Early Christian Studies series. New York, NY: Oxford University Press, 2019.

Crowe, Brandon D. *The Obedient Son: Deuteronomy and Christology in the Gospel of Matthew.* Vol. 188, Beihefte zur Zeitschrift für die Neutestamentliche Wissenschaft. Berlin, Germany: De Gruyter, 2012.

Cuddy, Cajetan OP. "Sixteenth-Century Reception of Aquinas by Cajetan." In *The Oxford Handbook of The Reception of Aquinas*, edited by Matthew Levering and Marcus Plested, 144-158. Oxford, UK: Oxford University Press, 2021.

Culpepper, R. Alan. *Matthew: A Commentary.* The New Testament Library. Louisville, KY: Westminster John Knox Press, 2021.

Danielou, Jean. *From Shadows to Reality: Studies in the Biblical Typology of the Fathers.* 1960. Reprint, Jackson, MI: Ex Fontibus Company, 2018.

Davidson, Richard M. *Typology in Scripture: A Study of Hermeneutical τύπος Structures.* Vol. 2, Andrews University Seminary Doctoral Dissertation Series. Berrein Springs, MI: Andrews University Press, 1981.

Davies, W.D. and D.C. Allison. *The Gospel According to Saint Matthew.* Vol. 3, The International Critical Commentary on the

Holy Scriptures of the Old and New Testaments, Matthew. Reprint, New York, NY: Bloomsbury T&T Clark, 2012.

"The Didache." In *The Apostolic Fathers: Greek Texts and English Translations*, edited and translated by Michael W. Holmes, 334-369. 3rd ed. Grand Rapids, MI: Baker Academic, 2007.

Diodati, John. *Pious and Learned Annotations upon the Holy Bible: Plainly Expounding the most difficult places thereof.* 2nd ed. London: Miles Flesher, 1648.

Donaldson, Terence L. *Jesus on the Mountain: A Study in Matthean Theology.* Vol. 8, Journal for the Study of New Testament Supplement Series. Sheffield, England: 1985.

Doriani, Daniel M. *Matthew Volume 2: Chapters 14-28.* Reformed Expository Commentary. Phillipsburg, NJ: P&R Publishing, 2008.

Dorsey, David A. *The Literary Structure of the Old Testament: A Commentary on Genesis–Malachi.* Grand Rapids, MI: Baker Academic, 2005.

Ephrem the Syrian. *Saint Ephrem's Commentary on Tatian's Diatessaron: An English Translation of Chester Beatty Syriac MS 709 with Introduction and Notes.* Journal of Semitic Studies Supplement 2. Translated by Carmel McCarthy. 1993. Reprint, Oxford, UK: Oxford university Press, 2000.

Elder, Nicholas A. *The Media Matrix of Early Jewish and Christian Narrative.* Library of New Testament Studies, 612. New York, NY: T&T Clark, 2019.

Ellis, Gretchen. "Form Criticism." In *Social & Historical Approaches to the Bible.* Vol. 3, Lexham Methods Series. Edited by Douglas Mangum and Amy Balogh. Bellingham, WA: Lexham Press, 2017.

Ellis, Peter F. *Matthew: His Mind and Message.* Collegeville, MN: The Liturgical Press, 1985.

————. *The Genius of John: A Composition-Critical Commentary on the Fourth Gospel.* Collegeville, MN: The Liturgical Press, 1985.

Eloff, Mervyn. "ἀπὸ ... ἕως and Salvation History in Matthew's Gospel." In *Built Upon The Rock: Studies in the Gospel of Matthew*, edited by Daniel M. Gurtner and John Nolland, 85-107. Grand Rapids, MI: William B. Eerdmans Publishing Company, 2008.

Eubank, Nathan. *Wages of Cross-Bearing and Debt of Sin: The Economy of Heaven in Matthew's Gospel.* Vol. 196, Beihefte zur Zeitschrift für die Neutestamentliche Wissenschaft. Berlin, Germany: De Gruyter, 2013.

Eusebius of Caesarea. *The Ecclesiastical History: English Translation.* Vol. 1, Loeb Classical Library, no. 153. Edited by T. E. Page, E. Capps, W. H. D. Rouse, L. A. Post, and E. H. Warmington. Translated by Kirsopp Lake. London: William Heinemann, 1974.

————. *The Proof of the Gospel.* Vol. 1. Translated by W. J. Ferrar. Edited by W. J. Sparrow-Simpson and W. K. L. Clarke. London: Society for Promoting Christian Knowledge; The Macmillan Company, 1920.

————. *The Theophany or Divine Manifestation of our Lord and Savior Jesus Christ.* Translated by Samuel Lee. London: The University Press at Cambridge, 1843.

Evans, Craig A. *Matthew.* New Cambridge Bible Commentary. New York, NY: Cambridge University Press, 2012.

Farley, Lawrence R. *The Gospel of Matthew: Torah for the Church.* The Orthodox Bible Study Companion Series. Chesterton, IN: Ancient Faith Publishing, 2009.

Feuillet, Andre. "Le sens du mot Parousie dans l'Evangile de Matthieu. Comparaison entre Matth. xxiv et Jac. V. 1-11." In *The Background of the New Testament and its Eschatology: Studies in*

Honour of C. H. Dodd, edited by W.D. Davies and D. Daube, 261-280. Cambridge, NY: Cambridge University Press, 1954.

Fiddes, Paul S. *The Promised End: Eschatology in Theology and Literature.* Oxford, UK: Blackwell Publishers, 2000.

Fletcher-Louis, Crispin H. T. "Jesus, the Temple and the Dissolution of Heaven and Earth." In *Apocalyptic in History and Tradition*, edited by Christopher Rowland and John Barton, 117-141. London: Sheffield Academic Press, 2002.

————. "The Destruction of the Temple and the Relativization of the Old Covenant: Mark 13:31 and Matthew 5:18" in *'The Reader Must Understand': Eschatology in Bible and Theology*, edited by K. E. Brower and M. W. Elliott, 145-169. Downers Grove, IL: Intervarsity Press, 1997.

Foster, P. "The Hebrew Bible / LXX and the Development of Ideas on Afterlife in Matthew." In *Life Beyond Death in Matthew's Gospel: Religious Metaphor or Bodily Reality?* Vol. 13, Biblical Tools and Studies, edited by Wim Weren, Huub van de Sandt, Joseph Verheyden, 3-25. Leuven: Peeters, 2011.

France, R. T. *The Gospel of Matthew.* The New International Commentary on the New Testament. Grand Rapids, MI: William B. Eerdmans Publishing Company, 2007.

————. "Matthew and Jerusalem." In *Built Upon The Rock: Studies in the Gospel of Matthew*, edited by Daniel M. Gurtner and John Nolland, 108-127. Grand Rapids, MI: William B. Eerdmans Publishing Company, 2008.

France, R. T. and John Nolland. "Reflections on the Writing of a Commentary on the Gospel of Matthew." In *Built Upon The Rock: Studies in the Gospel of Matthew*, edited by Daniel M. Gurtner and John Nolland, 270-289. Grand Rapids, MI: William B. Eerdmans Publishing Company, 2008.

Franklin, Eric. *Luke: Interpreter of Paul, Critic of Matthew.* Journal for the Study of the New Testament Supplement Series, no. 92. Sheffield, England: Sheffield Academic Press, 1994.

Frost, Samuel M. *Why I Left Full Preterism.* Powder Springs, GA: American Vision Press, 2012.

Gage, Warren Austin. *A Literary Guide to the Life of Christ in Matthew, Mark, and Luke-Acts.* Ft. Lauderdale, FL: St Andrews House, LLC, 2014.

———. *Essays in Biblical Theology.* Ft. Lauderdale, FL: St Andrews House, LLC, 2010.

———. *Theological Poetics: Typology, Symbol and the Christ.* Fort Lauderdale, FL: Warren A. Gage, 2010.

———. *There is No Greater Love: How Jesus is Greater Than All Who Came Before Him.* Ft. Lauderdale, FL: St Andrews House, LLC, 2013.

———. *The Romance of Redemption: Biblical Types of the Bride of Christ.* Ft. Lauderdale, FL: St Andrews House, LLC, 2014.

———. *Typological Poetics: Typology, Symbol, and the Christ.* Ft. Lauderdale, FL: St Andrews House, LLC, 2010.

Gage, Warren Austin and Christopher Barber. *The Story of Joseph and Judah.* Vol. 1, The Masterpiece Study Series. 2nd ed. Ft. Lauderdale, FL: St Andrews House, LLC, 2010.

Gale, Aaron M. *Redefining Ancient Borders: The Jewish Scribal Framework of Matthew's Gospel.* New York, NY: T&T Clark International, 2005.

Garland, David E. *Reading Matthew: A Literary and Theological Commentary.* Macon, GA: Smyth & Helwys, 2001.

———. *The Intention of Matthew 23.* Vol. 52, Supplement to Novum Testamentum. Leiden, Netherlands: E. J. Brill, 1979.

Garrow, Alan J. P. *The Gospel of Matthew's Dependance on the Didache.* Vol. 254, Library of New Testament Studies & Journal for the Study of New Testament Supplement Series. New York, NY: T&T Clark International, 2004.

Gärtner, Bertil. *The Temple and the Community in Qumran and the New Testament: A Comparative Study in the Temple Symbolism of the Qumran Texts and the New Testament.* Society for New Testament Studies Monograph Series 1. 1965. Reprint, Cambridge, UK: Cambridge University Press, 2005.

Gaston, Lloyd. *No Stone On Another: Studies in the Significance of the Fall of Jerusalem in the Synoptic Gospels.* Leiden, Netherlands: E.J. Brill, 1970.

George, Timothy. *Reading Scripture with the Reformers.* Downers Grove, IL: IVP Academic, 2011.

Geigenfeind, Matthias. "The Apocalypse of Thomas: A New Translation and Introduction." In *New Testament Apocrypha: More Noncanonical Scriptures,* vol. 2, edited by Tony Burke, 580-604. Grand Rapids, MI: William B. Eerdmans Publishing Company, 2020.

Gentry, Kenneth L. Jr. *The Olivet Discourse Made Easy.* 2010. Reprint, Chesnee, SC: Victorious Hope Publishing, 2021.

———. *Have We Missed the Second Coming? A Critique of the Hyper-Preterist Error.* Fountain Inn, SC: Victorious Hope Publishing, 2016.

Gibbs, Jeffrey A. *Jerusalem and Parousia: Jesus' Eschatological Discourse in Matthew's Gospel.* St. Louis, MO: Concordia Publishing House, 2000.

Goodman, Martin. *The Ruling Class of Judaea: The Origins of the Jewish Revolt against Rome, A.D. 66-70.* Reprint, New York, NY: Cambridge University Press, 1993.

Goulder, M.D. *Midrash and Lection in Matthew*. London: S.P.C.K. 1974.

Gray, Sherman W. *The Least of My Brothers, Matthew 25:31-46, A History of Interpretation*. Atlanta, GA: Scholars Press, 1989.

Groves, Beatrice. *The Destruction of Jerusalem in Early Modern English Literature*. Cambridge, UK: Cambridge University Press, 2015.

Gumerlock, Francis X. *Revelation and the First Century: Preterist Interpretations of the Apocalypse in Early Christianity*. Powder Springs, GA: American Vision Press; 2012.

Gundry, Robert H. "Matthean Foreign Bodies in Agreements of Luke with Matthew Against Mark: Evidence that Luke used Matthew." In *The Four Gospels: Festschrift Frans Neirynck*. Edited by F. Van Segbroeck, C.M. Tuckett, G. Van Belle, and J. Verheyden, 1467-1495. Bibliotheca Ephemeridum Theologicarum Lovaniensium C. Leuven, Belgium: Leuven University Press, 1992.

———. *Matthew: A Commentary on His Literary and Theological Art*. Reprint, Grand Rapids, MI: William B. Eerdmans Publishing Company, 1983.

Gurtner, Daniel M. "Matthew's Theology of the Temple and the 'Parting of the Ways': Christian Origins and the First Gospel." In *Built Upon The Rock: Studies in the Gospel of Matthew*, edited by Daniel M. Gurtner and John Nolland, 128-153. Grand Rapids, MI: William B. Eerdmans Publishing Company, 2008.

Haak, Theodore, trans. *The Dutch Annotations Upon the Whole Bible: Or, all the Holy Canonical Scriptures of the Old and New Testament, together with, and according to their own Translation of all the Text*. London, 1657.

Haar Romeny, Baster. "Hypotheses on the Development of Judaism and Christianity in Syria in the Period after 70 C.E." In *Matthew and the Didache: Two Documents from the Same Jewish-Christian*

Milieu?, edited by Huub van de Sandt, 13-33. Minneapolis, MN: Fortress Press, 2005.

Hagner, Donald A. *Matthew 14–28. Word Biblical Commentary.* Vol. 33B. Nashville, TN: Nelson Reference, 1995.

—. "The *Sitz im Leben* of the Gospel of Matthew." In *Treasures New and Old: Contributions to Matthean Studies.* Society of Biblical Literature Symposium Series, no 1, edited by David R. Bauer and Mark Allan Powell, 27-68. Atlanta, GA: Scholars Press, 1996.

Hagner, Donald A, and Stephen E. Young. "The Historical-Critical Method and the Gospel of Matthew." In *Methods for Matthew*, Methods in Biblical Interpretation Series, edited by Mark Allan Powell, 11-43. New York, NY: Cambridge University Press, 2009.

Hammond, Henry. *A Paraphrase and Annotations Upon all the Books of the New Testament, Briefly Explaining all the Difficult Places Thereof.* Oxford: The University Press, 1845.

Hare, Douglas R. A. *Matthew.* Interpretation: A Bible Commentary for Teaching and Preaching. Louisville, KY: Westminster John Knox Press, 2009.

—. *The Theme of Jewish Persecution of Christians in the Gospel According to St. Matthew.* Society for New Testament Studies Monograph Series, no. 6. London: Cambridge University Press, 1967.

Harrington, Daniel. *The Gospel of Matthew.* Vol. 1, Sacra Pagina Series. Collegeville, MN: Liturgical Press, 2007.

Hart, David Bentley. *That All Shall Be Saved: Heaven, Hell, & Universal Salvation.* New Haven and London: Yale University Press, 2019.

Hatina, Thomas R. "From History to Myth and Back Again: The Historicizing Function of Scripture in Matthew 2." In *Biblical*

Interpretation in Early Christian Gospels: Volume 2: the Gospel of Matthew. Vol. 310, Library of New Testament Studies, edited by Thomas R. Hatina, 98-119. New York, NY: 2008.

Haydock, George L. *The Holy Bible, Translated from the Latin Vulgate with Useful Notes, Critical, Historical, Controversial, and Explanatory*. New York: Edward Dunigan and Brother, 1852.

Hays, Christopher M., Brandon Gallaher, Julia S. Konstantinovsky, Richard J. Ounsworth, OP, and C.A. Strine. *When the Son of Man Didn't Come: A Constructive Proposal on the Delay of the Parousia*. Minneapolis, MN: Fortress Press, 2016.

Hays, Richard B. "'Why do you stand looking up toward heaven?' New Testament Eschatology at the Turn of the Millennium." In *Theology and Eschatology at the Turn of the Millennium*, edited by James Buckley and L. Gregory Jones, 113-133. Oxford, UK: Blackwell Publishers, 2001.

Heil, John Paul. *The Death and Resurrection of Jesus: A Narrative-Critical Reading of Matthew 26-28*. Reprint, Eugene, OR: Wipf & Stock, 2003.

Heine, Ronald E. "Origen's Gospel Commentaries." In *The Oxford Handbook of Origen*, edited by Ronald E. Heine and Karen Jo Torjesen, 211-228. Oxford, UK: Oxford University Press, 2022.

———. *Origen: Scholarship in the Service of the Church*. Christian Theology in Context Series. New York, NY: Oxford University Press, 2010.

Hendriksen, William. *The Gospel of Matthew*. Grand Rapids, MI: Baker Book House, 1973.

Henry, Matthew. *Commentary on the whole Bible: complete and unabridged in one volume*. Peabody: Hendrickson, 1994.

Herr, William A. *Catholic Thinkers in the Clear: Giants of Catholic Thought from Augustine to Rahner*. Vol. 2, Basics of Christian Thought. Chicago, IL: The Thomas More Press, 1985.

Hetherington, William M. *History of the Westminster Assembly of Divines*. 1856. Reprint, Edmonton, AB: Still Waters Revival Books, 1993.

Hilary of Poitiers. *Commentary on Matthew*. Vol. 125, Fathers of the Church. Translated by D. H. Williams. Washington, DC: The Catholic University of America Press, 2012.

Hill, Charles E. *The First Chapters: Dividing the Text of Scripture in Codex Vaticanus and its Predecessors*. New York, NY: Oxford University Press, 2022.

Holford, George Peter. *The Destruction of Jerusalem: An Absolute Irresistible Proof of the Divine Origin of Christianity*. 1814. Reprint, Nacogdoches, TX: Covenant Media Press, 2001.

Holmes, Michael W. *The Greek New Testament, SBL Edition*. Bellingham, WA: Lexham Press, 2013.

Hood, Jason. "Matthew 23-25: The Extent of Jesus' Fifth Discourse". In the *Journal of Biblical Literature*, vol. 128, no. 3, 527-543. Philadelphia, PA: Society of Biblical Literature, Fall 2009.

Hrynkiw, Gregory. *Cajetan on Sacred Doctrine*. Washington, DC: The Catholic University of America Press, 2020.

Ignatius of Antioch. "The Letters of Ignatius." In *The Apostolic Fathers: Greek Texts and English Translations*, edited and translated by Michael W. Holmes, 182-271. 3rd edition. Grand Rapids, MI: Baker Academic, 2007.

Jacobson, David M. *Agrippa II: The Last of the Herods*. Routledge Ancient Biography Series. 2019. Reprint, New York, NY: Routledge, 2021.

Jenkins, Allan K. and Patrick Preston. *Biblical Scholarship and the Church: A Sixteenth-Century Crisis of Authority*. Ashgate New Critical Thinking in Religion, Theology, and Biblical Studies Series. Burlington, VT: Ashgate Publishing Company, 2007.

Jerome of Stridon. *Commentary on Matthew*. Vol. 117, Fathers of the Church. Translated by Thomas P. Scheck. Washington, DC: The Catholic University of America Press, 2008.

Jindráček, Efrem. "The Western Reception of Aquinas in the Fifteenth Century." In *The Oxford Handbook of The Reception of Aquinas*, edited by Matthew Levering and Marcus Plested, 93-102. Oxford, UK: Oxford University Press, 2021.

Jordan, James B. *Matthew 23-25 A Literary, Historical, and Theological Commentary*. Powder Springs, GA: American Vision, 2022.

———. *Structures of The Gospel According to Matthew*, BH Occasional Paper, no. 38, 2-16. Niceville, FL: Biblical Horizons, Dec. 2010.

———. *Through New Eyes: Developing a Biblical View of the World*. Reprint, Eugene, OR: Wipf & Stock, 1999.

Josephus, Flavius. *The Fall of Jerusalem*. Translated by G. A. Williamson. London: Penguin Group, 2006.

———. *The Works of Josephus: Complete and Unabridged*. Translated by William Whiston. Peabody, MA: Hendrickson Publishers, 1987.

Kahl, Werner. "The Gospel of Luke as Narratological Improvement of Synoptic Pre-Texts: The Narrative Introduction to the Jesus Story (Mark 1.1 - 8 Parr.)." In *Gospel Interpretation and the Q-Hypothesis*, edited by Mogens, Muller, and Heike Omerzu, 223-244. Library of New Testament Studies, no. 573. New York, NY: T&T Clark, 2020.

Kampen, John. *Matthew within Sectarian Judaism*. New Haven, CT: Yale University Press, 2019.

Kee, H. C. "Testaments of the Twelve Patriarchs." In *The Old Testament Pseudepigrapha*. Vol. 1, edited by James H. Charlesworth, 775-828. New York, NY: Doubleday, 1983.

Keener, Craig S. *The Gospel of Matthew: A Socio-Rhetorical Commentary.* Grand Rapids, MI: William B. Eerdmans Publishing Company, 2009.

———. *The Historical Jesus of the Gospels.* Grand Rapids, MI: William B. Eerdmans Publishing Company, 2009.

Kellerman, James A. *Incomplete Commentary on Matthew (Opus imperfectum). Ancient Christian Texts.* Vol. 2. Translated by James A. Kellerman. Downers Grove, IL: IVP Academic, 2010.

Klawans, Jonathan. *Heresy, Forgery, Novelty: Condemning, Denying, and Asserting Innovation in Ancient Judaism.* Oxford, UK: Oxford University Press, 2019.

———. *Josephus and the Theologies of Ancient Judaism.* New York, NY: Oxford University Press, 2012.

———. *Purity, Sacrifice, and the Temple: Symbolism and Supersessionism in the Study of Ancient Judaism.* New York, NY: Oxford University Press, 2006.

Klijn, A. F. J. "2 (Syriac Apocalypse of) Baruch." In *The Old Testament Pseudepigrapha.* Vol. 1, edited by James H. Charlesworth, 615-652. New York, NY: Doubleday, 1983.

Knowles, Michael. *Jeremiah in Matthew's Gospel: The Rejected-Prophet Motif in Matthaean Redaction.* Journal for the Study of the New Testament Supplement Series 68. Sheffield, England: Sheffield Academic Press, 1993.

Kok, Michael J. *Tax Collector to Gospel Writer: Patristic Traditions about the Evangelist Matthew.* Minneapolis, MN: Fortress Press, 2023.

Konradt, Matthias. *The Gospel according to Matthew: A Commentary.* Waco, TX: Baylor University Press, 2020.

Lactantius. *The Divine Institutes, Books I-VII.* Vol. 49, Fathers of the Church. Translated by Sister Mary Francis McDonald, O.P. Washington, DC: The Catholic University of America Press, 1964.

Lampe, G. W. H. and K.J. Woollcombe. *Essays on Typology*. London: SCM Press, 1957.

Lapide, Cornelius A. *The Great Commentary: S. Matthew's Gospel—Chaps. XXII to XXVIII. S. Mark's Gospel–Complete*. Vol. 3. Translated by Thomas W. Mossman. 3rd ed. London: John Hodges, 1891.

Lee, Jason K. and William M. Marsh, eds. *Matthew*. Vol. 1, Reformation Commentary on Scripture: New Testament. Downers Grove, IL: IVP Academic, 2021.

Leigh, Edward. *Annotations upon the New Testament Philologicall and Theologicall: The Gospel according to St Matthew*. London: W.W. and E.G, 1650.

Leithart, Peter J. *A House For My Name: A Survey of the Old Testament*. Moscow, ID: Canon Press, 2000.

————. *A Son To Me: An Exposition of 1 & 2 Samuel*. Moscow, ID: Canon Press, 2003.

————. *BI111 Typological Hermeneutics: Finding Christ in the Whole Bible*. Logos Mobile Education. Bellingham, WA: Lexham Press, 2016.

————. *Deep Exegesis: The Mystery of Reading Scripture*. Waco, TX: Baylor University Press, 2009.

————. "Jesus as Israel: *The Typological Structure of Matthew's Gospel*." In *Biblical Horizons Occasional Paper No. 38*, 1-37. Niceville, FL: Biblical Horizons, Dec. 2010.

————. *The Four: A Survey of the Gospels*. Moscow, ID: Canon Press, 2010.

————. *The Gospel of Matthew Through New Eyes, Volume 1: Jesus as Israel*. Monroe, LA: Athanasius Press, 2017.

————. *Theopolitan Reading*. West Monroe, LA: Theopolis Books, 2020.

———. *The Theopolitan Vision.* West Monroe, LA: Theopolis Books, 2019.

———. *1 & 2 Kings.* Brazos Theological Commentary on the Bible. Grand Rapids, MI: Brazos Press, 2006.

———. *1 & 2 Chronicles.* Brazos Theological Commentary on the Bible. Grand Rapids, MI: Brazos Press, 2019.

Lenski, R. C. H. *The Interpretation of St. Matthew's Gospel.* Columbus, OH: Wartburg Press, 1943.

Levenson, Jon D. "Cosmos and Microcosm." In *Cult and Cosmos: Tilting Toward a Temple-Centered Theology,* edited by L. Michael Morales, 227-247. Leuven: Peeters, 2014.

Levy, Ian Christopher. *Introducing Medieval Biblical Interpretation: The Senses of Scripture in Premodern Exegesis.* Grand Rapids, MI: Baker Academic, 2018.

Ley, John. "The Gospel of Matthew." In *Annotations upon all the books of the Old and New Testament: wherein the text is explained, doubts resolved, scriptures paralleled, and various readings observed.* Edited by John Downame. London: John Legatt and John Raworth, 1645.

Liew, Tat-siong Benny. *Politics of Parousia: Reading Mark Inter(con)textually.* Vol. 42, Biblical Interpretation Series. Leiden, Netherlands: Brill, 1999.

Lightfoot, John. *A Commentary on the New Testament from the Talmud and Hebraica, Matthew-1 Corinthians, Matthew-Mark.* Vol. 2. Bellingham, WA: Logos Bible Software, 2010.

Lim, Timothy H. *The Formation of the Jewish Canon.* New Haven, CT: Yale University Press, 2013.

Lobrichon, Guy. "The Early Schools, c. 900–1100." In *The New Cambridge History of the Bible, Volume 2: From 600 to 1450,* edited by Richard Marsden and E. Ann Matter, 536-554. Cambridge, UK: Cambridge University Press, 2017.

Lövestam, Evald. *Jesus and 'this Generation': A New Testament Study.* Coniectanea Biblica New Testament Series 25. Translated by Moira Linnarud. Stockholm, Sweden: Almqvist & Wiksell International, 1995.

Lund, Nils W. *Chiasmus in the New Testament: A Study in the Form and Function of Chiastic Structures.* Peabody, MA: Hendrickson Publishers, 1992.

Luther, Martin. *Sermons on the Gospel of St. Matthew: Chapters 19–24.* Edited by B. T. G. Mayes and C. B. Brown. Vol. 68, Luther's Works. Saint Louis, MO: Concordia Publishing House, 2014.

Luz, Ulrich. *Matthew 21–28: A Commentary.* Hermeneia–A Critical and Historical Commentary on the Bible, Vol. 3 of Matthew. Translation by James E. Crouch. Minneapolis, MN: Fortress Press, 2005.

———. "The Final Judgment (Matt. 25:31-46): An Exercise in 'History of Influence' Exegesis." In *Treasures New and Old: Contributions to Matthean Studies,* Society of Biblical Literature Symposium Series, no. 1, edited by David R. Bauer and Mark Allan Powell, and translated by Dorothy Jean Weaver, 271-310. Atlanta, GA: Scholars Press, 1996.

———. *The Theology of the Gospel of Matthew.* Translated by J. B. Robinson. Cambridge: Cambridge University Press, 1995.

Macaskill, Grant. *Revealed Wisdom and Inaugurated Eschatology in Ancient Judaism and Early Christianity.* Vol. 115, Supplements to the Journal for the Study of Judaism. Leiden, Netherlands: Brill, 2007.

MacEwen, Robert K. *Matthean Posteriority: An Exploration of Matthew's Use of Mark and Luke as a Solution to the Synoptic Problem.* New York, NY: Bloomsbury T&T Clark, 2016.

Madigan, Kevin. *Olivi and the Interpretation of Matthew in the High Middle Ages.* Notre Dame, Indiana: University of Notre Dame Press, 2003.

Makrakis, Apostolos. *Interpretation of the Entire New Testament, Volume One – The Four Gospels, Book One: The Gospel According to St. Matthew.* Reprint, Sheridan, WY: Eastern Light Publishing, 2020.

Maldonado, Juan. *A Commentary of the Holy Gospels.* Translated by George J. Davie. London: John Hodges, 1888.

Mare, W. Harold. "A Study of the New Testament Concept of the Parousia." In *Current Issues in Biblical and Patristic Interpretation: Studies in Honor of Merrill C. Tenney Presented by His Former Students,* edited by Gerald F. Hawthorne, 336-345. Grand Rapids, MI: William B. Eerdmans Publishing Company, 1975.

Mason, Steve. *Josephus, Judea, and Christian Origins: Methods and Categories.* Peabody, MA: Hendrickson Publishers, 2009.

Mason, Steve and Tom Robinson. *Early Christian Reader: Christian texts from the first and second centuries in contemporary English translations including the New Revised Standard Version of the New Testament.* Atlanta, GA: Society of Biblical Literature, 2013.

Maximus of Turin. *The Sermons of St. Maximus of Turin.* Ancient Christian Writings: The Works of the Fathers in Translation, no. 50. Translated and annotated by Boniface Ramsey, O.P. Mahwah, NJ: Newman Press, 1989.

McDonald, Lee Martin. *The Biblical Canon: Its Origin, Transmission, and Authority.* Peabody, MA: Hendrickson Publishers, 2007.

McGinn, Bernard. *Antichrist: Two Thousand Years of the Human Fascination with Evil.* New York, NY: HarperCollins Publishers, 1994.

———. *Visions of the End: Apocalyptic Traditions in the Middle Ages.* New York, NY: Columbia University Press, 1979.

McGuckin, John Anthony. "Origen's Eschatology." In *The Oxford Handbook of Origen*, edited by Ronald E. Heine and Karen Jo Torjesen, 410-426. Oxford, UK: Oxford University Press, 2022.

———. *The Path of Christianity: The First Thousand Years.* Downers Grove, IL: IVP Academic, 2017.

McNeile, Alan Hugh. *The Gospel According to St. Matthew: The Greek Text with Introduction, Notes, and Indices.* Thornapple Commentaries. Reprint, Grand Rapids, MI: Baker Book House, 1980.

McNicol, Allan J. *Jesus' Directions for the Future: A Source and Redaction-History Study of the Use of the Eschatological Traditions in Paul and in the Synoptic Accounts of Jesus' Last Eschatological Discourse.* New Gospel Studies 9. Macon, GA: Mercer University Press, 1996.

Meade, John D. *The Biblical Canon Lists from Early Christianity: Texts and Analysis.* Oxford, UK: Oxford University Press, 2017.

Metzger, Bruce. *A Textual Commentary on the Greek New Testament.* 2nd ed. Stuttgart, Germany: United Bible Societies, 1994.

Mitch, Curtis and Edward Sri. *The Gospel of Matthew.* Catholic Commentary on Sacred Scripture. Grand Rapids, MI: Baker Academic, 2010.

Mitchell, Margaret M. "Concerning περὶ δέ in 1 Corinthians" in *Novum Testamentum*, vol. 31, no. 3, 229-256. Netherlands: Brill, 1989.

Moffitt, David M. *Rethinking the Atonement: New Perspectives on Jesus's Death, Resurrection, and Ascension.* Grand Rapids, MI: Baker Academic, 2022.

Morales, L. Michael, ed. *Cult and Cosmos: Tilting Toward a Temple-Centered Theology.* Leuven-Paris-Walpole, MA: Peeters, 2014.

———. *The Tabernacle Pre-Figured: Cosmic Mountain Ideology in Genesis and Exodus.* Leuven-Paris-Walpole, MA: Peeters, 2012.

Morris, Leon. *The Gospel According to Matthew.* Reprint, Grand Rapids, MI: William B. Eerdmans Publishing Company, 1995.

Moscicke, Hans M. *Goat for Yahweh, Goat for Azazel: The Impact of Yom Kippur on the Gospels.* Lanham, MD: Lexington Books, 2021.

———. *The New Day of Atonement: A Matthean Typology.* Wissenschaftliche Untersuchungen zum Neuen Testament 2. 517. Tubingen, Germany: Mohr Siebeck, 2020.

Neujhar, Matthew. *Predicting the Past in the Ancient Near East: Mantic Historiography in Ancient Mesopotamia, Judah, and the Mediterranean World.* Providence, RI: Brown Judaic Studies, 2012.

Newton, Thomas. *Dissertations on The Prophecies, which have remarkably been fulfilled, and at this time are fulfilling in the world.* London: J. F. Dove, 1825.

Nichols, Aidan. *The Theology of Joseph Ratzinger: An Introductory Study.* Edinburgh, Scotland: T&T Clark, 1988.

Nickelsburg, George W. E. *Resurrection, Immortality, and Eternal Life in Intertestamental Judaism and Early Christianity.* Harvard Theological Studies, 57. Cambridge, MA: Harvard University Press, 2006.

Njeri, George. "Surprise on the Day of Judgment in Matthew 25:31-46 and The Book of Watchers." In *Neotestamentica.* Vol. 54, Journal of the New Testament Society of Southern Africa, no. 1, 87-104. 2020.

Nolland, John. *The Gospel of Matthew: A Commentary on the Greek Text.* Grand Rapids, MI: William B. Eerdmans Publishing Company, 2005.

———. "The Gospel of Matthew and Anti-Semitism." In *Built Upon The Rock: Studies in the Gospel of Matthew,* edited by Daniel M. Gurtner & John Nolland, 154-169. Grand Rapids, MI: William B. Eerdmans Publishing Company, 2008.

Norris, Frederick W. "Eusebius on Jesus as Deceiver and Sorcerer." In *Eusebius, Christianity, and Judaism*, edited by Harold W. Attridge and Gohei Hata, 523-540. Detroit, MI: Wayne State University Press, 1992.

O'Callaghan, Paul. *Christ our Hope: An Introduction to Eschatology.* Washington, DC: The Catholic University of America Press, 2011.

———. "Reception of Thomas Aquinas in the Area of Eschatology." In *The Oxford Handbook of The Reception of Aquinas*, edited by Matthew Levering and Marcus Plested, 705-716. Oxford, UK: Oxford University Press, 2021.

O'Connor, Michael. *Cajetan's Biblical Commentaries: Motive and Method*. St. Andrews Studies in Reformation History. Leiden: Brill, 2017.

Omanson, Roger L. *A Textual Guide to the Greek New Testament.* Stuttgart, Germany: German Bible Society, 2012.

Origen of Alexandria. *The Commentary of Origen on the Gospel of St Matthew*. Vol. 2. Translated by Ronald E. Heine. Oxford, UK: Oxford University Press, 2018.

Paget, James Carleton. *Jews, Christians and Jewish Christians in Antiquity.* Wissenschaftliche Untersuchungen zum Neuen Testament. 251. Tubingen, Germany: Mohr Siebeck, 2010.

———. "Some Observations on the Problem of the Delay of the Parousia in the Historiography of Its Discussion." In *The "Delay of the Parousia." Early Christianity,* vol. 9, 9-36. Tubingen, Germany: Mohr Siebeck, 2018.

Parry, Robin A. *The Biblical Cosmos.* Eugene, OR: Cascade Books, 2014.

Pattarumadathil, Henry. "Pharisees and Sadducees Together in Matthew." In *The Pharisees,* edited by Joseph Sievers and Amy-Jill

Levine, 136-147. Grand Rapids, MI: William B. Eerdmans Publishing Company, 2021.

Patton, Matthew H. *Hope for a Tender Sprig: Jehoiachin in Biblical Theology.* Bulletin for Biblical Research Supplement 16; Winona Lake, IN: Eisenbrauns, 2017.

Peabody, David B. *One Gospel from Two: Mark's use of Matthew and Luke.* Edited by *David B. Peabody, Lamar Cope, & Allan J. McNicol.* Harrisburg, PA: Trinity Press International, 2002.

Perriman, Andrew. *The Coming of the Son of Man: New Testament Eschatology for an Emerging Church.* Eugene, OR: Wipf & Stock, 2005.

Pitre, Brant J. *The Historical Jesus, The Great Tribulation, and the End of Exile: Restoration Eschatology and the Origin of the Atonement.* Doctoral dissertation submitted to the Graduate School of the University of Notre Dame, April 2004.

Plested, Marcus. "Eutychianism: Is Jesus Christ divine and human or a hybrid, a third thing that is neither fully one nor the other?" In *Heresies and How to Avoid Them: Why it matters what Christians believe,* edited by Ben Quash and Michael Ward, 41-49. Peabody, MA: Hendrickson Publishers, 2007.

Plummer, Alfred. *An Exegetical Commentary on the Gospel According to S. Matthew.* New York, NY: Charles Scribner's Sons, 1909.

Poole, Matthew. *Annotations upon the Holy Bible.* Vol. 3. New York: Robert Carter and Brothers, 1853.

Porteus, Bielby. *Lectures on the Gospel of St. Matthew; Delivered in the Parish Church of St. James, Westminster, In the Years 1798, 1799, 1800, and 1801.* Philadelphia: Thomas Kite, 1829.

Postell, Seth D. *Adam as Israel: Genesis 1-3 as the Introduction to the Torah and Tanakh.* Eugene, OR: Pickwick Publications, 2011.

Pregeant, Russell. "The Wisdom Passages in Matthew's Story." In *Treasures New and Old: Contributions to Matthean Studies,* Society of Biblical Literature Symposium Series, no. 1, edited by David R. Bauer and Mark Allan Powell, 197-232. Atlanta, GA: Scholars Press, 1996.

Price, Charles. *Matthew: The King and His Kingdom.* Reprint, Scotland, UK: Christian Focus Publications Ltd., 2020.

Quarles, Charles, L. *Matthew.* Evangelical Biblical Theology Commentary. Bellingham, WA: Lexham Academic, 2022.

Quesnel, Pasquier. *The Gospels; with Moral Reflections on Each Verse.* Vol. 1. 1671. Reprint, Glasgow: William Collins, 1830.

Ratzinger, Joseph. *Eschatology: Death and Eternal Life.* Washington, DC: The Catholic University of America Press, 1988.

Regev, Eyal. *The Temple in Early Christianity: Experiencing the Sacred.* The Anchor Yale Bible Reference Library. New Haven, CT: Yale University Press, 2019.

Resseguie, James L. *Narrative Criticism of the New Testament: An Introduction.* Grand Rapids, MI: Baker Academic, 2005.

Richter, Amy E. *Enoch and the Gospel of Matthew.* Princeton Theological Monograph Series. Eugene, OR: Pickwick Publications, 2012.

Roberts, Alastair J. & Wilson, Andrew. *Echoes of Exodus: Tracing Themes of Redemption through Scripture.* Wheaton, IL: Crossway, 2018.

Robinson, John A.T. *Redating the New Testament.* Reprint, Eugene, OR: Wipf & Stock, 2000.

Roukema, Riemer. "Origen, the Jews, and the New Testament." In *The 'New Testament' as a Polemical Tool: Studies in Ancient Christian Anti-Jewish Rhetoric and* Beliefs, edited by Riemer Roukema and Hagit Amirav, 241-253. Gottingen: Vandenhoeck & Ruprecht Gmbh & Co., 2018.

Runesson, Anders. *Divine Wrath and Salvation in Matthew: The Narrative World of the First Gospel.* Minneapolis, MN: Fortress Press, 2016.

Runesson, Anders, Donald D. Binder, and Birger Olsson. *The Ancient Synagogue from Its Origins to 200 C.E.: A Sourcebook.* Leiden, Netherlands: Brill, 2010.

Saldarini, Anthony J. "Reading Matthew without Anti-Semitism." In *The Gospel of Matthew in Current Study: Studies in Memory of William G. Thompson, S.J.,* edited by David E. Aune, 166-184. Grand Rapids, MI: William B. Eerdmans Publishing Company, 2001.

Schafer, Peter. *Jesus in the Talmud.* Princeton, NJ, Princeton University Press, 2007.

Schneiders, Sandra M. "The Gospels and the reader." In *The Cambridge Companion to the Gospels,* edited by Stephen C. Barton, 97-118. New York, NY: Cambridge University Press, 2006.

Schreiner, Patrick. *Matthew, Disciple and Scribe: The First Gospel and Its Portrait of Jesus.* Grand Rapids, MI: Baker Academic, 2019.

Schweizer, Eduard. *The Good News According to Matthew.* Translated by David E. Green. Atlanta, GA: John Knox Press, 1977.

Scrivener, Frederick H. A. *A Plain Introduction to the Criticism of the New Testament.* Reprint, New York, NY: Cambridge University Press, 2009.

Shoemaker, Stephen J. "The Tiburtine Sibyl: A New Translation and Introduction." In *New Testament Apocrypha: More Noncanonical Scriptures,* vol. 1, edited by Tony Burke and Brent Landau, 510-525. Grand Rapids, MI: William B. Eerdmans Publishing Company, 2016.

Sigvartsen, Jan A. *Afterlife and Resurrection Beliefs in the Apocrypha and Apocalyptic Literature.* Vol. 29, T&T Clark Jewish and Christian Texts Series. New York, NY: Bloomsbury T & T Clark, 2019.

———. *Afterlife and Resurrection Beliefs in the Pseudepigrapha.* Vol. 30, T&T Clark Jewish and Christian Texts Series. New York, NY: Bloomsbury T & T Clark, 2019.

Sim, David C. *Apocalyptic Eschatology in the Gospel of Matthew.* Society for New Testament Studies Monograph Series 88. Reprint, Cambridge, UK: Cambridge University Press, 2005.

———. "Life after Death? The Question of Immediate Life after Death in the Dead Sea Scrolls and in the Gospel of Matthew." In *Matthew Within Judaism: Israel and the Nations in the First Gospel,* Early Christianity And Its Literature, no. 27, edited by Anders Runesson and Daniel M. Gurtner, 329-344. Atlanta, GA: SBL Press, 2020.

———. "Reconstructing the Social and Religious Milieu of Matthew: Methods, Sources, and Possible Results." In *Matthew, James, and Didache: Three Related Documents in Their Jewish and Christian Settings,* Society of Biblical Literature Symposium Series, no. 45, edited by Huub van de Sandt and Jurgen K. Zangenberg, 13-32. Atlanta, GA: Society of Biblical Literature, 2008.

———. *The Gospel of Matthew and Formative Judaism: The History and Social Setting of the Matthean Community.* Studies of the New Testament and Its World Series. Edinburgh, Scotland: T&T Clark LTD, 1998.

Simmonds, Andrew R. "'Woe to you …Hypocrites!' Re-reading Matthew 23:13-36." In *Bibliotheca Sacra, Volume 166* (2009), 336-349.

Smalley, Stephen S. "The Delay of the Parousia." In the *Journal of Biblical Literature*, vol. 83, 41-54. Philadelphia, PA: Society of Biblical Literature, March 1964.

Smith, Lesley. "The Glossed Bible." In *The New Cambridge History of the Bible, Volume 2: From 600 to 1450,* edited by Richard Marsden and E. Ann Matter, 363-379. Cambridge, UK: Cambridge University Press, 2017.

Smith, Ralph Allan. *Hear, My Son: An Examination of the Fatherhood of Yahweh in Deuteronomy.* Monroe, LA: Athanasius Press, 2011.

Smith, Steven C. *The House of the Lord: A Catholic Biblical Theology of God's Temple Presence in the Old and New Testaments.* Steubenville, OH: Franciscan University Press, 2017.

Stanton, Graham N. *A Gospel for a New People: Studies in Matthew.* Louisville, KY: Westminster/John Knox Press, 1993.

Staples, Jason A. *The Idea of Israel in Second Temple Judaism: A New Theory of People, Exile, and Israelite Identity.* Cambridge, UK: Cambridge University Press, 2021.

Stoldt, Hans-Herbert. *History and Criticism of the Markan Hypothesis.* Translated by Donald L. Niewyk. Macon, GA: Mercer University Press, 1980.

Stone, Timothy J. *The Compilational History of the Megilloth: Canon, Contoured Intertextuality and Meaning in the Writings.* Tübingen, Germany: Mohr Siebeck, 2013.

Stine, Philip C. & Newman, Barclay M. *A Handbook on The Gospel of Matthew.* New York, NY: United Bible Societies, 1988.

Sturz, Harry A. *The Byzantine Text-Type & New Testament Textual Criticism.* Nashville, TN: Thomas Nelson Publishers, 1984.

Sumner, John B. *A Practical Exposition of the Gospels of St. Matthew and St. Mark in the form of Lectures, intended to assist the practice of domestic instruction and devotion.* London: J. Hatchard and Son, 1831.

Sytsma, David S. "Sixteenth-Century Reformed Reception of Aquinas." In *The Oxford Handbook of The Reception of Aquinas,* edited by Matthew Levering and Marcus Plested, 121-143. Oxford, UK: Oxford University Press, 2021.

Tacitus. *The Histories: A New Translation*. Translated by Kenneth Wellesley. Reprint, New York, NY: Penguin Books, 1978.

Terry, Milton S. *Biblical Apocalyptics: A Study of the Most Notable Revelations of God and of Christ in the Canonical Scriptures*. New York, NY: Eaton & Mains, 1898.

———. *The Sibylline Oracles*. New York, NY: Eaton & Mains, 1899.

Theodoret of Cyrus. *Commentary on Daniel. Writings from the Greco-Roman World*. Translated by Robert C. Hill. Atlanta: Society of Biblical Literature, 2006.

Trapp, Johanis. *A Commentary or Exposition upon all the Books of the New Testament*. London: R. W., 1656.

Turner, David L. "His Glorious Throne: Israel and the Gentiles in Mission and Judgment in the Gospel of Matthew." In *Matthew Within Judaism: Israel and the Nations in the First Gospel*, Early Christianity And Its Literature, no. 27, edited by Anders Runesson and Daniel M. Gurtner, 135-168. Atlanta, GA: SBL Press, 2020.

———. *Israel's Last Prophet: Jesus and the Jewish Leaders in Matthew 23*. Minneapolis, MN: Fortress Press, 2015.

Valdés, Juan. *Commentary upon the Gospel of St. Matthew: Now for the first time translated from the Spanish, and never before published in English*. Translated by John T. Betts. London: Turner & Co., 1882.

Van Bruggen, Jakob. *The Ancient Text of the New Testament*. Winnipeg: Premier Publishing, 1936.

VanderKam, James C. *From Joshua to Caiaphas: High Priests after the Exile*. Minneapolis, MN: Fortress Press, 2004.

Varkey, Mothy. *Salvation in Continuity: A Reconsideration of Matthew's Soteriology*. Emerging Scholars Series. Minneapolis, MN: Fortress Press, 2017.

Vicchio, Stephen J. *The Legend of The Anti-Christ: A History.* Eugene, OR: Wipf & Stock, 2009.

Walck, Leslie W. *The Son of Man in the Parables of Enoch and in Matthew.* Vol. 9, T&T Clark Jewish and Christian Texts Series. New York, NY: Bloomsbury T & T Clark, 2011.

Walsh, Jeremy T. *Style & Structure in Biblical Hebrew Narrative.* Collegeville, MN: The Liturgical Press, 2001.

Watson, Francis. *An Apostolic Gospel: The "Epistula Apostolorum" in Literary Context.* Society for New Testament Studies Monograph Series 179. Cambridge, UK: Cambridge University Press, 2020.

Watson, Richard. *An Exposition of the Gospels of St. Matthew and St. Mark, and of some other detached parts of Holy Scripture.* London: John Mason, 1833.

Watts, Rikki E. *Isaiah's New Exodus in Mark.* Reprint, Grand Rapids, MI: Baker Academic, 2000.

Welch, John W. *The Sermon on the Mount in the Light of the Temple.* Society for Old Testament Study Monographs. New York, NY: Routledge, 2016.

Wenham, David. "The Rock on Which to Build: Some Mainly Pauline Observations about the Sermon on the Mount." In *Built Upon The Rock: Studies in the Gospel of Matthew,* edited by Daniel M. Gurtner and John Nolland, 187-206. Grand Rapids, MI: William B. Eerdmans Publishing Company, 2008.

Wenham, John. *Redating Matthew, Mark & Luke.* Downers Grove, IL: Intervarsity Press, 1992.

Wesley, John. *Explanatory Notes Upon the New Testament.* 12th ed. New York: Carlton & Porter, 1754.

Wilkin, Robert Louis, ed., and D.H. Williams, ed. and trans. *The Church's Bible: Matthew Interpreted by Early Christian Commentators.* Grand Rapids, MI: William B. Eerdmans Publishing Company, 2018.

Wilson, Alistair I. *When Will These Things Happen? A Study of Jesus as Judge in Matthew 21-25.* Paternoster Biblical Monographs. Reprint, Eugene, OR: Wipf & Stock Publishers, 2006.

Wilson, Walter T. *The Gospel of Matthew.* Vols. 1 and 2, Eerdmans Critical Commentary. Grand Rapids, MI: William. B. Eerdmans Publishing Company, 2022.

Winn, Adam. *Mark and the Elijah-Elisha Narrative: Considering the Practice of Greco-Roman Imitation in the Search for Markan Source Material.* Eugene, OR: Pickwick Publications, 2010.

Wright, Brian J. *Communal Reading in the Time of Jesus: A Window into Early Christian Reading Practices.* Minneapolis, MN: Fortress Press, 2017.

Wright, N. T. *History and Eschatology: Jesus and the Promise of Natural Theology.* Waco, TX: Baylor University Press, 2019.

———. "Hope Deferred? Against the Dogma of Delay." In *The "Delay of the Parousia." Early Christianity,* vol. 9, 37-82. Tubingen, Germany: Mohr Siebeck, 2018.

———. "In Grateful Dialogue: A Response." In *Jesus & The Restoration of Israel: A Critical Assessment of N. T. Wright's Jesus and the Victory of God,* edited by Carey C. Newman, 244-277. Downers Grove, IL: InterVarsity Press, 1999.

———. *Jesus and the Victory of God. V*ol. 2, Christian Origins and the Question of God. Minneapolis, MN: Fortress Press, 1996.

———. *The New Testament and the People of God.* Vol. 1, Christian Origins and the Question of God. Minneapolis, MN: Fortress Press, 1992.

Wright, N. T. and Michael F. Bird. *The New Testament in Its World: An Introduction to the History, Literature, and Theology of the First Century Christians.* Grand Rapids, MI: Zondervan, 2019.

Wycliffe, John. *Select English Works of John Wyclif.* Vol. 1, edited by T. Arnold. Oxford: Clarendon Press, 1869.

Yarbro-Collins, Adela. "Polemic against the Pharisees in Matthew 23." In *The Pharisees,* edited by Joseph Sievers and Amy-Jill Levine, 148-169. Grand Rapids, MI: William B. Eerdmans Publishing Company, 2021.